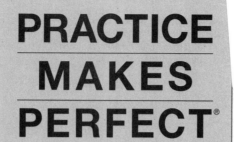
PRACTICE
MAKES
PERFECT®

Complete
Italian
All-in-One

Edited by

Marcel Danesi

Mc
Graw
Hill

New York   Chicago   San Francisco   Athens   London   Madrid
Mexico City   Milan   New Delhi   Singapore   Sydney   Toronto

5 6 7 8 9   LOV   24 23 22

ISBN   978-1-260-45512-0
MHID   1-260-45512-2

e-ISBN   978-1-260-45513-7
e-MHID   1-260-45513-0

McGraw-Hill Language Lab App

Audio recordings of conversations and answers to many of the exercises in this book are available to support your study. Go to www.mhlanguagelab.com to access the online version of the application, or to locate links to the mobile app for iOS and Android devices. (Note: Internet access is required to access streaming audio via app.)

McGraw-Hill books are available at special quantity discounts to use as premiums or for use in corporate training programs. To contact a representative, please e-mail at bulksales@mheducation.com.

Note: This book is a compilation of content from five Practice Makes Perfect titles: *Italian Conversation* (by Marcel Danesi), *Complete Italian Grammar* (by Marcel Danesi), *Italian Verb Tenses* (by Paola Nanni-Tate), *Italian Sentence Builder* (by Paola Nanni-Tate), and *Italian Problem Solver* (by Alessandra Visconti).

Contents

Preface

Practice Makes Perfect: Complete Italian All-in-One is a complete overview of the Italian language, from its basic conversation techniques to its advanced grammar, vocabulary, and usage. It is aimed especially at self-taught learners, providing a user-friendly way to learn or review the language, at different levels. It can also be used in classrooms for various purposes, from review to in-depth treatment.

This book is a compilation of five *Practice Makes Perfect* titles: *Italian Conversation* (by Marcel Danesi), *Complete Italian Grammar* (by Marcel Danesi), *Italian Verb Tenses* (by Paola Nanni-Tate), *Italian Sentence Builder* (by Paola Nanni-Tate), and *Italian Problem Solver* (by Alessandra Visconti).

There are five parts that follow the above texts, with the selected chapters laid out in such a way that you will be building up your competence gradually and comprehensively, starting almost "from scratch" and working towards an all-inclusive knowledge and control of the Italian language.

PART I: Conversation
This part introduces you to the basics of Italian conversation, while teaching you how to use main grammatical and vocabulary items that will allow you to carry out conversations in specific contexts knowingly.

PART II: Basic Grammar
This part provides an overview of basic Italian grammar in a simple yet exhaustive way, with many illustrations of how the parts of the language can be used in specific situations.

PART III: Verb Tenses
Learning to control Italian verbs always presents a particularly troublesome area of learning. So, this part goes into great depth on verb tenses—how to conjugate them, use them, etc.

PART IV: Sentence Building
Putting all the parts together to construct effective Italian sentences is an important goal in learning a language proficiently. This part allows you to go over all the parts of grammar in an interconnected fashion so that you can become adept at this important aspect of Italian sentence formation.

PART V: Problem Solver
In this final part, you will encounter all those tricky areas of grammar and usage that confront every learner of Italian, with many opportunities to "solve the problems" that you typically encounter in using the language. This is an overall review section that will allow you to put everything together.

In all the chapters you will find an abundance of practice material. The answers, which contain detailed charts and tables, as well as two glossaries (Italian-English, English-Italian) are provided at the end of the book.

This is a unique book, given its comprehensiveness and exhaustiveness. You have everything you will ever need here between two covers!

Buon divertimento!

Marcel Danesi
University of Toronto, 2019

CONVERSATION

Introduction to Part I

This part has one aim—to teach you how to converse in Italian and thus to get by in everyday situations. The emphasis is on how language is used in communication, not on the mechanics of the language in isolation, although there is plenty of that as well.

This part is made up of eight chapters. Each chapter revolves around a specific communication function and is subdivided into three themes. Each theme is constructed as follows:

- Two dialogues illustrate typical conversations related to the theme. English glosses are provided to enhance comprehension. This conversational material will help you to grasp how typical conversations are carried out in Italian. Reading these dialogues will enhance your conversation skills.
- Each dialogue is followed by a summary of the new vocabulary that it contains and a *Memory* section that allows you to check if you have learned important new words and structures.
- A *Language Notes* section explains and expands upon the grammatical and communicative material that the dialogue introduces.
- At the end of each thematic section there is an exercise section. This contains two types of activities—one that allows you to practice the new language forms and one that allows you to try out your conversation skills.

Here is a list of all abbreviations used:

-a = corresponding feminine ending
ess. = conjugated with **essere** in compound tenses

f. = feminine
fam. = familiar, informal
inv. = invariable
isc. = conjugated with **isc** in present tenses
m. = masculine
pl. = plural
pol. = polite, formal
sing. = singular

Pronunciation guide

Following are basic guidelines for pronouncing Italian words. Use these as you work your way through the book.

Vowels

The Italian vowels are **a**, **e**, **i**, **o**, **u**. They are pronounced as follows:

LETTERS	PRONUNCIATION	AS IN . . .	EXAMPLES	MEANINGS
a	ah	*bah*	**ma**	*but*
e	eh	*bet*	**bene**	*well*
i	eeh	*beet*	**mio**	*my*
o	oh	*bought*	**ora**	*hour*
u	ooh	*boot*	**uno**	*one*

When **i** and **u** come before or after another vowel (in the same syllable), they are pronounced instead as follows:

LETTERS	PRONUNCIATION	AS IN . . .	EXAMPLES	MEANINGS
i	y	*yes*	**ieri**	*yesterday*
i	y	*say*	**sai**	*you know*
u	w	*way*	**uomo**	*man*
u	w	*cow*	**autista**	*driver*

Single consonants

Italian has both single and double consonants. Single consonants are pronounced as follows:

LETTERS	PRONUNCIATION	AS IN . . .	EXAMPLES	MEANING
b	b	*bat*	**bello**	*beautiful*
c (before a, o, u)	k	*cat*	**come**	*how*
ch (before e, i)			**chi**	*who*
c (before e, i)	ch	*chin*	**cinema**	*cinema*
ci (before a, o, u)			**ciao**	*hi/bye*
d	d	*dip*	**dentro**	*inside*
f	f	*fair*	**fare**	*to do*

continued

LETTERS	PRONUNCIATION	AS IN ...	EXAMPLES	MEANING
g (before a, o, u)	g	*gas*	**gomma**	*tire*
gh (before e, i)			**paghi**	*you pay*
g (before e, i)	j	*gym*	**gente**	*people*
gi (before a, o, u)			**giacca**	*jacket*
gli	ly	*million*	**figlio**	*son*
gn	ny	*canyon*	**gnocchi**	*dumplings*
l	l	*love*	**latte**	*milk*
m	m	*man*	**madre**	*mother*
n	n	*name*	**nome**	*name*
p	p	*pen*	**pane**	*bread*
q	k(w)	*quick*	**qui**	*here*
r	r	*Brrrrr . . .*	**rosso**	*red*
s (unvoiced)	s	*sip*	**suo**	*his/her*
		spin	**studente**	*student*
s (voiced)	z	*zip*	**casa**	*house*
			sbaglio	*mistake*
sc (before a, o, u)	sk	*skill*	**scuola**	*school*
sch (before e, i)			**fresche**	*fresh (pl.)*
sc (before e, i)	sh	*shave*	**ascensore**	*elevator*
sci (before a, o, u)			**piscina**	*pool*
t	t	*tent*	**tanto**	*a lot*
v	v	*vine*	**vero**	*true*
z	ts or ds	*cats or lads*	**zio**	*uncle*

Double consonants

Double consonants are not pronounced as such in English, even though there are double letters in the language. The Italian double consonants last approximately twice as long as corresponding single ones and are pronounced with more intensity. They occur between vowels or between a vowel and **l** or **r**.

EXAMPLES	MEANINGS
arrivederci	*good-bye*
bello	*beautiful*
caffè	*coffee*
camminare	*to walk*
formaggio	*cheese*
nonno	*grandfather*
occhio	*eye*

Spelling peculiarities

Generally, there is a one-to-one correspondence between a sound and the letter (or letters) used to represent it. The main exceptions are as follows:

- Words with a stressed final vowel are written with an accent mark on the vowel. The mark is usually grave. But in some, especially those ending in **-ché**, the acute accent mark may be used.

EXAMPLES	MEANINGS
caffè	*coffee*
città	*city*
perché	*why, because*
ventitré	*twenty-three*

- The letter **h** is used only in several present indicative tense forms of the verb **avere** *to have*. It is always silent.

EXAMPLES	MEANINGS
io ho	*I have*
tu hai	*you have* (fam.)
Lei ha	*you have* (pol.)
lui/lei ha	*he/she has*
loro hanno	*they have*

- As in English, capital letters are used at the beginning of sentences and to write proper nouns (names of people, countries, etc.). However, there are differences: the pronoun **io** (*I*), titles, months of the year, days of the week, and adjectives and nouns referring to languages and nationalities are not capitalized.

EXAMPLES	MEANINGS
dottore	*Dr.*
professore	*Professor*
signora	*Ms., Mrs.*
cinese	*Chinese*
inglese	*English*
italiano	*Italian*
gennaio	*January*
settembre	*September*
ottobre	*October*
lunedì	*Monday*
martedì	*Tuesday*

- On the other hand, the polite pronoun **Lei** (*you*), and other corresponding polite forms, are capitalized.

Making contact

Knowing how to make contact and to take leave of people is a vital conversational skill, as is knowing how to introduce people to each other and to ask for assistance. These are the topics of Italian conversation covered in this chapter.

Hellos and good-byes

Dialogo

Here's how two people, a man (**uomo**) and a woman (**donna**), might greet and take leave of each other formally:

Uomo:	Buongiorno, signora Verdi.	*Good morning, Mrs. Verdi.*
Donna:	Buongiorno, signor Marchi.	*Good morning, Mr. Marchi.*
Uomo:	Come va?	*How's it going?*
Donna:	Bene, grazie. E Lei?	*Well, thanks. And you?*
Uomo:	Molto bene. Ci vediamo domani.	*Very well. See you tomorrow.*
Donna:	Sì, arrivederLa. A domani.	*Yes, good-bye. Till tomorrow.*

NEW VOCABULARY

a domani	see you tomorrow		**e**	and
arrivederLa	good-bye (*pol.*)		**grazie**	thank you
bene	well		**Lei**	you (*pol.*)
buongiorno	good morning, good day, hello		**molto**	very
ci vediamo	see you		**sì**	yes
come	how		**signora**	Mrs., madam, lady
Come va?	How's it going?		**signore**	Mr., sir, gentleman
domani	tomorrow		**uomo**	man
donna	woman			

Memory practice

After each new dialogue you will be given the opportunity to memorize important new forms with a simple fill-in-the-blanks exercise. Do this exercise from memory, and then go back and check your answers.

_____Buongiorno_____ , signora Verdi.
Buongiorno, _____signor_____ Marchi.
Come va?
Bene, _____Grazie_____ . E Lei?
_____Molto_____ bene. Ci vediamo
_____A domani.____ .
Sì, _____Ci vediamo_____ . A domani.

Language notes

The expression **buongiorno** is used in the *morning* to greet and take leave of people, especially if they are on formal terms. In the *afternoon*, Italians now use **buon pomeriggio** and in the *evening*, **buonasera**. *Good night* is **buonanotte**. These can also be written as separate words: **buon giorno**, **buona sera**, **buona notte**.

Note that the complete form for *Mr.* or *sir* is **signore**. Before a name, however, the **-e** is dropped: **signor Marchi**. This applies to all masculine titles ending in **-e**. Note as well that the title is not capitalized, unless it is the first word in a sentence. Here are two other common titles used in conversations. Note that there is a different form for each gender.

MASCULINE TITLES	FEMININE TITLES
Professor	*Professor*
professore	professoressa
professor Bruni	professoressa Bruni
Dr.	*Dr.*
dottore	dottoressa
dottor Santucci	dottoressa Santucci

Most other titles are the same in the masculine and femininte: **avvocato** *lawyer* for example is used before a masculine or feminine name: **Buongiorno, avvocato Verdi** (a female) and **Buongiorno, avvocato Marchi** (a male).

Dialogo

Here's how two friends—Giovanni, a young man, and Franca, a young woman—might greet and take leave of each other informally:

GIOVANNI:	Ciao, Franca!	*Hi, Franca!*
FRANCA:	Ah! Ciao, Giovanni!	*Ah! Hi, John!*
GIOVANNI:	Come stai?	*How are you?*
FRANCA:	Non c'è male. E tu?	*Not bad. And you?*
GIOVANNI:	Benissimo, grazie!	*Very well, thanks!*
FRANCA:	Ci vediamo presto, va bene?	*See you soon, OK?*
GIOVANNI:	Certo. A presto. Ciao!	*Certainly. See you soon. Bye!*
FRANCA:	Ciao!	*Bye!*

a presto	see you soon	**non**	not
benissimo	very well	**non c'è male**	not bad
certo	certainly, of course	**presto**	soon, early
ciao	hi, bye (*fam.*)	**stare**	to stay, to be
Come stai?	How are you? (*fam.*)	**tu**	you (*fam.*)
male	bad		

Memory practice

Fill in the blanks with the appropriate words and expressions. Do this from memory, and then go back and check your answers.

_____Ciao_____ , Franca!

Ah! Ciao, Giovanni!

Come _____stai_____ ?

Non c'è male. E

_____tu_____ ?

_____benissimo_____ , grazie!

Language notes

Italians address family, friends, children, pets, and anyone with whom they are on a first-name basis with familiar forms. Otherwise they would use formal or polite forms. Here are the relevant greeting forms according to level of formality:

FORMAL	INFORMAL
buongiorno, buon pomeriggio, buonasera	ciao [*the formal forms can also be used for informal speech if one is referring to actual time of day*]
Lei [*Note that it is always capitalized*]	tu
Come sta?	Come stai?
arrivederLa	ciao, arrivederci

Note the different pronouns (**Lei, tu**) and different verb forms (**sta, stai**) that reflect differences in formality.

ArrivederLa (written in this way!) is the polite form and **Arrivederci** the familiar one. **Ciao** can be used instead of **arrivederci**. And, as you have seen, **ciao** can mean both *hi* and *bye*.

Adding on -**issimo** to some words to mean *very* is common in Italian: **benissimo** (*very well*), **malissimo** (*very bad*).

Give the corresponding English or Italian word or expression.

ENGLISH	ITALIAN
1. man	*bene*
2. *Uomo*	signor Verdi
3. yes	*MR Verdi*
4. *Si*	professoressa Marchi
5. soon	*Proffesor Marchi*
6. *Presto*	dottor Bruni
7. and	*Doctor Bruni*
8. *e*	professor Santucci
9. you (*pol.*)	*Professor*
10. *Lei*	signora Marchi
11. woman	_____
12. *donna*	dottoressa Santucci
13. of course	*Doctor*
14. *Certo*	come
15. tomorrow	_____
16. *domani*	grazie
17. you (*fam.*)	*Thanks*
18. *tu*	molto
19. well	*Very*

Carry out the following conversation tasks.

20. Greet someone formally in the morning.
    Buongiorno

21. Say good afternoon to someone politely.
    _____

22. How would you say "See you tomorrow"?
    Ci

23. Say good-bye to someone formally.
    ArrivederLa

24. Say good-bye to a good friend.

Ciao

25. Ask someone "How's it going?"

Come va / Come

26. Say hi to a friend.

Ciao

27. Greet Mrs. Verdi in the morning.

Buongiorno signorina Verdi

28. Greet Mr. Marchi in the evening.

Buonasera Mr Marchi

29. Greet Professor Santucci (a female) in the afternoon.

30. Greet your friend Marcello.

Ciao Marcello

31. Say good night.

Buonasera

Introductions

Dialogo

Here's how two strangers might introduce themselves to each other formally:

UOMO: Buonasera. Mi presento. Mi chiamo Tom Smith.	*Good evening. Allow me to introduce myself. My name is Tom Smith.*
DONNA: Molto lieta! Mi presento anch'io. Mi chiamo Maria Morelli.	*Delighted! Allow me also to introduce myself. My name is Maria Morelli.*
UOMO: Molto lieto!	*Delighted!*
DONNA: Lei è americano?	*Are you American?*
UOMO: Sì, sono americano. E Lei?	*Yes, I'm American. And you?*
DONNA: Io sono italiana.	*I'm Italian.*
UOMO: Piacere di fare la Sua conoscenza.	*A pleasure to make your acquaintance.*
DONNA: Anch'io.	*Me too.*

NEW VOCABULARY

americano	American	**lieto**	delighted
anche (anche io *or* **anch'io)**	also, too	**mi chiamo**	my name is

essere	to be	**mi presento**	let me introduce myself
io	I	**piacere di fare la Sua conoscenza**	a pleasure to make your acquaintance
italiano	Italian		

Memory practice

Fill in the blanks with the appropriate words and expressions. Do this from memory, and then go back and check your answers.

Buonasera. Mi presento. Mi ___chiamo___ Tom Smith.

Molto ___lieta___! Mi presento anch'io. Mi chiamo Maria Morelli.

___Molto___ lieto!

Lei è ___Americano___?

Sì, sono americano. E Lei?

Io sono ___Italiano___.

___Piacere___ di fare la Sua conoscenza.

Anch'io.

Language notes

You will have noticed that the ending on some words (nouns and adjectives) changes if the speaker (or the one spoken about) is a male or a female. If you are an American male you are **americano**; if you are an American female, then you are **americana**. More technically, regular forms ending in **-o** are masculine; those ending in **-a** are feminine. Note that there is no capitalization in Italian of nationalities (unless the word starts a sentence). Some nouns and adjectives end in **-e** (as you have seen). These may be either masculine or feminine.

MASCULINE	FEMININE
americano	americana
italiano	italiana
lieto	lieta
professore	professoressa
signore	signora
dottore	dottoressa

The expression **mi chiamo** (*My name is*) translates literally as *I call myself*.

In this and previous dialogues, you have encountered a very important verb: **essere** (*to be*). Learn the forms below, which make up its conjugation in the present indicative. Note also that the pronouns (*I*, *you*, *he*, and so on) are optional in Italian when it is clear who the subject is: **io sono = sono**, **tu sei = sei**, and so on. Note also that **io** is not capitalized, unless it is the first word in a sentence.

(io) sono	*I am*
(tu) sei	*you are* (fam.)
(Lei) è	*you are* (pol.)
(lui) è	*he is*

(lei) è	*she is*
(noi) siamo	*we are*
(voi) siete	*you are* (pl.)
(loro) sono	*they are*

Dialogo

Here's how two young people might introduce themselves using an informal style of speech:

CLAUDIA: Come ti chiami?	*What's your name?*
BILL: Mi chiamo Bill Jones.	*My name is Bill Jones.*
CLAUDIA: Piacere!	*A pleasure!*
BILL: E tu?	*And you?*
CLAUDIA: Mi chiamo Claudia Santucci.	*My name is Claudia Santucci.*
BILL: Piacere di conoscerti! Sei italiana?	*A pleasure to know you! Are you Italian?*
CLAUDIA: Sì. E tu sei americano, vero?	*Yes. And you are American, right?*
BILL: Sì, sono americano.	*Yes, I'm American.*
CLAUDIA: Devo andare. A presto.	*I have to go. See you soon.*
BILL: Ciao, ciao.	*Bye-bye.*

NEW VOCABULARY

Come ti chiami?	What's your name?	**devo andare**	*I have to go*
piacere	a pleasure	**vero**	*true, right*
piacere di conoscerti (koh-nóh-sher-tee)	a pleasure to know you		

Memory practice

Fill in the blanks with the appropriate words and expressions. Do this from memory, and then go back and check your answers.

Come ti _chiami_ ?

Mi _chiamo_ Bill Jones.

Piacere!

E tu?

Mi chiamo Claudia Santucci.

Piacere di conoscerti! Sei italiana?

Sì. E tu sei americano, vero?

Sì, _sono_ americano.

Devo _andare_ . A presto.

Ciao, ciao.

Language notes

Note a few more differences between formal and informal speech.

FORMAL	INFORMAL
Lei è (*you are*)	tu sei (*you are*)
Come si chiama (Lei)? (*What's your name?*)	Come ti chiami (tu)? (*What's your name?*)

ESERCIZIO
1·2

Circle the correct word or expression.

1. Mi presento. Mi chiamo Maria Rossini.

    Molto lieto.

    Anch'io.

2. E io mi chiamo Gina Dorelli.

    A presto.

    Piacere di fare la Sua conoscenza.

3. Maria è (*Maria is*) _____ .

    italiano

    italiana

4. Tom è _____ .

    americano

    americana

5. Io _____ americana.

    sono

    è

6. Anche tu _____ italiana, vero?

    siete

    sei

7. Anche Marco _____ italiano, vero?

    siamo

    è

Carry out the following conversation tasks.

8. Ask a stranger what his/her name is, using formal speech.

    Come si chiama _____

9. Ask a little boy what his name is, using informal speech.

Come ti chiami

10. Tell someone informally that you are glad to make his/her acquaintance.

Piacere

11. Say that you (yourself) are Italian.

Io sono Italiana

12. Say that you have to go.

A questo

Assistance

Dialogo

Here's how someone might ask for assistance or directions in finding a place:

SIGNORINA:	Scusi, mi può aiutare?	*Excuse me, can you help me?*
SIGNORE:	Certo, signorina!	*Of course, Miss!*
SIGNORINA:	Dov'è via Nazionale?	*Where is National Street?*
SIGNORE:	Qui, a destra. È a due isolati.	*Here, to the right. It's two blocks away.*
SIGNORINA:	Grazie.	*Thank you.*
SIGNORE:	Non c'è problema!	*No problem!*

NEW VOCABULARY

a	at, to		**non**	not
a destra	to the right		**non c'è problema**	no problem
dove	where		**qui**	here
due	two		**scusi**	excuse me (*pol.*)
isolato	block		**signorina**	Miss, Ms.
mi può aiutare	can you help me (*pol.*)		**via**	street

Memory practice

Fill in the blanks with the appropriate words and expressions. Do this from memory, and then go back and check your answers.

_____Scusi_____ , mi può aiutare?

Certo, _____Signorina_____ !

_____Dove_____ è via Nazionale?

Qui, a _____destra_____ . È a due isolati.

Grazie.

Non c'è _____problema_____ !

Language notes

Here are a few more differences between formal and informal speech:

FORMAL	INFORMAL
scusi	scusa
mi può aiutare	mi puoi aiutare

When asking for assistance, you will need to know the following question words.

che (cosa)	*what*
chi	*who*
come	*how*
dove	*where*
perché	*why*
Che (cosa) è?	*What is it?*
Chi è?	*Who is it?*
Come stai?	*How are you?*
Dov'è via Nazionale?	*Where's National Street?*
Perché non mi puoi aiutare?	*Why can't you help me?*

To ask a question that requires a yes/no response, all you have to do is put a question mark at the end (or raise your tone of voice if speaking). More commonly, do the same but put the subject at the end.

STATEMENT	QUESTION
Via Nazionale è qui a destra.	È qui a destra, via Nazionale?
National Street is here to the right.	*Is National Street here to the right?*
Maria è italiana.	È italiana, Maria?
Maria is Italian.	*Is Maria Italian?*

To make a verb negative, just put **non** before the verb.

AFFIRMATIVE	NEGATIVE
Via Nazionale è qui a destra.	Via Nazionale **non** è qui a destra.
National Street is here to the right.	*National Street is not here to the right.*
Maria è italiana.	Maria **non** è italiana.
Maria is Italian.	*Maria is not Italian.*

Note the following:

a destra	*to the right*	a sinistra	*to the left*

Finally, note that **isolati** (*blocks*) is the plural of **isolato** (*block*). In general, if the noun or adjective ends in **-o**, its plural form is obtained by changing it to **-i**.

SINGULAR	PLURAL
isolato (*block*)	isolati (*blocks*)
italiano (*Italian*)	italiani (*Italians*)
americano (*American*)	americani (*Americans*)
lieto (*delighted*)	lieti (*delighted*)

There are exceptions, of course. One of these is **uomo** (*man*) whose plural form is **uomini** (*men*).

Dialogo

Here's how one might ask for help in a bookstore:

CLIENTE:	Ho bisogno di un libro da leggere.	*I need a book to read.*
COMMESSO:	Le piacciono i romanzi d'avventura?	*Do you like adventure novels?*
CLIENTE:	Sì, molto. Perché?	*Yes, a lot. Why?*
COMMESSO:	Perché abbiamo un nuovo romanzo.	*Because we have a new novel.*
CLIENTE:	Dov'è?	*Where is it?*
COMMESSO:	In vetrina. Ecco il romanzo.	*In the window. Here's the novel.*
CLIENTE:	Mi piace molto.	*I like it a lot.*
COMMESSO:	Va bene.	*OK.*

NEW VOCABULARY

avventura	adventure	**molto**	a lot
cliente	customer	**nuovo**	new
commesso (-a)	clerk	**perché**	because
da leggere (léh-jjeh-reh)	to read	**piacere**	to like, to be pleasing to
di	of	**prendere (préhn-deh-reh)**	to take
ecco	here is	**romanzo**	novel
ho bisogno di	I need (I have need of)	**va bene**	OK
in	in	**vetrina**	store window
libro	book		

Memory practice

Fill in the blanks with the appropriate words and expressions. Do this from memory, and then go back and check your answers.

Ho ___bisogno___ di un libro da leggere.

Le ___piacciono___ i romanzi d'avventura?

Sì, molto. Perché?

___Perché___ abbiamo un nuovo romanzo.

Dov'è?

In vetrina. ___Ecco___ il romanzo.

Mi ___piace___ molto.

Va bene.

Language notes

In this dialogue you have come across another key verb: **avere** (*to have*). Here are its present indicative forms. Note that you do not pronounce the **h**. It is silent, as it is in English words such as *hour* and *honor*.

(io) ho	*I have*
(tu) hai	*you have* (fam.)
(Lei) ha	*you have* (pol.)
(lui) ha	*he has*
(lei) ha	*she has*
(noi) abbiamo	*we have*
(voi) avete	*you have* (pl.)
(loro) hanno	*they have*

In this dialogue, you have also come across your first articles in Italian. You will learn about them in bits and pieces. In front of a masculine noun beginning with a consonant (except **z** and **s** plus a consonant) or a vowel, the form for the *indefinite* article is **un**.

un libro	*a book*	un romanzo	*a novel*
un uomo	*a man*	un italiano	*an Italian*
un signore	*a gentleman*	un isolato	*a block*

The corresponding masculine *definite* article form is **il**. But it occurs only before consonants, other than **z** or **s** plus consonant. It does not occur before a vowel.

il libro	*the book*
il signore	*the gentleman*
il romanzo	*the novel*

The plural of **il** is **i**. And, as you know, to make a masculine noun plural, just change the **-o** (and **-e** for that matter) to **-i**.

i libri	*the books*
i signori	*the gentlemen*
i romanzi	*the novels*

For the time being, note that to say *I like*, you must use **mi piace** followed by a singular noun and **mi piacciono** (pyáh-choh-noh) followed by a plural noun.

SINGULAR	PLURAL
Mi piace il romanzo.	Mi piacciono i romanzi.
I like the novel.	*I like the novels.*
Mi piace il libro.	Mi piacciono i libri.
I like the book.	*I like the books.*

Finally, note that **perché** means both *why* and *because*.

ESERCIZIO 1·3

Do the following. Ask . . .

1. what it is

   Cosa   e

2. who it is

   Chi   e

3. where the (male) clerk is

   Dov   e   Commesso

4. your friend why he cannot help you

   _____

Make each noun plural.

5. isolato   _isoluti_

6. libro   _libri_

7. italiano   _italiani_

8. romanzo   _romanzi_

9. uomo (*be careful!*)   _uomoini_

10. dottore   _dottori_

11. professore   _jr_

Give the correct form of **avere**.

12. io   _ho_

13. tu   _hai_

14. il commesso   _ha_

15. noi   _abbiumo_

16. voi   _avete_

17. i commessi   _____

Say that you like the following.

EXAMPLE: the book

   Mi piace il libro.

18. the new novel

   mi piace il nouvo romanzo

19. the books   _A libri_

20. the (male) doctor _____ il dottore _____

21. the (male) professors

_____ i professori _____

Carry out the following conversation tasks.

22. Say that you need a new book to read.

_____

23. Ask someone politely if he/she likes adventure novels.

_____

24. Say that the book is in the store window.

_____

25. Say "Here is an adventure novel."

_____

26. Say "OK."

_____

27. Excuse yourself and ask a clerk if he/she can help you.

_____

28. Now do the same, but this time you are speaking to a friend.

_____

29. Say that National Street is here to the left, not to the right.

_____

30. Say "Of course, Miss."

_____

31. Say that it's two blocks away.

_____

32. Say "no problem."

_____

33. Say that Maria is not American.

_____

34. Ask if Maria is Italian.

_____

Numbers, time, dates

Knowing how to use numbers, how to tell the time, and how to ask for the date, among other basic notions, constitutes a critical conversational skill, wouldn't you agree? That's what this chapter is all about.

Numbers

Dialogo

Here's how someone might order at a café (**un bar**), using numerical concepts:

CLIENTE:	Vorrei un caffè espresso, per favore.	*I would like an espresso coffee, please.*
BARISTA:	Subito. Altro?	*Right away. Anything else?*
CLIENTE:	Sì, anche due o tre cornetti. Ho molta fame.	*Yes, also two or three croissants. I am very hungry.*
BARISTA:	Va bene. Altro?	*OK. Anything else?*
CLIENTE:	Sì, vorrei comprare dieci o undici panini da portare via. C'è una festa stasera a casa mia. Grazie.	*Yes, I would like to buy ten or eleven buns to take out. There's a party tonight at my house. Thanks.*
BARISTA:	Prego.	*You're welcome.*

NEW VOCABULARY

a casa mia	at my house	**da portare via**	to take out
altro	anything else, other	**espresso**	espresso
avere fame	to be hungry	**esserci**	to be there
bar	coffee place, bar	**festa**	party
barista	bartender	**panino**	bun sandwich
caffè	coffee	**per favore**	please
casa	house	**prego**	you're welcome
cliente	customer	**stasera**	tonight
comprare	to buy	**subito (sóoh-beeh-toh)**	right away
cornetto	croissant	**vorrei**	I would like

Memory practice

Fill in the blanks with the appropriate words and expressions. Do this from memory, and then go back and check your answers.

_____Vorrei_____ un caffè espresso, per favore.

Subito. _____altro_____ ?

Sì, anche due o tre cornetti. Ho _____Molta_____ fame.

Va bene. Altro?

Sì, vorrei _____Comprare_____ dieci o undici panini da portare via. C'è una

_____festa_____ stasera a casa mia. Grazie.

Prego.

Language notes

The form **c'è** is from the verb **esserci**, which is really **essere** (as you know from the previous chapter), and **ci** (*there, here*). It is used to say *there/here is* (**c'è**) and *there/here are* (**ci sono**).

SINGULAR	PLURAL
C'è un bar qui.	**Ci sono** due bar qui.
There is a bar here.	*There are two bars here.*
Non **c'è** il barista.	Non **ci sono** i baristi.
The bartender is not here.	*The bartenders are not here.*

If you wish to point to something or someone, then **ecco** (which you came across in the previous chapter) is to be used.

C'è il barista?	Sì, **ecco** il barista.
Is the bartender here/there?	*Yes, there/here is the bartender.* (pointing him out)

Note that **caffè** ends with an accented vowel. This is rare in Italian. It means that the voice stress falls on that vowel. Also, note that the noun is masculine: **il caffè** (*the coffee*), **un caffè** (*a coffee*).

As used above, **molto** is an adjective. It agrees with the noun. This means that the ending changes according to the gender of the noun. For now, just notice that the masculine form of the adjective ends in **-o**, the feminine in **-a**. Note as well that the feminine form of the indefinite article is **una**, which is used before any consonant but not a vowel.

MASCULINE	FEMININE
molto caffè	molta fame
a lot of coffee	*very hungry* (= literally, *a lot of hunger*)
un nuovo libro	una nuova casa
a new book	*a new house*

The expression **avere fame** means, literally, "to have hunger": **Ho fame** = *I am hungry* ("I have hunger").

There were a few numbers used in the previous dialogue. Here are the first ten numbers in Italian:

1 uno	6 sei
2 due	7 sette
3 tre	8 otto
4 quattro	9 nove
5 cinque	10 dieci

Dialogo

Here's what someone might say when buying commemorative stamps, using numbers:

CLIENTE: Vorrei ventidue francobolli commemorativi, per favore.

I would like twenty-two commemorative stamps.

COMMESSA: Ecco i francobolli.

Here are the stamps.

CLIENTE: Quanto costano?

How much do they cost?

COMMESSA: Ogni francobollo costa trentacinque euro.

Each stamp costs 35 euros.

CLIENTE: Allora, ne prendo solo dieci.

Then, I'll take only ten of them.

COMMESSA: Belli, no?

Beautiful, aren't they?

CLIENTE: Molto.

Very.

NEW VOCABULARY

allora	then, thus	**ne prendo**	I'll take . . . of them
bello	beautiful	**no**	no
commemorativo	commemorative	**ogni**	each, every
costare	to cost	**quanto**	how much
euro	euro	**solo**	only
francobollo	stamp		

Memory practice

Fill in the blanks with the appropriate words and expressions. Do this from memory, and then go back and check your answers.

Vorrei ventidue francobolli _Commemorative_ , per favore.

Ecco i _francobolli_ .

Quanto costano?

Ogni francobollo _costa_ trentacinque euro.

Allora, ne prendo _solo_ dieci.

Belli , no?

Molto.

Language notes

The numbers from 11 to 20 are as follows:

11 undici (óohn-dee-cheeh)	16 sedici (séh-deeh-cheeh)
12 dodici (dóh-deeh-cheeh)	17 diciassette (deeh-chahs-séh-teh)
13 tredici (tréh-deeh-cheeh)	18 diciotto (deeh-chóht-toh)
14 quattordici (kwáh-tohr-deeh-cheeh)	19 diciannove (deeh-chah-nóh-veh)
15 quindici (kwéehn-deeh-cheeh)	20 venti

Counting from twenty on is systematic. Just add on the numbers from one to ten to the twenties, thirties, etc., numerical part. If two vowels are involved in the combination, drop the first vowel. Here are the numbers from 21 to 29 fully constructed:

21 = venti + uno = ventuno (*Note the dropped vowel*)
22 = venti + due = ventidue
23 = venti + tre = ventitré (*Note the accent*)
24 = venti + quattro = ventiquattro
25 = venti + cinque = venticinque
26 = venti + sei = ventisei
27 = venti + sette = ventisette
28 = venti + otto = ventotto (*Note the dropped vowel*)
29 = venti + nove = ventinove

Here are the categories from 30 on:

30 trenta	200 duecento
40 quaranta	300 trecento
50 cinquanta	. . .
60 sessanta	1000 mille
70 settanta	2000 duemila (*Note the **mila** form in the plural*)
80 ottanta	3000 tremila
90 novanta	1.000.000 un milione
100 cento	2.000.000 due milioni

Note that the verb **costare** has a singular form, **costa** (*it costs*), and a plural form, **costano** (kóhs-tah-noh) (*they cost*).

SINGULAR	PLURAL
Il libro costa 30 euro.	I libri costano 300 euro.
The book costs 30 euros.	*The books cost 300 euros.*
Il panino costa molto.	I francobolli costano molto.
The bun costs a lot.	*The stamps cost a lot.*

Note that **molto** has various functions. Just remember that as an adjective it agrees with the noun, as you have seen.

The plural form **belli** is derived from the singular **bello** (*beautiful, handsome*). The feminine forms are **bella** (singular) and **belle** (plural). Note that the adjective follows the noun. This is a general principle, even though some adjectives can come before, as you will discover.

SINGULAR	PLURAL
un uomo bello	due uomini belli
a handsome man	*two handsome men*
una donna bella	due donne belle
a beautiful woman	*two beautiful women*

Finally, note that **euro** does not change in the plural: **un euro** (*a euro*), **due euro** (*two euros*).

ESERCIZIO
2·1

Make the entire phrase plural.

EXAMPLE: il caffè

i caffè (the coffees)

SINGULAR	PLURAL
1. il francobollo	i francobolli
2. il cornetto	i cornetti
3. il libro	i libri
4. il panino	i panini
5. il romanzo	i romanzi

How do you say . . . ?

6. a house	una casa
7. a new house	una nuova casa
8. a beautiful woman	una bella donna
9. two euros	due euro
10. three buns	tre panini
11. four novels	quattro romanzi
12. five croissants	cinque cornetti
13. six espressos	sei espresi
14. seven men	sette uomini
15. eight beautiful books	otto bella libri — otto libri belli
16. nine euros	nove euros
17. ten commemorative stamps	dieci commem
18. thirteen handsome men	tredici uomini belli
19. fourteen beautiful women	
20. fifteen beautiful houses	

21. sixteen, seventeen, eighteen   _Seidici diciew_

22. nineteen, thirty-eight   _____

23. two hundred and fifty-three   _____

24. nine hundred and sixty-two   _____

25. two thousand and eighty   _____

Carry out the following conversation tasks.

26. Say you would like an espresso coffee, please.

    Vorrei un caffe espresso per favore

27. Ask someone if they would like something else.

    Altro

28. Say that you would like two or three croissants right away.

    Vorrie due o tre panini

29. Say that you are very hungry.

    Io sono fame

30. Say, OK, you would like to buy two buns to take out.

    _____

31. Say that there is a party at your house tonight.

    _____

32. Give an appropriate answer when someone says "**Grazie.**"

    _____

33. Say that there is a new café-bar on (**in**) National Street.

    _____

34. Say that there are no new books in the store window.

    _____

35. Point to an espresso and indicate that it is there.

    _____

36. Ask how much the stamps cost.

    _____

37. Say that each bun costs eleven euros.

    _____

38. Say: "Then, I'll take only twelve of them."

    _____

Time

Dialogo

The following dialogue illustrates how one might ask what the time is:

MARIA: Giovanni, che ore sono?	*Giovanni, what time is it?*
GIOVANNI: È l'una e mezzo. No, è l'una e quarantacinque.	*It's half past one. No, it's one forty-five.*
MARIA: È tardi.	*It's late.*
GIOVANNI: Perché?	*Why?*
MARIA: Abbiamo un appuntamento col nostro professore.	*We have an appointment with our professor.*
GIOVANNI: A che ora?	*At what time?*
MARIA: Alle due.	*At two.*
GIOVANNI: Precise?	*Exactly?*
MARIA: Sì, alle due in punto.	*Yes, at two on the dot.*
GIOVANNI: Andiamo!	*Let's go!*

NEW VOCABULARY

andiamo	let's go	**mezzo**	half
appuntamento	appointment, date	**nostro**	our
Che ore sono?	What time is it?	**ora**	hour, time
con	with	**preciso**	precise (precisely)
in punto	on the dot	**tardi**	late

Memory practice

Fill in the blanks with the appropriate words and expressions. Do this from memory, and then go back and check your answers.

Giovanni, che ___ore___ sono?

È l'una e ___mezzo___. No, è ___l'una___ e quarantacinque.

È ___tardi___.

Perché?

Abbiamo un ___appuntamento___ col nostro professore.

A che ___ora___?

___Alle___ due.

Precise?

Sì, alle due in ___punto___.

Andiamo!

Language notes

To ask for the time you can use either of the following formulas:

Che ora è? (literally: *What hour is it?*)   Che ore sono? (literally: *What hours are they?*)

To tell time, colloquially, all you have to do is count the hours, as in English, and add on the minutes. For one o'clock the verb is singular (è), while for the other hours it is plural (sono). Here are a few examples:

È l'una.	*It's one o'clock.*
Sono le due e dieci.	*It's two ten.*
Sono le cinque e venti.	*It's five twenty.*

Note that the form **alle** is a contracted form: **a + le = alle**. For one o'clock it is **a + l' = all'**. By the way, you have just come across another form of the definite article, namely, **l'**, which is used before nouns beginning with vowels: **l'appuntamento** (*the appointment*), **l'ora** (*the hour*), **l'avventura** (*the adventure*).

All'una.	*At one o'clock.*
Alle due e dieci.	*At two ten.*
Alle cinque e venti.	*At five twenty.*

Note that **un quarto** means *a quarter*, and **mezzo** *half*. Note also that to distinguish the morning hours from the afternoon and evening ones, you can use **della mattina** (*in the morning*), **del pomeriggio** (*in the afternoon*), and **della sera** (*in the evening*), respectively. Note that the forms **del** and **della** are contractions: **d + il = del, di + la = della**.

Sono le sette e un quarto.	*It's a quarter past seven.*
Alle undici e mezzo.	*At half past eleven.*
Sono le otto e quaranta della mattina.	*It's eight forty a.m.*
Alle nove e venticinque della sera.	*At nine twenty-five p.m.*
Sono le tre e tredici del pomeriggio.	*It's three thirteen in the afternoon.*

By the way, the word for *noon* is **mezzogiorno**, and the word for *midnight* is **mezzanotte**: È mezzogiorno (*It's noon*); È mezzanotte (*It's midnight*).

Notice that **preciso** is an adjective agreeing with **ore**. That's why its form is **precise**.

Finally, note that **col professore** is again a contracted form: **con + il**. You will learn more about such forms in due course.

Dialogo

Here's the kind of brief conversation someone might have with a tour guide involving times of the day and night:

GUIDA: Il giro comincia oggi alle sedici e quaranta.	*The tour begins today at four forty.*
TURISTA: Quando finisce?	*When does it end?*
GUIDA: Alle diciotto circa.	*At around six.*
TURISTA: Troppo tardi! Ho un appuntamento alle venti.	*Too late! I have an appointment at eight.*

GUIDA: C'è un giro anche domani alla stessa ora.   *There's a tour tomorrow, too, at the same time.*

TURISTA: Allora, torno domani.   *Then, I'll be back tomorrow.*

NEW VOCABULARY			
circa	around, nearly	**oggi**	today
cominciare	to begin, to start	**quando**	when
domani	tomorrow	**stesso**	same
finire	to finish	**tornare**	to return, to come back
giro	tour	**troppo**	too, too much
guida	guide	**turista**	tourist (*male or female*)

Memory practice

Fill in the blanks with the appropriate words and expressions. Do this from memory, and then go back and check your answers.

Il giro _comincia_ oggi alle sedici e quaranta.

Quando finisce?

Alle _diciotto_ circa.

Troppo tardi! Ho un appuntamento alle venti.

C'è un giro anche domani alla _stessa_ ora.

Allora, _torno_ domani.

Language notes

In Italy, the tendency is to use the twenty-four-hour clock. This is certainly the case for schedules of any kind (bus, train, TV, etc.). So, after twelve noon, you just continue counting to twenty-four.

Sono le quattordici e trenta.	*It's two thirty (afternoon).*
Sono le diciannove.	*It's seven (evening).*
Sono le ventitré e dieci.	*It's eleven ten (evening).*

Note that **alla** is a contraction of **a + la** and that **stesso** is an adjective that agrees with the noun: **alla stessa ora** (*at the same hour*).

You have encountered three verb forms in the present indicative in this dialogue—**comincia**, **finisce**, and **torno**. We will deal with verbs like **finisce** later. The other two verbs are present indicative forms of **cominciare** (*to begin*) and **tornare** (*to return, to come back*). To conjugate verbs such as these, called first-conjugation verbs ending in **-are**, drop the **-are** ending and add the following endings according to person. Here's **tornare** fully conjugated:

(io) torn**o**	*I return, am returning*
(tu) torn**i**	*you return, are returning* (fam.)
(Lei) torn**a**	*you return, are returning* (pol.)
(lui) torn**a**	*he returns, is returning*
(lei) torn**a**	*she returns, is returning*

(noi) torn**iamo**	*we return, are returning*
(voi) torn**ate**	*you return, are returning (pl.)*
(loro) torn**ano** (tóhr-nah-noh)	*they return, are returning*

In the case of verbs like **cominciare**, which end in **-ciare**, do not keep the **-i** in front of another **-i**: **io comincio, tu cominci, Lei comincia, noi cominciamo, voi cominciate, loro cominciano.**

ESERCIZIO
2·2

Give the indicated times following the example.

EXAMPLE: 2:25 (P.M.)

Sono le due e venticinque del pomeriggio./Sono le quattordici e venticinque.

1. 1:10 (P.M.) _____

2. 3:30 (P.M.) _____

3. 4:12 (P.M.) _____

4. 9:10 (A.M.) _____

5. 10:15 (A.M.) _____

6. 7:35 (P.M.) _____

7. 9:48 (P.M.) _____

8. noon _____

9. midnight _____

Say that the indicated person is coming back or starting something at the given time. Use only official time. Follow the examples.

EXAMPLES: Maria/tornare/2:25 (P.M.)

Maria torna alle quattordici e venticinque.

Io/cominciare/6:30 (A.M.)

Io comincio alle sei e trenta/mezzo.

10. tu/tornare/7:15 (P.M.) _____

11. la donna/cominciare/8:38 (A.M.)

_____

12. noi/cominciare/10:30 (A.M.) _____

13. voi/tornare/10:20 (P.M.) _____

14. loro/cominciare/11:10 (A.M.) _____

15. io/cominciare/1:05 (P.M.) _____

Carry out the following conversation tasks.

16. Ask someone what time it is.

_____

17. Tell someone that, no, it's not late.

_____

18. Say that you have an appointment at precisely 4 P.M. with the professor.

_____

19. Say that Maria is coming back at 8 P.M. on the dot.

_____

20. Ask when something is finishing.

_____

21. Say that it is finishing at around ten in the evening.

_____

22. Say that the tour is beginning too late.

_____

23. Ask if there is a tour that (**che**) begins at (**a**) noon?

_____

24. Say that, then, you are coming back tomorrow at the same hour.

_____

Dates

Dialogo

Here's a typical conversation that might unfold between friends discussing dates and birthdays:

MARCO: Dina, quanti ne abbiamo oggi?	*Dina, what's today's date?* (literally: *How many of them* [days] *do we have?*)
DINA: Oggi è il due novembre.	*Today, it's November 2.*
MARCO: Allora, se non sbaglio, è il tuo compleanno?	*Then, if I'm not mistaken, it's your birthday?*
DINA: Sì.	*Yes.*
MARCO: Buon compleanno! Quanti anni hai?	*Happy birthday! How old are you?*
DINA: Ho ventitré anni.	*I'm twenty-three years old.*
MARCO: Sembri ancora una bambina!	*You still look like a little girl!*

ancora	still, yet	**compleanno**	birthday
anno	year	**sbagliare**	to make a mistake
avere… anni	to be…old	**se**	if
bambino/bambina	little boy/girl, child	**sembrare**	to seem
Buon compleanno!	Happy birthday!	**tuo**	your (*fam.*)

Memory practice

Fill in the blanks with the appropriate words and expressions. Do this from memory, and then go back and check your answers.

Dina, _____ ne abbiamo oggi?

Oggi è _____ due novembre.

Allora, se non _____ , è il tuo compleanno?

Sì.

_____ compleanno! Quanti anni hai?

_____ ventitré anni.

Sembri _____ una bambina!

Language notes

Note that **quanto** can function as an adjective, agreeing with the noun of course. We will discuss adjectives more completely later. Note again the difference between familiar and polite speech.

Quant**i** anni hai? (*fam.*)	*How old are you?*
Quant**i** anni ha? (*pol.*)	*How old are you?*
Quant**o** caffè prendi?	*How much coffee are you having?*
Quant**e** case nuove ci sono?	*How many new houses are there?*

Note the expression **quanti ne abbiamo**, which means, literally, *how many of them* (days) *do we have*?

Also note that to indicate age, Italian uses the expression **avere… anni**, meaning, literally, *to have . . . years.*

Ho trentadue anni.	*I am thirty-two years old.* (literally: *I have thirty-two years.*)
La bambina ha dieci anni.	*The little girl is ten years old.* (literally: *The little girl has ten years.*)

To talk about birthdays, you'll need to know the months of the year. Here they are:

gennaio	*January*	luglio	*July*
febbraio	*February*	agosto	*August*
marzo	*March*	settembre	*September*
aprile	*April*	ottobre	*October*
maggio	*May*	novembre	*November*
giugno	*June*	dicembre	*December*

Here's how to indicate dates. Note that the definite article is used and that the number precedes the month.

il quattro luglio	*July 4*
il dieci agosto	*August 10*
il tre maggio	*May 3*
il venticinque dicembre	*December 25*
l'otto marzo	*March 8*
il primo luglio	*July 1*

Be careful with the eighth day of the month. It starts with a vowel, so the appropriate form of the article is **l'otto**. Note also that for the first day of each month you must use the ordinal number **primo: il primo luglio**.

Dialogo

Here's a conversation between a husband and wife involving dates. The dialogue is a little tongue in cheek!

MARITO:	Che giorno è, cara?	*What day is it, dear?*
MOGLIE:	Lunedì.	*Monday.*
MARITO:	È terribile! Dimentico sempre tutto!	*It's terrible. I always forget everything.*
MOGLIE:	Ma ricordi in che anno sono nata, no?	*But you do remember the year in which I was born, don't you?*
MARITO:	Sì. Nel 1985 (mille novecento ottantacinque).	*Yes, in 1985.*
MOGLIE:	Meno male!	*Thank goodness!*

NEW VOCABULARY

caro (-a)	dear	**moglie**	wife
dimenticare	to forget	**ricordare**	to remember
essere nato (-a)	to be born	**sempre**	always
ma	but	**terribile**	terrible
marito	husband	**tutto**	everything
Meno male!	Thank goodness!		

Memory practice

Fill in the blanks with the appropriate words and expressions. Do this from memory, and then go back and check your answers.

Che _____ è, cara?

Lunedì.

È terribile! Dimentico _____ tutto!

Ma _____ in che anno sono _____ , no?

Sì. _____ 1985 (mille novecento ottantacinque).

_____ !

Language notes

Knowing the days of the week is essential to many conversations.

lunedì	*Monday*
martedì	*Tuesday*
mercoledì	*Wednesday*
giovedì	*Thursday*
venerdì	*Friday*
sabato (sáh-bah-toh)	*Saturday*
domenica (doh-méh-neeh-kah)	*Sunday*

Note that **nel** is a contraction of **in + il**. Note also that the year is preceded by the article or the contracted article as follows:

il mille novecento novantaquattro (1994)

nel duemila sette (*in* 2007)

Note the expression **essere nato** (-**a**), which varies according to gender.

(Io) sono nato (-a) nel 1992.	*I was born in 1992.*
Marco è nato nel 1989.	*Marco was born in 1989.*
Maria è nata nel 2000.	*Maria è nata nel duemila.*

Finally, note that in conjugating the verb **dimenticare** in the present indicative, you have to add an **h** before the **i** ending to retain the hard sound of the **c**.

(io) dimentico	*I forget*

But:

(tu) dimentichi (deeh-méhn-teeh-keeh)	*you forget*
(noi) dimentichiamo	*we forget*

ESERCIZIO
2·3

Using a complete sentence, give the following dates.

EXAMPLE: Friday, October 12

Oggi è venerdì, il dodici ottobre.

1. Monday, January 1

_____

2. Tuesday, February 8

_____

3. Wednesday, March 10

_____

4. Thursday, April 12

_____

5. Friday, May 28

_____

6. Saturday, June 23

_____

7. Sunday, July 4

_____

Put the correct form of **quanto** *in front of the following nouns.*

8. _____ anni hai, Maria?

9. _____ euro ha, signor Marchi?

10. _____ caffè prendi, Marco?

11. _____ donne ci sono qui?

Say that the following were born in the indicated year.

EXAMPLE: Sara/1998

             Sara è nata nel 1998.

12. Alessandro/1994

_____

13. la moglie/1987

_____

14. il marito/1984

_____

Carry out the following conversation tasks.

15. Ask someone what today's date is.

_____

16. Say that, if you are not mistaken, it is Maria's birthday (**il compleanno di Maria**).

_____

17. Wish someone a happy birthday.

_____

18. Ask a friend how old he/she is.

_____

19. Ask someone formally how old he/she is.

_____

20. Say that you are thirty-six years old.

_____

21. Tell a friend that he still looks like a little boy.

_____

22. Ask someone what day it is.

_____

23. Say that it's terrible.

_____

24. Say that the husband always forgets everything.

_____

25. Say "But we, too, always forget everything."

_____

26. Say that you remember the year in which someone was born.

_____

Getting information

Needless to say, knowing how to get the information you might need, to ask for directions, or simply to chat on the phone or to text someone, constitutes an important ability in everyday life. This chapter shows you how to acquire this skill in Italian.

Information

Dialogo

Here's what a conversation between two friends who haven't seen each other for a while might sound like, especially if they want to catch up on things:

FRANCA: Maria, dove abiti adesso?	*Maria, where do you live now?*
MARIA: Qui a Bari. E tu, Franca?	*Here in Bari. And you, Franca?*
FRANCA: Anch'io abito a Bari.	*I also live in Bari.*
MARIA: Dove?	*Where?*
FRANCA: In via Dante.	*On Dante Street.*
MARIA: Io abito molto vicino a te, in via Machiavelli.	*I live very near you, on Machiavelli Street.*
FRANCA: Ottimo! Qualcuno mi ha detto che sei sposata. È vero?	*Excellent! Someone told me that you are married. Is it true?*
MARIA: No. E tu?	*No. And you?*
FRANCA: Non ancora. Mi piace la libertà, per adesso!	*Not yet. I like freedom, for now.*

NEW VOCABULARY

abitare	to live, to dwell	**ottimo** (óh-teeh-moh)	excellent
adesso	now	**per**	for, through
che	that, which, who	**qualcuno**	someone
essere sposato (-a)	to be married	**vicino**	near
libertà	liberty		

Memory practice

Fill in the blanks with the appropriate words and expressions. Do this from memory, and then go back and check your answers.

Maria, dove abiti _____ ?

Qui _____ Bari. E tu, Franca?

Anch'io _____ a Bari.

Dove?

_____ via Dante.

Io abito molto _____ a te, in via Machiavelli.

Ottimo! Qualcuno mi ha detto che sei _____ . È vero?

No. E tu?

Non ancora. Mi piace la _____ , per adesso!

Language notes

To say *in + city* use **a + città**; to say *in + country*, use **in + paese**.

a Bari	*in Bari*
a Roma	*in Rome*
a Firenze	*in Florence*
in Italia	*in Italy*
in Francia	*in France*

Note that *in the United States* is **negli Stati Uniti**. The reason is that *United States* is in the plural.

In this conversation, for now just note that **ha detto** is a past tense. We will deal with this tense later on.

Note, also, that **che** is a relative pronoun in the dialogue. In this function it means *that, which, who*.

La donna **che** abita a Bari si chiama Maria.	*The name of the woman who lives in Bari is Maria.*
Il libro **che** vorrei comprare è molto bello.	*The book that I would like to buy is very beautiful.*

Dialogo

Now, here's a similar conversation to the previous one. Again, two friends are chatting and catching up on things.

VANESSA: Gina! Come stai? E come sta tuo fratello che non vedo da molto?	*Gina! How are you? And how is your brother whom I haven't seen for a while?*
GINA: Tutti bene. È sposato, sai? E ha bambini.	*All (of us) well. He's married, you know? And he has children.*
VANESSA: Che bello! Quanti?	*How nice! How many?*
GINA: Tre.	*Three.*
VANESSA: Dove abita adesso?	*Where does he live now?*
GINA: A Perugia. Ma viene spesso qui.	*In Perugia. But he comes here often.*
VANESSA: Quando verrà la prossima volta?	*When will he be coming next time?*
GINA: Non sono sicura.	*I'm not sure.*

da	from (for)	**stare**	to stay, to be
fratello	brother	**tutti**	everyone
prossimo (próhs-seeh-moh)	next	**vedere**	to see
sapere	to know	**venire**	to come
sicuro	sure	**verrà**	he/she will come
spesso	often	**volta**	time (occurrence)

Memory practice

Fill in the blanks with the appropriate words and expressions. Do this from memory, and then go back and check your answers.

Gina! Come stai? E come _____ tuo fratello che non vedo da molto?

_____ bene. È sposato, sai? E ha bambini.

Che bello! Quanti?

Tre.

Dove abita _____ ?

A Perugia. Ma _____ spesso qui.

Quando verrà la _____ volta?

Non sono _____ .

Language notes

You've come across the verb **stare** a few times already. It is used to ask how someone is, although it really means *to stay*. It is an irregular verb (like **essere** and **avere**). Here is its conjugation in the present indicative:

(io) sto	*I am, stay*
(tu) stai	*you are, stay* (fam.)
(Lei) sta	*you are, stay* (pol.)
(lui) sta	*he is, stays*
(lei) sta	*she is, stays*
(noi) stiamo	*we are, stay*
(voi) state	*you are, stay* (pl.)
(loro) stanno	*they are, stay*

The dialogue contains two other irregular verbs (that is, verbs whose forms are not derived systematically)—**venire** and **sapere**. Needless to say, they are important verbs if you want to converse in Italian. Here are their present indicative forms:

venire (*to come*)	
(io) vengo	*I come, I am coming*
(tu) vieni	*you come, you are coming* (fam.)
(Lei) viene	*you come, you are coming* (pol.)
(lui) viene	*he comes, he is coming*

(lei) viene	she comes, she is coming
(noi) veniamo	we come, we are coming
(voi) venite	you come, you are coming (pl.)
(loro) vengono (véhn-goh-noh)	they come, they are coming

sapere (to know)	
(io) so	I know
(tu) sai	you know (fam.)
(Lei) sa	you know (pol.)
(lui) sa	he knows
(lei) sa	she knows
(noi) sappiamo	we know
(voi) sapete	you know (pl.)
(loro) sanno	they know

Previously you have come across a different kind of *knowing—knowing* or *meeting someone*. The verb was **conoscere**. It is a regular verb of the second conjugation—namely, verbs ending in -**ere**. To conjugate such verbs, drop the -**ere** and add the following endings:

(io) conosc**o**	I know
(tu) consosc**i**	you know (fam.)
(Lei) conosc**e**	you know (pol.)
(lui) conosc**e**	he knows
(lei) conosc**e**	she knows
(noi) conosc**iamo**	we know
(voi) conosc**ete**	you know (pl.)
(loro) conosc**ono** (koh-nóhs-koh-noh)	they know

Note that the endings -**sci**, -**sce**, -**sciamo,** and -**scete** are pronounced with a soft "sh" sound: **conosci** = koh-nóh-shee; **conosce** = koh-nóh-sheh; **conosciamo** = koh-noh-shyámoh; **conoscete** = koh-noh-shéh-teh. Otherwise it is "sk" as in **conosco** = koh-nóhs-koh and **conoscono** = koh-nóhs-koh-noh.

In the dialogue, you have come across another second-conjugation verb—**vedere**; and in a previous chapter, **prendere** (*to take*) and **leggere** (*to read*). These are conjugated with the same endings.

It is time to summarize the system of regular nouns, before we proceed. As you know by now, if the noun ends in -**o** it is normally masculine; to form its plural, change the -**o** to -**i**. If the noun ends in -**a** it is usually feminine; to form its plural change the -**a** to -**e**.

SINGULAR	PLURAL
Masculine	
anno (*year*)	anni (*years*)
francobollo (*stamp*)	francobolli (*stamps*)
Feminine	
donna (*woman*)	donne (*women*)
casa (*house*)	case (*houses*)

Nouns ending in -**e** can be either masculine or feminine (you will have to look this up if you are unsure). In either case, the plural is formed by changing the -**e** to –**i**.

SINGULAR	PLURAL
Masculine	
professore (*professor*)	professori (*professors*)
dottore (*doctor*)	dottori (*doctors*)
Feminine	
moglie (*wife*)	mogli (*wives*)
madre (*mother*)	madri (*mothers*)

ESERCIZIO
3·1

Put the following nouns into their plural forms.

1. americano _____

2. appuntamento _____

3. avventura _____

4. bambino _____

5. bambina _____

6. dottoressa _____

7. romanzo _____

8. sera _____

9. moglie _____

10. dottore _____

Ask how the following people are.

EXAMPLE: tu

Come stai (tu)?

11. tuo fratello _____

12. voi _____

13. Lei _____

14. i bambini _____

Give the corresponding forms of each verb according to person.

	VENIRE	SAPERE	CONOSCERE
15. io	_____	_____	_____
16. tu	_____	_____	_____
17. lui/lei	_____	_____	_____
18. noi	_____	_____	_____

19. voi   _____   _____   _____

20. loro   _____   _____   _____

Carry out the following conversation tasks.

21. Ask a friend where he/she is living now.

   _____

22. Ask Mrs. Marchi where she is living now. (*Don't forget to use the polite form of the verb.*)

   _____

23. Say that you live in Florence.

   _____

24. Say that Mrs. Marchi (**la signora Marchi**) lives in Italy. (*Note the use of the article with a title when talking about someone.*)

   _____

25. Say that Mr. Verdi (**il signor Verdi**) lives on Dante Street.

   _____

26. Say that you live near Maria.

   _____

27. Say that you live in the United States.

   _____

28. Say that someone said that you are married.

   _____

29. Say that, for now, you like freedom.

   _____

30. Say that the novel you are reading is new.

   _____

31. Ask a friend how his/her brother is.

   _____

32. Say that he is married and has children.

   _____

33. Say that you are not sure when he will be coming the next time.

   _____

34. Say that he comes often to Rome.

   _____

35. Say that you know how to read in Italian (**italiano**).

_____

36. Say that you do not know the professor of Italian (**d'italiano**).

_____

Directions

Dialogo

Here's how someone might ask for directions:

SIGNORE:	Scusi, mi sa dire dov'è via Dante?	_Excuse me, can you tell me where Dante Street is?_
SIGNORINA:	Certo! Vada a sinistra per due isolati.	_Certainly. Go left for two blocks._
SIGNORE:	E poi?	_And then?_
SIGNORINA:	Giri a destra al semaforo.	_Turn right at the traffic lights._
SIGNORE:	Devo attraversare la strada?	_Should I cross the street?_
SIGNORINA:	Sì, e vada diritto per ancora due isolati.	_Yes, and go straight ahead for two more blocks._
SIGNORE:	Lì, c'è via Dante?	_Is Dante Street there?_
SIGNORINA:	Sì.	_Yes._

NEW VOCABULARY

andare	to go	**girare**	to turn
attraversare	to cross	**lì**	there
dire	to tell, to say	**poi**	then
diritto	straight ahead	**semaforo (seh-máh-foh-roh)**	traffic lights
dovere	to have to, must	**strada**	road, street

Memory practice

Fill in the blanks with the appropriate words and expressions. Do this from memory, and then go back and check your answers.

Scusi, mi sa _____ dov'è via Dante?

Certo! _____ a sinistra per due isolati.

E _____ ?

Giri a destra al _____ .

_____ attraversare la strada?

Sì, e vada _____ per ancora due isolati.

_____ , c'è via Dante?

Sì.

Language notes

This dialogue introduces you to three new and very useful verbs. Here are their conjugations in the present indicative:

dovere (*to have to, must*)

(io) devo	*I have to, I must*
(tu) devi	*you have to, you must* (fam.)
(Lei) deve	*you have to, you must* (pol.)
(lui) deve	*he has to, he must*
(lei) deve	*she has to, she must*
(noi) dobbiamo	*we have to, we must*
(voi) dovete	*you have to, you must* (pl.)
(loro) devono (déh-voh-noh)	*they have to, they must*

dire (*to tell, to say*)

(io) dico	*I say, I am saying*
(tu) dici	*you say, you are saying* (fam.)
(Lei) dice	*you say, you are saying* (pol.)
(lui) dice	*he says, he is saying*
(lei) dice	*she says, she is saying*
(noi) diciamo	*we say, we are saying*
(voi) dite	*you say, you are saying* (pl.)
(loro) dicono (déeh-koh-noh)	*they say, they are saying*

andare (*to go*)

(io) vado	*I go, I am going*
(tu) vai	*you go, you are going* (fam.)
(Lei) va	*you go, you are going* (pol.)
(lui) va	*he goes, he is going*
(lei) va	*she goes, she is going*
(noi) andiamo	*we go, we are going*
(voi) andate	*you go, you are going* (pl.)
(loro) vanno	*they go, they are going*

The forms **vada** and **giri** are imperative forms. Just note this for now. The form **al** is a contraction of **a + il**. We will complete the discussion of contractions in the next chapter. Now it is time to summarize both the forms of the indefinite article and the forms of adjectives.

The indefinite article has the following forms:

- **uno** before a masculine noun (or adjective) beginning with **z** or **s** + consonant: **uno zio** (*an uncle*), **uno studente** (*a student*)
- **un** before all other masculine nouns (or adjectives): **un bambino** (*a little boy*), **un uomo** (*a man*)
- **una** before feminine nouns (or adjectives) beginning with any consonant: **una zia** (*an aunt*), **una studentessa** (*a female student*)
- **un'** before feminine nouns or adjectives beginning with any vowel: **un'americana** (*an American woman*), **un'avventura** (*an adventure*)

Adjectives end in **-o** or **-e**: **alto** (*tall*), **grande** (*big*). The ending changes according to the noun, as you have seen several times. Most adjectives are placed after the noun. Here are all the possibilities:

SINGULAR	PLURAL
Masculine	
il bambino alt**o**	i bambini alt**i**
the tall boy	*the tall boys*
il padre alt**o**	i padri alt**i**
the tall father	*the tall fathers*
il bambino grand**e**	i bambini grand**i**
the big boy	*the big boys*
il padre grand**e**	i padri grand**i**
the big father	*the big fathers*
Feminine	
la bambina alt**a**	le bambine alt**e**
the tall girl	*the tall girls*
la madre alt**a**	le madri alt**e**
the tall mother	*the tall mothers*
la bambina grand**e**	le bambine grand**i**
the big girl	*the big girls*
la madre grand**e**	le madri grand**i**
the big mother	*the big mothers*

Dialogo

Here's another dialogue showing you how someone might ask for directions:

SIGNORA: Scusi, sa dov'è un bancomat?	*Excuse me, do you know where there's an automatic teller?*
VIGILE: In via Boccaccio.	*On Boccaccio Street.*
SIGNORA: Come si fa per andarci?	*How does one get there?*
VIGILE: Vada a sud per un po'.	*Go south for a bit.*
SIGNORA: È vicino alla chiesa?	*Is it near the church?*
VIGILE: Sì. È proprio davanti. Non può sbagliare!	*Yes. Right in front of it. You can't go wrong!*

NEW VOCABULARY

andarci (andare + ci)	to go there	**potere**	to be able to, can
bancomat (*m.*)	automatic teller	**proprio**	just, right
chiesa	church	**un po'**	a bit
davanti	in front	**vigile** (véeh-jeeh-leh) (*m.*)	traffic policeman
fare	to do, to make		

Memory practice

Fill in the blanks with the appropriate words and expressions. Do this from memory, and then go back and check your answers.

Scusi, sa dov'è un _____ ?

In _____ Boccaccio.

Come si fa per _____ ?

Vada a _____ per un po'.

È vicino alla _____ ?

Sì. È proprio _____ . Non può sbagliare!

Language notes

In this dialogue, you have come across yet another two important irregular verbs, **fare** and **potere**. In the present indicative they are conjugated as follows:

fare (*to do, to make*)	
(io) faccio	*I do, I am doing*
(tu) fai	*you do, you are doing* (fam.)
(Lei) fa	*you do, you are doing* (pol.)
(lui) fa	*he does, he is doing*
(lei) fa	*she does, she is doing*
(noi) facciamo	*we do, we are doing*
(voi) fate	*you do, you are doing* (pl.)
(loro) fanno	*they do, they are doing*

potere (*to be able to, to can*)	
(io) posso	*I can, I am able to*
(tu) puoi	*you can, you are able to* (fam.)
(Lei) può	*you can, you are able to* (pol.)
(lui) può	*he can, he is able to*
(lei) può	*she can, she is able to*
(noi) possiamo	*we can, we are able to*
(voi) potete	*you can, you are able to* (pl.)
(loro) possono (póhs-soh-noh)	*they can, they are able to*

Note that **si** is the generic person *one*. So, **si fa** means *one does*. When asking for directions, you'll need to know the following:

nord	*north*
sud	*south*
est	*east*
ovest	*west*

Indicate the correct form of the verbs **dovere, andare, dire, fare,** *and* **potere.**

EXAMPLE: io   *devo*   *vado*   *dico*   *faccio*   *posso*

1. tu   _____   _____   _____   _____   _____

2. lui   _____   _____   _____   _____   _____

3. noi   _____   _____   _____   _____   _____

4. voi   _____   _____   _____   _____   _____

5. loro   _____   _____   _____   _____   _____

6. io   _____   _____   _____   _____   _____

Put the appropriate form of the indefinite article before the following nouns.

7. _____ semaforo

8. _____ strada

9. _____ studente

10. _____ studentessa

11. _____ zio

12. _____ zia

Give the corresponding singular or plural form of each phrase as the case may be.

SINGULAR	PLURAL
13. il bambino bello	_____
14. _____	le donne belle
15. il vigile alto	_____
16. _____	le madri alte
17. la casa grande	_____
18. _____	i bambini grandi

Carry out the following conversation tasks.

19. Ask someone if they can tell you where Dante Street is.

_____

20. Tell someone to go right for a block and then to turn left at the traffic lights.

_____

21. Ask if you have to cross the road.

_____

22. Tell someone to go straight ahead for three more blocks.

_____

23. Ask if Macchiavelli Street is there.

_____

24. Point out an automatic teller to someone (*Remember* **ecco**?)

_____

25. Ask "How does one get there?"

_____

26. Tell someone to go north for a bit.

_____

27. Tell someone that it is near the church.

_____

28. Tell someone that it is right in front of the church.

_____

29. Tell someone that he/she cannot go wrong.

_____

30. Tell someone to go south and then east for a bit.

_____

On the phone and mobile devices

Dialogo

Here's how a phone conversation might sound in Italian:

LAURA:	Pronto! Chi parla?	*Hello! Who's speaking?*
VINCENZO:	Laura, sono Vincenzo.	*Laura, it's Vincenzo.*
LAURA:	Ciao, Vincenzo. Che vuoi?	*Hi, Vincenzo. What do you want?*
VINCENZO:	C'è tuo fratello?	*Is your brother there?*
LAURA:	No, non c'è.	*No, he's not here.*
VINCENZO:	Non importa. Telefono più tardi.	*It doesn't matter. I'll phone later.*
LAURA:	Arrivederci.	*Good-bye.*

NEW VOCABULARY

non importa	it doesn't matter	**Pronto!**	Hello!
parlare	to speak	**telefonare**	to phone
più	more	**volere**	to want

Memory practice

Fill in the blanks with the appropriate words and expressions. Do this from memory, and then go back and check your answers.

Pronto! Chi _____ ?
Laura, _____ Vincenzo.
Ciao, Vincenzo. Che _____ ?
C'è tuo _____ ?
No, non _____ .
Non importa. _____ più tardi.
Arrivederci.

Language notes

Note that to say who you are on the phone you say **sono...** (*I am*), not *it is*, as in English.

In the previous dialogue you have come across another useful irregular verb: **volere**. Here's its conjugation in the present indicative:

volere (*to want*)	
(io) voglio	*I want*
(tu) vuoi	*you want* (fam.)
(Lei) vuole	*you want* (pol.)
(lui) vuole	*he wants*
(lei) vuole	*she wants*
(noi) vogliamo	*we want*
(voi) volete	*you want* (pl.)
(loro) vogliono (vóh-lyoh-noh)	*they want*

Dialogo

Here is an example of what you might say if you wanted to send a text message:

MARCO: Maria, ti chiamo col mio cellulare stasera. Va bene?

MARIA: È meglio mandarmi un SMS.

MARCO: Non ho il mio dispositivo mobile.

MARIA: Allora, manda un messaggino col cellulare, va bene?

MARCO: D'accordo.

Maria, I'll call you on my cell tonight, OK?

It's better to send me a text.

I don't have my mobile device.

Then send me a text with your cell, OK?

Fine (I agree).

NEW VOCABULARY

cellulare	cell phone	**mandarmi** (= mandare + mi)	to send me
chiamare	to call	**meglio**	better
d'accordo	fine, I agree	**messaggino**	text, message
dispositivo	device	**mobile** (móh-beeh-leh)	mobile
mandare	to send	**SMS**	text message

Memory practice

Fill in the blanks with the appropriate words and expressions. Do this from memory, and then go back and check your answers.

Maria, ti _____ col mio cellulare stasera. Va bene?

È _____ mandarmi un SMS.

Non ho il mio dispositivo _____ .

Allora, manda un messaggino col _____ , va bene?

D'accordo.

Language notes

Note that **manda** is yet another imperative form.

It is now time to summarize the forms of the definite article:

- **lo** before a masculine noun (or adjective) beginning with **z** or **s** + consonant: **lo zio** (*the uncle*), **lo studente** (*the student*)
- **il** before all other masculine nouns (or adjectives) beginning with any other consonant: **il bambino** (*the little boy*), **il vigile** (*the traffic policeman*).
- **la** before feminine nouns (or adjectives) beginning with any consonant: **la zia** (*the aunt*), **la studentessa** (*the female student*)
- **l'** before masculine and feminine nouns (or adjectives) beginning with any vowel: **l'americano** (*the American man*), **l'americana** (*the American woman*)

The corresponding plural forms are as follows.

SINGULAR	PLURAL
lo	**gli**
lo zio	gli zii
il	**i**
il vigile	i vigili
la	**le**
la casa	le case
l' (*m.*)	**gli**
l'americano	gli americani
l' (*f.*)	**le**
l'americana	le americane

ESERCIZIO
3·3

Give the corresponding singular or plural form of each phrase as the case may be.

SINGULAR	PLURAL
1. il bambino	_____
2. _____	le strade
3. lo studente	_____
4. _____	le avventure
5. l'anno	_____

6. _____ gli euro

7. il caffè

   _____

8. _____ gli uomini

*Indicate the appropriate form of **volere** according to the given person.*

9. (io) _____

10. (loro) _____

11. (tu) _____

12. (lui/lei) _____

13. (noi) _____

14. (voi) _____

Carry out the following conversation tasks.

15. Tell Giovanni that you will call him tonight on your cell.

    _____

16. Say that it's better to send you a text message.

    _____

17. Say that you do not have a mobile device.

    _____

18. Say hello on the phone.

    _____

19. Ask who's speaking.

    _____

20. Say that it is you (speaking).

    _____

21. Ask Laura what she wants.

    _____

22. Now ask Mrs. Verdi, politely of course, what she wants.

    _____

23. Say that he's not in.

    _____

24. Say that it doesn't matter.

    _____

25. Say that you'll call later.

    _____

People

Knowing how to describe people, flirt a bit, portray character, and talk about family relationships adds up to an important conversation skill. This chapter will show you how to hone that skill in Italian.

Describing and flirting

Dialogo

Here's how one might describe an attractive person:

SARA: Natalia, guarda che uomo bello!

Natalia, look at the handsome man!

NATALIA: Troppo alto per me! E poi, non mi piacciono gli uomini biondi!

Too tall for me! And then, I don't like blond men.

SARA: Non il biondo! Il bruno, con gli occhi blu.

Not the blond one. The dark-haired one with blue eyes.

NATALIA: Non sembra intelligente!

He doesn't seem intelligent!

SARA: Sei troppo fastidiosa! Sembra molto simpatico!

You're too fussy! I bet that he's very charming!

NATALIA: Allora, che cosa aspetti?

Then what are you waiting for?

SARA: Ci provo.

I'm going to try.

NEW VOCABULARY

aspettare	to wait for	**intelligente**	intelligent
biondo	blond	**occhio (óhk-kyoh)**	eye
blu	dark blue	**provarci**	to go ahead
bruno	dark-haired	(= **provare + ci**)	and try
fastidioso	fussy	**provare**	to try
guardare	to look at, to watch	**simpatico**	nice, charming

50

Memory practice

Fill in the blanks with the appropriate words and expressions. Do this from memory, and then go back and check your answers.

Natalia, _____ che uomo bello!

Troppo alto per me! E poi, non mi piacciono gli uomini _____ !

Non il biondo! Il bruno, con gli _____ blu.

Non sembra _____ !

Sei troppo _____ ! Sembra molto simpatico!

Allora, che cosa _____ ?

Ci provo.

Language notes

In this dialogue you have come across a number of new adjectives, which are useful for describing people. They are treated just like the other ones you learned about, except **blu**, which is invariable: **l'occhio blu** (*the blue eye*), **gli occhi blu** (*the blue eyes*).

Descriptive adjectives are best learned in contrasting pairs. Here are a few:

TRAIT	OPPOSITE
alto (*tall*)	basso (*short*)
bello (*nice, beautiful*)	brutto (*ugly*)
grande (*big*)	piccolo (péehk-koh-loh) (*little, small*)
intelligente (*intelligent*)	stupido (stóoh-peeh-doh) (*stupid*)
timido (*timid, shy*)	sicuro (*secure, sure*)

It is now time to summarize prepositional contractions. The prepositions that always contract before the definite article are: **a** (*to, at*), **di** (*of*), **da** (*from*), **in** (*in*), and **su** (*on*). The following chart summarizes the contractions:

+	IL	I	LO	L'	GLI	LA	LE
a	al	ai	allo	all'	agli	alla	alle
da	dal	dai	dallo	dall'	dagli	dalla	dalle
di	del	dei	dello	dell'	degli	della	delle
in	nel	nei	nello	nell'	negli	nella	nelle
su	sul	sui	sullo	sull'	sugli	sulla	sulle

Contraction does not apply to the other prepositions, except for **con** for which they are optional. In practice only the form **col = con + il** is used commonly.

Dialogo

Here is an analogous conversation to the previous one.

MARCELLO: Giovanni, guarda quella donna bella!   *Giovanni, look at that beautiful woman!*

GIOVANNI: Sì. È proprio bella!   *Yes. She's really beautiful!*

MARCELLO: È senz'altro sposata!   *She's likely married!*

GIOVANNI: Forse no, perché non porta l'anello.   *Maybe not, because she's not wearing a ring.*

MARCELLO:	È vero. Ma sono un po' timido per presentarmi.		*It's true. But I'm a little shy to introduce myself.*
GIOVANNI:	Non ci credo. Sei sempre così sicuro di te.		*I don't believe it. You're always so sure of yourself.*
MARCELLO:	Va bene. Ci provo.		*OK. I'll try.*

NEW VOCABULARY

anello	finger ring	**presentarmi** (= **presentare + mi**)	to introduce myself
così	so		
crederci (= **credere + ci**)	to believe it	**proprio**	really
		senz'altro	without doubt, likely
credere	to believe	**senza**	without
forse	maybe	**sicuro**	sure
portare	to wear	**timido (téeh-meeh-doh)**	timid, shy
presentare	to present, to introduce	**un po'**	a bit

Note: The descriptions in the previous dialogues apply to any romantic situation involving persons of any type of sexual orientation. In Italian the word for *gay* is **gay**.

Memory practice

Fill in the blanks with the appropriate words and expressions. Do this from memory, and then go back and check your answers.

Giovanni, guarda _____ donna bella!

Sì. È _____ bella!

È, _____ , sposata!

Forse no, perché non _____ l'anello.

È vero. Ma sono un po' _____ per presentarmi.

Non ci _____ . Sei sempre così sicuro di te.

Va bene. Ci _____ .

Language notes

The word **quella** is part of the demonstrative system of Italian. The system has two parts. First, there is the demonstrative indicating relative nearness: the forms of **questo** (*this, these*). Here are its forms. Note that like the article it precedes the noun, agreeing with it in gender and number.

SINGULAR	PLURAL
Masculine	
quest**o** cornetto	quest**i** cornetti
this croissant	*these croissants*
Feminine	
quest**a** commessa	quest**e** commesse
this female clerk	*these female clerks*

The second part of the demonstrative system is that indicating distance: the forms of **quello** (*that, those*). It takes the following forms. Note that they vary in the same way that the definite article does.

SINGULAR	PLURAL
Masculine	
[Before **z** or **s + consonant**]	
quello	quegli
quello studente	quegli studenti
that student	*those students*
[Before any other consonant]	
quel	quei
quel bambino	quei bambini
that boy	*those boys*
[Before any vowel]	
quell'	quegli
quell'americano	quegli americani
that American	*those Americans*
Feminine	
[Before any consonant]	
quella	quelle
quella commessa	quelle commesse
that female clerk	*those female clerks*
[Before any vowel]	
quell'	quelle
quell'italiana	quelle italiane
that female Italian	*those female Italians*

ESERCIZIO 4·1

Give the opposite phrase.

EXAMPLE: quel bambino grande   *quel bambino piccolo*

1. questo uomo timido _____

2. quello studente intelligente _____

3. questi commessi alti _____

4. quegli uomini brutti _____

5. questo signore intelligente _____

6. quell'americano piccolo _____

7. quegli italiani alti _____

8. questa donna bella _____

9. queste bambine sicure _____

10. quella casa grande _____

11. quelle case belle _____

12. quell'americana alta _____

13. quelle americane basse _____

Now complete each phrase with the appropriate form of the prepositional contraction.

EXAMPLE: *in the* strada   *nella strada*

14. *at the* semaforo _____

15. *from the* commessi _____

16. *of the* zio _____

17. *in the* occhio _____

18. *on the* SMS (*Be careful!*) _____

19. *to the* donne _____

20. *in the* strada _____

21. *of the* bambini _____

22. *of the* uomini _____

Carry out the following conversation tasks.

23. First, tell your lady friend to look at the handsome man.

_____

24. Now tell your male friend to look at the beautiful woman.

_____

25. Say that the man is too tall for you.

_____

26. Say that you like blond men with blue eyes.

_____

27. Say that you do not like dark-haired men who are too tall.

_____

28. Say that he doesn't seem intelligent, but he seems very charming.

_____

29. Tell your friend that she is too fussy.

_____

30. Ask your friend, then, what she's waiting for.

_____

31. Say OK that you'll give it a try.

_____

32. Say that this woman here is really beautiful.

_____

33. Say that that woman is likely to be married, because she is wearing a ring.

_____

34. Say that maybe the woman is a little shy.

_____

35. Say that you don't believe it, because she is always sure of herself (**di sé**).

_____

Character

Dialogo

The following dialogue is also about a potential amorous encounter. More importantly, it shows how character can be talked about; and from it you will learn a few more ways to describe people.

BRUNA: Mio fratello è molto noioso!

My brother is really annoying!

MARISA: No, io lo trovo molto simpatico e vivace.

No, I find him (to be) very nice and vivacious.

BRUNA: Non lo conosci come me!

You don't know him like I do!

MARISA: A me, sembra un ragazzo sincero, educato e anche assai carino!

To me, he seems like a sincere, well-mannered guy and also quite cute!

BRUNA: Capisco. Ti sei innamorata, vero?

I get it (I understand). You've fallen in love, haven't you?

MARISA: Sì, un po'!

Yes, a bit!

NEW VOCABULARY			
assai	quite	**noioso**	annoying
capire	to understand	**ragazzo**	boy, youth
carino	cute	**sincero**	sincere
come	like	**trovare**	to find
educato	well-mannered	**vivace**	lively, vivacious
essere innamorato	to be/fall in love		

Memory practice

Fill in the blanks with the appropriate words and expressions. Do this from memory, and then go back and check your answers.

Mio fratello è molto _____!

No, io lo trovo molto simpatico e _____.

Non lo _____ come me!

A me, sembra un _____ sincero, educato e anche assai _____!

_____. Ti sei _____, vero?

Sì, un po'!

Language notes

In this chapter you have come across a third-conjugation verb: **capire** (*to understand*). Recall that first-conjugation verbs end in **-are**, second in **-ere**. There are no others to learn about, especially in a brief introduction to the language. There are two types of third-conjugation verbs. Verbs such as **capire** and **finire** belong to the first type in which an **-isc** is added to all the persons except the first (**noi**) and second (**voi**) plural. The other type does not have this. A typical verb for this second type is **dormire** (*to sleep*). Compare their present indicative conjugations:

capire (*to understand*)		**dormire** (*to sleep*)	
(io) capisco	*I understand*	(io) dormo	*I sleep, I am sleeping*
(tu) capisci	*you understand (fam.)*	(tu) dormi	*you sleep, you are sleeping (fam.)*
(Lei) capisce	*you understand (pol.)*	(Lei) dorme	*you sleep, you are sleeping (pol.)*
(lui) capisce	*he understands*	(lui) dorme	*he sleeps, he is sleeping*
(lei) capisce	*she understands*	(lei) dorme	*she sleeps, she is sleeping*
(noi) capiamo	*we understand*	(noi) dormiamo	*we sleep, we are sleeping*
(voi) capite	*you understand (pl.)*	(voi) dormite	*you sleep, you are sleeping (pl.)*
(loro) capiscono	*they understand*	(loro) dormono	*they sleep, they are sleeping*

You will have to simply consult a dictionary or glossary to find out which verb is conjugated in which way. Don't forget how to pronounce **–sc** in two ways: as "sh" in **capisci** and **capisce**, and as "sk" in **capisco** and **capiscono**.

Also note that **ragazzo**, as we saw in the previous dialogue, means a boy or adolescent, and the corresponding feminine form is **ragazza**.

Incidentally, you have been using **di** as a genitive preposition throughout. It generally translates as the *'s* of English possession. Note that it may have to be contracted.

| il fratello **di** Maria | *Maria's brother* (literally: *the brother of Maria*) |
| la zia **della** donna | *the woman's aunt* |

Dialogo

This dialogue is very similar to the previous one. It's all about character portrayal and falling in love.

ALESSANDRO:	Mi piace molto la tua amica!	*I like you're friend a lot!*
BRUNA:	Chi? Marisa?	*Who? Marisa?*
ALESSANDRO:	Sì, proprio lei. È una ragazza molto amichevole e sincera.	*Yes, precisely her. She's a very friendly and sincere girl.*
BRUNA:	Sei innamorato?	*Are you in love?*

ALESSANDRO: No, mi piacciono le ragazze ottimiste e felici.

No, I like optimistic and happy girls.

BRUNA: Capisco. Siete tutti e due innamorati.

I get it. You're both in love.

NEW VOCABULARY			
amichevole (ah-meeh-kéh-voh-leh)	friendly	**ottimista**	optimistic
amico (-a)	friend	**tutti e due**	both
felice	happy		

Memory practice

Fill in the blanks with the appropriate words and expressions. Do this from memory, and then go back and check your answers.

Mi piace molto la tua _____ !

Chi? Marisa?

Sì, proprio lei. È una _____ molto amichevole e sincera .

Sei _____ ?

No, mi piacciono le ragazze ottimiste e _____ .

Capisco. Siete _____ e due innamorati.

Language notes

Note that the plural of **amico** (*male friend*) is **amici** (ah-méeh-cheeh), with the soft sound of **c**; whereas for **amica** (*female friend*), it is **amiche** (ah-méeh-keh), with the hard sound of **c**.

The word **ottimista** is both masculine and feminine, as is **barista** (which you came across previously). The plural forms of each, however, change according to gender, namely to **-i** (*masculine*) and **-e** (*feminine*). This applies to all forms ending in **-ista**. There are not many of these.

SINGULAR	PLURAL
Masculine	
l'ottimista	gli ottimist**i**
il barista	i barist**i**
Feminine	
l'ottimista	le ottimist**e**
la barista	le barist**e**

Throughout this and previous chapters you have come across snippets of the possessive: *my, your,* and so on. The time has come to summarize its forms. Note that the definite article is part of the possessive and that the possessive is an adjective agreeing in number and gender with the noun.

	MASCULINE		FEMININE	
	SINGULAR	PLURAL	SINGULAR	PLURAL
my	il mio (amico)	i miei (amici)	la mia (amica)	le mie (amiche)
your (fam.)	il tuo (cornetto)	i tuoi (cornetti)	la tua (casa)	le tue (case)

continued

	MASCULINE		FEMININE	
	SINGULAR	PLURAL	SINGULAR	PLURAL
your (pol.)	il Suo (cornetto)	i Suoi (cornetti)	la Sua (casa)	le Sue (case)
his/her	il suo (amico)	i suoi (amici)	la sua (amica)	le sue (amiche)
our	il nostro (libro)	i nostri (libri)	la nostra (casa)	le nostre (case)
your (pl.)	il vostro (amico)	i vostri (amici)	la vostra (amica)	le vostre (amiche)
their	il loro (professore)	i loro (professori)	la loro (dottoressa)	le loro (dottoresse)

Note that the **loro** form is invariable. Also, when used with a family member or a relative in the singular, the article is dropped. If the noun is plural or modified (by an adjective), the article is restored.

mio padre	*my father*
nostro zio	*our uncle*
sua madre	*his/her mother*
tua zia	*your aunt*

But:

il mio padre alto	*my tall father*
i nostri zii	*our uncles*
la sua madre bella	*his/her beautiful mother*
le tue zie	*your aunts*

The exception is, again, **loro**, which must be used with the article: **il loro padre**. This is changing, however, so that nowadays it also can be used without: **loro padre**.

Finally, note that the **suo** forms translate as either *his* or *her*, according to context. Thus, **suo fratello** can be either *his brother* or *her brother*, as you can see below:

Marco è il fratello di Maria?	*Is Marco Maria's brother?*
Sì, è suo fratello.	*Yes, he is her brother.*
Marco è il fratello di Giovanni?	*Is Marco Giovanni's brother?*
Sì, è suo fratello.	*Yes, he is his brother.*

ESERCIZIO
4·2

Translate the following sentences into Italian.

1. He understands a lot.

_____

2. We finish at five o'clock, and then we will be going to Maria's house.

_____

3. Maria's brother sleeps till (**fino a**) noon.

_____

Put the appropriate ending on each verb.

4. Loro non cap _____ .

5. Le amiche di Maria dorm _____ sempre fino a tardi.

6. Quei ragazzi non fin _____ fino alle sette.

7. Tu non cap _____ , vero?

Give the appropriate possessive as indicated, and then turn the whole phrase into the plural. Follow the example.

EXAMPLE: *my* amica   *la mia amica*   *le mie amiche*

8. *my* amico   _____   _____

9. *your (fam.)* zia   _____   _____

10. *your (fam.)* zio   _____   _____

11. *his* amica   _____   _____

12. *her* amica   _____   _____

13. *our* padre   _____   _____

14. *our* professore   _____   _____

15. *your (pl.)* fratello   _____   _____

16. *your (pol.)* casa   _____   _____

17. *their* aunt   _____   _____

18. *their* amico   _____   _____

Carry out the following conversation tasks.

19. Say that your brother is annoying but that he is quite cute.

_____

20. Say that you find your female friend charming and vivacious.

_____

21. Say that you do not know your brother's male friend.

_____

22. Say that your female friend's brother seems to be a sincere and well-mannered youth.

_____

23. Say that you get it!

_____

24. Ask a female friend if she is in love.

_____

25. Now ask a male friend if he is in love.

_____

26. Now ask both your friends if they are in love.

_____

27. Say that you like happy and optimistic guys. (use **ragazzo**)

_____

28. Say that you also like happy and optimistic girls. (use **ragazza**)

_____

Family relationships

Dialogo

Here is the type of brief conversation that may take place in a typical household:

SORELLA:	Alessandro, mi presti dei soldi?	_Alessandro, can you lend me some money?_
FRATELLO:	No, non posso!	_No, I can't!_
SORELLA:	Sei proprio come la mamma!	_You're just like Mom!_
FRATELLO:	E tu come il papà!	_And you're like Dad!_
SORELLA:	Perché non chiedi al nonno o alla nonna?	_Why don't you ask Granddad or Grandma?_
FRATELLO:	Hai ragione! Loro sono generosi!	_You're right! They're generous!_

NEW VOCABULARY

avere ragione	to be right		**prestare**	to lend
chiedere (kyéh-deh-reh)	to ask for		**soldi**	money
generoso	generous			

Memory practice

Fill in the blanks with the appropriate words and expressions. Do this from memory, and then go back and check your answers.

Alessandro, mi _____ dei soldi?

No, non _____ !

Sei proprio come la _____ !

E tu come il _____ !

Perché non _____ al nonno o alla nonna?

Hai _____ ! Loro sono generosi!

Language notes

Note that **avere ragione** is like **avere fame**. It means, literally, _to have reason_: **ho ragione** (_I am right_), **lui ha ragione** (_he is right_).

Note that to say *some*, just use the prepositional contraction **di** + definite article.

del caffè	*some coffee*
dei soldi	*some money*
degli amici	*some friends*
delle case	*some houses*
delle donne	*some women*

Here is a list of the words for common family members, some of which you have already come across:

MALE	FEMALE
nonno (*grandfather*)	nonna (*grandmother*)
padre (*father*)	madre (*mother*)
fratello (*brother*)	sorella (*sister*)
mamma (*mom*)	papà (*dad*)
zio (*uncle*)	zia (*aunt*)
cugino (*cousin*)	cugina (*cousin*)
figlio (*son*)	figlia (*daughter*)
marito (*husband*)	moglie (*wife*)

Note that some adjectives, like **piccolo** or **grande**, can come before or after the noun: **il piccolo bambino/il bambino piccolo, la casa nuova/la nuova casa**. This also applies to **bello**, but there are changes in this case to the form, which will be discussed later.

Dialogo

Here is some more in-family chatter:

SARA: Alessandro, che pensi della nostra piccola cugina che è nata ieri?	*Alessandro, what do you think of our little cousin who was born yesterday?*
ALESSANDRO: Lei assomiglia a suo padre, nostro zio.	*She looks like her father, our uncle.*
SARA: E anche un po' a sua madre, nostra zia.	*And also a bit like her mother, our aunt.*
ALESSANDRO: Sì, hai ragione. È molto carina.	*Yes, you're right. She's very cute.*
SARA: Come tutta la nostra famiglia.	*Like our whole family.*

NEW VOCABULARY

assomigliare a	to look like	**ieri**	yesterday
famiglia	family	**pensare**	to think

Memory practice

Fill in the blanks with the appropriate words and expressions. Do this from memory, and then go back and check your answers.

Alessandro, che _____ della nostra piccola cugina
che è _____ ieri?
Lei _____ a suo padre, nostro zio.

E anche un po' a _____ madre, nostra zia.

Sì, hai _____ . È molto carina.

Come tutta la nostra _____ .

Language notes

Note that **tutto** is an adjective in **tutta la famiglia** (*all the family*), **tutte le case** (*all the houses*), and so on. Recall that it is also part of the formula for *both*: **tutti e due**. In this case the ending reflects the gender.

tutt**i** e due i ragazzi   *both the boys*

tutt**e** e due le ragazze   *both the girls*

ESERCIZIO

4·3

Ask for some of the following items. Follow the example.

EXAMPLE: cornetti   *Vorrei dei cornetti.* (I would like some croissants.)

1. anelli _____

2. cellulari _____

3. francobolli _____

4. libri _____

5. panini _____

Describe each family member as indicated. Follow the example.

EXAMPLE: my intelligent aunt   *la mia zia intelligente*

6. his beautiful wife _____

7. her cute brother _____

8. their big son _____

9. their tall daughter _____

10. our charming grandfather _____

11. your (*fam.*) lively mom _____

12. my well-mannered dad _____

13. her handsome husband _____

14. our little cousin (*f.*) _____

15. their short cousin (*m.*) _____

Carry out the following conversation tasks.

16. Ask your brother, Alessandro, to lend you some money.

_____

17. Say that you cannot.

_____

18. Tell your brother that he is just like his dad.

_____

19. Tell your sister that she is just like her mom.

_____

20. Ask your brother why he doesn't ask Granddad or Grandma.

_____

21. Tell your sister that she's right and that she's also very generous.

_____

22. Ask your brother if your little female cousin was born yesterday.

_____

23. Say that she looks like her mother.

_____

24. Say that your whole family is nice.

_____

 **·I-5·**

Jobs and homes

Knowing how to speak about jobs, what to say at a job interview, and how to talk about homes is an obvious conversational skill to be acquired. This chapter will show you how to do so.

Jobs

Dialogo

Choosing a career is the theme of the following brief conversation. Take special note of the words for various professions.

MARCO: Maria, conosci un bravo dentista?	*Maria, do you know a good dentist?*
MARIA: Perché? Hai mal di denti?	*Why? Do you have a toothache?*
MARCO: No, voglio diventare dentista o medico e allora voglio qualche consiglio.	*No, I want to be a dentist or a doctor, and thus I want some advice.*
MARIA: Dentista, tu? Impossibile! Forse avvocato o anche architetto, ma non ti vedo come dentista.	*You, a dentist? Maybe a lawyer or even an architect, but I don't see you as a dentist.*
MARCO: Forse hai ragione.	*Maybe you're right.*

NEW VOCABULARY

architetto	architect	**diventare**	to become
avvocato	lawyer	**impossibile**	impossible
bravo	good (*at something*)	**mal di denti**	toothache
consiglio	advice	**medico**	medical doctor
dentista (*m./f.*)	dentist	(méh-deeh-koh)	
		o	or

Memory practice

Fill in the blanks with the appropriate words and expressions. Do this from memory, and then go back and check your answers.

Maria, conosci un _____ dentista?

Perché? Hai mal di _____ ?

No, voglio diventare dentista o _____ e allora voglio _____ consiglio.

Dentista, tu? Impossibile! Forse _____ o anche architetto, ma non ti _____ come dentista.

Forse hai _____ .

Language notes

As mentioned previously, some adjectives can be placed before a noun. When they are, two things can happen, either separately or in tandem: (1) there is a meaning change, and/or (2) they change in form. An example of (1) is **grande**. When it is placed after a noun it means *big*, and when in front it can also mean *great*:

un libro grande	*a big book* (*in size*)
un grande libro	*a great book*

Buono has analogous forms to the indefinite article. In addition, it has plural forms. Notice that the article in front of **buono** has to be adapted as well to agree with it. So, for example, the **uno** in **uno zio** is changed to **un** because it is now in front of the **b** of **buono**.

The adjectives **buono** (*good*) and **bello** (*beautiful*) are examples of (2). Appearing after a noun, they are regular adjectives ending in **-o**. But before nouns, they change as follows:

- ◆ **buono** before a masculine noun beginning with **z** or **s** + consonant: **un buono zio** (*a good uncle*), **un buono studente** (*a good student*). The plural form is **buoni**: **i buoni zii** (*the good uncles*), **i buoni studenti** (*the good students*).
- ◆ **buon** before all other masculine nouns: **un buon bambino** (*a good child*), **un buon uomo** (*a good man*). Again the plural is **buoni**: **i buoni bambini** (*the good children*), **i buoni uomini** (*the good men*).
- ◆ **buona** before feminine nouns beginning with any consonant: **una buona zia** (*a good aunt aunt*), **una buona studentessa** (*a good female student*). The plural form is **buone**: **le buone zie** (*the good aunts*), **le buone studentesse** (*the good students*).
- ◆ **buon'** before feminine nouns beginning with any vowel: **una buon'americana** (*a good American woman*), **una buon'avventura** (*a good adventure*). Again, the plural form is **buone**: **le buone americane** (*the good American women*), **le buone avventure** (*the good adventures*).

The forms of **bello** change in an analogous fashion to the definite article and the demonstrative **quello**.

SINGULAR	PLURAL
Masculine	
[Before **z** or **s** + **consonant**]	
bello	begli
il bello studente	i begli studenti
the handsome student	*the handsome students*
[Before any other consonant]	
bel	bei

continued

SINGULAR	PLURAL
il bel bambino	i bei bambini
the beautiful child	*the beautiful children*
[Before any vowel]	
bell'	begli
il bell'amico	i begli amici
the handsome friend	*the handsome friends*
Feminine	
[Before any consonant]	
bella	belle
la bella donna	le belle donne
the beautiful woman	*the beautiful women*
[Before any vowel]	
bell'	belle
la bell'italiana	le belle italiane
the beautiful Italian woman	*the beautiful Italian women*

Note that **qualche** means *some*, and it is followed by a singular noun even if it is a plural concept. It is an alternative to the **di + article** contraction you learned about in the previous chapter.

dei consigli = qualche consiglio	*some advice*
dei bambini = qualche bambino	*some children*
degli amici = qualche amico	*some friends*
delle case = qualche casa	*some houses*

Dialogo

The previous conversation continues. Take particular notice of the words for the professions and jobs mentioned.

MARCO: Maria, pensi che è forse meglio fare qualcosa di più pratico, come elettricista o barbiere?

Maria, do you think it is perhaps better to do something more practical, like an electrician or a barber?

MARIA: Sei impossibile, Marco! Secondo me, tu sei nato per essere insegnante.

You're impossible, Marco! In my opinion, you're a born teacher.

MARCO: No, non mi piace la scuola. Preferisco fare l'impiegato o anche un meccanico, piuttosto che insegnante.

No, I don't like school. I prefer to be an office worker or even a mechanic, rather than a teacher.

MARIA: Fa' quello che vuoi!

Do, whatever you want!

NEW VOCABULARY

barbiere (*m.*)	barber	**pratico** (práh-teeh-koh)	practical
elettricista (*m./f.*)	electrician	**preferire** (isc)	to prefer
impiegato (-a)	office worker	**qualcosa**	something
insegnante (*m./f.*)	teacher	**quello che**	that which, whatever

meccanico	mechanic	scuola	school
(meh-káh-neeh-koh)		secondo	according to
piuttosto	rather		

Memory practice

Fill in the blanks with the appropriate words and expressions. Do this from memory, and then go back and check your answers.

Maria, pensi che è forse meglio fare _____ di più pratico, come elettricista o

_____ ?

Sei impossibile, Marco! _____ me, tu sei nato per essere insegnante.

No, non mi piace la _____ . Preferisco fare _____ o anche

un meccanico, piuttosto che _____ .

Fa' _____ che vuoi!

Language notes

The form **Fa'** is an imperative. You have already come across imperative forms in previous chapters. To form the imperative of first-conjugation verbs, drop the **-are** and add the following endings:

> **girare** (*to turn*)
> (tu) gir**a**   *turn* (fam.)
> (Lei) gir**i**   *turn* (pol.)
> (noi) gir**iamo**   *let's turn*
> (voi) gir**ate**   *turn* (pl.)
> (Loro) gir**ino** (jéeh-reeh-noh)   *turn* (pol. pl.)

Note that there is a polite plural form (**Loro**). More will be said about it in due course. For now, just note that it is the plural of **Lei** forms; for example:

Signor Marchi, giri a destra!   *Mr. Marchi, turn right!*

Signori, girino a destra!   *Gentlemen, turn right!*

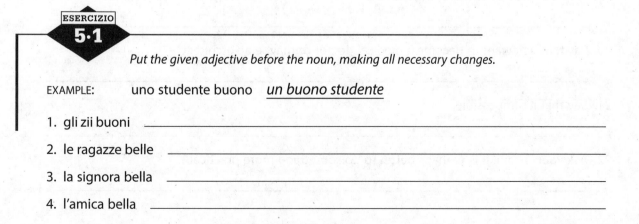

ESERCIZIO
5·1

Put the given adjective before the noun, making all necessary changes.

EXAMPLE: uno studente buono   *un buono studente*

1. gli zii buoni   _____

2. le ragazze belle   _____

3. la signora bella   _____

4. l'amica bella   _____

5. gli amici belli _____

6. l'uomo bello _____

7. l'uomo buono _____

8. lo zio bello _____

9. il panino buono _____

*Now give the equivalent for some. If you are given **dei panini**, the equivalent would be **qualche panino**; if instead, you are given **qualche amico**, give **degli amici**.*

10. delle amiche _____

11. qualche studente _____

12. dei cornetti _____

13. qualche libro _____

Tell the following people to do the indicated things.

14. Tell Marco to speak Italian.

_____

15. Tell Mr. Verdi to speak Italian.

_____

16. Tell Giovanni and Maria (together) to wait here.

_____

17. Tell a group of young ladies to wait here.

_____

Carry out the following conversation tasks.

18. Ask your sister if she knows a good lawyer or a good dentist.

_____

19. Ask your brother if he has a toothache.

_____

20. Say that you want to become a medical doctor or maybe an architect.

_____

21. Say that it's impossible.

_____

22. Ask your sister if it is perhaps better to do something more practical.

_____

23. Tell your brother that in your opinion, he is born to be a teacher.

_____

24. Say that you prefer to be a mechanic rather than an office worker.

_____

25. Tell your brother to do whatever he wants.

_____

Job interviews

Dialogo

The following dialogue exemplifies what someone looking for a job might say

BRUNA: Scusi, cerco lavoro nella Sua ditta.

Excuse me, I am looking for a job in your company.

SIGNORE: Ha mai lavorato in una ditta di informatica?

Have you ever worked for a computer (informatics) company?

BRUNA: No, ma ho una laurea in matematica. E ho creato diversi programmi all'università.

No, but I have a degree in mathematics. And I created several (computer) programs at the university.

SIGNORE: Ottimo. Ha qualche esperienza di lavoro?

Excellent. Do you have any work experience?

BRUNA: Sì, ho lavorato per una banca due anni fa.

Yes, I worked for a bank two years ago.

SIGNORE: Per il momento va bene così. Torni domani per un'intervista ufficiale, va bene?

For the time being this is all (it's OK like this). Come back tomorrow for an official interview, OK?

BRUNA: Certo. Grazie.

Of course. Thank you.

NEW VOCABULARY

banca	bank	**laurea**	degree
cercare	to search for, to look for	**lavorare**	to work
creare	to create	**lavoro**	work, job
ditta	company (*business*)	**mai**	ever, never
diverso	diverse, various, several	**matematica**	mathematics
esperienza	experience	**momento**	moment
fa	ago	**programma** (*m.*)	program
informatica	computer, informatics	**ufficiale**	official
intervista	interview	**università** (*f.*)	university

Memory practice

Fill in the blanks with the appropriate words and expressions. Do this from memory, and then go back and check your answers.

Scusi, _____ lavoro nella Sua ditta.

Ha mai _____ in una ditta di informatica?

No, ma ho una laurea in matematica. E ho _____ diversi programmi all'università.

Ottimo. Ha qualche esperienza di _____?

Sì, ho _____ per una banca due anni fa.

Per il momento va bene così. _____ domani per un'intervista ufficiale, va bene?

Certo. _____.

Language notes

The verb **cercare** retains the hard sound in its conjugations. So an **h** is added before an **-i** ending. In the present indicative, this is required for these two forms: **tu cerchi** and **noi cerchiamo**; in the imperative, it is required for these three forms: **(Lei) cerchi**, **(noi) cerchiamo**, **(Loro) cerchino**.

Note that you have come across your first past tense—the present perfect of first-conjugation verbs. It is made up of two parts: an auxiliary verb and a past participle. To form the past participle, drop the **-are** and add **–ato**.

parl**are** (*to speak*)	parl**ato** (*spoken*)
gir**are** (*to turn*)	gir**ato** (*turned*)

The auxiliary verb is either **avere** or **essere** in the present indicative (which you already know). For now, you have come across verbs using **avere**. Here is **lavorare** completely conjugated for you. You will learn more about this tense in subsequent chapters.

(io) ho lavorato	*I have worked, I worked*
(tu) hai lavorato	*you have worked, you worked* (fam.)
(Lei) ha lavorato	*you have worked, you worked* (pol.)
(lui) ha lavorato	*he has worked, he worked*
(lei) ha lavorato	*she has worked, she worked*
(noi) abbiamo lavorato	*we have worked, we worked*
(voi) avete lavorato	*you have worked, you worked* (pl.)
(loro) hanno lavorato	*they have worked, they worked*

Note that the plural of **banca** is **banche**, showing that the hard sound is retained. This applies to all nouns and adjectives ending in **-ca**.

Finally, **programma**, and any noun ending in **-amma**, is a masculine noun. Its plural form is **programmi**.

il nuovo programma	i nuovi programmi
the new program	*the new programs*

Dialogo

The following conversation is Bruna's interview. Note that in Italy it is not unusual to be asked your age and marital status in a job interview.

BRUNA:	Eccomi di nuovo.	*Here I am again.*
SIGNORE:	Va bene. Le faccio una serie di domande. Quanti anni ha?	*OK. I am going to ask you a series of questions. How old are you?*
BRUNA:	Ho ventinove anni.	*I am twenty-nine.*
SIGNORE:	Qual è il Suo indirizzo?	*What's your address?*
BRUNA:	Abito in centro, in via Petrarca, numero trentasei.	*I live downtown at 36 Petrarch Street.*
SIGNORE:	Qual è il Suo stato civile?	*What's your marital status?*
BRUNA:	Sono single.	*I'm single.*
SIGNORE:	Va bene così. La chiamo la prossima settimana.	*OK for now. I'll call you next week.*

NEW VOCABULARY

centro	downtown, center of town		**prossimo**	next
di nuovo	again		**quale**	which, what
domanda	question		**serie**	series
indirizzo	address		**settimana**	week
numero (nóoh-meh-roh)	number		**stato civile**	marital status

Memory practice

Fill in the blanks with the appropriate words and expressions. Do this from memory, and then go back and check your answers.

_____ di nuovo.

Va bene. Le _____ una serie di _____ . Quanti anni ha?

_____ ventinove anni.

Qual è il Suo _____ ?

Abito in _____ , in via Petrarca, numero trentasei.

Qual è il Suo _____ civile?

_____ single.

Va bene così. La chiamo la _____ settimana.

Language notes

Let's continue with the imperative—this time of the second-conjugation verbs. Again, drop the infinitive ending of **-ere**, and add the following endings:

leggere (*to read*)	
(tu) legg**i** (léh-jeeh)	*read* (fam.)
(Lei) legg**a** (léh-gah)	*read* (pol.)
(noi) legg**iamo** (leh-jáh-moh)	*let's read*
(voi) legg**ete** (leh-jéh-teh)	*read* (pl.)
(Loro) legg**ano** (léh-gah-noh)	*read* (pol. pl.)

Note that before **è** you simply drop the -**e** of **quale** without adding an apostrophe: **qual è**. With this dialogue, you have also come across a number of object pronouns (**mi, Le, La**), as you have in other chapters. These will be discussed in due course.

ESERCIZIO
5·2

Put the given infinitives in the present perfect tense.

EXAMPLE: Io *parlare* al professore due giorni fa. *ho parlato*

1. Tu *aspettare* la mia amica, vero? _____

2. Lei, signora Verdi, *lavorare* già? _____

3. Mio fratello *mandare* un SMS a Bruna. _____

4. Noi *prestare* dei soldi al nonno. _____

5. Voi *sbagliare* tutto! _____

6. I miei amici *telefonare* due minuti fa. _____

Tell the following people to do the indicated things.

7. Tell Maria to read the beautiful novel.

_____

8. Tell Mrs. Verdi to ask for a coffee.

_____

9. Tell Marco and Maria (together) to take a little coffee.

_____

10. Tell a group of gentlemen to read the new book.

_____

Carry out the following conversation tasks.

11. Tell an employer that you are looking for a job in his/her company.

_____

12. Say that you have never worked in a computer (informatics) company.

_____

13. Say that you have a mathematics degree.

_____

14. Say that you have created several programs at the university.

_____

15. Say that you have some work experience.

_____

16. Say that you worked for a bank several years ago.

_____

17. Tell someone (politely) to come back next week for an official interview.

_____

18. Say "Here I am again."

_____

19. Ask someone (formally) how old he/she is.

_____

20. Say that you want to ask a series of questions.

_____

21. Ask someone (formally) what his/her address is.

_____

22. Say that you live downtown.

_____

23. Ask someone (formally) what his/her marital status is.

_____

24. Say that you like those nice (beautiful) programs.

_____

25. Ask your brother if he is looking for the bank.

_____

Homes

Dialogo

Here's how a conversation between a husband and a wife who are house hunting might unfold:

MOGLIE: Questa casa è molto piccola.	*This house is very small.*
MARITO: Ma ha una bella cucina, due camere e un bagno grande.	*But it has a nice kitchen, two bedrooms, and a big bathroom.*
MOGLIE: Sì, e anche un salotto magnifico e una sala da pranzo eccezionale.	*Yes, and also a magnificent living room and an exceptional dining room.*
MARITO: Il garage, però, è un po' troppo piccolo.	*The garage, however, is a bit too small.*
MOGLIE: Ma ha un'entrata assai grande!	*But it has a rather large entrance!*

bagno	bathroom	**garage** (*m.*)	garage
camera (káh-meh-rah)	bedroom	**magnifico (mah-nyéh-feeh-koh)**	magnificent
cucina	kitchen	**però**	however
eccezionale	exceptional	**sala da pranzo**	dining room
entrata	entrance	**salotto**	living room

Memory practice

Fill in the blanks with the appropriate words and expressions. Do this from memory, and then go back and check your answers.

Questa casa è _____ piccola.

Ma ha una bella _____ , due camere e un _____ grande.

Sì, e anche un salotto _____ e una sala da pranzo _____ .

Il garage, _____ , è un po' troppo piccolo.

Ma ha un'_____ assai grande!

Language notes

To form the imperative of **-ire** verbs, drop the **-ire** ending and add the following endings. Note that some verbs (as you know) require the change to **-isc**.

dormire (*to sleep*)

(tu) dorm**i**	*sleep* (fam.)
(Lei) dorm**a**	*sleep* (pol.)
(noi) dorm**iamo**	*let's sleep*
(voi) dorm**ite**	*sleep* (pl.)
(loro) dorm**ano** (dóhr-mah-noh)	*sleep* (pol. pl.)

finire (*to finish*)

(tu) fin**isci**	*finish* (fam.)
(Lei) fin**isca**	*finish* (pol.)
(noi) fin**iamo**	*let's finish*
(voi) fin**ite**	*finish* (pl.)
(loro) fin**iscano** (feeh-néehs-kah-noh)	*finish* (pol. pl.)

Dialogo

The house hunting continues:

MOGLIE: Se prendiamo questa casa, dobbiamo comprare tanti mobili nuovi.

If we get this house, we will have to buy a lot of new furniture.

MARITO: Sì, è vero, ma abbiamo già un bel divano e una poltrona bellisima.

Yes, it's true, but we already have a beautiful sofa and a very beautiful armchair.

MOGLIE: Sì, ma dobbiamo comprare un nuovo frigorifero e un nuovo tavolo per la sala da pranzo.

Yes, but we have to buy a new refrigerator and a new table for the dining room.

MARITO: D'accordo.

I agree.

MOGLIE: E anche un nuovo letto per la nostra camera.

And also a new bed for our bedroom.

MARITO: Forse conviene rimanere nel nostro condominio!

Maybe it is better to remain in our condo!

NEW VOCABULARY

condominio	condo	**letto**	bed
convenire	to be better to	**mobile (móh-beeh-leh)**	piece of furniture
divano	sofa	**poltrona**	armchair
frigorifero (freeh-goh-réeh-feh-roh)	refrigerator	**rimanere**	to remain
		tanto	many, a lot
già	already	**tavolo (táh-voh-loh)**	table

Memory practice

Fill in the blanks with the appropriate words and expressions. Do this from memory, and then go back and check your answers.

Se prendiamo questa casa, dobbiamo comprare tanti _____ nuovi.

Sì, è vero, ma abbiamo _____ un bel _____ e una

_____ bellisima.

Sì, ma dobbiamo comprare un nuovo _____ e un nuovo

_____ per la sala da pranzo.

D'accordo.

E anche un nuovo _____ per la nostra _____.

Forse _____ rimanere nel nostro condominio!

Language notes

Note that **tanto** is a synonym of **molto**. And note that **convenire** is conjugated like **venire**.

ESERCIZIO
5·3

Tell the following people to do the indicated things.

1. Tell Giovanni to sleep.

_____

2. Tell Mr. Verdi to sleep.

_____

3. Tell Marco and Maria (together) to finish the coffee.

_____

4. Tell a group of young ladies to finish the book.

_____

5. Tell Bruna to finish the croissant.

_____

6. Tell Mrs. Verdi to finish the sandwich.

_____

7. Tell Marco and Maria (together) to sleep till (**fino a**) late.

_____

Carry out the following conversation tasks.

8. Say that this house is very small, but it has a beautiful kitchen, a beautiful bedroom, and a big bathroom.

_____

9. Say that the house has a magnificent living room and an exceptional dining room.

_____

10. Say that, however, the garage is very small.

_____

11. Say that the entrance is quite big.

_____

12. Say that you will have to buy many new pieces of furniture.

_____

13. Say that you already have a beautiful sofa and a beautiful armchair.

_____

14. Say that you want to buy a new refrigerator, a new bed for the bedroom, and a new table.

_____

15. Say that it is better to remain in your condo.

_____

Daily life

Shopping and banking are part of everyday life. Knowing how to converse in the relevant situations (at stores, at banks, and so on) is an obvious vital linguistic skill. This chapter will show you how to use that skill.

At the supermarket

Dialogo

Here's the kind of conversation that might take place at a supermarket, while shopping for food (**fare la spesa**). Note that the metric system is used in Italy for weights and measures.

COMMESSO: Quante mele desidera?	*How many apples do you want?*
CLIENTE: Una dozzina. Poi vorrei un mezzo chilo di quelle fragole.	*A dozen. Then I would like a half kilo of those strawberries.*
COMMESSO: Non prenda quelle! Queste sono più fresche.	*Don't take those! These are more fresh.*
CLIENTE: Vorrei anche dei piselli, dei fagioli e qualche pera.	*I would also like some peas, some beans, and a few pears.*
COMMESSO: Abbiamo anche delle pesche fresche.	*We also have some fresh peaches.*
CLIENTE: No, grazie. Basta così.	*No, thanks. This is enough.*

NEW VOCABULARY

bastare	to be enough	**fresco**	fresh
chilo	kilogram	**mela**	apple
desiderare	to desire, to want	**pera**	pear
dozzina	dozen	**pesca**	peach
fagiolo	bean	**pisello**	pea
fragola (fráh-goh-lah)	strawberry		

Memory practice

Fill in the blanks with the appropriate words and expressions. Do this from memory, and then go back and check your answers.

_____ mele desidera?

Una dozzina. Poi vorrei un mezzo chilo di quelle _____ .

Non _____ quelle! Queste sono più fresche.

Vorrei anche dei piselli, dei fagioli e _____ pera.

Abbiamo anche _____ pesche fresche.

No, grazie. _____ così.

Language notes

Recall that **di** + definite article or **qualche** + singular noun allows you to express *some*, known technically as the partitive.

delle mele	*some apples*
qualche pera	*some pears*

Recall also that **quanto** is an adjective that changes according to the gender and number of the noun.

Quante mele?	*How many apples?*
Quanti piselli?	*How many peas?*

Note that **non prenda** is a negative imperative. As in all other cases, the negative is formed simply by putting **non** before the imperative verb. However, for the singular familiar (**tu**) form, the verb is changed to the infinitive.

	AFFIRMATIVE	NEGATIVE
Tu-forms:	Prendi! (*Take!*)	Non **prendere**! (*Don't take!*)
Lei-forms:	Prenda! (*Take!*)	Non prenda! (*Don't take!*)

Finally, here are the names of some common stores where food is sold:

il negozio di generi alimentari	*grocery/food store*
il panificio	*bakery*
il mercato	*market*
il supermercato	*supermarket*
la pizzicheria (peeh-tseeh-keh-réeh-ah)	*delicatessen*

Dialogo

Here is a similar conversation:

COMMESSA:	Desidera, signore?	*May I help you, sir?*
CLIENTE:	Vorrei dieci fette di prosciutto.	*I would like ten slices of prosciutto.*
COMMESSA:	Il prosciutto che abbiamo è freschissimo. Altro?	*The prosciutto we have is very fresh. Anything else?*
CLIENTE:	Un po' di salame.	*A bit of salami.*
COMMESSA:	Abbiamo anche del formaggio buonissimo.	*We also have some very good cheese.*
CLIENTE:	No, grazie. Va bene così.	*No thanks. That's it.*

fetta	slice	**prosciutto**	prosciutto ham
formaggio	cheese	**salame** (*m.*)	salami

Memory practice

Fill in the blanks with the appropriate words and expressions. Do this from memory, and then go back and check your answers.

_____ , signore?

Vorrei dieci _____ di prosciutto.

Il prosciutto che abbiamo è _____ . Altro?

Un po' di _____ .

Abbiamo anche del _____ buonissimo.

No, grazie. Va bene _____ .

Language notes

Note that the expression **Desidera?** is translated as *May I help you?* But, literally, it means *Do you want (something)?*

In previous chapters, you have come across irregular imperative verbs. Three of the most common are the following:

essere (*to be*)	**avere** (*to have*)	**fare** (*to do, to make*)
(tu) sii (*be*)	(tu) abbi (*have*)	(tu) fa' (*do*)
(Lei) sia (*be*)	(Lei) abbia (*have*)	(Lei) faccia (*do*)
(noi) siamo (*let's be*)	(noi) abbiamo (*let's have*)	(noi) facciamo (*let's do*)
(voi) siate (*be*)	(voi) abbiate (*have*)	(voi) fate (*do*)
(Loro) siano (*be*)	(Loro) abbiano (*have*)	(Loro) facciano (*do*)

And don't forget that the negative imperative of **tu**-forms is the infinitive.

Marco, fa' questo!   Marco, non fare questo!

Marco, do this!   *Marco, don't do this!*

Here are the names of some common food items, which will come in handy when shopping for food:

la carne	*meat*	il latte	*milk*
il pesce	*fish*	il vino	*wine*
il pane	*bread*	la frutta	*fruit*
l'acqua	*water*	la verdura	*vegetables*

Note that with these nouns, called mass nouns (because they have mainly a singular form), the partitive consists of **di** + singular definite article. The **qualche** form is never used with these nouns.

della carne	*some meat*
del pesce	*some fish*

As you know, adding **-issimo** to the end of an adjective translates as *very*.

bellissimo   *very beautiful*
freschissimo   *very fresh*

Note that the hard **c** of adjectives like **fresco** is retained by adding an **h**.

ESERCIZIO
6·1

Say that you want some of each item mentioned.

EXAMPLE: mele   *Vorrei delle mele.*

1. fragole _____

2. piselli _____

3. pere _____

4. pesche _____

5. fagioli _____

6. formaggio _____

7. prosciutto _____

8. carne _____

9. pesce _____

10. pane _____

11. acqua _____

12. latte _____

13. vino _____

14. frutta _____

15. verdura _____

*Put the following commands in the negative. Remember to use the infinitive for **tu**-forms.*

EXAMPLE: Signora, prenda queste mele!

             Signora, non prenda queste mele!

16. Maria, torna domani!

_____

17. Signor Marchi, faccia questo!

_____

18. Marco, fa' quella domanda al professore!

_____

19. Giovanni e Bruna, siate vivaci!

_____

20. Maria, abbi fretta (*hurry*)!

_____

Carry out the following conversation tasks.

21. Ask someone how many strawberries they would like.

_____

22. Say that you would like a dozen (**dozzina di**) apples and a kilogram of peaches.

_____

23. Say that these strawberries are more fresh.

_____

24. Say "This is enough."

_____

25. As a store employee, ask a customer if you can help him/her.

_____

26. Say that you would like a dozen slices of prosciutto.

_____

27. Say that you would also like a bit of salami.

_____

28. Say that the cheese is very good and very fresh.

_____

29. Say that you want to buy some prosciutto at the delicatessen on National Street.

_____

30. Say that you want to buy some bread at the bakery on Dante Street.

_____

Shopping

Dialogo

The following conversation is characteristic of what one would say at a women's clothing store while shopping (**fare delle spese**):

COMMESSA: Buongiorno. Mi dica!	*Good day. May I help you?* (literally: *Tell me!*)
CLIENTE: Vorrei una giacca alla moda.	*I would like a fashionable jacket.*
COMMESSA: Che taglia porta?	*What's your size?*

CLIENTE: Il quarantadue.	I'm a 42.
COMMESSA: Vuole provarsi questa?	Would you like to try this one on?
CLIENTE: Sì. Ha dei pantaloni che vanno insieme?	Yes. Do you have pants that go together?
COMMESSA: Sì, questi azzurri.	Yes, these blue ones.
CLIENTE: Belli! Dov'è il camerino?	Beautiful! Where's the changing room?
COMMESSA: Vada lì, a destra.	Go there, to the right.

NEW VOCABULARY

alla moda	in style, fashionable	**pantaloni** (*m., pl.*)	pants
camerino	changing room	**portare**	to wear
giacca	jacket	**provarsi (provare + si)**	to try on
insieme	together	**taglia**	size

Memory practice

Fill in the blanks with the appropriate words and expressions. Do this from memory, and then go back and check your answers.

Buongiorno. Mi _____ !

Vorrei una giacca _____ .

Che _____ porta?

Il quarantadue.

Vuole _____ questa?

Sì. Ha dei _____ che vanno insieme?

Sì, questi _____ .

Belli! Dov'è il _____ ?

_____ lì, a destra.

Language notes

The forms **vada** and **dica** are imperatives of **andare** and **dire**, irregular verbs that you have come across in previous chapters. Another common verb that is irregular in the imperative is **venire**. Here are their conjugations:

andare (*to go*)	**dire** (*to say, to tell*)	**venire** (*to come*)
(tu) va' (*go*)	(tu) di' (*tell*)	(tu) vieni (*come*)
(Lei) vada (*go*)	(Lei) dica (*tell*)	(Lei) venga (*come*)
(noi) andiamo (*let's go*)	(noi) diciamo (*let's tell*)	(noi) veniamo (*let's come*)
(voi) andate (*go*)	(voi) dite (*tell*)	(voi) venite (*come*)
(Loro) vadano (*go*)	(Loro) dicano (*tell*)	(Loro) vengano (*come*)

Here are the names of some common colors in Italian. These will come in handy when shopping for clothes. Recall that **blu** is an invariable adjective. So are **arancione**, **marrone**, and **viola**. They never change in form, no matter what the gender and number of the noun they modify.

arancione (*inv.*)	*orange*	marrone (*inv.*)	*brown*
azzurro	*blue*	nero	*black*
bianco	*white*	rosso	*red*
giallo	*yellow*	verde	*green*
grigio	*gray*	viola (*inv.*)	*purple*

And here are the names of some common clothing items:

il vestito	*dress*	la camicia	*shirt*
la gonna	*skirt*	la cravatta	*tie*
la camicetta	*blouse*	l'abito	*suit*
la cintura	*belt*	la borsa	*purse*
la maglia	*sweater*		

Dialogo

Now let's put the spotlight on a conversation in a footwear store:

COMMESSO: Desidera, signore?	*May I help you, sir?*
CLIENTE: Quanto costano questi stivali?	*How much do these boots cost?*
COMMESSO: Duecento euro. Sono in saldo.	*Two hundred euros. They're on sale.*
CLIENTE: E queste scarpe?	*And these shoes?*
COMMESSO: Costano trecento euro.	*They cost three hundred euros.*
CLIENTE: Posso provarle?	*May I try them on?*
COMMESSO: Certo. Che numero porta?	*Of course. What's your size (literally, number)?*
CLIENTE: Il trentotto.	*Size thirty-eight.*
COMMESSO: Le stanno proprio bene!	*They really look good on you!*

NEW VOCABULARY

in saldo	on sale	**stare bene**	to look good on
scarpa	shoe	**stivale**	boot

Memory practice

Fill in the blanks with the appropriate words and expressions. Do this from memory, and then go back and check your answers.

Desidera, signore?

Quanto costano questi _____ ?

Duecento euro. Sono _____ .

E queste _____ ?

_____ trecento euro.

Posso provarle?

Certo. Che _____ porta?

Il trentotto.

Le _____ proprio _____ !

Language notes

In the previous chapter, you learned to form and use first-conjugation verbs in the present perfect. Recall that the verbs discussed were conjugated with **avere** as the auxiliary and that the past participle was formed by changing -**are** to -**ato**, for example:

(io) ho lavorato	*I have worked, I worked*
(tu) hai cercato	*you have searched, you searched*

and so on.

The same pattern applies to second- and third-conjugation verbs. In the case of the second conjugation, the past participle is formed by replacing -**ere** with -**uto**, and in the case of the third conjugation, by replacing -**ire** with -**ito**. Here are **credere** and **finire** completely conjugated:

credere (*to believe*)

(io) ho creduto	*I have believed, I believed*
(tu) hai creduto	*you have believed, you believed (fam.)*
(Lei) ha creduto	*you have believed, you believed (pol.)*
(lui) ha creduto	*he has believed, he believed*
(lei) ha creduto	*she has believed, she believed*
(noi) abbiamo creduto	*we have believed, we believed*
(voi) avete creduto	*you have believed, you believed (pl.)*
(loro) hanno creduto	*they have believed, they believed*

finire (*to finish*)

(io) ho finito	*I have finished, I finished*
(tu) hai finito	*you have finished, you finished (fam.)*
(Lei) ha finito	*you have finished, you finished (pol.)*
(lui) ha finito	*he has finished, he finished*
(lei) ha finito	*she has finished, she finished*
(noi) abbiamo finito	*we have finished, we finished*
(voi) avete finito	*you have finished, you finished (pl.)*
(loro) hanno finito	*they have finished, they finished*

ESERCIZIO
6·2

Tell the following people to do the things indicated.

EXAMPLE: Tell Maria to go downtown.

Maria, va' in centro!

1. Tell Professor Giusto (*a male*) to go downtown.

_____

2. Tell Marco and Bruna to go downtown.

_____

3. Tell Maria to tell the truth (**la verità**).

_____

4. Tell Dr. Marinelli (*a female*) to tell the truth.

_____

5. Tell Giovanni and Maria to tell the truth.

_____

6. Tell Marco to come here.

_____

7. Tell Mrs. Martini to come here.

_____

8. Tell Marco and Maria to come here.

_____

Say that you bought the following yesterday.

EXAMPLE: an orange dress and a blue skirt

            Ieri ho comprato un vestito arancione e una gonna azzurra.

9. a white blouse and a yellow belt

_____

10. two gray sweaters and a brown shirt

_____

11. a purple tie, a red purse, a green suit, and a black jacket

_____

Say that the following people did not do the indicated things.

EXAMPLE: (tu) finire di leggere quel libro

            (Tu) non hai finito di leggere quel libro.

12. (il professore) avere tempo (*time*)

_____

13. (noi) dovere comprare quell'abito

_____

14. (voi) potere comprare quegli stivali

_____

15. (tu) volere leggere quel libro

_____

16. (io) capire la verità

_____

17. (tu) dormire fino a tardi

_____

18. (il ragazzo) preferire il cornetto

_____

19. (noi) finire di lavorare (*working*)

_____

20. (voi) capire il libro

_____

Carry out the following conversation tasks.

21. Say that you would like to buy a jacket in style.

_____

22. Ask someone (*politely*) what his or her (*clothing*) size is.

_____

23. Ask someone (*politely*) if she wants to try on a blue dress.

_____

24. Say that you would like pants that go together with the green jacket.

_____

25. Ask where the changing room is.

_____

26. Tell someone (*politely*) to go there, to the right.

_____

27. Ask a store clerk how much the boots and the shoes cost.

_____

28. Say that the shoes are on sale.

_____

29. Ask someone (*politely*) what his/her shoe size is.

_____

30. Tell someone (*politely*) that they (*the shoes*) look really good on him/her.

_____

Banking

Dialogo

Here's what a typical conversation in a bank might sound like:

IMPIEGATO:	Che cosa desidera, signorina?	*May I help you with something, Miss?*
SIGNORINA:	Vorrei depositare questi soldi nel mio conto.	*I would like to deposit this money in my account.*
IMPIEGATO:	Altro?	*Anything else?*
SIGNORINA:	Vorrei prelevare del denaro da quest'altro conto.	*I would like to withdraw some money from this other account.*
IMPIEGATO:	Quanto?	*How much?*
SIGNORINA:	Cinquecento euro, per favore.	*Five hundred euros, please.*
IMPIEGATO:	EccoLe! Firmi questo modulo.	*Here you are. Sign this form.*
SIGNORINA:	Grazie.	*Thank you.*

NEW VOCABULARY

conto	account	**firmare**	to sign
denaro	money	**modulo (móh-dooh-loh)**	form
depositare	to deposit	**prelevare**	to withdraw

Memory practice

Fill in the blanks with the appropriate words and expressions. Do this from memory, and then go back and check your answers.

Che cosa _____ , signorina?

Vorrei _____ questi soldi nel mio _____ .

Altro?

Vorrei _____ del _____ da quest'altro conto.

Quanto?

Cinquecento _____ , per favore.

EccoLe! _____ questo modulo.

Grazie.

Language notes

So far you have been working with verbs conjugated with **avere** as the auxiliary in the present perfect. There are a small number of verbs, however, that are conjugated with **essere**. The best way to determine which verbs are conjugated with **essere** is to look it up. In this book this fact will be shown with (**ess.**) when the verb is first introduced and in the glossary. Of the verbs you have come across so far, the following are conjugated with **essere: andare, bastare, costare, convenire, diventare, essere, piacere, rimanere, sembrare, stare, tornare, venire.**

In this case, the past participle agrees with the subject (**io**, **tu**, and so on), as if it were an adjective.

Marco è andat**o** in centro ieri.   *Marco went downtown yesterday.*
Maria è andat**a** in centro ieri.   *Maria went downtown yesterday.*

Here is **andare** fully conjugated for you in the present perfect:

andare (*to go*)

(io) sono andato (-a)	*I have gone, I went*
(tu) sei andato (-a)	*you have gone, you went* (fam.)
(Lei) è andato (-a)	*you have gone, you went* (pol.)
(lui) è andato	*he has gone, he went*
(lei) è andata	*she has gone, she went*
(noi) siamo andati (-e)	*we have gone, we went*
(voi) siete andati (-e)	*you have gone, you went* (pl.)
(loro) sono andati (-e)	*they have gone, they went*

Dialogo

The bank conversation continues:

Impiegato:	Come le vuole?	*How would you like them (the money)?*
Signorina:	In biglietti di taglio piccolo.	*In small bills.*
Impiegato:	Va bene. Ha bisogno di altro?	*OK. Do you need anything else?*
Signorina:	Mi può cambiare in spiccioli questo biglietto?	*Can you change this bill into small change?*
Impiegato:	Certo!	*Of course.*

NEW VOCABULARY

avere bisogno di	to have need of	**spicciolo**	coin, small change
biglietto	bill	**taglio piccolo**	small
cambiare	to change, to exchange		

Memory practice

Fill in the blanks with the appropriate words and expressions. Do this from memory, and then go back and check your answers.

Come le _____ ?
In biglietti di _____ piccolo.
Va bene. Ha _____ di altro?
Mi può _____ in _____ questo biglietto?

Language notes

As you know, the present perfect (and all compound tenses) are formed with an auxiliary verb and the past participle. Needless to say, some verbs have irregular past participles. Of the verbs you have come across so far, the following have irregular past participles:

VERB	PAST PARTICIPLE
chiedere	chiesto
convenire	convenuto
dire	detto
essere	stato
fare	fatto
leggere	letto
prendere	preso
rimanere	rimasto
stare	stato
vedere	visto
venire	venuto

ESERCIZIO
6·3

Say that the following people did not do the indicated things.

EXAMPLE: (tu) andare in centro

(Tu) non sei andato (-a) in centro. [Note: the **tu** can be either a male or female, hence the need to show both endings in the past participle.]

1. (io) andare al supermercato

_____

2. (tu) venire con loro in centro

_____

3. (quell'uomo) tornare dal centro

_____

4. (quella donna) tornare dal centro

_____

5. (noi) stare in Italia

_____

6. (voi) venire in centro

_____

7. (gli studenti) rimanere in classe (*in class*)

_____

8. (le donne) essere al bar

_____

9. (quegli stivali) costare molto

_____

10. (quelle scarpe) costare tanto

_____

11. (Marco) chiedere quelle domande al professore

_____

12. (Maria) dire la verità

_____

13. (io) fare la spesa ieri

_____

14. (mio fratello) leggere quel libro

_____

15. (io) prendere il caffè al bar

_____

16. (tu) vedere Maria ieri

_____

17. (loro) venire con noi

_____

Carry out the following conversation tasks.

18. Say that you would like to deposit some money in your account.

_____

19. Say that you would like to withdraw some money from your other account.

_____

20. Tell someone (*politely*) to sign this form.

_____

21. Say that you want small bills.

_____

22. Ask the teller (*politely, of course*) to change these bills into small change.

_____

Weather, seasons, and holidays

The weather, the change of seasons, and, of course, holidays are common topics in conversation. This chapter will show you how to carry out conversations in this area of everyday life.

Weather

Dialogo

The following conversation is all about the weather:

AMICO:	Fa troppo freddo!	*It's too cold.*
AMICA:	Ma c'è un bel sole e non tira vento.	*But there's a beautiful sun, and it's not windy.*
AMICO:	Preferisco andare al mare.	*I prefer going to the sea.*
AMICA:	Non io. Preferisco la montagna.	*Not I. I prefer the mountains.*
AMICO:	Ma nevica sempre d'inverno.	*But it always snows in the winter.*
AMICA:	Non sei mai contento!	*You're never happy!*
AMICO:	Neanche tu!	*Nor are you!*

NEW VOCABULARY

contento	happy, content	**nevicare**	to snow
freddo	cold	**sole** (*m.*)	sun
inverno	winter	**tirare vento**	to be windy
mare (*m.*)	sea	**vento**	wind
montagna	mountain(s)		

Memory practice

Fill in the blanks with the appropriate words and expressions. Do this from memory, and then go back and check your answers.

_____ troppo freddo!

Ma c'è un bel sole e non _____ vento.

Preferisco andare al _____ .

Non io. Preferisco la _____ .

Ma _____ sempre d'inverno.

Non sei mai _____ !

_____ tu!

Language notes

Italian uses double negatives in sentence construction. This simply means that **non** is used with adverbs such as **mai** (*ever*) to produce *never*. Here are the most common double negatives:

non... mai	*never*
non... più	*no more, no longer*
non... niente	*nothing*
(*also*: non... nulla)	
non... neanche	*neither*
non... nessuno	*no one*
non... né... né	*neither . . . nor*

The **non** is dropped when used at the beginning of a sentence or for emphasis.

Neanche tu!   *Nor (neither) you!*

Note the use of **fare** with weather expressions: **fare freddo** (*to be cold*), **fare caldo** (*to be hot*).

Dialogo

The previous conversation continues:

AMICO:	Andiamo in centro oggi, va bene?	*Let's go downtown today, OK?*
AMICA:	Non vedi che piove forte?	*Don't you see that it's raining hard?*
AMICO:	Non importa. Fa caldo e ho voglia di uscire.	*It doesn't matter. It's warm, and I feel like going out.*
AMICA:	Va bene. Andiamo al cinema.	*OK. Let's go to the movies.*
AMICO:	D'accordo.	*I agree.*

NEW VOCABULARY

avere voglia di	to feel like	**forte**	strong, hard
caldo	hot, warm	**piovere** (pyóh-veh-reh)	to rain
cinema (*m., inv.*)	cinema, movies	**uscire** (ess.)	to go out

---

Memory practice

Fill in the blanks with the appropriate words and expressions. Do this from memory, and then go back and check your answers.

_____ in centro oggi, va bene?

Non vedi che _____ forte.

Non importa. Fa _____ e ho _____ di uscire.

Va bene. Andiamo al _____ .
D'accordo.

Language notes

In this and previous chapters, you have come across object pronouns (*me*, *him*, *her*, and so on). The time has come to learn them formally. Here are the direct object pronouns in Italian:

me	mi
you (fam., sing.)	ti
you (pol., sing.)	La
him	lo
her	la
us	ci
you (fam., pl.)	vi
them (m.)	li
them (f.)	le

Note that in a sentence these come before the verb.

Marco **mi** chiama ogni sera.	*Marco calls **me** every night.*
Maria, chi **ti** chiama spesso?	*Maria, who calls **you** often?*
Signorina, chi **La** chiama spesso?	*Miss, who calls **you** often?*
Il professore **lo** chiama spesso.	*The professor calls **him** often.*
Lui non **la** chiama mai.	*He never calls **her**.*
Marco **ci** aspetta.	*Marco is waiting **for us**.*
Maria non **vi** capisce.	*Maria does not understand **you**.*
Io non **li** conosco.	*I do not know **them** (m.).*
Lui non **le** conosce.	*He does not know **them** (f.).*

The verb **uscire** (*to go out*) is found in this dialogue. It is a very useful verb, and it is irregular. Here are its present indicative forms:

(io) esco	*I am going out*
(tu) esci	*you are going out* (fam.)
(Lei) esce	*you are going out* (pol.)
(lui) esce	*he is going out*
(lei) esce	*she is going out*
(noi) usciamo	*we are going out*
(voi) uscite	*you are going out* (pl.)
(loro) escono (éhs-koh-noh)	*they are going out*

Now, here are its imperative forms:

(tu) esci	*go out* (fam.)
(Lei) esca	*go out* (pol.)
(noi) usciamo	*let's go out*
(voi) uscite	*go out* (pl.)
(loro) escano (éhs-kah-noh)	*go out* (pol. pl.)

Finally, note that it is conjugated with **essere** in the present perfect:

Io sono uscito (-a) ieri.	*I went out yesterday.*
Mio fratello è uscito con Bruna.	*My brother went out with Bruna.*
Mia sorella non è uscita ieri.	*My sister did not go out yesterday.*

ESERCIZIO
7·1

Rewrite each statement in the negative.

EXAMPLE: Marco conosce tutti.

Marco non conosce nessuno.

1. Il tuo amico va sempre al cinema.

   _____

2. La sua amica sa tutto.

   _____

3. Loro vanno ancora in montagna.

   _____

4. Maria conosce tutti.

   _____

5. Io voglio la carne e il pesce.

   _____

Using appropriate direct object pronouns, identify the people Maria never calls.

EXAMPLE: me

Maria non mi chiama mai.

6. you (*fam., sing.*)

   _____

7. us

   _____

8. you (*pl.*)

_____

9. him

_____

10. her

_____

11. them (*all males*)

_____

12. them (*all females*)

_____

Translate the following sentences into Italian.

13. I never go out.

_____

14. The girls have gone out already.

_____

15. Marco, go out with Maria!

_____

16. Mrs. Verdi, go out with your husband!

_____

17. My brother went out a few moments ago.

_____

18. Marco, do you often go out?

_____

Carry out the following conversation tasks.

19. Say that it's too cold.

_____

20. Now say that it's too hot.

_____

21. Say that you prefer to go to the mountains rather than (**piuttosto che**) to the sea.

_____

22. Say that it always snows in the winter.

_____

23. Tell someone (*informally*) that he/she is never happy.

   _____

24. Tell a friend to go downtown with you.

   _____

25. Say that you do not want to go downtown because it is raining hard.

   _____

26. Say that you feel like going out.

   _____

27. Suggest to someone to go to the movies (*together*).

   _____

Seasons

Dialogo

The next conversation involves talking about the seasons:

AMICA:	Amo la primavera e l'autunno, e tu?	*I love spring and fall, and you?*
AMICO:	Io preferisco l'estate perché amo il caldo.	*I prefer summer because I love the heat.*
AMICA:	A primavera sbocciano le piante.	*In spring, the plants blossom.*
AMICO:	Come il mio amore per te.	*Like my love for you.*
AMICA:	Sei sempre romantico!	*You are always romantic!*

NEW VOCABULARY

amare	to love		**primavera**	spring
amore (*m.*)	love		**romantico**	romantic
autunno	autumn, fall		**(roh-máhn-teeh-koh)**	
estate (*f.*)	summer		**sbocciare**	to blossom
pianta	plant			

Memory practice

Fill in the blanks with the appropriate words and expressions. Do this from memory, and then go back and check your answers.

Amo la _____ e l'autunno, e tu?

Io preferisco l'_____ perché amo il caldo.

A primavera _____ le piante.

Come il mio _____ per te.

Sei sempre _____ !

Language notes

Let's continue with the object pronouns. Here are the indirect object pronouns (*to me*, *to her*, *to him*, and so on).

to me	mi
to you (fam., sing.)	ti
to you (pol., sing.)	Le
to him	gli
to her	le
to us	ci
to you (fam., pl.)	vi
to them (m.)	gli
to them (f.)	gli

Note that these also come before the verb. As you can see, you will have to be very careful when using these pronouns at first, until you become familiar with them.

Marco **mi** ha detto la verità.	*Marco told **me** the truth.*
Maria, che cosa **ti** ha detto lui?	*Maria, what did he say **to you**?*
Signorina, che cosa **Le** ha detto lui?	*Miss, what did he say **to you**?*
Il professore non **gli** ha detto la verità.	*The professor did not tell **him** the truth.*
Lui non **le** ha mandato un messaggino.	*He did not send a text **to her**.*
Marco **ci** ha mandato un messaggino.	*Marco sent a text **to us**.*
Maria non **vi** ha detto tutto.	*Maria did not tell **you** everything.*
Io non **gli** ho parlato.	*I did not speak **to them** (m./f.).*

Dialogo

The previous conversation continues:

AMICO:	Odio l'inverno e il freddo, e tu?	*I hate winter and the cold, and you?*
AMICA:	Io invece lo amo, perché mi piace la neve.	*I, instead, love it, because I like the snow.*
AMICO:	Non io. Ma mi piace molto l'autunno.	*Not I, but I really like the fall.*
AMICA:	Perché cadono le foglie?	*Because the leaves fall?*
AMICO:	Come il tuo amore per me?	*Like your love for me?*

NEW VOCABULARY

cadere (ess.)	to fall		**neve** (*f.*)	snow
foglia	leaf		**odiare**	to hate
invece	instead			

Memory practice

Fill in the blanks with the appropriate words and expressions. Do this from memory, and then go back and check your answers.

_____ l'inverno e il freddo, e tu?

Io _____ lo amo, perché mi piace la _____ .

Non io. Ma mi piace molto l'_____ .

Perché cadono le _____ ?

Come il tuo _____ per me?

Language notes

Sometimes, you might need to use stressed pronouns in place of the ones discussed above. These come after the verb for emphasis. And they are the only ones possible after prepositions.

me	me
you (fam., sing.)	te
you (pol., sing.)	Lei
him	lui
her	lei
us	noi
you (fam., pl.)	voi
them (m.)	loro
them (f.)	loro
Marco ha chiamato me, non te!	*Marco called me, not you!*
Venite con noi, va bene?	*Come with us, OK?*
Lui parla a me spesso.	*He talks to me often.*
Noi parliamo di lei spesso.	*We speak of her often.*

ESERCIZIO
7·2

Using appropriate indirect object pronouns, identify the people Maria has not spoken to.

EXAMPLE: to me

Maria non mi ha parlato.

1. to you (*fam., sing.*)

_____

2. to us

_____

3. to you (*pl.*)

_____

4. to him

_____

5. to her

_____

6. to them (*all males*)

_____

7. to them (*all females*)

_____

Now, using appropriate stressed object pronouns, identify the people with whom Maria went out or to whom she spoke as indicated.

EXAMPLE: **me**/uscire

Maria è uscita con me.

me/parlare

Maria ha parlato a me.

8. **you** (*fam., sing.*)/uscire

_____

9. **us**/parlare

_____

10. **you** (*pl.*)/uscire

_____

11. **him**/parlare

_____

12. **her**/uscire

_____

13. **them** (*all males*)/parlare

_____

14. **them** (*all females*)/uscire

_____

Carry out the following conversation tasks.

15. Say that you love the spring but that you hate winter.

_____

16. Say that you prefer summer because you love the heat.

_____

17. Say that in the spring the plants are in bloom.

   _____

18. Tell your romantic partner that he/she is romantic.

   _____

19. Say that your love for him/her is very strong (**forte**).

   _____

20. Say that you like the snow.

   _____

21. Say that you love autumn because the leaves fall.

   _____

Holidays

Dialogo

The following conversation deals with major holidays in Italy. Note that Christmas and Easter are national holidays.

AMICA:	È già Natale!	*It's already Christmas!*
AMICO:	Io amo le feste natalizie, e tu?	*I love the Christmas holidays, and you?*
AMICA:	Io preferisco la Pasqua.	*I prefer Easter.*
AMICO:	Perché?	*Why?*
AMICA:	Fa bel tempo e tutto comincia a crescere.	*The weather is beautiful, and everything begins to grow.*

NEW VOCABULARY

crescere (kréh-sheh-reh)	to grow	natalizio	of Christmas
festa	feast, holiday, party	Pasqua	Easter
Natale (*m.*)	Christmas	tempo	weather

Memory practice

Fill in the blanks with the appropriate words and expressions. Do this from memory, and then go back and check your answers.

È già _____ !

Io amo le _____ natalizie, e tu?

Io preferisco la _____ .

Perché?

Fa _____ tempo e tutto comincia a crescere.

Language notes

The object pronouns **lo**, **la**, **li**, and **le** also stand for things and are thus translated as *it* and *they*. As you know by now, the pronoun form agrees in gender and number with the noun phrase it replaces.

Compro **il romanzo** domani.	*I am buying **the novel** tomorrow.*
Lo compro domani.	*I am buying **it** tomorrow.*
Compro **quegli stivali** domani.	*I am buying **those boots** tomorrow.*
Li compro domani.	*I am buying **them** tomorrow.*
Non prendo **quella giacca**.	*I am not taking **that jacket**.*
Non **la** prendo.	*I am not taking **it**.*
La mia amica non vuole **le scarpe**.	*My friend doesn't want **the shoes**.*
La mia amica non **le** vuole.	*My friend doesn't want **them**.*

One more thing. If the verb is in the present perfect (or any other compound tense), then the past participle agrees with the preceding pronoun.

Ho comprato **il romanzo** ieri.	*I bought **the novel** yesterday.*
Lo ho (l'ho) comprat**o** ieri.	*I bought **it** yesterday.*
Ho comprato **quegli stivali** ieri.	*I bought **those boots** yesterday.*
Li ho comprat**i** ieri.	*I bought **them** yesterday.*
Non ho preso **quella giacca**.	*I didn't take **that jacket**.*
Non **la** ho (l'ho) pres**a**.	*I didn't take **it**.*
La mia amica non ha voluto **le scarpe**.	*My friend didn't want **the shoes**.*
La mia amica non **le** ha volut**e**.	*My friend didn't want **them**.*

Dialogo

The previous conversation continues:

AMICA: È già Ferragosto!	*It's already Ferragosto (August 15)!*
AMICO: Vero. Tutti vanno in vacanza.	*True. Everybody's going on vacation.*
AMICA: Sì, ma purtroppo io devo lavorare.	*Yes, but unfortunately, I have to work.*
AMICO: Non importa. Quando vai in ferie andiamo in vacanza anche noi.	*It doesn't matter. We'll also go on vacation when you are off.*
AMICA: Sei un vero amico!	*You're a real friend!*

NEW VOCABULARY

in ferie	on vacation, off work	**vacanza**	vacation
purtroppo	unfortunately		

Memory practice

Fill in the blanks with the appropriate words and expressions. Do this from memory, and then go back and check your answers.

È _____ Ferragosto!

Vero. Tutti vanno in _____ .

Sì, ma _____ io devo lavorare.

Non importa. Quando vai in _____ andiamo in vacanza anche noi.

Sei un _____ amico!

Language notes

Sometimes, the direct and indirect pronouns are required in the same sentence. In that case, the indirect pronouns come first and are changed as follows:

mi	*is changed to*	me
ti	*is changed to*	te
gli	*is changed to*	glie
le	*is changed to*	glie
ci	*is changed to*	ce
vi	*is changed to*	ve

Note that the only direct object pronouns used in double pronoun constructions are **lo, la, li,** and **le.** All double pronouns are written as separate words, except the ones formed with **glie,** which are written as single words.

Marco **mi** dice sempre **la verità**.	*Marco always tells **me the truth**.*
Marco **me la** dice sempre.	*Marco always tells **it to me**.*
Maria **gli** dice sempre **la verità**.	*Maria always tells **him the truth**.*
Maria **gliela** dice sempre.	*Maria always tells **it to him**.*
Io ho comprato **le scarpe a mia sorella**.	*I bought **my sister the shoes**.*
Io **gliele** ho comprate.	*I bought **them for her**. [Recall that the past participle agrees with **lo, la, li, le**.]*
Nostro padre **ci** ha comprato **gli stivali**.	*Our father bought **us the boots**.*
Nostro padre **ce li** ha comprati.	*Our father bought **them for us**.*

ESERCIZIO
7·3

*Replace each phrase in italics with the appropriate direct object pronoun (**lo, la, li, le**), rewriting the sentence and making any necessary changes.*

EXAMPLE: Marco ha comprato *gli stivali* ieri.

 Marco li ha comprati ieri.

1. Io ho preso *l'espresso* a quel bar.

2. Noi abbiamo letto *quel romanzo* già.

   _____

3. Mia sorella ha comprato *le scarpe nuove* ieri.

   _____

4. La sua amica ha fatto *la spesa* ieri.

   _____

5. Mia cugina non ha voluto *i pantaloni nuovi*.

   _____

6. Non ho ancora finito *quel libro*.

   _____

7. Maria non ha mai detto *la verità*.

   _____

8. Ho finito *i piselli*.

   _____

9. Non ho mai preferito *le mele*.

   _____

*Now replace the italicized direct object with an appropriate pronoun (**lo, la, li, le**), and then rewrite the whole sentence, making the necessary adjustments. Note that you will have to use double pronouns throughout.*

EXAMPLE: Maria mi ha detto *la verità*.

   Maria me la ha (l'ha) detta.

10. Io ti ho comprato *i cornetti*.

    _____

11. Mio fratello gli ha chiesto *le domande* ieri.

    _____

12. Mio fratello le ha comprato *gli stivali nuovi* ieri.

    _____

13. Tu ci hai mandato *i messaggini*, vero?

    _____

14. Io vi ho preso *un caffè*, va bene?

    _____

Carry out the following conversation tasks.

15. Say that it is already Christmas.

   _____

16. Say that you love the Christmas holidays.

   _____

17. Say that you do not like Easter because it is always raining.

   _____

18. Say that you love spring because the weather is beautiful and everything starts to grow.

   _____

19. Say that everyone goes on vacation in August.

   _____

20. Say that unfortunately you have to work.

   _____

21. Tell someone that he/she is a real friend.

   _____

Traveling

Everybody loves to travel these days. Knowing how to carry out conversations at airports, train stations, and bus stations, not to mention at hotels, is a vital skill. This chapter will show you how to do so in Italian.

Trains and buses

Dialogo

The following conversation involves getting a train ticket:

PASSEGGERA:	Vorrei fare il biglietto per Firenze.	*I would like to purchase a ticket for Florence.*
BIGLIETTAIO:	Di andata e ritorno?	*Round-trip ticket?*
PASSEGGERA:	Sì.	*Yes.*
BIGLIETTAIO:	Quale classe?	*What class?*
PASSEGGERA:	La prima, per favore.	*First, please.*
BIGLIETTAIO:	Il treno partirà dal binario numero cinque.	*The train will be departing from track number five.*
PASSEGGERA:	Grazie.	*Thank you.*

NEW VOCABULARY

andata e ritorno	round-trip	**fare il biglietto**	to buy a (travel) ticket
bigliettaio (-a)	ticket agent	**partire (ess.)**	to leave, to depart
binario	track	**passeggero (-a)**	passenger
classe (*f.*)	class	**treno**	train

Memory practice

Fill in the blanks with the appropriate words and expressions. Do this from memory, and then go back and check your answers.

Vorrei ＿＿＿＿＿＿＿ il biglietto per Firenze.

Di ＿＿＿＿＿＿＿ e ritorno?

Sì.

Quale ＿＿＿＿＿＿＿?

La prima, per favore.

Il treno _____ dal _____ numero
cinque.

Grazie.

Language notes

The verb form **partirà** is a future form. Let's start with first-conjugation, **-are**, verbs. To form the future, drop the **-re**, change the **a** to **e**, and add the following endings:

parlare (*to speak*)	
(io) parler**ò**	*I will speak*
(tu) parler**ai**	*you will speak* (fam.)
(Lei) parler**à**	*you will speak* (pol.)
(lui) parler**à**	*he will speak*
(lei) parler**à**	*she will speak*
(noi) parler**emo**	*we will speak*
(voi) parler**ete**	*you will speak* (pl.)
(loro) parler**anno**	*they will speak*

Note that if the verb ends in **-ciare** or **-giare**, the ending is changed to **-cer** and **-ger**, respectively.

(io) comin**cer**ò	*I will begin*
(loro) man**ger**anno	*they will eat*

If it ends in **-care** or **-gare**, as in **pagare** (*to pay*), then an **h** is added to indicate that the hard sound is to be retained.

(tu) cer**ch**erai	*you will look for*
(loro) pa**gh**eranno	*they will pay*

Here is some useful vocabulary related to the theme of this section:

arrivare	*to arrive*	la partenza	*departure*
l'arrivo	*arrival*	il posto	*seat*
l'orario	*schedule, timetable*	la stazione	*station*

Dialogo

Here's the kind of conversation you might hear at a bus depot:

PASSEGGERO:	Scusi, l'autobus per Firenze è in orario?	*Excuse me, is the bus for Florence on time?*
BIGLIETTAIO:	È in anticipo di qualche minuto.	*It's early by a few minutes.*
PASSEGGERO:	Ho ancora tempo. C'è un'edicola qui vicino?	*I still have some time. Is there a newsstand nearby?*
BIGLIETTAIO:	È alla fermata.	*It's at the bus stop.*
PASSEGGERO:	Grazie.	*Thank you.*

autobus (*m., inv.*)	bus	**in orario**	on time
edicola (eh-déeh-koh-lah)	newsstand	**minuto**	minute
fermata	stop	**tempo**	time
in anticipo (ahn-téeh-cheeh-poh)	early		

Memory practice

Fill in the blanks with the appropriate words and expressions. Do this from memory, and then go back and check your answers.

Scusi, l'autobus per Firenze è in _____ ?

È in _____ di qualche minuto.

Ho ancora tempo. C'è un'_____ qui vicino?

È alla _____ .

Grazie.

Language notes

To form the future of second- and third-conjugation verbs, just drop the **-re** and add the same endings as those required for first-conjugation verbs.

leggere (*to read*)

(io) legger**ò**	*I will read*
(tu) legger**ai**	*you will read* (fam.)
(Lei) legger**à**	*you will read* (pol.)
(lui) legger**à**	*he will read*
(lei) legger**à**	*she will read*
(noi) legger**emo**	*we will read*
(voi) legger**ete**	*you will read* (pl.)
(loro) legger**anno**	*they will read*

finire (*to finish*)

(io) finir**ò**	*I will finish*
(tu) finir**ai**	*you will finish* (fam.)
(Lei) finir**à**	*you will finish* (pol.)
(lui) finir**à**	*he will finish*
(lei) finir**à**	*she will finish*
(noi) finir**emo**	*we will finish*
(voi) finir**ete**	*you will finish* (pl.)
(loro) finir**anno**	*they will finish*

Put each italicized verb into the future tense.

1. Maria *arrivare* domani. _____

2. Noi *parlare* solo italiano in Italia. _____

3. Noi *pagare* il conto. _____

4. Voi non *mangiare* la carne. _____

5. Io *cominciare* a mangiare presto. _____

6. Anche tu *cercare* un posto in prima. _____

7. Tu *chiedere* un posto in prima, vero? _____

8. Io *credere* tutto quello che mi dici. _____

9. Noi *prendere* il treno delle sedici. _____

10. Domani *piovere* molto. _____

11. Loro *leggere* quel nuovo romanzo. _____

12. Io *capire* tutto quello che mi dici. _____

13. Loro *finire* alle diciassette. _____

14. Noi *partire* domani per Torino. _____

15. Voi *dormire* fino a tardi, vero? _____

16. Mio fratello *uscire* con Bruna stasera. _____

Carry out the following conversation tasks.

17. Say that you would like to purchase a round-trip ticket to Rome.

_____

18. Say that you would like a first-class ticket.

_____

19. Say that the train will be departing from track number 12.

_____

20. Say that you will arrive at the station on time.

_____

21. Say that your friend will arrive early by a few minutes.

_____

22. Say that bus departure is at 2 P.M. and that arrival is at 5 P.M. (*Use official time.*)

_____

23. Say that you still have some time.

_____

24. Ask if there is a newsstand nearby.

_____

Accommodations

Dialogo

The next conversation takes place at a hotel check-in counter:

IMPIEGATA: Scusi, ha fatto la prenotazione?	*Excuse me, did you make a reservation?*
TURISTA: Sì, per una camera che dà sulla Piazza della Signoria.	*Yes, for a room that looks onto Piazza della Signoria.*
IMPIEGATA: Vediamo! Abbiamo una camera singola.	*Let' see! We have a single room.*
TURISTA: Va bene! A quanto viene?	*That's fine! How much does it come to?*
IMPIEGATA: A quattrocento dollari americani a notte.	*Four hundred American dollars a night.*
TURISTA: La prendo.	*I'll take it.*

NEW VOCABULARY

dare	to give	**dollaro (dóh-lah-roh)**	dollar
dare su	to look onto	**singolo (séehn-goh-loh)**	single

Memory practice

Fill in the blanks with the appropriate words and expressions. Do this from memory, and then go back and check your answers.

Scusi, ha fatto la _____ ?

Sì, per una camera che _____ sulla Piazza della Signoria.

Vediamo! Abbiamo una camera _____ .

Va bene! A quanto _____ ?

A quattrocento _____ americani a notte.

La prendo.

Language notes

The form **dà** is from the verb **dare** (*to give*), which is irregular throughout the conjugations. It is a very useful verb to know. Here are the conjugations of **dare** in the tenses covered so far in this book:

Present indicative

(io) do	*I give*
(tu) dai	*you give* (fam.)
(Lei) dà	*you give* (pol.)
(lui) dà	*he gives*
(lei) dà	*she gives*
(noi) diamo	*we give*
(voi) date	*you give* (pl.)
(loro) danno	*they give*

Imperative

(tu) da'	*give* (fam.)
(Lei) dia	*give* (pol.)
(noi) diamo	*let's give*
(voi) date	*give* (fam., pl.)
(Loro) diano (déeh-ah-noh)	*give* (pol., pl.)

Imperfect

(io) davo	*I used to give, I was giving*
(tu) davi	*you used to give, you were giving* (fam.)
(Lei) dava	*you used to give, you were giving* (pol.)
(lui) dava	*he used to give, he was giving*
(lei) dava	*she used to give, she was giving*
(noi) davamo	*we used to give, we were giving*
(voi) davate	*you used to give, you were giving* (pl.)
(loro) davano (dáh-vah-noh)	*they used to give, they were giving*

Future

(io) darò	*I will give*
(tu) darai	*you will give* (fam.)
(Lei) darà	*you will give* (pol.)
(lui) darà	*he will give*
(lei) darà	*she will give*
(noi) daremo	*we will give*
(voi) darete	*you will give* (pl.)
(loro) daranno	*they will give*

The past participle is **dato**, and the verb is conjugated with **avere: ho dato, hai dato**, and so on. The present participle is **dando: sto dando, stavo dando**, and so on.

Needless to say, there are verbs that have irregular forms in the future. Of the verbs you have come across so far, the following are the most useful to know. Note that you do not need to memorize them all. Just look at how they are formed, and you will see a pattern in most, namely, that you drop two vowels from the infinitive. They are conjugated here as a kind of reference section for you:

andare (*to go*)

(io) andr**ò**	*I will go*
(tu) andr**ai**	*you will go* (fam.)
(Lei) andr**à**	*you will go* (pol.)
(lui) andr**à**	*he will go*
(lei) andr**à**	*she will go*
(noi) andr**emo**	*we will go*
(voi) andr**ete**	*you will go* (pl.)
(loro) andr**anno**	*they will go*

avere (*to have*)

(io) avr**ò**	*I will have*
(tu) avr**ai**	*you will have* (fam.)
(Lei) avr**à**	*you will have* (pol.)
(lui) avr**à**	*he will have*
(lei) avr**à**	*she will have*
(noi) avr**emo**	*we will have*
(voi) avr**ete**	*you will have* (pl.)
(loro) avr**anno**	*they will have*

bere (*to drink*)

(io) berr**ò**	*I will drink*
(tu) berr**ai**	*you will drink* (fam.)
(Lei) berr**à**	*you will drink* (pol.)
(lui) berr**à**	*he will drink*
(lei) berr**à**	*she will drink*
(noi) berr**emo**	*we will drink*
(voi) berr**ete**	*you will drink* (pl.)
(loro) berr**anno**	*they will drink*

dire (*to say*)

(io) dir**ò**	*I will say*
(tu) dir**ai**	*you will say* (fam.)
(Lei) dir**à**	*you will say* (pol.)
(lui) dir**à**	*he will say*
(lei) dir**à**	*she will say*
(noi) dir**emo**	*we will say*
(voi) dir**ete**	*you will say* (pl.)
(loro) dir**anno**	*they will say*

dovere (*to have to*)

(io) dov**rò**	*I will have to*
(tu) dov**rai**	*you will have to* (fam.)
(Lei) dov**rà**	*you will have to* (pol.)
(lui) dov**rà**	*he will have to*
(lei) dov**rà**	*she will have to*
(noi) dov**remo**	*we will have to*
(voi) dov**rete**	*you will have to* (pl.)
(loro) dov**ranno**	*they will have to*

essere (*to be*)

(io) sar**ò**	*I will be*
(tu) sar**ai**	*you will be* (fam.)
(Lei) sar**à**	*you will be* (pol.)
(lui) sar**à**	*he will be*
(lei) sar**à**	*she will be*
(noi) sar**emo**	*we will be*
(voi) sar**ete**	*you will be* (pl.)
(loro) sar**anno**	*they will be*

fare (*to do, to make*)

(io) far**ò**	*I will do*
(tu) far**ai**	*you will do* (fam.)
(Lei) far**à**	*you will do* (pol.)
(lui) far**à**	*he will do*
(lei) far**à**	*she will do*
(noi) far**emo**	*we will do*
(voi) far**ete**	*you will do* (pl.)
(loro) far**anno**	*they will do*

potere (*to be able to*)

(io) pot**rò**	*I will be able to*
(tu) pot**rai**	*you will be able to* (fam.)
(Lei) pot**rà**	*you will be able to* (pol.)
(lui) pot**rà**	*he will be able to*
(lei) pot**rà**	*she will be able to*
(noi) pot**remo**	*we will be able to*
(voi) pot**rete**	*you will be able to* (pl.)
(loro) pot**ranno**	*they will be able to*

sapere (*to know*)

(io) sap**rò**	*I will know*
(tu) sap**rai**	*you will know* (fam.)

(Lei) saprà	you will know (pol.)
(lui) saprà	he will know
(lei) saprà	she will know
(noi) sapremo	we will know
(voi) saprete	you will know (pl.)
(loro) sapranno	they will know

venire (*to go*)

(io) verrò	I will go
(tu) verrai	you will go (fam.)
(Lei) verrà	you will go (pol.)
(lui) verrà	he will go
(lei) verrà	she will go
(noi) verremo	we will go
(voi) verrete	you will go (pl.)
(loro) verranno	they will go

volere (*to want*)

(io) vorrò	I will want
(tu) vorrai	you will want (fam.)
(Lei) vorrà	you will want (pol.)
(lui) vorrà	he will want
(lei) vorrà	she will want
(noi) vorremo	we will want
(voi) vorrete	you will want (pl.)
(loro) vorranno	they will want

Here is some useful vocabulary related to the theme of this section:

l'ascensore	*elevator*	l'ingresso	*entrance*
l'atrio	*lobby*	il piano	*floor*
la chiave	*key*	l'uscita	*exit*

Dialogo

The following conversation shows how one might complain about poor hotel service:

TURISTA: Non tornerò mai più in quest'albergo!	*I'll never come back to this hotel!*
IMPIEGATA: Perché?	*Why?*
TURISTA: La colazione non è buona e le camere sono sporche!	*The breakfast is not good, and the rooms are dirty!*
IMPIEGATA: Non capisco!	*I don't understand!*
TURISTA: E l'ascensore non funziona quasi mai!	*And the elevator almost never works!*
IMPIEGATA: Si calmi, signore! Le faremo uno sconto.	*Stay calm, sir! We will work out a discount for you.*

albergo	hotel		**quasi**	almost
calmarsi	to stay calm		**sconto**	discount
colazione (*f.*)	breakfast		**sporco**	dirty
funzionare	to work (function)			

Memory practice

Fill in the blanks with the appropriate words and expressions. Do this from memory, and then go back and check your answers.

Non _____ mai più in quest'albergo!

Perché?

La _____ non è buona e le camere sono _____ !

Non capisco!

E l'_____ non funziona quasi mai!

Si calmi, signore! Le faremo uno _____ .

Language notes

You have come across the form **vorrei** often in this book. It is a conditional tense form. The conditional is formed exactly like the future. The only difference is the set of endings. So, drop the **-re** of all three conjugations, changing the **a** of the first-conjugation verbs to **e**, just as you do with the future tense, then add these endings instead of the future endings:

parlare (*to speak*)

(io) parler**ei**	*I would speak*
(tu) parler**esti**	*you would speak* (fam.)
(Lei) parler**ebbe**	*you would speak* (pol.)
(lui) parler**ebbe**	*he would speak*
(lei) parler**ebbe**	*she would speak*
(noi) parler**emmo**	*we would speak*
(voi) parler**este**	*you would speak* (pl.)
(loro) parler**ebbero**	*they would speak*

leggere (*to read*)

(io) legger**ei**	*I would read*
(tu) legger**esti**	*you would read* (fam.)
(Lei) legger**ebbe**	*you would read* (pol.)
(lui) legger**ebbe**	*he would read*
(lei) legger**ebbe**	*she would read*
(noi) legger**emmo**	*we would read*
(voi) legger**este**	*you would read* (pl.)
(loro) legger**ebbero**	*they would read*

finire (to finish)	
(io) finir**ei**	*I would finish*
(tu) finir**esti**	*you would finish* (fam.)
(Lei) finir**ebbe**	*you would finish* (pol.)
(lui) finir**ebbe**	*he would finish*
(lei) finir**ebbe**	*she would finish*
(noi) finir**emmo**	*we would finish*
(voi) finir**este**	*you would finish* (pl.)
(loro) finir**ebbero**	*they would finish*

The same verbs that are irregular in the future are also irregular in the conditional. Here are a few examples:

FUTURE	CONDITIONAL
io avrò (*I will have*)	io avrei (*I would have*)
tu sarai (*you will be*)	tu saresti (*you would be*)
lui andrà (*he will go*)	lui andrebbe (*he would go*)
noi vorremo (*we will like*)	noi vorremmo (*we would like*)
voi saprete (*you will know*)	voi sapreste (*you would know*)
loro verranno (*they will come*)	loro verrebbero (*they would come*)

ESERCIZIO
8·2

Give the present indicative forms of **dare** *as indicated.*

1. Noi *dare* questo al professore. _____

2. Anch'io *dare* qualcosa al professore. _____

3. Anche tu gli *dare* qualcosa? _____

4. Mia sorella *dare* molte cose alle amiche. _____

5. Anche voi *dare* molte cose agli amici. _____

6. Loro non ci *dare* mai niente. _____

Translate the following sentences into Italian.

7. I gave those shoes to my brother.

_____

8. You used to give your sister many things.

_____

9. He will give me some money to go out tonight.

_____

10. They would give me some money, but they can't.

_____

Give the corresponding conditional form for each future form.

FUTURE	CONDITIONAL
11. lui mangerà	_____
12. io cercherò	_____
13. noi partiremo	_____
14. tu verrai	_____
15. voi saprete	_____
16. io pagherò	_____
17. tu sarai	_____
18. lei avrà	_____
19. io vorrò	_____
20. loro diranno	_____
21. io farò	_____

Carry out the following conversation tasks.

22. Say that you have not made a reservation.

_____

23. Say that you would like a room that looks onto the square (**la piazza**).

_____

24. Say that you would like a single room, not a double room (**camera doppia**).

_____

25. Ask how much it comes to per night.

_____

26. Ask if you could have two keys.

_____

27. Say that the elevator doesn't work.

_____

28. Ask if you could have a room on the sixth floor.

_____

29. Ask where the lobby is.

_____

30. Say that the exit is here.

_____

31. Ask where the hotel entrance is.

_____

32. Say that you will never come back to this hotel.

_____

33. Say that the breakfast is almost never good.

_____

34. Say that your room is dirty.

_____

35. Say that you would like a discount.

_____

At the airport

Dialogo

The next conversation typifies what one might say at an airport check-in counter:

IMPIEGATO:	Il Suo biglietto, per favore.	*Your ticket, please.*
PASSEGGERO:	Eccolo!	*Here it is!*
IMPIEGATO:	Il volo partirà tra mezz'ora.	*The flight is leaving in half an hour.*
PASSEGGERO:	Meno male!	*Thank goodness!*
IMPIEGATO:	Ecco la Sua carta d'imbarco!	*Here's your boarding pass!*
PASSEGGERO:	Dov'è l'uscita?	*Where's the gate?*
IMPIEGATO:	Laggiù, davanti a quel segnale.	*Down there, in front of that sign.*

NEW VOCABULARY

carta d'imbarco	boarding pass		**tra**	within
laggiù	down there		**uscita**	gate, exit
Meno male!	Thank goodness!		**volo**	flight
segnale (*m.*)	sign			

Memory practice

Fill in the blanks with the appropriate words and expressions. Do this from memory, and then go back and check your answers.

Il Suo _____ , per favore.

Eccolo!

Il _____ partirà _____ mezz'ora.

Meno _____ !

Ecco la Sua _____ d'imbarco!

Dov'è l'_____ ?

_____ , davanti a quel segnale.

Language notes

Note that pronouns are attached to **ecco**.

Ecco**lo**.	*Here **it** is/Here **he** is.*
Ecco**mi**.	*Here **I** am.*

The preposition **tra** can also be written and pronounced as **fra**. And it also means *between*. Here is some useful vocabulary related to the theme of this section:

il bagaglio	*baggage*	un posto al finestrino	*window seat*
il posto	*seat*	la valigia	*suitcase*
un posto al corridoio	*aisle seat*		

Dialogo

Here's the type of announcement that is usually given at takeoff:

ASSISTENTE: Signore e signori, siete pregati di allacciare la cintura di sicurezza. Il decollo è previsto tra qualche minuto. A decollo compiuto, serviremo il pasto. Il comandante e l'intero equipaggio, vi augurano un buon viaggio!

Ladies and gentleman, please (you are asked) fasten your seat belts. Takeoff is expected in a few minutes. After takeoff, we will serve the meal. The captain and the entire crew wish you a good trip!

NEW VOCABULARY

allacciare	to fasten	**essere pregato**	to be asked
augurare	to wish	**essere previsto**	to be expected
cintura di sicurezza	seat belt	**intero**	entire
comandante (*m./f.*)	captain	**pasto**	meal
compiuto	completed	**servire**	to serve
decollo	takeoff	**viaggio**	trip
equipaggio	crew		

Memory practice

Fill in the blanks with the appropriate words and expressions. Do this from memory, and then go back and check your answers.

Signore e signori, siete _____ di allacciare la _____ di

sicurezza. Il _____ è previsto tra qualche minuto. A decollo

_____, serviremo il pasto. Il _____ e l'intero

_____, vi augurano un _____ viaggio!

Language notes

In previous chapters you have come across three particles: **ne, ci, si**. All three come before the verb. **Ne** usually replaces a partitive phrase. Note that in compound tenses the past participle agrees with **ne**.

Vuoi **dei piselli**?	*Would you like **some peas**?*
Sì, **ne** voglio.	*Yes, I would like **some**.*
Quanti **libri** hai comprato?	*How many **books** did you buy?*
Ne ho comprati due.	*I bought **two (of them)**.*
Hai **delle mele**?	*Do you have **some apples**?*
No, non **ne** ho.	*No, I do not have **any**.*

Ci means *there* and is an alternative to **lì** and other place adverbs.

| Quando vai **in centro**? | *When are you going **downtown**?* |
| **Ci** vado domani. | *I am going (**there**) tomorrow.* |

Si is used to mean the impersonal *one*. Note that the verb is singular or plural according to what the sentence is about.

| **Si compra** quel vestito in centro. | ***One buys** that dress downtown.* |
| **Si comprano** quegli stivali in centro. | ***One buys** those dresses downtown.* |

ESERCIZIO
8·3

Replace the italicized phrases with an appropriate pronoun, and then rewrite the entire sentence, making all necessary changes.

EXAMPLE: Ecco *le vostre carte d'imbarco.*

Eccole. (Here they are.)

1. Ecco *il Suo biglietto.*

   _____

2. Ecco *i vostri bagagli.*

   _____

3. Ecco *le mie valige.*

   _____

4. Ecco *la Sua valigia.*

   _____

*Now replace the italicized phrase with **ne**, **ci**, or **si** as the case may be, and then rewrite the entire sentence, making all necessary changes.*

5. Prendo *delle pere.*

   _____

6. Ho mangiato *dei fagioli.*

   _____

7. Vado *in l'Italia* domani.

_____

8. Andrò *in centro* nel pomeriggio.

_____

9. *Uno* (personal "one") deve dire sempre la verità.

_____

10. *Uno* (personal "one") compra quelle cose in centro.

_____

Carry out the following conversation tasks.

11. Give your ticket to the agent pointing it out. (*Here is my ticket.*)

_____

12. Say that the flight will be departing in half an hour.

_____

13. Say "Thank goodness!"

_____

14. Say "Here's your boarding pass."

_____

15. Ask where the gate is.

_____

16. Say that it's down there in front of that sign.

_____

17. Say that you would like a window seat, not an aisle seat.

_____

18. Pretend you are a flight attendant and inform the passengers to fasten their seat belt.

_____

19. Say that takeoff is expected in a few minutes.

_____

20. Say that the captain and the entire crew wish the passengers a good trip.

_____

COMPLETE ITALIAN GRAMMAR

Introduction to Part II

In this part, you will be introduced to basic Italian grammar. The more intricate aspects, such as certain verb conjugations, are treated later. By concentrating on areas of grammar for making sentences and conversations, this part is designed to improve your ability to communicate effectively in Italian.

Each chapter presents the main points related to a topic which is followed by an **Esercizio**. Along the way, information boxes provide further detail on some topics, offer tips, or introduce related vocabulary

At the end of each chapter is a **Grammar in culture** section that links a grammar topic to culture or usage, with a related exercise. This section underscores the relevance of grammar to the study of culture.

Nouns and titles

Simple Italian sentences, like English sentences, are composed of a subject, a verb, and an object. The subject consists of a noun or noun phrase. It is what the sentence is about and around which the rest of the sentence revolves. The subject is, more generally, the performer of some action. Many types of objects also consist of a noun (or noun phrase). In this case the noun is the person, concept, thing, etc., toward which the action of the verb is directed or to which a preposition expresses some relation. This unit and the next one describe nouns.

Mio nipote studia la matematica.	*My grandson studies math.* (subject noun phrase)
L'**amore** esiste dappertutto.	*Love exists everywhere.* (subject noun)
Ieri sera io ho chiamato **mia nipote**.	*Last night I called my granddaughter.* (object noun phrase)
Lui è un **amico caro**.	*He's a dear friend.* (object noun phrase)
Lei vive **in periferia**.	*She lives in the suburbs.* (object noun phrase)
Abbiamo comprato un **televisore plasma**.	*We bought a plasma TV.* (object noun phrase)

Nouns can be regular or irregular. Regular ones have predictable endings in the singular and plural. Nouns are also classified as either common or proper. The former refer to persons, objects, places, concepts, and all the other things that make up the world. Proper nouns are the actual names and surnames given to people, geographical places and formations, brands, and the like.

Common nouns

A common noun can generally be recognized by its vowel ending, which indicates if it is masculine or feminine. This is called grammatical gender. Gender is important because it determines the form of both the articles and adjectives that accompany nouns in sentences and phrases. Generally, nouns ending in **-o** are masculine. They are made plural by changing the **-o** to **-i**.

MASCULINE SINGULAR		MASCULINE PLURAL	
figlio	*son*	**figli**	*sons*
gatto	*cat*	**gatti**	*cats*
libro	*book*	**libri**	*books*
ragazzo	*boy*	**ragazzi**	*boys*
zio	*uncle*	**zii**	*uncles*

Nouns ending in **-a** are generally feminine. They are made plural by changing the **-a** to **-e**.

FEMININE SINGULAR		FEMININE PLURAL	
casa	*house*	**case**	*houses*
figlia	*daughter*	**figlie**	*daughters*
penna	*pen*	**penne**	*pens*
ragazza	*girl*	**ragazze**	*girls*
zia	*aunt*	**zie**	*aunts*

Lastly, nouns ending in **-e** are either masculine or feminine. This is not an option; gender is fixed by the grammar of Italian. To find out if a noun ending in **-e** is masculine or feminine, you will have to consult a dictionary, or else you will have to infer it by observing the form (article, adjective, etc.) that accompanies it. Such nouns are made plural by changing the **-e** to **-i**, no matter what their gender is.

MASCULINE SINGULAR		MASCULINE PLURAL	
(il) cane	*(the) dog*	**(i) cani**	*(the) dogs*
(il) cellulare	*(the) cell phone*	**(i) cellulari**	*(the) cell phones*
(il) padre	*(the) father*	**(i) padri**	*(the) fathers*
(il) portatile	*(the) laptop*	**(i) portatili**	*(the) laptops*

FEMININE SINGULAR		FEMININE PLURAL	
(la) madre	*(the) mother*	**(le) madri**	*(the) mothers*
(la) nazione	*(the) nation*	**(le) nazioni**	*(the) nations*
(la) notte	*(the) night*	**(le) notti**	*(the) nights*
(la) parete	*(the) wall (partition)*	**(le) pareti**	*(the) walls (partitions)*

Here's a tip. Most nouns ending in **-ione**, especially in **-zione** and **-sione**, are feminine.

la stazione	*the (train) station*
la regione	*the region*
la riunione	*the meeting*

Useful common nouns

anno	*year*	**gonna**	*skirt*
giorno	*day*	**macchina**	*car*
vestito	*dress, suit*		
casa	*house*	**chiave** (*f.*)	*key*
cosa	*thing*	**cognome** (*m.*)	*surname, family name*
cravatta	*necktie*	**giornale** (*m.*)	*newspaper*
donna	*woman*	**nome** (*m.*)	*name*

(m. = masculine, f. = feminine)

Common nouns are not capitalized unless they occur at the beginning of a sentence. Unlike English, nouns referring to languages, speakers of a language, or inhabitants of an area are not normally capitalized.

L'italiano è una bellissima lingua.	*Italian is a very beautiful language.*
Lui è italiano, ma lei non è italiana.	*He is Italian, but she is not Italian.*
Lui invece è americano, e anche lei è americana.	*He, instead, is American, and she, too, is American.*
Ci sono tanti siciliani in questo posto.	*There are a lot of Sicilians in this place.*

Note: The noun **gente** (*people*) is singular in Italian.

La gente parla troppo.	*People talk too much.*
Lui conosce tanta gente.	*He knows a lot of people.*

Note: The plural of **l'uomo** (*the man*) is irregular; it is **gli uomini** (*the men*).

Lui è un bravo uomo.	*He is a good man.*
Chi sono quegli uomini?	*Who are those men?*

Also, note that some nouns ending in -**ione** are masculine. Those ending in -**one** are all masculine.

il copione	*the script*
il cordone	*the rope*
il mattone	*the brick*

ESERCIZIO

1·1

A. *Provide the singular or plural form of each noun, as required.*

SINGULAR	PLURAL
1. zio	_____
2. _____	ragazzi
3. libro	_____
4. _____	gatti
5. figlio	_____

6. _____ zie

7. ragazza _____

8. _____ penne

9. figlia _____

10. _____ case

11. cane _____

12. _____ cellulari

13. padre _____

14. _____ pareti

15. madre _____

16. _____ nazioni

17. notte _____

18. _____ cose

19. casa _____

20. _____ anni

21. giorno _____

22. _____ vestiti

23. cravatta _____

24. _____ donne

25. gonna _____

26. _____ macchine

27. chiave _____

28. _____ cognomi

29. giornale _____

30. _____ nomi

31. copione _____

32. _____ riunioni

33. cordone _____

34. _____ mattoni

B. *Provide the missing endings to the common nouns in the following sentences.*

1. A suo nipot_____ piace la matematic_____ .

2. L'amor_____ conquista *(conquers)* tutto.

3. Quella donn_____ ha chiamato mia nipot_____ .

4. Marco è un caro amic_____ .

5. La mia amic_____ vive in periferi_____ .

6. I miei amic_____ hanno comprato un televisor_____ plasma.

7. L'italian_____ è una lingu_____ facile.

8. Lui è italian_____ , ma lei è american_____ .

9. Dov'è quella region_____ ?

10. A che ora c'è la riunion_____ ?

C. *There is an error in each sentence. Spot it and rewrite the sentence to correct it. You might have to make adjustments to the other words as well.*

1. Quei due uomi sono italiani.

_____

2. La gente parlano troppo.

_____

3. Sara è Siciliana.

_____

4. Alessandro parla Francese.

_____

Gender patterns

Every noun in Italian is marked for gender—that is to say, it is classified as either masculine or feminine. In the case of nouns referring to people (or animals), the grammatical gender of the noun usually matches the biological sex of the person (or animal).

With few exceptions, nouns that refer to males (people or animals) are masculine, and those that refer to females (people or animals) are feminine.

MASCULINE (MALES)		FEMININE (FEMALES)	
l'americano	*the male American*	l'americana	*the female American*
l'amico	*the male friend*	l'amica	*the female friend*
l'italiano	*the male Italian*	l'italiana	*the female Italian*
il gatto	*the male cat*	la gatta	*the female cat*

There are exceptions. For example, **il soprano** (*soprano*) is a masculine noun but it refers to a female person, and **la guardia** (*guard*) is a feminine noun but it can refer to either a male or female person.

Nouns ending in -a and referring to both males and females

la persona	*person (male or female)*
la spia	*spy (male or female)*
la stella	*star (male or female)*

Some nouns ending in -**e** refer to males or females. Note that with these nouns any other forms (articles, adjectives, etc.) that accompany the nouns must indicate the correct grammatical gender.

MASCULINE (MALES)		FEMININE (FEMALES)	
il cantante	*the male singer*	**la cantante**	*the female singer*
il francese	*the French man*	**la francese**	*the French woman*
il nipote	*the grandson; nephew*	**la nipote**	*the granddaughter; niece*
il padre	*the father*	**la madre**	*the mother*
l'inglese	*the English man*	**l'inglese**	*the English woman*

Some masculine nouns ending in -**e** correspond to feminine nouns ending in -**a**.

MASCULINE (MALES)		FEMININE (FEMALES)	
il cameriere	*the waiter*	**la cameriera**	*the waitress*
il signore	*the gentleman*	**la signora**	*the lady*
l'infermiere	*the male nurse*	**l'infermiera**	*the female nurse*

Note: The plural ending -**i** is used when the noun refers to both male *and* female beings taken together as a group, whereas the plural ending -**e** refers only to a group of females.

SINGULAR		PLURAL	
l'italiano	*the (male) Italian*	**gli italiani**	*the Italians (males only or males and females together)*
l'italiana	*the (female) Italian*	**le italiane**	*the Italians (females only)*
l'americano	*the (male) American*	**gli americani**	*the Americans (males only or males and females together)*
l'americana	*the (female) American*	**le americane**	*the Americans (females only)*

A. *Provide the corresponding nouns referring to males and females. The first one is done for you.*

	MALE	FEMALE
1. American	*americano*	*americana*
2. Italian		
3. friend		
4. soprano		
5. guard		
6. star		
7. spy		
8. person		
9. English		
10. French		
11. singer		
12. nurse		

B. *How do you say the following in Italian?*

1. grandson or nephew   il _____
2. Americans (in general)   gli _____
3. female Italians   le _____
4. granddaughter or niece   la _____
5. waiters (in general)   i _____
6. waitresses   le _____
7. gentleman   il _____
8. lady   la _____

Spelling adjustments in the plural

The consonants in the noun endings **-co**, **-go**, **-ca**, and **-ga** represent hard sounds. There are two possibilities for changing the **-co** and **-go** endings to the plural.

If the hard sounds are to be retained, the masculine plural endings are spelled respectively **-chi** and **-ghi**. To remember that **ch** and **gh** represent hard sounds in Italian, think of English words that use them in the same way: *chemistry, ache, school, charisma, ghost.*

SINGULAR		PLURAL	
gioco	*game*	**giochi**	*games*
tedesco	*German*	**tedeschi**	*Germans*
lago	*lake*	**laghi**	*lakes*
luogo	*place*	**luoghi**	*places*

If the corresponding soft sounds are required instead, the masculine plural endings are spelled respectively **-ci** and **-gi**.

SINGULAR		PLURAL	
amico	*friend*	**amici**	*friends*
greco	*Greek*	**greci**	*Greeks*
biologo	*biologist*	**biologi**	*biologists*
antropologo	*anthropologist*	**antropologi**	*anthropologists*

So, when do you use one or the other plural form? In general, if **-co** is preceded by **e** or **i** (as in **amico** and **greco**), the noun is pluralized to **-ci** (**amici**, **greci**). Otherwise the hard sound is retained (**-chi**). In the case of **-go**, the tendency is to retain the hard sound. However, when the noun ends in the suffix **-logo** and refers to a profession, career, or activity, then the appropriate plural suffix is **-logi**.

il teologo	*the theologian*	**i teologi**	*the theologians*

These rules should be considered "rules of thumb" rather than strict grammatical rules (covering a large number of cases, however).

Exceptions to the rules of thumb

il porco	*the pig*	**i porci**	*the pigs*
il fico	*the fig*	**i fichi**	*the figs*
il sindaco	*the mayor*	**i sindaci**	*the mayors*
il monaco	*the monk*	**i monaci**	*the monks*

The endings **-ca** and **-ga** are always changed to **-che** and **-ghe**, which represent hard sounds.

SINGULAR		PLURAL	
banca	*bank*	**banche**	*banks*
greca	*female Greek*	**greche**	*female Greeks*
riga	*straight ruler*	**righe**	*straight rulers*

The consonants in the endings **-cio** and **-gio** represent soft sounds. Note that the **i** is not pronounced. It is put there simply to indicate that the consonants are to be pronounced softly. There is only one way to change such nouns to the plural, which is to retain the soft sounds with the endings: **-ci** and **-gi**.

SINGULAR		PLURAL	
bacio	*kiss*	**baci**	*kisses*
orologio	*watch*	**orologi**	*watches*

If the **i** in **-io** is stressed, it is retained in the plural; otherwise, it is not retained. To be sure if it is stressed or not, consult a dictionary.

SINGULAR		PLURAL	
zio (stressed)	*uncle*	**zii**	*uncles*
occhio (unstressed)	*eye*	**occhi**	*eyes*

There are two possibilities for changing nouns ending in **-cia** and **-gia** to the plural. If the **i** in the ending is stressed, it is pronounced in the plural and, thus, retained in spelling.

SINGULAR		PLURAL	
farmacia	*pharmacy*	**farmacie**	*pharmacies*
bugia	*lie*	**bugie**	*lies*

If the **i** indicates that the preceding consonant represents a soft sound in the singular but is not stressed in the pronunciation, it is not retained in the plural spelling.

SINGULAR		PLURAL	
valigia	*suitcase*	**valige**	*suitcases*
faccia	*face*	**facce**	*faces*

To know if the **i** is stressed or not, consult a dictionary. The only exception to these rules applies to the word for *shirt*.

SINGULAR		PLURAL	
camicia	*shirt*	**camicie**	*shirts*

ESERCIZIO
1·3

A. *Provide the plural forms of the following nouns.*

1. luogo _____

2. tedesco _____

3. antropologo _____

4. greco _____

5. amico _____

6. gioco _____

7. biologo _____

8. lago _____

9. monaco _____

10. fico _____

11. sindaco _____

12. porco _____

13. riga   _____

14. greca   _____

15. banca   _____

16. camicia   _____

B. *Now, do the reverse. Provide the singular forms of the given plural nouns.*

1. baci   _____

2. occhi   _____

3. zii   _____

4. orologi   _____

5. farmacie   _____

6. bugie   _____

7. facce   _____

8. valige   _____

Mass nouns

There are two types of common nouns: count and mass. Count nouns refer to persons, things, etc., that can be counted (as their designation suggests). They have both singular and plural forms. The nouns you have been using so far are count nouns.

Mass nouns refer instead to things that cannot be counted and therefore generally have only a singular form.

l'acqua	*water*
la fame	*hunger*
la sete	*thirst*
lo zucchero	*sugar*

Mass nouns can, of course, be used in a figurative or poetic way. In such cases they can be put in the plural.

le acque del mare	*the waters of the sea*

Common mass nouns

la carne	*meat*	**il riso**	*rice*
il latte	*milk*	**il sale**	*salt*
il pane	*bread*	**l'uva**	*grapes*
il pepe	*pepper*		

A few nouns have only a plural form. They refer to things made up of more than one part.

i baffi	*mustache*
le forbici	*scissors*
gli occhiali	*(eye)glasses*
le mutande	*underwear*
i pantaloni	*pants*

ESERCIZIO
1·4

A. *Can you figure out what each clue refers to?*

1. È dolce. (*It is sweet.*) _____

2. Si usano per vedere. (*They are used for seeing.*) _____

3. Crescono sopra le labbra. (*They grow above the lips.*) _____

4. È un liquido bianco. (*It's a white liquid.*) _____

5. Si usa per fare il vino. (*It is used to make wine.*) _____

B. *How do you say the following in Italian?*

1. salt and pepper _____

2. meat, bread, and rice _____

3. hunger and thirst _____

4. water _____

5. the waters of the sea _____

6. pants and underwear _____

7. scissors and eyeglasses _____

Proper nouns and titles

The same gender patterns described above apply to proper nouns. However, such nouns generally have only a singular form, with some exceptions. For example, *the United States*, as in English, is plural in Italian, even though it is a proper noun: **gli Stati Uniti**. Note that a proper noun is capitalized.

MASCULINE		FEMININE	
Alessandro	*Alexander*	**Alessandra**	*Alexandra*
Franco	*Frank*	**Franca**	*Franca*
Giovanni	*John*	**Maria**	*Mary*
Paolo	*Paul*	**Paola**	*Paula*
Pasquale	*Pat*	**l'Italia**	*Italy*
il Natale	*Christmas*	**la Pasqua**	*Easter*
il Tevere	*the Tiber*	**Giovanna**	*Joanne*

Italians use more titles than Americans do to address people. Here are a few common ones.

MALE TITLE	FEMALE TITLE	MEANING
signore	**signora, signorina**	*Mr.; Mrs./Ms., Miss*
dottore	**dottoressa**	*Doctor*
professore	**professoressa**	*Professor*
avvocato	**avvocato**	*Lawyer*
geometra	**geometra**	*Draftsperson*
ragioniere	**ragioniera**	*Accountant (Bookkeeper)*
architetto	**architetto**	*Architect*

Title peculiarities

The title of **dottore/dottoressa** is used to address both a medical doctor and any university graduate.

The title of **professore/professoressa** is used to address both a university professor and any junior high and high school teacher.

Capitalizing titles is optional.

Note: The final **-e** of a masculine title is dropped before a name. This rule does not apply to feminine titles. This is a rule of style, rather than strict grammar. So, it is not technically wrong to keep the **-e**, but very few Italians do so.

MASCULINE TITLE		USED BEFORE A NAME	
il signore	*the gentleman*	**il signor Verdi**	*Mr. Verdi*
il professore	*the professor*	**il professor Rossi**	*Professor Rossi*
il dottore	*the doctor*	**il dottor Bianchi**	*Dr. Bianchi*

FEMININE TITLE		USED BEFORE A NAME	
la signora	*the lady*	**la signora Verdi**	*Mrs. Verdi*
la professoressa	*the professor*	**la professoressa Rossi**	*Professor Rossi*
la dottoressa	*the doctor*	**la dottoressa Bianchi**	*Dr. Bianchi*

Note as well that the title is preceded by the definite article. The article is dropped in direct speech (talking to someone and using the title):

TITLE	DIRECT SPEECH	
il dottor Giusti	«Buongiorno, **dottor Giusti**.»	*"Good morning, Dr. Giusti."*
la professoressa Dini	«Salve, **professoressa Dini**.»	*"Hello, Prof. Dini."*

A. *Provide the corresponding male or female form.*

MALE	FEMALE
1. Paolo	_____
2. _____	Franca
3. Alessandro	_____
4. _____	Giovanna
5. nipote	_____
6. _____	signora
7. professore	_____
8. _____	dottoressa
9. geometra	_____
10. _____	ragioniera
11. il dottor Totti	_____
12. _____	la professoressa Nardini
13. architetto	_____
14. _____	avvocato

B. *How do you say the following in Italian?*

1. Luke, Andrew, and Nicholas are friends.

_____

2. I love Christmas and Easter in Italy.

_____

3. Mr. Rossi is a friend of the family (*famiglia*).

_____

4. "Hello, Mr. Rossi."

_____

5. Mrs. Rossi is a friend of the family.

_____

6. "Good morning, Mrs. Rossi."

_____

C. *Use check marks to indicate the categories to which each given noun belongs.*

NOUN	COMMON	PROPER	COUNT	MASS	MASC.	FEM.	SING.	PL.
1. ragazzo	_____	_____	_____	_____	_____	_____	_____	_____
2. Giovanna	_____	_____	_____	_____	_____	_____	_____	_____
3. libri	_____	_____	_____	_____	_____	_____	_____	_____
4. camicie	_____	_____	_____	_____	_____	_____	_____	_____
5. Tevere	_____	_____	_____	_____	_____	_____	_____	_____
6. casa	_____	_____	_____	_____	_____	_____	_____	_____
7. pane	_____	_____	_____	_____	_____	_____	_____	_____
8. antropologi	_____	_____	_____	_____	_____	_____	_____	_____

D. *Rewrite each sentence by changing it from the masculine to the feminine, or vice versa, as required by the noun(s) in parentheses.*

EXAMPLE   Maria è un'amica. (Giovanni)
Giovanni è un amico.

1. Il signor Rossini è italiano. (la signora Binni)

_____

2. Giovanni e Luca sono due uomini. (Maria e Paola)

_____

3. I ragazzi sono francesi. (le ragazze)

_____

4. La professoressa Smith è americana. (il professor Jones)

_____

5. Maria è mia zia. (Pasquale)

_____

Grammar in culture

Many nouns have cultural and social naming functions. Among these are the names of the 20 Italian regions (**le regioni**) and their capital cities (**i capoluoghi**). Locate these regions and cities on a map of Italy, and try to commit the names and relative geographical locations to memory.

REGIONE	CAPOLUOGO
Abruzzo	L'Aquila
Basilicata	Potenza
Calabria	Catanzaro
Campania	Napoli
Emilia-Romagna	Bologna
Friuli-Venezia Giulia	Trieste
Lazio	Roma
Liguria	Genova
Lombardia	Milano
Marche	Ancona
Molise	Campobasso
Piemonte	Torino
Puglia	Bari
Sardegna	Cagliari
Sicilia	Palermo
Toscana	Firenze
Trentino-Alto Adige	Trento
Umbria	Perugia
Valle d'Aosta	Aosta
Veneto	Venezia

ESERCIZIO
1·6

There is incorrect information in each sentence. Rewrite the sentence with the correct information.

1. Trento è il capoluogo della Lombardia.

   _____

2. La Sardegna, l'Umbria e la Valle d'Aosta sono capoluoghi.

   _____

3. Venezia è il capoluogo del Piemonte.

   _____

4. Firenze e Aosta sono regioni.

   _____

5. La Basilicata è il capoluogo del Friuli-Venezia Giulia.

   _____

·II-2·

More about nouns

In the languages of the world, nouns make up from 70 to 80 percent of all words. In Italian it is almost 85 percent. Obviously, knowing as much as possible about nouns is an important aspect of learning Italian grammar. So, a second unit is devoted to this topic.

In the previous unit, we dealt with basic noun forms and gender patterns. In this unit we will go a little more in depth, completing the "grammatical story" of Italian nouns.

More gender patterns

Let's start with a few more gender patterns.

Nouns ending in **-ista** refer to both male and female persons, and are thus both masculine and feminine. Many of these nouns are used to indicate occupations, professions, etc.

MASCULINE (MALES)		FEMININE (FEMALES)	
il musicista	*the male musician*	**la musicista**	*the female musician*
il dentista	*the male dentist*	**la dentista**	*the female dentist*
il pianista	*the male pianist*	**la pianista**	*the female pianist*
il farmacista	*the male pharmacist*	**la farmacista**	*the female pharmacist*

Their plural forms vary according to gender. If the noun is used to indicate a group of males or a mixed group of males and females, then the masculine plural is formed by changing the final vowel to **-i**. If it is used to indicate a group of females, then the feminine plural is formed by changing the final vowel to **-e**.

MASCULINE SINGULAR		MASCULINE PLURAL	
il musicista	*the male musician*	**i musicisti**	*the male musicians / the musicians (in general)*
il dentista	*the male dentist*	**i dentisti**	*the male dentists / the dentists (in general)*

FEMININE SINGULAR		FEMININE PLURAL	
la musicista	*the female musician*	**le musiciste**	*the female musicians*
la dentista	*the female dentist*	**le dentiste**	*the female dentists*

Masculine nouns ending in **-tore** often correspond to feminine nouns ending in **-trice**.

138

MASCULINE (MALES)		FEMININE (FEMALES)	
l'attore	*the male actor*	**l'attrice**	*the female actor*
il pittore	*the male painter*	**la pittrice**	*the female painter*
l'autore	*the male author*	**l'autrice**	*the female author*
lo scultore	*the male sculptor*	**la scultrice**	*the female sculptor*

Some masculine nouns, generally ending in **-e**, correspond to feminine nouns ending in **-essa**.

MASCULINE (MALES)		FEMININE (FEMALES)	
il dottore	*the male doctor*	**la dottoressa**	*the female doctor*
l'elefante	*the male elephant*	**l'elefantessa**	*the female elephant*
il leone	*the lion*	**la leonessa**	*the lioness*
il professore	*the male professor*	**la professoressa**	*the female professor*
lo studente	*the male student*	**la studentessa**	*the female student*

Some feminine forms have been eliminated in Italy, especially in the area of the professions.

l'architetto	*male or female architect*
l'avvocato	*male or female lawyer*
lo scultore	*male or female sculptor*

The names of trees are generally masculine, whereas the names of the fruits they bear are usually feminine.

TREE = MASCULINE		FRUIT = FEMININE	
l'arancio	*the orange tree*	**l'arancia**	*the orange*
il ciliegio	*the cherry tree*	**la ciliegia**	*the cherry*
il melo	*the apple tree*	**la mela**	*the apple*
il pero	*the pear tree*	**la pera**	*the pear*
il pesco	*the peach tree*	**la pesca**	*the peach*

Exceptions

Il limone (*the lemon*), **il fico** (*the fig*), and **il mandarino** (*the mandarin*) refer to both the tree and the fruit.

ESERCIZIO
2·1

A. *Provide the singular form of each noun.*

SINGULAR	PLURAL
1. _____	pianiste
2. _____	dentisti
3. _____	farmacisti
4. _____	musiciste

B. *Provide the corresponding male or female form of each noun.*

MALE	FEMALE
1. attore	_____
2. _____	scultrice
3. autore	_____
4. _____	pittrice
5. farmacista	_____
6. _____	dottoressa
7. leone	_____
8. _____	professoressa
9. elefante	_____
10. _____	avvocato
11. studente	_____

C. *You are given the name of either a tree or a fruit. Provide the other as required.*

TREE	FRUIT
1. ciliegio	_____
2. _____	pera
3. melo	_____
4. _____	arancia
5. pesco	_____
6. _____	limone
7. mandarino	_____
8. _____	fico

Nouns of Greek origin

Some Italian nouns are of Greek origin. Some end in **-ema** and **-amma**, which correspond to English nouns ending in *-em* and *-am*. They are all masculine.

il diagramma	*the diagram*
il dramma	*the drama*
il problema	*the problem*
il programma	*the program*
il sistema	*the system*
il teorema	*the theorem*

As masculine nouns, the final -**a** changes to -**i** in the plural.

SINGULAR		PLURAL	
il diagramma	*the diagram*	**i diagrammi**	*the diagrams*
il problema	*the problem*	**i problemi**	*the problems*
il programma	*the program*	**i programmi**	*the programs*

Nouns ending in -**si** in the singular are also of Greek origin. They correspond to English nouns ending in -*sis*. They are all feminine.

l'analisi	*the analysis*
la crisi	*the crisis*
l'ipotesi	*the hypothesis*
la tesi	*the thesis*

Note: There is an exception to this rule; **il brindisi** (*drinking toast*) is masculine and is of Germanic origin.

The singular -**si** ending for all these words is not changed in the plural.

SINGULAR		PLURAL	
il brindisi	*the toast*	**i brindisi**	*the toasts*
la crisi	*the crisis*	**le crisi**	*the crises*
l'ipotesi	*the hypothesis*	**le ipotesi**	*the hypotheses*
la tesi	*the thesis*	**le tesi**	*the theses*

ESERCIZIO
2·2

A. *Provide the plural forms of the following nouns.*

SINGULAR   PLURAL

1. ipotesi _____

2. tesi _____

3. programma _____

4. problema _____

5. sistema _____

B. *Now, provide the singular forms.*

1. _____ brindisi

2. _____ crisi

3. _____ diagrammi

4. _____ teoremi

5. _____ drammi

6. _____ analisi

Other types of nouns

Nouns ending in an accented **-à** or **-ù** are feminine; those ending in other accented vowels are masculine.

MASCULINE		FEMININE	
il caffè	*the coffee*	**la città**	*the city*
il lunedì	*Monday*	**la gioventù**	*youth*
il tassì	*the taxi*	**l'università**	*the university*
il tè	*the tea*	**la virtù**	*virtue*

Exceptions

Il papà (*dad*), **il menù** (*menu*), and **il ragù** (*meat sauce*) are masculine.

These endings are not changed in the plural.

SINGULAR		PLURAL	
il caffè	*the coffee*	**i caffè**	*the coffees*
la città	*the city*	**le città**	*the cities*
il tassì	*the taxi*	**i tassì**	*the taxis*
il tè	*the tea*	**i tè**	*the teas*
l'università	*the university*	**le università**	*the universities*

A few nouns ending in **-o** are feminine, because they are shortened forms and thus retain their original feminine gender.

FEMININE NOUN		SHORTENED FORM	
la fotografia	*the photograph*	**la foto**	*the photo*
la motocicletta	*the motorcycle*	**la moto**	*the motorcycle*
la radiofonia	*the radio transmission*	**la radio**	*the radio*

A few nouns ending in **-a** are masculine because they are, analogously, shortened forms and thus retain their original masculine gender.

MASCULINE NOUN		SHORTENED FORM	
il cinematografo	*the movie theater*	**il cinema**	*the movies*

Shortened nouns are not changed in the plural.

SINGULAR		PLURAL	
il cinema	*the movie theater*	**i cinema**	*the movie theaters*
la foto	*the photo*	**le foto**	*the photos*
la moto	*the motorcycle*	**le moto**	*the motorcycles*
la radio	*the radio*	**le radio**	*the radios*

Nouns that have been borrowed from other languages, primarily English, are generally masculine. These typically end in a consonant.

l'autobus	the bus
il clacson	the car horn
il computer	the computer
lo sport	the sport
il tennis	tennis
il tram	the streetcar, trolley

Exceptions

The following are feminine.

la chat	chatroom
la mail (l'e-mail)	e-mail, e-mail message

Such nouns are invariable—that is, they are not changed in the plural.

SINGULAR		PLURAL	
il clacson	the car horn	i clacson	the car horns
il computer	the computer	i computer	the computers
la mail	the e-mail	le mail	the e-mails
lo sport	the sports	gli sport	the sports

Like the English nouns *memorandum* and *compendium*, which have the plural forms *memoranda* and *compendia*, Italian also has a few nouns whose plural forms end in -**a**. These derive from Latin words that were pluralized in this way. In Italian, these nouns are masculine in the singular but feminine in the plural.

SINGULAR		PLURAL	
il braccio	arm	le braccia	arms
il dito	the finger	le dita	the fingers
il ginocchio	the knee	le ginocchia	the knees
il labbro	the lip	le labbra	the lips
il paio	the pair	le paia	the pairs

There are not too many of these nouns, and most refer to parts of the human body. In some cases, the regular plural form is used when the noun is used with an extended or figurative meaning.

i bracci della croce	the arms of a cross
i labbri della ferita	the lips of a wound

Note: There are also some nouns which are simply irregular and don't follow a rule or pattern.

il bue	the ox
la mano	the hand
il pianeta	the planet
il vaglia	the money order

They are also irregular in the plural.

SINGULAR		PLURAL	
il bue	*the ox*	i buoi	*the oxen*
la mano	*the hand*	le mani	*the hands*
il pianeta	*the planet*	i pianeti	*the planets*
il vaglia	*the money order*	i vaglia	*the money orders*

ESERCIZIO 2·3

A. *Indicate if the noun is masculine or feminine.*

NOUN	MASCULINE	FEMININE
1. città	_____	_____
2. lunedì	_____	_____
3. papà	_____	_____
4. tè	_____	_____
5. menù	_____	_____
6. ragù	_____	_____
7. caffè	_____	_____
8. gioventù	_____	_____
9. virtù	_____	_____
10. università	_____	_____
11. tassì	_____	_____
12. tram	_____	_____
13. autobus	_____	_____

B. *Provide the singular or plural form of each noun, as required.*

SINGULAR	PLURAL
1. caffè	_____
2. _____	città
3. foto	_____
4. _____	cinema
5. moto	_____
6. _____	computer
7. vaglia	_____

8. _____   mail

9. dito   _____

10. _____   braccia

11. paio   _____

12. _____   ginocchia

13. il braccio della croce   _____

14. _____   i labbri della ferita

15. bue   _____

16. _____   radio

17. mano   _____

18. _____   pianeti

19. clacson   _____

20. _____   sport

Altered nouns

Suffixes are forms with set meanings that are attached after a noun (or other part of speech), altering its meaning in some specific way. Such nouns are called, logically enough, altered nouns. Common suffixes are as follows.

The suffixes **-ino**, **-etto**, and **-ello**, with corresponding feminine forms **-ina**, **-etta**, and **-ella**, are often used to add a nuance of "littleness" or "smallness" to the meaning of the noun.

NOUN		ALTERED NOUN	
ragazzo	*boy*	**ragazzino**	*small boy*
ragazza	*girl*	**ragazzina**	*little girl*
gallo	*rooster*	**galletto**	*little rooster*
asino	*donkey*	**asinello**	*small donkey*

Be careful!

There are a number of exceptions. For example: **il libretto** does not mean *small book* but *opera libretto* or *bankbook*. The appropriate suffix is **il libricino** (*the little book*). Also **la manina** means *little hand*, but **la manetta** means *handcuff*.

The suffix **-one/-ona** is sometimes used to add a nuance of "bigness" or "largeness" to the meaning of the noun.

NOUN		ALTERED NOUN	
libro	*book*	**librone**	*big book*
ragazza	*girl*	**ragazzona**	*big girl*
ragazzo	*boy*	**ragazzone**	*big boy*

The suffix **-uccio/-uccia** (also **-uzzo/-uzza**) is sometimes used to add a nuance of "smallness" with a tinge of criticism or, on the contrary, "dearness" to the meaning of the noun. The suffix **-accio/-accia** is used instead to add a nuance of "badness" or "ugliness" to the meaning of the noun.

NOUN		ALTERED NOUN	
affare	*business transaction*	**affaraccio**	*hollow business transaction*
corpo	*body*	**corpaccio**	*ugly body*
Sara	*Sarah*	**Saruccia**	*dear little Sarah*

There is no steadfast rule as to when such suffixes can be used and with which nouns they can be used. Their use is more a matter of style than it is of grammar. Only through exposure and practice will you develop facility with them.

ESERCIZIO
2·4

A. *Add a suffix to each noun as indicated, altering its meaning accordingly.*

NOUN	SMALLNESS SUFFIX	LARGENESS SUFFIX
1. asino	_____	_____
2. ragazza	_____	_____
3. libro	_____	_____
4. mano	_____	_____

B. *How would you say the following, using appropriate suffixes?*

1. a big arm   un _____

2. an ugly body   un _____

3. a handcuff   una _____

4. a small problem   un _____

5. a big problem   un _____

6. un ugly, bad problem   un _____

7. a hollow business transaction   un _____

8. a big business transaction   un _____

9. cute little Mary   _____

Compound nouns

Compound nouns are nouns made of two parts of speech. For example, in English, the compound noun *handkerchief* is made up of two nouns *hand* + *kerchief*. Here are some common Italian compound nouns.

CONSTITUENT PARTS	COMPOUND NOUN	
arco + baleno	l'arcobaleno	*rainbow*
caccia + vite	il cacciavite	*screwdriver*
capo + luogo	il capoluogo	*capital of a region*
capo + reparto	il caporeparto	*head of a department*
cassa + forte	la cassaforte	*safe (for valuables)*
ferro + via	la ferrovia	*railroad*
franco + bollo	il francobollo	*postage stamp*
piano + forte	il pianoforte	*piano*
salva + gente	il salvagente	*life jacket*

To form the plural of such nouns, observe the following guidelines.

Most compound nouns are pluralized in the normal fashion, by changing the final vowel.

SINGULAR		PLURAL	
l'arcobaleno	*the rainbow*	gli arcobaleni	*the rainbows*
la ferrovia	*the railroad*	le ferrovie	*the railroads*

But there are exceptions. In some cases, the final vowels of both parts of the word are changed.

SINGULAR		PLURAL	
la cassaforte	*safe (for valuables)*	le casseforti	*safes (for valuables)*

If the compound noun has a verb as one of its parts, it does not change at all in traditional grammar. Today, however, there is a tendency to pluralize such a noun in the normal fashion. The following examples conform to tradition.

SINGULAR		PLURAL	
il cacciavite	*the screwdriver*	i cacciavite	*the screwdrivers*
il salvagente	*the life jacket*	i salvagente	*the life jackets*

To be certain of the correct plural form, you will need to look up such nouns in a good dictionary (as do most native speakers, by the way).

ESERCIZIO
2·5

A. *Provide the singular or plural form of each noun, as required.*

SINGULAR	PLURAL
1. arcobaleno	_____
2. _____	salvagente
3. ferrovia	_____

4. _____   casseforti

5. pianoforte   _____

B. *Can you figure out what compound noun corresponds to each clue?*

EXAMPLE   Ci passa sopra il treno. (*The train goes over it.*)
               la ferrovia

1. Si chiama anche «manager» oggi. (*He/She is also called "manager" today.*)

   _____

2. È un utensile. (*It's a utensil/tool.*)

   _____

3. Si mette sulla busta. (*It's put on an envelope.*)

   _____

4. È lo strumento di Chopin. (*It's Chopin's instrument.*)

   _____

5. È la città principale di una regione. (*It's the main city of a region.*)

   _____

C. *Choose the appropriate form that corresponds to each phrase.* (*Note:* **piccolo** = *little, small;* **caro** = *dear;* **grande** = *big;* **plurale** = *plural;* **frutta** = *fruit.*)

1. il piccolo Marcello

   a. Marcellino   b. Marcellone

2. la piccola e cara Teresa

   a. Teresina   b. Teresuccia

3. il grande Alessandro

   a. Alessandrone   b. Alessandruccio

4. un piccolo gallo

   a. una gallina   b. un galletto

5. il plurale di **problema**

   a. problemi   b. problema

6. la frutta del pesco

   a. la pesca   b. il pesco

7. la frutta del limone

   a. la limonata   b. il limone

8. il plurale di **ipotesi**

   a. ipotesi   b. ipotesina

D. *Complete the chart with the missing noun forms.*

MASC. SING.	MASC. PL.	FEM. SING.	FEM. PL.
1. pianista	_____	_____	_____
2. _____	farmacisti	_____	_____
3. _____	_____	attrice	_____
4. _____	_____	_____	scultrici
5. elefante	_____	_____	_____
6. _____	studenti	_____	_____

E. *You are given eight nouns in their singular form. However, the sentences provided require that they be inserted in their plural form. So, complete each sentence with the appropriate noun in its plural form (which, of course, might be the same form as the singular).*

autobus   sport   caffè   tennis
foto   città   paio   dito

1. Bevo sempre troppi _____ . (*I always drink too many . . . .*)

2. Voglio vedere tante _____ in Italia. (*I want to see many . . . in Italy.*)

3. Dove sono le _____ delle vacanze? (*Where are the . . . from vacation?*)

4. Mio nipote pratica tanti _____ . (*My grandson plays a lot of . . . .*)

5. Il mio sport preferito è il _____ . (*My favorite sport is . . . .*)

6. Iero ho preso l'_____ per andare a scuola. (*Yesterday I took the . . . to go to school.*)

7. Lui ha le _____ lunghe. (*He has long . . . .*)

8. Ieri lei ha comprato due _____ di scarpe. (*Yesterday she bought two . . . of shoes.*)

Grammar in culture

Many Italian nouns associated with the Internet, social media, and mobile devices are borrowed from English.

l'app	*app*
il blog	*blog*
Facebook	*Facebook*
il file	*file*
Instagram	*Instagram*
Internet	*Internet*
Twitter	*Twitter*
il wiki	*wiki*
YouTube	*YouTube*

Other computer-related terms are not English borrowings.

il caricamento	*uploading*
la navigazione	*navigation (of the Web)*
la piattaforma	*platform*
la rete sociale (social network)	*social network*
lo scaricamento	*downloading*
il sito web	*website*

ESERCIZIO

2·6

Choose the appropriate word.

1. È una piattaforma web.

    a. app   b. YouTube

2. È un servizio di rete sociale (*social network*).

    a. Facebook   b. scaricamento

3. È un servizio di rete sociale che permette di scattare (*to take*) foto.

    a. Instagram   b. caricamento

4. È un particolare tipo di sito.

    a. sito web   b. blog

5. È un servizio gratuito (*free*) di rete sociale e microblogging.

    a. Twitter   b. navigazione

Articles

Articles are "function words" that mark nouns as specific or nonspecific, that is, as referring to something in particular or in general. A function word is a form that has grammatical meaning or value.

SPECIFIC REFERENCE		NONSPECIFIC REFERENCE	
il bambino	*the child*	**un bambino**	*a child*
la porta	*the door*	**una porta**	*a door*

The indefinite article

The indefinite article, **un** (the form listed in the dictionary), corresponds to both English indefinite article forms *a* and *an*. It has only singular forms that vary according to the gender and initial letter of the noun they precede.

The form **uno** is used before a masculine singular noun beginning with **z**, **s** + **consonant**, **gn**, or **ps**.

uno zio	*an uncle*
uno studente	*a student*
uno gnocco	*a dumpling*
uno psicologo	*a psychologist*

The form **un** is used before a masculine singular noun beginning with any other letters (consonants or vowels).

un amico	*a friend*
un orologio	*a watch*
un portatile	*a laptop*
un ragazzo	*a boy*

The form **una** is used before a feminine singular noun beginning with any consonant (including **z**, **s** + **consonant**, **gn**, or **ps**).

una porta	*a door*
una zia	*an aunt*
una studentessa	*a student*
una psicologa	*a psychologist*

Lastly, the form **un'** is used before a feminine singular noun beginning with any vowel.

un'americana	*an American*
un'amica	*a friend*
un'isola	*an island*
un'ora	*an hour*

Be careful!

When an adjective precedes the noun, it is necessary to adjust the indefinite article according to the beginning letters of the adjective.

un'amica	*a friend*	una cara amica	*a dear friend*	
uno zio	*an uncle*	un caro zio	*a dear uncle*	

ESERCIZIO 3·1

A. *You are given some nouns taken from the above lists and from previous units. Provide the appropriate form of the indefinite article for each one.*

1. _____ americano
2. _____ americana
3. _____ studente
4. _____ zia
5. _____ studentessa
6. _____ ora
7. _____ gnocco
8. _____ portatile
9. _____ tesi
10. _____ brindisi
11. _____ problema
12. _____ programma
13. _____ caffè
14. _____ foto
15. _____ computer
16. _____ mano
17. _____ radio
18. _____ pianoforte
19. _____ isola
20. _____ porta
21. _____ psicologo
22. _____ psicologa
23. _____ orologio

B. *Now you are given some noun phrases consisting of the indefinite article, an adjective, and a noun. Provide the corresponding masculine or feminine noun phrase as required. Again, the words are taken from this and previous units.* (Note: **bravo** = *good;* **grande** = *big, important.*)

MASCULINE	FEMININE
1. un caro amico	_____
2. _____	una piccola zia
3. un bravo figlio	_____
4. _____	una brava cantante

5. un grande professore   _____

6. _____   una brava signora

7. un bravo musicista   _____

8. _____   una grande scultrice

The definite article

The definite article has both singular and plural forms.

The form **lo** is used before a masculine singular noun beginning with **z**, **s** + **consonant**, **gn**, or **ps**. It corresponds to the previously described uses of **uno**.

The singular forms are as follows.

lo zio	*the uncle*
lo studente	*the student*
lo gnocco	*the dumpling*
lo psicologo	*the psychologist*

The form **il** is used before a masculine singular noun beginning with any other consonant. It corresponds to the previously described uses of **un**.

il bambino	*the child*
il cellulare	*the cell phone*
il portatile	*the laptop*
il ragazzo	*the boy*

The form **la** is used before a feminine singular noun beginning with any consonant. It corresponds to the previously described uses of **una**.

la porta	*the door*
la zia	*the aunt*
la studentessa	*the student*
la psicologa	*the psychologist*

The form **l'** is used before a masculine or feminine singular noun beginning with any vowel. It corresponds in the feminine to the previously described uses of **un'** and in the masculine to the previously described uses of **un**.

l'amico	*the (male) friend*
l'isola	*the island*
l'ora	*the hour*
l'orologio	*the watch*

The form **gli** is used before a masculine plural noun beginning with **z**, **s** + **consonant**, **gn**, **ps**, or any vowel. It is the plural of both **lo** and **l'**.

The corresponding plural forms of the definite article are as follows.

SINGULAR		PLURAL	
lo zio	*the uncle*	**gli zii**	*the uncles*
lo studente	*the student*	**gli studenti**	*the students*
lo gnocco	*the dumpling*	**gli gnocchi**	*the dumplings*
lo psicologo	*the psychologist*	**gli psicologi**	*the psychologists*
l'amico	*the friend*	**gli amici**	*the friends*
l'orologio	*the watch*	**gli orologi**	*the watches*

The form **i** is used before a masculine plural noun beginning with any other consonant. It is the plural of **il**.

SINGULAR		PLURAL	
il bambino	*the child*	**i bambini**	*the children*
il cellulare	*the cell phone*	**i cellulari**	*the cell phones*
il portatile	*the laptop*	**i portatili**	*the laptops*
il ragazzo	*the boy*	**i ragazzi**	*the boys*

The form **le** is used before a feminine plural noun beginning with any sound (consonant or vowel). It is the plural of both **la** and **l'**.

SINGULAR		PLURAL	
l'isola	*the island*	**le isole**	*the islands*
l'ora	*the hour*	**le ore**	*the hours*
la porta	*the door*	**le porte**	*the doors*
la zia	*the aunt*	**le zie**	*the aunts*

Once again, be careful!

When an adjective precedes the noun, it is necessary to adjust the definite article according to the beginning letters of the adjective.

l'amica	*the friend*	**la cara amica**	*the dear friend*
gli amici	*the friends*	**i cari amici**	*the dear friends*
lo zio	*the uncle*	**il caro zio**	*the dear uncle*

ESERCIZIO
3·2

A. *You are given some noun phrases composed of the indefinite article and a noun. Provide the corresponding noun phrase with the definite article for each one. Then, make the new phrase plural.*

EXAMPLE   un ragazzo

   il ragazzo _____   *i ragazzi* _____

	SINGULAR	PLURAL
1. un vestito	_____	_____
2. una studentessa	_____	_____
3. uno psicologo	_____	_____
4. una psicologa	_____	_____
5. una tesi	_____	_____
6. un tedesco	_____	_____
7. uno sport	_____	_____

8. un problema   _____   _____

9. un orologio   _____   _____

10. un'ora   _____   _____

11. un amico   _____   _____

12. un'amica   _____   _____

13. uno zio   _____   _____

14. una zia   _____   _____

15. un bambino   _____   _____

16. una bambina   _____   _____

17. uno gnocco   _____   _____

18. uno studente   _____   _____

B. *Now you are given a phrase that is either in the singular or the plural. Provide its corresponding form as required.*

SINGULAR	PLURAL
1. lo zio	_____
2. _____	i vaglia
3. la valigia	_____
4. _____	le virtù
5. l'uomo	_____
6. _____	i tè
7. lo gnocco	_____
8. _____	i sistemi
9. lo scultore	_____
10. _____	i programmi
11. la radio	_____
12. _____	le università
13. il paio	_____
14. _____	gli orologi
15. il musicista	_____
16. _____	le infermiere

Uses of the indefinite article

English and Italian use the articles in similar ways. However, there are differences. They are described in this and the remaining sections of this unit.

The indefinite article is omitted in exclamations of the type shown below.

Che buon caffè!	*What a good coffee!*
Che macchina bella!	*What a beautiful car!*

It is also omitted in the expression **mal di…** .

mal di denti	*a toothache*
mal di gola	*a sore throat*
mal di stomaco	*a stomachache*
mal di testa	*a headache*

In Italian, the indefinite article must be repeated before every noun, while the article is often used only before the first noun in English.

un amico e uno studente	*a friend and (a) student*
un ragazzo e una ragazza	*a boy and (a) girl*
una zia e uno zio	*an aunt and (an) uncle*

ESERCIZIO
3·3

A. *Provide the appropriate indefinite article forms for the following sentences. If no article is required, leave the space blank. (Note:* **anche** *= also, too;* **e** *= and;* **film** *= movie;* **grande** *= great;* **o** *= or;* **sempre** *= always;* **simpatico** *= nice;* **solo** *= only;* **studiare** *= to study.)*

1. Mia madre aveva (*had*) _____ mal di denti ieri.

2. Anch'io ho _____ mal di gola.

3. Che _____ bella musica!

4. Mio padre ha _____ mal di testa o _____

   mal di stomaco.

5. Che _____ bella macchina!

6. In questa classe conosco (*I know*) solo _____ studente

   e _____ studentessa.

7. Lui è _____ persona simpatica; e anche lei è _____

   persona simpatica.

8. Io studio sempre _____ ora ogni giorno (*every day*).

B. *How do you say the following in Italian?*

1. I have only an aunt and uncle.

   _____

2. I bought (**ho comprato**) a car.

   _____

3. What a nice house!

   _____

4. What a great movie!

   _____

Uses of the definite article

The definite article is normally used in front of a mass noun, especially if it is the subject of a sentence.

L'acqua è un liquido.	*Water is a liquid.*
Lui beve solo **il caffè**.	*He drinks only coffee.*
La pazienza è una virtù.	*Patience is a virtue.*

It is also used with nouns in the plural that express generalizations.

Gli americani sono simpatici.	*Americans are nice.*
Oggi tutti hanno **i cellulari**.	*Today everybody has cell phones.*

The definite article is used in front of geographical names (continents, countries, states, rivers, islands, mountains, etc.), except the names of cities.

le Alpi	*the Alps*
il Belgio	*Belgium*
la California	*California*
l'Italia	*Italy*
il Mediterraneo	*the Mediterranean*
il Piemonte	*Piedmont*
la Sicilia	*Sicily*
gli Stati Uniti	*the United States*
il Tevere	*the Tiber*

But:

Firenze	*Florence*
Napoli	*Naples*
Roma	*Rome*
Venezia	*Venice*

It is usually dropped after the preposition **in** plus an unmodified geographical noun.

Vado **in** Italia.	*I'm going to Italy.*
Vivo **in** Francia.	*I live in France.*

But when the noun is modified, the definite article must be restored. (Note, if you have forgotten: **nell'** = in + **l'**; **nella** = in + **la**; **nel** = in + **il**; **nei** = in + **i**; **negli** = in + **gli**; **nelle** = in + **le**.)

Vado **nell'Italia centrale**.	*I'm going to central Italy.*
Vivo **nella Francia meridionale**.	*I live in southern France.*

Like the indefinite article, the definite article must be repeated before each noun.

l'amico e lo studente	*the friend and the student*
il ragazzo e la ragazza	*the boy and the girl*

Useful expressions

settentrionale	*northern*
centrale	*central*
meridionale	*southern*
orientale	*eastern*
occidentale	*western*

The definite article is commonly used in place of possessive adjectives if referring to family members, parts of the body, and clothing.

Oggi vado in centro con **la zia**.	*Today I'm going downtown with my aunt.*
Mi fa male **la testa**.	*My head hurts.*
Lui non si mette mai **la giacca**.	*He never puts his jacket on.*

The definite article is used with the days of the week to indicate a habitual action.

Il lunedì gioco sempre a tennis.	*On Mondays I always play tennis.*
La domenica vado regolarmente in chiesa.	*On Sundays I go regularly to church.*

Days of the week

lunedì (*m.*)	*Monday*
martedì (*m.*)	*Tuesday*
mercoledì (*m.*)	*Wednesday*
giovedì (*m.*)	*Thursday*
venerdì (*m.*)	*Friday*
sabato (*m.*)	*Saturday*
domenica (*f.*)	*Sunday*

Note that **domenica** is the only day of the week that is feminine.

The definite article is used with titles, unless the person bearing the title is being spoken to directly.

Il dottor Rossi è italiano.	*Dr. Rossi is Italian.*
La professoressa Bianchi è molto brava.	*Professor Bianchi is very good.*

But:

«**Dottor Rossi**, come va?»	*"Dr. Rossi, how is it going?"*
«**Professoressa Bianchi**, come sta?»	*"Professor Bianchi, how are you?"*

The definite article is used before the names of languages and nouns referring to school subjects.

Amo **lo spagnolo**.	*I love Spanish.*
Mi piace solo **la matematica**.	*I only like mathematics.*

School subjects

la biologia	*biology*	**la lingua**	*language*
la chimica	*chemistry*	**la matematica**	*math*
la fisica	*physics*	**la musica**	*music*
il francese	*French*	**la scienza**	*science*
la geografia	*geography*	**lo spagnolo**	*Spanish*
l'italiano	*Italian*	**la storia**	*history*

However, it is dropped when the prepositions **di** and **in** precede the school subject.

Ecco il mio libro **di spagnolo**.	*Here is the Spanish book.*
Lui è molto bravo **in matematica**.	*He is very good in math.*

But the definite article is restored if the noun is plural or modified.

Lei è molto brava **nelle lingue moderne**.	*She is very good in modern languages.*

The definite article is used with **scorso** (*last*) and **prossimo** (*next*) in time expressions.

la settimana scorsa	*last week*
il mese prossimo	*next month*

Time vocabulary

oggi	*today*
ieri	*yesterday*
domani	*tomorrow*
la settimana	*week*
il mese	*month*
l'anno	*year*

But, it is not used in some other common expressions.

a destra	*to/on the right*
a sinistra	*to/on the left*
a casa	*at home*

A. *Complete each sentence with the appropriate form of the definite article (if required).*

1. _____ acqua è necessaria per vivere (*to live*).

2. _____ caffè è buono.

3. _____ italiani sono simpatici.

4. _____ pazienza è la virtù più importante.

5. Anche _____ americani sono simpatici.

6. Mi piacciono (*I like*) _____ lingue e _____ storia.

7. _____ Sicilia è una bella regione.

8. _____ anno prossimo vado in _____ Piemonte.

9. Forse vado (in) _____ Italia settentrionale.

10. Mia zia vive (a) _____ Roma.

11. Lei si mette sempre _____ giacca per andare (*to go*) in centro.

12. _____ venerdì, io gioco sempre a tennis.

13. _____ domenica vado regolarmente in chiesa.

14. _____ martedì o _____ mercoledì guardo (*I watch*) la televisione.

15. _____ giovedì o _____ sabato vado in centro.

16. Come si chiama (*What is the name of*) _____ professoressa d'italiano?

17. Come sta, _____ professoressa Bianchi?

18. Mi fa male _____ testa.

B. *How do you say the following in Italian?*

1. I drink only tea.

   _____

2. I love (**amo**) spaghetti.

   _____

3. I have only an aunt and uncle in Italy.

   _____

4. He lives in southern Italy.

   _____

5. She lives in the eastern United States.

   _____

6. I instead (**invece**) live in the western United States.

   _____

7. I like (**Mi piacciono**) biology, chemistry, science, geography, math, and physics.

   _____

8. She is very good in music and in languages.

   _____

9. Last month I bought (**ho comprato**) a car.

   _____

10. Next year I am going (**vado**) to Italy.

    _____

11. Next week I am going downtown.

    _____

12. He lives to the left and she lives to the right.

    _____

C. *Provide the corresponding indefinite or definite article, as required.*

INDEFINITE ARTICLE	DEFINITE ARTICLE
1. un ragazzo	_____
2. _____	l'anno
3. una settimana	_____
4. _____	il mese
5. un caffè	_____
6. _____	lo psicologo

D. *Rewrite each phrase in the plural.*

SINGULAR	PLURAL
1. il ragazzo	_____
2. lo spagnolo	_____
3. la scienza	_____
4. la giacca	_____
5. l'amico	_____
6. l'amica	_____
7. il cellulare	_____
8. la virtù	_____

E. *Complete each sentence with the article or word required, if one is necessary.*

1. Che _____ bel film! (*What a nice movie!*)

2. Ho _____ mal di stomaco. (*I have a stomachache.*)

3. Loro hanno un cane e _____ gatto. (*They have a dog and cat.*)

4. Sono la zia e _____ zio dall'Italia. (*They're the aunt and uncle from Italy.*)

5. Io amo _____ carne. (*I love meat.*)

6. _____ italiani sanno vivere. (*Italians know how to live.*)

7. Loro vanno spesso _____ Italia. (*They go often to Italy.*)

8. _____ Francia è un bel paese. (*France is a beautiful country.*)

9. Oggi vado in centro con _____ zio. (*Today I am going downtown with my uncle.*)

10. _____ venerdì vanno spesso al cinema. (*On Fridays they often go to the movies.*)

11. Conosci _____ professor Martini? (*Do you know Professor Martini?*)

12. Mio fratello ama _____ matematica. (*My brother loves math.*)

13. Lei è andata al cinema _____ settimana scorsa. (*She went to the movies last week.*)

14. Loro vivono _____ destra. (*They live on the right.*)

F. *Match the words and expressions in the left column with those in the right column to make complete logical sentences.*

1. Lui è _____   a. dottoressa Rossi, come va?

2. Lui va spesso _____   b. il mio libro.

3. Buongiorno, _____   c. i miei libri.

4. Mio fratello è bravo _____   d. le mie amiche.

5. Questo è _____   e. nell'Italia settentrionale.

6. Quelli sono _____   f. un caro zio.

7. Quelle sono _____   g. in matematica.

Grammar in culture

In the changing world of technology, grammar follows suit. Today, the Italian article is rarely used with a noun that refers to the Internet or to a specific social media site.

Vado spesso su Internet.	*not*	Vado spesso su**l** Internet.
Non sono su Facebook.	*not*	Non sono su**l** Facebook.
Amo Twitter.	*not*	Amo **il** Twitter.
Mi piace molto Instagram.	*not*	Mi piace molto **l'**Instagram.

Otherwise, the article is used.

Mi piace molto **il** sito del tuo amico.   *not*   Mi piace molto sito del tuo amico.

ESERCIZIO 3·5

Complete each sentence with the appropriate article, if one is needed.

1. Non leggo mai _____ blog di quel giornalista.

2. Non mi piace _____ Facebook; preferisco _____ Twitter.

3. Anche tu usi spesso _____ Instagram?

4. Questo è _____ sito della mia professoressa.

5. Oggi _____ Internet ha cambiato (*changed*) tutto.

Adjectives

Adjectives are words that modify or describe nouns and other parts of speech.

È una macchina **nuova**.	*It's a new car.*
Mi piacciono solo le macchine **italiane**.	*I only like Italian cars.*

In general, adjectives are identifiable by changes in the vowel endings, which show agreement with the nouns they modify.

lo studente americano	*the (male) American student*
gli studenti americani	*the American students*
la studentessa italiana	*the (female) Italian student*
le studentesse italiane	*the (female) Italian students*

Descriptive adjectives

The most common type of adjective is called descriptive. As its name implies, it is a word that describes the noun it modifies—that is, it indicates whether someone is tall or short, something is good or bad, and so on. What does modifying a noun mean grammatically? For most intents and purposes, it means that the final vowel of an adjective must change to match the gender and number of the noun.

There are two main types of descriptive adjectives, as listed in the dictionary:

1. the type that ends in **-o**

alto	*tall*

2. the type that ends in **-e**

intelligente	*intelligent*

As with masculine singular nouns which end in **-o** or **-e**, the masculine plural forms of both of these types of adjectives end in **-i**.

SINGULAR		PLURAL	
l'uomo alto	*the tall man*	**gli uomini alti**	*the tall men*
l'uomo intelligente	*the intelligent man*	**gli uomini intelligenti**	*the intelligent men*
il cantante alto	*the tall singer*	**i cantanti alti**	*the tall singers*
il cantante intelligente	*the intelligent singer*	**i cantanti intelligenti**	*the intelligent singers*

The corresponding feminine singular forms of these two types of adjectives end, as you may expect, in -**a** and -**e**, respectively. The feminine plural forms of type (1) adjectives end in -**e**; the feminine plural forms of type (2) adjectives end in -**i**.

SINGULAR		PLURAL	
la donna alta	*the tall woman*	**le donne alte**	*the tall women*
la donna intelligente	*the intelligent woman*	**le donne intelligenti**	*the intelligent women*
la scultrice alta	*the tall (female) sculptor*	**le scultrici alte**	*the tall sculptors*
la scultrice intelligente	*the intelligent sculptor*	**le scultrici intelligenti**	*the intelligent sculptors*

Common descriptive adjectives

alto	*tall*	**basso**	*short*
bello	*beautiful*	**brutto**	*ugly*
grande	*big*	**piccolo**	*small*
magro	*skinny*	**grasso**	*fat*
nuovo	*new*	**vecchio**	*old*
ricco	*rich*	**povero**	*poor*

Invariable adjectives

A few adjectives are invariable; that is, their ending does not change. The most common are the color adjectives: **arancione** (*orange*), **blu** (*dark blue*), **marrone** (*brown*), **rosa** (*pink*), and **viola** (*violet, purple*).

SINGULAR		PLURAL	
la giacca arancione	*the orange jacket*	**le giacche arancione**	*the orange jackets*
il vestito blu	*the blue dress*	**i vestiti blu**	*the blue dresses*
la camicia marrone	*the brown shirt*	**le camicie marrone**	*the brown shirts*
la sciarpa rosa	*the pink scarf*	**le sciarpe rosa**	*the pink scarves*
lo zaino viola	*the purple backpack*	**gli zaini viola**	*the purple backpacks*

Other color adjectives

These are regular color adjectives, that is, their endings change according to the normal rules for adjectives.

azzurro	*blue*
bianco	*white*
celeste	*sky blue*
giallo	*yellow*
grigio	*gray*
nero	*black*
rosso	*red*
verde	*green*

Note: Adjectives ending in **-co**, **-go**, **-cio**, and **-gio** undergo the same spelling changes when pluralized that the nouns with these endings do (see Unit 1).

SINGULAR		PLURAL	
l'uomo simpatico	*the nice man*	**gli uomini simpatici**	*the nice men*
la camicia bianca	*the white shirt*	**le camicie bianche**	*the white shirts*
il bambino stanco	*the tired child*	**i bambini stanchi**	*the tired children*
la gonna lunga	*the long skirt*	**le gonne lunghe**	*the long skirts*
il vestito grigio	*the gray suit*	**i vestiti grigi**	*the gray suits*

When two nouns are modified by an adjective, the adjective must be in the plural. If the two nouns are feminine, then the appropriate feminine plural ending is used; if the two nouns are both masculine, or of mixed gender, then the appropriate masculine plural ending is used.

Two feminine nouns

La camicia e la gonna sono rosse.   *The shirt and (the) skirt are red.*

Two masculine nouns

Il cappotto e l'impermeabile sono rossi.   *The coat and (the) raincoat are red.*

Mixed gender nouns

La camicia e il cappotto sono rossi.   *The shirt and (the) coat are red.*

ESERCIZIO
4·1

A. *Provide the missing ending for each adjective.*

1. la bambina ricc_____
2. i ragazzi alt_____
3. la casa grand_____
4. le case grand_____
5. gli uomini stanc_____
6. le donne pover_____
7. la bambina bell_____
8. i cantanti brutt_____
9. le cantanti magr_____
10. la giacca ross_____
11. le giacche bl_____
12. le sciarpe verd_____
13. le sciarpe viol_____
14. la camicia bianc_____
15. le camicie marron_____
16. gli zaini celest_____
17. le gonne grig_____
18. i vestiti ros_____
19. l'impermeabile azzurr_____
20. gli impermeabili giall_____
21. i cappotti arancion_____
22. la camicia e la sciarpa bianc_____
23. la gonna e il cappotto ross_____

B. *Provide the corresponding singular or plural phrase, as required.*

SINGULAR	PLURAL
1. lo zio vecchio	_____
2. _____	le studentesse intelligenti
3. la valigia grande	_____
4. _____	le città piccole
5. l'uomo ricco	_____
6. _____	le donne stanche
7. il ragazzo simpatico	_____
8. _____	le cantanti simpatiche
9. il vestito lungo	_____
10. _____	le sciarpe lunghe

C. *Rewrite each phrase with the opposite adjective.*

EXAMPLE   l'uomo alto

l'uomo basso

1. la macchina nuova   _____
2. gli uomini alti   _____
3. le donne povere   _____
4. il cane grande   _____
5. i cantanti grassi   _____
6. i professori belli   _____
7. le ragazze povere   _____
8. il vestito nero   _____

Position

Descriptive adjectives generally come after the noun or nouns they modify.

una camicia bianca	*a white shirt*
un libro interessante	*an interesting book*

Some adjectives, however, can come either before or after.

È una **bella camicia**.	(or)	È una **camicia bella**.	*It's a beautiful shirt.*
Giulia è una **ragazza simpatica**.	(or)	Giulia è una **simpatica ragazza**.	*Julie is a nice girl.*

Be careful!

As discussed in Unit 3, you will have to adjust the form of the article to the adjective that is put before a noun.

lo zio simpatico	but	il simpatico zio
l'amico povero	but	il povero amico
un'amica simpatica	but	una simpatica amica
gli studenti nuovi	but	i nuovi studenti

You will have to learn which descriptive adjectives can come before through practice and use. As you listen to someone speak or as you read something, make a mental note of the position of the adjective. Some common adjectives that can come before or after a noun are the following.

bello	*beautiful*
brutto	*ugly*
buono	*good*
caro	*dear; expensive*
cattivo	*bad*
giovane	*young*
grande	*big, large; great*
nuovo	*new*
povero	*poor*
simpatico	*nice, charming*
vecchio	*old*

A few of these adjectives change in meaning depending on their position. Needless to say, when you are unsure of the meaning and use of an adjective, check a dictionary. Here are the four most common adjectives whose meaning changes depending on their position before or after the noun.

	BEFORE THE NOUN	AFTER THE NOUN
caro	*dear*	*expensive*
	Lui è un **caro amico**.	È una **giacca cara**.
	He's a dear friend.	*It's an expensive jacket.*
grande	*great*	*big*
	È un **grande libro**.	È un **libro grande**.
	It's a great book.	*It's a big book.*
povero	*poor (deserving of pity)*	*poor (not wealthy)*
	Lui è un **povero uomo**.	Lui è un **uomo povero**.
	He is a poor man (pitiable).	*He is a poor man (not wealthy).*
vecchio	*old (known for many years)*	*old (in age)*
	Lei è una **vecchia amica**.	Lei è una **donna vecchia**.
	She is an old friend.	*She is an old woman.*

Note: Descriptive adjectives can also be separated from the nouns they modify by a linking verb. The most common linking verbs are: **essere** (*to be*), **sembrare** (*to seem*), and **diventare** (*to become*).

Quella giacca **è** nuova. *That jacket is new.*
Quell'uomo **sembra** intelligente. *That man seems intelligent.*
Questa macchina **sta diventando** vecchia. *This car is becoming old.*

Adjectives used in this way are known as predicate adjectives, because they occur in the predicate slot, after the verb that links them to the noun or nouns they modify.

One final word about the position of descriptive adjectives. When these adjectives are accompanied by an adverb, another adjective, or some other part of speech, they must follow the noun.

Lui è un **simpatico uomo**. *He is a nice man.*

But:

Lui è un **uomo molto simpatico**. *He is a very nice man.*
Lui è un **uomo simpatico e bravo**. *He is a nice and good man.*

ESERCIZIO
4·2

A. *Rewrite each sentence by changing the position of the adjective—if it is before the noun, move it after and vice versa—and by making any other changes that are then required.*

1. Lui è uno studente simpatico.

_____

2. È un nuovo zaino.

_____

3. Ho comprato un orologio nuovo.

_____

4. Marco e Maria sono amici simpatici.

_____

5. Lei è un'amica ricca.

_____

B. *Match each sentence to its correct English equivalent.*

1. Lei è una donna vecchia.

   a. *She's an elderly woman.*   b. *She is a woman whom I have known for a while.*

2. Loro sono vecchi amici.

   a. *They are elderly friends.*   b. *They are friends whom we have known for ages.*

3. Noi siamo persone povere.

   a. *We are impoverished people.*   b. *We are unfortunate people.*

4. Lui è un povero cantante.

   a. *He is an impoverished singer.*   b. *He is a pitiable singer.*

5. La Ferrari è una macchina cara.

    a. *The Ferrari is an expensive car.*   b. *The Ferrari is a dear car.*

6. Giulio è un caro amico.

    a. *Giulio is an expensive friend.*   b. *Giulio is a dear friend.*

7. Quello è un grande film.

    a. *That is a big movie (long in length).*   b. *That is a great movie.*

8. Alessandro è un ragazzo grande.

    a. *Alexander is a big boy.*   b. *Alexander is a great boy.*

Form-changing adjectives

The adjectives **buono** (*good, kind*), **bello** (*beautiful, nice, handsome*), **grande** (*big, large, great*), and **santo** (*saint*) undergo changes in form when they are placed before a noun.

Let's start with **buono**. Before masculine nouns beginning with **z**, **s** + **consonant**, **gn**, and **ps**, its forms are as follows (remember that the partitive **dei** = *some*).

SINGULAR		PLURAL	
buono		**buoni**	
un buono zio	*a kind uncle*	**dei buoni zii**	*(some) kind uncles*
un buono studente	*a kind student*	**dei buoni studenti**	*(some) kind students*

Before masculine nouns beginning with any other consonant or any vowel, its forms are as follows.

SINGULAR		PLURAL	
buon		**buoni**	
un buon ragazzo	*a good boy*	**dei buoni ragazzi**	*(some) good boys*
un buon amico	*a good friend*	**dei buoni amici**	*(some) good friends*

Before feminine nouns beginning with any consonant, its forms are as follows (remember that the partitive **delle** = *some*).

SINGULAR		PLURAL	
buona		**buone**	
una buona bambina	*a good child*	**delle buone bambine**	*(some) good children*
una buona pizza	*a good pizza*	**delle buone pizze**	*(some) good pizzas*

Before feminine nouns beginning with any vowel, the forms are as follows.

SINGULAR		PLURAL	
buon'		**buone**	
una buon'amica	*a good friend*	**delle buone amiche**	*(some) good friends*
una buon'infermiera	*a good nurse*	**delle buone infermiere**	*(some) good nurses*

Tips!

Note that the singular forms undergo the same kinds of form changes as the indefinite article (see Unit 3).

uno	→	buono
un	→	buon
una	→	buona
un'	→	buon'

Note also that the apostrophe is used only with the feminine form (**buon'**), as is the case with the indefinite article.

When referring to people, **buono** means *good* in the sense of *good in nature, kind*. If *good at doing something* is intended, then the adjective **bravo** is more appropriate.

È un **buon ragazzo**.	*He is a good (natured) boy.*
È un **bravo studente**.	*He is a good student. (He is good at being a student.)*

When **buono** is placed after the noun, it is treated as a normal type (1) descriptive adjective ending in **-o** (remember the forms of the partitive: **di + i = dei, di + gli = degli, di + le = delle**).

BEFORE THE NOUN		AFTER THE NOUN	
un buon amico	*a good friend (m.)*	**un amico buono**	*a good friend (m.)*
una buon'amica	*a good friend (f.)*	**un'amica buona**	*a good friend (f.)*
un buono zio	*a kind uncle*	**uno zio buono**	*a kind uncle*
dei buoni amici	*good friends (m.)*	**degli amici buoni**	*good friends (m.)*
delle buone amiche	*good friends (f.)*	**delle amiche buone**	*good friends (f.)*
dei buoni zii	*kind uncles*	**degli zii buoni**	*kind uncles*

Be careful!

As discussed above and in Unit 3, you will have to adjust the form of the article (or partitive) to the adjective that is put before a noun.

uno zio buono	but	un buono zio
l'amico buono	but	il buon amico
un'amica buona	but	una buon'amica
degli studenti buoni	but	dei buoni studenti

Now, let's consider **bello**. Before masculine nouns beginning with **z**, **s** + **consonant**, **gn**, and **ps**, its forms are as follows.

SINGULAR		PLURAL	
bello		**begli**	
un bello zaino	*a nice backpack*	**dei begli zaini**	*(some) nice backpacks*
un bello sport	*a nice sport*	**dei begli sport**	*(some) nice sports*

Before masculine nouns beginning with any other consonant, its forms are as follows.

SINGULAR		PLURAL	
bel		**bei**	
un bel cane	*a beautiful dog*	**dei bei cani**	*(some) beautiful dogs*
un bel gatto	*a beautiful cat*	**dei bei gatti**	*(some) beautiful cats*

Before masculine nouns beginning with any vowel, its forms are as follows.

SINGULAR		PLURAL	
bell'		**begli**	
un bell'uomo	*a handsome man*	**dei begli uomini**	*(some) handsome men*
un bell'orologio	*a beautiful watch*	**dei begli orologi**	*(some) beautiful watches*

Before feminine nouns beginning with any consonant, its forms are as follows.

SINGULAR		PLURAL	
bella		**belle**	
una bella donna	*a beautiful woman*	**delle belle donne**	*(some) beautiful women*
una bella camicia	*a nice shirt*	**delle belle camicie**	*(some) nice shirts*

Before feminine nouns beginning with any vowel, the forms are as follows.

SINGULAR		PLURAL	
bell'		**belle**	
una bell'amica	*a beautiful friend*	**delle belle amiche**	*(some) beautiful friends*
una bell'attrice	*a beautiful actress*	**delle belle attrici**	*(some) beautiful actresses*

Tip!

Note that **bello** undergoes the same kinds of form changes as the definite article (see Unit 3).

lo	→	**bello**
l'	→	**bell'**
gli	→	**begli**
il	→	**bel**
i	→	**bei**
la	→	**bella**
le	→	**belle**

If placed after the noun, **bello** is treated like a normal type (1) descriptive adjective ending in **-o**.

BEFORE		AFTER	
un bell'uomo	*a handsome man*	**un uomo bello**	*a handsome man*
una bell'attrice	*a beautiful actress*	**un'attrice bella**	*a beautiful actress*
un bello zaino	*a nice backpack*	**uno zaino bello**	*a nice backpack*
dei begli uomini	*handsome men*	**degli uomini belli**	*handsome men*
delle belle attrici	*beautiful actresses*	**delle attrici belle**	*beautiful actresses*
dei begli zaini	*nice backpacks*	**degli zaini belli**	*nice backpacks*

Once again, be careful!

As discussed above and in Unit 3, you will have to adapt the form of the article (or partitive) to the adjective that is put before a noun.

uno zaino bello	but	un bello zaino
l'amico bello	but	il bell'amico
l'amica bella	but	la bell'amica
degli studenti belli	but	dei begli studenti

Grande has the optional forms **gran** (before a masculine singular noun beginning with any consonant except **z**, **s + consonant**, **ps**, and **gn**), and **grand'** (before any singular noun beginning with a vowel). Otherwise, it is treated as a normal type (2) adjective ending in **-e**.

un gran film	(or)	un grande film	*a great movie*
un grand'amico	(or)	un grande amico	*a great friend*
una grand'attrice	(or)	una grande attrice	*a great actress*

But in all other cases, only **grande** is allowed. And there is only one plural form: **grandi**.

un grande scrittore	*a great writer*
una grande donna	*a great woman*
dei grandi amici	*great friends*
delle grandi attrici	*great actresses*

Finally, consider **santo**. It undergoes changes only before proper names. Before masculine singular proper names beginning with **z**, **s + consonant**, **gn**, and **ps**, the form used is **Santo**.

Santo Stefano	*St. Stephen*
Santo Spirito	*Holy Spirit*

Before masculine singular proper names beginning with any other consonant, the form used is **San**.

San Paolo	*St. Paul*
San Giovanni	*St. John*

Before masculine and feminine proper names beginning with any vowel, the form used is **Sant'**.

Sant'Anna	*St. Ann*
Sant'Antonio	*St. Anthony*
Sant'Elisabetta	*St. Elizabeth*
Sant'Eugenio	*St. Eugene (Eugenius)*

Before feminine proper names beginning with any consonant, the form used is **Santa**.

Santa Maria	*St. Mary*
Santa Caterina	*St. Catherine*

With common nouns, **santo** is treated like a normal type (1) adjective ending in **-o**.

un santo bambino	*a saintly child*
una santa donna	*a saintly woman*

A. *Rewrite each phrase by putting the adjective before the noun and by making any other necessary changes.*

EXAMPLE   amico buono

buon amico

1. zio buono   _____
2. zia buona   _____
3. amico buono   _____
4. amica buona   _____
5. padre buono   _____
6. ragazzi buoni   _____
7. amiche buone   _____
8. zaino bello   _____
9. libro bello   _____
10. orologio bello _____
11. zaini belli   _____
12. libri belli   _____
13. orologi belli   _____
14. donna bella   _____
15. donne belle   _____
16. attrice bella   _____
17. attrici belle   _____

B. *Rewrite each phrase by putting the adjective after the noun. Don't forget to make any necessary changes to the article or partitive.*

BEFORE   AFTER

1. un bello zaino   _____
2. dei grandi scultori   _____
3. un buon caffè   _____
4. dei buoni ragionieri _____
5. un bell'uomo   _____
6. un buon portatile   _____
7. dei bei programmi   _____
8. un buono psicologo   _____

9. una buona psicologa   _____

10. un gran problema   _____

11. una buona pesca   _____

12. delle grandi autrici   _____

13. un buon orologio   _____

14. un gran musicista   _____

15. una bella donna   _____

16. un buon affare   _____

C. *Each of the following is the name of a saint. Add the appropriate form of* **santo** *to each name.*

1. _____ Marco

2. _____ Isabella

3. _____ Bernardo

4. _____ Francesco

5. _____ Agnese (*f.*)

6. _____ Alessio

Comparison of adjectives

Someone or something can have a comparatively equal, greater, or lesser degree of some quality (as specified by some adjective). These degrees are called: positive, comparative, and superlative.

For the positive degree either **così... come** or **tanto... quanto** are used. (Note: **felice** = *happy*.)

Alessandro è **così** felice **come** sua sorella.	*Alexander is as happy as his sister.*
Loro sono **tanto** simpatici **quanto** intelligenti.	*They are as nice as they are intelligent.*

The first words in these constructions are optional in colloquial or informal speech.

Alessandro è felice **come** sua sorella.
Loro sono simpatici **quanto** intelligenti.

For the comparative degree, **più** (*more*) or **meno** (*less*) is used, as the case may be.

Marco è **intelligente**.	*Mark is intelligent.*	Maria è **più intelligente**.	*Mary is more intelligent.*
Lui è **simpatico**.	*He's nice.*	Lei è **meno simpatica**.	*She is less nice.*
Sara è **alta**.	*Sarah is tall.*	Alessandro è **più alto**.	*Alexander is taller.*

For the superlative degree, the definite article is used (in its proper form, of course!) followed by **più** or **meno**, as the case may be. The English preposition *in* is rendered by **di** in this case. (Note: **costoso** = *costly, expensive*. Recall that **di** + **il** = **del**; **di** + **la** = **della**, etc.)

Maria è **la più alta della** sua classe.	*Mary is the tallest in her class.*
Lui è **il più simpatico della** famiglia.	*He is the nicest in the family.*
Quelle macchine sono **le meno costose**.	*Those cars are the least expensive.*

In superlative constructions, the definite article is not repeated if it is already in front of a noun.

Maria è **la** ragazza **più alta** della classe.	*Mary is the tallest girl in the class.*
Bruno è **il** ragazzo **meno intelligente** della classe.	*Bruno is the least intelligent boy in the class.*

Note the following

In comparative constructions, the word *than* is rendered in one of two ways.

- If two forms (nouns or noun phrases) are compared by one adjective, the preposition **di** is used.

Giovanni è più alto **di** Marco.	*John is taller than Mark.*
Maria è meno ricca **di** sua sorella.	*Mary is less rich than her sister.*

- If two adjectives are used to compare the same form, **che** is used instead.

Lui è più simpatico **che** intelligente.	*He is nicer than he is intelligent.*
Maria è meno elegante **che** simpatica.	*Mary is less elegant than she is nice.*

The construction **di quello che** (also **di quel che** or **di ciò che**) corresponds to the English form *than* before a dependent clause (a clause that generally follows the main one).

Marco è più intelligente **di quel che** crede.	*Mark is more intelligent than what he believes.*
Maria è meno elegante **di quello che** pensa.	*Mary is less elegant than what she thinks.*

Some adjectives have both regular and irregular comparative and superlative forms.

buono	*good*	**più buono** (or) **migliore**	*better*
cattivo	*bad*	**più cattivo** (or) **peggiore**	*worse*
grande	*big*	**più grande** (or) **maggiore**	*bigger (older)*
piccolo	*small*	**più piccolo** (or) **minore**	*smaller (younger)*

Questo pane è **buono**, ma quello è **migliore**.	*This bread is good, but that one is better.*
Questo caffè è **cattivo**, ma quello è **peggiore**.	*This coffee is bad, but that one is worse.*
Lui è **il** fratello **maggiore**.	*He is the oldest brother.*
Lei è **la** sorella **minore**.	*She is the youngest sister.*

To express *very* as part of the adjective, just drop the final vowel of the adjective and add **-issimo**. These adjectives are then treated like normal type (1) adjectives ending in **-o**.

alto → alt- + -issimo = **altissimo**	*very tall*
buono → buon- + -issimo = **buonissimo**	*very good*
facile → facil- + -issimo = **facilissimo**	*very easy*
grande → grand- + -issimo = **grandissimo**	*very big*

Marco è **intelligentissimo**.	*Mark is very intelligent.*
Anche Claudia è **intelligentissima**.	*Claudia is also very intelligent.*
Quelle ragazze sono **bravissime**.	*Those girls are very good.*
Quelle lezioni sono **facilissime**.	*Those classes are very easy.*

A. *Say the following things using complete sentences.*

EXAMPLE   Mark is _____ than Claudia.

taller → *Marco è più alto di Claudia.*

1. John is as _____ as Mary.

   a. tall _____

   b. intelligent _____

   c. nice _____

   d. happy _____

2. Mr. Sabatini is _____ than the students.

   a. happier _____

   b. richer _____

   c. nicer _____

   d. more tired _____

3. Mrs. Sabatini is less _____ than the students.

   a. happy _____

   b. rich _____

   c. nice _____

   d. tired _____

4. The jackets are _____ than the coats.

   a. more expensive _____

   b. longer _____

   c. more beautiful _____

   d. newer _____

5. The raincoats are _____ than the dresses.

   a. less expensive _____

   b. longer _____

   c. less beautiful _____

   d. older _____

B. *Complete each sentence with the appropriate form. If no form is necessary, leave the space blank.*

1. Lui è _____ professore più bravo _____ università.

2. Lei è _____ più intelligente _____ tutti *(everyone)*.

3. Giovanni è più bravo _____ intelligente.

4. Giovanni è più bravo _____ Pasquale.

5. Gli studenti sono più simpatici _____ intelligenti.

6. Maria è più intelligente _____ crede.

C. *Provide an equivalent form.*

1. più buoni   _____

2. più grande   _____

3. più cattiva   _____

4. più piccole   _____

5. più grandi   _____

6. molto ricco   _____

7. molto rossi   _____

8. molto facile   _____

9. molto belle   _____

10. molto simpatici   _____

11. molto simpatiche   _____

12. molto buona   _____

D. *Provide the corresponding masculine or feminine form of each noun phrase, as required.*

MASCULINE	FEMININE
1. l'uomo intelligente	_____
2. _____	l'amica elegante
3. lo zio alto	_____
4. _____	la bella studentessa
5. il fratello simpaticissimo	_____
6. _____	la buon'amica
7. il ragazzo francese	_____
8. _____	una bravissima professoressa
9. un buono zio	_____
10. _____	una bella ragazza

11. un bell'amico   _____

12. _____ Santa Maria

E. *Choose the correct response.*

1. To refer to a man who is not wealthy, you would say _____.

   a. un povero uomo   b. un uomo povero

2. To refer to a friend who is old in age, you would say _____.

   a. un vecchio amico   b. un amico vecchio

3. Sara è così brava _____ il fratello.

   a. tanto   b. come

4. Alessandro è più simpatico _____ Maria.

   a. di   b. che

5. Marco è più simpatico _____ intelligente.

   a. di   b. che

6. Maria è più intelligente _____ quel che crede.

   a. di   b. che

Grammar in culture

Adjectives have many social functions. One of these is talking about the weather (**il tempo**). The following sentences use weather-related adjectives.

Il tempo è bello. / Fa bel tempo.	*The weather is nice.*
Il tempo è brutto. / Fa brutto tempo.	*The weather is bad.*
Il tempo è cattivo. / Fa cattivo tempo.	*The weather is awful.*
È sereno.	*It's clear.*
È nuvoloso.	*It's cloudy.*
È umido.	*It's humid.*
È piovoso.	*It's rainy.*
È burrascoso.	*It's stormy.*
È ventoso.	*It's windy.*

Some weather-related expressions require nouns rather than adjectives in Italian, even though the nouns are treated like adjectives in English.

Fa caldo.	*It is hot.*
Fa fresco.	*It is cool.*
Fa freddo.	*It is cold.*

How do you say the following in Italian?

1. It's hot and it's rainy.

_____

2. It's always cold here (**qui**) and it's always cloudy.

_____

3. The weather is nice today. It's clear and cool.

_____

4. It's rainy today. The weather is awful.

_____

Pronouns

Pronouns are words used in place of nouns, substantives (words taking on the function of nouns), or noun phrases (nouns accompanied by articles, demonstratives, adjectives, etc.).

Giovanni è italiano.	*John is Italian.*
Lui è italiano.	*He is Italian.*

We will deal with several types of pronouns in other units, including demonstrative, possessive, interrogative, indefinite, and relative pronouns. The discussion in this and the next unit will thus focus on personal pronouns (*I, me, you, us, them,* etc.).

Subject pronouns

Personal pronouns are classified as subject, object, or reflexive pronouns. They are also classified according to the person(s) speaking (first person), the person(s) spoken to (second person), or the person(s) spoken about (third person). The pronoun can, of course, be in the singular (referring to one person) or in the plural (referring to more than one person).

Subject pronouns are used as the subjects of verbs.

Io parlo italiano e **lui** parla francese.	*I speak Italian and he speaks French.*
Anche **loro** andranno in Italia.	*They, too, will be going to Italy.*

The Italian subject pronouns are (*fam.* = *familiar*; *pol.* = *polite*):

	SINGULAR		PLURAL	
FIRST PERSON	**io**	*I*	**noi**	*we*
SECOND PERSON	**tu**	*you* (*fam.*)	**voi**	*you* (*fam.*)
THIRD PERSON	**lui**	*he*	**loro**	*they*
	lei	*she*	**Loro**	*you* (*pol.*)
	Lei	*you* (*pol.*)		

Note that **io** is not capitalized unless it is the first word of a sentence.

Pronouns are optional in simple affirmative sentences, because it is easy to tell from the verb which person is the subject.

Io non capisco.	(or)	Non **capisco**.	*I do not understand.*
Loro vanno in Italia.	(or)	**Vanno** in Italia.	*They are going to Italy.*

181

However, they must be used for emphasis, to avoid ambiguity, or if more than one subject pronoun is required.

Devi parlare **tu**, non **io**!	*You have to speak, not I!*
Non è possibile che l'abbiano fatto **loro**.	*It's not possible that they did it.*
Mentre **lui** guarda la TV, **lei** ascolta la radio.	*While he watches TV, she listens to the radio.*
Lui e **io** vogliamo che **tu** dica la verità.	*He and I want you to tell the truth.*

Note

Subject pronouns must also be used after the following words.

anche	*also, too*
neanche	*neither, not even* (synonyms are **neppure** and **nemmeno**)
proprio	*really*

Anche **tu** devi venire alla festa.	*You, too, must come to the party.*
Non è venuto neanche **lui**.	*He didn't come either.*
Signor Rossini, è proprio **Lei**?	*Mr. Rossini, is it really you?*

The subject pronoun *it* is not usually stated in Italian.

È vero.	*It is true.*
Sembra che sia vero.	*It appears to be true.*

However, if this subject is required, then the following can be used.

esso (*m., sing.*)	**essi** (*m., pl.*)
essa (*f., sing.*)	**esse** (*f., pl.*)

È una buona ragione, ma neanche **essa** sarà creduta.	*It's a good reason, but not even it will be believed.*
Sono buone ragioni, ma neanche **esse** saranno credute.	*They are good reasons, but not even they will be believed.*

You has both familiar and polite forms.

Maria, anche **tu** studi l'italiano?	*Mary, are you also studying Italian?*
Signora Giusti, anche **Lei** studia l'italiano?	*Mrs. Giusti, are you also studying Italian?*

In writing, the polite forms (**Lei, Loro**) are capitalized in order to distinguish them from **lei**, meaning *she*, and **loro**, meaning *they*, but this is not obligatory. In the plural, there is a strong tendency in current Italian to use **voi** as the plural of both **tu** and **Lei**. **Loro** is restricted to very formal situations.

The forms **lui** and **lei** are used in ordinary conversation and for most purposes. However, there are two more formal pronouns: **egli** and **ella**, respectively. These are used especially in reference to famous people.

Dante scrisse la *Divina Commedia*. **Egli** era fiorentino.	*Dante wrote the* Divine Comedy. *He was Florentine.*
Chi era Natalia Ginzburg? **Ella** era una grande scrittrice.	*Who was Natalia Ginzburg? She was a great writer.*

A. *Provide the missing pronouns.*

1. Anch'_____ voglio andare in Italia.

2. Devi chiamare _____ , non io!

3. Non è possibile che siano stati _____ .

4. Mio fratello guarda sempre la TV. _____ guarda sempre programmi interessanti.

5. Mia sorella legge molto. _____ vuole diventare professoressa d'università.

6. Anche _____ siamo andati in centro ieri.

7. Siete proprio _____ ?

8. Galileo era un grande scienziato (*scientist*). _____ era toscano.

9. Elsa Morante è una grande scrittrice. _____ è molto famosa.

10. Maria, vai anche _____ alla festa?

11. Signora Marchi, va anche _____ al cinema?

12. Signore e signori, anche _____ siete/sono felici?

B. *Rewrite each sentence by making each verb plural and adjusting the rest of the sentence accordingly.*
(Note: **importante** = *important;* **interessante** = *interesting.)*

1. Anche esso è un problema importante.

_____

2. Anche essa è una tesi interessante.

_____

3. Io andrò in Italia quest'anno.

_____

4. Lui è italiano.

_____

5. Lei è italiana.

_____

Object pronouns

Object pronouns are used as objects of verbs and other structures. Their main use is to replace direct or indirect objects.

Direct object

Marco sta leggendo **quel libro** adesso.	*Marco is reading that book now.*
Marco **lo** sta leggendo.	*Marco is reading it.*

Indirect object

Marco darà quel libro **a sua sorella**.   *Marco will give that book to his sister.*
Marco **le** darà quel libro domani.   *Marco will give her that book tomorrow.*

Italian object pronouns generally come right before the verb. There are some exceptions, however, as will be discussed later on. The direct and indirect object pronouns are as follows.

DIRECT		INDIRECT	
mi	*me*	**mi**	*to me*
ti	*you (fam., sing.)*	**ti**	*to you (fam., sing.)*
La	*you (pol., sing.)*	**Le**	*to you (pol., sing.)*
lo	*him; it*	**gli**	*to him*
la	*her; it*	**le**	*to her*
ci	*us*	**ci**	*to us*
vi	*you (fam., pl.)*	**vi**	*to you (fam., pl.)*
li	*them (m.)*	**gli**	*to them (m.)*
le	*them (f.)*	**gli**	*to them (f.)*

Notice that the plural of the indirect object pronouns **gli** (*to him*) and **le** (*to her*) is **gli** (*to them*). This means that you will have to be very careful when determining which meaning is intended by the context of the sentence.

Dove sono i tuoi amici?   *Where are your (male) friends?*
Gli voglio parlare.   *I want to speak to them.*
Dove sono le tue amiche?   *Where are your (female) friends?*
Gli voglio parlare.   *I want to speak to them.*

Third-person forms

The English direct object pronouns *it* and *them* are expressed by the third-person direct object pronouns. Be careful! Choose the pronoun according to the gender and number of the noun it replaces. And, again, these go before the verb.

Masculine singular

Il ragazzo comprerà **il gelato** domani.   *The boy will buy the ice cream tomorrow.*
Il ragazzo **lo** comprerà domani.   *The boy will buy it tomorrow.*

Masculine plural

Quella donna comprerà **i biglietti** domani.   *That woman will buy the tickets tomorrow.*
Quella donna **li** comprerà domani.   *That woman will buy them tomorrow.*

Feminine singular

Mio fratello comprerà **la rivista** domani.   *My brother will buy the magazine tomorrow.*
Mio fratello **la** comprerà domani.   *My brother will buy it tomorrow.*

Feminine plural

Sua sorella comprerà **le riviste** domani.   *His sister will buy the magazines tomorrow.*
Sua sorella **le** comprerà domani.   *His sister will buy them tomorrow.*

A. *Complete each sentence with the appropriate direct or indirect pronoun, as required.*
Use the English pronouns given as a guide. (Note: **va bene** *= OK;* **indirizzo** *= address.)*

1. *(to) me*

   a. Giovanni _____ chiama ogni sera.

   b. Giovanni _____ ha dato la sua penna.

2. *(to) you (fam., sing.)*

   a. La sua amica _____ ha telefonato, non è vero?

   b. Lui vuole che io _____ chiami stasera.

3. *(to) you (pol., sing.)*

   a. Professoressa, _____ chiamo domani, va bene?

   b. Professoressa, _____ do il mio compito domani, va bene?

4. *(to) him*

   a. Conosci Marco? Mia sorella _____ telefona spesso.

   b. Sì, io _____ conosco molto bene.

5. *(to) her*

   a. Ieri ho visto Maria e _____ ho dato il tuo indirizzo.

   b. Anche tu hai visto Maria, no? No, ma forse _____ chiamo stasera.

6. *(to) us*

   a. Marco e Maria, quando _____ venite a visitare?

   b. Signor Verdi e signora Verdi, quando _____ telefonerete?

7. *(to) you (fam., pl.)*

   a. Claudia e Franca, _____ devo dire qualcosa.

   b. Claudia e Franca, non _____ ho dato niente ieri.

8. *(to) them (m.)*

   a. Conosci quegli studenti? No, non _____ conosco.

   b. Scrivi mai a quegli studenti? No, non _____ scrivo mai.

9. *(to) them (f.)*

   a. Conosci quelle studentesse? No, non _____ conosco.

   b. Scrivi mai a quelle studentesse? No, non _____ scrivo mai.

B. *Rewrite each sentence by replacing the italicized object with the appropriate pronoun. (Note:* **volentieri** *= gladly;* **stivale** *[m.] = boots.)*

EXAMPLE   Io comprerò *quella camicia* domani.

              Io la comprerò domani.

1. Marco guarda sempre *la televisione* ogni sera.

   _____

2. Anche lei preferisce *quel programma.*

   _____

3. Mangeremo *gli spaghetti* volentieri in quel ristorante.

   _____

4. Anche Maria vuole *le patate.*

   _____

5. Compreremo *le scarpe* domani.

   _____

6. Loro compreranno *gli stivali* in centro.

   _____

7. Anch'io prendo *l'espresso,* va bene?

   _____

8. Vuoi *la carne* anche tu?

   _____

Stressed pronouns

There is a second type of personal object pronoun that goes after the verb. It is known as a stressed or tonic pronoun.

DIRECT OBJECT PRONOUNS

BEFORE, UNSTRESSED		AFTER, STRESSED	
mi	*me*	**me**	*me*
ti	*you (fam.)*	**te**	*you (fam.)*
La	*you (pol.)*	**Lei**	*you (pol.)*
lo	*him*	**lui**	*him*
la	*her*	**lei**	*her*
ci	*us*	**noi**	*us*
vi	*you (fam., pl.)*	**voi**	*you (fam., pl.)*
li	*them (m.)*	**loro**	*them*
le	*them (f.)*	**loro**	*them*

INDIRECT OBJECT PRONOUNS

BEFORE, UNSTRESSED		AFTER, STRESSED	
mi	*to me*	**a me**	*to me*
ti	*to you (fam., sing.)*	**a te**	*to you (fam., sing.)*
Le	*to you (pol., sing.)*	**a Lei**	*to you (pol., sing.)*
gli	*to him*	**a lui**	*to him*
le	*to her*	**a lei**	*to her*
ci	*to us*	**a noi**	*to us*
vi	*to you (fam., pl.)*	**a voi**	*to you (fam., pl.)*
gli	*to them (m.)*	**a loro**	*to them*
gli	*to them (f.)*	**a loro**	*to them*

For most purposes, the two types can be used alternatively, although the unstressed pronouns are more common in most types of discourse. The stressed pronouns are more appropriate when emphasis is required or in order to avoid ambiguity.

Marco lo darà **a me**, non **a te**!	*Mark will give it to me, not to you!*
Ieri ho scritto **a te**, e solo **a te**!	*Yesterday I wrote to you, and only you!*

These are the only object pronouns you can use after a preposition.

Maria viene **con noi**.	*Mary is coming with us.*
Il professore parla **di te**.	*The professor is speaking about you.*
L'ha fatto **per me**.	*He did it for me.*

ESERCIZIO
5·3

A. *Complete each sentence with the appropriate stressed direct or indirect object pronoun, as required. Use the English pronouns given as a guide.*

1. *(to) me*

   a. Claudia chiama solo _____ ogni sera, non la sua amica.

   b. Giovanni ha dato la sua penna _____ , non al suo amico.

2. *(to) you (fam., sing.)*

   a. Claudia ha telefonato _____ , non è vero?

   b. Lui vuole che io chiami anche _____ stasera.

3. *(to) you (pol., sing.)*

   a. Dottor Marchi, chiamo _____ , non l'altro medico, domani, va bene?

   b. Professoressa Verdi, do il mio compito _____ domani, va bene?

4. *(to) him*

   a. Conosci il professor Giusti? Mia sorella telefona solo _____ per studiare per gli esami.

   b. Sì, io conosco proprio _____ molto bene.

5. *(to) her*

   a. Ieri ho visto la tua amica e ho dato il tuo indirizzo anche _____ .

   b. Anche tu hai visto Paola, no? No, ma forse esco con _____ stasera.

6. *(to) us*

   a. Marco e Maria, quando uscirete con _____ ?

   b. Signor Verdi e signora Verdi, quando telefonerete _____ ?

7. *(to) you (fam., pl.)*

   a. Marco e Maria, parlerò di _____ alla professoressa.

   b. Claudia e Franca, non ho dato niente _____ ieri.

8. *(to) them (m.)*

   a. Conosci quegli studenti? Sì, e domani parlerò di _____ al professore.

   b. Scrivi mai a quegli studenti? No, non scrivo mai _____ .

9. *(to) them (f.)*

   a. Conosci quelle studentesse? Sì, e domani parlerò di _____ al professore.

   b. Scrivi mai a quelle studentesse? No, non scrivo mai _____ .

B. *How do you say the following in Italian?*

1. Mark will give your address to me, not to him!

   _____

2. Yesterday I wrote to you *(fam., sing.)*, and only you!

   _____

3. Mary is coming with us, not with them, to the movies tomorrow.

   _____

4. The professor is always speaking about you *(fam., pl.)*, not about us!

   _____

5. Mary, I did it for you!

   _____

6. Mrs. Verdi, I did it for you!

   _____

Other pronouns

Words such as **molto**, **tanto**, etc., can also function as pronouns.

Lui mangia **assai**.	*He eats quite a lot.*
Tuo fratello dorme **molto**, no?	*Your brother sleeps a lot, doesn't he?*
Ieri ho mangiato **troppo**.	*Yesterday I ate too much.*

When referring to people in general, use the plural forms **alcuni**, **molti**, **parecchi**, **pochi**, **tanti**, **tutti**, etc.

Molti vanno in Italia quest'anno.	*Many (people) are going to Italy this year.*
Tutti sanno quello.	*Everyone knows that.*

Use the corresponding feminine forms (**molte**, **alcune**, etc.) when referring to females.

Di quelle ragazze, **molte** sono italiane.	*Of those girls, many are Italian.*
Di tutte quelle donne, **alcune** sono americane.	*Of all those women, some are American.*

The pronoun **ne** has four main functions. It is placed before the verb when used to replace the following structures:

- partitives

Comprerai anche **delle patate**?	*Will you also buy some potatoes?*
Sì, **ne** comprerò.	*Yes, I'll buy some.*

- numbers and quantitative expressions

Quanti **libri** devi leggere?	*How many books do you have to read?*
Ne devo leggere tre.	*I have to read three (of them).*

- indefinite expressions

Leggi molti **libri** di solito, non è vero?	*You usually read a lot of books, don't you?*
Sì, **ne** leggo molti di solito.	*Yes, I usually read a lot (of them).*

- topic phrases introduced by **di**

Ha parlato **di matematica**, vero?	*He spoke about mathematics, didn't he?*
Sì, **ne** ha parlato.	*Yes, he spoke about it.*

The locative (place) pronoun **ci** means *there*. It also is placed before the verb.

Andate **in Italia**, non è vero?	*You are going to Italy, aren't you?*
Sì, **ci** andiamo domani.	*Yes, we are going there tomorrow.*
Marco vive **a Perugia**, non è vero?	*Marco lives in Perugia, doesn't he?*
Sì, **ci** vive da molti anni.	*Yes, he has been living there for many years.*

Ne is used instead to express *from there*.

Sei arrivato **dall'Italia** ieri, non è vero?	*You arrived from Italy yesterday, didn't you?*
Sì, **ne** sono arrivato proprio ieri.	*Yes, I came from there just yesterday.*

A. *Rewrite each sentence by replacing the italicized word or phrase with either* **ne** *or* **ci.**

1. Sì, comprerò *delle matite.*

_____

2. Mio fratello comprerà *degli zaini* domani.

_____

3. Devo guardare due *programmi* stasera.

_____

4. Di solito leggo molte *riviste* ogni settimana.

_____

5. Anche lei ha parlato *di Dante.*

_____

6. Andiamo *in Italia* domani.

_____

7. Mia sorella vive *a Chicago* da molti anni.

_____

8. Loro arrivano *dalla Francia* tra poco.

_____

B. *How do you say the following in Italian?*

1. My brother eats quite a lot.

_____

2. Does your sister sleep a lot?

_____

3. Yesterday we ate too much.

_____

4. Only a few are going to Italy this year. But many went last year.

_____

5. Of those women, many are Italian and a few are American.

_____

C. *Choose the appropriate pronoun to complete each sentence.*

1. Giovanni è andato anche _____ in Italia.

    a. lui   b. egli

2. Petrarca era anche _____ un fiorentino.

    a. lui   b. egli

3. Claudia, quando _____ hai chiamato?

    a. mi   b. me

4. Marco, è vero che _____ hai parlato già?

    a. gli   b. lui

5. Noi abbiamo parlato a tuo fratello ieri. Non _____ abbiamo detto proprio niente.

    a. gli   b. le

6. Noi abbiamo parlato a quella donna ieri. Non _____ abbiamo detto proprio niente.

    a. gli   b. le

7. Vieni con _____ in centro!

    a. mi   b. me

D. *Rewrite each sentence by replacing the italicized object pronoun words or phrases with the appropriate unstressed pronouns and by making all necessary changes.*

1. Claudia darà *il libro* a me domani.

   _____

2. Io darò *le matite* a te dopo.

   _____

3. Io ho dato le scarpe *alla loro amica*.

   _____

4. Voglio *gli gnocchi* anch'io.

   _____

5. Lui chiama spesso *il fratello e sua sorella*.

   _____

6. Lui vuole *delle scarpe*.

   _____

7. Non voglio *la carne*.

   _____

8. Prendo due *matite*.

   _____

9. Marco andrà *in Italia* domani.

_____

10. Lei comprerà *molte cose* per la festa.

_____

11. Prendo quattro *tazze di caffè* di solito.

_____

Grammar in culture

Familiar vs. polite address in Italian is an important social distinction. Grammatically, this involves using appropriate pronouns and verb forms. Use the third-person plural polite forms with strangers and those with whom you are on a formal social basis; otherwise, use the second-person familiar forms (with family, friends, children, colleagues, and animals).

FAMILIAR	POLITE
tu	**Lei**
Anche **tu** sei italiana, Maria, vero? *Maria, you're Italian as well, right?*	Anche **Lei** è italiana, dottoressa Verdi, vero? *Dr. Verdi, you're Italian as well, right?*
voi	**Loro**
Venite anche **voi**, Marco e Maria? *You're coming too, Marco and Maria?*	Vengono anche **Loro**, signor e signora Rossi? *You're coming too, Mr. and Mrs. Rossi?*
ti	**La**
Maria, **ti** chiamo domani. *Maria, I'll call you tomorrow.*	Professore, **La** chiamo domani. *Professor, I'll call you tomorrow.*
ti / a te	**Le / a Lei**
Maria, **ti** ho detto tutto. *Mary, I told you everything.*	Signore, **Le** ho detto tutto. *Sir, I told you everything.*
Maria, ho dato il mio cellulare **a te**. *Maria, I gave my cell phone to you.*	Signore, ho dato il mio cellulare **a Lei**. *Sir, I gave my cell phone to you.*

Rewrite each sentence, using the addressee in parentheses and making all necessary changes.

EXAMPLE   Maria, vieni anche tu? (Signora Verdi)

Signora Verdi, viene anche Lei?

1. Professore, La chiamo domani, va bene? (Gina)

   _____

2. Mamma, ti ho dato il regalo (*gift*) per Natale. (Professore)

   _____

3. Signor e signora Marchi, partono anche Loro domani? (Gina e Claudia)

   _____

4. Ragazzino (*little boy*), chi sei tu? (Signore)

   _____

5. Marco, ho dato quella cosa a te ieri. (Professoressa)

   _____

More pronouns

As you saw in the previous unit, pronouns constitute a fairly complex part of Italian grammar. And there is more to know about them, as you may recall from previous study. In this unit, we will conclude the treatment of these pesky pronouns.

Object pronouns with compound tenses

The past participle of verbs in compound tenses agrees with the object pronouns **lo**, **la**, **li**, **le**, and **ne**.

Agreement with lo

Hanno visto **il nuovo film**?	*Did they see the new movie?*
Sì, **lo** hanno visto (**l'**hanno vist**o**).	*Yes, they saw it.*

Agreement with la

Hai comprato **la camicia**?	*Did you buy the shirt?*
Sì, **la** ho comprat**a** (**l'**ho comprat**a**) ieri.	*Yes, I bought it yesterday.*

Agreement with li

Avete finito **gli spaghetti**?	*Did you finish the spaghetti?*
Sì, **li** abbiamo finit**i**.	*Yes, we finished them.*

Agreement with le

Hai mangiato **le mele**?	*Did you eat the apples?*
Sì, **le** ho mangiat**e**.	*Yes, I ate them.*

Agreement with ne (when used to replace quantitative expressions only)

Quante **mele** hai mangiato?	*How many apples did you eat?*
Ne ho mangiat**e** quattro.	*I ate four of them.*
Quanti **panini** hai mangiato?	*How many sandwiches did you eat?*
Ne ho mangiat**i** tanti.	*I ate a lot.*

Note: Only the singular forms **lo** and **la** can be elided with the auxiliary forms of **avere**.

Agreement with the other direct object pronouns—**mi**, **ti**, **ci**, **vi**—is optional.

Claudia **ci** ha chiamato. (or)	*Claudia called us.*
Claudia **ci** ha chiamati.	

There is no agreement with indirect object pronouns.

Giovanni **gli** ha scritto. *John wrote to him (to them).*
Giovanni **le** ha scritto. *John wrote to her.*

So, be careful!

Direct object pronoun: agreement

Lui ha già mangiato **le patate**. *He already ate the potatoes.*
Lui **le** ha già mangiate. *He already ate them.*

Indirect object pronoun: no agreement

Lui ha scritto **a sua sorella**. *He wrote to his sister.*
Lui **le** ha scritto. *He wrote to her.*

ESERCIZIO
6·1

A. *Rewrite each sentence by replacing each italicized object word or phrase with the appropriate unstressed object pronoun and by making all other necessary changes.*

1. Mio fratello ha comprato *quello zaino* ieri.

   _____

2. Abbiamo dato quello zaino *a mio fratello*.

   _____

3. Loro hanno preso *quegli stivali* ieri.

   _____

4. Ho dato quegli stivali *ai miei amici* ieri.

   _____

5. Mia sorella ha comprato *quella borsa* ieri.

   _____

6. Mia madre ha dato quella borsa *a mia sorella*.

   _____

7. Abbiamo visto *quelle scarpe* in centro.

   _____

8. Abbiamo dato quelle scarpe *alle nostre amiche* ieri.

   _____

9. Ho mangiato tre *patate*.

   _____

10. Abbiamo comprato molte *cose* in centro ieri.

   _____

B. *Answer each question affirmatively, using the appropriate unstressed pronoun and making any necessary adjustment to the past participle.*

EXAMPLE   Hai preso quella matita?

Sì, l'ho presa.

1. Hai preso quello zaino?

_____

2. Hai comprato quelle scarpe?

_____

3. Hai visto la tua amica?

_____

4. Hai chiamato i tuoi amici?

_____

5. Hai mangiato delle patate?

_____

Double pronouns

When both direct and indirect object pronouns are used, the following rules apply:

- The indirect object pronoun always precedes the direct object pronoun (the only possible forms are **lo, la, li, le**) and the pronoun **ne**.

Claudia **mi** darà **il libro** domani.	*Claudia will give the book to me tomorrow.*
Claudia **me lo** darà domani.	*Claudia will give it to me tomorrow.*
Giovanni **mi** comprerà **delle matite**.	*John will buy me some pencils.*
Giovanni **me ne** comprerà.	*John will buy me some.*

- The indirect pronouns **mi, ti, ci**, and **vi** are changed to **me, te, ce**, and **ve**, respectively.

Lei **mi** darà **il libro** domani.	*She is giving me the book tomorrow.*
Lei **me lo** darà domani.	*She is giving it to me tomorrow.*
Maria **vi** darà **quelle scarpe** per Natale.	*Mary will give you those shoes for Christmas.*
Maria **ve le** darà per Natale.	*Mary will give you them for Christmas.*

Note that the rule regarding agreement between the direct object pronoun and the past participle still applies.

Lui **ci** ha dato **la sua bella penna** ieri.	*He gave his beautiful pen to us yesterday.*
Lui **ce l'**ha data ieri.	*He gave it to us yesterday.*
Giovanni **ti** ha dato **i suoi libri** già.	*John has already given his books to you.*
Giovanni **te li** ha dati già.	*John has already given them to you.*

◆ The indirect pronouns **gli** and **le** are both changed to **glie** and combined with **lo, la, li, le,** or **ne** to form one word: **glielo, gliela, glieli, gliele, gliene.**

Claudia dà **il libro a Paolo** domani.	*Claudia will give the book to Paul tomorrow.*
Claudia **glielo** dà domani.	*Claudia will give it to him tomorrow.*
Maria darà **quella borsa a sua sorella**.	*Mary will give her sister that purse.*
Maria **gliela** darà.	*Mary will give it to her.*

Note again the agreement between the past participle and the direct object pronoun, even though it is part of the combined word.

Io ho dato **i miei orologi ad Alessandro**.	*I gave my watches to Alexander.*
Io **glieli** ho dat**i**.	*I gave them to him.*
Io ho dato **le mie chiavi a Marco**.	*I gave my keys to Mark.*
Io **gliele** ho dat**e**.	*I gave them to him.*
Io ho comprato **due matite a mio zio**.	*I bought my uncle two pencils.*
Io **gliene** ho comprat**e** due.	*I bought him two (of them).*

ESERCIZIO
6·2

A. *Rewrite each sentence by replacing the italicized object words or phrases with the appropriate double object pronouns and by making all other necessary changes.*

1. Mia sorella *mi* ha comprato *quello zaino* ieri.

   _____

2. *Gli* ho dato *quello zaino* ieri.

   _____

3. Loro *ti* hanno preso *quegli stivali* ieri.

   _____

4. *Le* ho dato *quegli stivali* ieri.

   _____

5. Nostra madre *ci* ha comprato *quella macchina* qualche anno fa.

   _____

6. Mia madre *le* ha dato *quella borsa*.

   _____

7. *Vi* abbiamo comprato *quelle scarpe* in centro.

   _____

8. *Gli* abbiamo dato *quelle scarpe* ieri.

   _____

9. *Gli* ho dato tre *patate*.

   _____

10. *Le* abbiamo comprato molte *cose* in centro ieri.

    _____

B. *Answer each question affirmatively, using the appropriate double pronoun and making any necessary adjustment to the past participle.*

EXAMPLE   Mi hai preso quella matita?

Sì, te l'ho presa.

1. Ci hai preso quello zaino?

_____

2. Gli hai comprato quelle scarpe?

_____

3. Ti ho dato le mie matite?

_____

4. Le hai detto quelle cose?

_____

5. Mi hai preso delle patate?

_____

Attached pronouns

Object pronouns are attached to an infinitive or gerund. Double pronouns are both attached. Note that the final **-e** of the infinitive is dropped when a single or double pronoun is attached.

Prima di mangiare **il gelato**, voglio i ravioli.	*Before eating the ice cream, I want ravioli.*
Prima di mangiar**lo**, voglio i ravioli.	*Before eating it, I want ravioli.*
Vedendo **Maria**, l'ho chiamata.	*Seeing Mary, I called her.*
Vedendo**la**, l'ho chiamata.	*Seeing her, I called her.*

They are also attached to the form **ecco** (see Unit 7).

Ecco **la matita**.	*Here is the pencil.*
Ecco**la**.	*Here it is.*
Ecco **Giovanni e Claudia**.	*Here are John and Claudia.*
Ecco**li**.	*Here they are.*
Ecco **le chiavi per te**.	*Here are the keys for you.*
Ecco**tele**.	*Here they are for you.*

All double pronouns are written as one unit when attached to a verb.

With the modal verbs (**potere, dovere, volere**), you can either attach the object pronouns to the infinitive or put them before the modal verb.

Non posso mangiare **la carne**.	*I cannot eat meat.*
Non posso mangiar**la**. (or) Non **la** posso mangiare.	*I cannot eat it.*
Lei **gli** vuole dare **il suo portatile**.	*She wants to give him her laptop.*
Lei vuole dar**glielo**. (or) Lei **glielo** vuole dare.	*She wants to give it to him.*

Object pronouns with imperative verbs

The object pronouns (single and double) are also attached to the familiar forms of the imperative (**tu, noi, voi**). They are not attached to the polite **Lei** and **Loro** forms.

Familiar

Giovanni, mangia **la mela**!	*John, eat the apple!*
Giovanni, mangia**la**!	*John, eat it!*
Sara, scrivi **l'e-mail a tuo fratello**!	*Sarah, write the e-mail to your brother!*
Sara, scrivi**gliela**!	*Sarah, write it to him!*
Marco e Maria, date **la vostra penna a me**!	*Mark and Mary, give your pen to me!*
Marco e Maria, date**mela**!	*Mark and Maria, give it to me!*

Polite

Signor Marchi, mangi **la mela**!	*Mr. Marchi, eat the apple!*
Signor Marchi, **la** mangi!	*Mr. Marchi, eat it!*
Signor Dini, scriva **l'e-mail a Suo fratello**!	*Mr. Dini, write the e-mail to your brother!*
Signor Dini, **gliela** scriva!	*Mr. Dini, write it to him!*

When attaching pronouns to familiar forms ending with an apostrophe **da', di', fa', sta',** and **va'** (see Unit 15), you must double the first letter of the pronoun. There is, of course, no double **gl**.

Da' la penna a me!	*Give the pen to me!*
Dammi la penna!	*Give me the pen!*
Dammela!	*Give it to me!*
Di' la verità a lui!	*Tell him the truth!*
Dilla a lui!	*Tell it to him!*
Digliela!	*Tell it to him!*
Fa' quel compito per lui!	*Do that task for him!*
Fallo per lui!	*Do it for him!*
Faglielo!	*Do it for him!*
Da' due matite a me!	*Give me two pencils!*
Danne due a me!	*Give me two (of them)!*
Dammene due!	*Give me two (of them)!*
Va' in Italia!	*Go to Italy!*
Vacci!	*Go there!*

With the second-person singular negative infinitive form, you can either attach the pronouns to the infinitive or put them before.

AFFIRMATIVE		NEGATIVE			
Mangia**lo**!	*Eat it!*	Non mangiar**lo**!	(or)	Non **lo** mangiare!	*Don't eat it!*
Manda**mela**!	*Send it to me!*	Non mandar**mela**!	(or)	Non **me la** mandare!	*Don't send it to me!*

A. *Rewrite each sentence by replacing the italicized words with single or double object pronouns, as necessary, and by making all necessary changes. (Note:* **favore** *[m.] = favor.)*

1. Prima di bere *la bibita*, voglio mangiare.

   _____

2. Vedendo *i miei amici*, li ho chiamati.

   _____

3. Ecco *le tue amiche.*

   _____

4. Ecco *gli stivali nuovi per te.*

   _____

5. Non voglio mangiare *gli spaghetti.*

   _____

6. Potremo andare *in Italia* tra poco.

   _____

7. Vogliamo scrivere molte *cose a lui.*

   _____

8. Giovanni, bevi *il caffè!*

   _____

9. Alessandro da' *la tua penna a me!*

   _____

10. Maria, fa' *questo favore a tua madre!*

    _____

11. Signora Marchi, dica *la verità a me!*

    _____

12. Franco, di' *la verità a me!*

    _____

B. *How do you say the following in Italian?*

1. John, give the pen to me! Don't give it to her!

   _____

2. Doctor Verdi, tell him the truth! But don't tell it to them (*f.*)!

   _____

3. Mom, do that task for me! But don't do it for him!

_____

4. Mark, do me a favor! But don't do it for them (_m._)!

_____

5. Mary, go downtown with us! Don't go there with him!

_____

6. Mrs. Verdi, go downtown with us! Don't go there with her!

_____

C. _Rewrite each sentence by replacing the italicized object pronoun words or phrases with the appropriate unstressed pronouns and by making all other necessary changes._

1. Marco _mi_ darà _il portatile_ domani.

_____

2. Io _ti_ ho dato _le scarpe_ ieri.

_____

3. Loro hanno dato _le matite alla loro amica._

_____

4. Prima di mangiare _gli gnocchi_, voglio mangiare l'antipasto.

_____

5. Ecco _il fratello e sua sorella._

_____

6. Lui ha comprato _le scarpe nuove_ ieri.

_____

7. Non voglio mangiare _la carne._

_____

8. Claudia, mangia _le patate_!

_____

9. Giovanni, dammi due _matite_!

_____

10. Mio fratello è andato _in Italia_ ieri.

_____

11. Lei ha comprato molte _mele_ ieri.

_____

12. Ci sono quattro _matite_ nello zaino.

_____

D. *Rewrite each sentence by replacing each italicized phrase with the appropriate unstressed object pronoun. Then, rewrite the sentence again by making the italicized phrase plural and resubstituting the appropriate unstressed object pronoun. Make all other necessary changes.*

EXAMPLE   Io ho sempre detto *la stessa cosa.*

                     Io l'ho sempre detta.

                     Io ho sempre detto le stesse cose.

                     Io le ho sempre dette.

1. Bruno mi ha comprato *quell'orologio.*

2. Marco, mangia *quella mela*!

3. Paola vi darà *quel libro* domani.

4. Anche tu mi hai comprato *quella camicia* nello stesso negozio, vero?

5. Lui ha bevuto *quel caffè* volentieri.

Grammar in culture

Whether a pronoun comes before or after the verb depends on the structure of the sentence. In some cases, however, as in the negative imperative, the pronoun may come before or after; this is a matter of style or emphasis. The difference between **Marco, non lo mangiare** and **Marco, non mangiarlo** (*Marco, don't eat it!*) is that the latter command stresses the verb more, thus giving the action more emphasis.

ESERCIZIO
6·4

Provide the emphatic or nonemphatic version of each sentence.

EMPHATIC	NONEMPHATIC
1. Gina, non darmela!	_____
2. _____	Luca, non ci andare!
3. Posso darti questo libro?	_____
4. _____	Ti voglio chiamare subito.

Demonstratives

Demonstratives are special kinds of adjectives (see Unit 4). They mark nouns as referring to someone or something that is relatively near or far from someone or something else.

RELATIVELY NEAR		RELATIVELY FAR	
questo bambino	*this child*	**quel bambino**	*that child*
questa porta	*this door*	**quella porta**	*that door*

The demonstrative of nearness

As listed in the dictionary, the demonstrative indicating *nearness* is **questo** (*this*). Like any adjective, it modifies the noun—that is, it changes in form to indicate the gender and number of the noun. Its forms are given below.

The form **questo** is used before a masculine noun. Its plural form is **questi**.

SINGULAR		PLURAL	
questo amico	*this friend*	**questi amici**	*these friends*
questo cane	*this dog*	**questi cani**	*these dogs*
questo ragazzo	*this boy*	**questi ragazzi**	*these boys*
questo studente	*this student*	**questi studenti**	*these students*
questo zio	*this uncle*	**questi zii**	*these uncles*

And the form **questa** is used before a feminine noun. Its plural form is **queste**.

SINGULAR		PLURAL	
questa amica	*this friend*	**queste amiche**	*these friends*
questa camicia	*this shirt*	**queste camicie**	*these shirts*
questa ragazza	*this girl*	**queste ragazze**	*these girls*
questa studentessa	*this student*	**queste studentesse**	*these students*
questa zia	*this aunt*	**queste zie**	*these aunts*

The form **quest'** can be used (optionally) in front of a singular noun (masculine or feminine) beginning with a vowel.

questo orologio	(or)	**quest'orologio**	*this watch*
questa amica	(or)	**quest'amica**	*this friend*

Be careful!

Unlike in English, in Italian you must repeat the demonstrative before each noun.

questo zio e **questa zia**   *this uncle and aunt*
questi ragazzi e **queste ragazze**   *these boys and girls*

ESERCIZIO
7·1

A. *Rewrite each of the following phrases in the plural. If you have forgotten the meanings of the nouns used in this and the next Esercizio, look them up in the glossary at the back of this book.*

1. quest'affare   _____

2. quest'attrice   _____

3. questo biologo   _____

4. questa bugia   _____

5. questo cameriere   _____

6. questa cameriera   _____

B. *Now, rewrite each phrase in the singular. Some of the items are tricky, although you have come across the grammar behind them in previous units. So, be careful!*

1. questi diagrammi   _____

2. queste dita   _____

3. questi francesi   _____

4. queste francesi   _____

5. questi giornali   _____

The demonstrative of farness

The demonstrative adjective indicating farness is **quello** (*that*). Its forms vary as follows.

- The form **quello** is used before a masculine noun beginning with **z**, **s** + **consonant**, **gn**, or **ps**. Its plural form is **quegli**.

SINGULAR		PLURAL	
quello zio	*that uncle*	**quegli zii**	*those uncles*
quello studente	*that student*	**quegli studenti**	*those students*
quello gnocco	*that dumpling*	**quegli gnocchi**	*those dumplings*
quello psicologo	*that psychologist*	**quegli psicologi**	*those psychologists*

- The form **quel** is used before a masculine noun beginning with any other consonant. Its plural form is **quei**.

SINGULAR		PLURAL	
quel cane	*that dog*	quei cani	*those dogs*
quel giornale	*that newspaper*	quei giornali	*those newspapers*
quel giorno	*that day*	quei giorni	*those days*
quel ragazzo	*that boy*	quei ragazzi	*those boys*

◆ The form **quell'** is used before a masculine noun beginning with any vowel. Its plural form is **quegli**.

SINGULAR		PLURAL	
quell'amico	*that friend*	quegli amici	*those friends*
quell'avvocato	*that lawyer*	quegli avvocati	*those lawyers*
quell'impermeabile	*that raincoat*	quegli impermeabili	*those raincoats*
quell'orologio	*that watch*	quegli orologi	*those watches*

◆ The form **quella** is used before a feminine noun beginning with any consonant. Its plural form is **quelle**.

SINGULAR		PLURAL	
quella camicia	*that shirt*	quelle camicie	*those shirts*
quella ragazza	*that girl*	quelle ragazze	*those girls*
quella studentessa	*that student*	quelle studentesse	*those students*
quella zia	*that aunt*	quelle zie	*those aunts*

◆ And the form **quell'** is used before a feminine noun beginning with any vowel. Its plural form is also **quelle**.

SINGULAR		PLURAL	
quell'amica	*that friend*	quelle amiche	*those friends*
quell'attrice	*that actress*	quelle attrici	*those actresses*
quell'infermiera	*that nurse*	quelle infermiere	*those nurses*
quell'ora	*that hour*	quelle ore	*those hours*

Tips and reminders!

As with the articles, when an adjective precedes a noun, you will have to change the demonstrative according to the adjective's initial sound.

quello zio	*that uncle*	but	**quel simpatico zio**	*that nice uncle*
quegli amici	*those friends*	but	**quei simpatici amici**	*those nice friends*

Remember to repeat the demonstratives before every noun:

quel ragazzo e **quella ragazza**   *that boy and girl*

As was the case with **bello** (see Unit 4), **quello** undergoes the same kinds of form changes as the definite article (see Unit 3).

lo	→	quello
l'	→	quell'
gli	→	quegli
il	→	quel
i	→	quei
la	→	quella
le	→	quelle

A. *Rewrite each of the following phrases in the plural. If you have forgotten the meanings of the nouns and adjectives used in this and the next Esercizio, look them up in the glossary at the back of this book.*

1. quell'architetto _____

2. quell'autrice _____

3. quel braccio _____

4. quella cameriera _____

5. quello zaino _____

6. quell'ipotesi _____

7. quella macchina _____

8. quel simpatico bambino _____

9. quel bel ragazzo _____

10. quella bella ragazza _____

B. *Now, rewrite each phrase in the singular.*

1. quei programmi _____

2. quei problemi _____

3. quegli inglesi _____

4. quelle inglesi _____

5. quei nomi _____

6. quelle notti _____

7. quegli occhi _____

8. quelle paia _____

9. quegli spagnoli simpatici _____

10. quei teoremi e quelle tesi _____

Demonstrative pronouns

Demonstrative pronouns replace noun phrases formed with demonstrative adjectives.

Questa ragazza è americana.	*This girl is American.*
Questa è americana.	*This one is American.*
Quel ragazzo è italiano.	*That boy is Italian.*
Quello è italiano.	*That one is Italian.*

The pronouns retain the gender and number of the demonstratives they replace. However, once you do this you will have to make adjustments. Here are all the possibilities.

MASCULINE DEMONSTRATIVES

SINGULAR ADJECTIVE FORM		CORRESPONDING PRONOUN FORM	
questo (or) **quest'**		**questo**	
questo zaino	*this backpack*	**questo**	*this one* (*referring to* zaino)
quest'uomo	*this man*	**questo**	*this one* (*referring to* uomo)
quel, quello, (or) **quell'**		**quello**	
quel ragazzo	*that boy*	**quello**	*that one* (*referring to* ragazzo)
quello psicologo	*that psychologist*	**quello**	*that one* (*referring to* psicologo)
quell'orologio	*that watch*	**quello**	*that one* (*referring to* orologio)

PLURAL ADJECTIVE FORM		CORRESPONDING PRONOUN FORM	
questi		**questi**	
questi zaini	*these backpacks*	**questi**	*these ones* (*referring to* zaini)
questi uomini	*these men*	**questi**	*these ones* (*referring to* uomini)
quei (or) **quegli**		**quelli**	
quei ragazzi	*those boys*	**quelli**	*those ones* (*referring to* ragazzi)
quegli psicologi	*those psychologists*	**quelli**	*those ones* (*referring to* psicologi)
quegli orologi	*those watches*	**quelli**	*those ones* (*referring to* orologi)

FEMININE DEMONSTRATIVES

SINGULAR ADJECTIVE FORM		CORRESPONDING PRONOUN FORM	
questa (or) **quest'**		**questa**	
questa ragazza	*this girl*	**questa**	*this one* (*referring to* ragazza)
quest'amica	*this friend*	**questa**	*this one* (*referring to* amica)
quella		**quella**	
quella ragazza	*that girl*	**quella**	*that one* (*referring to* ragazza)
quell'amica	*that friend*	**quella**	*that one* (*referring to* amica)

PLURAL ADJECTIVE FORM		CORRESPONDING PRONOUN FORM	
queste		**queste**	
queste ragazze	*these girls*	**queste**	*these ones* (*referring to* ragazze)
queste amiche	*these friends*	**queste**	*these ones* (*referring to* amiche)
quelle		**quelle**	
quelle ragazze	*these girls*	**quelle**	*those ones* (*referring to* ragazze)
quelle amiche	*these friends*	**quelle**	*those ones* (*referring to* amiche)

A. *Provide the appropriate demonstrative pronoun for each phrase.*

1. quel vestito rosa _____
2. quelle sciarpe rosse _____
3. quell'uomo alto _____
4. quegli zaini marrone _____
5. quel fratello simpatico _____
6. quegli zii _____
7. quegli psicologi simpatici _____
8. quegli orologi _____
9. quelle isole _____
10. questa macchina _____
11. quest'ora _____
12. queste amiche _____
13. questo bambino _____
14. quest'impermeabile _____
15. questi bambini _____
16. questi ingegneri _____

B. *You are asked if you want this item or these items nearby. Answer that, no, you want that one or those ones farther away.*

EXAMPLE   Desidera questa macchina?

No, quella.

Desidera...

1. quest'orologio? _____
2. questi impermeabili? _____
3. questa camicia? _____
4. queste sciarpe? _____
5. questo libro? _____
6. questi zaini? _____
7. questo vestito? _____
8. quest'arancia? _____

Indicating words and expressions

The adverbs **qui** (*here*), **qua** (*right here*), **lì** (*there*), and **là** (*over there*) can be used alone, of course, or with demonstratives to emphasize the nearness or farness of someone or something, or to indicate their relative farness or nearness.

questo ragazzo	*this boy*	**questo ragazzo qui**	*this boy here*
questa ragazza	*this girl*	**questa ragazza qua**	*this girl right here*
quei libri	*those books*	**quei libri lì**	*those books there*
quelle sciarpe	*those scarves*	**quelle sciarpe là**	*those scarves over there*

The verb **essere** (*to be*) combined with **ci** (*there*) produces the construction **esserci** (*to be there*). It is conjugated like **essere** with **ci** before the verb. Note, however, that it can only be used in the third person (singular and plural). The conjugations of **essere** are found in the irregular verb section at the back of this book.

C'è troppo zucchero nel caffè.	*There is too much sugar in the coffee.*
Ci sono molte persone alla festa.	*There are many people at the party.*

Ecco means *here is, here are, there is,* or *there are.* But it is used to indicate or point out something or someone directly. **Essere, esserci,** and **ecco** are often confusing to learners. Note the differences between them.

SINGULAR		PLURAL	
Che cosa **è**?	*What is it?*	Che cosa **sono**?	*What are they?*
È un libro.	*It's a book.*	**Sono** dei libri.	*They are books.*
C'è Dino?	*Is Dino there?*	**Ci sono** Dino e Maria?	*Are Dino and Mary there?*
Sì, **c'è**.	*Yes, he is (there/here).*	Sì, **ci sono**.	*Yes, they are (there/here).*
No, **non c'è**.	*No, he is not (there/here).*	No, **non ci sono**.	*No, they are not (there/here).*
Dov'è Dino?	*Where is Dino?*	Dove **sono** Dino e Maria?	*Where are Dino and Mary?*
Ecco Dino.	*Here/There is Dino.*	**Ecco** Dino e Maria.	*Here/There Dino and Mary are.*

ESERCIZIO
7·4

A. *You are asked if you want this item or these items nearby. Answer that, no, you want that item or those items farther away.*

EXAMPLE   Desidera questa penna qui?

No, quella penna lì.

Desidera...

1. quest'orologio qui? _____

2. questi impermeabili qui? _____

3. questa camicia qua? _____

4. queste sciarpe qua? _____

5. questo libro qui? _____

6. questi zaini qua? _____

B. *Answer each question with an appropriate form of* **essere**, **esserci**, *or* **ecco**, *as required. If you have forgotten how to conjugate* **essere** *look it up in the irregular verb section at the back of this book.*

1. Dov'è la penna? _____

2. C'è un'americano qui? _____

3. È uno studente d'italiano? _____

4. Dove sono quelle persone? _____

5. Ci sono persone italiane lì? _____

6. Sono amici? _____

C. *Provide the corresponding demonstrative of nearness or farness, as required. Note that you could be given an adjective or pronoun form of the demonstrative. If you have forgotten the meanings of the nouns and adjectives in this and the next sets of exercises, look them up in the glossary at the back of this book.*

NEARNESS	FARNESS
1. questo ragazzo	_____
2. _____	quella nuova macchina
3. questo qui	_____
4. _____	quegli studenti là
5. queste amiche simpatiche	_____
6. _____	quei simpatici psicologi
7. questi gnocchi lì	_____
8. _____	quelle paia di pantaloni

D. *A friend says that he or she wants, buys, needs, etc., this or these. Indicate instead that you want, will buy, need, etc., that or those of the same item or items.*

EXAMPLE   Voglio (*I want*) questa sciarpa.

           Io, invece, voglio quella sciarpa.

1. Voglio questo impermeabile.

   _____

2. Voglio questi libri.

   _____

3. Voglio questa camicia.

   _____

4. Voglio queste giacche.

   _____

5. Voglio questo zaino.

   _____

6. Voglio questi orologi.

_____

7. Voglio queste foto.

_____

E. *How do you say the following in Italian? (Note:* **dove** *= where;* **che cosa** *= what.)*

1. John and Mary are not here.

_____

2. Where are those shirts? Here are the shirts.

_____

3. What is it? It is a new car.

_____

4. Where are the students? There are the students.

_____

5. Are they right here? No, they are over there.

_____

Grammar in culture

The form **ecco** has many social and conversational uses. Here are a few:

- ◆ As a conversational hedge or support:

  Ecco, quello che voglio dire è questo.　　*Well, what I want to say is this.*
  Eccoci finalmente arrivati.　　*Well, we have arrived at last.*

- ◆ With the meaning *this is*:

  Ecco perché ho fatto questo.　　*This is why I did it.*

- ◆ To indicate that something is done or complete:

  Ecco fatto.　　*All done. / It's done.*
  Ecco tutto.　　*This is all of it. / That's all.*

How do you say the following in Italian?

1. This is why he didn't do it.

   _____

2. Well, this is the truth (**la verità**).

   _____

3. This is all of it. There is nothing else (**altro**) to (**da**) say.

   _____

4. Well, here we are at last.

   _____

 **·II-8·**

Possessives

Possessives are adjectives that indicate ownership of, or relationship to, something or someone. Like all other adjectives, they modify nouns.

il mio libro	*my book (ownership of)*	**i miei libri**	*my books*
la nostra amica	*our friend (relationship to)*	**le nostre amiche**	*our friends*

Possessive adjective forms

Like descriptive adjectives (see Unit 4), demonstratives (see Unit 7), and ordinal number words (see Unit 19), possessives agree in number and gender with the noun or nouns they modify. One of the possessives, however, is invariable: **loro**. Unlike most descriptive adjectives, however, they come before the noun (as do demonstratives and ordinals).

Unlike English, the definite article is part of the possessive. It is not optional. Here are the forms of the possessive adjective:

- **mio**   *my*

	SINGULAR		PLURAL	
MASCULINE	**il mio amico**	*my (male) friend*	**i miei amici**	*my (male) friends*
FEMININE	**la mia amica**	*my (female) friend*	**le mie amiche**	*my (female) friends*

- **tuo**   *your* (*fam., sing.*)

	SINGULAR		PLURAL	
MASCULINE	**il tuo orologio**	*your watch*	**i tuoi orologi**	*your watches*
FEMININE	**la tua giacca**	*your jacket*	**le tue giacche**	*your jackets*

214

- **suo** *his/her, its*

	SINGULAR		PLURAL	
MASCULINE	**il suo espresso**	*his/her espresso*	**i suoi espressi**	*his/her espressos*
FEMININE	**la sua bibita**	*his/her soft drink*	**le sue bibite**	*his/her soft drinks*

- **Suo** *your (pol., sing.)*

	SINGULAR		PLURAL	
MASCULINE	**il Suo espresso**	*your espresso*	**i Suoi espressi**	*your espressos*
FEMININE	**la Sua bibita**	*your soft drink*	**le Sue bibite**	*your soft drinks*

- **nostro** *our*

	SINGULAR		PLURAL	
MASCULINE	**il nostro amico**	*our friend*	**i nostri amici**	*our friends*
FEMININE	**la nostra amica**	*our friend*	**le nostre amiche**	*our friends*

- **vostro** *your (fam., pl.)*

	SINGULAR		PLURAL	
MASCULINE	**il vostro orologio**	*your watch*	**i vostri orologi**	*your watches*
FEMININE	**la vostra giacca**	*your jacket*	**le vostre giacche**	*your jackets*

- **loro** *their (invariable)*

	SINGULAR		PLURAL	
MASCULINE	**il loro espresso**	*their espresso*	**i loro espressi**	*their espressos*
FEMININE	**la loro bibita**	*their soft drink*	**le loro bibite**	*their soft drinks*

- **Loro** *your (pol., pl., invariable)*

	SINGULAR		PLURAL	
MASCULINE	**il Loro cellulare**	*your cell phone*	**i Loro cellulari**	*your cell phones*
FEMININE	**la Loro macchina**	*your car*	**le Loro macchine**	*your cars*

Note: The possessive adjective can be put after the noun for emphasis.

È **il mio cane**.	*It's my dog.*	È **il cane mio**!	*It's my dog!*
Chiama **il tuo amico**.	*Call your friend.*	Chiama **l'amico tuo**!	*Call your friend!*

When preceded by the indefinite, rather than the definite, article, the possessive adjective renders the same concept as can be found in English phrases such as *of mine, of yours,* etc.

un mio zio	*an uncle of mine*
una sua amica	*a friend of his/hers*

To express *(very) own*, use the adjective **proprio**.

il mio proprio cane	*my (very) own dog*
la sua propria motocicletta	*his/her (very) own motorcycle*
il loro proprio indirizzo	*their (very) own address*
la nostra propria casa	*our (very) own house*

A. *Complete the chart as indicated, providing the appropriate forms of the indicated possessives. The first one is done for you.*

	MY	YOUR (FAM., SING.)	OUR	THEIR
1. bibita	*la mia bibita*	*la tua bibita*	*la nostra bibita*	*la loro bibita*
2. cappuccino	_____	_____	_____	_____
3. bicchieri	_____	_____	_____	_____
4. braccia (*Be careful!*)	_____	_____	_____	_____
5. cappotto	_____	_____	_____	_____
6. cravatta	_____	_____	_____	_____
7. dita (*Be careful!*)	_____	_____	_____	_____
8. diagrammi	_____	_____	_____	_____

B. *You are asked a question. Answer in the negative, providing the correct information indicated in parentheses, which tells you which possessive to use.*

EXAMPLE   È la sua macchina? (*your, fam., pl.*)

No, è la vostra macchina. _____

1. È il suo espresso? (*their*)

_____

2. Sono i vostri figli? (*her*)

_____

3. Sono le vostre figlie? (*his*)

_____

4. È il tuo giornale? (*their*)

_____

5. È la sua professoressa? (*your, fam., sing.*)

_____

6. Sono i vostri amici? (*his*)

_____

7. Sono le sue chiavi? (*my*)

_____

The third-person forms

Both *his* and *her* are expressed by the same possessive form **suo** (which takes on its appropriate form before the noun). This is a constant source of blunders for many learners.

HIS		HER	
il suo orologio	*his watch*	**il suo orologio**	*her watch*
i suoi orologi	*his watches*	**i suoi orologi**	*her watches*
la sua bibita	*his soft drink*	**la sua bibita**	*her soft drink*
le sue bibite	*his soft drinks*	**le sue bibite**	*her soft drinks*

To avoid making potential blunders, keep this simple rule in mind—make the possessive adjective agree with the noun, without worrying about what it means in English. Otherwise, you will confuse its form with its meaning.

You can also figure out the meaning by using a corresponding genitive phrase, which is introduced by **di**. This is equivalent to English forms such as *John's, the boy's,* etc. If you have forgotten how to contract the preposition **di** with the definite article, jump forward to Unit 9. The genitive phrase provides information on the meaning, not the form of the possessive.

GENITIVE		CORRESPONDING POSSESSIVE	
il cappotto di Marco	*Mark's coat*	**il suo cappotto**	*his coat*
il cappotto di Maria	*Mary's coat*	**il suo cappotto**	*her coat*
la giacca del ragazzo	*the boy's jacket*	**la sua giacca**	*his jacket*
la giacca della ragazza	*the girl's jacket*	**la sua giacca**	*her jacket*
i libri di Marco	*Mark's books*	**i suoi libri**	*his books*
i libri di Maria	*Mary's books*	**i suoi libri**	*her books*
le giacche del ragazzo	*the boy's jackets*	**le sue giacche**	*his jackets*
le giacche della ragazza	*the girl's jackets*	**le sue giacche**	*her jackets*

Notice that there are familiar and polite possessives that correspond to the English possessive *your*. As these terms imply, you must use familiar forms with the people you know well and with whom you are on familiar terms; otherwise, you must use the polite forms.

Basically, you use the familiar forms (**tuo** in the singular and **vostro** in the plural) with people with whom you are on a first-name basis (family members, friends, children, colleagues, etc.). Otherwise, you use the polite forms (**Suo** in the singular and **Loro** in the plural) with anyone else (strangers, store clerks, etc.).

The polite forms are identical to the **suo** forms in the singular, and to the **loro** forms in the plural. To keep the two types distinct in writing, the polite forms are often capitalized, as has been done here.

HIS/HER		YOUR (POL., SING.)	
il suo cane	*his/her dog*	**il Suo cane**	*your dog*
i suoi cani	*his/her dogs*	**i Suoi cani**	*your dogs*
la sua bibita	*his/her soft drink*	**la Sua bibita**	*your soft drinks*
le sue bibite	*his/her soft drinks*	**le Sue bibite**	*your soft drinks*

THEIR		YOUR (POL., PL.)	
il loro amico	*their friend*	**il Loro amico**	*your friend*
i loro amici	*their friends*	**i Loro amici**	*your friends*
la loro fotografia	*their photograph*	**la Loro fotografia**	*your photograph*
le loro fotografie	*their photographs*	**le Loro fotografie**	*your photographs*

Thus, when you see or hear these forms, you will have to figure out what they mean from the context.

In current Italian, it is not unusual to find the **vostro** forms used as the plural of both the familiar and polite forms. The use of **Loro** as the polite plural possessive is restricted to very formal situations.

A. *Answer each question affirmatively, using the appropriate form of the possessive.*

EXAMPLE   È la macchina di Maria?

Sì, è la sua macchina.

1. È la macchina di Paolo?

_____

2. È il caffè di quell'uomo?

_____

3. È il caffè di quella donna?

_____

4. Sono gli amici del bambino?

_____

5. Sono gli amici della bambina?

_____

6. Sono le amiche del bambino?

_____

7. Sono le amiche della bambina?

_____

8. È la foto di quella donna?

_____

9. Sono le foto di quell'uomo?

_____

B. *Complete each question with the missing possessive adjective. Insert the familiar or polite form of the appropriate possessive, as required.*

EXAMPLE 1   Marco, è _____*il tuo*_____ libro?

EXAMPLE 2   Signor Dini, è _____*il Suo*_____ libro?

1. Maria, è _____ caffè?

2. Signora Rossi, è _____ caffè?

3. Gino, è _____ cappuccino?

4. Signor Bruni, è _____ cappuccino?

5. Claudia, sono _____ amiche?

6. Signorina Verdi, sono _____ amiche?

7. Giovanni, sono _____ forbici?

8. Professor Marchi, sono _____ forbici?

9. Maria e Claudia, è _____ caffè?

10. Signora Rossi e signorina Verdi, è _____ caffè?

11. Gino e Marco, è _____ cappuccino?

12. Signor Bruni e dottor Rossini, è _____ cappuccino?

13. Claudia e Maria, sono _____ amiche?

14. Signorina Verdi e dottoressa Dini, sono _____ amiche?

15. Giovanni e Claudia, sono _____ forbici?

16. Professor Marchi e dottoressa Bruni, sono _____ forbici?

Possessives with kinship nouns

The definite article is dropped from all forms except **loro** when the noun to which the possessive refers is a singular, unmodified kinship noun (**padre**, **madre**, etc.).

The most common kinship terms

il padre	*father*
la madre	*mother*
il figlio	*son*
la figlia	*daughter*
il fratello	*brother*
la sorella	*sister*
il nonno	*grandfather*
la nonna	*grandmother*
lo zio	*uncle*
la zia	*aunt*
il cugino / la cugina	*cousin*
il genero	*son-in-law*
il suocero / la suocera	*father-in-law / mother-in-law*
la nuora	*daughter-in-law*
il cognato / la cognata	*brother-in-law / sister-in-law*

SINGULAR KINSHIP NOUN		PLURAL KINSHIP NOUN	
tuo cugino	*your cousin*	**i tuoi cugini**	*your cousins*
sua zia	*his/her aunt*	**le sue zie**	*his/her aunts*
mia sorella	*my sister*	**le mie sorelle**	*my sisters*
nostro fratello	*our brother*	**i nostri fratelli**	*our brothers*

SINGULAR KINSHIP NOUN		MODIFIED OR ALTERED KINSHIP NOUN	
tuo cugino	*your cousin*	**il tuo cugino americano**	*your American cousin*
sua zia	*his/her aunt*	**la sua zia vecchia**	*his/her old aunt*
mia sorella	*my sister*	**la mia sorella minore**	*my little sister*
nostra cugina	*our cousin*	**la nostra cugina italiana**	*our Italian cousin*

The article is always retained with **loro**, even in the singular possessive forms.

il loro figlio	*their son*
la loro figlia	*their daughter*
il loro fratello	*their brother*
la loro sorella	*their sister*

The above set of rules are optional in the case of the following kinship nouns (when singular and unmodified, of course).

nonno	*grandfather*			
nonna	*grandmother*			
mamma	*mom*			
papà (or) **babbo**	*dad*			
mia mamma	*my mom*	(or)	**la mia mamma**	*my mom*
tuo papà / tuo babbo	*your dad*	(or)	**il tuo papà / il tuo babbo**	*your dad*
mio nonno	*my grandfather*	(or)	**il mio nonno**	*my grandfather*
mia nonna	*my grandmother*	(or)	**la mia nonna**	*my grandmother*

Be careful!

As in the case of articles and demonstratives, you must repeat the possessive before each noun.

mio zio e **mia sorella**	*my uncle and sister*
tuo fratello e **la tua amica**	*your brother and friend*

ESERCIZIO
8·3

A. *How do you say the following in Italian?*

1. Marco è...

a. *my cousin* _____

b. *her younger brother* _____

c. *your (fam., sing.) father* _____

d. *our Italian uncle* _____

e. *their friend* _____

2. Maria è...

   a. *my cousin* _____

   b. *his older sister* _____

   c. *your (fam., sing.) mother* _____

   d. *your (fam., pl.) aunt* _____

   e. *their friend* _____

3. Il signor Verdi e la signora Verdi sono...

   a. *my grandfather and grandmother* _____

   b. *his Italian uncle and aunt* _____

   c. *your (fam., sing.) father-in-law and mother-in-law* _____

   d. *your (fam., pl.) son-in-law and daughter-in-law* _____

   e. *their Italian brother-in-law and sister-in-law* _____

B. *Rewrite each phrase in the plural.*

1. mio cugino   _____

2. mia nonna   _____

3. tuo fratello   _____

4. tua sorella   _____

5. suo zio   _____

6. sua zia   _____

7. nostro genero   _____

8. nostra suocera   _____

9. vostro cognato   _____

10. vostra cognata   _____

11. il loro fratello   _____

12. la loro sorella   _____

Possessive pronouns

A possessive pronoun replaces a noun phrase containing a possessive adjective. The pronouns correspond to English *mine, yours, his, hers, ours,* and *theirs.* There is a perfect match between the adjective and pronoun forms of the possessive.

mio

Il mio amico è italiano.
My friend is Italian.
La mia amica è simpatica.
My friend is nice.
I miei professori sono italiani.
My professors are Italian.
Le mie professoresse sono italiane.
My professors (f.) are Italian.

Il mio è italiano.
Mine is Italian.
La mia è simpatica.
Mine is nice.
I miei sono italiani.
Mine are Italian.
Le mie sono italiane.
Mine are Italian.

tuo

Il tuo amico è italiano.
Your friend is Italian.
La tua amica è simpatica.
Your friend is nice.
I tuoi professori sono italiani.
Your professors are Italian.
Le tue professoresse sono italiane.
Your professors (f.) are Italian.

Il tuo è italiano.
Yours is Italian.
La tua è simpatica.
Yours is nice.
I tuoi sono italiani.
Yours are Italian.
Le tue sono italiane.
Yours are Italian.

suo

Il suo amico è italiano.
His/Her friend is Italian.
La sua amica è simpatica.
His/Her friend is nice.
I suoi professori sono italiani.
His/Her professors are Italian.
Le sue professoresse sono italiane.
His/Her professors (f.) are Italian.

Il suo è italiano.
His/Hers is Italian.
La sua è simpatica.
His/Hers is nice.
I suoi sono italiani.
His/Hers are Italian.
Le sue sono italiane.
His/Hers are Italian.

nostro

Il nostro amico è italiano.
Our friend is Italian.
La nostra amica è simpatica.
Our friend is nice.
I nostri professori sono italiani.
Our professors are Italian.
Le nostre professoresse sono italiane.
Our professors (f.) are Italian.

Il nostro è italiano.
Ours is Italian.
La nostra è simpatica.
Ours is nice.
I nostri sono italiani.
Ours are Italian.
Le nostre sono italiane.
Ours are Italian.

vostro

Il vostro amico è italiano.
Your friend is Italian.
La vostra amica è simpatica.
Your friend is nice.
I vostri professori sono italiani.
Your professors are Italian.
Le vostre professoresse sono italiane.
Your professors (f.) are Italian.

Il vostro è italiano.
Yours is Italian.
La vostra è simpatica.
Yours is nice.
I vostri sono italiani.
Yours are Italian.
Le vostre sono italiane.
Yours are Italian.

loro

Il loro amico è italiano.	**Il loro** è italiano.
Their friend is Italian.	*Theirs is Italian.*
La loro amica è simpatica.	**La loro** è simpatica.
Their friend is nice.	*Theirs is nice.*
I loro professori sono italiani.	**I loro** sono italiani.
Their professors are Italian.	*Theirs are Italian.*
Le loro professoresse sono italiane.	**Le loro** sono italiane.
Their professors (f.) are Italian.	*Theirs are Italian.*

The article is always used with the pronoun forms, even when the noun phrase replaced contains singular, unmodified, kinship nouns.

Sua sorella è simpatica.	*His/Her sister is pleasant.*
La sua è simpatica.	*His/Hers is pleasant.*
Nostro zio è giovane.	*Our uncle is young.*
Il nostro è giovane.	*Ours is young.*

The article can be dropped if the pronoun occurs as a predicate; that is, if it occurs after the verb **essere** (*to be*) or some other linking verb.

Questo cappotto **è mio.**	*This coat is mine.*
È tua questa camicia?	*Is this shirt yours?*
Quei libri **sono suoi.**	*Those books are his/hers.*

ESERCIZIO
8·4

A. *Answer each question affirmatively using the appropriate possessive pronoun.*

EXAMPLE   Giovanni è tuo fratello? (*Is John your brother?*)

            Sì, è il mio.

1. Maria è la tua amica?   _____

2. La signora Verdi è la loro nonna?   _____

3. Io sono il vostro amico?   _____

4. Tu sei sua zia?   _____

5. Lui è suo zio?   _____

6. Marco è il loro amico?   _____

7. Quegli uomini sono i tuoi cugini?   _____

8. Quelle donne sono le vostre cugine?   _____

B. *Answer each question as suggested by the italicized word in parentheses.*

EXAMPLE   Di chi è questo cappotto? (*Whose coat is it?*) (*mine*)

          È il mio.

1. Di chi è questa giacca? (*mine*) _____

2. Di chi è questo impermeabile? *(his)* _____

3. Di chi è quella macchina? (*hers*) _____

4. Di chi è quello zaino? (*ours*) _____

5. Di chi sono quei vestiti rossi? (*theirs*) _____

6. Di chi sono quelle sciarpe verdi? (*mine*) _____

7. Di chi sono questi bicchieri? (*his*) _____

8. Di chi sono quelle bibite? (*hers*) _____

C. *Provide the corresponding singular or plural form, as required.*

SINGULAR	PLURAL
1. il mio orologio	_____
2. _____	le nostre amiche
3. la mia camicia	_____
4. _____	i nostri libri
5. il tuo cane	_____
6. _____	le vostre amiche
7. la tua macchina	_____
8. _____	i vostri amici
9. il suo gatto	_____
10. _____	le sue amiche
11. il loro amico	_____
12. _____	le loro case

D. *Complete each sentence with the appropriate form of the indefinite or definite article, if needed. If the article is not needed, leave the space blank.*

1. Lui è _____ mio fratello. (*He is my brother.*)

2. Lei è _____ nostra sorella maggiore. (*She is our older sister.*)

3. Quel ragazzo è _____ loro figlio. (*That boy is their son.*)

4. Lei è _____ sua figlia più grande. (*She is his oldest daughter.*)

5. Signora Marchi, come si chiama _____ Sua figlia? (*Mrs. Marchi, what's*

   your daughter's name?)

6. Signora e signor Marchi, come si chiama _____ Loro figlio? (*Mrs. and Mr. Marchi, what's your son's name?*)

7. Lui è _____ mio amico, tra molti amici. (*He is one of my friends, among many friends.*)

8. Anche lei è _____ mia amica, tra molte amiche. (*She is also one of my friends, among many friends.*)

9. Questo libro è mio. Dov'è _____ tuo? (*This book is mine. Where is yours?*)

Grammar in culture

The omission of the article in kinship possessives is probably due to convention and frequency of usage. The article is used, in fact, with other people to whom you have a social or emotional attachment.

amico (*friend*)	il mio amico, il tuo amico...
amica (*friend*)	la mia amica, la tua amica...
fidanzato (*fiancé*)	il mio fidanzato, il tuo fidanzato...
fidanzata (*fiancée*)	la mia fidanzata, la tua fidanzata...
ragazzo (*boyfriend*)	il mio ragazzo, il tuo ragazzo...
ragazza (*girlfriend*)	la mia ragazza, la tua ragazza...
amante (*m./f.*) (*lover*)	il mio amante, la mia amante...

ESERCIZIO
8·5

How do you say the following in Italian?

1. She's my sister, not my lover!

_____

2. Here's my boyfriend and your brother.

_____

3. She's my girlfriend, not yet my fiancée.

_____

4. My sister is also my friend.

_____

Partitives

Partitives are forms used with nouns to indicate a part of something as distinct from its whole.

l'acqua	*water*	**dell'**acqua	*some water*
un esame	*an exam*	**degli** esami	*some exams*
un'amica	*a (female) friend*	**delle** amiche	*some friends*
lo zucchero	*sugar*	**dello** zucchero	*some sugar*

Partitives with count nouns

Before count nouns (nouns that have a plural form), the partitive functions grammatically as the plural of the indefinite article. The most commonly used type of partitive in this case consists of the preposition **di** + *the appropriate plural forms of the definite article.*

Contractions of di with the masculine plural forms of the definite article

di + i → dei	di + i libri → dei libri	*some books*
di + gli → degli	di + gli studenti → degli studenti	*some students*

Contractions of di with the feminine plural forms of the definite article

di + le → delle	di + le penne → delle penne	*some pens*

MASCULINE SINGULAR		MASCULINE PLURAL	
uno, un (*before a vowel*)		**degli**	
uno sbaglio	*a mistake*	**degli sbagli**	*some mistakes*
un albero	*a tree*	**degli alberi**	*some trees*
un		**dei**	
un bicchiere	*a glass*	**dei bicchieri**	*some glasses*
un coltello	*a knife*	**dei coltelli**	*some knives*

FEMININE SINGULAR		FEMININE PLURAL	
una		**delle**	
una forchetta	*a fork*	**delle forchette**	*some forks*
una sedia	*a chair*	**delle sedie**	*some chairs*
un'		**delle**	
un'automobile	*an automobile*	**delle automobili**	*some automobiles*
un'arancia	*an orange*	**delle arance**	*some oranges*

As always, be careful when an adjective precedes the noun. You must adjust the form of the partitive accordingly.

degli zii	*some uncles*	**dei simpatici zii**	*some nice uncles*
degli zaini	*some backpacks*	**dei nuovi zaini**	*some new backpacks*

Useful vocabulary

The following words, referring to items in the house, will come in handy. They are used in the Esercizio that follows.

il bagno	*bathroom*	**la cucina**	*kitchen*
il bicchiere	*drinking glass*	**la forchetta**	*fork*
la bottiglia	*bottle*	**il salotto**	*living room*
la camera	*bedroom*	**la sedia**	*chair*
il coltello	*knife*	**la stanza**	*room*
il cucchiaino	*teaspoon*	**la tavola**	*eating table*
il cucchiaio	*spoon*		

ESERCIZIO
9·1

A. *Provide the singular or plural form of each phrase, as required.*

SINGULAR	PLURAL PARTITIVE
1. un coltello	_____
2. _____	degli sbagli
3. una forchetta	_____
4. _____	dei salotti
5. uno zio	_____
6. _____	delle cucine
7. uno psicologo	_____
8. _____	dei bagni
9. una camera	_____
10. _____	delle bottiglie

11. una sedia   _____

12. _____   delle tavole

13. un bicchiere   _____

14. _____   dei cucchiai

15. un cucchiaino   _____

16. _____   delle forchette

17. un coltello   _____

18. _____   degli gnocchi

19. un'automobile   _____

20. _____   degli amici

B. *For each question provide an answer in the plural, using the indicated adjective.*

EXAMPLE   È un coltello? (nuovo)

         Sono dei coltelli nuovi. / Sono dei nuovi coltelli.

1. È un'automobile? (italiano) _____

2. È una sedia? (nuovo) _____

3. È uno psicologo? (bravo) _____

4. È un amico? (vecchio) _____

5. È un'amica? (vecchio) _____

6. È un bagno? (grande) _____

7. È una camera? (piccolo) _____

8. È un salotto? (bello) _____

9. È una cucina? (bello) _____

Alternative forms

In place of **di** + *definite article*, the pronouns **alcuni** (*m.*, *pl.*) and **alcune** (*f.*, *pl.*) can be used to correspond more precisely to the idea of *several*.

degli zii	*some uncles*	**alcuni zii**	*several (a few) uncles*
dei bicchieri	*some glasses*	**alcuni bicchieri**	*several (a few) glasses*
delle forchette	*some forks*	**alcune forchette**	*several (a few) forks*
delle amiche	*some friends*	**alcune amiche**	*several (a few) friends*

The invariable pronoun **qualche** can also be used to express the partitive with count nouns. But be careful with this one! It must be followed by a singular noun, even though the meaning is plural.

degli zii	*some uncles*	**qualche zio**	*some uncles*
dei bicchieri	*some glasses*	**qualche bicchiere**	*some glasses*
delle forchette	*some forks*	**qualche forchetta**	*some forks*
delle amiche	*some friends*	**qualche amica**	*some friends*

The pronoun forms (**qualche** or **alcuni/alcune**) are often used at the start of sentences, rather than the partitive forms with **di**. Once again, be careful with **qualche**. It requires a singular verb!

Alcuni studenti studiano il francese.	*Some students study French.*
Qualche studente studia il francese.	*Some students study French.*

ESERCIZIO
9·2

A. *Provide the equivalent partitive phrase with* **alcuni/alcune**.

1. dei coltelli   _____

2. delle sedie   _____

3. degli gnocchi   _____

4. delle automobili   _____

5. dei cucchiai   _____

6. degli amici   _____

B. *Now, provide the equivalent partitive phrase with* **qualche**.

1. dei cucchiaini   _____

2. delle tavole   _____

3. degli zaini   _____

4. delle automobili   _____

5. dei bicchieri   _____

6. degli sbagli   _____

C. *Complete each sentence with the appropriate form of the verb* **essere**, **è** *(is) or* **sono** *(are), as required.*

1. Alcuni amici nostri _____ italiani.

2. Qualche amico nostro _____ italiano.

3. Alcune ragazze _____ americane.

4. Qualche ragazza _____ americana.

Partitives with mass nouns

With mass nouns (nouns that do not, normally, have a plural form), the partitive is rendered by either **di** + *the singular forms of the definite article* or by the expression **un po' di** (*a bit of*).

Contractions of di with the masculine singular forms of the definite article

di + il → del	di + il pane → del pane	*some bread*
di + lo → dello	di + lo zucchero → dello zucchero	*some sugar*
di + l' → dell'	di + l'orzo → dell'orzo	*some barley*

Contractions of di with the feminine singular forms of the definite article

di + la → della	di + la carne → della carne	*some meat*
di + l' → dell'	di + l'acqua → dell'acqua	*some water*

PARTITIVE FORM		ALTERNATIVE FORM	
del pane	*some bread*	**un po' di pane**	*a little bread*
dell'orzo	*some barley*	**un po' d'orzo**	*a little barley*
dello zucchero	*some sugar*	**un po' di zucchero**	*a little sugar*
della pasta	*some pasta*	**un po' di pasta**	*a little pasta*
dell'acqua	*some water*	**un po' d'acqua**	*a little water*

Useful vocabulary

Mass nouns		**Count nouns**	
l'acqua	*water*	la carota	*carrot*
la carne	*meat*	il fagiolino	*string bean*
l'insalata	*salad*	il fagiolo	*bean*
la minestra	*soup*	la patata	*potato*
l'orzo	*barley*	il pomodoro	*tomato*
la pasta	*pasta*		
il pesce	*fish* (*as a food*)		
il riso	*rice*		
l'uva	*grapes*		
lo zucchero	*sugar*		

A. *Provide the corresponding partitive phrase.*

PARTITIVE	ALTERNATIVE FORM
1. dell'insalata	_____
2. _____	un po' d'uva
3. del pesce	_____
4. _____	un po' di carne
5. della minestra	_____
6. _____	un po' di riso
7. dello zucchero	_____
8. _____	un po' d'orzo
9. della pasta	_____
10. _____	un po' d'acqua

B. *Say that you want both the items indicated. Follow the example, using only partitive forms (not their alternatives).*

EXAMPLE   meat and potatoes

Voglio della carne e delle patate.

1. fish and beans _____
2. salad and carrots _____
3. pasta and string beans _____
4. meat and apples _____
5. coffee and sugar _____
6. grapes and potatoes _____

Partitives in the negative

In negative sentences, the partitive is omitted.

AFFIRMATIVE SENTENCE		NEGATIVE SENTENCE	
Ho dei biglietti.	*I have some tickets.*	**Non ho biglietti.**	*I don't have (any) tickets.*
Ho alcune riviste.	*I have some magazines.*	**Non ho riviste.**	*I don't have (any) magazines.*

The negative partitive can also be rendered by **non... nessuno**. Notice that **nessuno** is made up of **ness** + *indefinite article*. It renders the idea of *not . . . any*. This means that in Italian the noun is always in the singular, even though the meaning is plural.

Non ho nessun biglietto.	*I don't have any tickets.*
Non ho nessuna rivista.	*I don't have any magazines.*

This cannot be used with mass nouns.

AFFIRMATIVE SENTENCE		NEGATIVE SENTENCE	
Prendo dello zucchero.	*I'll take some sugar.*	**Non prendo zucchero.**	*I don't take sugar.*
Mangio un po' di pasta.	*I'll eat a little pasta.*	**Non mangio pasta.**	*I don't eat pasta.*

ESERCIZIO
9·4

A. *Rewrite each sentence in the negative, as required. Do not use **nessuno** in this exercise.*

1. Mario mangia delle patate.

   _____

2. Io voglio dei fagiolini.

   _____

3. Il ragazzo prende un po' di carne.

   _____

4. La ragazza vuole dello zucchero.

   _____

5. Anch'io voglio alcuni biglietti.

   _____

6. Maria prende qualche pomodoro. (*Be careful!*)

   _____

B. *Now, rewrite each phrase in the negative with **nessuno**.*

1. delle carote   _____

2. dei fagiolini   _____

3. dei cucchiai   _____

4. delle patate   _____

5. degli zaini   _____

6. delle arance   _____

Adjectives indicating quantity

In addition to descriptive, demonstrative, ordinal, and possessive adjectives there are certain words that have various adjectival functions. Some grammar texts classify them as adjectives (as we do here), others as different types of structures. Here are the most common. Most of these indicate quantity of some sort. Notice also that these come before the noun they modify.

abbastanza	*enough*
assai	*quite a lot, enough*
certo	*certain*
molto	*much, a lot*
ogni	*each, every*
parecchio	*several, quite a few, a lot*
poco	*little, few*
qualsiasi	*whichever, any*
qualunque	*whichever, any*
stesso	*the same*
tanto	*much, a lot*
troppo	*too much*
tutto	*all*
ultimo	*last*

The adjectives **abbastanza**, **assai**, **ogni**, **qualsiasi**, and **qualunque** are invariable (that is, they do not change).

Non ho **abbastanza soldi**.	*I do not have enough money.*
Lui mangia **assai carne**.	*He eats quite a lot of meat.*
Ogni mattina legge il giornale.	*Every morning he reads the newspaper.*
Possiamo andare a **qualsiasi ristorante**.	*We can go to any restaurant.*

The others are treated like any regular adjective.

Conosco un **certo signore** che si chiama Roberto.	*I know a certain gentleman named Robert.*
Lui mangia **molti (tanti) dolci**.	*He eats a lot of sweets.*
Ci sono **poche studentesse** in questa classe.	*There are few female students in this class.*
Parecchi turisti visitano Venezia.	*A lot of tourists visit Venice.*
Abbiamo mangiato **troppa carne**.	*We ate too much meat.*
Questa è **l'ultima volta** che ti chiamo.	*This is the last time I'm going to call you.*

Notice that **tutto** is separated from the noun by the definite article.

Lei ha mangiato **tutto il formaggio**.	*She ate all the cheese.*
Giovanni ha mangiato **tutta la minestra**.	*John ate all the soup.*

A. *Provide the missing adjective ending for each phrase.*

1. l'ultim_____ donna

2. poc_____ studenti

3. tutt_____ la minestra

4. parecch_____ bambini

5. una cert_____ signora

6. qualsias_____ città

7. qualunqu_____ ristorante

8. abbastanz_____ soldi

9. assa_____ studenti

10. ogn_____ settimana

B. *Write a sentence to indicate that you need much, many, little, etc., of the item or items indicated.*

EXAMPLE   dei fagioli / molto

         Ho bisogno di (I need) *molti fagioli.*

1. delle patate / poco   _____

2. dei fagioli / tutto   _____

3. delle carote / tanto   _____

4. alcuni fagiolini / molto   _____

5. qualche mela / poco   _____

6. un po' di minestra / tutto   _____

7. della pasta / tanto   _____

8. dei cucchiai / molto   _____

C. *Provide the equivalent partitive noun phrases for each item. The first item is done completely for you.*

1. ___*dei bambini*___   alcuni bambini   ___*qualche bambino*___

2. delle patate   _____   _____

3. _____   _____   qualche fagiolo

4. _____   alcune mele   _____

5. degli zaini   _____   _____

6. _____   _____   qualche forchetta

D. *Choose the correct response to complete each sentence.*

1. Non ho _____.

   a. degli amici   b. amici

2. Non ho mangiato _____.

   a. delle patate   b. nessuna patata

3. Prendo _____ zucchero.

   a. qualche   b. un po' di

4. Non prendo _____.

   a. nessun pane   b. pane

5. Voglio _____.

   a. dell'acqua   b. qualche acqua

6. Ecco _____ buono zucchero.

   a. del   b. dello

Grammar in culture

Classifying a noun as count or mass is a matter of cultural convention, even though there is a great deal of correspondence between lists of English and Italian nouns in this respect. This correspondence deviates for the following important Italian nouns.

◆ **Informazione** (*information*) is a count noun when it refers to a piece of information or similar item; as a general concept, **informazione** is a mass noun.

◆ **Comunicazione** (*communication*) is a count noun when it refers to correspondence or a message of some sort; as a general concept, **comunicazione** is a mass noun.

AS A COUNT NOUN	AS A MASS NOUN
Ho ricevuto poche informazioni da lui. *I received little information from him.*	L'informazione oggi controlla tutto. *Information controls everything today.*
Tutte le sue comunicazioni sono brevi. *All his messages are brief.*	La comunicazione scritta è importante. *Written communication is important.*

◆ **Uva** (*grapes*) is a mass noun. **Chicco** is used to refer to a single grape.

Quest'uva è molto buona.   Questo chicco d'uva è marcio.
These grapes are very good.   *This grape is rotten.*

How do you say the following in Italian?

1. I love grapes.

   _____

2. She sent me a few messages yesterday.

   _____

3. This grape is blue!

   _____

4. He always sends me little information.

   _____

Present tenses

Verbs are words that convey the action performed by the subject of a sentence. For this reason, they agree with the subject's person (first, second, or third) and number (singular or plural). Verbs are also marked for tense (present, past, future, etc.) to indicate the time an action occurred—now (present tense), before (past tense), or after (future tense); and they are marked for mood (indicative, imperative, conditional, etc.).

io mangio	*I eat*	**tu mangi**	*you eat*
io ho mangiato	*I ate*	**tu hai mangiato**	*you ate*
io mangerò	*I will eat*	**tu mangerai**	*you will eat*

The infinitive is the verb form that you will find in a dictionary. It is the "default" form of the verb. Italian verbs are divided into three main conjugations according to their infinitive endings. Verbs of the first conjugation end in **-are**, those of the second in **-ere**, and those of the third in **-ire**.

FIRST CONJUGATION		SECOND CONJUGATION		THIRD CONJUGATION	
parlare	*to speak*	**vendere**	*to sell*	**dormire**	*to sleep*
arrivare	*to arrive*	**cadere**	*to fall*	**finire**	*to finish*

The present indicative of regular verbs

The indicative mood is used to express or indicate facts. It is the most commonly used mood in everyday conversation. The **present indicative**, as its name implies, is used to express or indicate facts in the present or related to the present in some way.

To conjugate regular verbs in the present indicative, drop the infinitive ending, and add the appropriate ending according to person and number shown below.

First conjugation

parlare *to speak, talk* → **parl-**

io	par**lo**	*I speak, am speaking, do speak*
tu	par**li**	*you (fam., sing.) speak, are speaking, do speak*
Lei	par**la**	*you (pol., sing.) speak, are speaking, do speak*
lui/lei	par**la**	*he/she speaks, is speaking, does speak*
noi	par**liamo**	*we speak, are speaking, do speak*
voi	par**late**	*you (fam., pl.) speak, are speaking, do speak*
Loro	par**lano**	*you (pol., pl.) speak, are speaking, do speak*
loro	par**lano**	*they speak, are speaking, do speak*

Second conjugation

vendere *to sell* → **vend-**

io	vend**o**	*I sell, am selling, do sell*
tu	vend**i**	*you (fam., sing.) sell, are selling, do sell*
Lei	vend**e**	*you (pol., sing.) sell, are selling, do sell*
lui/lei	vend**e**	*he/she sells, is selling, does sell*
noi	vend**iamo**	*we sell, are selling, do sell*
voi	vend**ete**	*you (fam., pl.) sell, are selling, do sell*
Loro	vend**ono**	*you (pol., pl.) sell, are selling, do sell*
loro	vend**ono**	*they sell, are selling, do sell*

Third conjugation (type 1)

dormire *to sleep* → **dorm-**

io	dorm**o**	*I sleep, am sleeping, do sleep*
tu	dorm**i**	*you (fam., sing.) sleep, are sleeping, do sleep*
Lei	dorm**e**	*you (pol., sing.) sleep, are sleeping, do sleep*
lui/lei	dorm**e**	*he/she sleeps, is sleeping, does sleep*
noi	dorm**iamo**	*we sleep, are sleeping, do sleep*
voi	dorm**ite**	*you (fam., pl.) sleep, are sleeping, do sleep*
Loro	dorm**ono**	*you (pol., pl.) sleep, are sleeping, do sleep*
loro	dorm**ono**	*they sleep, are sleeping, do sleep*

Third conjugation (type 2)

finire *to finish* → **fin-**

io	fin**isco**	*I finish, am finishing, do finish*
tu	fin**isci**	*you (fam., sing.) finish, are finishing, do finish*
Lei	fin**isce**	*you (pol., sing.) finish, are finishing, do finish*
lui/lei	fin**isce**	*he/she finishes, is finishing, does finish*
noi	fin**iamo**	*we finish, are finishing, do finish*
voi	fin**ite**	*you (fam., pl.) finish, are finishing, do finish*
Loro	fin**iscono**	*you (pol., pl.) finish, are finishing, do finish*
loro	fin**iscono**	*they finish, are finishing, do finish*

Note that there are two sets of endings for third-conjugation verbs, and this fact is a constant source of blunders for learners. Essentially, you will have to learn to which category (type 1 or 2) a third-conjugation verb belongs. This information is contained in a good dictionary.

Type 1 verbs		**Type 2 verbs**	
aprire	*to open*	**capire**	*to understand*
dormire	*to sleep*	**finire**	*to finish*
partire	*to leave*	**preferire**	*to prefer*

The subject pronouns are optional. The reason for this is obvious: the endings generally make it clear which person is the subject of the verb.

Second-person forms are used for familiar (informal) address; third-person forms are used instead for polite (formal) address. The pronouns for the latter are normally capitalized in writing (**Lei**, **Loro**) to keep them distinct from the pronouns standing for *she* (**lei**) and *they* (**loro**).

Familiar

| Maria, (**tu**) cosa preferisci? | *Mary, what do you prefer?* |
| Marco e Maria, capite (**voi**)? | *Mark and Mary, do you understand?* |

Polite

Professore, (**Lei**) cosa preferisce? *Professor, what do you prefer?*
Signor Marchi e Signora Verdi, *Mr. Marchi and Mrs. Verdi, do you understand?*
    capiscono (**Loro**)?

The English subject pronouns *it* and *they* are not normally expressed in Italian.

Apre a mezzogiorno. *It opens at noon.*
Chiudono alle sei. *They close at six.*

Verbs that undergo spelling changes

If a verb ends in -**care** or -**gare**, the hard sound is preserved by inserting an **h** before the endings -**i** and -**iamo**.

cercare *to look for* → **cerc-**

io	cerco	*I look for, am looking for, do look for*
tu	cer**chi**	*you (fam., sing.) look for, are looking for, do look for*
Lei	cerca	*you (pol., sing.) look for, are looking for, do look for*
lui/lei	cerca	*he/she looks for, is looking for, does look for*
noi	cer**chiamo**	*we look for, are looking for, do look for*
voi	cercate	*you (fam., pl.) look for, are looking for, do look for*
Loro	cercano	*you (pol., pl.) look for, are looking for, do look for*
loro	cercano	*they look for, are looking for, do look for*

pagare *to pay* → **pag-**

io	pago	*I pay, am paying, do pay*
tu	pag**hi**	*you (fam., sing.) pay, are paying, do pay*
Lei	paga	*you (pol., sing.) pay, are paying, do pay*
lui/lei	paga	*he/she pays, is paying, does pay*
noi	pag**hiamo**	*we pay, are paying, do pay*
voi	pagate	*you (fam., pl.) pay, are paying, do pay*
Loro	pagano	*you (pol., pl.) pay, are paying, do pay*
loro	pagano	*they pay, are paying, do pay*

If a verb ends in -**ciare** or -**giare**, the -**i** of these endings is dropped before adding the conjugated endings -**i** and -**iamo**.

cominciare *to start, begin* → **cominci-**

io	comincio	*I start, am starting, do start*
tu	cominc**i**	*you (fam., sing.) start, are starting, do start*
Lei	comincia	*you (pol., sing.) start, are starting, do start*
lui/lei	comincia	*he/she starts, is starting, does start*
noi	cominc**iamo**	*we start, are starting, do start*
voi	cominciate	*you (fam., pl.) start, are starting, do start*
Loro	cominciano	*you (pol., pl.) start, are starting, do start*
loro	cominciano	*they start, are starting, do start*

mangiare *to eat* → **mangi-**

io	mangio	*I eat, am eating, do eat*
tu	mang**i**	*you (fam., sing.) eat, are eating, do eat*
Lei	mangia	*you (pol., sing.) eat, are eating, do eat*
lui/lei	mangia	*he/she eats, is eating, does eat*
noi	mang**iamo**	*we eat, are eating, do eat*
voi	mangiate	*you (fam., pl.) eat, are eating, do eat*
Loro	mangiano	*you (pol., pl.) eat, are eating, do eat*
loro	mangiano	*they eat, are eating, do eat*

Uses

The present indicative is used mainly to state facts in the present, to indicate an ongoing action, to refer to a continuous or habitual action, or to indicate an immediate future action.

Facts in the present

Studio l'italiano.	*I study Italian.*
Finisco di lavorare alle sei.	*I finish working at six.*

Ongoing actions

In questo momento **mangio** una pizza.	*At this moment I am eating a pizza.*
Loro **guardano** la TV.	*They are watching TV.*

Continuous or habitual actions

Il lunedì **mangio** sempre la pizza.	*On Mondays I always eat pizza.*
Ogni giorno **studio** l'italiano.	*Every day I study Italian.*

Immediate future actions

Domani **mangio** gli spaghetti.	*Tomorrow I am going to eat spaghetti.*
Loro **arrivano** la settimana prossima.	*They are arriving next week.*

As you will see in Unit 17, the present indicative can also be used with the preposition **da**, meaning both *since* and *for*, to correspond to English progressive tenses such as those below.

Aspetto da lunedì.	*I have been waiting since Monday.*
Aspetto da due giorni.	*I have been waiting for two days.*
Lui **dorme** da ieri.	*He has been sleeping since yesterday.*
Lui **dorme** da 48 ore.	*He has been sleeping for 48 hours.*

ESERCIZIO
10·1

A. *Provide the complete present indicative conjugation for each verb.*

1. First-conjugation verbs

   a. arrivare _____

   _____

   b. cercare _____

   _____

   c. cominciare _____

   _____

   d. mangiare _____

   _____

   e. pagare _____

   _____

2. Second-conjugation verbs

   a. chiedere _____

   _____

   b. rispondere _____

   _____

   c. vendere _____

   _____

   d. leggere _____

   _____

   e. chiudere _____

3. Third-conjugation verbs type 1

   a. aprire _____

   _____

   b. dormire _____

   _____

   c. partire _____

   _____

4. Third-conjugation verbs type 2

   a. capire _____

   _____

   b. finire _____

   _____

   c. preferire _____

   _____

B. *Rewrite each sentence by changing the verb to indicate that the subject in parentheses also does the same thing. Be careful! If the sentence is affirmative, the appropriate form to use is* **anche**; *if it is negative, the form is* **neanche** *(or* **nemmeno** *or* **neppure***).*

EXAMPLE 1   Giovanni mangia la pizza. (io)

           Anch'io mangio la pizza.

EXAMPLE 2   I miei amici non giocano a tennis. (noi)

           Neanche (Nemmeno/Neppure) noi giochiamo a tennis.

1. Marco non capisce la lezione. (io)

_____

2. Loro partono domani. (noi)

_____

3. La ragazza gioca a calcio da molti anni. (tu)

_____

4. I miei cugini non aspettano mai. (voi)

_____

5. Io telefono spesso a mia sorella. (Luigi)

_____

6. Tu giochi sempre a tennis. (le mie amiche)

_____

C. *Rewrite each question by changing the verb to direct the question to the subject in parentheses. Remember to use the polite form when appropriate.*

EXAMPLE Maria, mangi la pizza stasera? (Signora Marchi)
Signora Marchi, mangia la pizza stasera?

1. Alessandro, capisci la lezione? (Signor Verdi)

_____

2. Signora Rossini, cerca qualcosa? (Sara)

_____

3. Marco e Maria, partite domani? (Signori [*Gentlemen*])

_____

4. Signore (*Ladies*), cominciano a studiare la matematica? (Ragazze)

_____

Irregular verbs in the present indicative

Irregular verbs—that is, verbs that are not conjugated according to the pattern indicated above—are always problematic, since they have to be learned by memory. It is not possible to cover all the irregular verbs here. Below are the most commonly used and their present indicative conjugations.

andare (*to go*)	vado	vai	va	andiamo	andate	vanno
avere (*to have*)	ho	hai	ha	abbiamo	avete	hanno
bere (*to drink*)	bevo	bevi	beve	beviamo	bevete	bevono
dare (*to give*)	do	dai	dà	diamo	date	danno
dire (*to say, tell*)	dico	dici	dice	diciamo	dite	dicono

dovere (*to have to*)	**devo**	**devi**	**deve**	**dobbiamo**	**dovete**	**devono**
essere (*to be*)	**sono**	**sei**	**è**	**siamo**	**siete**	**sono**
fare (*to do, make*)	**faccio**	**fai**	**fa**	**facciamo**	**fate**	**fanno**
potere (*to be able to*)	**posso**	**puoi**	**può**	**possiamo**	**potete**	**possono**
sapere (*to know*)	**so**	**sai**	**sa**	**sappiamo**	**sapete**	**sanno**
stare (*to stay*)	**sto**	**stai**	**sta**	**stiamo**	**state**	**stanno**
tenere (*to hold, keep*)	**tengo**	**tieni**	**tiene**	**teniamo**	**tenete**	**tengono**
uscire (*to go out*)	**esco**	**esci**	**esce**	**usciamo**	**uscite**	**escono**
venire (*to come*)	**vengo**	**vieni**	**viene**	**veniamo**	**venite**	**vengono**
volere (*to want*)	**voglio**	**vuoi**	**vuole**	**vogliamo**	**volete**	**vogliono**

Special uses of avere, fare, and stare

avere caldo	*to be (feel) hot*	**stare bene**	*to be (feel) well*
avere freddo	*to be (feel) cold*	**stare male**	*to be (feel) bad*
fare bel tempo	*to be good weather*	**stare così così**	*to be so-so*
fare brutto tempo	*to be bad weather*		
fare cattivo tempo	*to be awful weather*		

ESERCIZIO
10·2

A. *Provide the appropriate present indicative forms for each verb.*

	IO	TU	LUI/LEI	NOI	VOI	LORO
1. volere						
2. venire						
3. uscire						
4. tenere						
5. stare						
6. sapere						
7. potere						
8. fare						
9. essere						
10. dovere						
11. dire						
12. dare						
13. bere						
14. avere						
15. andare						

B. *Complete the following dialogue between Maria and Marco with the missing forms of the verbs* **avere,** **fare,** *and* **stare.** *Note that* **ciao** *means both* hi *and* bye *in informal speech.*

1. Marco: Ciao, Maria, come _____?

2. Maria: Ciao, Marco, io _____ molto bene. E tu?

3. Marco: Io _____ così così. Anzi, _____ male.

4. Maria: Perché?

5. Marco: _____ male quando _____ cattivo o brutto tempo.

   _____ freddo!

6. Maria: Domani, per fortuna, dovrebbe (*it should*) _____ bel tempo.

7. Marco: Meno male! (*Thank heavens!*) E allora spero di (*I hope to*) _____ caldo!

C. *Rewrite each question by changing the form of the verb to direct the question to the subject in parentheses. Remember to use the polite form when appropriate.*

1. Marco, dove vai? (Signor Rossi)

   _____

2. Signora, come sta? (Maria)

   _____

3. Alessandro, cosa vuoi? (Signorina Verdi)

   _____

4. Signor Rossini, quando viene alla festa? (Giovanni)

   _____

5. Marco e Maria, quando uscite stasera? (Signor Verdi e Signora Verdi)

   _____

VERB TENSES

Introduction to Part III

In this part, you will be working with verbs. You were introduced to the indicative in Part II. So, before delving into the following chapters, review Chapter II-10. Learning how to conjugate verbs correctly is a difficult task in every language but more so in Italian because of the many tenses and irregular verbs. Correctly conjugating a verb is a very important part of speaking and writing well, but one must also understand the need to use one verb over another and the reason for choosing each verb. It can be difficult; however, with time, dedication, practice, and consistency, one can achieve excellent results.

Each chapter is complete with explanations and exercises that reinforce the learning of each tense. By following the lessons and completing the exercises, students will progress in their knowledge and understanding of Italian.

More on the present tense (*presente indicativo*) ·III-1·

The progressive tense (*gerundio*)

In Italian often the present and the imperfect tenses are used to express continuing actions, while in English the progressive tense is generally used.

Mangiano.	*They are eating.*
Leggo una lettera importante.	*I am reading an important letter.*
Parlavamo.	*We were speaking.*

In Italian the progressive tense is used to emphasize that the action coincides with the speaking. The progressive tense, also called the present continuous or gerund tense, is formed by the present or the imperfect tense of **stare** + the gerund. The gerund is formed from the infinitive of the verb, by omitting the ending and adding -**ando** or -**endo** to the root.

> **andare** (*to go*), and**ando** (*going*)

The progressive tense is used to express an action that is going on at the same time as the person who is speaking or doing the action.

The endings of the progressive tense are:

INFINITIVE	GERUND	INFINITIVE-GERUND
-are	-**ando**	parlare, parl**ando**
-ere	-**endo**	vedere, ved**endo**
-ire	-**endo**	sentire, sent**endo**

sto andando	*I am going*
stai vedendo	*you are seeing*
sta sentendo	*he/she is hearing*
stavo parlando	*I was speaking*

Some verbs form the gerund from the first-person singular of the present tense.

> **bevo** (*I drink*), **bevendo** (*drinking*)
> **faccio** (*I do, make*), **facendo** (*making*)
> **dico** (*I say*), **dicendo** (*saying*)

stare + gerundio

PRESENT PROGRESSIVE (*Gerundio Presente*)

io	sto	andando	*I am going*
tu	stai	scrivendo	*you are writing*
lui, lei	sta	sentendo	*he/she is listening*
noi	stiamo	capendo	*we are understanding*
voi	state	cantando	*you are singing*
loro	stanno	leggendo	*they are reading*

PAST PROGRESSIVE (*Gerundio Passato*)

io	stavo	andando	*I was going*
tu	stavi	scrivendo	*you were writing*
lui, lei	stava	sentendo	*he/she was hearing*
noi	stavamo	capendo	*we were understanding*
voi	stavate	cantando	*you were singing*
loro	stavano	leggendo	*they were reading*

Present:	Io **telefono** a mia sorella tutte le settimane.	I *call* my sister every week.
Progressive:	Io **sto telefonando** a mia sorella (adesso).	I *am calling* my sister (just now).
Present:	Voi **partite** alle sei.	You *leave* at six.
Progressive:	Voi **state partendo** (adesso).	You *are leaving* (just now).

ESERCIZIO 1·1

Complete the sentences using the gerund form of the verbs in parentheses.

1. Il fornaio _____ (preparare) il pane.

2. La mamma _____ (leggere) il libro.

3. Il vigile _____ (fare) la multa.

4. Il fioraio _____ (vendere) i fiori.

5. Il ragazzo _____ (fare) la doccia.

6. Mio padre _____ (andare) a letto.

7. I miei genitori _____ (arrivare) con i miei cugini.

8. Il treno _____ (partire) in ritardo.

9. Oggi _____ (piovere) forte.

10. Io _____ (mangiare) il gelato con i miei amici.

11. Tu _____ (salire) sull'aereo.

12. Lui _____ (bere) una birra fredda.

13. Noi _____ (finire) la lettera.

14. La gente _____ (camminare) per la strada.

15. Voi _____ (ascoltare) la musica.

ESERCIZIO

1·2

A. *Complete the sentences using the gerund of the verbs in parentheses.*

1. Io _____ (andare) al cinema con i miei amici.

2. Tu e tua sorella _____ (cucinare) per tutti gli amici.

3. Il mio amico _____ (arrivare) da Parigi con la sua famiglia.

4. Noi _____ (portare) le valige in macchina.

5. Voi _____ (finire) i compiti.

6. Loro _____ (fare) molto rumore.

7. Io _____ (mangiare) troppo.

8. Lei _____ (parlare) con le sue amiche.

9. I nostri cugini _____ (ritornare) dal loro viaggio.

B. *Change the sentences below from the present to the gerund.*

1. Io parto per Firenze.   Io _____ .

2. Tu dormi in albergo.   Tu _____ .

3. Lui scrive la lettera.   Lui _____ .

4. Lei finisce di mangiare.   Lei _____ .

5. Noi scriviamo un libro.   Noi _____ .

6. Voi parlate al telefono.   Voi _____ .

7. Loro ascoltano la musica.   Loro _____ .

8. Io non mangio la carne.   Io _____ .

9. Tu non arrivi con il treno.   Tu _____ .

Essere (to be) and avere (to have)

Essere and **avere** are the two most common Italian verbs. They are both irregular in all their forms.

Essere (to be)

io	**sono**	*I am*
tu	**sei**	*you are*
lui, lei	**è**	*he/she is*
noi	**siamo**	*we are*
voi	**siete**	*you are*
loro	**sono**	*they are*

The **io** and **loro** forms have the same spelling: **sono**. This is seldom confusing since the correct meaning is obvious from the context.

Essere is used to express:

Relationships:	Loro sono i miei genitori.	*They are my parents.*
	Lei è mia nipote.	*She is my niece.*
	Lei è mia moglie.	*She is my wife.*
Physical characteristics:	Lui è un uomo alto.	*He is a tall man.*
	Paola è bruna.	*Paola is a brunette.*
Personal traits:	Lui è un uomo intelligente.	*He is an intelligent man.*
	Voi siete gentili.	*You are kind.*
Date and time:	Oggi è il 25 dicembre.	*Today is the 25th of December.*
	Domani è domenica.	*Tomorrow is Sunday.*
	Che ora sono?	*What time is it?*
Profession:	Loro sono studenti.	*They are students.*
	Lui è un professore.	*He is a professor.*
Nationality:	Io sono americano.	*I am American.*
	Lei è italiana.	*She is Italian.*
Mood:	Maria è felice.	*Mary is happy.*
	Tu sei di cattivo umore.	*You are in a bad mood.*
Physical status:	Noi siamo stanchi.	*We are tired.*
	Voi siete giovani.	*You are young.*
Unusual conditions:	Il cielo è nuvoloso.	*The sky is cloudy.*
	Il suo vestito è sporco.	*Her dress is dirty.*
Colors to describe things:	L'erba è verde.	*The grass is green.*
	Il sangue è rosso.	*The blood is red.*
Location:	Io sono a letto.	*I am in bed.*
	Tu non sei a casa.	*You are not at home.*

*Complete the sentences with the correct form of **essere**. Then translate the sentences into English.*

1. Noi _____ da Maria.

_____

2. Loro _____ felici perchè possono viaggiare.

_____

3. Io _____ ansioso perchè non capisco bene.

_____

4. Ci _____ molte persone in casa.

_____

5. Dove _____ tu?

_____

6. Le pere _____ verdi.

_____

7. Il gatto _____ ammalato.

_____

8. La donna _____ alta.

_____

9. Tu _____ molto bella.

_____

Change the following sentences into the interrogative and then into the negative.

1. Io sono a scuola. _____

2. Tu sei al cinema. _____

_____

3. Lui è con i suoi amici. _____

_____

4. Lei è molto bella. _____

_____

5. Noi siamo ricchi. _____

_____

6. Voi siete a casa. _____

_____

7. Loro sono ammalati. _____

_____

Avere (to have)

io	**ho**	*I have*
tu	**hai**	*you have*
lui, lei	**ha**	*he/she has*
noi	**abbiamo**	*we have*
voi	**avete**	*you have*
loro	**hanno**	*they have*

The **h-** in **ho**, **hai**, **ha**, and **hanno** is never pronounced. It is used to distinguish between the verb form and other words with the same pronunciation but different meanings. For example: **ho** (*I have*) and **o** (*or*), and **ha** (*he/she has*) or **a** (*at, to*).

Avere is often used in Italian, where **essere** would be used in English. In English *to be* is used when telling or asking one's age, but in Italian *to have* is used. In Italian people say "How many years do you/does he or she have?" instead of "How old are you/is he or she?"

Quanti anni **hai**?	*How old **are** you?*
Quanti anni **ha** Giovanni?	*How old **is** Giovanni?*
La ragazza **ha** venti anni.	*The girl **is** twenty years old.*

ESERCIZIO
1·5

Translate the following into Italian using complete sentences.

1. How old are you? _____

2. I am twenty years old. _____

3. You are twelve years old. _____

4. How old is she? _____

5. Lidia is thirty years old. _____

6. My cat is seven years old. _____

7. Her brother is fifteen years old. _____

8. How old are the boys? _____

9. They are nine years old. _____

Other instances when **avere** is used in Italian and **essere** is used in English are:

Io	**ho fame.**	*I am hungry.*
Tu	**hai sete.**	*You are thirsty.*
Lui	**ha sonno.**	*He is sleepy.*
Lei	**ha fretta.**	*She is in a hurry.*
Noi	**abbiamo caldo.**	*We are warm.*
Voi	**avete paura.**	*You are afraid.*
Loro	**hanno molta fortuna.**	*They are very lucky.*

ESERCIZIO
1·6

Translate the following sentences into Italian.

1. I am hungry. _____

2. You are hungry. _____

3. He is sleepy. _____

4. She is afraid. _____

5. We are cold. _____

6. You are in a hurry. _____

7. They are lucky. _____

8. I am very hungry. _____

9. You are very thirsty. _____

10. He is very sleepy. _____

11. She is not afraid. _____

12. We are not cold. _____

13. Are you in a hurry? _____

14. They are not lucky. _____

Fare (to do, to make)

The verb **fare** (*to do, to make*) is an irregular verb, but it is used a lot. The **io** and **noi** forms follow the Latin infinitive "facere." The third-person plural **fanno** doubles the -n- as it does in verbs like **dare** (**danno**), **stare** (**stanno**), and **sapere** (**sanno**).

The following is the complete conjugation of the present tense of fare:

io	**faccio**	*I make, do*
tu	**fai**	*you make, do*
lui, lei	**fa**	*he/she makes, does*
noi	**facciamo**	*we make, do*
voi	**fate**	*you make, do*
loro	**fanno**	*they make, do*

In the right context, to state someone's profession, the verb **fare** followed by the definite article and the profession is used.

Faccio il dottore.   *I am* a doctor.
Faccio l'idraulico.   *I am* a plumber.

ESERCIZIO 1·7

Fill in the spaces with the correct form of **fare**.

1. Che cosa (tu) _____ oggi?

2. Io _____ il dottore.

3. Tu _____ il bagnino.

4. Lui non _____ niente.

5. I ragazzi _____ molti progetti per l'avvenire.

6. Lei _____ la cuoca.

7. Voi _____ la villeggiatura al mare.

8. Loro _____ gli esercizi.

9. Noi non _____ il pranzo per tutti.

When asked what he/she does, a student could reply:

Io studio. Or just, **Studio.**   *I study.*

To state what kind of school he/she attends, the student would reply:

Faccio il liceo.   *I attend* high school.
Faccio l'università.   *I go* to college.

To indicate a major in college, one would say:

Faccio italiano.   *I am majoring* in Italian.
Fai scienze politiche.   *You are majoring* in political science.

ESERCIZIO 1·8

Complete the following sentences with the correct form of **fare**.

1. Che scuola fai quest'anno? (io) _____ il liceo.

2. Che anno fa tuo cugino? (lui) _____ il terzo anno di università.

3. Lei _____ l'università a Pisa.

4. Lui _____ medicina.

5. Noi _____ l'ultimo anno di scuola tecnica.

6. Voi non _____ l'università.

7. Loro non _____ italiano.

8. Vuoi _____ l'università?

9. Vogliamo _____ informatica.

Sapere and conoscere (to know)

Both **sapere** and **conoscere** mean to *know*, but they are used differently. First, we will look at **sapere**—its meaning and uses.

Sapere

Sapere means *to know something, facts, information*. If followed by an infinitive, it means *to know how*. It is an irregular verb.

The following is the complete conjugation of the present tense of **sapere**:

io	**so**	*I know*
tu	**sai**	*you know*
lui, lei	**sa**	*he/she knows*
noi	**sappiamo**	*we know*
voi	**sapete**	*you (pl.) know*
loro	**sanno**	*they know*

Sai che cosa desidero?	***Do you know*** *what I would like?*
No, non lo **so**.	*No, I don't **know** it.*
So il tuo numero di telefono.	*I **know** your telephone number.*
Mio marito **sa** giocare a tennis.	*My husband **knows how** to play tennis.*

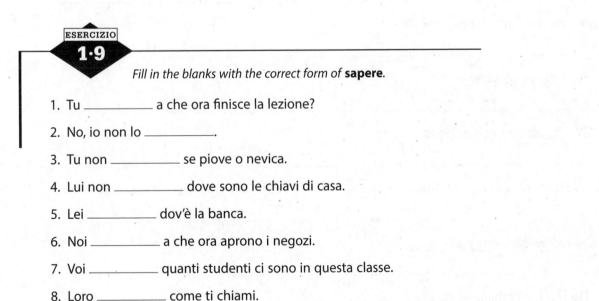

ESERCIZIO
1·9

*Fill in the blanks with the correct form of **sapere**.*

1. Tu _____ a che ora finisce la lezione?

2. No, io non lo _____.

3. Tu non _____ se piove o nevica.

4. Lui non _____ dove sono le chiavi di casa.

5. Lei _____ dov'è la banca.

6. Noi _____ a che ora aprono i negozi.

7. Voi _____ quanti studenti ci sono in questa classe.

8. Loro _____ come ti chiami.

Conoscere

Conoscere (*to know*) states familiarity or acquaintance with places, things, and people. It is always followed by a direct object. It also means *to make the acquaintance* or *to meet*.

Conoscere + a location (*to know a place*), + a person (*to know someone*): Whether you know a place or a person very well or very little, **conoscere** has to be used. If you know a place well, you will add **molto bene** to your sentence. If you do not know it well, you will add **poco** or **non molto bene**.

Io **conosco** bene quella ragazza.	*I know that girl very well.*
Io **non conosco** molto bene Firenze.	*I don't know Florence well.*
Vorrei conoscere quella ragazza.	*I would like to meet that girl.*

The following is the complete conjugation of the present tense of **conoscere**:

io	**conosco**	*I know*
tu	**conosci**	*you know*
lui, lei	**conosce**	*he/she knows*
noi	**conosciamo**	*we know*
voi	**conoscete**	*you (pl.) know*
loro	**conoscono**	*they know*

ESERCIZIO
1·10

Translate the following sentences into Italian.

1. I know Maria.

_____

2. I know a good tennis coach.

_____

3. My brother knows many people.

_____

4. She knows my sister.

_____

5. We do not know your friend.

_____

6. You (pl.) know Mary and Albert.

_____

7. You know him very well.

_____

8. Do you know them well?

_____

9. I know New York.

_____

10. I don't know Chicago.

_____

11. You know Africa well.

_____

12. Does she know Africa?

_____

13. We know our city.

_____

14. You (pl.) know this restaurant well.

_____

15. They know his story.

_____

16. They don't know his story.

_____

The imperative
(*imperativo*)

The imperative is used to give advice, warnings, orders, and exhortations. It does not have the **io** (*I*) form. In Italian there are two different types of imperative: familiar and formal.

First, let's take a look at the familiar imperative. The forms of the familiar imperative of regular verbs are the same as the ones of the present indicative, except in the **tu** form of the -**are** verbs. These change the final -**i** of the present to -**a** (**Guarda** cosa fai! *Watch what you are doing!*).

The following is the complete conjugation of the familiar imperative forms of -**are**, -**ere**, and -**ire** verbs in the positive and negative forms:

	PARLARE (*to speak*)	SCRIVERE (*to write*)	SENTIRE (*to hear*)	FINIRE (*to finish*)
tu	parl**a!**	scriv**i!**	sent**i!**	fin**isci!**
noi	parl**iamo!**	scriv**iamo!**	sent**iamo!**	fin**iamo!**
voi	parl**ate!**	scriv**ete!**	sent**ite!**	fin**ite!**

Parla con lei!	Speak with her!
Scrivi a Maria!	Write Maria!
Finite la lezione!	Finish the lesson!

The **noi** form of the imperative is the same as the **noi** form of the present tense, and it corresponds to the English *let's* + verb.

Mandiamo una cartolina ai nostri amici!	*Let's send a postcard to our friends!*

In the negative, the **non** stands in front of the verb. (**Non andate!** *Don't go!*). The negative imperative of the **tu** form uses the infinitive of the verb. The **non** precedes the verb. (**Non mangiare** troppo! *Do not eat too much!*). The negative imperative for **noi** and **voi** forms places **non** in front of the **noi** and **voi**.

tu	**non** parl**are!**	**non** scriv**ere!**	**non** sent**ire!**	**non** fin**ire!**
noi	**non** parl**iamo!**	**non** scriv**iamo!**	**non** sent**iamo!**	**non** fin**iamo!**
voi	**non** parl**ate!**	**non** scriv**ete!**	**non** sent**ite!**	**non** fin**ite!**

Non parlare con lei!   *Don't speak with her!*
Non scrivete a Maria!   *Don't write Maria!*
Non finiamo la lezione!   *Don't finish the lesson!*

ESERCIZIO
2·1

Complete the sentences by conjugating the verbs in parentheses.

1. Giovanni, _____ (tu-scrivere) il libro!

2. _____ (noi-prendere) un espresso!

3. Ragazzi, _____ (voi-leggere) la lettera!

4. Ragazzi, _____ (voi-scrivere) la cartolina!

5. Ragazzi, _____ (voi-parlare) piano!

6. Ragazze, _____ (non-parlare) ascoltate la musica!

7. _____ (tu-guardare) la partita di tennis oggi!

8. _____ (non-guardare) la televisione!

The following verbs have irregular forms in the familiar imperative of tu and voi:

INFINITIVE	FAMILIAR SINGULAR (TU-*YOU*)	FAMILIAR PLURAL (VOI-*YOU*)
andare (*to go*)	**Vai** or **Và!**	**Andate!**
dare (*to give*)	**Dai** or **Dà!**	**Date!**
stare (*to stay*)	**Stai** or **Stà!**	**State!**
avere (*to have*)	**Abbi!**	**Abbiate!**
essere (*to be*)	**Sii!**	**Siate!**
dire (*to say, tell*)	**Dì!**	**Dite!**
fare (*to do, make*)	**Fai** or **Fà!**	**Fate!**
sapere (*to know*)	**Sappi!**	**Sappiate!**

ESERCIZIO
2·2

Translate the following sentences into Italian.

1. Be kind to the elderly! (tu) _____

2. Don't tell lies! (tu) _____

3. Don't tell lies! (voi) _____

4. Be quiet! (tu) _____

5. Be quiet! (voi) _____

6. Give bread to the poor! (tu) _____

7. Stay at home! It is too cold. (tu) _____

8. Be patient with the students! (tu) _____

9. Don't be too patient with the students! (tu) _____

ESERCIZIO
2·3

Change the following commands into the negative.

1. Vieni a casa! _____

2. Venite a casa! _____

3. Mangia tutta la pasta! _____

4. Leggi il libro! _____

5. Dormi di più! _____

6. Dormite di più! _____

7. Guarda la televisione! _____

8. Mangiamo in fretta! _____

9. Vendi la tua casa! _____

ESERCIZIO
2·4

Translate the first sentence; then in the sentences that follow, change the infinitives into the imperative of the familiar singular **tu**. *Explain how I can help you plan your father's birthday party.*

Domenica prossima è il compleanno di tuo padre e vuoi fare una festa. Ecco che cosa devo

fare per aiutarti: _____

_____

1. Mandare gli inviti agli amici. _____

2. Andare al supermercato. _____

3. Comprare le bibite. _____

4. Preparare i panini. _____

5. Mettere tutto nel frigorifero. _____

6. Fare la torta. _____

7. Mettere le sedie in giardino. _____

8. Ricevere gli ospiti. _____

9. Dopo la festa, pulire tutto. _____

Use the irregular verbs in parentheses in the correct form of the imperative, to give advice to your friend.

1. _____ (avere) pazienza!

2. _____ (stare) attenta!

3. _____ (stare) calma!

4. Non _____ (essere) nervosa!

5. _____ (fare) attenzione!

6. Non _____ (dare) l'idea che sei stanca!

7. _____ (essere) sicura di quello che dici!

8. _____ (fare) tutto quello che puoi!

9. Non _____ (dare) l'idea di sapere tutto!

The verbs that add **-isc** in the present indicative also add **-isc** to the stem of the second-person singular of the imperative.

	FINIRE (*to finish*)	CAPIRE (*to understand*)
tu	**finisci!**	**capisci!**
noi	**finiamo!**	**capiamo!**
voi	**finite!**	**capite!**

Tu **finisci** la lezione.   *You **finish** the lesson.*
Finisci la lezione!   ***Finish** the lesson!*

Change the following verbs from the present indicative to the positive and negative imperative in the correct forms.

	POSITIVE	NEGATIVE
1. Tu dimentichi.	_____!	_____!
2. Tu spendi.	_____!	_____!
3. Noi spendiamo.	_____!	_____!
4. Tu lavori.	_____!	_____!
5. Voi lavorate.	_____!	_____!
6. Noi ricordiamo.	_____!	_____!
7. Tu leggi.	_____!	_____!

8. Tu entri. _____! _____!

9. Noi entriamo. _____! _____!

10. Tu pulire. _____! _____!

Formal commands

Formal commands are used with **Lei** and **Loro**. You use these forms with people you do not know well or with people who are older than you. They are formed from the root of the first-person singular of the present indicative, which serves as the root for the formal commands. The formal pronouns **Lei** and **Loro** are usually omitted.

INFINITIVE	SINGULAR FORMAL COMMAND (LEI)	PLURAL FORMAL COMMAND (LORO)
cantare	**Canti!**	**Cantino!**
parlare	**Parli!**	**Parlino!**
guardare	**Guardi!**	**Guardino!**
scrivere	**Scriva!**	**Scrivano!**
vendere	**Venda!**	**Vendano!**
dormire	**Dorma!**	**Dormano!**
sentire	**Senta!**	**Sentano!**
finire	**Finisca!**	**Finiscano!**

In the negative form the non is placed in front of the verb.

Non guardi!   *Don't look!*

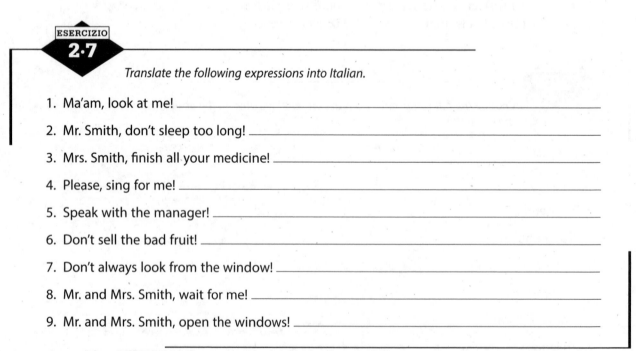

ESERCIZIO
2·7

Translate the following expressions into Italian.

1. Ma'am, look at me! _____

2. Mr. Smith, don't sleep too long! _____

3. Mrs. Smith, finish all your medicine! _____

4. Please, sing for me! _____

5. Speak with the manager! _____

6. Don't sell the bad fruit! _____

7. Don't always look from the window! _____

8. Mr. and Mrs. Smith, wait for me! _____

9. Mr. and Mrs. Smith, open the windows! _____

The imperative with object pronouns and reflexive pronouns

Object pronouns and reflexive pronouns are attached to the end of the verb in **tu**, **noi**, and **voi** forms.

Scrivi**la**!	*Write **it**!*
Scriviamo**la**!	*Let's write **it**!*
Scrivete**la**!	*Write **it**! (pl.)*
Sveglia**ti**!	*Wake up!*
Svegliamo**ci**!	***Let's** wake up!*
Svegliate**vi**!	*Wake up! (pl.)*
Leggi**lo**!	*Read **it**!*
Leggiamo**lo**!	***Let's** read it!*
Leggete**lo**!	*Read **it**! (pl.)*

Object pronouns and reflexive pronouns come before the verb in the **Lei** and **Loro** forms.

La scriva!	*Write **it**!*
La scrivano!	*Write **it**!*
Si svegli!	*Wake up!*
Si sveglino!	*Wake up!*
Lo legga!	*Read **it**!*
Lo leggano!	*Read **it**!*

In the negative, object pronouns and reflexive pronouns remain unchanged in the **Lei** and **Loro** forms but are placed either before the verb or attached to the end of the verb in the informal commands.

Non la scriva!	***Don't** write it!*
Non si svegli!	***Don't** wake up!*

But you say:

Non la scrivere! *or* **Non** scriver**la**!
Non ti svegliare! *or* **Non** svegliar**ti**!
Non la scrivete! *or* **Non** scrivete**la**!
Non vi svegliate! *or* **Non** svegliate**vi**!

When **dà**, **dì**, **fà**, **stà**, and **và** are followed by an object pronoun (**la**, **le**, **mi**, **ti**, **ci**), except for **gli** (*to him*), the consonant of the pronoun is doubled as follows: da**lle** (*give **her***), not da**le**; di**lle** (*tell **her***), not di**le**; fa**mmi** (*do . . . **me***), not fa**mi**; va**mmi** (*go . . . **me***), not **vami**; but do not double the following: da**gli**, di**gli**, fa**gli**, sta**gli**, va**gli**.

Da**gli** il libro!	*Give **him** the book!*
Di**gli** la storia!	*Tell **him** the story!*
Fa**gli** la cortesia!	*Do **him** the courtesy!*
Sta**gli** vicino!	*Stay near **him**!*
Va**gli** a portare il libro!	*Go and bring **him** the book!*

With the **tu** form, the pronoun can be attached or can precede the infinitive. The consonant is not doubled.

Non dar**mi** quel libro! *or* **Non mi** dare quel libro!   ***Don't give me** that book!*

Additional ways of using the imperative

Following are additional rules to help when using the imperative:

- Infinitives are often used when giving instructions, recipes, notices, etc.

  Scaldare il forno!   ***Preheat** the oven!*
  Spegnere il motore!   ***Turn off** the motor!*

- **È vietato** + infinitive

  È vietato parcheggiare!   *Parking **is forbidden**!*
  È vietato entrare!   *Entering **is forbidden**!*

- **Divieto** + a noun

  Divieto di sosta!   *Stopping **not allowed**!*
  Divieto di sorpasso!   ***No** passing!*

ESERCIZIO
2·8

Translate the following expressions into Italian.

1. Eat in that restaurant! (tu) _____

2. Return home early! (tu) _____

3. Do not dance! (tu) _____

4. Do not dance! (voi) _____

5. Let's pack! _____

6. Be patient! (tu) _____

7. Be patient! (voi) _____

8. Eat quickly! (tu) _____

9. Let's eat quickly! _____

Rewrite the following negative commands in the positive.

1. Non dire tutto! _____

2. Non telefonate tardi! _____

3. Non leggete il giornale! _____

4. Non essere sgarbato! _____

5. Non ritornare tardi! _____

6. Non urlare! _____

7. Non urliamo! _____

8. Non scrivere a mia nonna! _____

9. Non bevete acqua ghiacciata! _____

Rewrite the following sentences in the negative.

1. Parla piano! _____

2. Parli piano! _____

3. Parlate piano! _____

4. Parlino piano! _____

5. Stà zitto! _____

6. Fai il caffè! _____

7. Fate il caffè! _____

8. Dammi la mano! _____

9. Dagli i soldi! _____

Change the following sentences from informal to formal commands.

1. Vieni qui! _____

2. Scrivi la lezione! _____

3. Credi in te stesso! _____

III-2 The imperative (*imperativo*)   **265**

4. Parla poco! _____

5. Svegliati presto! _____

6. Finisci la colazione! _____

7. Lavora di più! _____

8. Scendi dalle scale! _____

9. Dammi quella mela! _____

ESERCIZIO
2·12

Translate the following sentences into Italian.

1. You need money. Go to the bank!

   _____

2. You have a headache. Take an aspirin!

   _____

3. You are afraid to travel by plane. Go by train!

   _____

4. It is your mother's birthday. Buy her a gift!

   _____

5. You walk for ten minutes a day. Walk more!

   _____

6. You eat too late at night. Eat earlier!

   _____

7. You get up late on Saturdays. Get up earlier!

   _____

8. You are tired. Rest!

   _____

9. You are not hungry. Don't eat!

   _____

ESERCIZIO
2·13

Carlo is leaving for a business trip. He needs his wife's help. Complete the sentences below.

Wife: _____ (ascoltare) Carlo, non (dimenticare) _____ di prendere il passaporto!

Carlo: Va bene, grazie.

Wife: Non _____ (dimenticare) le cravatte!

Carlo: Va bene! Ma adesso (dare) una mano, altrimenti faccio tardi! Per favore _____ (tu-mettere) i pantaloni, le camice, e i calzini in valigia! _____ (Preparare) la colazione per favore!

Wife: Va bene, e poi che cosa devo fare?

Carlo: Mentre io faccio colazione, _____ (tu-chiamare) un tassì. Dopo che io sono partito, _____ (tu sedersi), (chiamare) le tue amiche, _____ (bere) il caffè con loro e (andare) al cinema!

Reflexive verbs (*verbi riflessivi*)

Reflexive verbs are transitive verbs that express an action reflecting back to the subject. The subject and the object are the same. In this unit you will study the simple tense reflexive verbs or reflexive verbs made up of only one word and the pronoun. (Later in this book you will study the compound reflexive verbs.)

Many verbs that are reflexive in English are also reflexive in Italian, but not all are reflexive in both languages. The infinitive endings of the reflexive verbs are: **-are, arsi; -ere, -ersi;** and **-ire, -irsi** (the **-si** means *oneself*): alzar**si** (*to get up*), seder**si** (*to sit down*), divertir**si** (*to have fun*). As you can see, the final vowel **-e** of the infinitive is dropped from the infinitive of the reflexive verbs.

Following are some common reflexive verbs (they are not all reflexive in English):

abituarsi	*to get used to*	**lavarsi**	*to wash*
addormentarsi	*to fall asleep*		*(oneself)*
alzarsi	*to get up*	**meravigliarsi**	*to be amazed*
annoiarsi	*to get bored*	**mettersi**	*to put on, wear*
chiamarsi	*to be called,*	**mettersi a**	*to begin to*
	be named	**prepararsi**	*to get ready*
divertirsi	*to have fun*	**presentarsi**	*to introduce*
domandarsi	*to wonder*		*oneself*
farsi la barba	*to shave*	**ricordarsi**	*to remember*
fermarsi	*to stop (oneself)*	**riposarsi**	*to rest*
girarsi	*to turn around*	**sedersi**	*to sit down*
guardarsi	*to look at oneself*	**sentirsi**	*to feel*
lamentarsi	*to complain*		

Reflexive verbs are conjugated like the verbs ending in **-are, -ere,** and **-ire.** The reflexive pronouns must be used when conjugating a verb, unlike the non-reflexive verbs that can omit the pronouns. They are:

mi	*myself*
ti	*yourself*
si	*himself, herself; yourself (form. sing.)*
ci	*ourselves*
vi	*yourselves*
si	*themselves; yourself (form. pl.)*

Following is the complete conjugation of the present simple tense of some reflexive verbs:

	ALZARSI (to get up)	**METTERSI** (to put on, wear)	**DIVERTIRSI** (to have fun)
mi	alzo	metto	diverto
ti	alzi	metti	diverti
si	alza	mette	diverte
ci	alziamo	mettiamo	divertiamo
vi	alzate	mettete	divertite
si	alzano	mettono	divertono

Positioning of reflexive pronouns

The reflexive pronouns **mi, ti, si, ci, vi,** and **si** always precede the indicative form. The endings of the verb are not affected by the reflexive pronouns in the simple tenses.

> Io **mi alzo** presto.   *I **get up** early.*

ESERCIZIO 3·1

Write the correct form of the following reflexive verbs, using the words in parentheses.

1. alzarsi (tu, lei, voi) _____

2. svegliarsi (Giovanni, noi, loro) _____

3. addormentarsi (i bambini, io, tu) _____

4. lavarsi (Carlo, Maria, i nostri cugini) _____

5. vestirsi (io, tu, loro) _____

6. riposarsi (Rita, Giovanni, noi) _____

7. svegliarsi (Edoardo) _____

8. divertirsi (noi) _____

9. vestirsi (loro) _____

If the infinitive is preceded by **dovere, potere,** or **volere,** the reflexive pronoun may precede or be attached to the infinitive.

> **Mi** voglio **svegliare** presto.   *I want **to get up** early.*
> Voglio **svegliarmi** presto.   *I want **to get up** early.*

ESERCIZIO 3·2

Translate these sentences into Italian, following both examples shown above.

1. I have to wake up early.

_____

2. We have to wake up early.

_____

3. You want to have fun with your friends.

_____

4. He wants to take a shower every morning.

_____

5. She must comb her hair.

_____

6. I have to get dressed.

_____

7. The kids can get up late.

_____

8. You (pl.) have to wash your hands often.

_____

9. They cannot fall asleep.

_____

Reciprocal reflexives

Reciprocal reflexives express a reciprocal action. More than one person is involved. The phrase **l'un l'altro a** or **a vicenda** (*one another, each other*) may be used to clarify the meaning of the reflexive pronoun.

Here is a list of the most commonly used reciprocal reflexives:

abbracciarsi	*to embrace one another (each other)*
amarsi	*to love one another (each other)*
baciarsi	*to kiss one another (each other)*
conoscersi	*to know one another (each other)*
incontrarsi	*to meet one another (each other)*
innamorarsi	*to fall in love with each other*
rispettarsi	*to respect one another (each other)*
rivedersi	*to see each other again*
salutarsi	*to greet one another (each other)*
sposarsi	*to get married to each other*
vedersi	*to see one another (each other)*
visitarsi	*to visit one another (each other)*

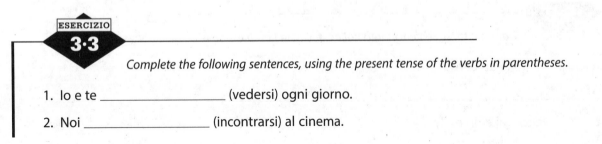

ESERCIZIO
3·3

Complete the following sentences, using the present tense of the verbs in parentheses.

1. Io e te _____ (vedersi) ogni giorno.

2. Noi _____ (incontrarsi) al cinema.

3. Carlo e Maria _____ (sposarsi) il mese prossimo.

4. I nonni _____ (volersi) bene.

5. Loro _____ (aiutarsi) sempre.

6. Voi non _____ (vedersi) spesso.

7. Tu e Maria non _____ (conoscersi) bene.

8. Io e Giovanna _____ (visitarsi) ogni settimana.

9. I miei amici _____ (amarsi) molto.

Reflexive versus non-reflexive

Some verbs can be used reflexively and non-reflexively, and their meaning is also different.

Reflexive	**Non-Reflexive**
Io **mi lavo** le mani.	Io **lavo** la macchina.
*I **wash my** hands.*	*I **wash** the car.*
Tu **ti addormenti** al cinema.	Tu **addormenti** la bambina.
*You **fall asleep** at the movies.*	*You **put** the baby to sleep.*

Following is a list of verbs that can be used reflexively or non-reflexively. Note their change in meaning.

REFLEXIVE		NON-REFLEXIVE	
addormentarsi	to fall asleep	**addormentare**	to put to sleep
alzarsi	to get up	**alzare**	to lift
chiamarsi	to be called	**chiamare**	to call
farsi il bagno	to take a bath	**fare il bagno**	to give a bath
lavarsi	to get washed	**lavare**	to wash
pettinarsi	to comb one's hair	**pettinare**	to comb somebody's hair
pulirsi	to get cleaned	**pulire**	to clean up
sentirsi	to feel	**sentire**	to hear, listen
svegliarsi	to wake up	**svegliare**	to wake up someone
vestirsi	to get dressed	**vestire**	to dress someone

ESERCIZIO 3·4

Complete the following sentences, using reflexive pronouns when required.

1. Io _____ diverto molto.

2. Tu _____ chiami Roberto.

3. Tu _____ chiami i bambini.

4. Lei _____ lava le mani.

5. Lui _____ lava la macchina.

6. Noi _____ puliamo la casa.

7. Noi _____ puliamo.

8. Loro _____ sentono la musica.

9. Loro non _____ sentono bene oggi.

ESERCIZIO
3·5

Fill in the spaces with the correct form of the reflexive verb. Then translate into English.

La domenica _____ (alzarsi) sempre tardi. Mi piace molto dormire. Quando _____

(alzarsi), faccio la doccia, _____ (vestirsi) e _____ (prepararsi) per uscire e

andare al parco con il mio cagnolino. Quando ritorno a casa, io e la mia famiglia _____

(mettersi) a tavola. Mia madre prepara il pranzo e mio padre _____ (occuparsi) del

vino. Dopo pranzo vengono i nostri parenti a _____ (visitarsi). Noi (divertirsi) molto

quando _____ (riunirsi) e stiamo tutti insieme.

_____

_____

_____

_____

_____

_____

_____

_____

ESERCIZIO
3·6

Choose the reflexive verbs from the list below and insert them in the sentences in the appropriate forms.

alzarsi   ricordarsi   incontrarsi   riposarsi   truccarsi
lavarsi   divertirsi   vestirsi   farsi

1. Carlo _____ bene.

2. Non (tu) _____ dove sono le chiavi della macchina?

3. Io _____ i capelli tre volte alla settimana.

4. Loro _____ quando vengono a casa nostra.

5. Se sei stanca, _____ !

6. Io e Carlo _____ davanti alla stazione.

7. La tua amica _____ troppo.

8. Mio marito _____ la barba tutte le mattine.

9. La domenica _____ molto tardi.

The future tense (*futuro semplice*)

In English as well as in Italian, the future tense is used to express an action that will take place in the future, regardless of whether it is in the near future or distant future.

The future tense in Italian consists of a single verb, while in English two different words can be used: the auxiliaries *shall* or *will*, and the infinitive of the verb. The future tense of regular verbs in Italian is formed by putting the future endings on the infinitive of the verb without the final **-e-**. In the first conjugation (**-are** verbs), the **-a-** of the infinitive ending changes to **-e-** in the future tense. The endings for the **-are**, **-ere**, and **-ire** verbs are: **-ò**, **-ai**, **-à**, **-emo**, **-ete**, and **-anno**.

parlare	**scrivere**	**sentire**
Parlerò.	Scriverò.	Sentirò.
I will speak.	*I will write.*	*I will hear.*

Below is the complete conjugation of the future of the **-are**, **-ere**, and **-ire** verbs.

	PARLARE	SCRIVERE	SENTIRE
io	parlerò	scriverò	sentirò
tu	parlerai	scriverai	sentirai
lui/lei	parlerà	scriverà	sentirà
noi	parleremo	scriveremo	sentiremo
voi	parlerete	scriverete	sentirete
loro	parleranno	scriveranno	sentiranno

Note: The first- and the third-person singular have an accent on the ending. This means that the last syllable needs to be stressed.

The verbs that add **-isc**, such as **finire** (*to finish*), **preferire** (*to prefer*), and **pulire** (*to clean*), in the present tense form the future like any other regular verb.

Write the future tense of the verbs in parentheses in the correct forms.

1. La campana _____ (suonare) a mezzogiorno.

2. Oggi noi non _____ (guardare) la televisione.

3. Io _____ (studiare) la lezione.

4. Domani tu _____ (portare) il computer a scuola.

5. Il mese prossimo mio padre _____ (comprare) una macchina nuova.

6. Maria _____ (ascoltare) la radio.

7. Io _____ (leggere) il giornale.

8. A che ora _____ (arrivare) il treno da Roma?

9. Dove _____ (voi-dormire) questa notte?

10. Con chi _____ (voi-pranzare) oggi?

11. Noi _____ (finire) tutto il pane.

12. Voi _____ (prendere) una tazza di caffè.

13. Con chi _____ (loro-parlare) l'italiano?

14. Io non _____ (cantare) in chiesa.

Translate the following sentences into Italian.

1. Tomorrow I will receive the book. _____

2. We will dine in a good restaurant. _____

3. I will answer your letter next week. _____

4. At what time will you arrive? _____

5. At what time will you leave? _____

6. You will sell the house. _____

7. You will not sell the house. _____

8. How many people will you invite? _____

9. I will invite only my friends. _____

10. I will visit many cities. _____

Following are additional examples of when the future tense is used:

- In Italian the future tense can be replaced by the present tense when the time of the action will take place in the near future.

   Partiamo domani mattina.   *We'll leave tomorrow morning.*

- When a dependent clause referring to something that will happen in the near future is introduced by **se** (*if*), **quando** (*when*), or **appena** (*as soon as*), the future tense is used in Italian, while in English the present tense is used.

   Scriverò **quando avrò** tempo.   *I will write **when I have** time.*

- In verbs ending in -**gare** (**pagare**, *to pay*) and -**care** (**cercare**, *to look for*), an -**h**- is added to the future tense to preserve the hard sound of the infinitive.

INFINITIVE: ROOT OF THE FUTURE TENSE:	CERCARE CERCHER-	PAGARE PAGHER-
io	cercherò	pagherò
tu	cercherai	pagherai
lui/lei	cercherà	pagherà
noi	cercheremo	pagheremo
voi	cercherete	pagherete
loro	cercheranno	pagheranno

- The verbs ending in -**ciare** (**cominciare**, *to start, begin*) and -**giare** (**mangiare**, *to eat*) drop the -**i**- before the endings of the future tense.

INFINITIVE: ROOT OF THE FUTURE TENSE:	MANGIARE MANGER-	COMINCIARE COMINCER-
io	mangerò	comincerò
tu	mangerai	comincerai
lui/lei	mangerà	comincerà
noi	mangeremo	cominceremo
voi	mangerete	comincerete
loro	mangeranno	cominceranno

- As in English, the idea of the future can also be expressed in Italian by using the present tense.

   Il treno **parte** tra dieci minuti.   *The train **leaves** in ten minutes.*
   or Il treno **partirà** tra dieci minuti.   *The train **will leave** in ten minutes.*

- The future is also used to express probability or possibility.

   Che ora **sarà?**   *What time **can it be?***
   Saranno le otto.   *It is **probably** eight o'clock.*

   Chi è quella signora?   *Who **is** that lady?*
   Sarà la nuova inquilina.   *She **might be** the new tenant.*

Complete each sentence with the correct form of the verb in parentheses.

1. Quando i turisti _____ (arrivare), andranno all'albergo.

2. Quando verrà tuo cugino, _____ (noi-andare) al cinema.

3. Se tu _____ (visitare) tua zia, sarà molto contenta.

4. Quando _____ (noi-vedere) i nostri amici, parleremo del viaggio.

5. Quando _____ (tu-venire) a casa mia, ti mostrerò le foto.

6. Se _____ (io-andare) in vacanza, mi riposerò molto.

7. Se _____ (voi-spendere) molti soldi, sarete contenti.

8. Se _____ (loro-venire), saremo molto contenti.

9. Se _____ (fare) cattivo tempo, staremo a casa.

Translate the following sentences into Italian.

1. The girls are probably at the park.

_____

2. When are you going to Italy?

_____

3. When I go to Italy, I will see the Vatican.

_____

4. When the tourists arrive, the restaurants will be very busy.

_____

5. If you visit your mother, she will be very happy.

_____

6. When I go home, I will put on my pajamas.

_____

7. If you come home late, the dinner will be cold.

_____

8. When we arrive, everybody will be in bed.

_____

9. If it snows, we'll make a snowman.

_____

ESERCIZIO

4·5

Complete each sentence with the correct form of the future tense.

1. Io _____ (mangiare) a casa dei nonni.

2. Tu _____ (noleggiare) una macchina piccola.

3. Lui _____ (viaggiare) in aereo.

4. Lei _____ (cominciare) a parlare.

5. Io non _____ (cercare) un albergo in centro.

6. Noi _____ (cercare) un albergo in centro.

7. Voi _____ (pagare) con la carta di credito.

8. Loro _____ (cercare) la banca.

9. Io non _____ (pagare) con un assegno.

ESERCIZIO

4·6

Answer the following questions, using the words in parentheses to express possibility.

1. Dove saranno le chiavi? (in casa) _____

2. Che ore saranno? (13,30) _____

3. Costa molto questa casa? (No) _____

4. A che ora rientrerai questa sera? (tardi) _____

5. Dove saranno le tue amiche? (al cinema) _____

6. Quanti anni ha quel ragazzo? (20 anni) _____

7. Quanti ragazzi ci saranno alla festa? (20) _____

8. Che tempo farà domani? (brutto) _____

9. Quante parole nuove imparerai? (molte) _____

- The prepositions **tra** (*in*) and **per** (*by*) always refer to something that is about to happen. They are often used with the future tense.

    Le **parlerò tra** una settimana.   *I **will talk** to you **in** a week.*
    Lo **finirai per** la fine di marzo.   *You **will finish** it by the end of March.*

- There are some verbs that have irregular roots in the future tense. But their endings are the same as they are for the future tense of the regular verbs. Following are some commonly used verbs that have irregular roots in the future tense. Note that the endings are the same as the regular future endings.

INFINITIVE	FUTURE STEM	CONJUGATION
andare (*to go*)	**andr**	andrò, andrai, andrà, ecc.
avere (*to have*)	**avr**	avrò, avrai, avrà, ecc.
bere (*to drink*)	**berr**	berrò, berrai, berrà, ecc.
cadere(*to fall*)	**cadr**	cadrò, cadrai, cadrà, ecc.
dare (*to give*)	**dar**	darò, darai, darà, ecc.
dovere (*to have to*)	**dovr**	dovrò, dovrai, dovrà, ecc.
essere (*to be*)	**sar**	sarò, sarai, sarà, ecc.
fare (*to do, make*)	**far**	farò, farai, farà, ecc.
porre (*to put*)	**porr**	porrò, porrai, porrà, ecc.
potere (*to be able to*)	**potr**	potrò, potrai, potrà, ecc.
rimanere (*to remain*)	**rimarr**	rimarrò, rimarrai, rimarrà, ecc.
sapere (*to know*)	**sapr**	saprò, saprai, saprà, ecc.
tenere (*to keep*)	**terr**	terrò, terrai, terrà, ecc.
vedere (*to see*)	**vedr**	vedrò, vedrai, vedrà, ecc.
venire (*to come*)	**verr**	verrò, verrai, verrà, ecc.
vivere (*to live*)	**vivr**	vivrò, vivrai, vivrà, ecc.

Note: The verbs **andare** (*to go*), **avere** (*to have*), **cadere** (*to fall*), **dovere** (*to have to*), **potere** (*to be able to*), **sapere** (*to know*), **vedere** (*to see*), and **vivere** (*to live*) have a shorter root in the future. They drop the vowels **-a-** and **-e-** from the infinitive.

The verbs **bere** (*to drink*), **volere** (*to want*), **tenere** (*to keep*), **rimanere** (*to stay*), and **venire** (*to come*) have a double **-r-** (**-rr-**) in the future tense. Refer to the list above.

ESERCIZIO
4·7

Translate the following sentences into Italian.

1. Tomorrow we'll go to visit our aunt. _____

2. Next year my parents will go to Italy. _____

3. You will have an important job. _____

4. I will see them tomorrow. _____

5. We will live in Italy. _____

6. We will see our friends in a few days. _____

7. He will come to my house. _____

8. She will stay for a week. _____

9. They will not drink very much beer. _____

10. I will live for many years. _____

11. Terry will come to the office late. _____

12. We will drink mineral water. _____

13. You will see many monuments. _____

The future tense of *essere*

All forms of **essere** are irregular in the future. The root is **sar-** and to this the future tense endings are added.

INFINITIVE: ROOT OF THE FUTURE TENSE:	ESSERE SAR-
io	**sarò**
tu	**sarai**
lui/lei	**sarà**
noi	**saremo**
voi	**sarete**
loro	**saranno**

ESERCIZIO 4·8

*Supply the correct future forms of **essere**.*

1. Io _____ a casa domani.

2. Tu _____ molto contento.

3. Lui _____ al parco.

4. Noi _____ contenti di rivederti.

5. Voi _____ in Italia per due anni.

6. Loro _____ i primi ad arrivare.

7. Io non _____ a scuola domani.

8. Tu non _____ in chiesa domenica.

9. Tu _____ in ritardo domani?

ESERCIZIO 4·9

Supply the correct forms of the future tense for the verbs suggested.

Il mese prossimo _____ (noi-andare) in vacanza. Mi piacerebbe andare alle

isole Maldive. Domani (io-andare) all'agenzia di viaggi e _____ (io-prenotare)

il volo e l'albergo. Se non _____ (costare) troppo, (io-stare) in un albergo di

lusso e _____ (io-andare) tutti i giorni a fare lo scuba. _____

(io-vedere) tanti pesci colorati e tipici di quei posti. Se non (essere) possibile andare alle

Maldive, _____ (rimanere) in Italia e _____ (io-fare) le mie

vacanze sulla spiaggia di Rimini, che è una delle più famose stazioni balneari

italiane. _____ (io-fare) il bagno tutti i giorni e _____ (stare) molto

tempo al sole, così _____ (io-ritornare) in città molto abbronzata.

The present perfect tense (*passato prossimo*)

The present perfect tense in Italian is a compound tense, made up of more than one word, and used to express an action or an event recently completed at a definite moment in the past. It literally corresponds to the English simple past, present perfect, and emphatic past. It expresses what you have done, what has happened.

Io ho parlato con Maria.	*I spoke with Maria.*
	I have spoken with Maria.
	I did speak with Maria.

It is the tense used in conversational Italian. It is often preceded or followed by such time expressions as **ieri** (*yesterday*), **domenica scorsa** (*last Sunday*), **l'anno scorso** (*last year*), **un anno fa** (*a year ago*), and **un'ora fa** (*an hour ago*).

Ieri ho mangiato da mia mamma.	*Yesterday I ate at my mother's.*

The present perfect is formed by combining the present tense of **avere** or **essere** and the past participle of the verb.

We will start studying the verbs using **avere** in the present perfect, since the majority of Italian verbs use **avere**. When the present perfect is formed with **avere**, the past participle doesn't agree in gender and number with the subject. Later, we'll explore the times when this rule has to be modified.

The present perfect with *avere*

Verbs that take **avere** as the helping, or auxiliary, verb are in most cases transitive verbs or verbs that take a direct object and answer the question **chi?** (*whom?*) or **che cosa?** (*what?*).

Io ho mangiato la cioccolata. (che cosa?)	*I ate chocolate.* (*what?*)

The past participle of regular verbs is formed by dropping the infinitive ending and adding the ending for the present perfect to the root.

INFINITIVE	ENDINGS	PAST PARTICIPLE
parl**are**	**-ato** for **-are** verbs	parl**ato**
vend**ere**	**-uto** for **-ere** verbs	vend**uto**
dorm**ire**	**-ito** for **-ire** verbs	dorm**ito**

Ieri ho parlato con la tua amica.	*Yesterday I spoke with your friend.*

Verbs that add **-isc** in the present tense and are conjugated like **finire** have the past participle like **dormire**.

Ho capito tutto.   *I **understood** everything.*

Following are the complete conjugations of the **passato prossimo** of **-are**, **-ere**, and **-ire** verbs:

	PARLARE (I [have] spoken, etc.)	VENDERE (I [have] sold, etc.)	DORMIRE (I [have] slept, etc.)
io	**ho parlato**	**ho venduto**	**ho dormito**
tu	**hai parlato**	**hai venduto**	**hai dormito**
lui/lei	**ha parlato**	**ha venduto**	**ha dormito**
noi	**abbiamo parlato**	**abbiamo venduto**	**abbiamo dormito**
voi	**avete parlato**	**avete venduto**	**avete dormito**
loro	**hanno parlato**	**hanno venduto**	**hanno dormito**

All verbs ending in **-are** have regular past participle endings except for **fare: fatto** (and compounds). Note that a compound is a verb like **fare** with the addition of a prefix like **rifatto** (*remade*).

INFINITIVE	PAST PARTICIPLE
ballare (*to dance*)	**ballato**
camminare (*to walk*)	**camminato**
cantare (*to sing*)	**cantato**
fare (*to make, do*)	**fatto**
giocare (*to play*)	**giocato**
preparare (*to prepare*)	**preparato**
provare (*to try*)	**provato**
rifare (*to remake*)	**rifatto**

ESERCIZIO
5·1

Complete the following sentences with the correct forms of the present perfect for the verbs suggested.

1. Io _____ (parlare) con lui questa mattina.

2. Tu _____ (cantare) in chiesa.

3. Lei _____ (provare) le scarpe.

4. Lui _____ (giocare) alle carte.

5. Noi _____ (provare) i vestiti.

6. Voi _____ (camminare) sulla neve.

7. I nostri amici _____ (preparare) un ottimo pranzo.

8. Ieri _____ (io-ballare) molto.

9. I bambini _____ (giocare) con la neve.

The negative is formed by putting **non** in front of the auxiliary.

Non ho mangiato niente.   *I didn't eat anything.*

The majority of verbs ending in **-ire** are regular with the exception of **dire** (*to say, tell*), **detto**; **morire** (*to die*), **morto**; **venire** (*to come*), **venuto**; **scomparire** (*to disappear*), **scomparso**; **aprire** (*to open*), **aperto**; **offrire** (*to offer*), **offerto**.

Io **ho detto** tutta la verità.   *I told the truth.*

Note: **morire** and **venire** form the present perfect with **essere**.

There are large numbers of verbs that have irregular past participles. The following list is for you to use as a general guideline and to help you group together the verbs with irregular past participles.

Verbs ending in **-durre** follow the pattern of **tradurre** (*to translate*): **tradotto**.
Verbs ending in **-arre** follow the pattern of **attrarre** (*to attract*): **attratto**.
Verbs ending in **-orre** follow the pattern of **comporre** (*to compose*): **composto**.
Verbs ending in **-endere** follow the pattern of **prendere** (*to take*): **preso**.
Verbs ending in **-eggere** follow the pattern of **leggere** (*to read*): **letto**.
Verbs ending in **-idere** follow the pattern of **ridere** (*to laugh*): **riso**.
Verbs ending in **-udere** follow the pattern of **chiudere** (*to close*): **chiuso**.

Verbs ending in **-scere** and **-cere** have the past participle **-iuto** as in **conosciuto** (*known*) and **piaciuto** (*liked*). Some exceptions include **nascere** (*to be born*), **nato**, and **vincere** (*to win*), **vinto**.

ESERCIZIO
5·2

Complete the following sentences with the present perfect of the verb in parentheses.

1. Io _____ (tradurre) la lettera.

2. Tu _____ (comporre) della musica molto bella.

3. Lui _____ (prendere) un caffè.

4. Lei _____ (leggere) molti libri.

5. Noi _____ (ridere) tutta la sera.

6. Voi _____ (chiudere) la porta e le finestre.

7. Loro _____ (conoscere) la vostra amica.

8. I nostri amici _____ (vincere) la partita.

9. Io _____ (non leggere) il giornale.

10. Tu _____ (non chiudere) la porta.

Note: **nascere** forms the present perfect with **essere**.

Many Italian verbs, especially **-ere** verbs, have irregular past participles. Following is a list of the ones most commonly used:

accendere	*to turn on*	**acceso**
aggiungere	*to add*	**aggiunto**
appendere	*to hang*	**appeso**
assumere	*to hire*	**assunto**
bere	*to drink*	**bevuto**
chiedere	*to ask*	**chiesto**
chiudere	*to close*	**chiuso**
comprendere	*to understand*	**compreso**
confondere	*to confuse*	**confuso**
conoscere	*to know*	**conosciuto**
convincere	*to convince*	**convinto**
correggere	*to correct*	**corretto**
correre	*to run*	**corso**
cuocere	*to cook*	**cotto**
decidere	*to decide*	**deciso**
discutere	*to discuss*	**discusso**
dividere	*to divide*	**diviso**
eleggere	*to elect*	**eletto**
leggere	*to read*	**letto**
mettere	*to put*	**messo**
nascondere	*to hide*	**nascosto**
perdere	*to lose*	**perso**
piangere	*to cry*	**pianto**
prendere	*to take, get*	**preso**
promettere	*to promise*	**promesso**
ridere	*to laugh*	**riso**
rispondere	*to answer*	**risposto**
scrivere	*to write*	**scritto**
spegnere	*to turn off*	**spento**
vedere	*to see*	**visto**
vincere	*to win*	**vinto**
vivere	*to live*	**vissuto**

ESERCIZIO
5·3

Translate the following sentences into Italian, using the present perfect.

1. I answered your letter. _____

2. You drank a glass of wine. _____

3. You cooked a good dinner. _____

4. We elected a new president. _____

5. He has read the newspaper. _____

6. The dog hid the ball. _____

7. She cried all day long. _____

8. He didn't answer my letter. _____

9. She laughed all day long. _____

10. You (pl.) turned off the television. _____

11. We won the soccer game. _____

Rewrite the following sentences in the present perfect.

1. Maria canta bene. _____

2. Leggiamo il libro. _____

3. Mangio con i miei genitori. _____

4. Voi scrivete una storia molto lunga. _____

5. Il bambino piange sempre. _____

6. Noi facciamo molte cose. _____

7. Voi capite bene la lezione. _____

8. Loro ballano tutta la sera. _____

9. Tu non accendi la luce. _____

10. Lui prende il raffreddore. _____

Agreement of the past participle with verbs conjugated with *avere* in the present perfect

Following are the rules to remember when using the past participle of a verb used with **avere**:

- The past participle must agree with the direct object pronoun **lo** (*him*), **la** (*her*), **li** (*them*), or **le** (**them**) preceding the verb.

  Avete comprato il pane? No, non **lo** abbiamo comprat**o**.
  *Did you buy the bread? No, we didn't buy **it**.*

  Avete comprato i fiori? Sì, **li** abbiamo comprat**i**.
  *Did you buy the flowers? Yes, we bought **them**.*

  Hai visto mia sorella? No, non **l'**(la) ho vist**a**.
  *Have you seen my sister? No, I haven't seen **her**.*

  Hai visto le mie amiche? No, non **le** ho vist**e**.
  Did you see my friends? No, I didn't see them.

- The past participle must agree with the pronoun **ne** when it means some or part of.

> Avete mangiato molte mele? Si, **ne** abbiamo mangiat**e** molt**e**.
> *Did you eat many apples? Yes, we ate many (**of them**).*

- The agreement is optional with the direct object pronouns **mi**, **ti**, **ci**, and **vi** and when a sentence is introduced by **che**, **la quale**, **i quali**, or **le quali**.

> Non **ci** hanno portat**o**/portat**i** al cinema.
> *They didn't take **us** to the movies.*

> I film **che** abbiamo vist**o**/vist**i** sono interessanti.
> *The movies (**that**) **we saw** were interesting.*

- The past participle never agrees with the indirect object.

> **Le abbiamo mandato** un telegramma.
> *We **sent her** a telegram.*

ESERCIZIO
5·5

Translate the following sentences into Italian.

1. I have never seen him. _____

2. You have seen them (m.). _____

3. He saw her. _____

4. He didn't see her. _____

5. Have you received the letter? No, I didn't receive it. _____
   _____

6. I said good-bye to my aunts. I said good-bye to them. _____
   _____

7. We opened the windows. We opened them. _____
   _____

8. They didn't bring us the bread. They didn't bring it. _____
   _____

9. I bought many apples. You bought some of them. _____
   _____

10. We sent her a fax. _____

Using the suggested verbs, describe how you and your family spent last weekend. Then translate it into English.

pulire	fare	lavare	telefonare
ascoltare	andare	leggere	preparare
dormire	guardare	giocare	

Sabato, io _____ fino a tardi. _____ colazione, poi _____

la musica country. Mio fratello _____ in piscina e io e mia sorella _____

al tennis. Mio padre _____ la televisone e _____ il giornale. Nel

pomeriggio _____ la nostra macchina. Mia madre _____ la

casa, _____ alla nonna e _____ una cena speciale per tutti noi.

_____

_____

_____

_____

_____

_____

_____

_____

_____

The present perfect with *essere*

The present perfect of intransitive verbs—those that do not take a direct object—is formed by combining the present tense of **essere** and the past participle of the verb. Most of these verbs usually express movement (**arrivare**, *to arrive*), lack of movement (**stare**, *to stay*), a mental or physical state (**arrossire**, *to blush*), or some process of change (**invecchiare**, *to age*).

Regular past participles of verbs conjugated with **essere** are formed like those conjugated with **avere**.

Past participles conjugated with **essere** agree in gender and number with the subject of the verb.

Antonio **è uscito** alle due.	*Antonio **went out** at two.*
Maria **è uscita** alle due.	*Maria **went out** at two.*

	ARRIVARE (to arrive)	CADERE (to fall)	USCIRE (to go out)
io	sono arrivato/a	sono caduto/a	sono uscito/a
tu	sei arrivato/a	sei caduto/a	sei uscito/a
lui/lei	è arrivato/a	è caduto/a	è uscito/a
noi	siamo arrivati/e	siamo caduti/e	siamo usciti/e
voi	siete arrivati/e	siete caduti/e	siete usciti/e
loro	sono arrivati/e	sono caduti/e	sono usciti/e

Below is a list of commonly used verbs conjugated with **essere** in the present perfect:

INFINITIVE	PAST PARTICIPLE
andare (*to go*)	**andato**
apparire (*to appear*)	**apparso**
arrivare (*to arrive*)	**arrivato**
cadere (*to fall*)	**caduto**
diventare (*to become*)	**diventato**
entrare (*to enter*)	**entrato**
essere (*to be*)	**stato**
morire (*to die*)	**morto**
nascere (*to be born*)	**nato**
partire (*to depart, leave*)	**partito**
restare (*to remain*)	**restato**
rimanere (*to stay, remain*)	**rimasto**
ritornare (*to return*)	**ritornato**
salire (*to go up*)	**salito**
scendere (*to go down*)	**sceso**
stare (*to stay*)	**stato**
tornare (*to return, come back*)	**tornato**
uscire (*to go out*)	**uscito**
venire (*to come*)	**venuto**
vivere (*to live*)	**vissuto**

ESERCIZIO
5·7

Translate the following sentences into Italian.

1. I went to the movies. _____

2. You arrived late. _____

3. He entered the restaurant. _____

4. She died last month. _____

5. I was born in a small town. _____

6. We left by ship. _____

7. You (pl.) became American citizens. _____

8. They returned home in time for supper. _____

9. They went on the bus. _____

Rewrite the following sentences in the present perfect.

1. Paola va al mercato. _____

2. Tu non esci con i tuoi amici. _____

3. Lui ritorna a casa sua. _____

4. Maria entra nel negozio. _____

5. Voi partite per l'Africa. _____

6. Noi siamo dagli zii. _____

7. Le ragazze arrivano alla stazione. _____

8. Loro crescono molto. _____

9. Tu non cadi quando pattini. _____

Following are additional rules you need to remember when using **essere** + the past participle:

- **Essere** is also used when referring to the weather, even though it is common today to hear people use **avere**.

È piovuto tutto il giorno.	*It has rained all day long.*
Ha piovuto tutto il giorno.	*It has rained all day long.*

- Some verbs use either **essere** or **avere**, depending on whether they are used transitively or intransitively.

Intransitive: I prezzi della frutta **sono aumentati**.	*The prices for fruit have increased*.
Transitive: I padroni **hanno aumentato** i prezzi.	*The owners have increased the prices.*

- With the modal verbs **dovere**, **potere**, and **volere**, it is more correct to use **essere** if the following infinitive takes **essere**. This rule is particularly used in writing. But when speaking, **avere** is heard more frequently.

Siamo dovuti stare a casa tutto il giorno.	*We had to stay home all day.*
Non siamo potuti venire perchè eravamo senza macchina.	*We couldn't come because we were without a car.*

- Impersonal verbs require the use of **essere** in the present perfect: **accadere** (*to happen*), **bastare** (*to be enough*), **capitare** (*to happen*), **costare** (*to cost*), **dispiacere** (*to regret*), **sembrare** (*to seem*), **succedere** (*to happen*).

Che cosa **è successo**?	*What has happened?*
Mi è **dispiaciuto** molto.	*I have regretted it a lot.*

- All reflexive verbs use **essere** in the present perfect.

Mi sono alzata tardi ieri.   *I woke up* late yesterday.
Vi siete divertiti al parco?   *Did you have* a good time at the park?

ESERCIZIO
5·9

Translate the following sentences into Italian.

1. I don't know what happened to Peter. _____

2. It seemed to me too late to call you. _____

3. We went skiing, but there was no snow. _____

4. The prices for fruit have increased a lot. _____

5. It took three hours to get home. _____

6. Yesterday it snowed all day. _____

7. We had a great time at the beach. _____

8. They went on the plane. _____

9. My relatives left at three o'clock. _____

ESERCIZIO
5·10

Translate the following paragraph into Italian.

Last summer I went to Italy with some friends. Once in Italy, we took the train from one city to another. We liked traveling by train. It is very comfortable, and we did not have to look for parking. We walked a lot. We visited many museums, and we ate a lot of Italian ice cream. Italian ice cream is famous all over the world. We spent two weeks in Italy. We had a great time, and we will remember this trip for a long time!

_____

_____

_____

_____

_____

_____

_____

_____

_____

_____

VOCABOLARIO			
comfortable	**comodo**	summer	**estate**
once	**una volta**	trip	**viaggio**
spend	**trascorrere**	world	**mondo**

ESERCIZIO
5·11

Last year Angela went to the United States. Describe her vacation by putting the following sentences in the present perfect.

1. Angela va negli Stati Uniti.

_____

2. Parte da Milano alle otto.

_____

3. Rimane a New York per qualche giorno.

_____

4. Va a visitare le chiese e i musei di New York.

_____

5. La sera va a teatro.

_____

6. Dopo tre o quattro giorni va a Chicago.

_____

7. Fa delle piacevoli camminate lungo il lago.

_____

8. Visita i musei e va a fare molte spese.

_____

292   PRACTICE MAKES PERFECT   Complete Italian All-in-One

9. Da Chicago va a San Francisco.

_____

10. San Francisco è la città che preferisce.

_____

11. Ritorna in Italia dopo tre settimane.

_____

12. Le piace molto la vacanza negli Stati Uniti.

_____

The imperfect tense (*imperfetto*)

The imperfect tense in Italian expresses a recurrent event in the past. It is used to express continuity or actions in the past that are customary or habitual. There is no indication of the beginning or the end of the action or whether it was finished or not. It is very easy to learn but not so easy to use. It is much less commonly used in English than in Italian.

The imperfect indicative of:

- **-are** verbs is formed by dropping the infinitive ending **-are** and adding the following endings to the root: **-avo, -avi, -ava, -avamo, -avate, -avano**.

  mangiare (*to eat*) Mangi**avo**. (*I used to eat.*)

- **-ere** verbs is formed by dropping the infinitive ending **-ere** and adding the following endings to the root: **-evo, -evi, -eva, -evamo, -evate, -evano**.

  leggere (*to read*) Legg**evo**. (*I used to read.*)

- **-ire** verbs is formed by dropping the infinitive ending **-ire** and adding the following endings to the root: **-ivo, -ivi, -iva, -ivamo, -ivate, -ivano**.

  partire (*to leave*) Part**ivo** (*I used to leave.*)

The imperfect corresponds to the English expressions formed by:

used to + the infinitive: She **used to live** in New York.

was/were + the gerund: They **were living** in Italy.

would + the infinitive: He **would go** to the library every day.

The following is the complete conjugation of the imperfect tense of **-are**, **-ere**, and **-ire** regular verbs:

INFINITIVE: ROOT:	PENSARE (*to think*) PENS-	LEGGERE (*to read*) LEGG-	PARTIRE (*to leave*) PART-
io	pens**avo**	legg**evo**	part**ivo**
tu	pens**avi**	legg**evi**	part**ivi**
lui/lei	pens**ava**	legg**eva**	part**iva**
noi	pens**avamo**	legg**evamo**	part**ivamo**
voi	pens**avate**	legg**evate**	part**ivate**
loro	pens**avano**	legg**evano**	part**ivano**

The verbs **fare** (*to do, to make*), **dire** (*to say*), **bere** (*to drink*), **produrre** (*to produce*), and **porre** (*to place*) take their root for the imperfect from the original Latin infinitives, but the conjugation is regular. (All the compounds of these verbs follow the same pattern.)

INFINITIVE: ROOT:	FARE FAC-	DIRE DIC-	BERE BEV-	PRODURRE PRODUC-	PORRE PON-
io	fac**evo**	dic**evo**	bev**evo**	produc**evo**	pon**evo**
tu	fac**evi**	dic**evi**	bev**evi**	produc**evi**	pon**evi**
lui/lei	fac**eva**	dic**eva**	bev**eva**	produc**eva**	pon**eva**
noi	fac**evamo**	dic**evamo**	bev**evamo**	produc**evamo**	pon**evamo**
voi	fac**evate**	dic**evate**	bev**evate**	produc**evate**	pon**evate**
loro	fac**evano**	dic**evano**	bev**evano**	produc**evano**	pon**evano**

The present perfect is used to express an action that started and was completed in the recent past; the imperfect, however, is used with a past action without any reference to when it started or ended. It is used to express ongoing actions in the past, to describe a past action in progress, or to indicate a state of mind, age, time, or weather.

Il mio amico **veniva** sempre tardi alla lezione di italiano.	*My friend always **used to come** late to the Italian lesson.*
Quando **abitavamo** in Italia, **andavamo** sempre in montagna.	*When we **lived** in Italy, we always **went** to the mountains.*

The following are some adverbial expressions that indicate continuity and are associated with the use of the imperfect:

continuamente	continuously
costantemente	constantly
di frequente	frequently
di solito	usually
di tanto in tanto	from time to time
la domenica (il lunedì, ecc.)	on Sundays (on Mondays, etc.)
mentre	while
ogni giorno	every day
ogni giorno, ogni notte	each day, each night
ogni tanto	once in a while
qualche volta	sometime
quando	when
sempre	always
spesso	often
tutti i giorni	every day

ESERCIZIO
6·1

Rewrite the following sentences in the imperfect.

1. Di solito Maria cena presto. _____

2. I ragazzi vanno spesso in biblioteca. _____

3. I bambini piangono sempre. _____

4. Ogni tanto vado al cinema. _____

5. Vado alla spiaggia tutti i giorni. _____

6. Voi andate spesso a sciare. _____

7. Il lunedì vado a scuola. _____

8. La domenica andiamo in chiesa. _____

9. Mentre mangiate, guardate la televisione. _____

Now look at the following additional rules used with the imperfect:

- The imperfect is used when two or more actions are going on simultaneously.

Io **parlavo** e mio fratello **studiava**.	*I **was speaking** and my brother **was studying**.*
Mia mamma **cucinava**, tu **studiavi**,	*My mother **was cooking**, you **were studying**,*
e mio padre **leggeva il giornale**.	*and my father **was reading** the newspaper.*

- The imperfect is frequently used to describe people or things in the past with color, size, and personal qualities.

Tua nonna **era** molto intelligente.	*Your grandmother **was** very intelligent.*
Le strade **erano** coperte di neve.	*The streets **were covered** with snow.*

- The imperfect expresses the time of day, age, and weather in the past.

Che ore **erano**?	*What time **was** it?*
Faceva bel tempo.	*The weather **was** good.*
Era l'una e **pioveva**.	*It **was** one o'clock and it **was raining**.*

- The imperfect is used with the preposition **da** to express an event in the past. In English this requires the past perfect tense.

Nevicava da una settimana.	*It **had been snowing** for a week.*
Non **uscivamo da** tre giorni.	*We **had not gone out** for three days.*

ESERCIZIO
6·2

Rewrite the following using the correct forms of the imperfect.

1. La bambina è brava. _____

2. Gli insegnanti sono pazienti. _____

3. Le camicie sono sporche. _____

4. Le strade sono larghe. _____

5. Tu sei stanco. _____

6. Voi siete alti. _____

7. Tu sei molto magro. _____

8. Io sono molto studiosa. _____

9. Il cielo è nuvoloso. _____

Translate the following sentences into Italian.

1. I was sixteen years old. _____

2. It was very windy. _____

3. What was the weather like? _____

4. How old was your grandfather? _____

5. He was ninety years old. _____

6. The weather was very bad. _____

7. It was early. _____

8. It was very late. _____

9. It was snowing very hard. _____

Complete each sentence with the correct form of the imperfect.

1. Noi lo _____ (sapere) da molti giorni.

2. La squadra di calcio non _____ (vincere) da molte settimane.

3. Noi _____ (essere) in America da sette anni.

4. Il bambino _____ (piangere) da diverse ore.

5. Caterina _____ (vivere) a San Francisco da tre anni.

6. Da quanto tempo _____ (tu-studiare) l'italiano?

7. Loro _____ (viaggiare) da tre mesi.

8. Carlo _____ (andare) a nuotare da due settimane.

9. L'orologio non _____ (funzionare) da diversi giorni.

Answer the following questions positively with complete sentences in the imperfect.

1. Leggevate dei bei libri in classe? _____

2. Uscivi di frequente con i tuoi amici? _____

3. Andavi al mare ogni estate? _____

4. Voi preferivate il mare o la montagna? _____

5. Avevi molti amici? _____

6. Capivano bene l'italiano? _____

7. Visitavate spesso i vostri parenti? _____

8. Ti piaceva giocare al calcio? _____

9. Andavate spesso in Italia? _____

ESERCIZIO
6·6

Translate into Italian the following letter.

Dear Maria,

I just returned from a vacation in Rome. The weather was beautiful, and the sun was shining every day. I would get up early and take a walk in the park. The city was very quiet in the morning. At the end of the park there was a nice café, and I would stop there for a hot cappuccino. I would sit and read the Italian newspaper. I did not like to read it because it was full of bad news. Afterwards, I would return to the hotel, take a shower, and go to museums and churches. When I was tired I would go back to the hotel, sit under the umbrella by the pool, and I would write postcards. It was a beautiful and unforgettable vacation, but too short.

_____

_____

_____

_____

_____

_____

VOCABOLARIO

afterwards	**dopodichè**		postcards	**cartoline**
to get up	**alzarsi**		shining	**splendeva**
newspaper	**giornale**		shower	**doccia**
pool	**piscina**		unforgettable	**indimenticabile**

Comparison of the present perfect and the imperfect

Both the present perfect and the imperfect are past tenses and are often used together in the narration of past events. However, they express different kinds of actions and cannot be used interchangeably. Look at the following:

- The present perfect states events or actions that happened at a specific time.

Ieri sera siamo usciti alle otto.   *Last night we went out at eight.*

- The imperfect describes ongoing actions or events in the past.

  Uscivamo tutte le sere alle otto.   *We went out every night at eight.*

- The present perfect expresses an action or an event that went on or was repeated a definite number of times.

  Lei ha studiato sabato e domenica.   *She studied Saturday and Sunday.*

- The imperfect describes repeated or habitual actions in the past.

  Lei studiava tutti i sabati e le domeniche.   *She used to study every Saturday and Sunday.*

- The imperfect is used to describe two different actions going on at the same time in the past.

  Io parlavo al telefono **mentre lui guardava** la partita.   *I was talking on the phone while he was watching the game.*

- The imperfect describes an action that was going on in the past, when another action or event took place. This last action or event is in the present perfect.

  Voi **dormivate quando** lei **è venuta** a casa.   *You were sleeping when she came home.*

ESERCIZIO
6·7

Translate the following sentences into Italian, using the correct forms of the present perfect and imperfect.

1. I ate at the restaurant./I used to eat at the restaurant.

   _____

2. I traveled a lot./I used to travel a lot.

   _____

3. I went to the doctor./I used to go to the doctor.

   _____

4. You called Marco on Saturday./You called Marco every Saturday.

   _____

5. They finished working late./Usually they finished working late.

   _____

6. I swam all morning long./I used to swim every morning.

   _____

7. Last night we went to a party./We went to a party every weekend.

   _____

8. Last summer he went to the zoo./He went to the zoo every summer.

_____

9. You (pl.) went to the park./You (pl.) used to go to the park.

_____

Complete the sentences below, using the imperfect or the present perfect as necessary.

1. _____ (andare) molto veloce quando la polizia lo (l')
   _____ (fermare).

2. Io _____ (mangiare) le lasagne quando _____
   (trovare) un insetto nel piatto.

3. Tu _____ (essere) a casa quando io _____ (chiamare).

4. Che tempo _____ (fare) quando _____ (tu-uscire)
   di casa questa mattina?

5. Quanti anni _____ (tu-avere) quando _____ (cominciare) l'università?

6. Mentre _____ (io-studiare) _____ (loro-suonare)
   alla porta e _____ (portare) una bella pianta.

7. _____ (io-avere) vent'anni quando _____ (cominciare) a sciare.

8. Non _____ (io-avere) la penna e non _____ (potere) scriverti.

9. _____ (Loro-essere) preoccupati perchè non _____ (io-chiamare).

Translate the following sentences into Italian, using the imperfect and the present perfect.

1. We were eating dessert when you arrived.

_____

2. While I was studying, somebody rang the doorbell.

_____

3. Were you tired when you came home?

_____

4. What was the weather like in Italy?

_____

5. It was not raining when I went out.

_____

6. She was taking a shower when I called her.

_____

7. They were playing golf when it started to rain.

_____

8. While I was studying, you went to the movies.

_____

9. Were you waiting for the bus when he saw you?

_____

Translate the following paragraphs into Italian, using the vocabulary words provided on the next page.

It was a beautiful day. The sun was shining, and it was a warm spring day. Carlo was happy because he had a date with a beautiful girl. He wanted to take her to the soccer game and then to a nice restaurant.

Unfortunately, the girl did not come, the weather changed, and it started to thunder and rain very hard. He got all wet. He returned home, turned on the television, and watched the game on TV. His team lost. This day did not turn out very well. He went to bed in a bad mood.

_____

_____

_____

_____

_____

_____

VOCABOLARIO

appointment/date	**appuntamento**	spring	**primaverile**
mood	**umore**	thunder	**tuonare**
soccer	**calcio**	weather	**tempo**

The preterite
(*passato remoto*)

The preterite is a past tense, also called the historical past. It is mostly used in narrative writing of one-time events in the past. It is quite often seen in books, newspapers, documents, etc. In speech and informal letter writing, it has been replaced by the present perfect. In northern Italy, people seem to use the present perfect more frequently when expressing past events; however, the preterite is more frequently used in southern and central Italy even when speaking of recent happenings.

Both the present perfect and preterite are commonly translated into English by the simple past (*I bought, you wrote*).

The preterite of regular verbs is formed by dropping the infinitive endings **-are**, **-ere**, and **-ire** and adding to the root the following endings:

- Verbs ending in **-are**: **-ai**, **-asti**, **-ò**, **-ammo**, **-aste**, **-arono**

- Verbs ending in **-ere**: **-ei**, **-esti**, **-è**, **-emmo**, **-este**, **-erono** (**io**, **lui**, **lei**, and **loro** forms have an alternate ending **-etti**, **-ette**, and **-ettero**)

- Verbs ending in **-ire**: **-ii**, **-isti**, **-ì**, **-immo**, **-iste**, **-irono**

	COMPRARE (*to buy*)	VENDERE (*to sell*)	SENTIRE (*to hear*)
io	compr**ai**	vend**ei** (vend**etti**)	sent**ii**
tu	compr**asti**	vend**esti**	sent**isti**
lui/lei	compr**ò**	vend**è** (vend**ette**)	sent**ì**
noi	compr**ammo**	vend**emmo**	sent**immo**
voi	compr**aste**	vend**este**	sent**iste**
loro	compr**arono**	vend**erono** (vend**ettero**)	sent**irono**

ESERCIZIO
7·1

Complete the following sentences with the correct endings of the preterite.

1. Io arriv _____ tardi a scuola.

2. Tu parl _____ troppo.

3. Il bambino gioc _____ tutto il giorno.

4. Lei and _____ a scuola.

5. Mia mamma prepar _____ un ottimo pranzo.

6. Voi lavor _____ fino a tardi.

7. Noi parl _____ al telefono con loro.

8. Tu non parl _____ al telefono.

9. Voi non cant _____ molte canzoni.

ESERCIZIO
7·2

Complete the following sentences with the correct forms of the verbs in parentheses
in the preterite.

1. Io _____ (invitare) i miei amici alla festa.

2. Tu _____ (camminare) molto lentamente.

3. Lei _____ (comprare) molti bei vestiti.

4. Noi _____ (preparare) le valige.

5. Voi _____ (pagare) il conto.

6. Loro _____ (cenare) in un ristorante molto famoso.

7. Io _____ (andare) in Italia con mio marito.

8. Tu non _____ (telefonare) ai tuoi fratelli.

9. Voi non _____ (ascoltare) i buoni consigli.

ESERCIZIO
7·3

Rewrite the following sentences in the preterite.

1. Tu viaggi molto. _____

2. Io mangio con le mie sorelle. _____

3. Lei aspetta suo marito. _____

4. Lui visita il museo. _____

5. Noi telefoniamo a Carlo. _____

6. Voi comprate molti libri. _____

7. Loro comprano una casa nuova. _____

8. Io non preparò il letto per gli ospiti. _____

9. Tu non lavi la maglia. _____

Complete the following sentences with the required form of the preterite, using the verbs in parentheses.

1. Io _____ (sedere) con i miei amici.

2. Tu _____ (ripetere) bene le parole.

3. Lui _____ (dovere) ritornare a casa.

4. Lei _____ (vendere) l'automobile.

5. Noi _____ (ricevere) le cartoline.

6. Voi _____ (credere) tutti.

7. Loro _____ (ripetere) quello che avevano sentito.

8. Noi non _____ (battere) alla finestra.

9. Loro non _____ (credere) Giovanna.

Rewrite the following sentences in the preterite.

1. Io ricevo la lettera da mio figlio. _____

2. Tu vendi la tua casa. _____

3. Lei siede da sola nel suo grande giardino. _____

4. Noi crediamo a tutti. _____

5. Il pappagallo ripete quello che sente. _____

6. Voi ricevete una buona notizia. _____

7. Loro abbattono l'albero. _____

8. Giovanni e Carla vendono la loro casa. _____

9. Lo studente deve studiare molto. _____

The following are some common expressions that are often used with the preterite:

ieri	*yesterday*
ieri pomeriggio	*yesterday afternoon*
ieri sera	*last night*
l'altro giorno	*the other day*
la settimana scorsa	*last week*
il mese/l'anno scorso	*last month, year*
l'estate/l'inverno scorso	*last summer, winter*
poco fa	*a little while ago*
per molto tempo	*for a long time*
all'improvviso	*all of a sudden*

Complete the following sentences with the correct forms of the preterite.

1. L'estate scorsa io _____ (leggere) un bellissimo libro.

2. Carlo, dove _____ (passare) le vacanze?

3. All'improvviso tutti se ne _____ (andare).

4. Il mese scorso tu non _____ (venire) alla riunione.

5. Ieri sera lui _____ (venire) a casa molto tardi.

6. Poco fa loro _____ (partire) per l'Europa.

7. Da molto tempo io non _____ (andare) a fare yoga.

8. L'altro giorno io _____ (vedere) un topo in casa.

9. Ieri pomeriggio io _____ (riposare) per due ore.

Irregular verbs in the preterite

Many Italian verbs that are irregular in the preterite have the **-ere** ending in the infinitive. They can be grouped together according to their irregularities. You will notice that the verbs ending in **-ere** are regular in the **tu**, **noi**, and **voi** forms. The infinitive ending is dropped to form the root of the verb. But in the **io**, **lui**, **lei**, and **loro** forms, the root is modified.

> **chiudere** (*to close*): **chiusi**, chiudesti, **chiuse**, chiudemmo, chiudeste, **chiusero**

The following **-ere** verbs will be grouped according to their root irregularities.

Verbs with a single -s-

Many verbs ending in **-ere** have an irregular root in the **io**, **lui**, **lei**, and **loro** forms of the preterite. They have regular roots in the other forms.

> **chiedere** (*to ask*): **chiesi**, chiedesti, **chiese**, chiedemmo, chiedeste, **chiesero**
> **cogliere** (*to gather*): **colsi**, cogliesti, **colse**, cogliemmo, coglieste, **colsero**
> **concludere** (*to conclude*): **conclusi**, concludesti, **concluse**, concludemmo, concludeste, **conclusero**
> **decidere** (*to decide*): **decisi**, decidesti, **decise**, decidemmo, decideste, **decisero**
> **dividere** (*to divide*): **divisi**, dividesti, **divise**, dividemmo, divideste, **divisero**
> **mettere** (*to put*): **misi**, mettesti, **mise**, mettemmo, metteste, **misero**
> **prendere** (*to take*): **presi**, prendesti, **prese**, prendemmo, prendeste, **presero**
> **ridere** (*to laugh*): **risi**, ridesti, **rise**, ridemmo, rideste, **risero**
> **rimanere** (to stay): **rimasi**, rimanesti, **rimase**, rimanemmo, rimaneste, **rimasero**
> **scendere** (*to descend*): **scesi**, scendesti, **scese**, scendemmo, scendeste, **scesero**
> **spegnere** (*to turn off*): **spensi**, spegnesti, **spense**, spegnemmo, spegneste, **spensero**
> **spendere** (*to spend*): **spesi**, spendesti, **spese**, spendemmo, spendeste, **spesero**
> **vincere** (*to win*): **vinsi**, vincesti, **vinse**, vincemmo, vinceste, **vinsero**

-ere verbs that double the -s- (-ss-)

The following -ere verbs double the -s- in the **io**, **lui**, **lei**, and **loro** forms:

discutere (*to discuss*): **discussi**, discutesti, **discusse**, discutemmo, discuteste, **discussero**
leggere (*to read*): **lessi**, leggesti, **lesse**, leggemmo, leggeste, **lessero**
scrivere (*to write*): **scrissi**, scrivesti, **scrisse**, scrivemmo, scriveste, **scrissero**
vivere (*to live*): **vissi**, vincesti, **visse**, vincemmo, vinceste, **vissero**

-ere verbs with a double consonant other than -ss-

The following verbs double the consonant of the infinitive root in the **io**, **lui**, **lei**, and **loro** forms:

cadere (*to fall*): **caddi**, cadesti, **cadde**, cademmo, cadeste, **caddero**
conoscere (*to know*): **conobbi**, conoscesti, **conobbe**, conoscemmo, conosceste, **conobbero**
rompere (*to break*): **ruppi**, rompesti, **ruppe**, rompemmo, rompeste, **ruppero**
sapere (*to know*): **seppi**, sapesti, **seppe**, sapemmo, sapeste, **seppero**
tenere (*to keep*): **tenni**, tenesti, **tenne**, tenemmo, teneste, **tennero**
volere (*to want*): **volli**, volesti, **volle**, volemmo, voleste, **vollero**

Bere uses the root from the original Italian infinitive **bevere**. It doubles the -v- in the **io**, **lui**, **lei**, and **loro** forms.

bere (*to drink*): **bevvi**, bevesti, **bevve**, bevemmo, beveste, **bevvero**

ESERCIZIO 7·7

Complete the following sentences with the preterite in the correct forms of the verbs in parentheses.

1. Le pere _____ (cadere) dagli alberi.

2. Io non _____ (chiedere) niente a nessuno.

3. Tu _____ (chiudere) la porta.

4. Lui _____ (decidere) di andare in Italia.

5. Lei _____ (discutere) con i suoi fratelli.

6. Noi _____ (prendere) un caffè al bar.

7. Voi _____ (leggere) tutto il giornale.

8. Loro _____ (scrivere) una lunga lettera.

9. Io non _____ (vivere) in Italia per molto tempo.

Complete the following sentences with the preterite of the following irregular **-ere** verbs.

1. Io _____ (conoscere) molte persone importanti.

2. Il bambino _____ (cadere) dalla sedia.

3. Io _____ (volere) parlare con il direttore.

4. Lei _____ (sapere) arrivare a casa tua.

5. Noi _____ (rompere) il ghiaccio.

6. Voi _____ (dovere) andare all'ambasciata.

7. Loro non _____ (tenere) la porta chiusa.

8. Tu non _____ (conoscere) le mie sorelle.

9. Carlo non _____ (volere) vedere il risultato.

Dire doubles the -s- in the **io**, **lui**, **lei**, and **loro** forms as follows:

> **Dire** (*to tell, to say*): **dissi**, dicesti, **disse**, dicemmo, diceste, **dissero**

Venire and **divenire** double the -n- of the infinitive in the **io**, **lui**, **lei**, and **loro** forms:

> **Venire** (*to come*): **venni**, venisti, **venne**, venimmo, veniste, **vennero**
> **Divenire** (*to become*): **divenni**, divenisti, **divenne**, divenimmo, diveniste, **divennero**

Complete the following sentences with the irregular **-ire** verbs in the preterite in the correct forms.

1. Io _____ (dire) molte cose a mia mamma.

2. Tu non _____ (dire) niente a nessuno.

3. Chi _____ (venire) a casa vostra?

4. I miei amici _____ (venire) a prendere il tè.

5. Noi _____ (venire) a casa tardi.

6. Voi _____ (venire) al cinema con noi.

7. Loro _____ (divenire) molto alti.

8. Noi _____ (dire) tutto alla polizia.

9. Lui non _____ (venire) con i suoi amici.

-ere verbs with -qu-

Nascere (*to be born*) and **piacere** (*to like*) have a -**qu**- in the **io**, **lui**, **lei**, and **loro** forms of the preterite. **Nascere** also drops the -**s**- in the same forms.

	NASCERE (*to be born*)	PIACERE (*to like*)
io	**nacqui**	**piacqui**
tu	**nascesti**	**piacesti**
lui/lei	**nacque**	**piacque**
noi	**nascemmo**	**piacemmo**
voi	**nasceste**	**piaceste**
loro	**nacquero**	**piacquero**

The preterite of *fare*

Fare takes the root for the preterite from the Latin infinitive **facere** from which it originates.

	FARE (*to make, do*)
io	**feci**
tu	**facesti**
lui/lei	**fece**
noi	**facemmo**
voi	**faceste**
loro	**fecero**

ESERCIZIO 7·10

Complete the following sentences with the required forms of the preterite using the verbs in parentheses.

1. Io _____ (nascere) in Italia.

2. Anche tu _____ (nascere) in Italia.

3. Quando _____ (nascere) mio fratello, io avevo due anni.

4. Lui _____ (piacere) ai miei genitori.

5. Il vostro modo di fare _____ (dispiacere) ai vostri amici.

6. Loro _____ (fare) una bellissima festa.

7. Mi _____ (piacere) andare in aereo.

8. Tu _____ (fare) molti dolci.

9. La commedia non _____ (piacere) a nessuno.

The preterite of *essere* and *avere*

Essere and **avere** have irregular forms in the preterite as shown below.

	ESSERE	AVERE
io	**fui**	**ebbi**
tu	**fosti**	**avesti**
lui/lei, Lei	**fu**	**ebbe**
noi	**fummo**	**avemmo**
voi	**foste**	**aveste**
loro, Loro	**furono**	**ebbero**

ESERCIZIO 7·11

Complete the following sentences with the correct forms of the preterite using the verbs in parentheses.

1. Dante _____ (nascere) nel 1215.

2. L'anno scorso noi _____ (andare) in Cina.

3. Mio nonno _____ (essere) ammalato per molto tempo.

4. Ti _____ (piacere) la sfilata di moda?

5. Tre mesi fa tu _____ (fare) gli esami di maturità.

6. Voi _____ (essere) tutti promossi.

7. L'anno scorso noi _____ (fare) una bella vacanza.

8. Io non _____ (avere) molto tempo da perdere.

9. Noi _____ (fare) molte cose.

ESERCIZIO 7·12

Rewrite the following sentences in the preterite.

1. Io rispondo alla tua lettera. _____

2. Tua madre compra una collana di perle. _____

3. Lui rompe molti bicchieri. _____

4. Gli studenti sanno la poesia. _____

5. Tu compri un bel paio di scarpe. _____

6. I nonni vogliono restare a casa. _____

7. Maria non viene a scuola. _____

8. I bambini piangono tutto il giorno. _____

9. Le giornate sono molto lunghe. _____

Translate the following sentences into Italian using the preterite.

1. I arrived last night at nine. _____

2. We visited the museum two days ago. _____

3. I went to the mountains to ski. _____

4. You didn't finish the soup. _____

5. I didn't buy the purse at the market. _____

6. We arrived late at the station. _____

7. They asked me to go to the game with them. _____

8. Carlo spent his vacation in Hawaii. _____

9. He had a lot of fun. _____

Rewrite the following sentences replacing the preterite with the present perfect.

1. Tu arrivasti molto stanco. _____

2. Nessuno ci aiutò. _____

3. Leonardo fu un genio. _____

4. Noi non vedemmo niente di bello. _____

5. Non ricordano dove misero le chiavi. _____

6. Aprii la finestra, ma faceva freddo. _____

7. Giovanna rispose subito alla mia lettera. _____

8. Andai a comprare due francobolli. _____

9. L'estate scorsa fece molto caldo. _____

Translate the following paragraph into Italian.

In 1954 television arrived in Italy. Slowly, little by little, it came into every house.
Everybody wanted to buy it. Some programs were especially successful. People liked variety
shows and quiz programs. The news shows were very popular. The television allowed people
to gather and come together in homes and in bars. Italians made sacrifices to buy a television
of their own. The arrival of the television changed everyone's lives.

_____

_____

_____

_____

_____

_____

_____

_____

VOCABOLARIO

allowed	**permettere**	sacrifices	**sacrifici**
to gather	**riunirsi**	variety show	**programmi di varietà**
programs	**programmi**		

The past perfect (*trapassato prossimo*), preterite perfect (*trapassato remoto*), and future perfect (*futuro anteriore*)

These tenses are formed by combining the appropriate tense of the auxiliary verb **avere** or **essere** with the past participle of the verb. For each of the simple tenses, there is a corresponding compound tense.

SIMPLE TENSE		COMPOUND TENSE	
PRESENT	**io parlo** *I speak*	PRESENT PERFECT	**io ho parlato** *I have spoken*
IMPERFECT	**io parlavo** *I spoke* *I was speaking*	PAST PERFECT	**io avevo parlato** *I had spoken* *I had been* *speaking*
PRETERITE	**io parlai** *I spoke*	PRETERITE PERFECT	**io ebbi parlato** *I had spoken*
FUTURE	**io parlerò** *I will speak*	FUTURE PERFECT	**io avrò parlato** *I will have* *spoken*

You have already studied the present perfect. To decide which auxiliary to choose, the agreement of the past participle, and the formation of the negative, the other compound tenses follow the same rules as those already seen in the present perfect.

The past perfect (*trapassato prossimo*)

This tense is used to express an action in the past that happened before another one and was completed in the past. Its name means "more than perfect," or further back in the past. It is used in Italian the same way it is used in English. A more recent action can be expressed in the present perfect, preterite, or imperfect. The past perfect corresponds to the English *had + past participle (I had understood)*.

It is formed with the imperfect of the auxiliary **avere** or **essere** + the past participle of the verb.

Io avevo parlato con mia sorella.   *I had spoken* with my sister.
Io ero andato al cinema.   *I had gone* to the movies.

	PARLARE (*I had spoken*)	VENDERE (*I had sold*)	FINIRE (*I had finished*)	ANDARE (*I had gone*)
io	**avevo parlato**	**avevo venduto**	**avevo finito**	**ero andato/a**
tu	**avevi parlato**	**avevi venduto**	**avevi finito**	**eri andato/a**
lui/lei	**aveva parlato**	**aveva venduto**	**aveva finito**	**era andato/a**
noi	**avevamo parlato**	**avevamo venduto**	**avevamo finito**	**eravamo andati/e**
voi	**avevate parlato**	**avevate venduto**	**avevate finito**	**eravate andati/e**
loro	**avevano parlato**	**avevano venduto**	**avevano finito**	**erano andati/e**

Past participles conjugated with **essere** agree in gender and number with the subject.

Le ragazze **erano andate**.   *The girls **had gone**.*

The negative is formed by placing **non** in front of the auxiliary.

Io **non avevo mangiato**.   *I **had not eaten**.*

The past participles conjugated with **avere** agree in gender and number with the direct object pronouns **la**, **le**, and **li**. It is optional with **mi**, **ti**, **ci**, or **vi**.

Le avevo comprat**e**.   ***I had bought them.***

ESERCIZIO
8·1

Translate the following sentences into Italian, using the past perfect.

1. They had spoken with him. _____

2. They had eaten. _____

3. They had already eaten. _____

4. He had not returned yet. _____

5. They had arrived late. _____

6. I had not finished yet. _____

7. Rita had confirmed her flight. _____

8. We had traveled. _____

9. They had already eaten. _____

_____

ESERCIZIO
8·2

Translate the following sentences into English, using either the present perfect or past perfect.

1. Io ho visto. _____

2. Tu avevi visto. _____

3. Lui era andato. _____

4. Avevano letto. _____

5. Io ho giocato. _____

6. Io avevo giocato. _____

7. Non abbiamo letto. _____

8. Loro non avevano finito. _____

9. Avevate già mangiato? _____

The preterite perfect (*trapassato remoto*)

The preterite perfect is used in place of the past perfect but with the same meaning. It is used with the preterite of **essere** or **avere** and the *past participle* of the verb.

In conversation the preterite perfect is replaced by the past perfect. This tense is used mainly in writing and literature when the verb in the main clause is in the preterite. The meaning is the same as that of the past perfect.

| **Dopo che ebbi parlato** con lei, mi sentii meglio. | *After I talked* with her, I felt better. |

	PARLARE, VENDERE, FINIRE (*I had spoken, sold, finished*)	ANDARE (*I had gone*)
io	**ebbi parlato, venduto, finito**	**fui andato/a**
tu	**avesti parlato, venduto, finito**	**fosti andato/a**
lui/lei	**ebbe parlato, venduto, finito**	**fu andato/a**
noi	**avemmo parlato, venduto, finito**	**fummo andati/e**
voi	**aveste parlato, venduto, finito**	**foste andati/e**
loro	**ebbero parlato, venduto, finito**	**furono andati/e**

ESERCIZIO 8·3

Change the preterite into the preterite perfect.

1. Io lessi molti libri. _____

2. Tu partisti alle tre. _____

3. Gli ospiti partirono. _____

4. Voi cantaste bene. _____

5. Appena arrivai, io spensi la luce. _____

6. Noi uscimmo presto. _____

7. Lei piantò molti fiori. _____

8. Noi credemmo nel futuro. _____

9. Loro mangiarono troppo. _____

Translate the following sentences into Italian, using the preterite perfect.

1. The guests had eaten.

_____

2. I had slept.

_____

3. You had spoken.

_____

4. When they had arrived, we greeted them.

_____

5. As soon as he had finished his homework, he went out to play.

_____

6. After we had written the postcards, we mailed them.

_____

7. After you had taken a bath, you got dressed.

_____

8. After I had seen the children, I was happy.

_____

9. As soon as you had returned, many things went wrong.

_____

The future perfect (*futuro anteriore*)

The future perfect is used to express an action that will be completed in the future. It is formed by combining the future of the auxiliary **avere** or **essere** and the past participle of the verb.

Avrete finito i compiti prima di sabato?	***Will you have finished*** your homework before Saurday?

	PARLARE, VENDERE, FINIRE (*I will have spoken, sold, finished*)	ANDARE (*I will have gone*)
io	avrò parlato, venduto, finito	sarò andato/a
tu	avrai parlato, venduto, finito	sarai andato/a
lui/lei	avrà parlato, venduto, finito	sarà andato/a
noi	avremo parlato, venduto, finito	saremo andati/e
voi	avrete parlato, venduto, finito	sarete andati/e
loro	avranno parlato, venduto, finito	saranno andati/e

Very often the future perfect is used after such expressions as: **quando**, **appena**, **finchè**, or **finchè non**.

Ti telefonerò **appena sarò arrivato** in Italia.

*I will call you **as soon as I have arrived** in Italy.*

With **se**, the future perfect expresses an action that happens before another future action.

Se avrete pulito la vostra camera, potrete uscire.

***If you have cleaned** your room, you'll be able to go out.*

The future perfect is used to express possibility, doubt, or supposition when referring to the past.

Che cosa **sarà successo**?
Saranno già **arrivati**?

*What **could have happened**?*
***Could they have** already **arrived**?*

Translate the following sentences into Italian, using the future perfect.

1. I will have finished. _____

2. You (sing.) will have arrived. _____

3. He will have gotten married. _____

4. Everything will have changed. _____

5. We will have gone. _____

6. They will have closed the door. _____

7. Nothing will be changed. _____

8. She will have finished. _____

9. You (sing.) will have cleaned. _____

Change the future into the future perfect.

1. Io andrò a casa.

2. Tu studierai.

3. Lui parlerà con il direttore.

4. Lei andrà in Italia.

5. Noi partiremo.

6. Voi avrete molti bambini.

7. Loro costruiranno la casa.

8. Noi non arriveremo tardi.

9. Gli astronauti andranno sulla luna.

Translate the following paragraphs into Italian.

After we have visited Rome, we will go back to the United States. If we haven't spent all our money we will go back next summer. When we have seen all of the northern regions of Italy, we will start visiting the central part of the country.

When we went the last time, we visited Venice and its surroundings. We went to the beautiful wine country near Verona and to the lakes. I had never dreamed of seeing such beautiful sights. Many people had told us that Italy was very beautiful and we had wanted to see it, and now we never tire of going back there.

_____

_____

_____

_____

_____

_____

_____

_____

_____

_____

_____

VOCABOLARIO

country	**paese**	spent	**speso**
dreamed	**sognato**	surroundings	**dintorni**
lakes	**laghi**	sights	**vedute, panorami**
regions	**regioni**	tire	**stancare**

The present conditional (*condizionale presente*)

In Italian as in English, the present conditional tense is frequently used to express an action that depends on another fact expressed or implied, or to express a future hypothetical situation.

Comprerei una casa, ma non ho i soldi.	*I would buy a house, but I don't have the money.*

English forms the present conditional by using the auxiliary *would*; Italian forms the present conditional by adding appropriate endings to the end of the infinitive. The present conditional of regular verbs is formed by dropping the final -**e**- of the infinitive and adding the endings -**ei**, -**esti**, -**ebbe**, -**emmo**, -**este**, -**ebbero**. As with the future tense, the -**a**- of -**are** verbs changes to -**e**- (**parl**e**rei**).

	PARLARE (*I would speak*)	VENDERE (*I would sell*)	SENTIRE (*I would hear*)
io	parler**ei**	vender**ei**	sentir**ei**
tu	parler**esti**	vender**esti**	sentir**esti**
lui/lei	parler**ebbe**	vender**ebbe**	sentir**ebbe**
noi	parler**emmo**	vender**emmo**	sentir**emmo**
voi	parler**este**	vender**este**	sentir**este**
loro	parler**ebbero**	vender**ebbero**	sentir**ebbero**

ESERCIZIO 9·1

Complete the following sentences, using the correct forms of the present conditional tense for the verbs in parentheses.

1. Io _____ (cantare), ma ho mal di gola.

2. Tu _____ (visitare) i nonni, ma sei troppo stanco.

3. Lui _____ (comprare) una macchina nuova, ma non ha i soldi.

4. Lei _____ (preparare) la cena, ma non ha tempo.

5. Voi _____ (parlare) francese, ma non lo sapete.

6. Loro _____ (cenare) con voi, ma è troppo tardi.

7. Io _____ (ballare), ma mi fanno male i piedi.

8. Tu _____ (lavare) i piatti, ma non c'è acqua calda.

9. Lei _____ (camminare), ma piove.

*Complete the following sentences, putting the **-ere** and **-ire** verbs in the present conditional.*

1. Io _____ (leggere), ma ho sonno.

2. Tu _____ (aprire) le finestre, ma fa freddo.

3. Lui _____ (capire) ma, non ha studiato.

4. Lei _____ (ripetere) le parole, ma non le ha sentite bene.

5. Noi _____ (finire), ma dobbiamo andare a casa.

6. Loro _____ (friggere) le patate, ma non hanno l'olio.

7. Voi _____ (vendere) la macchina, ma nessuno la vuole.

8. Io _____ (servire) il tè, ma non piace a nessuno.

9. Tu _____ (chiudere), ma la porta è aperta.

Rewrite the following expressions in Italian, using the present conditional.

1. I would start _____

2. you (sing.) would speak _____

3. you (sing.) would not speak _____

4. he would eat _____

5. she would clean _____

6. we would not arrive _____

7. she would not think _____

8. we would swim _____

9. they would look _____

Verbs that are regular in the future are also regular in the present conditional. Verbs ending in **-ciare** and **-giare** drop the **-i-** and have **-ce-** and **-ge-** in the root of the present conditional. Verbs ending in **-care** and **-gare** add an **-h-** to keep the hard sound of the **-c-** (**che**) and **-g-** (**ghe**).

| **Io comincerei** a mangiare. | *I would start* eating. |
| **Io pagherei** il conto. | *I would pay* the bill. |

Complete the following sentences with the present conditional of the verbs in parentheses in the correct forms.

1. Io _____ (mangiare) molto, ma non voglio ingrassare.

2. Tu _____ (viaggiare), ma non ti piace.

3. Lui _____ (giocare) alle carte, ma non ha tempo.

4. Lei _____ (pagare), ma non ha i soldi.

5. Noi _____ (mangiare), ma non ci piace il pesce.

6. Voi _____ (cominciare) a camminare, ma non conoscete la strada.

7. Loro _____ (viaggiare), ma non ci sono treni.

8. Tu non _____ (mangiare) mai la trippa.

9. Tu _____ (cominciare) a guardare il film?

All direct and indirect object pronouns, including **ne**, precede the present conditional tense of the verb.

The same verbs that are irregular in the future are also irregular in the present conditional. The same root for these verbs is used for both the future and the present conditional. The following are the most commonly used verbs with irregular roots in the present conditional:

	DARE	STARE	FARE	ESSERE
io	darei	starei	farei	sarei
tu	daresti	staresti	faresti	saresti
lui/lei	darebbe	starebbe	farebbe	sarebbe
noi	daremmo	staremmo	faremmo	saremmo
voi	dareste	stareste	fareste	sareste
loro	darebbero	starebbero	farebbero	sarebbero

	ANDARE	AVERE	CADERE	DOVERE
io	andrei	avrei	cadrei	dovrei
tu	andresti	avresti	cadresti	dovresti
lui/lei	andrebbe	avrebbe	cadrebbe	dovrebbe
noi	andremmo	avremmo	cadremmo	dovremmo
voi	andreste	avreste	cadreste	dovreste
loro	andrebbero	avrebbero	cadrebbero	dovrebbero

	POTERE	SAPERE	VEDERE	VIVERE
io	potrei	saprei	vedrei	vivrei
tu	potresti	sapresti	vedresti	vivresti
lui/lei	potrebbe	saprebbe	vedrebbe	vivrebbe
noi	potremmo	sapremmo	vedremmo	vivremmo
voi	potreste	sapreste	vedreste	vivreste
loro	potrebbero	saprebbero	vedrebbero	vivrebbero

	BERE	RIMANERE	TENERE	VENIRE
io	berrei	rimarrei	terrei	verrei
tu	berresti	rimarresti	terresti	verresti
lui/lei	berrebbe	rimarrebbe	terrebbe	verrebbe
noi	berremmo	rimarremmo	terremmo	verremmo
voi	berreste	rimarreste	terreste	verreste
loro	berrebbero	rimarrebbero	terrebbero	verrebbero

	VOLERE
io	vorrei
tu	vorresti
lui/lei	vorrebbe
noi	vorremmo
voi	vorreste
loro	vorrebbero

Following is a list of how and when the present conditional should be used:

- The present conditional is used to express *would* when referring to actions that may never materialize.

  Sarebbe una buona idea,
  ma non so se ce la faremo.

  It would be a good idea,
  but I don't know if we can make it.

- The present conditional can be used as it is in English to soften a request or a command. It is also often used with dovere, potere, and volere to express a suggestion, a wish, a preference, etc.

  Mi **faresti** un grosso favore?
  Lui **dovrebbe** chiamare sua madre.

  Would you do me a big favor?
  He should call his mother.

- The present conditional is used in indirect speech.

  Si chiedeva quando
    potrebbe rivederla.

  He was asking himself when
  he could see her again.

- The present conditional is used to express doubt or uncertainty about information being given.

  Secondo lui, quell'uomo
    potrebbe essere un ladro.

  According to him that man
  could be a thief.

Rewrite the following sentences in English.

1. Comprerei molto pane.

_____

2. Vedresti tutti i tuoi amici e parenti.

_____

3. Lui sentirebbe le ultime notizie.

_____

4. Lei comprerebbe molti vestiti.

_____

5. Vorremmo andare al cinema.

_____

6. Tu e Paolo fareste molte camminate.

_____

7. Giocherebbero al pallone.

_____

8. Non leggeresti solo il giornale.

_____

9. Non piangerebbero sempre.

_____

10. Verreste a teatro con noi?

_____

11. Sareste contenti di venire a casa?

_____

12. Non sareste stanchi?

_____

13. Non saremmo in troppi?

_____

14. Fareste un favore alla signora?

_____

15. Secondo me, sarebbe meglio dormire.

_____

_____

Answer the following questions with complete sentences in the present conditional tense, using the suggestions given in parentheses.

1. Dove ti piacerebbe andare? (in montagna)

_____

2. Viaggeresti da solo/a? (sì)

_____

3. Avresti bisogno di aiuto per fare le prenotazioni? (no)

_____

4. Quando potresti partire? (fra una settimana)

_____

5. Vorresti noleggiare una macchina? (sì)

_____

6. Preferiresti un albergo o un agriturismo? (agriturismo)

_____

7. Quanti giorni vorresti stare in vacanza? (due settimane)

_____

8. Chi vorresti incontrare? (degli italiani)

_____

9. Dove vorresti mangiare? (in tipici ristoranti della montagna)

_____

You and your friend are writing to the coordinator of the Italian language school in Florence. Translate the following sentences into Italian.

1. My friend and I would like to study Italian in Italy this summer.

   _____

2. We would come at the beginning of summer.

   _____

3. We would like to spend two months in Florence.

   _____

4. We would like to find a small hotel.

   _____

5. If possible, we would prefer to live with an Italian family.

   _____

6. We would like to stay with a family where nobody speaks English.

   _____

7. When could we enroll?

   _____

8. How many students would be in each class?

   _____

9. How much would it cost for everything?

   _____

10. Where should we send the payment for the courses?

    _____

11. When could we call you?

    _____

12. Would we need a special permit to stay in Italy?

    _____

13. When would the courses start?

    _____

Translate the following paragraph into English.

Dovrei studiare ma non ne ho voglia. Penso all'estate e dove potrei andare in vacanza. Mentre faccio progetti per le vacanze, e penso dove preferirei andare, vorrei bere qualche cosa di fresco. Non c'è niente nel frigorifero. Sarebbe bene fare del tè freddo. I miei genitori vorrebbero andare in montagna, io preferirei andare in campeggio. Potremmo andare in Puglia o in Calabria. Mio padre potrebbe venire con il pulmino perchè la mia mini è troppo piccola e non ci si sta dentro. I miei genitori sono molto simpatici e sarebbe molto piacevole andare in vacanza con loro. Quando ritornano dal lavoro glielo chiederò. Adesso sarebbe meglio studiare perchè c'è ancora molto tempo prima che arrivi l'estate.

_____

_____

_____

_____

_____

_____

_____

_____

_____

VOCABOLARIO

adesso	now	**mini**	a small Italian car
avere voglia	to feel like	**pulmino**	van
campeggio	camping	**prima**	before
fresco	cool	**simpatico**	pleasant

The past conditional (*condizionale passato*)

The past conditional is a tense used to describe an action that would have been completed in the past if something else had happened. It corresponds to the English use of *would have + past participle* of the verb (*I would have spoken*).

The past conditional is a compound tense. It is formed by combining the conditional tense of the auxiliary **avere** and **essere** plus the past participle of the main verb. The past participle agrees with the subject when the verb is conjugated with the auxiliary **essere**.

	PARLARE, VENDERE, SENTIRE (*I would have spoken, sold, heard*)	ANDARE (*I would have gone*)
io	avrei parlato, venduto, sentito	sarei andato/a
tu	avresti parlato, venduto, sentito	saresti andato/a
lui/lei	avrebbe parlato, venduto, sentito	sarebbe andato/a
noi	avremmo parlato, venduto, sentito	saremmo andati/e
voi	avreste parlato, venduto, sentito	sareste andati/e
loro	avrebbero parlato, venduto, sentito	sarebbero andati/e

Io **avrei parlato** con il tuo amico.

*I **would have spoken** to your friend.*

Tu **non avresti venduto** la casa.

*You **wouldn't have sold** the house.*

The past conditional is used in dependent clauses to express a future action as seen from the past. In English the present conditional is used, but in Italian the past conditional is used.

Ha detto che **avrebbe scritto**.

*He said he **would write/would have written**.*

Remember the following rules for the past conditional:

- The past conditional is used after verbs of knowing, promising, and telling, such as **promettere** (*to promise*), **sapere** (*to know*), and **dire** (*to tell, to say*) in the past.

Hai detto che **avresti mangiato** tutto.

*You said that you **would have eaten** everything.*

- The past conditional is used to report a rumor or a fact that may or may not be true.

> L'aereo **sarebbe precipitato** sulle montagne.
>
> *It seems* that the plane **crashed** against the mountains.

- The past conditional is used to express what would have happened but didn't, or what shouldn't have happened but did.

> **Avresti dovuto mettere** un'inserzione sul giornale.
>
> You **should have put** an ad in the newspaper. (**But you didn't.**)
>
> **Non sarebbero andati** al teatro, ma erano stati invitati.
>
> They **wouldn't have gone** to the theater, but they had been invited.

- When the main clause is expressed with the past tense of verbs such as **credere**, **dire**, **immaginare**, **pensare**, **promettere**, and **sperare**, the past conditional is used in Italian. English uses the simple conditional with such verbs.

> **Pensavo** che **sarebbero arrivati** prima di sera.
>
> *I was thinking* they *would be* here before dark.

- When the dependent clause is introduced by **ma**, Italian uses the indicative in the dependent clause. If it is introduced by **se**, Italian uses the subjunctive, which you will study in the next chapter.

> **Sarei venuto ma non ho avuto** tempo.
>
> *I would have come, but I didn't have* time.
>
> **Sarei venuto se avessi avuto** tempo.
>
> *I would have come if I had had* time.

ESERCIZIO
10·1

Change the following sentences from the present conditional to the past conditional.

1. Io mangerei una mela. _____

2. Tu parleresti col dottore. _____

3. Lui penserebbe di venire domani. _____

4. Lei firmerebbe il documento. _____

5. Noi risponderemmo al telefono. _____

6. Voi scrivereste una cartolina. _____

7. Loro uscirebbero presto. _____

8. Io non comprerei le scarpe. _____

9. Verresti con noi? _____

10. Non inviterebbe molti amici. _____

11. Inviterebbero anche noi? _____

Translate the following sentences into Italian.

1. I would have taken the bus. _____

2. You would have danced all night. _____

3. He would have known. _____

4. We would have answered. _____

5. She would have understood the lesson. _____

6. You (pl.) would have waited. _____

7. They would have traveled. _____

8. You shouldn't have answered. _____

9. Should she have written? _____

10. They wouldn't have known. _____

11. Should they have known? _____

Complete the following sentences using the past conditional, showing what would have been done but couldn't be, with the words suggested.

andare in centro	**andare a ballare**	**andare a nuotare**
arrivare in ritardo	**cantare**	**ridere**
andare a dormire	**entrare**	**riparare**

1. La signora Nanni _____ ma non aveva la macchina.

2. Loro _____ ma hanno preso un tassì.

3. Io _____ ma dovevo ancora finire di stirare.

4. Voi _____ ma la piscina era sporca.

5. Mio fratello _____ ma non conosceva quella canzone.

6. Noi _____ ma la discoteca era chiusa.

7. Voi _____ ma non avete trovato le chiavi.

8. Io _____ ma la commedia non era molto comica.

9. Tu _____ la motocicletta ma non avevi tempo.

Supply the correct form of the verbs in parentheses in the past conditional and then translate the paragraphs into English.

Mussolini era un politico molto ambizioso. Secondo lui, l'Italia _____ (dovere) ritornare al passato glorioso dell'antico impero romano. Era convinto che sotto il suo commando l'Italia _____ (ritornare) ad essere un grande impero. Credeva che un'alleanza con la Germania lo _____ (aiutare) nella sua ambiziosa idea. Mussolini ha fatto tante cose buone per l'Italia, come la costruzione di scuole, strade, e ospedali. _____ (Dovere) ascoltare chi gli suggeriva che (essere) un errore allearsi con la Germania. Era troppo sicuro di sè. Molti italiani lo seguirono ed erano certi che Mussolini sapeva quello che faceva e che _____ (portare) l'Italia e gli italiani alla gloria del passato.

É salito al potere nel 1924. Nel 1943, quando la guerra è finita e l'Italia ha perso, la sua dittatura è caduta e lui è stato ucciso con la sua compagna in piazzale Loreto a Milano.

_____

_____

_____

_____

_____

_____

_____

VOCABOLARIO			
alleanza	alliance	**piazzale**	square
ambizioso	ambitious	**seguirono**	followed
dittatura	dictatorship	**suggeriva**	suggested
impero	empire		

Compound reflexive verbs (*verbi riflessivi composti*)

Compound tenses of reflexive verbs are formed by combining the auxiliary verb essere with the past participle of the verb.

	PRESENT PERFECT (*I woke up*)	PAST PERFECT (*I had woken up*)
io	mi sono svegliato/a	mi ero svegliato/a
tu	ti sei svegliato/a	ti eri svegliato/a
lui/lei	si è svegliato/a	si era svegliato/a
noi	ci siamo svegliati/e	ci eravamo svegliati/e
voi	vi siete svegliati/e	vi eravate svegliati/e
loro	si sono svegliati/e	si erano svegliati/e

	FUTURE PERFECT (*I will have woken up*)	PAST CONDITIONAL (*I would have woken up*)
io	mi sarò svegliato/a	mi sarei svegliato/a
tu	ti sarai svegliato/a	ti saresti svegliato/a
lui/lei	si sarà svegliato/a	si sarebbe svegliato/a
noi	ci saremo svegliati/e	ci saremmo svegliati/e
voi	vi sarete svegliati/e	vi sareste svegliati/e
loro	si saranno svegliati/e	si sarebbero svegliati/e

The past participle of reflexive verbs agrees in gender and number with the subject.

I ragazzi si erano già **lavati**.	*The boys had already washed themselves.*
Il ragazzo si era già **lavato**.	*The boy had already washed himself.*

In compound tenses the reflexive pronouns precede the helping verb. In the negative, **non** precedes the reflexive pronoun.

Giovanna **si è alzata** tardi.	*Giovanna woke up late.*
Giovanna **non si è alzata** tardi.	*Giovanna didn't wake up late.*

ESERCIZIO
11·1

Rewrite the following sentences, using the present perfect.

1. Carlo si fa la barba tutte le mattine. _____

2. I ragazzi si alzano tardi. _____

3. Io (f.) mi metto il vestito nuovo. _____

4. Paola si lava le mani. _____

5. Io (m.) mi siedo vicino alla porta. _____

6. Paolo si alza presto tutte le mattine. _____

7. Pietro e Anna si sposano. _____

8. Giovanna si diverte molto. _____

9. Giovanna e Teresa si divertono. _____

ESERCIZIO
11·2

Rewrite the following sentences, using the past perfect.

1. I ragazzi si divertono molto. _____

2. Carlo si veste molto bene. _____

3. Giovanna si pettina. _____

4. Pietro e Anna si innamorano. _____

5. Io (m.) non mi sento molto bene. _____

6. Le ragazze si coprono perchè fa freddo. _____

7. I bambini si divertono al parco. _____

8. Il signore si pulisce le scarpe. _____

9. Le signore si puliscono le scarpe. _____

ESERCIZIO
11·3

Rewrite the following sentences, using the future perfect.

1. Io (m.) mi siedo sulla poltrona. _____

2. Carlo si fa la barba. _____

3. Il bambino si addormenta. _____

III-11 Compound reflexive verbs (*verbi riflessivi composti*) **331**

4. Pietro e Anna si sposano. _____

5. Noi (m.) ci vestiamo. _____

6. Voi (f.) vi laureate. _____

7. Loro (m.) si spogliano. _____

8. Giovanna non si sveglia. _____

9. Carlo si dimentica. _____

Rewrite the following sentences, using the past conditional.

1. Quei ragazzi si alzano alle otto. _____

2. Luigi si sveglia presto. _____

3. Tu (m.) ti laurei in medicina. _____

4. Lei si fa la doccia. _____

5. Noi ci divertiamo molto. _____

6. Voi (f.) vi vestite di bianco. _____

7. Giovanna e Paola si mettono il cappotto. _____

8. Noi ci scusiamo. _____

9. Noi non ci scusiamo. _____

The subjunctive mood (*modo congiuntivo*)

Until now, except for the conditional, this book has covered the indicative mood of verbs. The word *mood* describes a subject's attitude. You will now learn how to use the subjunctive mood and how it allows the Italian speaker to express a variety of moods. It is used much more in Italian than in English.

The subjunctive mood expresses opinions, uncertainty, supposition, possibility, wishes, and doubts. It conveys the speaker's opinions and attitude.

It may seem difficult to remember these concepts, but there is a simple and basic rule that makes the subjunctive easier to master. The subjunctive implies subjectivity. If there is a chance that the action, feeling, or opinion being expressed has not or may not take place, use the subjunctive. If it is a fact that an action has been realized or will definitely be realized, the indicative is used. Take a look at the following sentences:

So che ti piace Roma.	*I know that you like Rome.*
Spero che ti piaccia Roma.	*I hope that you like Rome.*

The first sentence is in the indicative because the speaker expresses certainty that you like Rome. The second clause of the second sentence is in the subjunctive because the speaker doesn't know if you will like Rome, but he hopes that you do.

The subjunctive is mostly found in a dependent clause. It is used mainly after the following verbs: **pensare** (*to think*), **credere** (*to believe*), **sperare** (*to hope*), **dubitare** (*to doubt*), **non sapere** (*do not know*), **avere paura** (*to be afraid*), **volere** (*to want*), **desiderare** (*to wish*), and others that are expressed in the indicative. Therefore, the verb in the main clause is in the indicative, and the **che** clause is in the subjunctive.

Spero che tu **venga**.	*I **hope** that you **come**.*
Lui **desidera** che tu **venga**.	*He **wants** you to **come**.*

Exactly how and when to use the subjunctive will be explained in the next few units. If you follow the explanations and are diligent in doing the exercises that accompany them, you will soon be competent and comfortable in using the subjunctive.

As previously mentioned, the subjunctive is seldom used independently. It is usually preceded by a main clause connected by che.

	main clause	+	che	+	dependent clause
Io	**credo**		che		**lei canti** in italiano.
I	*think*		*that*		*she sings* in Italian.

The subjunctive has four tenses: present, past, imperfect, and pluperfect.

333

The present subjunctive (*congiuntivo presente*)

The present subjunctive states actions that may take place in the present or in the future.

È necessario che tu beva.	*It is necessary that you drink.* (now)
È possibile che arrivino tardi.	*It is possible they'll arrive late.* (**future**)

The present subjunctive is formed by adding the required endings to the root of the verbs. The root of the present subjunctive of most regular and irregular verbs is formed by:

- dropping the -**o**- of the first-person singular of the present indicative
- adding the endings of the present subjunctive for each conjugation to the root

	PARLARE (*to speak*)	SCRIVERE (*to write*)	SENTIRE (*to hear*)	CAPIRE (*to understand*)
che io	parli	scriva	senta	capisca
che tu	parli	scriva	senta	capisca
che lui/lei	parli	scriva	senta	capisca
che noi	parliamo	scriviamo	sentiamo	capiamo
che voi	parliate	scriviate	sentiate	capiate
che loro	parlino	scrivano	sentano	capiscano

Note that in the present subjunctive the endings of -**ere** and -**ire** verbs are the same.

The **noi** and **voi** endings are the same for all three conjugations. The third-person plural endings add -**no** to the singular ending. Verbs with spelling changes in the present indicative have the same spelling irregularities in the subjunctive. Because the first three persons of each conjugation are the same, if the subject is unclear, the personal pronoun is normally used to avoid confusion.

All -**are**, -**ere**, and -**ire** verbs that are regular in the present indicative are conjugated like **parlare**, **scrivere**, **sentire**, and **capire** in the present subjunctive.

ESERCIZIO
12·1

Complete the following sentences with the appropriate forms of the present subjunctive for the verbs in parentheses.

1. Io voglio che tu _____ (aprire) la porta.

2. Lei desidera che tu _____ (scrivere) spesso.

3. Ho paura che tu _____ (cadere) sul ghiaccio.

4. Mio padre vuole che io _____ (chiamare) tutte le settimane.

5. Voglio che tu _____ (sentire) bene quello che ti dico.

6. Desidero che tu _____ (ballare) con lui.

7. Credo che voi _____ (guardare) troppo la televisione.

8. Penso che loro _____ (camminare) molto in fretta.

9. Abbiamo paura che lei _____ (spendere) troppo.

The verbs ending in -**care** and -**gare** add an -**h**- in all forms of the present subjunctive.

	GIOCARE (to play)	PAGARE (to pay)
che io	gio**chi**	pa**ghi**
che tu	gio**chi**	pa**ghi**
che lui/lei	gio**chi**	pa**ghi**
che noi	gio**chiamo**	pa**ghiamo**
che voi	gio**chiate**	paghiate
che loro	gio**chino**	paghino

The verbs ending in -**ciare** and -**giare** do not repeat the -**i**-.

	COMINCIARE (to begin, start)	MANGIARE (to eat)
che io	cominc**i**	mang**i**
che tu	cominc**i**	mang**i**
che lui/lei	cominc**i**	mang**i**
che noi	cominc**iamo**	mang**iamo**
che voi	cominc**iate**	mang**iate**
che loro	cominc**ino**	mangino

Complete the following sentences with the appropriate forms of the present subjunctive for the verbs in parentheses.

1. Io voglio che tu _____ (pagare) i debiti.

2. Tu credi che la lezione _____ (cominciare) tardi tutte le sere.

3. Lei spera che tu _____ (mangiare) da lei questa sera.

4. Voglio che loro _____ (mangiare) la colazione tutte le mattine.

5. Dubito che loro _____ (giocare) a carte.

6. Il bambino vuole che io _____ (cercare) la palla.

7. Non voglio che nessuno _____ (toccare) il cristallo.

8. Dubitiamo che lui _____ (pagare) il conto.

9. Penso che voi _____ (cominciare) a lavorare troppo tardi.

Since the first-person singular of the present indicative is the root for the present subjunctive, most of the verbs with an irregular root in the first person of the present indicative will have an irregular root for the present subjunctive. Take a close look at the following verbs:

	BERE (to drink)	DIRE (to tell, say)	FARE (to do, make)	POTERE (to be able)
PRESENT INDICATIVE				
	bevo (io)	**dico**	faccio	**posso**
PRESENT SUBJUNCTIVE				
che io	beva	dica	faccia	possa
che tu	beva	dica	faccia	possa
che lui/lei	beva	dica	faccia	possa
che noi	beviamo	diciamo	facciamo	possiamo
che voi	beviate	diciate	facciate	possiate
che loro	bevano	dicano	facciano	possano

Note: **facci-** and **vogli-** drop the **-i-** before the noi ending of **-iamo** (**facciamo** and **vogliamo** and not **facciiamo** and **vogliiamo**).

Some verbs have an irregular present subjunctive in the **io, tu, lui, lei,** and **loro** forms (from the **io** form of the present indicative) but return to the **noi** and **voi** forms of the present indicative for the **noi** and **voi** forms of the subjunctive.

DOVERE (must)			
PRESENT INDICATIVE		PRESENT SUBJUNCTIVE	
io	devo (debbo)	che io	deva (debba)
tu	devi	che tu	deva (debba)
lui/lei	deve	che lui,lei	deva (debba)
noi	dobbiamo	che noi	dobbiamo
voi	dovete	che voi	dobbiate
loro	devono (debbono)	che loro	debbano

You will now study a few verbs that follow the same pattern as **dovere** in the present subjunctive.

	ANDARE (to go)	RIMANERE (to remain)	SALIRE (to go up)
che io	vada	rimanga	salga
che tu	vada	rimanga	salga
che lui/lei	vada	rimanga	salga
che noi	andiamo	rimaniamo	saliamo
che voi	andiate	rimaniate	saliate
che loro	vadano	rimangano	salgano

	TENERE (to keep)	VALERE (to be worth)	VENIRE (to come)
che io	tenga	valga	venga
che tu	tenga	valga	venga
che lui/lei	tenga	valga	venga
che noi	teniamo	valiamo	veniamo
che voi	teniate	valiate	veniate
che loro	tengano	valgano	vengano

	APPARIRE (to appear)	MORIRE (to die)	CUOCERE (to cook)
che io	appaia	muoia	cuocia
che tu	appaia	muoia	cuocia
che lui/lei	appaia	muoia	cuocia
che noi	appariamo	moriamo	cociamo/cuociamo
che voi	appariate	moriate	cociate/cuociate
che loro	appaiano	muoiano	cuociano

	SEDERE (to sit)	SUONARE (to play, ring)	USCIRE (to go out)
che io	sieda	suoni	esca
che tu	sieda	suoni	esca
che lui/lei	sieda	suoni	esca
che noi	sediamo	suoniamo	usciamo
che voi	sediate	suoniate	usciate
che loro	siedano	suonino	escano

ESERCIZIO 12·3

Translate the following sentences into Italian.

1. It is possible that they'll come right away. _____

2. Carlo wants you (pl.) to do your homework. _____

3. I think that you will understand the lesson. _____

4. I don't want you to keep the door open. _____

5. He hopes that we will come to his house. _____

6. She wants her to sit down. _____

7. I think that they must go. _____

8. He hopes that we tell the truth. _____

9. I think that it's time that they go home. _____

The verbs **avere**, **essere**, **sapere**, **dare**, and **stare** are all irregular in the present subjunctive. Study the following forms:

AVERE	ESSERE	SAPERE	DARE	STARE
abbia	sia	sappia	dia	stia
abbia	sia	sappia	dia	stia
abbia	sia	sappia	dia	stia
abbiamo	siamo	sappiamo	diamo	stiamo
abbiate	siate	sappiate	diate	stiate
abbiano	siano	sappiano	diano	stiano

Complete the following sentences with the appropriate forms of the verbs in parentheses, using the present subjunctive.

1. Io spero che tu _____ (sapere) la lezione.

2. Perchè vuoi che io ti _____ (dare) il suo indirizzo?

3. Penso che voi gli _____ (portare) tanti regali.

4. È possibile che tu non _____ (sapere) la notizia.

5. Desideriamo che voi _____ (avere) tutti i conforti.

6. Non voglio che voi _____ (avere) freddo.

7. Lui spera che voi _____ (stare) in America per tanto tempo.

8. Giovanna vuole che loro _____ (stare) a casa loro.

9. Carlo e Maria pensano che lei _____ (essere) molto dimagrita.

The subjunctive is used after verbs and expressions of command, demand, desire, permission, preference, request, and wishing. Some commonly used verbs requiring the subjunctive are listed below.

- Verbs of desire, hope, preference, and will

desiderare	*to wish*
sperare	*to hope*
preferire	*to prefer*
volere	*to want*

Desidero che tu **legga.**	*I want you to read.*
Spero che arrivino presto.	*I hope that they will arrive early.*
Preferite che io **vada** al ristorante?	*Do you prefer that I go to the restaurant?*
Tu non vuoi che noi ti **aspettiamo.**	*You don't want us to wait for you.*

- Verbs of emotion

arrabbiarsi	*to get angry*
avere paura	*to be afraid*
dispiacersi	*to be sorry*
essere contento, triste	*to be happy, sad*
temere	*to fear*

Ho paura che non trovino la strada.	*I am afraid that they will not find the road.*
Sono contenta che lei **sia arrivata.**	*I am happy that she has arrived.*
Mi dispiace che oggi **non ci sia** il sole.	*I am sorry that today there is no sun.*

- Verbs expressing command

esigere	to demand
ordinare	to order
pretendere	to demand, to claim
richiedere	to request, to demand

Io richiedo che vi togliate le scarpe quando **entrate**.	*I request that you take off your shoes when you come in.*
Pretendo che voi **mi aiutiate**.	*I demand that you help me.*
Esigo che usiate la massima attenzione.	*I demand that you use the maximum attention.*

- Verbs expressing permission or prohibition

lasciare	to let
consentire	to allow, to permit
impedire	to prevent
permettere	to allow
proibire	to forbid

| **Io permetto che voi parliate** in classe. | *I allow you to talk in class.* |
| **Tu proibisci che stiamo** fuori fino a tardi. | *You forbid us to stay out too late.* |

ESERCIZIO
12·5

*Rewrite the following sentences, using the subjunctive with **spero che**.*

1. Lui abita qui vicino. _____

2. Lui scrive una cartolina. _____

3. Lei cammina molto. _____

4. Noi arriviamo presto. _____

5. Voi studiate all'università. _____

6. Carlo impara a suonare il piano. _____

7. Maria non perde l'autobus. _____

8. Carlo e Maria non litigano. _____

9. Tu giochi al tennis. _____

ESERCIZIO
12·6

*Rewrite the following sentences, using the subjunctive with **mi dispiace che**.*

1. Tu stai poco bene. _____

2. Lui è troppo impegnato. _____

3. Lei ha il raffreddore. _____

4. Noi non possiamo venire da te. _____

5. Voi siete molto stanchi. _____

6. Loro mangiano troppo. _____

7. Tu non giochi al tennis. _____

8. Il bambino piange sempre. _____

9. Voi non potete venire a visitarci. _____

ESERCIZIO
12·7

*Rewrite the following sentences, using the subjunctive with **preferisco che**.*

1. Tu metti questo vestito. _____

2. Lei studia il francese. _____

3. Lui parla con il direttore. _____

4. Noi andiamo al cinema. _____

5. Voi dormite e vi riposate. _____

6. Tu ti alzi presto. _____

7. Voi andate in vacanza al mare. _____

8. Voi venite da noi. _____

9. Loro viaggiano in macchina. _____

ESERCIZIO
12·8

Rewrite the following sentences, using the present subjunctive or the infinitive of the verbs in parentheses.

1. Io voglio che tu (andare). _____

2. Dubitiamo che lui (arrivare). _____

3. Speri che io vi (visitare). _____

4. Speriamo che lui (capire). _____

5. Penso che tu (potere). _____

6. Dubito che tu (potere). _____

7. Carlo vuole che io (ascoltare). _____

8. Penso che Mario (comprare) la frutta. _____

9. Dubito che voi (studiare). _____

10. Spero di (finire). _____

11. Speriamo di (partire). _____

12. Dubitate di (finire). _____

The subjunctive with impersonal expressions

The subjunctive is used in a dependent **che** clause after impersonal expressions of possibility, opinion, and probability. Following are some impersonal expressions that require the use of the subjunctive:

È necessario che...	*It is necessary that . . .*
Basta che...	*It is enough that . . .*
È probabile che...	*It is probable that . . .*
È peccato che...	*It is a pity that . . .*
È opportuno che...	*It is opportune that . . .*
È raro che...	*It is rare that . . .*
È improbabile che...	*It is improbable that . . .*
È facile che...	*It is possible that . . .*
È bene che...	*It is good that . . .*
È difficile che...	*It is difficult that . . .*
È necessario che...	*It is necessary that . . .*
È meglio che...	*It is better that . . .*
Bisogna che...	*It is necessary that . . .*
È giusto che...	*It is right that . . .*
È importante che...	*It is important that . . .*
È possibile che...	*It is possible that . . .*
È impossibile che...	*It is impossible that . . .*
È preferibile che...	*It is preferable that . . .*
Non importa che...	*It is not important that . . .*

È probabile che piova domani.	***It is probable that it will rain** tomorrow.*
È facile che io vada al cinema.	***It is possible I will go** to the movie.*
Bisogna che voi studiate.	***It is necessary that you study.***

The impersonal expressions are followed by an infinitive instead of the subjunctive if no subject is expressed.

È importante che impariate la lingua inglese.   ***It is important that you learn** English.*

But:

È importante imparare l'inglese.   ***It is important to learn** English.*

If the impersonal expression states certainty, you have to use the indicative instead of the subjunctive. The following expressions require the indicative.

È certo che...	*It is certain that . . .*
È evidente che...	*It is obvious that . . .*
È ovvio che...	*It is obvious that . . .*
È chiaro che...	*It is clear that . . .*

Put each sentence in the subjunctive or the indicative as needed.

1. È importante che tu _____ (scrivere) una lettera o due.

2. È probabile che io _____ (ritornare) tardi.

3. È necessario che noi _____ (partire) domani.

4. È difficile che voi _____ (essere) molto in ritardo.

5. È meglio che tu _____ (stare) a casa tutto il giorno.

6. È raro che _____ (essere) rotta.

7. È giusto che _____ (io ti dare) i soldi.

8. È bene che voi _____ (mangiare) la frutta.

9. È possibile che noi _____ (venire) da voi.

10. È certo che noi _____ (parlare) con il padrone di casa.

11. È chiaro che voi _____ (volere) vedere i conti.

12. È ovvio che non vi _____ (piacere) quella persona.

The subjunctive is used with the following subordinate expressions:

a meno che	*unless*	**malgrado**	*although*
a patto che	*provided that*	**nonostante che**	*although*
affinché	*in order that*	**prima che**	*before*
benché	*although*	**purché**	*provided that*
cosí che	*so that*	**sebbene**	*although, even if*
dopo che	*after*	**senza che**	*without*
finché non	*until*		

It is also used with the following pronouns and adjectives:

chiunque	*whoever*	**ovunque**	*wherever*
dovunque	*wherever*	**qualunque**	*whatever*

Complete the following sentences with the appropriate form of the verbs in parentheses.

1. Vengo anch'io, purché ci _____ (essere) anche tu.

2. Benché _____ (nevicare) non fa molto freddo.

3. Malgrado ci _____ (essere) molta gente, è bello stare sulla spiaggia.

4. Chiunque _____ (volere) venire, dovrà comprare i biglietti.

5. Prima che Maria (partire), spero che mi _____ (venire) a salutare.

6. A meno che non _____ (fare) bel tempo, staremo a casa tutto il giorno.

7. Sebbene _____ (essere) già in aereo, non siete ancora partiti.

8. Dovunque voi _____ (andare), aspetto la vostra telefonata.

9. Benché _____ (arrivare) tardi, li aspettiamo con molta ansia.

The subjunctive is used with a clause that modifies a negative expression such as **non...nessuno** che, **non...niente** che.

ESERCIZIO
12·11

Complete the following negative expressions, using the appropriate form of the verbs in parentheses in the subjunctive.

1. Non c'è niente che lo _____ (svegliare).

2. In Svizzera non c'è nessun negozio che _____ (aprire) alla domenica.

3. Non c'è nessun posto che _____ (piacere) a tuo marito.

4. Non c'è niente che mi _____ (disturbare).

5. Non c'è nessun tesoro che _____ (valere) come la salute.

6. Non c'è nessun poliziotto che ti _____ (proteggere).

7. Non c'è niente che ti _____ (fare) cambiare idea.

8. Non c'è nessuno che ci _____ (aiutare).

9. Non cè niente che tu non _____ (sapere) fare.

The subjunctive is used with a relative superlative: **il/la, i/le...più...che**.

Lei è **la più** bella ragazza **che io conosca**.	*She is **the most** beautiful girl **that I know**.*
È la chiesa **più vecchia che** ci **sia**.	*It is **the oldest** church **that** there is.*

The subjunctive is used in relative clauses when the word that modifies it is indefinite. If it is definite, the indicative is used.

Conosco una traduttrice **che parla** cinque lingue.	*I know a translator **who speaks** five different languages.*
Ho bisogno di una traduttrice **che parli** cinque lingue.	*I need a translator **who speaks** five different languages. (I don't know one yet.)*

Complete the following sentences with the appropriate forms and tenses of the verbs in parentheses.

1. Abbiamo una casa che _____ (avere) molti piani.

2. Cerco una persona che _____ (fare) le pulizie.

3. Conosco molti studenti che _____ (studiare) sempre.

4. Abbiamo bisogno di studenti che _____ (studiare) molto.

5. Hanno un gatto che _____ (miagolare) continuamente.

6. Cerchiamo delle case che non _____ (avere) molti piani.

7. Cercano un negozio che _____ (vendere) articoli sportivi.

8. Conosciamo un negozio che _____ (vendere) articoli sportivi.

9. Lui ha bisogno di una cravatta che _____ (andare) con l'abito elegante.

10. È la segretaria più intelligente che io _____ (conoscere).

11. È il dottore più conosciuto che _____ (esistere).

12. È l'agenzia di viaggi più informata che ci _____ (essere) in questa città.

Fill in the spaces with the correct forms of the verbs in parentheses and translate the paragraph into English.

In Italia, quasi tutti i giorni c'è uno sciopero. Ho l'impressione che gli italiani non

_____ (avere) più voglia di lavorare. Con gli scioperi la gente spera di ottenere

degli aumenti di stipendio. È necessario che il governo e i sindacati _____

(ascoltare) i lavoratori. La gente dice che lavora molto ma non guadagna abbastanza. È

possibile che la gente _____ (esagerare), ma è certo che non

_____ (potere) continuare ad aumentare il costo delle merci senza aumentare

gli stipendi. Sembra che gli scioperi _____ (aiutare) la gente ad ottenere quello

che desidera, ma in realtà non si ottiene mai niente o abbastanza per giustificare tali scioperi

e perdite di ore lavorative.

_____

_____

_____

_____

_____

_____

_____

_____

_____

The imperfect subjunctive (*congiuntivo imperfetto*)

The imperfect subjunctive, like the present subjunctive, is used after certain verbs, impersonal expressions, and conjunctions. The main difference between these two tenses is the time of the action. If the action is in the present, the present subjunctive is used. If the action is related to the past, the imperfect subjunctive is used.

If the verb of the main clause is expressed in the past tense or conditional, the imperfect subjunctive is used in the dependent **che** clause.

Maria **pensa che io arrivi**.   *Maria **thinks that I will arrive**.*
Maria **pensava che io arrivassi**.   *Maria **thought I would arrive**.*

The imperfect subjunctive is used in sentences when the main clause requires the subjunctive and when the verb of the main clause is in the past indicative or in the conditional. The main clause can be in the imperfect indicative, preterite, perfect, and conditional. But the dependent clause will be in the imperfect subjunctive.

Speravo che tu venissi.   *I hoped that you would come.*
Sperai che tu venissi.   *I hoped that you would come.*
Ho sperato che tu venissi.   *I hoped that you would come.*
Spererei che tu venissi.   *I would hope that you come.*

The imperfect subjunctive for regular verbs is formed as follows:

- Verbs ending in **-are** form the imperfect subjunctive by dropping the infinitive ending and adding: **-assi, -assi, -asse, -assimo, -aste**, and **-assero** (parl**are**, parl**assi**).

- Verbs ending in **-ere** drop the infinitive ending and add: **-essi**, **-essi**, **-esse**, **-essimo**, **-este**, and **-essero** (ved**ere**, ved**essimo**).

- Verbs ending in **-ire** drop the infinitive ending and add: **-issi**, **-issi**, **-isse**, **-issimo**, **-iste**, and **-issero** (sent**ire**, sent**issimo**).

	PARLARE (to speak)	VEDERE (to see)	SENTIRE (to hear)
che io	parl**assi**	ved**essi**	sent**issi**
che tu	parl**assi**	ved**essi**	sent**issi**
che lui/lei	parl**asse**	ved**esse**	sent**isse**
che noi	parl**assimo**	ved**essimo**	sent**issimo**
che voi	parl**aste**	ved**este**	sent**iste**
che loro	parl**assero**	ved**essero**	sent**issero**

There are no irregular **-ire** verbs in the imperfect subjunctive. Very few verbs are irregular in the imperfect subjunctive. The ones that are irregular simply use the Latin or the old Italian infinitive to form the root for the imperfect subjunctive.

INFINITIVE	ROOT FOR THE IMPERFECT SUBJUNCTIVE	IMPERFECT SUBJUNCTIVE
bere	**bev** (*from* **bevere**)	che io bevessi, bevessi, bevesse, ecc.
dire	**dic** (*from* **dicere**)	che io dicessi, dicessi, dicesse, ecc.
fare	**fac** (*from* **facere**)	che io facessi, facessi, facesse, ecc.
condurre	**conduc** (*from* **conducere**)	che io conducessi, conducessi, conducesse, ecc.
tradurre	**traduc** (*from* **traducere**)	che io traducessi, traducessi, traducesse, ecc.

The following verbs are irregular in all the forms of the imperfect subjunctive:

	ESSERE (to be)	DARE (to give)	STARE (to stay)
che io	**fossi**	**dessi**	**stessi**
che tu	**fossi**	**dessi**	**stessi**
che lui/lei	**fosse**	**desse**	**stesse**
che noi	**fossimo**	**dessimo**	**stessimo**
che voi	**foste**	**deste**	**steste**
che loro	**fossero**	**dessero**	**stessero**

The same rules that apply to the use of present subjunctive are used for the imperfect subjunctive. When the verb in the main clause is in the imperfect indicative, perfect, or conditional, the dependent clause uses the imperfect subjunctive.

Speravo che tu **venissi** subito a casa.	*I hoped you **would come** home right away.*
Ho voluto che loro **studiassero**.	*I wanted them **to study**.*
Vorrei che tuo fratello **chiamasse**.	*I would like your brother **to call**.*

Complete the following sentences with the appropriate forms of the imperfect subjunctive for the verbs in parentheses.

1. Noi volevamo che i nostri figli _____ (dire) la verità.

2. Mio padre ha proibito che io _____ (andare) a ballare.

3. Io preferirei che voi _____ (tornare) indietro.

4. Era necessario che loro _____ (leggere) la lezione.

5. La maestra ordinò che gli studenti non _____ (fumare) in classe.

6. Noi volevamo che lei _____ (rimanere) in Italia.

7. Lei vorrebbe che io le _____ (regalare) un orologio d'oro.

8. Ho proibito che i bambini _____ (giocare) vicino al fiume.

9. Preferireste che loro _____ (comprare) un divano.

10. Io avevo paura che tu non lo _____ (comprare).

11. Speravamo che Carlo _____ (arrivare) con il treno delle otto.

12. Era impossibile che lui _____ (finire) il lavoro.

13. I miei amici volevano che io _____ (fare) una cena per tutti.

14. Volevo che ti _____ (lavare) bene la faccia.

15. Pensavo che lui _____ (potere) tradurre questo documento.

Rewrite the following sentences in Italian, using the imperfect subjunctive. Sometimes an infinitive will be needed.

1. I wanted you (sing.) to come. _____

2. I hoped you (sing.) would come. _____

3. I believed he would write a few letters. _____

4. He thought she would clean. _____

5. I didn't know she would come too. _____

6. It would be necessary for them to leave. _____

7. My father wanted us to work all day long. _____

8. She wished to sleep all day long. _____

9. You wanted us to go home. _____

10. She wanted to ask the doctor. _____

11. You (sing.) thought he would come. _____

12. You (sing.) thought that he could study. _____

13. They wanted me to cook. _____

14. I hoped she would be well for the wedding. _____

15. I would like to sleep all day long. _____

ESERCIZIO

12·16

Rewrite the following sentences, using the imperfect subjunctive.

1. Spera che voi studiate. _____

2. Desiderano che li chiamiamo. _____

3. Proibiscono che noi fumiamo in ufficio. _____

4. Ho paura che tu lo veda. _____

5. Preferisco che loro vengano a casa mia. _____

6. Insisto che tu finisca i compiti. _____

7. Penso che voi vi ricordiate. _____

8. Credo che tu venga. _____

9. Spero che tu parli. _____

10. Spero che tu non dica niente. _____

11. Dubito che comprino la casa. _____

12. Penso che lui sia americano. _____

13. Immagino che voi siate stanchi. _____

14. Non crede che voi viaggiate in macchina. _____

15. Non penso che voi vi ricordiate. _____

The imperfect subjunctive is used after adverbial expressions if the main clause is in the imperfect indicative, preterite, perfect, or conditional.

Refer to the list of adverbial expressions presented earlier in this unit in the section on the present subjunctive (**benché, a patto che, sebbene**, etc.).

Avevo paura che voi **non veniste.**	*I was afraid you would not come.*
C'era molta gente **benché fosse** molto freddo.	*There were many people, even if it was very cold.*

ESERCIZIO 12·17

Complete the following sentences with the appropriate forms of the imperfect subjunctive for the verbs in parentheses.

1. Benché ci _____ (essere) molta neve siamo andati a lavorare.

2. Saremmo andati a patto che _____ (venire) anche loro.

3. Non era difficile da trasportare sebbene _____ (essere) molto pesante.

4. Lei ha lavorato tutto il giorno sebbene _____ (avere) il raffreddore.

5. Dovevo andare nonostante che _____ (essere) molto stanco.

6. Non volevano aspettarmi a meno che _____ (portare) loro la cena.

7. Avevano pulito la casa affinché tu _____ (fare) bella figura.

8. Loro ascoltavano la radio, sebbene tu _____ (suonare) la chitarra.

9. Sono venuti prima che Giovanna li _____ (chiamare).

10. Benché _____ (avere) paura del buio, non ha acceso la luce.

ESERCIZIO 12·18

Complete the sentences with the correct forms of the imperfect subjunctive and then translate the paragraphs into English, using the vocabulary words that follow.

Giovanna ieri è andata in centro con la sua amica Maria. Si sono fermate davanti alle vetrine dei negozi e hanno sognato. Giovanna ha detto: «Se io _____ (avere) molti soldi, mi comprerei una camicetta di seta. Penso che se _____ (essere) possibile e non _____ (costare) molto, comprerei anche una gonna alla moda. _____ (comprare) anche le scarpe. Farei tutto questo se _____ (essere) possibile, ma non posso perchè sono una studentessa e non ho molti mezzi.» Maria ha detto: «Se io _____ (avere) molti soldi, andrei in un'agenzia di viaggi e chiederei degli opuscoli per andare in un'isola lontana da tutto e da tutti. Vorrei affittare una villetta. Vorrei che questa villetta (essere) vicino la spiaggia, ma _____ (avere) anche la piscina. Vorrei che ci _____ (essere) molte camere così potrei invitare degli amici. Assumerei delle persone che _____ (sapere) cucinare bene. Vorrei girare per poter conoscere bene l'isola. Insomma mi divertirei e mi riposerei.»

_____

_____

_____

_____

_____

_____

_____

_____

VOCABOLARIO

assumere	to hire	**opuscoli**	brochures
camicetta	blouse	**piscina**	pool
gonna	skirt	**seta**	silk
isola	island	**spiaggia**	beach
moda	fashion	**vetrine**	shop windows

The past subjunctive (*congiuntivo passato*)

The past subjunctive is used in a dependent **che** clause to express the speaker's feelings toward a recent past action when the verb in the main clause is in the present indicative. The present subjunctive of **avere** or **essere** + the past participle of the verb is used.

The action in the **che** clause is in the past, while the action in the main clause is in the present tense.

Credo che abbiano vinto la partita.   *I think that they won the game.*
Dubito che voi abbiate vinto.   *I doubt that you have won.*

	PARLARE (*to speak*)	VENDERE (*to sell*)	SENTIRE (*to hear*)
che io	**abbia parlato**	**abbia venduto**	**abbia sentito**
che tu	**abbia parlato**	**abbia venduto**	**abbia sentito**
che lui/lei	**abbia parlato**	**abbia venduto**	**abbia sentito**
che noi	**abbiamo parlato**	**abbiamo venduto**	**abbiamo sentito**
che voi	**abbiate parlato**	**abbiate venduto**	**abbiate sentito**
che loro	**abbiano parlato**	**abbiano venduto**	**abbiano sentito**

Following is the conjugation of the past subjunctive using **essere**:

	PARTIRE (to leave, to depart)	VESTIRSI (to get dressed)
che io	**sia partito/a**	**mi sia vestito/a**
che tu	**sia partito/a**	**ti sia vestito/a**
che lui/lei	**sia partito/a**	**si sia vestito/a**
che noi	**siamo partiti/e**	**ci siamo vestiti/e**
che voi	**siate partiti/e**	**vi siate vestiti/e**
che loro	**siano partiti/e**	**si siano vestiti/e**

As with the present subjunctive and the imperfect subjunctive, the past subjunctive is used after expressions of doubt, emotion, wishing, and impersonal expressions.

Dubito che tu **abbia parlato**.	*I doubt that you spoke.*
Sono contenta che tu **abbia lavorato**.	*I am happy that you worked.*
È impossibile che siano già **partiti**.	*It is impossible that they have already left.*

The past subjunctive is used to express a past action that has taken place before the action of the main verb. Notice the use of the present and past subjunctive in these sentences:

Spero che **Carlo legga** il libro.	*I hope Carlo **will read** the book.*
Spero che Carlo **abbia letto** il libro.	*I hope Carlo **read** the book.*

ESERCIZIO
12·19

Complete the following sentences with the appropriate forms of the past subjunctive.

1. Credo che loro _____ (arrivare) con il treno.

2. Non credo che voi _____ (essere) ammalati.

3. Carlo dubita che voi vi _____ (alzare) presto.

4. È impossibile che voi _____ (bussare) alla porta.

5. Giovanna pensa che lui _____ (svelare) il segreto.

6. Non credo che voi _____ (andare) in Italia.

7. Penso che _____ (fare) molto freddo.

8. Dubito che noi _____ (capire) dove andare.

9. È importante che voi _____ (arrivare) prima di tutti.

10. Loro credono che tu _____ (lavorare) tutto il fine settimana.

11. Lui crede che loro _____ (rubare) questa macchina.

12. Mi dispiace che tua sorella _____ (dire) quelle cose.

The past subjunctive is the equivalent of the present perfect in the indicative mood. Note the following examples:

So che **sei andato** al cinema con Maria.   *I know that you **went** to the movie with Maria.*
Penso che tu **sia andato** al cinema   *I think that you **went** to the movie with Maria.*
   con Maria.
So che **hai lavorato** molto.   *I know that you **worked** a lot.*
Penso che tu **abbia lavorato** molto.   *I think you **worked** a lot.*

ESERCIZIO
12·20

Complete the following sentences with the present perfect or the past subjunctive as necessary.

1. È bene che Paolo _____ (venire).

2. So che Paola _____ (venire).

3. Siamo certi che lei _____ (parlare).

4. Speriamo che lei _____ (parlare).

5. Sono sicura che voi _____ (nuotare).

6. Spero che voi _____ (nuotare).

7. È possibile che Carlo _____ (partire).

8. So che Carlo non _____ (partire).

9. Siete sicuri che lui non _____ (ricevere) la lettera?

10. Non siamo certi che lui _____ (ricevere) la lettera.

11. La maestra sa che gli studenti _____ (capire) tutto.

12. La maestra non crede che gli studenti _____ (capire) tutto.

ESERCIZIO
12·21

Fill in the spaces with the imperfect subjunctive and past subjunctive and then translate the paragraph into English.

Ieri pomeriggio dovevo fare una presentazione fotografica del mio ultimo viaggio. Avevo

preparato tutto la sera prima e pensavo che mio marito _____ (mettere) nella

scatola tutti i cavi necessari. I cavi non c'erano! Non pensavo che _____

(dimenticare) una cosa così importante. I miei amici pensavano che io _____

(scherzare) quando ho detto che non avevo le prolunghe. Ho preso la macchina e sono

andata a casa a prendere quello che mi occorreva. Quando sono arrivata lì, ho suonato il

campanello e aspettavo che qualcuno mi _____ (venire) ad aprire la porta.

Non c'era nessuno in casa! Speravo che mio marito _____ (lasciare) la porta del garage aperta. Era chiusa. Speravo che _____ (mettere) una chiave di riserva fuori. Niente da fare. Ero disperata! In quel momento ho sentito una macchina arrivare. Era mio figlio. Ho preso il necessario e sono ritornata a casa dei miei amici dove ho potuto finalmente fare la mia presentazione!

_____

_____

_____

_____

_____

_____

_____

_____

_____

_____

_____

_____

_____

VOCABOLARIO			
chiave	key	**presentazione**	presentation
disperata	desperate	**prolunghe**	extensions, cables
niente	nothing	**riserva**	extra
occorreva	to be needed	**scherzare**	to joke

The past perfect subjunctive (*congiuntivo trapassato*)

The past perfect subjunctive is used when the action of the verb in the dependent clause happened before the action of the verb in the main clause, which is in the past. The independent clause is in a past tense or in the conditional. It is formed by the imperfect subjunctive of **avere** and **essere** + the past participle of the verb.

PRESENT INDICATIVE	PERFECT SUBJUNCTIVE	IMPERFECT INDICATIVE	PAST PERFECT SUBJUNCTIVE
Credo che Mario *I think that* Mario	**sia venuto.** *came.*	**Credevo che** *I thought that*	Mario **fosse venuto.** *Mario **had come.***

The following chart shows the conjugations of the past perfect subjunctive with **essere** and **avere**:

	PARLARE	VENDERE	PARTIRE
che io	avessi parlato	avessi venduto	fossi partito/a
che tu	avessi parlato	avessi venduto	fossi partito/a
che lui/lei	avesse parlato	avesse venduto	fosse partito/a
che noi	avessimo parlato	avessimo venduto	fossimo partiti/e
che voi	aveste parlato	aveste venduto	foste partiti/e
che loro	avessero parlato	avessero venduto	fossero partiti/e

ESERCIZIO
12·22

Complete the following sentences with the past perfect subjunctive of the verbs in parentheses.

1. Tu eri contento che loro _____ (capire).

2. Lei credeva che loro _____ (arrivare).

3. Ero contenta che tu _____ (venire).

4. Avremmo preferito che voi _____ (andare) all'università.

5. Sembrava che io _____ (sapere) dove erano andati.

6. Speravamo che voi _____ (entrare) prima di noi.

7. Credevamo che lui _____ (cercare) lavoro.

8. Sembrava che _____ (imparare) solo lui.

9. Era impossibile che la lettera _____ (arrivare).

10. Ci aiutò senza che glielo _____ (chiedere).

After **come se** (*as if*), the imperfect and the past perfect subjunctive are always used, regardless of the tense of the main verb.

Parlavano **come se non fosse**
   successo niente.
Lo trattavano **come se fosse**
   stato un figlio.

*They were talking **as if** nothing*
   ***had happened**.*
*They treated him **as if***
   ***he had been** a son.*

ESERCIZIO
12·23

Translate the following sentences into Italian using the past perfect subjunctive.

1. I doubted that Maria had come.

_____

2. I hoped that you had found the keys.

_____

3. It was possible that he had arrived late.

_____

4. She thought that you had taken the money.

_____

5. You (pl.) doubted that I had looked for work.

_____

6. I had hoped that he had sold his motor scooter.

_____

7. It seemed to me that you had already read it.

_____

8. I didn't want the workers to have already left.

_____

9. This seemed to me the longest book that I had ever read.

_____

Fill in the spaces using the past perfect subjunctive of the verbs in parentheses, then translate the paragraph into English.

Se la tua casa _____ (essere) vicino ad una località sciistica, avresti avuto molti

ospiti. I tuoi amici si sarebbero aspettati che tu li _____ (invitare) a casa tua e

che _____ (chiedere) che _____ (rimanere) a dormire.

Speravano che tu li avessi invitati ad andare a sciare sulle meravigliose piste dove vai tu. La

tua casa non è vicino ad una località sciistica. Non hai potuto invitare gli amici, ma penso che

i tuoi parenti non sarebbero stati molto contenti se i tuoi amici _____ (venire),

_____ (dormire), _____ (mangiare) e _____

(sciare) per una settimana a casa tua.

_____

_____

_____

_____

_____

_____

_____

_____

_____

VOCABOLARIO

aspettarsi	expect	**piste**	runs
meravigliose	wonderful	**località sciistica**	ski resort
ospiti	guests		

The *se* clause and the subjunctive

To express a contrary-to-fact statement in the present or the future, the imperfect subjunctive is used in the **se** clause. The conditional tense is then normally used in the main clause to express a conclusion to the action.

Se potessi, verrei.   *If I could, I would come.*

To express a contrary-to-fact statement in the past, the past perfect subjunctive is used in the **se** clause and the past conditional is used in the main clause. The conditional is only used in the main clause; never in the **se** clause. Only the imperfect or the past perfect subjunctive is used after **se**. Never use the present subjunctive.

Se avessi saputo, sarei venuto.   *If I had known, I would have come.*

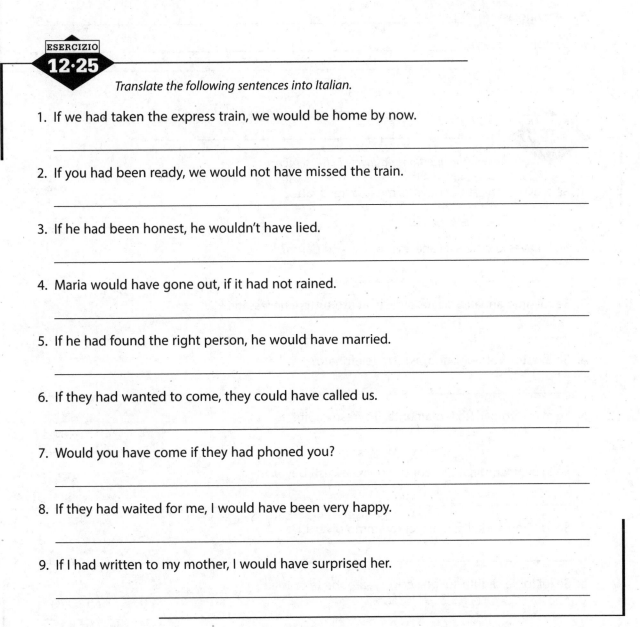

ESERCIZIO

12·25

Translate the following sentences into Italian.

1. If we had taken the express train, we would be home by now.

   _____

2. If you had been ready, we would not have missed the train.

   _____

3. If he had been honest, he wouldn't have lied.

   _____

4. Maria would have gone out, if it had not rained.

   _____

5. If he had found the right person, he would have married.

   _____

6. If they had wanted to come, they could have called us.

   _____

7. Would you have come if they had phoned you?

   _____

8. If they had waited for me, I would have been very happy.

   _____

9. If I had written to my mother, I would have surprised her.

   _____

   _____

ESERCIZIO

12·26

Change the following verbs into the past perfect subjunctive.

1. se ti chiedessi un favore _____

2. se vedessi un extraterrestre _____

3. se avessi una casa grande _____

4. se lui capisse _____

5. se lei leggesse _____

6. se noi bevessimo il vino rosso _____

7. se voi aspettaste _____

8. se mangiassero _____

9. se non capissero _____

Answer the questions positively in full sentences.

1. Se ti avessi chiesto un favore, me lo avresti fatto?

_____

2. Se lui avesse visto un cane, avrebbe avuto paura?

_____

3. Se fossimo andati a sciare, avreste avuto tutto il necessario?

_____

4. Se aveste avuto bisogno, avreste telefonato?

_____

5. Se avessero parlato lentamente, li avresti capiti?

_____

6. Se io avessi ordinato il cappuccino, lo avresti bevuto?

_____

7. Se fossimo andati al mare, ci saremmo divertiti?

_____

8. Se lui fosse caduto sul ghiaccio, si sarebbe fatto male?

_____

9. Se mi fossi sentito bene, saresti venuto a lavorare?

_____

The passive voice (*forma passiva*)

In the active voice studied so far, the subject performs the action. In the passive voice, the subject receives the action.

ACTIVE VOICE	PASSIVE VOICE
Maria **legge** il libro.	Il libro **è letto** da Maria.
*Maria **reads** the book.*	*The book **is read** by Maria.*

The passive in Italian is formed, as in English, with the verb **essere** and the past participle of the action verb. The passive voice of any transitive verb is formed with the conjugated forms of the auxiliary **essere** + the past participle of the verb, followed by the preposition **da**, if the agent is expressed. It is not always necessary to express the agent.

La macchina **è stata rubata** da delinquenti.	*The car **has been robbed by** delinquents.* (By whom is expressed.)
La macchina **è stata rubata**.	*The car **has been robbed**.* (By whom is not expressed.)

Verbs other than *essere* to express the passive voice

Venire is often used in place of **essere**. The use of either verb does not change the meaning of the sentence. In general, you use **venire** to express carrying out an action, while **essere** is used to emphasize a state of being.

I loro dipinti **vennero/furono ammirati** da tutto il mondo.	*Their paintings **were admired** by the entire world.*
La vostra macchina **verrà riparata** la settimana prossima.	*Your car will **be repaired** next week.* (action)
Le camicie **sono lavate**.	*The shirts **are washed**.* (state of being)

Answer the following questions, using the passive voice and the words suggested in parentheses.

1. Quando è stato pagato il conto? (ieri)

   _____

2. Da chi è stata scritta *La Divina Commedia*? (Dante Alighieri)

   _____

3. A che ora sono stati svegliati i ragazzi? (tardi)

   _____

4. Dove sono state fatte queste scarpe? (in Italia)

   _____

5. Quante fotografie sono state scattate? (molte)

   _____

6. Dove è stato pubblicato questo libro? (in America)

   _____

7. In che anno è stata scoperta l'America? (1492)

   _____

8. Dove sono stati portati i quadri? (in cantina)

   _____

*Translate the following sentences into Italian, using **venire** in the appropriate forms.*

1. The new statue will be admired in the museum's lobby.

   _____

2. Alessandro Manzoni's works have been studied by all Italian students.

   _____

3. The soccer team was honored for its excellent season.

   _____

4. The school's roof will be repaired during the summer.

   _____

5. The contract will be signed this evening.

   _____

6. The tax return will be completed by the middle of April.

_____

7. The museum will be closed for three months for remodeling.

_____

8. The drapes were taken down to be cleaned.

_____

9. The house was sold a long time ago.

_____

Modal verbs do not have a passive form. The infinitives that follow them must be put in the passive.

Il biglietto **deve essere emesso** entro la prossima settimana.	*The ticket **must be issued** by next week.*
Le spese della casa **possono essere pagate** piano piano.	*The house expenses **can be paid** little by little.*

Rimanere and **restare** are often used in place of **essere** when the past participle following it describes emotions such as: **deluso, stupito, meravigliato, sorpreso, chiuso,** and **aperto.**

Siamo rimasti molto delusi quando abbiamo saputo che non sareste venuti.	*We were very **disappointed** when we heard that you were not coming.*
La chiesa **resterà chiusa** al pubblico tutto il mese di giugno per restauro.	*The church **will remain closed** to the public throughout June for remodeling.*

ESERCIZIO
13·3

Translate the following sentences into Italian, using the passive voice.

1. The contract must be signed.

_____

2. The contract will have to be signed by your parents.

_____

3. The contract (venire) was signed by everybody.

_____

4. The contract (venire) was signed in court.

_____

5. We are surprised that the contract has not been signed yet.

_____

6. The airline ticket will be reimbursed.

_____

7. The airline ticket was reimbursed already.

_____

8. The airline ticket (venire) will be reimbursed as soon as possible.

_____

9. The house (venire) will be built in six months.

_____

10. This museum will remain closed all winter.

_____

Andare is often used in place of **essere** with verbs such as **perdere** (*to lose*), **smarrire** (*to lose*), and **sprecare** (*to waste*). Also, sometimes **andare** replaces **dovere** + **essere** when conveying a sense of necessity.

Molta frutta **va sprecata** perchè nessuno vuole raccoglierla.	*A lot of fruit **is wasted** because nobody wants to pick it.*
Tutte le fotografie **sono andate smarrite** durante la guerra. *or* Tutte le fotografie **sono state smarrite** durante la guerra.	*All the pictures **were lost** during the war.*
Va ricordato che non si può correre nei corridoi. *or* **Deve essere ricordato** che non si può correre nei corridoi.	*It **must be remembered** that one cannot run in the corridors.*

ESERCIZIO
13·4

Translate the following sentences into Italian, using the appropriate form of the verb in the passive voice.

1. Lots of food is wasted in restaurants.

_____

2. Very often I see signs that say, "A dog is lost."

_____

3. It must be remembered that one cannot go fishing without a permit.

_____

4. It must be remembered that smoking is prohibited in airplane lavatories.

_____

5. All the leftovers from the roof repair will have to be picked up and put in the containers.

_____

6. All my documents have been robbed.

   _____

7. All that gossip will have to be taken with a grain of salt.

   _____

8. So much space is wasted in her house!

   _____

9. All these ideas will have to be taken into consideration.

   _____

Alternatives to the passive voice

In Italian the passive voice is often used in written language such as in newspapers, magazines, and books. In the spoken language, you can choose a few alternatives that are usually preferred.

Si

Si is used to express the idea of *one*, and it is used much more in Italian than in English. It also has a variety of meanings, such as *we*, *you*, and *they*.

Si dice che i nostri amici siano pieni di soldi.	*It is said that our friends are rolling in money.*
Che cosa **si fa** oggi?	*What are we doing today?*

The **si passivante**

A very common way to avoid the passive in Italian is to use the passive **si** + the third-person singular or plural of the verb.

Dove **si comprano** questi libri?	*Where are these books bought?*

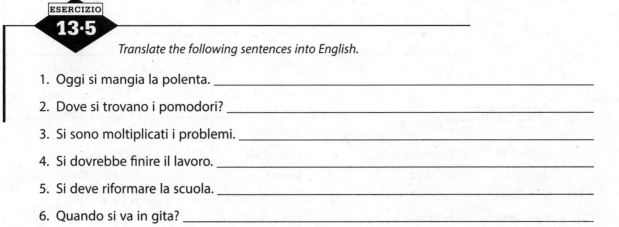

ESERCIZIO
13·5

Translate the following sentences into English.

1. Oggi si mangia la polenta. _____

2. Dove si trovano i pomodori? _____

3. Si sono moltiplicati i problemi. _____

4. Si dovrebbe finire il lavoro. _____

5. Si deve riformare la scuola. _____

6. Quando si va in gita? _____

7. Non si accettano le carte di credito. _____

8. Qui si parla Inglese. _____

9. Si deve abbattere quell'albero. _____

_____

ESERCIZIO
13·6

Read and translate the following paragraph into English.

Domenica prossima più di 36.000 persone di Milano dovranno lasciare le loro case per una giornata intera. La stazione centrale sarà chiusa e i treni non arriveranno o partiranno. La ferrovia all'entrata di Milano rimarrà bloccata con serie ripercussioni sul traffico ferroviario nazionale e internazionale. Tutto questo per permettere agli artificieri di neutralizzare e rimuovere una bomba caduta da un aereo nella seconda guerra mondiale ancora inesplosa sotto la strada. Questa bomba è stata trovata quando degli operai stavano scavando la strada per rifare le fognature e sono andati ad una certa profondità. Si pensa che questa sia una delle bombe più grandi ancora inesplose che si siano mai trovate a Milano. La zona sarà protetta da esperti e dalla polizia urbana.

_____

_____

_____

_____

_____

_____

_____

_____

VOCABOLARIO

artificieri	bomb experts	**inesplosa**	unexploded
bloccata	blocked	**intera**	whole/entire
ferroviario	railway (adj.)	**ripercussioni**	repercussions
fognatura	sewers	**scavare**	to dig

Idiomatic expressions (*espressioni idiomatiche*)

Idioms with *avere*

The verb **avere** is used in idiomatic expressions. Very often the infinitive of **avere** is abbreviated to **aver** before a noun or an adjective.

avere (aver)... anni	*to be . . . years old*
aver(e) bisogno di	*to need*
aver(e) caldo	*to feel (be) warm*
aver(e) fame	*to be hungry*
aver(e) freddo	*to be cold*
aver(e) fretta	*to be in a hurry*
aver(e) l'impressione (di)	*to have the impression*
aver(e) l'intenzione (di)	*to have the intention*
aver(e) mal (di)	*to have an ache*
aver(e) paura (di)	*to be afraid*
aver(e) ragione (di)	*to be right*
aver(e) sete	*to be thirsty*
aver(e) sonno	*to be sleepy*
aver(e) torto (di)	*to be wrong*
aver(e) vergogna (di)	*to be ashamed*
aver(e) voglia (di)	*to feel like doing*

ESERCIZIO
14·1

*Rewrite the following sentences in Italian, using the idiomatic expressions with **avere**.*

1. I need an umbrella. _____

2. You (sing.) are always in a hurry. _____

3. He is cold. _____

4. She has a headache. _____

5. We are thirsty. _____

6. I was wrong. _____

7. They need new shoes. _____

8. I had a headache. _____

9. You (sing.) are ashamed. _____

10. You (pl.) are sleepy. _____

11. We are very warm. _____

12. They are right. _____

Idioms with *fare*

The verb **fare** is also used in idiomatic expressions. Very often the infinitive of **fare** is abbreviated to **far** before a consonant.

fare attenzione	to pay attention
far(e) bella, brutta figura	to make a good, bad impression
far(e) benzina	to get gas
fa caldo, freddo	it is warm, cold
far(e) carriera	to be successful
far(e) colpo su qualcuno	to impress someone
far(e) colazione	to have breakfast
far(e) compere	to go shopping
far(e) esercizio	to exercise
far(e) fotografie	to take pictures
far(e) il bagno	to take a bath
far(e) la conoscenza (di)	to make the acquaintance
far(e) una crociera	to take a cruise
far(e) la doccia	to take a shower
far(e) il pieno	to fill up with gas
far(e) la spesa	to get groceries
far(e) male	to hurt, to ache
far parte (di)	to be part of
far(e) una passeggiata	to take a walk
far(e) presto	to hurry up
far(e) progresso	to progress
far(e) quattro chiacchiere	to chat
far(e) il campeggio	to go camping
far(e) un complimento	to pay a compliment
far(e) alla romana	to go Dutch
far(e) un discorso	to make a speech
fare la predica	to preach
fare una domanda	to ask a question
fare un giro	to take a tour
fare uno spuntino	to have a snack
fare un viaggio	to take a trip
fare un regalo	to give a gift
fare una visita	to pay a visit
farsi male	to get hurt
fare un favore (a)	to do a favor
fare un piacere (a)	to do a favor
far vedere a qualcuno	to show someone

Following are some common weather-related expressions:

Che tempo fa?	*How is the weather?*
Fa bel tempo (cattivo).	*The weather is good (bad).*
Fa caldo (freddo).	*It is warm (cold).*

ESERCIZIO 14·2

Rewrite the following sentences in Italian, using the idiomatic expressions with **fare**.

1. He pays attention. _____

2. We have breakfast. _____

3. They will take pictures. _____

4. I took a trip. _____

5. He has a snack. _____

6. I pay a visit. _____

7. It was very cold. _____

8. He will make a speech. _____

9. We will go Dutch. _____

10. He does me a favor. _____

11. We will take a cruise. _____

12. I have a snack. _____

13. She pays attention. _____

14. You (pl.) ask a question. _____

Special constructions with *fare*, *lasciare*, *metterci*, and *volerci*

Fare

The construction of **fare** + the infinitive is commonly used in Italian and corresponds to the English *to have something done or to make/have someone do something*. Direct and indirect object pronouns precede **fare** except when it is in the infinitive or is conjugated in the familiar forms of the imperative.

Il capo **fa lavorare** molto gli operai.   *The boss **is having** the workers **work** hard.*

Object pronouns usually precede the conjugated form of **fare**. They follow **fare** only when **fare** is in the infinitive or in the first or second person of the imperative.

Faccio pulire il tappeto.	*I am having the carpet cleaned.*
Lo faccio pulire ogni anno.	*I have it cleaned every year.*
Desidero **far cambiare** le tende.	*I wish to have the drapes changed.*
Desidero **farle cambiare**.	*I wish to have them changed.*

If there is only one object, it is a direct object.

La facciamo scrivere.	*We make her write it.*
Il capo **li fa lavorare** molto.	*The boss makes them work very hard.*
Abbiamo fatto partire la macchina.	*We started the car.*
Falli studiare!	*Make them study!*

When the person who completes the action and the action completed are expressed in a sentence, the result of the action is the direct object, and the person doing the action is the indirect object.

Faccio mandare la lettera a mia sorella.	*I am having my sister send the letter.*
Gliela **faccio mandare**.	*I'm having her send it.*

Sometimes, to clarify some ambiguity, the preposition **a** preceding the noun of the doer is replaced with **da**.

Faccio mandare il pacco da Giovanna a Carlo.	*I'm having the package sent to Carlo by Giovanna.*

The infinitive of **fare** may follow a conjugated form of the same verb.

Lei **fa fare** un vestito dal sarto.	*I had the tailor make me a suit.*

Very common in Italian is the expression formed by **farsi** + **fare** (or the infinitive of another verb). The doer of the action is preceded by the preposition **da**.

Mi sono fatto fare un vestito da un sarto.	*I had the dressmaker make me a dress.*

Lasciare

When the verb **lasciare** is followed by an infinitive, it means *to let*, *permit*, or *allow*. It is used in the same way as **fare** + infinitive. Verbs of perception like *seeing*, *watching*, and *hearing* follow the same rule.

Lasciate parlare il professore.	*Let the professor speak!*
Lasciate stare!	*Let it be!*
Maria non mi **lascia andare** sull'altalena!	*Maria doesn't let me go on the swing!*
Mio padre non mi **lascia andare** fuori.	*My father doesn't allow me to go out.*
Sento cadere la grandine.	*I hear the hail fall.*
Abbiamo visto partire i nostri amici.	*We saw our friends leave.*

Lasciare may also be followed by **che** + the subjunctive.

Perchè non lo **lasciate andare** al cinema?	*Why don't you let him go to the movie?*
Perchè non **lasciate che** lui **vada** al cinema?	*Why don't you let him go to the movie?*

A relative clause with **che** has the option of replacing the infinitive after a verb of perception.

L'ho vista **piangere**.	*I saw her* **cry**.
L'ho vista **che piangeva**.	*I saw her* **cry**.

Metterci and *volerci*

The expressions formed with **metterci** (**mettere** + **ci**) and **volerci** (**volere** + **ci**) are used with reference to time needed to do something or go somewhere. If the subject is clear, **metterci** is used. If it is not clearly expressed, **volerci** is used.

Quante ore di aereo **ci vogliono** per andare in Italia?	*How many hours on the plane* **are needed** *to go to Italy?*
Carlo, quanto tempo **ci metti** per arrivare al lavoro?	*Carlo, how long* **does it take** *you to get to work?*

ESERCIZIO
14·3

Translate the following sentences into Italian.

1. They make her work too many hours.

_____

2. I had my husband take me to the doctor.

_____

3. My grandmother used to make me dry the dishes every day.

_____

4. They will have us look at pictures for two hours.

_____

5. She made her kids go to bed very early.

_____

6. She will not let him go in the house.

_____

7. Grandparents let their grandchildren do everything they want.

_____

8. The school lets the students go home early.

_____

9. Let her laugh!

_____

10. Let them play!

_____

11. It will take several years for the trees to grow.

_____

12. How long will it take to do this translation?

_____

13. It took me only three days.

_____

14. How many days does it take for a letter to arrive from Italy?

_____

15. It takes a week.

_____

Read and translate the following paragraphs into English.

Ho una bella casa in campagna, ma è vecchia. Vorrei farla restaurare. Ho già fatto fare il progetto e il preventivo delle spese da un architetto conosciuto in questa zona. Farò fare i lavori da una ditta di costruzioni che conosco da tanto tempo. Ci vorranno molti mesi per finire questo progetto. Io non andrò a vederla fino a quando non sarà finita. Lascio che i muratori lavorino in pace. Sanno come fare il loro lavoro.

Ho già fatto riparare il caminetto e ci vorranno due o tre settimane prima di poterlo usare. Non appena i lavori saranno finiti inviterò i mei amici per una festa.

_____

_____

_____

_____

_____

_____

_____

_____

caminetto	fireplace	muratori	masons
campagna	country	preventivo	estimate
ditta	company	restaurare	to remodel

Idioms with *dare*

The verb **dare** is used in many idiomatic expressions. Very often the infinitive of **dare** is abbreviated to **dar** before a consonant.

dare ascolto	*to listen to someone*
dar(e) da mangiare (bere)	*to feed, to give something to eat (drink)*
dar(e) del tu	*to use the informal way of speaking*
dar(e) fastidio(a)	*to bother someone*
dare i saluti (a)	*to give regards, greetings*
dare il benvenuto (a)	*to welcome*
dar(e) la mano (a)	*to shake hands*
dar(e) ragione	*to admit someone is right*
dar(e) la colpa (a)	*to blame*
dar(e) su (il mare, la piazza, ecc.)	*to face (the sea, the square, etc.)*
dare un esame	*to take a test*
dare un film	*to show a movie*
dare un urlo	*to let out a yell*
dare un passaggio	*to give a lift*
dare un pugno	*to punch*
dare un calcio	*to kick*
dare una risposta	*to give an answer/response*
dare un sospiro (di)	*to sigh*
darsi da fare	*to get busy*
darsi per vinto	*to give up*
darsi agli studi	*to devote oneself to one's studies*

ESERCIZIO
14·5

Translate the following sentences into Italian, using the idiomatic expressions with **dare**.

1. I have to feed the dog.

_____

2. Don't bother them; they are sleeping.

_____

3. She welcomed me with affection.

_____

4. My sister always blames her friends.

_____

5. In Italy people shake hands.

_____

6. Don't listen to them!

_____

7. Tomorrow the students will take the final tests.

_____

8. Georgia's house faces the beach.

_____

9. I let out a scream when I saw the mouse.

_____

10. They give us a ride to the airport.

_____

11. Children like to kick the ball.

_____

12. I sighed when I finished the book on time.

_____

13. We did not give him an answer yet.

_____

14. I have to get busy, because I am leaving in two weeks.

_____

15. My son doesn't want to give up.

_____

Expressions with *andare*

Following are some commonly used expressions with **andare**. Most of the times **andare** is followed by a preposition. This is not the case if an adverb follows it.

andare a piedi	*to walk, to go by foot*
andare a teatro	*to go to the theater*
andare a braccetto	*to walk arm in arm*
andare a cavallo	*to go horseback riding*
andare a pescare	*to go fishing*
andare bene	*to go well*
andare male	*to go badly*
andare d'accordo	*to get along*
andare di giorno, di sera	*to go during the day, in the evening*

andare in macchina	*to go by car*
andare in aereo, in treno, in bicicletta	*to go by plane, train, bicycle*
andare per affari	*to go on business*
andare in vendita	*to go on sale*

ESERCIZIO
14·6

Translate the following sentences into Italian, using the idiomatic expressions with **andare**.

1. People in Italy often walk arm in arm.

   _____

2. Carlo wants to go fishing with his grandfather.

   _____

3. Their children always get along very well.

   _____

4. I would like to go horseback riding in the West.

   _____

5. Today, everything I did went well!

   _____

6. She is afraid to go by plane.

   _____

7. She prefers to go by train.

   _____

8. Why don't we go in the evening?

   _____

9. Everything will go on sale tomorrow.

   _____

ESERCIZIO
14·7

Read and translate the following paragraph into English.

I ragazzi erano al parco e giocavano al pallone. Ad un tratto uno di loro diede un calcio ad un ragazzo della squadra opposta. Il ragazzo diede un urlo di dolore e cadde per terra. Tutti gli andarono intorno per vedere se si era fatto veramente male. L'allenatore voleva che stessero lontani, ma nessuno lo ascoltava. Volevano dare una mano al loro compagno. Gli adulti hanno discusso per un po' e poi hanno dato ragione al ragazzo colpito. Quando chiesero all'altro il motivo delle sue azioni, lui non diede una risposta. L'allenatore l'ha sospeso dal gioco per due settimane. Può darsi che la prossima volta cerchi di essere più gentile, rispettoso e sportivo verso i compagni di gioco.

_____

_____

_____

_____

_____

_____

_____

_____

_____

VOCABOLARIO

allenatore	coach	**opposta**	opposite
colpito	hit	**motivo**	reason
discusso	discussed	**sospeso**	suspended
squadra	team	**rispettoso**	respectful

Expressions with *stare*

The verb **stare** is used in many idiomatic expressions. Very often the infinitive of **stare** is abbreviated to **star** before a consonant.

lasciare stare	*leave something or someone alone*
stare attento/a (a)	*to pay attention*
star(e) fermo/a	*to keep still*
stare a pennello	*to fit like a glove*
star(e) bene (male)	*to be well (sick); to fit well (badly)*
stare in casa	*to stay in the house*
stare in piedi	*to be standing*
star(e) seduto/a	*to be sitting*
star(e) zitto/a	*to be quiet*

star(e) da...	*to be at somebody's (home, office, etc.)*
star(e) con le mani in mano	*to do nothing*
star(e) con le mani in tasca	*to do nothing*
star(e) per...	*to be about to . . .*
stare a vedere	*to wait and see*

ESERCIZIO 14·8

Translate the following sentences into Italian, using the idiomatic expressions with **stare***.*

1. That dress fits her like a glove.

   _____

2. We will wait and see who will win the best picture award.

   _____

3. Giovanni is in bed. He is not well at all.

   _____

4. Erica never keeps still.

   _____

5. Why are you standing?

   _____

6. I was at the dentist for three hours.

   _____

7. Keep (you pl.) still and quiet. I am tired.

   _____

8. It is too cold. I'll stay in the house.

   _____

9. Be careful not to slip on the icy roads.

   _____

ESERCIZIO 14·9

Read and translate the following paragraph into English.

Questa mattina mi sono alzata presto e stavo per andare alla stazione ad incontrare Giovanna, quando mi ha telefonato per dirmi che la babysitter non stava bene e non poteva andare a casa sua e stare con i suoi bambini. Mi ha detto anche che i bambini avevano l'influenza e dovevano stare fermi a letto. Quando i bambini staranno bene e il tempo sarà bello andremo tutti insieme a cavallo. Per adesso Giovanna deve stare a casa per far stare fermi i bambini. Che peccato!

_____

_____

_____

_____

_____

_____

_____

_____

_____

_____

_____

VOCABOLARIO	
che peccato	what a pity
incontrare	to meet

Verbs and expressions followed by a preposition

In Italian many verbs and expressions are followed by a preposition. Following are the most commonly used prepositions.

Verbs and expressions followed by the preposition *a*

The preposition **a** is used before a noun or a pronoun with the following verbs:

assistere a	*to attend*
assomigliare a	*to resemble*
credere a	*to believe in*
dare da mangiare a	*to feed*
dare fastidio	*to bother*
dare la caccia a	*to chase*
dare noia a	*to bother*
dare retta a	*to listen to*
dare torto a	*to blame*
dare un calcio a	*to kick*
dare un pugno a	*to punch*
fare attenzione a	*to pay attention*
fare bene (male) a	*to be good (bad)*
fare piacere a	*to please*
far vedere a	*to show*
fare visita a	*to visit*
fare un regalo a	*to give a present to*
giocare a	*to play a game*
interessarsi a	*to be interested in*
partecipare a	*to participate in*
pensare a	*to think about*
raccomandarsi a	*to ask favors of*
ricordare a	*to remind*
rinunciare a	*to give up*
servire a	*to be good for*
stringere la mano a	*to shake hands with*
tenere a	*to care about*

Before an infinitive the preposition **a** is used with the following verbs:

abituarsi a	*to get used to*	**insegnare a**	*to teach*
affrettarsi a	*to hurry*	**invitare a**	*to invite to*
aiutare a	*to help*	**mandare a**	*to send*
cominciare a	*to begin*	**obbligare a**	*to oblige*
continuare a	*to continue*	**pensare a**	*to think about*
convincere a	*to convince*	**persuadere a**	*to convince*
costringere a	*to compel*	**preparare a**	*to prepare*
decidersi a	*to decide*	**provare a**	*to try*
divertirsi a	*to have fun*	**rinunciare a**	*to give up*
fare meglio a	*to be better off*	**riprendere a**	*to resume*
fare presto a	*to do fast*	**riuscire a**	*to succeed*
imparare a	*to learn*	**sbrigarsi a**	*to hurry*
incoraggiare a	*to encourage*	**servire a**	*to be good for*

With verbs of movement use **a** with the following verbs:

andare a	*to go*	**stare a**	*to stay*
correre a	*to run*	**tornare a**	*to return*
fermarsi a	*to stop*	**venire a**	*to come*
passare a	*to stop by*		

ESERCIZIO
15·1

Translate the following sentences into Italian.

1. They believe in everybody. _____

2. I try not to bother my sister. _____

3. The children don't listen to their teacher. _____

4. The cat chases the mouse. _____

5. Please pay attention to the road. _____

6. The boy punched his sister in the nose. _____

7. You (sing.) will please your mother. _____

8. He always thinks about you (sing.). _____

9. They like to play cards. _____

10. She looks like her father. _____

11. He doesn't shake his friend's hand. _____

12. We have to feed our pets. _____

Translate the following sentences into Italian.

1. I must get used to the new place.

   _____

2. She hurries to eat.

   _____

3. I will help you tie your shoes.

   _____

4. He decided to study Italian.

   _____

5. We have a lot of fun watching the monkeys at the zoo.

   _____

6. You (sing.) are better off not getting married.

   _____

7. We must learn how to ski.

   _____

8. The mother teaches the child to walk.

   _____

9. They invite us to dance.

   _____

10. I always think about buying something for my kids.

    _____

11. This instrument is good for blocking the door.

    _____

12. You (pl.) must give up your trip.

    _____

13. Don't keep on laughing!

    _____

14. They will send me to get the package.

    _____

15. We will resume learning Italian tomorrow.

    _____

Translate the following sentences into Italian.

1. We go to the movie.

   _____

2. I went to the cemetery.

   _____

3. He runs home because he is hungry.

   _____

4. She stops to buy the newspaper.

   _____

5. We will stop by your house.

   _____

6. They returned home very late.

   _____

7. We go to school with our friends.

   _____

8. Maria and Carlo are coming to visit us this afternoon.

   _____

9. He is running to catch the bus.

   _____

10. I stop to look at the flowers in the meadow.

    _____

11. They will stay at home all day.

    _____

12. She returned home with many books.

    _____

Verbs and expressions followed by the preposition *di*

Many verbs and expressions are followed by the preposition **di**. Following are the most commonly used verbs followed by **di**.

Before a noun or a pronoun:

accorgersi di	*to notice, realize*	**nutrirsi di**	*to feed on*
avere bisogno di	*to need*	**occuparsi di**	*to plan*
avere paura di	*to be afraid*	**pensare di**	*to think about*
dimenticarsi di	*to forget*	**preoccuparsi di**	*to worry about*
fidarsi di	*to trust*	**ricordarsi di**	*to remember*
innamorarsi di	*to fall in love*	**ridere di**	*to laugh at*
interessarsi di	*to be interested in*	**soffrire di**	*to suffer from*
lamentarsi di	*to complain*	**trattare di**	*to deal with*
meravigliarsi di	*to be surprised*	**vivere di**	*to live on*

Before an infinitive:

accettare di	*to notice, accept*	**finire di**	*to finish*
ammettere di	*to need*	**ordinare di**	*to order*
aspettare di	*to wait for*	**pensare di**	*to plan*
augurare di	*to wish*	**permettere di**	*to permit*
avere bisogno di	*to need*	**pregare di**	*to beg*
cercare di	*to try*	**proibire di**	*to prohibit*
chiedere di	*to ask*	**promettere di**	*to promise*
confessare di	*to confess*	**proporre di**	*to propose*
consigliare di	*to advise*	**ringraziare di**	*to thank*
contare di	*to plan*	**sapere di**	*to know*
credere di	*to believe*	**smettere di**	*to stop*
decidere di	*to decide*	**sperare di**	*to hope*
dimenticare di	*to forget*	**suggerire di**	*to suggest*
dubitare di	*to doubt*	**tentare di**	*to attempt*
fingere di	*to pretend*	**vietare di**	*to avoid*

ESERCIZIO 15·4

Translate the following sentences into Italian.

1. I didn't notice her. _____

2. You (sing.) need your friends. _____

3. Maria eats only fruit. _____

4. We are afraid of cats. _____

5. You (pl.) forgot me at home. _____

6. They worried about their old parents. _____

7. I trust you. _____

8. He doesn't remember you at all. _____

9. She has fallen in love with him. _____

10. They laugh at them. _____

11. We are surprised at his ability. _____

12. She suffers from migraine headaches. _____

13. They complain about everything. _____

14. You (pl.) cannot live on bread and water alone. _____

Translate the following sentences into Italian.

1. I admit that I am wrong.

   _____

2. You (sing.) have finished talking on the phone.

   _____

3. He ordered his troops to withdraw.

   _____

4. She is thinking about eating a steak.

   _____

5. I wish you a long and happy life.

   _____

6. We need to sleep.

   _____

7. I beg you to come quickly.

   _____

8. She prohibits you to touch the cake.

   _____

9. We ask you to close the door.

   _____

10. I plan to arrive on time.

    _____

11. They promised to bring me a nice toy.

    _____

12. We thank you (pl.) for watering the plants.

_____

13. He believes he will get out of the hospital in four days.

_____

14. I forgot to turn off the lights.

_____

15. You (sing.) have decided to travel by train.

_____

Verbs followed by the preposition *su*

Following are the most common verbs followed by the preposition **su**:

contare su	*to count on*	**riflettere su**	*to reflect on*
giurare su	*to swear on*	**scommettere su**	*to bet on*

Verbs followed directly by the infinitive

Some commonly used verbs are followed directly by the infinitive of a verb.

amare	*to love*	**piacere**	*to like*
desiderare	*to wish*	**potere**	*to be able*
dovere	*to have to, must*	**preferire**	*to prefer*
fare	*to make, do*	**sapere**	*to know how*
gradire	*to appreciate*	**volere**	*to want*
lasciare	*to let, allow*		

Impersonal verbs

The following verbs are called impersonal verbs. They are used in the third-person singular or the third-person plural.

basta	*it is enough*
bisogna	*it is necessary*
pare	*it seems*

ESERCIZIO
15·6

Translate the following sentences into Italian.

1. You can count on me. _____

2. I am reflecting on what to do. _____

3. The president swears on the Bible. _____

4. I wish I had a beautiful garden. _____

5. We allow the children to watch television. _____

6. We prefer eating outside. _____

7. I love having a beautiful house. _____

8. You (sing.) know how to live well. _____

9. That's enough talking. _____

10. It is necessary to speak with the director. _____

_____

ESERCIZIO
15·7

Translate the following sentences into Italian.

1. We learn to ski. _____

2. I start to understand. _____

3. I'm thinking of coming. _____

4. He needs to study. _____

5. They'll return to Italy. _____

6. You are afraid of the dark. _____

7. We don't trust him. _____

8. Stop talking. _____

9. We'll stay at home. _____

10. They forgot to study. _____

11. I need you. _____

12. She promised to come. _____

13. They give thanks for everything. _____

14. She used to teach driving. _____

15. Call me before you leave. _____

SENTENCE BUILDING

Introduction to Part IV

Writing skills can be difficult to acquire and use effectively in any language. This is particularly true when writing in a foreign language. This part will guide you through the many different structures in the Italian language and show you how to avoid the common pitfalls of writing in a foreign language.

In order to learn to write well, you need considerable practice. This part provides many exercises in which you will put to use the rules that are explained in each chapter.

Good sentence writing can be a difficult, but not impossible, task. It requires breaking the habit of translating word for word from your mother tongue and, instead, acquiring a feeling for the particulars of the new language.

Declarative sentences and word order

Phrases and sentences are different in nature and serve different purposes. A phrase is made up of more than one word but does not have a **subject + predicate** structure.

> one or more words → phrase subject + predicate → sentence

Phrases are used frequently in colloquial Italian and daily conversations.

A presto.	*See you soon.*
Buon giorno.	*Good morning.*

Below are examples of proverbs or short sayings commonly used in the Italian language. They are phrases because they do not have a subject-verb structure.

Meglio tardi che mai.	*Better later than never.*
A buon intenditor poche parole.	*A few words to the good listener.*

A sentence is an organized idea or thought. It is a grammatical unit consisting of different elements such as nouns, verbal structures, adverbs, modifiers, and object pronouns. Each element contributes to a sentence's structure. A sentence expresses a statement, a question, a command, a wish, or an exclamation. In writing, it generally begins with a capital letter and ends with the appropriate punctuation. In speaking, it is expressed with various stresses, pitches, and pauses. Following is an example of a simple sentence:

subject + predicate

Maria parla l'italiano.	*Maria speaks Italian.*

This sentence consists of a subject (**Maria**) and a predicate (**parla l'italiano**, including the verb **parla**). The subject, the "who" or "what" the sentence is about, is often the first element in a sentence. The predicate expresses the action of the subject.

Declarative sentences

Depending on the action they perform, sentences are classified into categories. First we will examine the declarative sentence. Declarative sentences are simple sentences with one verb in the indicative tense. They state a fact, an idea, or an argument. Declarative sentences make a statement and communicate information;

they do not ask questions, express exclamations, or give commands. These sentences use the following elements:

subject + verb + complement
Il volo 237 parte domani.   *Flight 237 will leave tomorrow.*

Take a look at the following sentences:

Il volo 237 **parte** alle dieci di mattina.   *Flight 237 **leaves** at ten in the morning.*
Il volo 237 **è partito** in ritardo ieri.   *Flight 237 **left** late yesterday.*
Oggi, il volo 237 **partirà** alle diciassette. *Today, flight 237 **will leave** at five in the evening.*

The verbs in these declarative sentences are in the indicative mode of the infinitive **partire**: present **parte**, past **è partito**, and future **partirà**.

ESERCIZIO
1·1

*Is it a phrase or a sentence? Write **P** for phrase or **S** for sentence.*

1. Maria ed io. _____

2. La porta è chiusa. _____

3. Noi leggiamo il giornale. _____

4. Buona notte. _____

5. Di niente. _____

6. Questo è certo. _____

7. Voi viaggiate. _____

8. Loro aspettano. _____

ESERCIZIO
1·2

Translate the following sentences into Italian.

1. My brother is very young.

_____

2. He is only eighteen.

_____

3. His name is Marco.

_____

4. I spoke to him yesterday.

_____

5. He is always on time.

   _____

6. He will call you soon.

   _____

7. She reads many books.

   _____

8. We like Rome.

   _____

9. We want to visit new places.

   _____

10. You (pl.) are interested in learning a new language.

    _____

Word order in declarative sentences

In every language, words must be arranged in the proper and logical order to express ideas clearly and to avoid misunderstandings. In Italian, as in English, the natural word order of simple sentences is:

> **subject + verb + direct object**
>
> **Giovanna compra il libro.**   *Giovanna is buying the book.*

This is the most frequent word order in Italian, but unlike English, Italian allows for more flexibility. Another pattern commonly used in Italian is:

> **verb + subject**
>
> **Venne un temporale.**   *A storm came.*

Some declarative sentences are expressed with an indirect object noun instead of a direct object noun.

> **subject + verb + indirect object**
>
> **Maria parlerà a Luigi.**   *Maria will speak to Luigi.*

Declarative sentences with direct and indirect object nouns

In English and Italian alike, some declarative sentences include both direct and indirect object nouns.

> **subject + verb + direct object + indirect object**
>
> **Renata ha comprato un libro a suo padre.**   *Renata has bought a book for her father.*

The word order is the same in the Italian and English sentences, but in English you can also say:

> *Renata has bought her father a book.*

This word order shows that English has more flexibility than Italian when direct and indirect object nouns are used in a sentence.

Declarative sentences with direct and indirect object pronouns

Although the word order in declarative sentences with object *nouns* is similar in both English and Italian, there is a significant difference between the word order in the two languages when using direct and indirect object *pronouns*. In Italian sentences, all object pronouns are placed before the verb.

subject + indirect object + direct object + verb

Renata gliel(o)' ha comprato.   *Renata bought it for him.*

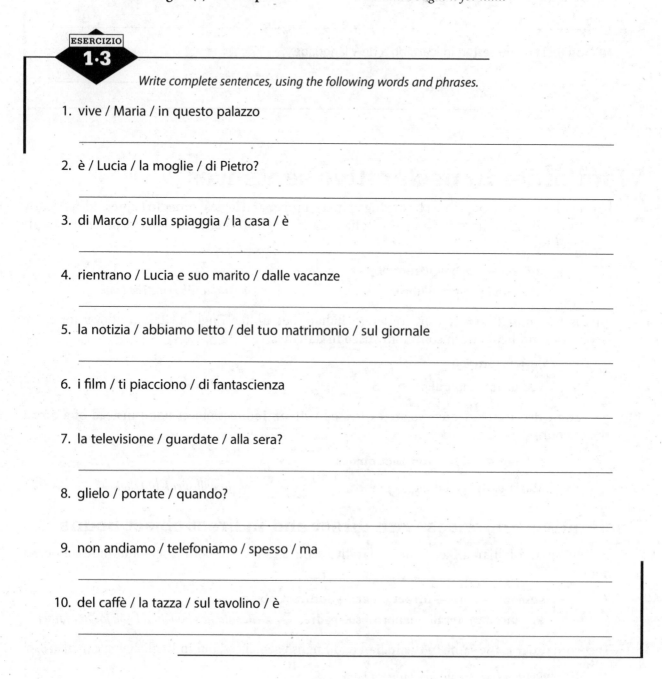

ESERCIZIO
1·3

Write complete sentences, using the following words and phrases.

1. vive / Maria / in questo palazzo

   _____

2. è / Lucia / la moglie / di Pietro?

   _____

3. di Marco / sulla spiaggia / la casa / è

   _____

4. rientrano / Lucia e suo marito / dalle vacanze

   _____

5. la notizia / abbiamo letto / del tuo matrimonio / sul giornale

   _____

6. i film / ti piacciono / di fantascienza

   _____

7. la televisione / guardate / alla sera?

   _____

8. glielo / portate / quando?

   _____

9. non andiamo / telefoniamo / spesso / ma

   _____

10. del caffè / la tazza / sul tavolino / è

   _____

Declarative sentences with prepositional phrases

Sentences may include a variety of prepositional phrases such as **di sera** (*in the evening*), **all'ombra** (*in the shade*), **per i tuoi amici** (*for your friends*). Generally, these phrases will occupy the same position in both Italian and English sentences. Compare the following:

Noi andiamo **ai corsi serali**.	*We attend **night classes**.*
Tu ti siedi **all'ombra**.	*You sit **in the shade**.*
Durante la cena, guardiamo la televisione.	***During dinner**, we watch television.*

Be aware of phrases such as **i corsi serali** (*the night classes*). Note how **corsi** (*classes*) comes before **serali** (*night*). Compound phrases such as this follow reversed word order in Italian, as opposed to how they are treated in English. When you encounter these phrases, remember that the Italian phrase will position the main idea (the fact that it is a class) first, followed by the detail (it is an evening class). These examples follow the same pattern:

il cucchiaino da caffè	*the coffee spoon*
la casa di campagna	*the country home*
gli occhiali da sole	*the sunglasses*
il tempo estivo	*the summertime*

Declarative sentences with adverbial phrases or adverbs

It is normal to use the same word order in Italian and in English when dealing with an adverbial phrase.

adverbial phrase + subject + verb

Tutte le sere noi usciamo.	*Every night we go out.*

Or:

subject + verb + adverbial phrase

Noi usciamo tutte le sere.	*We go out every night.*

Though an adverbial phrase such as **tutte le sere** (*every night*) can appear either before or after the subject-verb cluster in the Italian and English sentences, there are a few phrases, such as **a mano** (*by hand*), that only appear after the subject-verb cluster in both languages.

Noi cuciamo **a mano**.	*We sew **by hand**.*

Simple adverbs in Italian can have a variety of positions in a sentence. Longer adverbs (more than two syllables) can be found at the beginning or at the end of a sentence. When placed at the beginning of a sentence, an adverb is usually emphatic.

Adesso, ne ho abbastanza.	***Now**, I have had enough.*
Ne ho abbastanza **adesso**.	*I have had enough **now**.*

The most common position for an adverb, especially for short adverbs (no more than two syllables), is right after the verb in an Italian sentence. This is different from its most common position in English sentences, which is before the verb.

subject + verb + adverb + complement

Lei fa sempre il suo lavoro.	*She always does her work.*

Compare the positions of the adverbs in the following Italian and equivalent English sentences.

Tu parli **spesso** con tua sorella.
*You **often** speak with your sister.*

Lei studia **anche** l'inglese.
*She **also** studies English.*

As you can see, the adverb is placed before the verb in English but after it in Italian.

ESERCIZIO
1·4

Translate the following sentences into Italian.

1. Today we study Italian.

_____

2. We speak Italian well.

_____

3. We already finished reading.

_____

4. I rarely study.

_____

5. I will bring it to him tonight.

_____

6. We always talk about Italy.

_____

7. She gives me coffee, too.

_____

8. I bring a book to my sister.

_____

9. We often get together to have a party.

_____

10. You (sing.) live in the country, but love the city.

_____

Negative declarative sentences

To make an affirmative sentence negative in Italian, place the word **non** directly in front of the conjugated verb.

Leggiamo molto.	*We read a lot.*
→ **Non** leggiamo molto.	*We do **not** read a lot.*
Lei balla bene.	*She dances well.*
→ Lei **non** balla bene.	*She does **not** dance well.*
Il treno è arrivato.	*The train arrived.*
→ **Il treno non è arrivato.**	*The train did **not** arrive.*

There is no equivalent for the auxiliary words *do*, *does*, and *did* in Italian. Do not try to include them in a negative Italian sentence.

Other common negative words or phrases (adverbs) that are used to create negative declarative sentences are: **niente** (*nothing*), **mai** (*never*), **mai più** (*never again*), **neppure** (*neither*), **nè** (*neither, nor*), and **da nessun parte** (*nowhere*). Unlike English, two or three negative words can be used in a single Italian sentence.

Non so **niente**.	*I do **not** know **anything**. (I know **nothing**.)*
Noi **non** viaggiamo **mai** in inverno.	*We **never** travel in winter.*
Non vuole **più** fumare.	*He does **not** want to smoke **anymore**.*
Lei **non** mi invita **mai** alla festa.	*She **never** invites me to the party.*
Io **non** voglio **mai più** fare del male.	*I do **not** want to do **anything** bad **again**.*
Io **non** fumerò **mai più**.	*I will **never** smoke **again**.*
Elisa **non** viaggia **mai.**	*Elisa **never** travels.*

In Italian, the negative pronouns **nessuno** (*no one*) and **alcuno** (*someone*) also appear with other negative words.

Domani **non** viene **nessuno**.	*Tomorrow **no one** will come.*
Non c'è **alcun** problema.	*There is **no** problem.*
Lucia **non** chiede **niente**.	*Lucia does **not** ask for **anything**.*

In Italian, to be emphatic you may use redundant elements, or double negatives, in a sentence, especially in informal conversations.

Maria **non** verrà **mai** e poi **mai**.	*Maria will **never ever** come.*

ESERCIZIO
1·5

*Affirmative or negative? Write **A** for affirmative and **N** for negative.*

1. Le palme sono alte e belle. _____

2. La luna non brilla oggi. _____

3. Vedo molte stelle nel cielo. _____

4. Di notte, gli uccelli dormono sugli alberi. _____

5. Mai e poi mai starò a dormire in questo albergo. _____

6. Nessuno dice niente. _____

7. Non mi piace la gente che fuma. _____

8. Lui ha paura di viaggiare in aereo. _____

9. Abbiamo molto da fare. _____

10. Non c'è niente che io voglia comprare. _____

ESERCIZIO
1·6

Translate the sentences from Esercizio 1-5 into English.

1. _____

2. _____

3. _____

4. _____

5. _____

6. _____

7. _____

8. _____

9. _____

10. _____

ESERCIZIO
1·7

To form double negatives, add another negative word to the following sentences.

1. _____ e poi mai avremo un anno così prospero.

2. Non vediamo _____ molta gente dalla finestra.

3. Giulia non invita _____ a casa sua.

4. Non ho mangiato nè il pesce _____ la carne.

5. Non lo dice a _____ .

6. Io non faccio più _____ questa sera.

7. Non dire a _____ quello che ti ho raccontato.

8. Non fa _____ dalla mattina alla sera.

9. _____ mi piace nè mangiare nè bere nei ristoranti che non conosco.

10. _____ vengono all'ora giusta. _____ capiscono niente.

Write the following sentences in Italian, using only one negative word.

1. I never buy wine at this store.

   _____

2. The clerk is never very helpful.

   _____

3. Maria does not play with anybody.

   _____

4. I do not like to watch baseball or football on television.

   _____

5. Neither you nor I feel very well.

   _____

6. You never play tennis.

   _____

7. The children in this neighborhood never play outside.

   _____

8. The students in Italian schools do not have sports or theater.

   _____

9. This city is not near the sea or the mountains.

   _____

10. My job is never boring.

   _____

Interrogative sentences

Interrogative sentences ask a question. In English, an interrogative sentence can be formed by adding the helping verbs *do*, *does*, or *did* before the subject in a declarative sentence:

Marco likes good food.	→	***Does** Marco like good food?*
They just got married.	→	***Did** they just get married?*

In Italian a **declarative** sentence can become an **interrogative** sentence by placing the subject after the verb:

verb + subject

Legge Giovanni?   *Does Giovanni read?*

The auxiliary words *do*, *does*, or *did* used in English to form a question are not used in Italian. Italian has no such helping verbs.

Forming interrogative sentences

There are three types of interrogative sentences, those that:

◆ Elicit a yes-no response

Luisa è a casa?	*Is Luisa at home?*
Sì?/No?	*Yes?/No?*

These yes-no questions in Italian are formed by placing a question mark at the end of an affirmative sentence in written language. In spoken Italian, a different voice intonation is given to signify that a question is being asked. This type of interrogative sentence can also be formed by putting the subject at the end of a sentence.

Luisa è a casa? (asking tone in the voice)	*Is Luisa at home?*
È a casa **Luisa**? (subject at the end of the question)	*Is Luisa at home?*

◆ Ask for information

Di che nazionalità è Luisa?	*What nationality is Luisa?*

◆ Seek agreement or confirmation

Luisa dorme, non è vero?	*Luisa is sleeping, isn't she?*

396

In English as well as in Italian, you can change a statement into a question by adding a short phrase at the end of the statement. This short phrase is called a **tag question**, or tag, because it is tagged onto the end of a sentence. These questions are intended to elicit consent, agreement, confirmation, or verification. In Italian, the words **no** (*no*), **vero** (*true/right*), **non è vero** (*isn't it right/ isn't it correct*), and **giusto** (*right*) can be added or tagged onto a statement to change it into a question.

Luisa è una brava ragazza, **no**?	*Luisa is a nice girl, **isn't she**?*
Sei molto stanco, **vero**?	*You are very tired, **aren't you**?*
Oggi è venerdì, **non è vero**?	*Today is Friday, **isn't it**?*
Hai capito la lezione, **giusto**?	*You understood the lesson, **right**?*

When using the verbs **essere** (*to be*) and **avere** (*to have*), the question usually begins with the verb.

Sei ancora a casa?	***Are you** still at home?*
Hai un vestito nuovo?	***Do you have** a new dress?*
Sei stato a casa o sei andato a giocare a tennis?	***Did you stay** at home or did you go to play tennis?*
Hai visitato tutti i tuoi parenti in Italia?	***Have you visited/Did you visit** all your relatives in Italy?*

ESERCIZIO
2·1

Rewrite each sentence as a question.

1. I ragazzi cantano.

   _____

2. Luisa lavora.

   _____

3. La casa è grande.

   _____

4. Loro viaggiano molto.

   _____

5. Voi dormite sempre.

   _____

6. Le ragazze giocano a tennis.

   _____

7. I bambini piangono.

   _____

8. Tu fumi troppo.

   _____

9. Maria è andata a casa.

_____

10. La tua amica è ammalata.

_____

Translate the following questions into Italian.

1. Do you (sing.) play basketball?

_____

2. Do you (sing.) smoke a lot?

_____

3. Does Luigi live here?

_____

4. Do you (sing.) speak English?

_____

5. Do the ladies play bridge on Wednesday?

_____

6. Does she travel by train?

_____

7. Are you (sing.) happy in this house?

_____

8. Is your (sing.) father the gentleman whom I met the other night?

_____

9. Do you (sing.) have a lot of stress in your life?

_____

10. Have you (sing.) traveled to many parts of the world?

_____

Rewrite the following questions, changing them to Italian tag questions, using the suggestions in parentheses.

1. Tu studi molto (*right*)?

_____

2. Suo marito è un campione di tennis (*isn't it true*)?

_____

3. Loro sono in vacanza (*no*)?

_____

4. Il concerto è sabato (*isn't it*)?

_____

5. Preferisci il gelato al dolce (*true*)?

_____

6. Loro vanno in chiesa la domenica (*don't they*)?

_____

7. È molto scoraggiante perdere sempre (*right*)?

_____

8. Se uno non paga le tasse, potrebbe andare in prigione (*no*)?

_____

9. I parchi americani sono molto belli e spaziosi (*aren't they*)?

_____

10. Bisogna guidare per molte ore per attraversare gli Stati Uniti (*right*)?

_____

Interrogative words

Interrogative sentences eliciting information use the following words: **chi** (*who*), **che cosa** (*what*), **quando** (*when*), **dove** (*where*), **come** (*how*), **quanto** (*how much*), **quale** (*which*), and **perchè** (*why*). In general, Italian and English interrogative words are used in the same way.

Chi (*who*) is used in questions to inquire where or to inquire what one or more persons may be doing. It is a singular pronoun and requires a singular verb, even when it refers to a plural subject.

The main interrogative words in Italian are used as follows:

Maria abita in Italia.	*Maria lives in Italy.*
→ **Chi** abita in Italia?	**Who** *lives in Italy?*
I miei genitori vivono a Parigi.	*My parents live in Paris.*
→ **Chi** vive a Parigi?	**Who** *lives in Paris?*
Il dottore non è ancora arrivato.	*The doctor has not arrived yet.*
→ **Chi** non è ancora arrivato?	**Who** *has not arrived yet?*
Luisa e suo marito non conoscono tua madre.	*Luisa and her husband do not know your mother.*
→ **Chi** non conosce tua madre?	**Who** *does not know your mother?*

Chi is also frequently preceded by simple prepositions depending on the case of the noun that is being replaced.

a chi	*to whom*
con chi	*with whom*
da chi	*where*
di chi	*whose*
per chi	*for whom*

In the following examples, you can observe the use of a **preposition** + *chi*. The subject of the sentence is replaced by the pronoun **chi**.

A chi (*to whom*) is used to ask to whom something is being given, said, or brought.

A chi ha dato il libro?	**To whom** *did she give the book?*
Lei ha dato il libro alla sua amica.	*She gave the book to her friend.*

Di chi (*whose*) is used to show possession.

La nonna **di chi** viene in America?	**Whose** *grandmother will come to America?*
La nonna di Paola viene in America.	*Paola's grandmother will come to America.*

Da chi (*where*) is used to ask at whose house one is or is going to be.

Da chi sei?	**Where** *are you?* (**Whose house?**)
Sono a casa di Luisa.	*I am at Luisa's house.*
Sono da Luisa.	*I am at Luisa's.*
Da chi vai domani?	**Whose house** *are you going to tomorrow?*
Vado a casa di mia zia.	*I am going to my aunt's house.*
Vado da mia zia.	*I am going to my aunt's.*

Con chi (*with whom*) is used to ask with whom something is done.

Con chi vai in Italia?	**With whom** *will you go to Italy?*
Vado in Italia con la mia famiglia.	*I will go to Italy with my family.*

Per chi (*for whom*) is used to inquire for whom something is done.

Per chi sono questi regali?	**For whom** *are these presents?*
Questi regali sono per mio nipote.	*These presents are for my nephew.*

Rewrite the following sentences as questions and change the underlined words or phrases to the appropriate form of **chi** or *preposition* + **chi**.

1. Luisa ha un libro per i tuoi figli.

_____

2. La casa è di mia zia.

_____

3. Porto il pane alla mia amica.

_____

4. Vado al cinema con le mie amiche.

_____

5. Vogliono visitare la nonna.

_____

6. Quando vado in Florida sto da mio figlio.

_____

7. Penso spesso a mia mamma.

_____

8. Domani viene la mia amica.

_____

The interrogative words **che** and **che cosa** (*what*) are used to replace nouns referring to objects or a group of objects in a sentence. Even if the noun replaced by **che** or **che cosa** is plural, **che** and **che cosa** do not change.

Che cosa vuoi?	**What** do you want?
Io vorrei un gelato.	*I would like an ice cream.*
Che cosa compri?	**What** do you buy?
Compro molte riviste.	*I buy many magazines.*
Che vuoi mangiare?	**What** do you want to eat?
Vorrei mangiare una pizza.	*I would like to eat pizza.*

Come (*how*) is generally used to inquire into someone's name or their health.

Come si chiama quella signora?	**What** is that lady's name?
	(literally, **How** *is that lady called?*)
Quella signora si chiama Adriana.	*That lady's name is Adriana.*
Come sta tua zia?	**How** *is your aunt?*
Mia zia sta poco bene.	*My aunt is not feeling well.*

Dove (*where*) is used to inquire about a location.

Dove va lui?	**Where** *is he going?*
Lui va al mercato.	*He goes to the market.*

The prepositions **da** and **di** are sometimes placed in front of **dove**. *Da dove* + **verb** inquires into the origin or the motion of the subject. **Di** + **essere** (*to be*) inquires about the origin of the subject.

Da dove + verb

Da dove vieni?	**Where** *are you coming from?*

Di dove + essere

Di dove sei?	**Where** *do you come from?*
Di dov'è Angela?	**Where** *is Angela from?*
Angela è italiana.	*Angela is Italian.*
Di dove è Luisa?	**Where** *is Luisa from?*
Luisa è di Napoli.	*Luisa is from/was born in Naples.*

Here are some additional ways that **dove** is used in questions:

* **Dove** + location + subject → location (*Where?*)

Dove dorme tuo marito?	*Where is your husband sleeping?*

* **Dove** + verb of motion + subject → motion to a place (*Where to?*)

Dove vanno gli studenti?	*Where are the students going?*

* **Da dove** + verb of motion + subject → motion from a place (*Where from?*)

Da dove arriva il treno?	*Where is the train coming from?*

Quando (*when*) is used to ask when something is going to happen.

Quando arriva l'autobus?	**When** *will the bus come?*
L'autobus arriva fra dieci minuti.	*The bus will come in ten minutes.*

Quale (*which*) is used to make a distinction between two or more people, things, or animals. The endings change according to the number of the noun that **quale** modifies.

Quale professore è molto bravo?	**Which** *professor is very good?*
Il nuovo professore è molto bravo.	*The new professor is very good.*
Quali amici vedi oggi?	**Which** *friends will you see today?*
Oggi vedo i miei amici italiani.	*Today, I will see my Italian friends.*

Perchè (*why*) is used to ask about reasons or motives of actions.

Perchè va dal dottore Luisa?	**Why** *is Luisa going to the doctor?*
Luisa va dal dottore perchè non si sente bene.	*Luisa is going to the doctor because she is not feeling well.*

Quanto/a/i/e (*how much, how many*) is used to inquire about the quantity of the nouns it modifies. The endings change according to the gender and number of the noun that **quanto** modifies in a sentence.

Quanto caffè bevi durante il giorno?	*How much coffee do you drink during the day?*
Quanta pioggia è venuta?	*How much rain fell?*
Quanti fiori hai comprato?	*How many flowers did you buy?*
Quante piante hai comprato?	*How many plants did you buy?*

When used as a pronoun, **quanto** does not change gender or number.

Quanto leggi?	*How much do you read?*
Quanto camminate?	*How much do you walk?*

Note also that the final vowel of **cosa**, **come**, **dove**, **quando**, and **quanto** may be dropped when these words precede the verb form **è** to make: **cos'è/cosa è, com'è/come è, dov'è/dove è, quand'è/quando è, quant'è/quanto è**.

Quand'è il concerto?	*When is the concert?*
Quant'è un cappuccino?	*How much is a cappuccino?*

ESERCIZIO
2·5

*Compose four questions for each of the following items, using **quando**, **quale**, **perchè**, and a tag question. Use either **bevi** (you drink) or **mangi** (you eat).*

Example: il caffè

Quando bevi il caffè?

Quale caffè bevi?

Perchè bevi il caffè?

Bevi il caffè, vero?

1. il gelato

   a. _____

   b. _____

   c. _____

   d. _____

2. il succo di frutta

   a. _____

   b. _____

   c. _____

   d. _____

3. il formaggio

　a. _____

　b. _____

　c. _____

　d. _____

4. la pasta

　a. _____

　b. _____

　c. _____

　d. _____

5. la cioccolata calda

　a. _____

　b. _____

　c. _____

　d. _____

6. la torta

　a. _____

　b. _____

　c. _____

　d. _____

ESERCIZIO
2·6

Complete the following sentences with the appropriate question words suggested in parentheses.

1. _____ biciclette avete? (*how many*)

2. _____ andate in Italia? (*when*)

3. _____ andate in Italia? (*how*)

4. _____ vestito preferisci? (*which*)

5. _____ vedrai domani? (*who*)

6. _____ giorni starai in vacanza? (*how many*)

7. _____ sono i calzini e le scarpe? (*where*)

8. _____ sta la nonna di Maria? (*how*)

9. _____ è la signora che abita vicino a te? (*where from, born*)

10. _____ arrivano tutte quelle casse divino? (*where from*)

ESERCIZIO 2·7

Complete the sentences with the appropriate form, using **chi** *or* **preposition** + **chi**.

1. _____ è quella bella signora?

2. _____ sono queste scarpe?

3. _____ portate il dolce?

4. _____ andate in Italia?

5. _____ dormite quando siete in Italia?

6. _____ fate le lasagne?

7. _____ è quella macchina in garage?

8. _____ comprate la frutta, la pasta e il pane?

9. _____ sono i CD che ho trovato in macchina?

10. _____ dovete parlare oggi pomeriggio?

ESERCIZIO 2·8

Complete the following sentences with the appropriate interrogative words.

1. _____ viene la tua amica?

2. _____ desideri comprare al mercato?

3. _____ proviene questa bella statua?

4. _____ delle tue amiche parla l'italiano?

5. _____ vorresti mangiare questa sera?

6. _____ fratelli hai?

7. _____ ragazze giocano a tennis?

8. _____ stivali hai comprato?

9. _____ andate a visitare gli amici che abitano al mare?

10. _____ sono andati gli esami di maturità?

Questions and answers

In Chapter 2, you became familiar with the various ways of forming a question in Italian. Nearly every word in a sentence can become a cue for a question to ask and the answer to give.

Forming questions from sentences

Let's look at an English sentence and the questions that can originate from it.

> *Every day after they came home from school, the children played soccer with their friends at the park near their house.*

The following questions are just a few that can be formed from the various elements of this sentence:

> How often did the children play soccer?
> With whom did they play soccer?
> Did the children play soccer every day?
> When did the children play soccer?
> What did the children play every day after school?
> What happened every day after school?

In Italian, too, sentences can be separated into elements, and several questions can be formed. Here is an example:

> La madre e il padre di Giovanni vivevano in Italia con la loro figlia maggiore.
>
> *Giovanni's mother and father lived in Italy with their oldest daughter.*

Below are some questions you can form from this sentence. Some questions will:

- ◆ Ask about people

> Chi viveva in Italia con la figlia maggiore?
>
> *Who lived in Italy with the oldest daughter?*
>
> Con chi vivevano in Italia la madre e il padre di Giovanni?
>
> *With whom did Giovanni's mother and father live in Italy?*

- ◆ Inquire about location

> Dove vivevano la madre e il padre di Giovanni?
>
> *Where did Giovanni's mother and father live?*

Vivevano in Francia con la figlia maggiore la madre e il padre di Giovanni?

Did Giovanni's mother and father live in France with the oldest daughter?

◆ Differentiate between persons or things by using **quale** (*which*) or **che cosa** (*what*)

Quale figlia viveva in Italia con la madre e il padre?

***Which** daughter lived in Italy with her mother and father?*

Che cosa facevano la madre e il padre di Giovanni?

***What** were Giovanni's mother and father doing?*

◆ Use **di chi** (*whose*) to identify possession

La madre e il padre **di chi** viveva in Italia?

***Whose** mother and father lived in Italy?*

Some **sì-no** questions seek to clarify information.

La madre e il padre di Giovanni vivevano in Italia?

Did Giovanni's mother and father live in Italy?

By understanding how to form questions in this way, you can get all kinds of information. It will also enable you to understand the complexities of a sentence in order to better compose your own. Knowing how to do this effectively will be a great help in compiling proper sentences.

ESERCIZIO
3·1

Write a question for each of the underlined elements in the sentences that follow.

EXAMPLE: I bambini vogliono giocare a scacchi.

Chi vuole giocare a scacchi?

A che cosa vogliono giocare i bambini?

1. La nostra insegnante vuole andare in Italia.

   a. _____

   b. _____

2. Le banche sono chiuse il sabato e la domenica.

   a. _____

   b. _____

3. Il dizionario italiano costa troppo.

   a. _____

4. Io annaffio le piante tutte le sere.

   a. _____

5. Il cane è seduto accanto alla sua padrona.

   a. _____

   b. _____

6. Domani, vado al cinema con le mie amiche.

   a. _____

   b. _____

7. Maria vuole andare a visitare i suoi figli.

   a. _____

8. La macchina è parcheggiata davanti alla casa.

   a. _____

   b. _____

9. Mio marito vuole guardare il torneo di tennis.

   a. _____

   b. _____

10. Mia sorella, mi telefona tutti i giorni.

   a. _____

   b. _____

ESERCIZIO
3·2

Write a complete answer for each of the following questions, using the suggested words or phrases in parentheses.

1. Da dove vieni? (Roma)

_____

2. Quanti ne abbiamo oggi? (12)

_____

3. Che cosa hanno rubato i ladri? (la televisione)

_____

4. Come viaggiano i tuoi amici? (in macchina)

_____

5. Chi viene a visitarti la prossima settimana? (mia sorella)

_____

6. Che cosa fai prima di andare in Italia? (studiare l'italiano)

_____

7. Di chi sono questi documenti? (miei genitori)

_____

8. Quando arriva l'aereo? (fra un'ora)

_____

9. Quanti giornali leggi ogni giorno? (due)

_____

10. Per chi fai tutti questi costumi? (cantanti d'opera)

_____

Chi and *che cosa*

You have already encountered the interrogative pronouns **chi** (*who*) and **che cosa** (*what*), which are used in questions regarding people and things, respectively. Both pronouns are singular even when they refer to plural nouns.

Chi chiami?	**Who** are you calling?
Che cosa vogliono le tue amiche?	**What** do your friends want?

ESERCIZIO
3·3

Form questions using **chi** *and* **che cosa** *as appropriate, replacing the underlined words.*

EXAMPLE: Luigi parla con mia sorella.

Chi parla con mia sorella?

1. I bambini devono lavarsi le mani.

_____

2. Maria deve aspettare Luigi.

_____

3. Maria deve aspettare i suoi genitori.

_____

4. Lei ha comprato dei bei fiori.

_____

5. Ho letto molti libri interessanti.

_____

6. Mio zio ha perso il portafoglio.

   _____

7. Mia zia ha dimenticato dove ha messo la borsa.

   _____

8. Penso che questo ristorante sia molto buono.

   _____

9. Tutti hanno freddo in classe.

   _____

10. Margherita ha lasciato la borsa in classe.

    _____

ESERCIZIO
3·4

Write an appropriate answer for each of the following questions, using the suggested words or phrases in parentheses.

1. Chi abita con tuo nonno? (la nonna)

   _____

2. Che cosa fa tua nonna tutto il giorno? (guardare la televisione)

   _____

3. Chi ha telefonato oggi? (il falegname)

   _____

4. Che cosa ti ha detto Maria? (non viene a casa mia)

   _____

5. Quando va al mercato Carlo? (venerdì mattina)

   _____

6. Chi balla molto bene? (Eric)

   _____

7. Chi suona molto bene il piano? (il figlio della mia amica)

   _____

8. Che cosa vuoi mangiare questa sera? (gli spaghetti)

   _____

Use the following words and phrases to form a complete question.

1. viene / con sua sorella / lui / al cinema?

2. perchè / con i bambini / non giochi?

3. quanti / ha comprato / metri / la sarta / di stoffa?

4. quanto / il nuovo CD / costa?

5. quale / hai comprato / macchina?

6. avete mangiato / che cosa / questa sera?

7. al ristorante / a mangiare / siete andati?

8. da dove / è / questo libro / venuto?

ESERCIZIO
3·6

Write a question, using the words in parentheses. Then answer each question.

EXAMPLE: (Che cosa)

Che cosa hai comprato?

Ho comprato una macchina.

1. (Quando)

    a. _____

    b. _____

2. (Perchè)

    a. _____

    b. _____

3. (Da dove)

   a. _____

   b. _____

4. (Chi)

   a. _____

   b. _____

5. (Come)

   a. _____

   b. _____

6. (Da quanto)

   a. _____

   b. _____

7. (Quale)

   a. _____

   b. _____

8. (Quanto)

   a. _____

   b. _____

Imperatives

The imperative is the command form of a verb. It is used to give orders, advice, instructions, encouragements, directions, and suggestions.

Luigi, mangia la carne!	*Luigi, eat the meat!*
Maria, chiudi la finestra!	*Maria, close the window!*
Chiamami, quando hai tempo!	*Call me when you have time!*

In Italian there is a singular and plural form of informal commands (**tu** and **voi**). This is the equivalent of *you* in English. There is also a singular and plural form of formal commands (**Lei** and **Loro**), also equivalent to *you* in English.

(**tu**) + verb + ! → singular informal command

(Tu) cammina!   *Walk!*

(**voi**) + verb + ! → plural informal command

(Voi) camminate!   *Walk!*

Lei + verb + ! → singular formal command

Lei cammini!   *Walk!*

Loro + verb + ! → plural formal command

(Loro) camminino!   *Walk!*

-are verbs

First conjugation, or -**are**, verbs drop the infinitive ending -**are** and add the imperative endings, according to person and number. The imperative endings for the first conjugation verbs are: —, -**a**, -**i**, -**iamo**, -**ate**, -**ino**. There is, of course, no first person in the imperative.

	TU	VOI	LEI	LORO
cominciare (*to start, begin*)	comincia!	cominciate!	cominci!	comincino!
giocare (*to play*)	gioca!	giocate!	giochi!	giochino!
mangiare (*to eat*)	mangia!	mangiate!	mangi!	mangino!
pagare (*to pay*)	paga!	pagate!	paghi!	paghino!
parlare (*to speak*)	parla!	parlate!	parli!	parlino!

(Tu) Parla ai tuoi studenti!	Speak to your students!		
(Lei) Cominci a parlare!	Start speaking!		
(Voi) Mangiate tutto!	Eat everything!		
(Loro) Giochino!	Play!		

The accent on the third person plural does not fall on the last syllable, but on the first: PAR-li-no and not par-LI-no.

If the infinitive ends in **-ciare** or **-giare**, drop the **-are** and retain the **-i**. Note, however, that no double **-i** is used with the **-i**, **-iamo**, and **-ino** endings.

If the infinitive ending of the verb is **-care** or **-gare**, drop the **-are**, but add **h** before adding the endings **-i**, **-iamo**, and **-ino**. This is to retain the hard sound of the infinitive.

-ere verbs

Second conjugation, or **-ere**, verbs drop the infinitive ending **-ere** and add the imperative endings according to person and number. The imperative endings for the second conjugation verbs are: —, **-i**, **-a**, **-iamo**, **-ete**, **-ano**.

	TU	VOI	LEI	LORO
chiedere (to ask)	chiedi!	chiedete!	chieda!	chiedano!
scrivere (to write)	scrivi!	scrivete!	scriva!	scrivano!
vendere (to sell)	vendi!	vendete!	venda!	vendano!

(Tu) Chiedi un favore alla tua vicina!	Ask your neighbor a favor!
(Voi) Scrivete bene!	Write well!
(Lei) Venda la casa!	Sell your house!
(Loro) Chiedano le informazione alla guida!	Ask the guide for the information!

-ire verbs

For third conjugation, or **-ire**, verbs, a distinction has to be made between the regular **-ire** verbs and those that add **-isc**. The third conjugation of regular **-ire** verbs drops the infinitive ending **-ire** and adds the following endings according to the person and number: —, **-i**, **-a**, **-iamo**, **-ite**, **-ano**. The third conjugation verbs that insert **-isc** drop the infinitive ending **-ire** and add the following endings according to person and number: —, **-isci**, **-isca**, **-iamo**, **-ite**, **-iscano**.

	TU	VOI	LEI	LORO
finire (to finish)	finisci!	finite!	finisca!	finiscano!
pulire (to clean)	pulisci!	pulite!	pulisca!	puliscano!
sentire (to hear, listen)	senti!	sentite!	senta!	sentano!

(Tu) Senti quello che ti dice!	Listen to what he has to say!
(Lei) Finisca di parlare al telefono!	Stop talking on the phone!
(Voi) Pulite bene le scale!	Clean the stairway well!

The first person plural ending in **-iamo** is used more as an exhortation or a suggestion rather than a command.

Andiamo alla stazione!	Let's go to the station!
Compriamo una macchina nuova!	Let's buy a new car!
Finiamo di lavorare in giardino!	Let's stop working in the yard!

Irregular imperative forms

There are several irregular imperative forms. They can be confusing and need to be memorized.

	TU	LEI	NOI	VOI	LORO
andare (*to go*)	va' (vai)	vada	andiamo	andate	vadano
avere (*to have*)	abbi	abbia	abbiamo	abbiate	abbiano
bere (*to drink*)	bevi	beva	beviamo	bevete	bevano
dare (*to give*)	da' (dai)	dia	diamo	date	diano
dire (*to tell, say*)	di'	dica	diciamo	dite	dicano
essere (*to be*)	sii	sia	siamo	siate	siano
fare (*to do, make*)	fa' (fai)	faccia	facciamo	fate	facciano
rimanere (*to stay*)	rimani	rimanga	rimaniamo	rimanete	rimangano
salire (*to go up*)	sali	salga	saliamo	salite	salgano
sapere (*to know*)	sappi	sappia	sappiamo	sapete	sappiano
scegliere (*to choose*)	scegli	scelga	scegliamo	scegliete	scelgano
stare (*to stay*)	sta' (stai)	stia	stiamo	state	stiano
tenere (*to keep*)	tieni	tenga	teniamo	tenete	tengano
uscire (*to go out*)	esci	esca	usciamo	uscite	escano
venire (*to come*)	vieni	venga	veniamo	venite	vengano

ESERCIZIO

4·1

*Rewrite the following infinitives as imperatives in all the appropriate forms (**tu, Lei, Loro**).*

1. bere _____

2. aspettare _____

3. ordinare _____

4. stare _____

5. votare _____

6. leggere _____

7. mangiare _____

8. sapere _____

9. essere _____

10. mettere _____

Addressing groups

The infinitive of the verb is used to give instructions, warnings, notices, and messages to groups or people in general. These commands can appear on signs or be heard over loudspeakers. When giving a negative command, place **non** in front of the infinitive as shown below.

Non fumare!	*No smoking!*
Non gettare oggetti dal finestrino!	*Do not throw objects from the window!*
Accendere i fari in galleria!	*Turn on the lights in the tunnel!*
Parlare piano!	*Speak softly!*
Osservare il limite di velocitá!	*Mind the speed limit!*

ESERCIZIO 4·2

Translate the following commands into Italian, using the imperative form that addresses people or groups.

1. Push! _____

2. Pull! _____

3. Do not touch! _____

4. Keep off the grass! _____

5. Do not speak to the driver! _____

6. Do not take pictures! _____

7. No passing! _____

8. No parking! _____

9. Do not feed the animals! _____

10. Keep the door closed! _____

Lasciare in the imperative form

The verb *lasciare* (*to let*) + **the infinitive** often is used as a command. It is used with **tu, Lei, voi,** and **Loro.**

lasciare + infinitive + !

Lascia stare!	*Let it go!*
Lasciami dormire!	*Let me sleep!*
Lascia passare la signora!	*Let the lady go by!*
Lasci parlare gli altri!	*Let the others speak!*
Lasciate andare la corda!	*Let go of the rope!*
Ci lascino parlare!	*Let us speak!*

The **noi** form with **lasciare** is used in Italian but not in the English equivalent.

Lasciamoli andare a dormire!	*Let's let them go to sleep!*

*Translate the following sentences into English, using **let** or **let's** as appropriate.*

1. Andiamo al cinema!

   _____

2. Lascialo viaggiare in Europa!

   _____

3. Lasciala parlare!

   _____

4. Scriviamo una lettera alla nonna!

   _____

5. Lascia che faccia quel che vuole!

   _____

6. Lascia che parli io!

   _____

7. Andiamo a prendere un caffè!

   _____

8. Lasciami mangiare!

   _____

9. Ci lascino leggere!

   _____

10. Facciamo una foto!

    _____

11. Lasci parlare gli altri!

    _____

12. Lasciami stare!

    _____

Negative imperatives

To form the negative imperative, add **non** before the verb. All the imperative forms, except the **tu** form, use the same conjugations in the negative that are used in the affirmative. For example:

Non pianga!	*Do not cry!*
Non aspettate gli altri!	*Do not wait for the others!*
Non partiamo così in fretta!	*Let's not leave so fast!*

The **tu** form of the negative imperative, however, is formed by inserting **non** just before the infinitive of the verb.

non + infinitive + !

non cantare!   *Do not sing!*

Canta con il coro!	*Sing with the choir!*
→ Non cantare con il coro!	*Do not sing with the choir!*
Scrivi una lunga lettera!	*Write a long letter!*
→ Non scrivere sul muro!	*Do not write on the wall!*
Cammina lentamente!	*Walk slowly!*
→ Non camminare così velocemente!	*Do not walk so fast!*

Imperatives with object and reflexive pronouns

Object pronouns and reflexive pronouns are attached to the end of the **tu**, **noi**, and **voi** forms of the imperative.

Guarda**mi**!	*Look at me!*
Svegliamo**ci**!	*Let's wake up!*
Scrivete**la**!	*Write it!*

However, they are placed before the **Lei** and **Loro** imperative forms.

Mi scriva presto!	*Write to me soon!*
Si accomodino!	*Make yourself comfortable!*

When **Loro** is used with the meaning of *to them*, it is placed after the imperative, is never attached to it, and is not capitalized.

Da' loro la macchina!   *Give (to) them the car!*

When **da'**, **di'**, **fa'**, and **va'** are followed by an object pronoun, the initial consonant of the pronoun is doubled and the accent is dropped.

da**mmi**	*give me*
di**lle**	*tell her*
fa**cci**	*do us*
sta**mmi** vicina	*stay close to me*
va**cci** a prendere una birra	*go get us a beer*

Gli is an exception, however. **Dagli** (*give him*), not da**ggli**, and **digli** (*tell him*), not di**ggli**, are the correct forms.

In the negative forms of the imperative, the positions of the pronouns **Lei** and **Loro** would be before **non**. However, they are omitted and used only for emphasis.

(Lei) Non mi parli!	*Do not speak to me!*
(Loro) Non si fermino qui!	*Do not stop here!*

In the **tu** form, the object pronouns can either be attached to the infinitive or precede it.

Non **mi** aspettare!	*Do not wait for me!*
or Non aspettar**mi**!	
Non **mi** scrivere!	*Do not write me!*
or Non scriver**mi**!	

This is also possible with **noi** and **voi**, but the tendency is to place the pronouns at the end of the imperative. **Non scriveteci!** is preferable to **non ci scrivete!**

ESERCIZIO
4·4

Change the following sentences into the negative imperative.

1. Mangiate tutti i cioccolatini!

   _____

2. Compriamo le ciliege!

   _____

3. Fate la doccia!

   _____

4. Saluta il professore!

   _____

5. Facciamo gli esercizi!

   _____

6. Chiama un tassì!

   _____

7. Parla lentamente!

   _____

8. Mettete la giacca!

   _____

9. Comprate una giacca pesante!

   _____

10. Impara a usare il computer!

   _____

Complete the sentences below with the imperative forms of the verbs in parentheses.

1. Per favore, _____ a bassa voce! (Lei-parlare)

2. _____ ai tuoi genitori! (tu-scrivere)

3. Prima di uscire _____ le finestre! (voi-chiudere)

4. Signora, _____ le scarpe! (Lei-provare)

5. _____ perchè avete gli esami! (voi-studiare)

6. _____ la tavola! (tu-preparare)

7. _____ il riso per mezz'ora! (Lei-cuocere)

8. _____ il vino per gli ospiti! (tu-comprare)

9. _____ il dottore. Viene subito! (Loro-aspettare)

10. _____ se tutte le finestre sono chiuse! (tu-controllare)

Complete the following sentences with the imperative forms of the verbs in parentheses.

1. Mamma _____, oggi cucino io! (riposarsi)

2. Non _____ dal letto, sei ancora molto debole! (alzarsi)

3. _____ a cena da noi! (voi-fermarsi)

4. Signora, _____ allo sportello numero 5! (rivolgersi)

5. Mi raccomando _____ prima di uscire! (tu-pettinarsi)

6. Domani _____ prima, se volete andare a pescare! (voi-svegliarsi)

7. _____ bene, fa molto freddo! (voi-coprirsi)

8. _____ da questa parte! (Loro-accomodarsi)

9. Non _____ di dare da mangiare al cane! (voi-dimenticare)

10. Non _____ troppi vestiti! Li comprerà in Italia. (Lei-portare)

Rewrite the following sentences, replacing indirect and direct objects with indirect and direct object pronouns.

EXAMPLE: Da' a lei le matite colorate!

Dalle le matite colorate!

1. Di' a lei che lui l'ama!

   _____

2. Stai vicino a me!

   _____

3. Di' a noi chi viene alla festa!

   _____

4. Da' a me la borsa!

   _____

5. Da' a noi un colpo di telefono!

   _____

6. Fa' a noi un favore!

   _____

7. Fa' a lui un regalo per il suo compleanno!

   _____

8. Non dare a lui un orologio!

   _____

9. Da' a lei la macchina nuova!

   _____

10. Non dare a lei la macchina fotografica!

    _____

Coordinating conjunctions

Conjunctions show how words or phrases are related and allow us to express, in a logical way, a complex thought. If we did not use them, we would end up with a list of disjointed information.

Le pesche **e** le albicocche sono belle **e** buone.	*Peaches **and** apricots are beautiful **and** good.*
La tua casa è bella, **ma** è troppo grande.	*Your house is beautiful, **but** it is too big.*

A clause is made up of a group of words containing a subject and a predicate.

subject + predicate

La vita è bella.   *Life is beautiful.*

Coordinating conjunctions join words, phrases, or clauses of the same type. There are different types of coordinating conjunctions in Italian. They all, though, follow this basic pattern:

word/phrase/clause + conjunction + word/phrase/clause

Io visito le chiese e i musei.   *I visit the churches and the museums.*

Types of conjunctions

Positive coordinating conjunctions join words, phrases, and clauses of equal importance. They include **anche** (*also, too*), **cioè** (*in fact, that is*), **dunque** (*so, therefore*), **e** (*and*), **inoltre** (*besides*), **invece** (*instead*), **ma** (*but*), **perciò** (*so, for this reason*), **però** (*but*), and **pure** (*also*).

Maria compra patate **e** spinaci.	*Maria buys potatoes **and** spinach.*
Il dolce è buono, **ma** io non posso mangiarlo.	*The cake is good, **but** I cannot eat it.*
Ho finito di studiare, **perciò** vado a dormire.	*I finished studying **so** I am going to sleep.*
Io sto a casa **invece** tu vai a ballare.	*I stay at home; you, **instead**, will go dancing.*
Mi piacciono le pesche e **anche** le ciliege.	*I like peaches and cherries **too**.*
Io capisco quello che dici; **cioe'** ti capisco bene.	*I understand what you are saying; **in fact** I understand you well.*

Dunque, ditemi quando arriverete.	*So, tell me when you will arrive.*
Ci piace viaggiare, **pero'** non andiamo lontano.	*We like to travel, **but** we do not go very far.*

Negative coordinating conjunctions join words or phrases of equal importance in the negative: **nè... nè** (*neither ... nor*), **neanche** (*not even*), **nemmeno** (*not even*), and **neppure** (*nor*).

Non ti ho visto e **neppure** ti ho parlato.	*I did not see you, **nor** did I speak to you.*
Non ha bevuto **nè** vino **nè** birra.	*He drank **neither** wine **nor** beer.*
Non vuole andare in montagna e **nemmeno** al mare.	*He does not want to go to the mountains **or even** to the beach.*

Some conjunctions join words or phrases in contrast with each other: **o** (*or*), **altrimenti** (*otherwise*), **oppure** (*or*), and **ovvero** (*or*).

Uscirete questa sera, **oppure** starete a casa?	*Are you going out this evening, **or** will you stay at home?*
Prendete le chiavi di casa, **altrimenti** dovrete aspettare fuori.	*Take the house keys; **otherwise**, you will have to wait outside.*
Andrai all'università **o** andrai a lavorare?	*Are you going to college **or** will you work?*

Others join a phrase or an independent sentence that needs clarification: **cioè** (*that is*), **difatti** (*in fact*), **infatti** (*in fact*), **ossia** (*that is*), **in effetti** (*in reality*), and **vale a dire** (*exactly*).

Me ne andrò tra due giorni, **cioè** giovedì.	*I will leave within two days, **which is** Thursday.*
Non capisco la matematica, **infatti** ho preso un brutto voto nella verifica.	*I do not understand math; **in fact**, I did not do well on the test.*
Domani sarà un brutto giorno, **ossia** un giorno pieno di riunioni.	*Tomorrow is going to be a bad day; **in fact**, it is full of meetings.*

Some coordinating conjunctions join phrases or independent sentences that indicate a conclusion: **dunque** (*therefore*), **perciò** (therefore), **per questo** (*for this reason*), **pertanto** (*for this reason*), and **quindi** (*therefore*).

Ho finito di parlare, **quindi** me ne vado.	*I finished speaking; **therefore**, I will leave.*
Abbiamo mangiato tardi, **perciò** non abbiamo fame.	*We ate late; **for this reason/therefore**, we are not hungry.*
Ho un forte mal di testa, **per questo** non vengo alla festa.	*I have a bad headache; **for this reason**, I am not going to the party*
Oggi ho del tempo libero, **dunque** taglierò l'erba.	*Today I have some free time; **therefore**, I will cut the grass.*

Still others serve to emphasize the coordination between two words, phrases, or sentences: **entrambi** (*both*), **non solo... ma anche** (*not only . . . but also*), **sia... che** (*either . . . or*), **nè... nè** (*neither . . . nor*).

Entrambi Maria ed io andremo in Italia.	***Both** Maria and I will go to Italy.*
Sia mio marito **che** io possiamo portarti a scuola.	***Either** my husband **or** I can take you to school.*
Non solo è alto, **ma anche** robusto.	*He is **not only** tall **but also** stocky.*
Non voleva **nè** nuotare **nè** giocare a tennis.	*He **neither** wanted to swim **nor** play tennis.*

Conjunctions *ma* and *e*

The most commonly used coordinating conjunctions in Italian are **ma** (*but*) and **e** (*and*). Here you will find some practical suggestions for where to place a comma when using them.

- The coordinating conjunction **ma** must be preceded by a comma when it links two opposing sentences or phrases.

  Hai preparato la tavola, **ma** ti sei dimenticato i tovaglioli.

  *You set the table, **but** you forgot the napkins.*

- **Ma** is not preceded by a comma if it links two elements in the same sentence.

  Ho mangiato un panino piccolo **ma** buono.

  *I ate a small **but** good sandwich.*

- Finally, **ma** can never be used with **bensì** or **però**. You must use one construction or the other.

  È bello **però** caro.
  or È bello **ma** caro. (*never* **ma però**)

  *It is beautiful **but** expensive.*

- When listing several items in a sentence, a comma is used before the coordinating conjunction **e**.

  In questo bosco vivono cinghiali, cervi, volpi, **e** lepri.

  *Wild boars, deer, foxes, **and** hares live in these woods.*

- A comma is used after **e** when an incidental phrase is inserted into the sentence.

  In questa foresta è facile vedere il picchio **e**, se si è fortunati, si vede anche la civetta.

  *The woodpecker is easily seen in this forest, **and**, if one is lucky, one can see the owl, too.*

- If the word following **e** starts with a vowel, **e** becomes **ed** to make pronouncing it easier.

  Tu **ed** io andiamo al mercato.

  *You **and** I will go to the market.*

Be careful not to abuse the use of conjunctions. This could fragment your speech and make it less elegant and flowing. The repeated use of **cioè**, **va be'**, **però**, **quindi**, one after the other, is incorrect and not a good representation of spoken Italian.

ESERCIZIO
5·1

Complete each of the following sentences with the appropriate coordinating conjunction.

1. Gli spinaci sono nutrienti _____ contengono ferro.

2. Gli spinaci sono nutrienti, _____ non mi piacciono.

3. L'ho chiamato due volte, _____ non mi ha risposto.

4. L'ho chiamato due _____ tre volte.

5. Vado in vacanza, _____ vi penserò molto.

6. I compiti sono difficili, _____ proveremo a farli.

7. Non sto molto bene, _____ rimango a casa.

8. Il sole di agosto è molto forte, _____ devi mettere il cappello.

9. Gli amici _____ i parenti possono rendere la vita molto difficile.

10. Il vento ha alzato il tetto della casa, _____ dobbiamo ripararlo.

Combine the following sentences, linking each with the proper conjunction.

1. Ci sono tanti nostri amici. Vorremmo che venissi anche tu.

   _____

2. Ti ammonisco. Fa quel che vuoi.

   _____

3. Segui il tuo istinto. Non venire a piangere da me.

   _____

4. Filippo non è generoso. È molto tirchio.

   _____

5. Franco è un ragazzo molto intelligente. Franco è un genio.

   _____

6. Tu vuoi andare al cinema. Io non voglio andarci.

   _____

7. I miei genitori non vogliono comprarmi un cane. Non vogliono comprarmi un gatto.

   _____

8. Se tutto va bene mi comprerò la moto. Mi comprerò la macchina l'anno prossimo.

   _____

9. Abbiamo comprato la frutta e la carne. Abbiamo dimenticato il pane.

   _____

10. Lui non sta molto bene. Deve andare dal dottore per un controllo.

   _____

Circle the correct coordinating conjugation for each of the following sentences.

1. Sono contenta del tuo progresso, però / ma però devi studiare di più.

2. Chiudi la porta o / e la finestra.

3. Ti ho già detto di no, quindi / anzi non insistere.

4. Tua sorella arriva sempre in ritardo perciò / ma deve essere punita.

5. Domani arriveremo a Roma cioè / però partiamo oggi.

6. Giovanni è alto, bello, invece / e famoso.

7. È dimagrita molto però / anche mangia sempre.

8. Non riesco a concentrarmi ma / invece continuo a studiare.

9. La tigre si muove silenziosamente quindi / e velocemente.

10. Scivolò e / invece cadde sul pavimento di marmo.

Translate the following sentences into Italian, using the appropriate coordinating conjunctions.

1. Both Luigi and I will go to the party.

_____

2. Money and power do not bring happiness.

_____

3. She gave us presents, and she invited us to her house.

_____

4. He was tired, and he was not feeling well.

_____

5. I have finished my homework, therefore I can go out to play.

_____

6. I will see you all in two weeks, or for Christmas.

_____

7. The thief moved quickly and quietly.

_____

8. Neither you nor I will be able to go to the wedding.

_____

9. Today it was very cold, in fact it snowed.

_____

10. Will you go out with your friends or with your relatives?

_____

Subordinating conjunctions

Subordinating conjunctions join elements of unequal importance. They join a clause to the main clause; in other words, they subordinate one clause to another. In this chapter, we'll look at the most commonly used subordinating conjunctions grouped according to their use.

main + subordinating + verb + dependent
clause   conjunction   clause

Andiamo prima che cominci   *Let's go before it starts raining.*
piovere.

Common subordinating conjunctions

Conjunctions of cause express a relationship between the dependent and the main clauses.

dal momento che	*because*
dato che	*since, because*
giacchè	*since*
perchè	*because*
poichè	*since, because*
siccome	*since, because*

Sono arrivata in ritardo **perchè** c'era troppo traffico.	*I arrived late **because** there was lots of traffic.*
Dato che ritorno domani, non porto la valigia.	*__Since__ I will return tomorrow, I will not take a suitcase with me.*
Siccome piove, dobbiamo comprare un ombrello.	*__Because__ it is raining, we have to buy an umbrella.*
Dato che l'autobus è pieno, vado a piedi.	*__Because__ the bus is full, I will walk.*

Conjunctions of choice introduce a choice of action between the main and the dependent clauses.

anche se	*even if*
piuttosto che	*rather than*
sebbene	*even*

Giocano al calcio, **sebbene** piova.	*They play soccer, **even** in the rain.*
Ti aspetto **anche se** arrivi tardi.	*I will wait for you **even if** you arrive late.*

427

Piuttosto che andare in metropolitana, lei va con la bicicletta.	***Rather than*** *going on the subway, she's going to ride her bike.*

Conjunctions of comparison introduce a dependent clause that expresses a comparison between the main and the dependent clauses.

così... come	*as . . . as*
meglio... che	*better . . . than*
meno... di	*less/fewer than*
più... che	*more . . . than*
piuttosto che	*rather than*
tanto... quanto	*as much . . . as*

Vado a teatro **piuttosto che** il cinema.	*I will go to the theater **rather than** the movies.*
È **meglio** leggere **che** guardare la TV.	*It is **better** to read **than** watch TV.*
Il mare è **tanto** misterioso **quanto** incantevole.	*The sea is **as much** mysterious **as** it is enchanting.*
È **meglio** ridere **che** piangere.	*It is **better** to laugh **than** cry.*
Oggi sulla spiaggia c'è **meno** gente **di** ieri.	*Today at the beach there are **fewer** people **than** yesterday.*

Conjunctions of condition introduce a dependent clause that indicates the necessary conditions for the action expressed in the main clause to happen.

a meno che	*unless*
a patto che	*on condition that*
anche se	*even if*
purchè	*as long as*
qualora	*when*
se	*if*

Se vieni, ci divertiremo.	***If*** *you come, we'll have fun.*
Qualora tu voglia andare al cinema, fammelo sapere.	***When*** *you want to go to the movies, let me know.*
Vengo **purchè** tu mi aspetti.	*I will come **as long as** you wait for me.*
Anche se non c'e nessuno, io vado lo stesso.	***Even if*** *nobody is there, I'll go anyway.*

Conjunctions of contrast express a contrast between the main and the dependent clauses.

al contrario	*on the contrary*
anche se	*though, although*
invece	*while, instead*
ma	*but*
salvo che	*except, unless*

Compra tanti gioielli **anche se** non ha soldi.	*She buys a lot of jewelry, **although** she does not have any money.*
Anche se sarai lontana, ti verrò a trovare.	***Though*** *you will be far away, I will come to visit you.*
Tutti saranno in classe, **salvo che** nevichi.	*Everybody will be in class **unless** it snows.*

Interrogative conjunctions introduce a subordinating clause that expresses an indirect question or a doubt.

come	*how*
perchè	*why*
quando	*when*
quanto	*how much*
se	*if*

Vorrei sapere **come** si chiama quella ragazza.	*I would like to know what the name of that girl is.* (literally, **how** *that girl is called*)
Non so **quanto** disti il paese.	*I do not know **how far** it is to town.*

Conjunctions of location express the relative location discussed between the main and the dependent clauses.

dove	*where*
ovunque	*anywhere*
Ti raggiungerò, **ovunque** tu sia.	*I will reach you, **wherever** you are.*

Conjunctions of reason introduce an explanation between the main and the dependent clauses.

come	*as*
comunque	*anyhow*
dato che	*because*
perchè	*because, why*
quantunque	*though, although*
siccome	*since*

Bisogna fare **come** dicono i genitori.	*You must do **as** your parents say.*
Comunque vadano le elezioni, io sarò contento.	***However** the election goes, I will be happy.*
Vorrei sapere **perchè** ti sei fermato.	*I would like to know **why** you stopped.*
Se vuoi venire, vieni, **comunque** ti aspetto.	*If you want to come, come; **anyhow**, I will wait for you.*

Modal conjunctions introduce a subordinate clause that defines the way in which the action expressed in the main clause is carried out.

come	*as*
come se	*as if*
comunque	*whichever way*
nel modo che	*in the way which*
quasi	*almost*

Fai **come se** fossi a casa tua.	*Our home is your home.* (literally, *Do **as if** you were in your home.*)
Comunque tu parli, non ti capisco.	***Whichever way** you speak, I do not understand you.*

Conjunctions of result or effect establish the result between a main clause and the dependent clause.

affinchè	*so that*
a meno che	*unless*
così	*so*
così che	*so that*
in modo che	*in order that*

Ti dò la chiave, **in modo che** tu possa entrare.	*I will give you the key **so that** you can go in.*
Restavamo nascosti, **affinchè** non ci vedesse.	*We were hiding, **so that** he would not see us.*
Ti telefono **a meno che** non ci vediamo.	*I will call you, **unless** we see each other.*

Conjunctions of time show the relative time between the main and the dependent clauses.

allorchè	*when*
appena	*as soon as*
come	*as soon as*
da quando	*since*
dopo che	*after*
fino a che	*until*
mentre	*while*
ogni volta che	*every time that*
prima che	*before*
quando	*when*
una volta che	*once*

Arrivò a casa, **quando** già dormivamo tutti.	*He arrived home **when** we were all already asleep.*
Prima che si laurei, passerà tanto tempo.	***Before** he gets his degree, a long time will go by.*
Ogni volta che ti guardo, sorrido.	***Every time that** I look at you, I smile.*
Mentre voi studiate, noi ci riposiamo.	***While** you study, we will rest.*
Fino a che non studiate il congiuntivo, non saprete parlare bene l'italiano.	***Until** you study the subjunctive, you will not speak Italian well.*

As you may have noticed from the previous lists, many subordinating conjunctions assume different meanings depending on the context in which they are used. Let's take **come** as an example, first as a conjunction of time:

conjunction (time) + dependent clause + main clause

Come venisti da me andasti a dormire.	*As soon as you came to my house, you went to sleep.*
Come aprì la porta, fu accolto dagli amici esultanti.	***As soon as** he opened the door, he was greeted by his very happy friends.*
Come vennero a casa, andarono a dormire.	***As soon as** they came home, they went to sleep.*

Now let's use **come** as a subordinating indirect interrogative conjunction:

main + subordinating indirect + dependent
clause   interrogative conjunction   clause

Dimmi come riesci a capirli.	*Tell me how you can understand them.*
Dimmi **come** stai oggi.	*Tell me **how** you are feeling today.*
Vorrei sapere **come** vanno le cose.	*I would like to know **how** things are going.*

Here, **come** is used as a modal subordinating conjunction:

main + modal subordinating + dependent
clause   conjunction   clause

Ho risposto come mi hai suggerito.	*I answered as you suggested.*
Ho fatto **come** mi hai detto.	*I did **as** you asked me to.*

Subordinating conjunctions with indicative and subjunctive moods

Subordinating conjunctions require the verb to be in either the indicative or the subjunctive mood, depending on the circumstances. In the majority of cases, subordinating conjunctions of time (**allorché, mentre, quando**) and cause (**appena, dal momento che, dato che, ogni volta che, siccome**) use the verb in the indicative mood.

> **indicative verb + conjunction (time) + dependent clause**
>
> **Portami quei documenti quando puoi.**   *Bring me the documents when you can.*
>
> **Ogni volta che vado** a sciare, mi diverto molto.   ***Each time that I go** skiing, I have a lot of fun.*
>
> **Appena tu ritorni** dal tuo viaggio, vogliamo vedere le fotografie.   ***As soon as you come back** from your trip, we want to see the pictures.*
>
> Portami le fotografie **quando vieni.**   *Bring me the pictures **when you come.***

All of the following subordinating conjunctions require the verb to be in the subjunctive: **a condizione che, affinchè, benchè, nonostante, per quanto, purchè, qualora, sebbene.**

> **conjunction + subjunctive verb + independent clause**
>
> **Nonostante tu pulisca sempre, la casa è ancora sporca.**   *Even if you clean all the time, the house is still dirty.*
>
> **Benchè sia** intelligente, non si applica.   ***Although he is** intelligent, he does not apply himself.*
>
> **Qualora tu voglia** venire, fammelo sapere.   ***When you want** to come, let me know.*

ESERCIZIO 6·1

Complete the following sentences with the appropriate subordinating conjunctions suggested in parentheses.

1. Sono tutta bagnata _____ pioveva e non avevo l'ombrello. (*because*)

2. Decisi di andare a scuola _____ avessi il raffreddore. (*even if*)

3. Siamo andati via _____ finisse la partita. (*before*)

4. Andremo a casa _____ vi abbiamo accompagnati alla stazione. (*after*)

5. Vengo a casa tua _____ studiamo. (*as long as*)

6. _____ non chiude la porta disturberà tutti. (*if*)

7. Ci ha detto _____ era molto stanco. (*that*)

8. Sono andati via _____ si annoiavano. (*because*)

Complete the following sentences with the appropriate subordinating conjunctions.

1. Vorrei sapere _____ stanno i tuoi amici.

2. _____ abbia molto da studiare, trova il tempo per lo sport.

3. Dimmi _____ non riesci a studiare alla sera.

4. Alcuni studenti sono in ritardo _____ hanno perso l'autobus.

5. Lo spettacolo fu _____ bello _____ tutti uscirono dal teatro molto entusiasti.

6. Non riesco a concentrarmi _____ c'è molta confusione.

7. Mi sono scusata con loro _____ sia molto orgogliosa.

8. _____ la porta sia chiusa, la sentono tutti.

Circle the correct subordinating conjunction for each of the following sentences.

1. Se / E non chiudi la finestra, c'è troppa corrente.

2. Benchè / Perchè tu abbia molto da fare, esci tutte le sere con gli amici.

3. Sono soddisfatta del tuo progresso, ma / ma però devi continuare a migliorare.

4. Ti ho già detto di no ieri, quindi / anzi non me lo chiedere di nuovo.

5. Giovanni viene a casa tardi, perchè / anzi deve finire il suo lavoro.

6. Sebbene / Dopo che vi siete riposati, andremo al mercato.

7. Dimmi se / perchè non riesci a capire l'algebra.

8. Prima che / Dato che tu sei allergica alla polvere, è meglio togliere tutti i tappeti.

Complete the following sentences with the appropriate coordinating or subordinating conjunctions.

1. Io vado, _____ ti aspetto in macchina.

2. _____ tu sappia che sono in macchina ad aspettarti, tu non vieni.

3. Non ho comprato lo zaino _____ mi piacesse _____ costa troppo, _____ ho deciso di usare quello dell'anno scorso.

4. La squadra ha vinto il torneo di tennis _____ non lo meritasse.

5. Sono molto stanca _____ non mi reggo in piedi, _____ non posso andare a letto _____ ho molte cose da fare.

6. Domani vengono a pranzo i nostri amici, _____ voglio invitare _____ te e tuo marito.

7. Preferisci usare la bicicletta _____ la motocicletta?

8. _____ tu sia molto sportivo _____ ti piaccia competere, non vinci mai.

Relative pronouns

A relative pronoun joins a clause, the relative clause, with a larger one, the main clause. As a pronoun, it stands in place of a noun or another pronoun previously mentioned in the main clause (its antecedent). Relative pronouns may take the place of the subject, the indirect object, or the object of a preposition. There are fewer relative pronouns in Italian than in English, and determining which one to use depends on its function in the relative clause. Unlike in English, relative pronouns are never omitted in Italian: **che** (*that, who, whom, which*), **chi** (*who, the one who, she who, he who*), **cui** (*that, which, whom*), and **il quale** (*which*).

Che and *chi*

Che (*that, who, whom, which*) is the pronoun in Italian used for the subject or the direct object of the relative clause.

> **noun + relative pronoun (subject) + relative clause**

La macchina che ha vinto la corsa è mia.	*The car that has won the race is mine.*

> **noun + relative pronoun (direct object) + relative clause**

La macchina che hai visto ieri era mia.	*The car that you saw yesterday was mine.*

Che is the most common relative pronoun. It is invariable for gender and number and is used for persons, animals, and things. **Che** is never used with a preposition. It is placed after the noun that it modifies.

Gli amici **che** sono venuti a pranzo sono molto simpatici.	*The friends **who** came to lunch are very nice.*
La ragazza **che** hai incontrato è Americana.	*The girl **whom** you met is American.*
Il cane **che** abbaia è molto vecchio.	*The dog **that** is barking is very old.*
I biglietti **che** hai comprato sono cari.	*The tickets **that** you bought are expensive.*

Be careful not to confuse the different functions of **che**:

Relative pronoun	L'auto **che** passa è veloce.	*The car **that** is going by is fast.*
Interrogative pronoun	**Che** vuole il tuo amico?	***What** does your friend want?*

434

Interrogative adjective	**Che** partita hai visto?	**Which** game did you watch?
Exclamative adjective	**Che** meraviglia!	**How** wonderful!
Conjunction	Penso **che** verrò da te.	I think **that** I will come to your house.

Chi (*who, the one who, he who, she who, whoever*) is an invariable, singular pronoun used only for people.

Non so **chi** è al telefono.	I do not know **who** is talking on the phone.
Dobbiamo aiutare **chi** ha fame.	We must help **whoever** is hungry.
Chi viaggia in Italia mangerà molto bene.	**He/She who** travels to Italy will eat very well.

Cui

Cui (*that, which, whom*) is an invariable relative pronoun. It is used as an indirect object when it is preceded by the preposition **a**, or as the object of any other preposition. It is used for persons, animals, and things. If **cui** is used without a preposition, it means **a cui** (*to whom*).

relative clause + indirect object pronoun + main clause

Ecco lo studente a cui parlavo in classe.	Here is the student to whom I was speaking in class.
Ecco il libro **di cui** ti ho parlato.	Here is the book (**that**) I was speaking of.
Questa è la città **da cui** viene mio padre.	This is the city (**that**) my father comes from.
L'Italia è il paese **in cui** vivo.	Italy is the country where (**in which**) I live.
Il dottore **cui** (**a cui**) parlai è molto conosciuto.	The doctor **to whom** I spoke is very well known.

When **cui** is preceded by the definite article (**il cui, la cui, i cui, le cui**), it has a possessive implication: **definite article + *cui* = whose. Cui** is invariable, but the definite article must agree in gender and number with the noun that follows it.

possessor + definite article + cui + noun + main clause

Ecco la donna il cui figlio canta molto bene.	Here is the lady whose son sings very well.
Ecco la donna **il cui** braccialetto è stato rubato.	Here is the woman **whose** bracelet was stolen.
Questa è la mia amica **il cui** figlio ha avuto un incidente con la macchina.	This is my friend **whose** son had a car accident.

Il quale

Il quale, la quale, i quali, le quali (*who, which, that*) is a variable pronoun used for persons, animals, or things. This form is often replaced in colloquial Italian by **che**. It is used after prepositions for emphasis, for clarification, or to avoid repetition.

L'amica di Maria, **la quale** studia l'inglese, verrà a vivere in America.	Maria's friend, **who** studies English, will come to live in America.
L'uomo, **il quale** legge il giornale, è bene informato.	The man **who** reads the daily newspaper is well informed.
La ragazza **alla quale** porto il regalo, è mia cugina.	The girl **to whom** I bring the gift is my cousin.

Quello che, ciò che, and quanto

Quello che, **ciò che**, and **quanto**, meaning *that which* or *what*, are used when the antecedent is not clear or understood. They are used mostly for things and can be the subject or the direct object of the verb.

main clause + relative pronoun + dependent clause

So quello che è successo ieri a scuola.	*I know **what** happened yesterday in school.*
Non capisco **quello che** dici.	*I do not understand **what** you are saying.*
Fai **ciò che** ti dicono le persone amiche.	*Do **what** friends tell you to do.*
Ecco **quanto** mi ha dato.	*Here is **what** he gave me.*

If **tutto** precedes **ciò che** or **quello che**, it means *all that* or *everything that*.

Se passi gli esami, ti darò **tutto quello che** vuoi.	*If you pass the exams, I will give you **everything** you want.*
Non dice mai **tutto quello che** pensa.	*He never says **all that** he is thinking.*

ESERCIZIO 7·1

Complete the following sentences with the relative pronouns **che** *or* **chi**.

1. Il libro _____ mi hai dato, è appena stato pubblicato.

2. La vita _____ fai è molto faticosa.

3. Ti riporto i biglietti _____ non sono stati venduti.

4. Non conosco la ragazza _____ ti piace.

5. Non so _____ cosa vuoi vedere.

6. Mi dici _____ porti a casa domani?

7. Non parlare con _____ non conosci.

8. Fammi sapere _____ vuoi assumere.

ESERCIZIO 7·2

Complete the following sentences with the article or appropriate **preposition** + **cui**.

1. Il film _____ ti ho parlato, è appena uscito.

2. L'Italia è il paese _____ si fanno gli spaghetti.

3. Il ragazzo _____ padre lavora con tuo marito, gioca bene al calcio.

4. Questa è la casa _____ sono cresciuta.

5. L'esame _____ abbiamo studiato, era molto difficile.

6. La classe _____ ci troviamo, è sempre fredda.

7. La signora _____ vuoi fare il regalo, è andata via.

8. Il fatto _____ abbiamo parlato, deve rimanere un segreto.

ESERCIZIO
7·3

Complete the following sentences with the appropriate relative pronouns.

1. L'auto _____ passa è veloce.

2. Rispetto solo _____ stimo.

3. Condivido _____ hai affermato.

4. Potrai conoscere questa sera l'amico _____ ti ho parlato.

5. _____ non sta attento a scuola, non può fare bene i compiti.

6. Il giorno _____ ci siamo incontrati, era d'estate.

7. La fontana _____ ho bevuto, è in montagna.

8. L'uomo _____ mi insegna a sciare, è molto bravo.

Quanto, chiunque, and *dove*

Quanto in the singular form is used only for things and means *that which, what,* or *all that.* In the plural form, **quanti** and **quante** (*all those that, all those which*) refer to people and things.

Gli dò **quanto** gli spetta.	*I will give him **what** I owe him.*
Quanti verranno saranno i benvenuti.	***All those that** will come are welcome.*

Chiunque (*anybody, all those who*) is used only for people and always in the singular form.

Chiunque vada alla partita deve avere il biglietto.	*All those who go to the game must have a ticket.*

Dove is a relative pronoun when it is used to connect two sentences or phrases.

Abita nel palazzo **dove** (**in cui, nel quale**) c'è l'ufficio postale.	*The post office is in the building **where** he lives.*

Complete the following sentences with the relative pronouns **chi**, **quanto**, **chiunque**, **dove**, or the appropriate form of **quello che**.

1. Guadagna _____ vuole.

2. Abitano nella città _____ ci sono molti parchi.

3. _____ tace acconsente.

4. Andrà con _____ glielo chieda.

5. _____ va spesso in spiaggia, si abbronzerà.

6. _____ vanno spesso in spiaggia, si abbronzeranno.

7. _____ parli in classe sará punito.

8. Ti dò _____ vuoi.

ESERCIZIO

7·5

Complete the following sentences with the appropriate relative pronouns.

1. Il signore _____ è venuto a casa mia, è un collega di lavoro.

2. L'amico _____ mi ha portato in barca, vive molto bene.

3. Non so _____ vuole andare al cinema.

4. Se sapete _____ ha chiamato diteglielo.

5. Il libro _____ ti ho parlato, è molto interessante.

6. La signora _____ porto il regalo, è mia zia.

7. È una persona _____ puoi parlare liberamente.

8. Mangia _____ vuoi.

ESERCIZIO

7·6

Complete the following sentences with the appropriate relative pronouns.

1. _____ va piano, va lontano.

2. Il ragazzo _____ studia l'italiano con noi, viene dagli Stati Uniti.

3. Il ragazzo a _____ porto la palla, è molto sportivo.

4. La squadra di calcio _____ ha vinto la coppa del mondo, è italiana.

5. Ecco la signora con _____ parlavo.

6. _____ voglia venire, deve farmelo sapere.

7. Non so _____ volete vedere domani.

8. Questa è la casa _____ sono nato.

Present and past participles

The participle has two forms: present (or simple) and past.

È una donna **affascinante**.　　　　*She is a **fascinating** woman.*
Ho **trovato** il libro.　　　　　　*I have **found** the book.*

Present participles

In Italian, the present participle is formed by adding **-ante** to the stem of **-are** and **-ente** to the stem of **-ere** and **-ire** verbs. The present participle can be used as a noun, as an adjective, and, more infrequently, as a verb.

As a **noun**, the present participle is used in the singular or plural form. It is always preceded by the definite or indefinite article: **cantare** (*to sing*) → **il cantante** (*singer*); **amare** (*to love*) → **l'amante** (*lover*); **brillare** (*to shine*) → **il brillante** (*diamond*).

present participle (noun) + verb + direct object

La **cantante** ha avuto molto　　*The **singer** has had great success.*
　successo.

Il **cantante** ha lanciato una　　*The **singer** has launched a new song.*
　canzone nuova.
I **cantanti** hanno lanciato la loro　*The **singers** have launched their new*
　canzone nuova.　　　　　　　　*song.*
L'**amante** piangeva, perchè era　*The **lover** was crying because she had*
　stata lasciata.　　　　　　　　*been dumped.*
Il **brillante** luccicava sul suo dito　*The **diamond** was shining on her*
　affusolato.　　　　　　　　　　*slender finger.*

When the present participle functions as an **adjective**, it is used in the singular and plural forms and in the comparative and the superlative. As an adjective, it expresses a state or an inherent quality of the noun.

subject + verb + direct object + present participle (adjective)

Noi abbiamo visto dei piatti　　*We saw some flying saucers.*
　volanti.

Ho letto un libro **interessante**.　*I have read an **interesting** book.*
Ho letto dei libri **interessanti**.　*I have read some **interesting** books.*
Questo libro è più **interessante**　*This book is more **interesting** than*
　di quello.　　　　　　　　　　*that one.*
Ho letto un libro **interessantissimo**.　*I have read a **very interesting** book.*

The present participle is used also as a **verb**. However, is not very common in spoken language and tends to be used mainly in political and legal language. The use of a relative clause is usually preferred. A present participle used as a verb has the same value as a relative clause expressing an action contemporary to that indicated by the main verb.

subject + present participle (verb) + dependent clause

**I danni derivanti (che derivano)
dall'uragano sono enormi.**

*The damages caused by (coming from) the
hurricane are enormous.*

I soldati hanno trovato una scatola
contenente (che conteneva) una
bomba a mano.

*The soldiers found a box **containing** a hand
grenade.*

Parleremo con la persona **facente** funzione
(che svolge la funzione) di presidente.

*We'll speak with the person **functioning** as
president.*

È stato firmato il documento **comprovante
(che comprova)** l'accordo di vendita.
(*also:* Il documento **comprovante**
l'accordo di vendita è stato firmato.)

*The document **proving** the sale agreement
has been signed.*

ESERCIZIO
8·1

Write the present participles of the following verbs. Then translate them into English.

1. assistere _____ _____

2. commuovere _____ _____

3. dirigere _____ _____

4. mancare _____ _____

5. obbedire _____ _____

6. perdere _____ _____

7. riposare _____ _____

8. tollerare _____ _____

9. uscire _____ _____

10. vivere _____ _____

ESERCIZIO
8·2

Complete the following sentences with the appropriate forms of the present participle, using the verbs in parentheses.

1. L'acqua della doccia è _____. (bollire)

2. In questa casa non c'è l'acqua _____. (correre)

3. La ragazza è _____. (sorridere)

4. Mi piacciono i bambini _____. (obbedire)

5. Il mio _____ è una persona molto valida. (assistere)

6. Ha avuto una vita _____. (sconvolgere)

7. Abbiamo visto un film _____. (divertire)

8. L'esercizio è nella pagina _____. (seguire)

ESERCIZIO
8·3

Complete the following sentences with the present participle of the verbs in parentheses functioning as nouns.

1. I _____ di quel paese non sono molto civili. (governare)

2. Luigi è un _____ di una ditta multinazionale. (dipendere)

3. La vita degli _____ è molto dura. (emigrare)

4. I _____ degli autobus oggi sono in sciopero. (condurre)

5. Alcuni _____ hanno visto la rapina. (passare)

6. Questa bevanda è molto _____. (dissetare)

7. I _____ al convegno sono tutti stranieri. (partecipare)

8. Ha acceso gli _____. (abbagliare)

Past participles

Like the present participle, the past participle is used as an adjective, a noun, or a verb. The past participle is formed by changing the endings of regular -**are** verbs (**pagare**, *to pay*) to -**ato** (**pagato**, *paid*). Regular verbs ending in -**ere** (**vendere**, *to sell*) change to -**uto** (**venduto**, *sold*). Regular verbs ending in -**ire** (**capire**, *to understand*) change to -**ito** (**capito**, *understood*). If the verbs have an irregular past participle, it should be used. For example, **scegliere** (*to choose*) would change to the noun or adjective **scelto**.

As an **adjective**, the past participle is used without the auxiliary and agrees in gender and number with the noun it refers to. It is also used in the comparative and the superlative.

subject + past participle (adjective) + verb

I candidati scelti (che sono stati scelti) non piacciono alla popolazione.	*The people do not like the candidates that have been chosen.*
I bambini **viziati** sono molto antipatici.	***Spoiled** children are very unpleasant.*
La casa **restaurata** è stata affittata.	*The **renovated** home has been rented.*
La donna **affaticata** voleva riposarsi.	*The **tired** woman wanted to rest.*
L'opera **rappresentata**, ha suscitato molto entusiasmo.	*The opera that was **performed** generated much enthusiasm.*
Il cane è **più amato** del gatto.	*The dog is **loved more** than the cat.*
Il cane è **molto amato**.	*The dog is **loved very much**.*

The past participle used as an adjective is often changed to function as a noun. When it is used as a noun, the past participle does not accompany another noun as it would if it were functioning as an adjective. As a noun, it is used as a subject or as an object.

In this example, the past participle **invitati** functions as an adjective modifying a noun:

I giovani **invitati** sono arrivati tardi alla festa.	*The young people who had been invited arrived late at the party.*

In the example below, however, the past participle **gli immigrati** functions as a noun:

past participle (noun) + verb + direct object

Gli immigrati cercavano un posto per dormire.	*The immigrants looked for a place to sleep.*
Gli **invitati** sono arrivati tardi.	*The **guests** arrived late.*
I **laureati** cercavano tutti un lavoro.	*The **graduates** were all looking for a job.*

The past participle used as a **verb** is added to the auxiliary **avere** or **essere** to form the compound tenses of all the other verbs. It usually expresses actions or events prior to those in the main clause.

subject + avere/essere + past participle

Io ho visto.	*I have seen.*
Io sono venuto.	*I have come.*

The past participle is also used with the auxiliary **essere** to form the passive constructions.

subject + essere + past participle

Noi siamo stati lodati.	*We have been praised.*

Past participles standing alone

The past participle is also used by itself as a central element of dependent clauses.

past participle + object + main clause

Raggiunta (Dopo che avevamo raggiunto) **la meta facemmo uno spuntino.**	*Having reached our goal, we had a snack.*
Riposatosi (Dopo che si era riposato) un poco, era pronto per giocare a tennis.	*After resting for a while, he was ready to play tennis.*
Resosi conto che (Siccome si era reso conto) lo avevano riconosciuto, decise di fuggire.	*Realizing that he had been recognized, he decided to run away.*
Rallegrati (Poichè furono rallegrati) dalla notizia, fecero salti di gioia.	*Pleased by the news, they were jumping with joy.*

Often, in front of the past participle one can find the following conjunctions: **appena** (*as soon as*), **benchè** (*even if*), **se pur** (*even if*), **se anche** (*even if*), and **una volta** (*once, when*). These conjunctions help in identifying the type of secondary clause expressed by the participle.

Appena arrivata a casa, telefonò subito alla sua amica.	*As soon as she arrived home, she called her friend.* (appena = *conjunction of time*)
Benchè spaventato, non respinse il cane.	*Even if he was scared, he did not push the dog away.*

Generally, the main and the secondary clauses refer to the same subject. If this is not the case, then the subject must be placed directly after the past participle. The past participle must then agree with the subject of the secondary clause.

Persa la partita, i giocatori erano molto silenziosi.

Sfumati i soldi, Luigi e Mario decisero di ritornare a casa.

After losing the game, the players were very quiet.

Once the money was finished, Luigi and Mario decided to return home.

ESERCIZIO 8·4

Complete the following sentences, changing the verbs in parentheses to past participles used as adjectives.

1. A tutti piacciono molto le patatine _____. (friggere)

2. Con il mare _____ non è consigliabile andare in barca. (muovere)

3. Il corteo avanza _____ dalla banda locale. (precedere)

4. Il tennista _____ dal sole si è ritirato dal torneo. (accaldare)

5. L'acqua _____ del lago viene mandata all'acquedotto. (depurare)

6. Le persone anziane pagano tariffa _____ al cinema. (ridurre)

7. Firenze, una città molto _____ dagli italiani, è molto antica. (amare)

8. Il giocatore di calcio più _____ è brasiliano. (conoscere)

ESERCIZIO 8·5

Complete the following sentences, changing the verbs in parentheses to past participles used as nouns.

1. Li vedo spesso alla _____ dell'autobus. (fermare)

2. Gli studenti non hanno il _____ di parcheggio. (permettere)

3. È necessario il _____ del consolato per entrare negli Stati Uniti. (vedere)

4. All'inaugurazione dello stadio c'erano molti _____. (invitare)

5. Fare un _____ di cipolla, carote, e sedano. (soffriggere)

6. I _____ politici, spesso parlano troppo. (candidare)

7. Questa estate ho avuto molti _____ a casa mia. (ammalare)

8. Lui non sente bene. Ha perso l'_____. (udire)

Rewrite the following sentences, using a compound tense in place of the past participle.

EXAMPLE: Terminati gli esami, le bambine andranno in America.

Quando avranno terminato gli esami, le bambine andranno in America.

1. Una volta finito il concerto, ti riporteremo a casa.

   _____

2. Spente le luci, la bambina si addormenterà.

   _____

3. Finito il corso, gli studenti andranno al mare.

   _____

4. Una volta saliti sull'autobus, troveranno senz'altro un posto a sedere.

   _____

5. Lavati i piatti, puliranno la cucina.

   _____

6. Una volta presa la patente, potranno guidare.

   _____

7. Appena arrivati a destinazione, si riposeranno.

   _____

8. Finiti i compiti, potranno andare fuori a giocare.

   _____

Position of pronouns with the past participle

The pronouns **mi, ti, gli, lo, la, le**, and the reflexive pronouns **mi, ti, si, ci, vi, si**, are attached to the end of the participle.

Scritta la lettera e spedita**la**, si sentì molto soddisfatto.	*Once he wrote the letter and he mailed it, he felt satisfied.*
Addormentato**si** sul divano, si svegliò tutto infreddolito.	*After sleeping on the couch, he woke up cold.*

Remember that when the pronouns **lo, la, li, le** precede the compound tenses, the past participle must agree with them.

Li ho visti sulla metropolitana.	*I saw them on the subway.*
Le ho scritte e **le** ho spedite.	*I wrote them, and I mailed them.*

If the pronoun **ne** is used, the past participle must agree with the noun it refers to.

La torta era buonissima, **ne** ho mangiate   *The cake was excellent; I ate two slices of it.*
due fette.

ESERCIZIO
8·7

Rewrite each sentence and replace the underlined phrase with the appropriate pronoun and past participle. Remember where to place the pronoun.

1. Finita <u>la lettera</u>, mi sono sentita sollevata.

   _____

2. <u>Appena riposatosi</u>, viene a visitarvi.

   _____

3. Cercava la palla dappertutto, <u>trovata la palla</u> è uscito a giocare.

   _____

4. Ho letto tutte <u>le tue lettere</u> in questi giorni.

   _____

5. Vedo sempre <u>Marco e Cristina</u> quando ritornano a casa dal lavoro.

   _____

6. La cioccolata calda era squisita, ho bevuto <u>due tazze di cioccolata</u>.

   _____

7. Ho mangiato <u>una banana</u>, ma era acerba.

   _____

8. Ho comprato tante <u>piante</u>.

   _____

Adjectives

The word "adjective" comes from Latin *adiectivum*, meaning "word that is added." Adjectives are added to nouns to attribute special qualities to them or to specify some determining aspects of them. Their use makes sentences more interesting, clear, and effective. Adjectives can be attributive or predicative.

Attributive	Ho guidato una macchina **veloce**.	*I drove a **speedy** car.*
Predicative	La macchina è **veloce**.	*The car is **speedy**.*

Attributive adjectives

Attributive adjectives expand or limit the noun they modify. Sometimes these adjectives are placed before the noun, and other times they are placed after the noun. We'll look at this later in the unit.

subject + verb + object + attributive adjective

Maria vede gli uccelli affamati. *Maria sees the hungry birds.*

Ho visto **mio** zio. *I saw **my** uncle.*
Luisa ha visto un **bel** fiore. *Luisa saw a **beautiful** flower.*

The adjectives **mio** and **bel** are directly *attributed* to the nouns **zio** and **fiore**. They are placed next to them and have an attributive function.

Predicative adjectives

Predicative adjectives specify a quality or the characteristics of the subject. They refer to the noun indirectly through a verb.

subject + linking verb + predicative adjective

La casa è grande. *The house is big.*

La bicicletta è **nuova**. *The bicycle is **new**.*
Francesca sembra **felice**. *Francesca seems **happy**.*

The adjectives **nuova** and **felice** refer to the noun through the verbs **essere** and **sembrare**.

Adjectives agree in gender and number with the nouns they modify. They can express:

Color rosso (*red*), verde (*green*), giallo (*yellow*), nero (*black*), violaceo (*purplish*)

447

Dimension	lungo (*long*), largo (*large*), stretto (*narrow, tight*), grande (*big*), vasto (*wide*), piccolo (*small*), alto (*tall*)
Look	robusto (*stocky*), florido (*florid*), solido (*solid*), liquido (*liquid*), longilineo (*slender*)
Matter	bronzeo (*bronze*), marmoreo (*marble*), ligneo (*wooden*)
Personal feelings	felice (*happy*), triste (*sad*), curioso (*curious*), ansioso (*anxious*), malinconico (*melancolic*), stanco (*tired*), riposato (*rested*), rilassato (*relaxed*), nuovo (*new*)
Physical feelings	caldo (*warm*), freddo (*cold*), dolce (*sweet*), piccante (*spicy*), roccioso (*rocky*), pericoloso (*dangerous*)
Shape	quadrato (*square*), rotondo (*round*), triangolare (*triangular*)
Time	quotidiano (*daily*), diurno (*daytime*), notturno (*nighttime*), serale (*evening time*), invernale (*wintertime*), estivo (*summertime*)

ESERCIZIO
9·1

Write three adjectives to describe each noun, as shown in the example below.

EXAMPLE: finestra *quadrata, stretta, nuova*

1. libro _____

2. fiore _____

3. casa _____

4. gatto _____

5. montagna _____

6. giornale _____

7. neve _____

8. ragazzo _____

Position of adjectives

Attributive adjectives in Italian sentences can be placed either before or after the nouns they modify. Generally, when the adjective is placed before the noun, it emphasizes the noun it modifies. When it is placed after the noun, the adjective itself is emphasized.

Vidi in lontananza **stanchi** montanari.	*I saw from a distance **tired** mountaineers.*
Vidi in lontananza montanari **stanchi**.	*I saw from a distance mountaineers **who were tired**.*

Often, an adjective placed before the noun it modifies has purely a descriptive meaning. If it is placed after the noun, it is restrictive.

Usa sempre i **vecchi** giocattoli.	*He always uses the **old** toys.*
Usa sempre i giocattoli **vecchi**.	*He always uses the **old** toys.* (the **toys that are old**)

Sometimes the position of an adjective completely changes the meaning.

povero uomo (un uomo di basso livello)	*a man of low station*
uomo **povero** (un uomo senza soldi)	*a man without money*
diverse occasioni (molte occasioni)	*many (several) chances*
occasioni **diverse** (occasioni di vario tipo)	*occasions of different types*

Some adjectives have a fixed position. They are always found after the noun. They are adjectives of:

Color	vestito **blu** (*blue* dress), gonna **rossa** (*red* skirt)
Matter	terreno **sabbioso** (*sandy* soil), roccia **dolomitica** (*dolomite* rock)
Nationality	donna **messicana** (*Mexican* lady), uomo **tedesco** (*German* man)
Shape	cesto **ovale** (*oval* basket), tappeto **quadrato** (*square* rug)

Adjectives that must be altered or changed in form in order to improve a description are placed after the nouns they modify.

donna **magrolina** (*from* **magra**)	*thin* woman
ragazzo **grassotello** (*from* **grasso**)	*plump* boy

ESERCIZIO
9·2

Translate the following sentences into Italian, putting the adjective in the correct position.

1. I saw a poor woman trapped in the snow.

   _____

2. They are American children.

   _____

3. He is an Austrian citizen.

   _____

4. I like square tables.

   _____

5. In Michigan you find sandy soil everywhere.

   _____

6. She wears only black shoes.

   _____

7. I have a red scarf.

   _____

8. She is a sickly person.

   _____

Adjectives used as nouns

The usual function of adjectives is to accompany a noun in order to qualify or determine it better. Sometimes, however, adjectives themselves are used as nouns. In this case, they are preceded by the definite article.

Arrivano **le straniere**. (Arrivano **le donne straniere**.)   *The foreigners are arriving.*

Loro leggono **i gialli**. (Loro leggono **i libri gialli**.)   *They read **mystery books**.*

Just about any adjective can be used as a noun. Some adjectives are used so often as nouns that it is common to forget their adjectival origins. Here is a list of a few such adjectives:

i belli	*the beautiful*	il possibile	*the possible*
le buone	*good manners*	i poveri	*the poor*
le cattive	*bad manners*	il quotidiano	*the daily (newspaper)*
i deboli	*the weak*	i ricchi	*the rich*
i dolci	*sweets*	i salatini	*salty snacks*
il futuro	*the future*	gli studiosi	*the studious*
le giovani	*the young*	i temerari	*the fearless*
l'impossibile	*the impossible*	i timidi	*the shy*
i mondiali	*the World Cup*	i vecchi	*the old*

ESERCIZIO
9·3

Change the following adjectives into nouns.

1. incerto _____

2. bello _____

3. fiorito _____

4. difficile _____

5. veloce _____

6. nuovo _____

7. caldo _____

8. reale _____

9. velenoso _____

10. profumato _____

11. fresco _____

Complete the following sentences with the adjectives used as nouns suggested in parentheses.

1. I giocatori di calcio del Milan sono chiamati _____. (the red and blacks)

2. La gente spera di poter conoscere _____. (the future)

3. Ogni quattro anni si giocano _____ di calcio. (the World Cup)

4. Agli _____ piace molto l'Italia. (foreigners)

5. _____ e _____ sono molto ammirati. (The rich, the beautiful)

6. La professoressa elogia sempre _____. (the studious)

7. Spesso _____ ottengono più dei _____. (the fearless, weak)

8. _____ hanno sempre paura di tutto. (The shy)

Adverbial adjectives

An adjective that, instead of modifying a noun, modifies a verb is called an adverbial adjective. It is used to better qualify the verb. These include **chiaro** (*in a clear way*), **duro** (*the hard way*), **giusto** (*in the right way*), and **piano** (*in a slow way*). In English, these would be considered adverbs, but in Italian, they are called adjectives with adverbial value, or adverbial adjectives.

subject + verb + adverbial adjective

Lei mangia piano. (in modo lento)   *She eats slowly. (in a slow way)*

The following expressions are part of this group:

Cammina **piano**. (in modo lento)	*She walks **slowly**. (in a slow way)*
Lavorano **sodo**. (in modo sodo)	*They work **hard**. (in a hard way)*
Parla **forte**. (a voce alta)	*He speaks **loudly**. (with a loud voice)*
Parlate **chiaro**! (in modo chiaro)	*Speak **clearly**! (in a clear way)*

Underline the adjectives used as nouns and/or the adverbial adjectives in the following sentences.

1. Gli sportivi devono allenarsi per la gara.

2. Dimmi chiaro e tondo che cosa vuoi.

3. Il piatto toscano più famoso è la classica fiorentina.

4. C'è un proverbio che dice: "Chi va piano, va sano e lontano".

5. Coraggio, il peggio è passato.

6. L'italiano è una lingua difficile da imparare per gli stranieri.

7. Le cinesi lavorano duro nelle fabbriche.

8. Il futuro nessuno lo conosce.

Comparative and superlative forms of adjectives

An adjective used in its regular form is called positive. When an adjective is used to state the idea that someone or something has a relatively equal, greater, or lesser degree of a quality, it is called comparative or superlative.

The comparative is used to express a comparison between two people, animals, or things, in relation to a quality that they both have. The comparative can be of majority, minority, or equality.

The comparative of majority is used when the first term of comparison is greater than the second term of comparison. In this case, the adjective is introduced by **più** (*more*) and the second term is introduced by **di** or **che**.

subject + verb + comparative + adjective + **di** + second term
of majority   of comparison

Loro sono più affamati di noi.	*They are hungrier than we are.*
Luca è **più calmo di** Marco.	*Luca is **calmer than** Marco.*
Giovanni è **più studioso di** Marco.	*Giovanni is **more studious than** Marco.*
Noi abbiamo **più fame di** te.	*We are **hungrier than** you.*
Lei parla **più velocemente di** suo fratello.	*She speaks **faster than** her brother.*

In the comparative of majority, the second term of comparison is introduced by **che** when two nouns, or two noun phrases, are compared by one adjective, noun, or adverb.

subject + verb + comparative + adjective + **che** + second term
of majority   of comparison

Maria è più affamata che stanca.	*Maria is more hungry than tired.*
Siamo **più** assonnati **che** affamati.	*We are **more** tired **than** hungry.*

The second term of comparison is introduced by **che** in the comparative of majority when:

◆ The second term of comparison is a noun or a pronoun preceded by a compound preposition

Sei **più** interessato **allo** sport **che allo** studio.	*You are **more interested in** sports **than in** studying.*

◆ Comparing two qualities with the same subject

È un'occasione **più** unica **che** rara.	*It is an occasion **more** unique **than** rare.*

◆ Comparing two verbs

È **più** bello dare **che** ricevere.	*It is **better** to give **than** to receive.*

The **comparative of minority** is used when the first term of the comparison is of a lesser degree than the second term. In this case, the adjective is introduced by **meno** (*less*); the second term is introduced by **di** or **che**, and it follows the same rules as the comparative of majority.

Luca è **meno** alto **di** Marco.	*Luca is **less** tall **than** Marco. (shorter)*
Giulia è **meno** studiosa **che** intelligente.	*Giulia is **less** studious **than** intelligent.*

The **comparative of equality** is used when the quality expressed by the adjective is equally present in the two terms of comparison.

Luca è **tanto** alto **quanto** Marco.	*Luca is **as** tall **as** Marco.*
Lisa è (**così**) simpatica **come** te.	*Lisa is **as** nice **as** you.*

When the quality of the adjective is compared to a group of people or things, the **relative superlative** construction is used. It is formed by placing the definite article in front of **più** or **meno**.

subject + verb + definite + più/meno + adjective + second term
article **of comparison**

Il Sahara è il più grande dei deserti.	*The Sahara Desert is the largest of all deserts.*
Anna è **la più brava** della classe.	*Anna is **the best** of the class.*
Carla è **la meno brava** della classe.	*Carla is **the worst** of the class.*
La Sicilia è **la più vasta** delle isole italiane.	*Sicily is **the biggest** of the Italian islands.*

When the quality of the adjective is expressed in an absolute way, with no comparison, the **absolute superlative** is used. It is formed by adding the suffix **-issimo** to the root of the adjective: bell**o** (*beautiful*) → bell**issimo/a/i/e** (*very beautiful*); urgent**e** (*urgent*) → urgent**issimo/a/i/e** (*very urgent*).

subject + verb + absolute superlative

I pini in California sono altissimi.	*Pine trees in California are very tall.*
La Sicilia è **vastissima**.	*Sicily is **very vast**.*
Il lavoro è **urgentissimo**.	*The job is **very urgent**.*

Other ways to form the absolute superlative of an adjective is by placing the adverb of quality or quantity before the adjective, for example, **molto** (*very*), **davvero** (*really*), or **assai** (*very*).

Mia mamma è **molto stanca**.	*My mother is **very tired**.*

Sometimes the absolute superlative is obtained with prefixes such as:

arci-	arcicontento (*very happy*)
iper-	iperattivo (*hyperactive*), ipercritico (*overly critical*), ipersensibile (*overly sensitive*)
stra-	stragrande (*very big*), stracarico (*very loaded*), strapieno (*very full*)
super-	superaffollato (*overcrowded*), superconveniente (*very convenient*)

Besides the regular formation of comparatives and superlatives, four adjectives have another form that comes directly from Latin:

POSITIVE	COMPARATIVE OF MAJORITY	ABSOLUTE SUPERLATIVE	RELATIVE SUPERLATIVE
buono (*good*)	più buono/migliore	buonissimo/ottimo	il migliore di...
cattivo (*bad*)	più cattivo/peggiore	cattivissimo/pessimo	il peggiore di...
grande (*big*)	più grande/maggiore	grandissimo/massimo	il maggiore di...
piccolo (*small*)	più piccolo/minore	piccolissimo/minimo	il minore di...

The forms **migliore**, **ottimo**, **peggiore**, and **pessimo** are used when:

- Referring to something abstract

> Devi esercitare un **maggior autocontrollo**. (*not* ... un più grande autocontrollo)
>
> *You must have **more self-control**.*

- Using technical and scientific language

> Consideriamo **il lato minore** del triangolo.
>
> *Let's take a look at **the shorter side** of the triangle.*

Migliore, **peggiore**, **maggiore**, and **minore** are used with adjectives that describe the ability or the strength of a person.

> Ho scelto **il migliore** avvocato della città.
>
> *I chose **the best** lawyer in the city.*
>
> Raffaello è fra **i migliori** artisti italiani.
>
> *Raffaello is one of **the best** Italian artists.*

Six adjectives form the superlative with the suffix **-errimo** rather than the suffix **-issimo**:

acre (*sour*)	acerrimo	integro (*intact*)	integerrimo
aspro (*sour*)	asperrimo	misero (*miserable*)	miserrimo
celebre (*famous*)	celeberrimo	salubre (*healthy*)	saluberrimo

Six other adjectives form the superlative with the suffix **-ente**, which, when put next to **-issimo**, becomes **-entissimo**:

benefico (*beneficial*)	beneficentissimo	malefico (*evil*)	maleficentissimo
benevolo (*benevolent*)	benevolentissimo	malevolo (*malevolent*)	malevolentissimo
maledico (*cursed*)	maledicentissimo	munifico (*munificent*)	munificentissimo

However, the superlatives ending in **-errimo** and **-entissimo** are not commonly used in spoken Italian.

Generally, rather than using the superlative, an adverb precedes the adjective in a sentence.

> Le Marche sono una regione **molto salubre**.
>
> *Marche is a **very healthy** region.*
>
> La vitamina C è una vitamina **molto benefica**.
>
> *Vitamin C is a **very beneficial** vitamin.*

ESERCIZIO
9·6

Complete the following sentences in the comparative and the superlative, using the suggestions given in parentheses.

1. Matteo è _____ _____ _____ Mario.
   (*taller*)

2. Matteo è _____ _____. (*very tall*)

3. Lucia legge _____ _____ Giovanna. (*less than*)

4. Lucia legge _____. (*very little*)

5. La minestra è _____ salata _____ carne. (*more ... than*)

6. La minestra è _____ _____ . (*very salty*)

7. La neve è _____ fredda _____ pioggia. (*colder*)

8. La neve è _____ _____ . (*very cold*)

Using the adjectives and noun phrases provided, form sentences with a comparative, a relative superlative, and an absolute superlative, as shown in the example.

EXAMPLE:　　　La tua amica / simpatica / mia.

La tua amica è più simpatica della mia.

La tua amica è la più simpatica di tutti.

La tua amica è simpaticissima.

1. il gatto / il cane nero / piccolo

　　a. _____

　　b. _____

　　c. _____

2. buono / il dolce / il gelato

　　a. _____

　　b. _____

　　c. _____

3. alto / l'uomo / sua moglie

　　a. _____

　　b. _____

　　c. _____

4. freddo / l'inverno / l'autunno

　　a. _____

　　b. _____

　　c. _____

Complete the following sentences with an appropriate adjective.

1. La tua _____ amica adora la musica classica. (*very young*)

2. La macchina di mio figlio è _____ _____. (*very old*)

3. Questa rivista è _____ _____. (*very interesting*)

4. Sotto le feste di Natale sono _____ _____. (*very busy*)

5. Il ragazzo è _____ _____ _____ intelligente. (*more ambitious than*)

6. Questa città è _____ _____. (*very old*)

7. I miei _____ zii abitano vicino alla torre. (*very old*)

8. I miei vicini sono _____ _____. (*very rich*)

Replace the words in parentheses in each sentence with an adjective.

1. L'acqua (della pioggia) _____.

2. Un bambino (senza vestiti) _____.

3. Un cielo senza nuvole _____.

4. Una minestra (senza sale) _____.

5. Un uomo (privo di lavoro) _____.

6. Un fiore (della primavera) _____.

7. Una regione (senza acqua) _____.

8. Un giovane (senza genitori) _____.

Adverbs

The Italian word **avverbio** comes from the Latin *adverbium*, meaning "next to another word." Adverbial expressions can be a single word or a phrase. Adverbs indicate:

Intensity	Maria lavora **davvero molto**.	*Maria works **really hard**.*
Location	Maria lavora **laggiù**.	*Maria works **down there**.*
Manner	Maria lavora **seriamente**.	*Maria works **seriously**.*
Quantity	Maria lavora **troppo**.	*Maria works **too much**.*
Question	Maria, **perchè** lavori?	Maria, ***why** are you working?*
Time	Maria lavora **sempre**.	*Maria works **all the time**.*

Adverbs in Italian are invariable. This means that, unlike adjectives, they never change form to agree with gender or number.

Their function is to modify an adjective, a noun, a verb, or another adverb.

> **subject + verb + adverb + adjective**
>
> **Il quadro è piuttosto bello.**   *The painting is rather beautiful.*

> **adverb + noun + adjective + verb**
>
> **Solo l'attore principale è stato bravo.**   *Only the main actor was good.*

> **subject + verb + adverb**
>
> **Il ragazzo mangia molto.**   *The boy eats a lot.*

> **subject + verb + adverb + adverb**
>
> **Io ho dormito proprio bene.**   *I slept really well.*

Position of the adverb

When an adverb modifies a verb, it is usually placed after the verb it modifies. In compound tenses it can be placed between the auxiliary and the participle.

Camminava **speditamente**.	*He was walking **fast**.*
Ho **molto** gradito il tuo regalo.	*I have appreciated your present **a lot**.*

When an adverb modifies an adjective, a noun, or another adverb, it is usually placed before them in a sentence.

Sei **troppo** debole per fare la partita.	*You are **too** weak to play the game.*
La **quasi** sicurezza del tuo arrivo ci allieta.	*The **near** certainty of your arrival pleases us.*

457

When the adverb modifies a phrase, it can be placed either before or after the word it modifies.

Il ragazzo **voracemente** divorò la cena.	*The boy **voraciously** devoured dinner.*
Voracemente, il ragazzo divorò la cena.	***Voraciously**, the boy devoured dinner.*
	(not very common in English)

Ci (*there*) and **vi** (*there*), as adverbs of location, are placed before the verb.

Ci sono ospiti a casa mia.	***There** are guests at my house.*
Penso che non **vi** sia nessuno.	*I think that no one is **there**.*

The adverb **non** is placed before what needs to be negated.

L'acqua **non** è calda.	*The water **is not warm**.*

Modal adverbs

Modal adverbs express how an action is carried out by the verb. The majority of adverbs in this category add the suffix -**mente** to the feminine adjective of quality.

feminine adjective + -mente → modal adverb

FEMININE ADJECTIVE		ADVERB	
aperta	*open*	apertamente	*openly*
brillante	*brilliant*	brillantemente	*brilliantly*
certa	*certain*	certamente	*certainly*
forte	*strong*	fortemente	*strongly*
fortunata	*fortunate*	fortunatamente	*fortunately*
generosa	*generous*	generosamente	*generously*
rara	*rare*	raramente	*rarely*
sfortunata	*unfortunate*	sfortunatamente	*unfortunately*

Dobbiamo parlare **apertamente**.	*We have to talk **openly**.*
Fortunatamente, hanno abbastanza da mangiare.	***Fortunately**, they have enough to eat.*

When the adjective ends in -**le**, the final -**e** is omitted before adding the -**mente** ending.

FEMININE ADJECTIVE		ADVERB	
agile	*agile*	agilmente	*agilely*
banale	*banal*	banalmente	*banally*
casuale	*casual*	casualmente	*casually*
generale	*general*	generalmente	*generally*
regolare	*regular*	regolarmente	*regularly*

Other adverbs that end with the suffix -**oni** express positions of the body. They are usually preceded by the preposition **a**.

a bocconi	*facedown*
a carponi	*on all fours*
a cavalcioni	*astride*
a penzoloni	*hanging*

Il bambino gira per la casa **a carponi**.	*The child goes around the house **on all fours**.*
Giovanni siede **a cavalcioni** della poltrona.	*Giovanni sits **astride** the armchair.*

Still other adverbs are the same as the masculine singular of the equivalent adjective.

chiaro	*clearly*
piano	*slowly*
scuro	*dark*
sodo	*hard*
storto	*crookedly*

Lei parla **chiaro**.	*She speaks **clearly**.*
Per favore, fate **piano**!	*Please, go **slowly**!*

Some adverbs do not originate or coincide with adjectives at all.

bene	*well, fine*
così	*so*
insieme	*together*
invano	*in vain*
male	*badly*
volentieri	*willingly*

Il lavoro è fatto **bene**.	*The job is **well** done.*
Vado **volentieri** a scuola.	*I **willingly** go to school.*

Also included among the modal adverbs are the following expressions:

a dirotto	*hard* (as in *raining cats and dogs*)
in fretta e furia	*in a rush*

Adverbs of location

Adverbs of location are used to express where an action takes place or where something is found. Some adverbs in this category are:

davanti	*in front*	quassù	*up here*
dentro	*inside*	sopra	*on* (top)
fuori	*outside*	sotto	*underneath*
intorno	*around*	vicino	*near*
oltre	*further*		

Vieni **quassù**!	*Come **up here**!*
La casa è **vicino** alla strada.	*The house is **near** the street.*

Some useful adverbial expressions of location are:

a destra	*on the right*	di sotto	*under*
a sinistra	*on the left*	nei dintorni	*in the surroundings*
da lontano	*from far away*	per di là	*that way*
di quì	*this way*		

Io non vedo bene **da lontano**.	*I do not see well **from far away**.*
Ci sono molti cipressi in questi **dintorni**.	*There are many cypresses in these **surroundings**.*

Adverbs of time

Adverbs of time express the circumstances, the moment, and the duration of the action expressed by the verb.

adesso	*now*	ora	*now*
ancora	*again*	ormai	*by now*
domani	*tomorrow*	poi	*later, then*
dopo	*after*	recentemente	*recently*
già	*already*	sempre	*always*
giammai	*never*	sovente	*often*
ieri	*yesterday*	subito	*right away*
mai	*never*	tardi	*late*

Stasera andrò a letto **tardi**.　　　　　*Tonight I will go to bed **late**.*
Siamo arrivati **ieri**.　　　　　　　　*We arrived **yesterday**.*

Here are some helpful adverbial expressions of time:

di quando in quando	*once in a while*	tempo fa	*some time ago*
di solito	*usually*	una volta	*once*
per sempre	*for good*		

Sono stata in Cina **una volta**.　　　　*I was in China **once**.*
Leggemmo "La Divina Commedia"　　　*We read* The Divine Comedy ***some time ago**.*
　　tempo fa.

Adverbs of quantity

These adverbs express an indefinite quantity:

abbastanza	*enough*	più	*more*
almeno	*at least*	poco	*a little*
appena	*just*	quasi	*almost*
assai	*very much*	tanto	*a lot, much*
circa	*about*	troppo	*too much*
parecchio	*much, several*		

Abbiamo dormito **abbastanza**.　　　　*We slept **enough**.*
Questo vestito costa **parecchio**.　　　　*This dress is **fairly** costly.*

The following adverbial expressions of quantity are quite useful:

a bizzeffa	*a lot*	di più	*more*
all'incirca	*about*	press'a poco	*about*
di meno	*less*	su per giù	*more or less*

Ci sono **su per giù** venti studenti in　　*There are **more or less** twenty students in*
　　questa classe.　　　　　　　　　　*this class.*
Luisa ne vuole **di più**.　　　　　　　*Luisa would like **more** of it.*

Adverbs of affirmation, denial, and doubt

This type of adverb reinforces, contradicts, or shows doubt about what is expressed by the verb: It expresses a judgment. Examples of adverbs that reinforce or affirm the verb are:

certamente	*certainly*	proprio	*really*
certo	*sure*	sì	*yes*
esattamente	*exactly*	sicuramente	*surely*

È **certo** che finirò i compiti oggi.　　　*It is **certain** that I will finish my homework*
　　　　　　　　　　　　　　　　　today.

Vorrei **proprio** andare in centro.　　　*I would **really** like to go downtown.*

Some adverbs used to express denial regarding the verb are:

neanche	*not even*	no	*no*
nemmeno	*not even*	non	*not*
neppure	*neither*		

Non c'è **neanche** un giornale in questa casa.	*There is **not even** a newspaper in this house.*
Non hai lavato le mani.	*You did **not** wash your hands.*

There is no strict rule about the position of adverbs for affirming or denying, with the one exception of the adverb of denial **non**, which is always placed before the verb.

Some common adverbs used to express doubt are:

circa	*about*	possibilmente	*possibly*
eventualmente	*eventually*	presumibilmente	*presumably*
forse	*maybe*	probabilmente	*probably*
magari	*maybe*		

Probabilmente ci vedremo domani.	*We'll **probably** see each other tomorrow.*
Forse Patrizia starà in Italia per tre settimane.	***Maybe** Patrizia will stay in Italy for three weeks.*

Interrogative adverbs

Interrogative adverbs are used to introduce a direct question.

come	*how, what*	quando	*when*
dove	*where*	quanto	*how much*
perchè	*why*		

Come ti chiami?	*What is your name?*
Quando andrete in Italia?	*When will you go to Italy?*

Comparative and superlative of adverbs

Adverbs are compared in the same manner as adjectives; that is, they have three degrees: majority, minority, and equality. Furthermore, adverbs have the relative superlative and absolute superlative constructions, just as adjectives do.

Più, **meno**, **così tanto**, **come**, and **quanto** are used to form the **comparative of majority, minority, and equality**. In all cases they follow this pattern:

verb + più + adverb + second element of comparison

Partirò più tardi di te.	*I will leave later than you.*

Comparative of minority	Partirò **meno tardi** di lui.	*I will not leave **as late as** him.*
Comparative of equality	Partirò **tardi come** lui.	*I will leave **as late as** him.*
Comparative of equality	Partirò **tardi quanto** lui.	*I will leave **as late as** him.*

Molto, **assai**, and the suffixes **-issimo** and **-issimamente** are used to form the **superlative absolute** construction.

verb + adverb + suffix

Partirò tardissimo.	*I will leave very late.*

You could also say **Partirò molto tardi** or **Partirò assai tardi**.
Il più and **il meno** are placed before the adverb to form the **superlative relative**.

verb + il più + adverb + reinforcing element

Partirò il più (meno) tardi possibile.   *I will leave as late as possible.*

Adjectives with irregular forms in the comparative and superlative have the equivalent adverbs with the same irregularities.

ADJECTIVE	ADVERB	COMPARATIVE ADVERB	SUPERLATIVE ADVERB
buono	bene	meglio	benissimo, ottimamente
cattivo	male	peggio	malissimo, pessimamente
grande	grandemente	maggiormente	massimamente
molto	molto	più	moltissimo, assai
piccolo	poco	meno	pochissimo, minimamente

È **tardissimo**, la mamma ci sgriderà sicuramente!	*It is **very late**. Mother will scold us for sure!*
Farò **il meno possibile**.	*I will do **as little as possible**.*
Luigi sta **benissimo**.	*Luigi feels **very well**.*

ESERCIZIO
10·1

Change the following adjectives into adverbs.

1. esatto _____

2. doppio _____

3. ordinato _____

4. freddo _____

5. veloce _____

6. attivo _____

7. allegro _____

8. pacifico _____

ESERCIZIO
10·2

Complete the following sentences with an adjective or adverb as appropriate, using the words in parentheses.

1. I bambini sono _____ . *(happy)*

2. I bambini parlano _____ . *(happily)*

3. La matematica è una scienza _____ . (*exact*)

4. Lui lavora molto _____ . (*orderly*)

5. È un uomo molto _____ . (*cold*)

6. Parla molto _____ . (*coldly*)

7. La vecchia signora è molto _____ . (*active*)

8. Io lavoro _____ con i miei colleghi. (*actively*)

ESERCIZIO
10·3

Complete each of the following sentences with the appropriate adverb or adverbial phrase.

1. Oggi piove _____ .

2. I bambini sono _____ a giocare.

3. L'autobus si ferma _____ alla scuola.

4. Il cane _____ è tornato a casa.

5. Ti dirò _____ che cosa penso.

6. Tutto è _____ chiaro.

7. Qui nei _____ ci sono molti stranieri.

8. Ci sono _____ cento persone.

ESERCIZIO
10·4

Complete each of the following sentences with a modal adverb.

1. Ti ringrazio _____ .

2. Luisa legge _____ .

3. Maria studia _____ .

4. Lui è entrato in casa _____ .

5. Quel giornalista è _____ invadente.

6. Gli studenti ascoltano _____ .

7. Loro parlano _____ .

8. Lucia e Maria si vedono _____ .

Complete the following sentences with the comparative or superlative of the adverbs in parentheses.

1. Oggi hai fatto il compito _____ _____ di ieri.
(diligentemente)

2. Mi è piaciuto _____ lo spettacolo che abbiamo visto. (molto)

3. Stai _____. Che cosa hai fatto? (bene)

4. Vengo da te _____ _____. Adesso devo studiare. (tardi)

5. Vado _____ _____ in gita con i miei amici che con i miei
genitori. (volentieri)

6. Ho l'influenza e nonstante io prenda gli antibiotici, oggi sto _____ di ieri.
(male)

7. Per le feste sono stata _____. (male)

8. Maria si veste _____ _____. (elegantemente)

Pronouns

Pronouns are a variable part of speech that generally replace a noun. They often are used to refer to someone or something that has already been mentioned. Italian pronouns agree in gender and number with the nouns they replace.

> L'uomo → **lui**
> La donna → **lei**
> Il cane → **lui** (**esso**)
> Gli uomini → **loro**

In Italian there is no translation for the pronoun *it*. Instead, everything is considered masculine or feminine. In the "old days," people were referred to by using the pronoun **egli** for masculine nouns and **ella** for feminine nouns, and animals by using **esso/essa**. Today these forms are not used anymore in spoken language. They are found only in written language.

Let us now look at the **personal pronouns**:

SUBJECT PRONOUNS	STRONG PRONOUNS	WEAK PRONOUNS	
io	me	mi	*I, me, me*
tu	te	ti	*you, you, you* (sing.)
lui	lui	lo	*he, him, him* (*it*)
lei	sè	la	*she, her, her* (*it*)
noi	noi	ci	*we, us, us*
voi	voi	vi	*you, you, your* (pl.)
loro	loro	li/le	*they, them, them*

Subject pronouns

Keep in mind that the personal pronouns used as the subject of a sentence—**io, tu, lui, lei, noi, voi, loro**—are less frequently used in Italian than in English because the verb in an Italian sentence conveys the agent by its conjugation, making subject pronouns superfluous. Subject pronouns, however, are **not** omitted when:

- There is ambiguity about the gender of the subject (especially with the subjunctive)

  Lui/Lei gioca.   *He/She is playing.*

- One wants to emphasize something

   Voi siete una bella coppia.   *You make a nice couple.*

- There are several subjects

   Io lavoro e **lui** si diverte.   *I am working, and he is having fun.*

The subject pronouns **io**, **tu**, **noi**, and **voi** are invariable. They are used for the feminine or the masculine. **Io** and **tu** are used for singular forms, while **noi** and **voi** are for plural forms.

   Tu sei Alfredo, **tu** sei Luisa.   *You are Alfredo; you are Luisa.*
   Noi siamo ragazze, **voi** siete ragazzi.   *We are girls; you are boys.*

Esso/a (*it*) and **essi/e** (*they*) are almost never used.

   (Lui) Ha una macchina nuova.   *He has a new car.*
   È una Ferrari.   *It is a Ferrari.*

   Ha molti libri.   *She has many books.*
   Sono tutti nuovi.   *They are all new.*

There is no specific rule to this effect, but usually one does not say **Essa è una Ferrari** or **Essi sono tutti nuovi**.

Remember that Italian has informal versions of you, **tu** (sing.) and **voi** (pl.), as well as formal, **Lei** (sing.) and **Loro** (pl.). They are all used to refer to male or female nouns.

   Tu parli bene l'italiano.   *You speak Italian well.*
   Carlo, **tu** mi vedi?   *Carlo, do you see me?*
   Luisa, **tu** mi vedi?   *Luisa, do you see me?*

   Voi parlate bene l'italiano.   *You speak Italian well.*
   Carlo e Luigi, **voi** mi vedete?   *Carlo and Luigi, do you see me?*
   Luisa e Maria, **voi** mi vedete?   *Luisa and Maria, do you see me?*

   Signor Marchi, **Lei** conosce mia sorella?   *Mr. Marchi, do you know my sister?*
   Signora Marchi, **Lei** conosce mia sorella?   *Mrs. Marchi, do you know my sister?*

   (**Loro**) Si accomodino in quella poltrona!   (*You*) *Sit in that armchair!*

The formal pronouns **Lei** and **Loro** are always written with a capital letter. **Loro**, however, is only used for emphasis.

   Vengano con me!   *Come with me!*
   Loro, **vengano** con me!   *You, come with me!*

Personal pronouns as direct objects

Personal pronouns that replace a direct object noun are referred to as **direct object pronouns**.

They are labeled as *weak* (**debole** or **atono**) or *strong* (**forte** or **tonica**). Weak object pronouns are always placed close to the verb, usually in front of it. Strong object pronouns usually follow the verb, and they do not need to be placed close to it.

Weak object pronouns get their name because they do not have their own stress. They are pronounced almost in unison with the verb that precedes or follows it.

subject + weak object pronoun + verb

Lui la chiama.	*He calls her.*
Prendo il libro.	*I take the book.*
→ **Lo** prendo.	*I take **it**.*
Vediamo Maria e Giuseppe.	*We see Maria and Giuseppe.*
→ **Li** vediamo.	*We see **them**.*

A strong object pronoun has its own pronounced stress. Strong pronouns create a special strength in a sentence. They clarify and emphasize what the subject wants to convey. They are usually placed after the verb.

subject + verb + strong object pronoun

Luigi chiama lei.	*Luigi calls her.*
Maria chiama **me**.	*Maria calls **me**.*
Maria e Giuseppe chiamano **te**.	*Maria and Giuseppe call **you**.*

The choice between using a strong or weak object pronoun depends on what one wants to relate. If putting emphasis on the pronoun is important, the strong form must be used; otherwise, if no emphasis is needed, the weak pronoun is used.

Per quella partita hanno scelto **me**.	*I was the chosen one for that game.* (The person speaking wants to emphasize that he/she was preferred to others.)
Mi hanno scelto per quella partita.	*I have been chosen for that game.* (Using the weak pronoun, the person speaking wants only to inform that he/she was chosen.)

ESERCIZIO
11·1

Replace the underlined noun in each sentence with the appropriate object pronoun. Use both the weak and strong forms, as shown in the example.

EXAMPLE: Luisa vede <u>Giovanni</u> tutti i giorni.

Luisa lo vede tutti i giorni.

Luisa vede lui tutti i giorni.

1. Portano <u>mia sorella</u> al cinema.

   a. _____

   b. _____

2. Luisa porta <u>le bambine</u> in piscina tutti i pomeriggi.

   a. _____

   b. _____

3. Contatterò <u>il mio amico</u> appena posso.

   a. _____

   b. _____

4. Portiamo il <u>nostro amico</u> all'aereoporto e poi torniamo a casa.

a. _____

b. _____

5. Inviti <u>la professoressa e me</u> a cena a casa tua.

a. _____

b. _____

6. Luigi porta <u>i suoi figli</u> in vacanza.

a. _____

b. _____

7. Vediamo <u>i tuoi parenti</u> al mare.

a. _____

b. _____

8. Rivedo <u>Paolo</u> con molto piacere.

a. _____

b. _____

Indefinite pronouns

Indefinite pronouns refer to persons, things, or periods of time that are not well defined. The most commonly used indefinite pronouns are: **uno/una** (*someone*), **qualcuno** (*someone*), **ognuno** (*everyone*), **chiunque** (*whoever*), **chicchessia** (*whoever*), **qualcosa** (*something*), **niente** (*nothing*), **nulla** (*nothing*), **nessuno** (*nobody*).

Uno/una means **una persona** (*someone*). It expresses what people do in general, or is used to point out that the person carrying out an action is unknown. It is used:

◆ To refer to someone unknown

Ho fermato **uno** e gli ho chiesto dove era il museo.	*I stopped **someone**, and I asked him where the museum was.*

◆ To refer to a generic or unknown subject. In this case **uno** is followed by a verb in the third person singular

In certe situazioni, **uno** non sa cosa dire.	*In some instances, **one** does not know what to say.*

◆ Before a relative phrase

Ho incontrato **uno** che era perso, e l'ho aiutato.	*I met **someone** who was lost, and I helped him.*

◆ Before an indirect complement introduced by the prepositions **di, del, dello, della, dei, degli,** or **delle**

Mi ha telefonato **una della** parrocchia.   ***Someone from*** *the parish called me.*
Sei **uno dei** miei migliori amici.   *You are **one of** my best friends.*

ESERCIZIO
11·2

Rewrite the following sentences using **uno** *or* **una** *as appropriate.*

1. In treno ho parlato con un uomo che non conoscevo.

   _____

2. Una persona non sa mai cosa dire ai parenti dei morti.

   _____

3. Abbiamo conosciuto una signora che parla bene l'inglese.

   _____

4. Un signore ha avuto problemi di cuore mentre era in aereo.

   _____

5. Ho parlato con un impiegato dell'anagrafe.

   _____

6. Non c'è uno studente in questa classe che capisca la matematica.

   _____

7. Ho parlato con una ragazza che non mi piaceva affatto.

   _____

8. Maria è una donna che sa il fatto suo.

   _____

9. Teresa è fra le mie migliori amiche.

   _____

Qualcuno/a (*someone*), **ognuno/a** (*everyone*), **chiunque** (*whoever*), and **chicchessia** (*whoever*) refer to people. They can only be used as pronouns in the singular form.

Quello di cui parli potrebbe farlo **chiunque**.   ***Anybody*** *could do what you are talking about.*
Qualcuno vuole venire con me al cinema?   ***Someone*** *want to go to the movies with me?*

ESERCIZIO
11·3

Complete the following sentences with the pronouns **qualcuno**, **ognuno**, *or* **chiunque** *as appropriate.*

1. Prova a vendere questi libri a _____ che te li comprerà.

2. _____ di voi sa quello che deve fare.

3. _____ voglia venire a Roma con noi, sarà ben accetto.

4. _____ potrà darti precise informazioni quando arrivi alla stazione.

5. _____ pensi di non studiare e imparare, si sbaglia.

6. Voglio portare una rivista italiana a _____ degli studenti.

7. Spero che _____ mi chiami per andare al cinema.

8. Voglio parlare con _____ di voi.

Qualcosa (*something*), **niente** (*nothing*), and **nulla** (*nothing*) are also used only as pronouns and refer only to things.

Perchè mi sgridi? Non ho fatto **nulla**.   *Why do you scold me? I have not done **a thing**.*
C'è molta nebbia. Non vedo **niente**.   *It is very foggy. I cannot see **anything**.*

Nessuno (*nobody*) is used only in the singular. In Italian, unlike English, the double negative is frequently used. **Nessuno** is usually preceded by **non**.

Non c'è **nessuno** in casa.   ***Nobody** is at home.*

ESERCIZIO
11·4

Complete the following sentences with **qualcosa**, **niente**, **nulla**, *or* **nessuno** *as appropriate.*

1. Ti assicuro che non ho fatto _____ di male.

2. Sono andata in centro a fare delle compere, ma non ho trovato _____.

3. Vado al mercato perchè ho bisogno di _____ per la cena.

4. _____ vuole comprare i libri usati.

5. Non trovo mai _____ di interessante alla televisione.

6. Il libro di letteratura non piace a _____.

7. Hai comprato _____ di bello in Italia?

8. Non capisco _____.

470   PRACTICE MAKES PERFECT   Complete Italian All-in-One

Reflexive pronouns

When the subject and the object in a sentence are the same person or thing, reflexive pronouns are used. They convey the idea that the action expressed by the verb reflects back to the subject. The reflexive pronoun **si** is used with all the third person (singular and plural) reflexive verbs. Only in the first and second persons are other forms used.

SUBJECT PRONOUNS		REFLEXIVE PRONOUNS	
io	*I*	mi	*myself*
tu	*you*	ti	*yourself*
lui	*he*	si	*himself*
lei	*she*	si	*herself*
Lei	*you*	si	*yourself*
noi	*we*	ci	*ourselves*
voi	*you*	vi	*yourselves*
loro	*they*	si	*themselves*
Loro	*you*	si	*yourselves*

subject pronoun + reflexive pronoun + verb

Io mi lavo.	*I wash myself.*
Tu **ti** svegli presto tutte le mattine.	*You wake (**yourself**) up early every morning.*
Maria **si** veste molto in fretta.	*Maria gets (**herself**) dressed very fast.*
Luigi **si** prepara per andare a lavorare.	*Luigi gets (**himself**) ready to go to work.*

If the infinitive of a verb is preceded by a form of **dovere**, **potere**, or **volere**, the reflexive pronoun is either attached to the infinitive or placed before the conjugated verb.

Mi sveglio presto.	*I wake up early.*
Voglio svegliar**mi** presto.	*I want to wake up early.*
Mi voglio svegliare presto.	*I want to wake up early.*

In compound tenses, the auxiliary verb used with reflexive verbs is **essere**. The past participle agrees in gender and number with the subject. The reflexive pronoun is placed before the auxiliary.

subject + reflexive pronoun + essere + past participle

Lei si è svegliata.	*She woke up.*

ESERCIZIO 11·5

Complete each of the following sentences with the appropriate form of the reflexive pronoun.

1. Io _____ chiamo Giovanni e tu come _____ chiami?

2. Quelle ragazze _____ alzano tardi.

3. Lei _____ siede vicino al finestrino.

4. Noi _____ addormentiamo sui libri.

5. Voi _____ svegliate presto.

6. Voglio sposar _____ la prossima estate.

7. _____ devo alzare presto per andare al lavoro.

8. Loro _____ vogliono comprare un cappotto pesante.

Infinitives

An infinitive is the base form of a verb. In English, the infinitive is usually formed by using two words, **to** + **verb**: *to walk*, *to talk*, etc. In Italian, however, the infinitive is composed of only one word, a verb, which ends in **-are**, **-ere**, or **-ire**.

cant**are**	*to sing*
ved**ere**	*to see*
sent**ire**	*to hear*

In an Italian sentence, the infinitive form is used when a verb depends upon another verb other than **essere** (*to be*) or **avere** (*to have*). Usually the preposition **a** or **di** precedes the infinitive. The preposition **da**, however, is found after the verbs **avere** (*to have*), **dare** (*to give*), **fare** (*to make*), **offrire** (*to offer*), and **preparare** (*to prepare*).

verb + a + infinitive

Cominciò a nevicare.	*It started to snow.*
Loro cominciano **a capire** l'italiano.	*They are starting **to understand** Italian.*
Lei pensa di imparare **a volare**.	*She is thinking of learning **to fly**.*
Non pensiamo **di venire** da voi domani.	*We do not think we will **come** to your house tomorrow.*
Non ho niente **da darti**.	*I do not have anything **to give you**.*
Abbiamo molto **da fare**.	*We have a lot **to do**.*

The infinitive is used:

- In dependent clauses with verbs that usually require the subjunctive when the subject of the main and the dependent clause is the same

Spero **di vincere** il primo premio.	*I hope **to win** the first prize.*
Pensiamo **di andare** in vacanza in Italia.	*We are thinking **of going** on vacation in Italy.*

- In dependent clauses when the verb is in the present tense in the main clause and indicates that the action is going on at the same time or a later time with respect to the verb in the dependent clause

Same time	Spera di **vederlo**.	*She hopes **to see him**.*
Later time	Spera **di vincere** la partita.	*She hopes **she will win** the game.*

473

- When the imperative is preceded by the negative **non**

Non parlare!	*Do not talk!*
Non attraversare i binari!	*Do not cross the tracks!*

- As a noun preceded by the article **il**; it is always masculine

Il bere fa male alla salute.	*Drinking damages health.*
Il viaggiare è interessante ma faticoso.	*Traveling is interesting, but tiring.*

- With certain modal verbs

dovere	*must, to have to*
piacere	*to like*
potere	*to be able, can, to be allowed*
volere	*to want*

subject + modal verb + infinitive + complement

Maria deve stare a scuola.	*Maria has to stay in school.*
Devo aspettarlo fuori della scuola.	*I **have to wait for him** outside the school.*
Non possiamo parlare al telefono.	*We **cannot speak** on the telephone.*
Luisa **voleva fare** la modella.	*Luisa **wanted to be** a model.*
Ci **è piaciuto viaggiare** in prima classe.	*We **liked traveling** in first class.*

Tenses of the infinitive

The infinitive has two tenses: **simple** (or present) and **compound** (or past). The simple infinitive corresponds to the English *to* + **verb**.

present infinitive + object + main clause

Ascoltare la musica è rilassante.	*To listen to music is relaxing.*
Sciare è molto divertente.	***Skiing** is lots of fun.*
Giocare a tennis è un buon esercizio.	***Playing** tennis is good exercise.*
Imparare una lingua straniera fa bene alla mente.	***Learning** a foreign language is good for the mind.*

The **past infinitive** expresses an action or a condition valid in the past. It is formed by using the infinitive of the auxiliary **avere** or **essere** followed by the past participle of the verb. **Avere** or **essere** generally drops the final -**e**.

adverb + past infinitive + main clause

Dopo averlo ascoltato ero stanco.	*After having listened to him, I was tired.*
Dopo **esser tornato** dalle vacanze avevo molto da fare.	*After **I returned** from vacation, I had a lot to do.*

Rewrite the following sentences using **prima di** *and* **dopo**.

EXAMPLE: Prima telefono poi esco.

Prima di uscire, telefono.

Dopo aver telefonato, esco.

1. Prima chiediamo il prezzo, poi compriamo.

    a. _____

    b. _____

2. Prima chiamo un taxi, poi telefono a Marco.

    a. _____

    b. _____

3. Prima passo di qui, poi vado in chiesa.

    a. _____

    b. _____

4. Prima mi lavo le mani, poi mangio.

    a. _____

    b. _____

5. Prima pensa, poi agisce.

    a. _____

    b. _____

6. Prima mi vesto, poi vado a lavorare.

    a. _____

    b. _____

7. Prima scrive la lettera, poi va alla posta.

    a. _____

    b. _____

8. Prima studiamo, poi giochiamo.

    a. _____

    b. _____

Using the verbs in parentheses, complete each of the following sentences with the present infinitive.

1. Sono contenta di _____ i tuoi fratelli. (*to see*)

2. Questo libro comincia ad _____ noioso. (*to be*)

3. Ma quando imparerete a _____ a bridge? (*to play*)

4. Giovanni ha smesso di _____. (*to smoke*)

5. Abbiamo l'abitudine di _____ il caffè alle quattro del pomeriggio. (*to drink*)

6. Pensiamo di _____ al mare questa estate. (*to go*)

7. Io comincio a _____ le valige. (*to pack*)

8. Siamo spiacenti di non _____ vi. (*to see*)

Circle the correct form of the infinitive in each of the following sentences.

1. È stato terribile vedere / avere visto tutta quella povera gente.

2. Dopo pensarci / averci pensato bene, abbiamo deciso di non comprare una macchina nuova.

3. Per arrivare / essere arrivati in tempo alla stazione, dovreste uscire ora.

4. È stato necessario chiamare / aver chiamato il dottore.

5. Dopo aver finito / finire la scuola sono andati al mare.

6. Abbiamo fatto un'ora di coda per aver comprato / comprare i biglietti per il concerto.

7. Prima di passare / essere passati di qui, ci siamo fermati al bar.

8. Per passare / aver passato gli esami, è necessario studiare molto.

Complete the following sentences with the present or past infinitive of the verbs in parentheses.

1. Dopo _____ della morte del suo amico, si è chiuso in camera sua. (apprendere)

2. Per _____ medico, occorre studiare molti anni. (diventare)

3. Dopo _____ la sua lettera, gli ho telefonato. (leggere)

4. Prima di _____ al mercato, vai in banca. (andare)

5. Dopo _____ il discorso, è andato a comprare il giornale. (finire)

6. Dopo _____ molte volte, mi ha finalmente risposto. (telefonare)

7. Prima di _____ la televisione, finisco i lavori di casa. (guardare)

8. Per _____ un architetto, deve capire la matematica. (diventare)

ESERCIZIO

12·5

Rewrite the following sentences with the modal auxiliary **potere**, *as shown in the example.*

EXAMPLE: Non capisce niente.

Non può capire niente.

1. Sua madre non beve vino.

_____

2. La ragazza non legge mai.

_____

3. Dopo pranzo andiamo a riposare.

_____

4. Lei non apre la porta a nessuno.

_____

5. Noi parliamo con i nostri amici.

_____

6. Lei ha comprato i biglietti per l'aereo.

_____

7. Voi siete andati dal dottore.

_____

8. Io mi faccio la barba tutte le mattine.

_____

Infinitive constructions with *aiutare, imparare, leggere, sentire,* and *vedere*

The verbs **aiutare**, **imparare**, **leggere**, **sentire**, and **vedere** are conjugated in the present or the past tenses and are followed by an infinitive.

Maria mi aiuta a **scrivere** una lettera.	*Maria helps me **write** a letter.*
Hai sentito **cantare** il tenore?	*Did you hear the tenor **sing**?*
Abbiamo visto qualcuno **camminare** in giardino.	*We saw someone **walk** in the garden.*
Ho imparato ad **andare** in bicicletta.	*I learned **to ride** a bike.*

ESERCIZIO
12·6

Complete the following sentences using the verbs in parentheses.

1. Io imparo a _____ la lingua cinese. (*to speak*)

2. Aiuto le persone anziane a _____. (*to walk*)

3. Sento _____ il campanello. (*to ring*)

4. Devo _____ un albero di Natale. (*to buy*)

5. Lei mi aiuta a _____ la casa. (*to clean*)

6. La bambina vede _____ il suo papà. (*to arrive*)

7. Potete _____ un bel film domani. (*to see*)

8. Avete potuto _____ la segreteria. (*to listen*)

Passive voice

Verb constructions have two voices: active and passive. In the active voice, the *subject* performs the action indicated by the verb and the *object* undergoes this action. The active voice emphasizes who is doing the action.

Io **guido** la macchina.	I **drive** the car.
Giovanni **compra** il giornale.	Giovanni **buys** the newspaper.

In the passive voice, the *subject* undergoes the action. It emphasizes the fact, the action, or what has occurred. The performer, or agent, of the action is preceded by the preposition **da** (*by*) or its contractions: **dal, dallo, dalla, dai, dagli, dalle**. The active voice is almost always preferred in colloquial Italian. The passive voice is used in its place when one does not want to name or does not know the agent of the action.

subject + passive verb + da + agent

La finestra è chiusa da mia sorella.	*The window is being closed by my sister.*
La macchina è **guidata da** me.	*The car **is driven by** me.*
Il giornale è **comprato da** Giovanni.	*The newspaper **is bought by** Giovanni.*

An active sentence can be changed to passive only if the verb is transitive, that is, if it has a direct object. When this change occurs, the object of the active sentence becomes the subject of the passive one. The verb used is: ***essere*** + **the past participle** of the verb. The past participle in the passive sentence always agrees with the subject of the sentence.

subject + verb + object

Io mangio la mela.	*I eat the apple.*

subject + verb + da + agent

La mela è mangiata da me.	*The apple is eaten by me.*
La mia casa **è stata costruita** su una collina.	*My house **has been built** on a hill.*
Il presidente **è stato eletto** dalla popolazione.	*The president **was elected** by the people.*

479

Change the following sentences from the active into passive, using the words in parentheses.

1. Chi guarda il programma televisivo? (i bambini)

   _____

2. Chi gestisce questo bar? (Giovanni)

   _____

3. Chi compra la casa nuova? (mia figlia)

   _____

4. Chi scrive il libro? (il professore di italiano)

   _____

5. Chi legge il nuovo romanzo giallo? (gli studenti)

   _____

6. Chi costruisce questo bel palazzo? (un famoso architetto)

   _____

7. Chi fa il viaggio in Asia? (i miei amici)

   _____

8. Chi beve la birra? (Luigi)

   _____

Any tense can have a passive voice, for example:

Present

Molti giocattoli **sono dati** ai bambini per Natale.

*Many toys **are given** to children at Christmas.*

Future

Molti giocattoli **saranno dati** ai bambini per Natale.

*Many toys **will be given** to children at Christmas.*

Imperfect

Molti giocattoli **erano dati** ai bambini per Natale.

*Many toys **were given** to children at Christmas.*

Present perfect

Molti giocattoli **sono stati dati** ai bambini per Natale.

*Many toys **have been given** to children at Christmas.*

Pluperfect

Molti giocattoli **erano stati dati** ai bambini per Natale.

*Many toys **had been given** to children at Christmas.*

Conditional

Molti giocattoli **sarebbero dati** ai bambini per Natale.

*Many toys **would be given** to children at Christmas.*

Past conditional

Molti giocattoli **sarebbero stati dati** ai bambini per Natale.

*Many toys **would have been given** to children at Christmas.*

Venire with the passive voice

Instead of using the auxiliary verb **essere**, it is possible to use the verb **venire** to form the passive voice. **Venire** in the passive voice is used only with simple tenses, such as the present, imperfect, historical past, and future, and not with the compound tenses. If the agent performing the action is expressed after the verb, **da** precedes it.

subject + venire + past participle + da + agent

La casa viene imbiancata da suo padre. *The house is being painted by his father.*

I cittadini **eleggono** il presidente. *The citizens **elect** the president.*
→ Il presidente **viene eletto dai** cittadini. *The president **is elected by the** people.*

Molti turisti **visitano** Firenze. *Many tourists **visit** Florence.*
→ Firenze **viene visitata da** molti turisti. *Florence **is visited by** many tourists.*

ESERCIZIO
13·2

Rewrite the following questions in the passive, using the verb **venire**.

1. Chi prenota l'albergo?

_____

2. Chi indirizza le lettere?

_____

3. Chi interpreta il film?

_____

4. Chi organizza la festa?

_____

5. Chi invia questi pacchi?

_____

6. Chi firma il documento?

_____

7. Chi paga il conto?

_____

8. Chi prepara la cena?

_____

*Answer the questions in Esercizio 13-2 in the passive using the verb **venire** and the following suggestions.*

1. mio fratello

_____

2. segretaria

_____

3. Sofia Loren

_____

4. miei amici

_____

5. mamma

_____

6. notaio

_____

7. mio padre

_____

8. cuoca

_____

Andare with the passive voice

It is also possible to use *andare* + **the past participle** to form the passive voice. This implies an obligation or necessity and is synonymous with **dover essere** (*must be, has to be*).

subject + andare + past participle + adverb

La casa va pulita spesso.	*The house has to be cleaned often.*
Il cane **va portato** fuori tutti i giorni.	*The dog **must be taken** out every day.*
I bambini **vanno seguiti** sempre.	*Children **have to** (**must**) **be followed** all the time.*

Using the words in parentheses, complete the following sentences with the correct form of **andare** + *the past participle*.

1. La televisione _____ quando hai finito di guardarla. (spegnere)

2. La strada _____ dopo che ha finito di nevicare. (spalare)

3. Il giornale _____ quando hai finito di leggerlo. (buttare)

4. I vetri _____ dopo la pioggia. (asciugare)

5. Il motore della macchina _____ ogni tre mesi. (controllare)

6. I bambini _____ il più possibile. (lodare)

7. I vecchi _____ quando sono in difficoltà. (aiutare)

8. I piatti _____ dopo che si sono usati. (lavare)

Si with the passive voice

The pronoun **si** is also used to create the passive voice with the third person of the active verb. This construction is called **si passivante**.

> **si + verb + direct object + complement of location**

Si vedono le oche nel laghetto.	*The geese are seen in the small lake.*
La domenica **non si lavora**.	*On Sunday, **one does not work**.*
In Italia **si dà** troppa importanza alla moda.	*In Italy, too much importance **is given** to fashion.*

Sometimes you will see the use of the **si passivante** in newspaper advertisements, selling or renting signs, or newspaper articles. In this case, **si** is attached to the verb.

Affitta**si** monolocale ristrutturato.	*Remodeled apartment for rent.*
Vende**si** casa con giardino.	*Home with garden for sale.*

When using the **si passivante**, it is important to remember transitive verbs agree in gender and number with the subject when they following **si**. If the verb is followed by another verb or an intransitive verb, agreement is not necessary.

Abbiamo **visto molti musei**.	*We have **seen many museums**.*
Si sono **visti molti musei**.	***Many museums** have been **seen**.*
Dormiamo per riposare.	*We **sleep** to rest.*
Si dorme per riposare.	*One **sleeps** to rest.*

Rewrite the following sentences in the passive, using the **si passivante**.

1. Lavoriamo per vivere.

   _____

2. Abbiamo lavorato tanti anni per avere un certo benessere.

   _____

3. Hanno piantato tanti fiori per avere un bel giardino.

   _____

4. Di notte vediamo tante stelle.

   _____

5. Porteremo tante cose in Italia per le nostre nipoti.

   _____

6. In America viviamo bene.

   _____

7. In questa casa parliamo solo italiano.

   _____

8. Negli aeroporti vediamo tante cose strane.

   _____

Subjunctive mood

The subjunctive is used to express wishes, doubts, possibilities, and opinions, unlike the indicative, which expresses facts and conveys information. In contemporary Italian, there is a tendency to replace the subjunctive with the indicative, but a good speaker or writer does not let this happen. The subjunctive has four tenses: two simple (present and imperfect) and two compound (past and pluperfect). The subjunctive is generally used in dependent clauses introduced by **che**.

main clause + che + subjunctive tense

Credo che tu venga.   *I think that you will come.*

Present subjunctive

Assuming that you have already studied the subjunctive, this chapter will not dwell so much on its conjugation as on its use, which is rather complex. The present subjunctive expresses a present action with respect to the main verb. It is used in dependent clauses where there is a present or a future tense in the main clause.

present/future indicative + che + present subjunctive

Credi che io possa venire da te?	*Do you think that I can come to your house?*
Penso che **sia** una scelta giusta.	*I think **it is** the right choice.*
Penseranno che **tu sia** una persona importante.	*They will think that **you are** an important person.*
Il dottore vuole che **io mangi** molta frutta.	*The doctor wants **me to eat** a lot of fruit.*
Mi sembra che **tu abbia** molta pazienza.	*It seems to me that **you have** a lot of patience.*
Lei crede che **voi siate** sempre affamati.	*She believes that **you are** always hungry.*

Some important facts to keep in mind about the present subjunctive:

◆ It is necessary to use the subject pronoun with the **io**, **tu**, **lui/lei** verb forms, since the endings are often the same.

◆ In addition to the regular verbs in the third conjugation forms, there are those conjugated with **-isc**.

◆ In the first conjugation, with verbs ending in -**care** and -**gare**, in order to keep the hard sound of **c** and **g** before the **i**, it is necessary to add **h** before all endings.

    Bisogna che **voi paghiate** il conto.   *It is necessary that **you pay** the bill.*

◆ The verbs ending in -**ciare** and -**giare** drop the -**i** of the endings.

    Credo che il film **cominci** fra un'ora.   *I think that the movie **is going to start** in one hour.*
    Mi sembra che **mangiate** troppo.   *It seems to me that **you are eating** too much.*

ESERCIZIO 14·1

Complete the following sentences with the correct forms of the verbs in parentheses.

1. Tu credi che io _____ in tempo? (fare)

2. La professoressa vuole che tu _____ più attento. (stare)

3. È ora che io _____ di casa e _____ a lavorare. (uscire, andare)

4. Spero che lo spettacolo _____ divertente. (essere)

5. Penso che lui _____ domani pomeriggio. (arrivare)

6. Spero che non _____ troppo freddo. (fare)

7. Credo che voi _____ a casa. (ritornare)

8. Pensa che noi _____ poco. (dormire)

When the subject of the main sentence and the dependent sentence is the same, the infinitive is used instead of the subjunctive. The preposition **di** precedes the infinitive.

    present indicative + di + infinitive
    Crede di sapere tutto.   *He thinks he knows everything.*

Past subjunctive

The past subjunctive expresses a past action with respect to the main verb. It is used in dependent clauses when there is a future or a present tense in the main clause. It is formed by the present subjunctive of the auxiliary **essere** or **avere** followed by the past participle of the verb.

present indicative + che + past subjunctive

Sono felice che siate ritornati.	*I am happy that you returned.*
Sono contento che tu mi **abbia chiamato**.	*I am happy that you **called** me.*
È impossibile che lui **abbia comprato** una casa.	*It is impossible that **he bought** a house.*
Mi dispiace che loro **siano** già **partiti**.	*I am sorry that they **have** already **left**.*
Penserà che tu **abbia voluto** vederlo.	*He will think that you **wanted** to see him.*

ESERCIZIO
14·2

Complete the following sentences with the past subjunctive of the verbs in parentheses.

1. Tutti credono che io _____ il dolce. (fare)

2. Penso che loro _____ la lotteria. (vincere)

3. Luisa è la persona più colta che io _____. (conoscere)

4. Lei crede che voi _____ tutto. (mangiare)

5. Credo che quella donna _____ i suoi figli. (trascurare)

6. Penso che voi _____ un bel libro. (leggere)

7. Mi sembra che ieri _____. (nevicare)

8. Penso che voi _____ la mia lettera. (ricevere)

Imperfect subjunctive

The imperfect subjunctive is used in the dependent clause when the past tense is used in the main clause. It expresses a thought, a belief, or a hope in the past.

subject + imperfect indicative + che + imperfect subjunctive

Io pensavo che tu venissi da me.	*I thought you would come to my house.*
Luisa voleva che io parl**assi** con sua madre.	***Luisa wanted** me **to speak** to her mother.*
Pensavo che tu vend**essi** la tua casa.	***I thought you were selling** your home.*
Giovanni credeva che voi part**iste** con il treno.	***Giovanni thought you would leave** by train.*

The imperfect subjunctive is also used in a dependent clause when the present conditional appears in the main clause. It expresses a wish that may or may not be realized in the present.

verb in the conditional + che + imperfect subjunctive

Vorrei che tu parlassi di più.	*I wish you talked more.*
Vorrei che tu **scrivessi** a tua madre.	***I would like** you **to write** to your mother.*
Mi piacerebbe che lei **studiasse** medicina.	***I would like** her **to study** medicine.*
Vorrebbero che io **comprassi** una casa.	***They would like** me **to buy** a house.*

ESERCIZIO
14·3

Complete the following sentences with the imperfect subjunctive of the verbs in parentheses.

1. Tutti volevano che io _____ il dolce. (fare)

2. Desideravo che loro _____ la lotteria. (vincere)

3. Teresa era l'amica più cara che io _____. (avere)

4. Lei credeva che voi _____ tutto. (mangiare)

5. Mi sembrava che quella donna _____ i suoi figli. (trascurare)

6. Pensavo che vi _____ un bel libro. (piacere)

7. Volevano che _____ molto. (nevicare)

8. Pensavate che io _____ la vostra lettera prima di partire. (ricevere)

Pluperfect subjunctive

The pluperfect subjunctive is used to express a desire, a hope, or a thought that has not been realized in the past. It is also used in dependent clauses when the verb of the main clause is in the past.

The pluperfect subjunctive is formed with the imperfect subjunctive of the auxiliary verbs **essere** or **avere** and the past participle of the verb showing the action. Because the first and the second person singular have the same endings, it is preferable to use the subject pronouns to avoid ambiguity.

imperfect + che + pluperfect subjunctive

Pensavo che tu avessi dormito bene.   *I thought you had slept well.*

Credevo che tu **avessi parlato** con Maria.   *I believed that you **had spoken** with Maria.*
Non sapevo che lei **avesse comprato** la casa.   *I did not know that she **had bought** a house.*
Noi pensavamo che voi **foste** già **partiti**.   *We thought that you **had** already **left**.*
Pensavamo che voi non **foste arrivati**.   *We thought that you **had** not **arrived**.*

ESERCIZIO
14·4

Complete the following sentences with the pluperfect subjunctive of the verbs in parentheses.

1. Pensavamo che Mario _____ di più per gli esami. (studiare)

2. Temevamo che voi non _____ il biglietto. (fare)

3. Io avrei voluto che voi _____ con me in Africa. (venire)

4. Pensavo che loro _____ già _____ in Florida. (andare)

5. Pensavate che _____ con il treno? (io-arrivare)

6. Non sapevo che tu _____ la tua macchina. (vendere)

7. Non credevo che tu _____ senza salutare. (partire)

8. Mi sembrava che a Paolo non _____ il ristorante. (piacere)

Uses of the subjunctive in independent clauses

In a main or independent clause, the subjunctive may express:

- ◆ An exhortation or an order, instead of using the formal imperative; the present subjunctive is used in this instance

  Abbia pazienza!   *Be patient!*
  Stia zitto!   *Be quiet!*

- ◆ The giving of permission or an invitation

  Venga pure a trovarci!   *Of course, **come** and see us!*

- ◆ A doubt; the present or past subjunctive is used in this case

  Non è venuto! Che **si sia dimenticato**?   *He did not come! Could it be possible **that he forgot**?*

  Luisa non ha chiamato! Che **abbia perso** il numero di telefono?   *Luisa did not call! Could **she have lost** our phone number?*

- ◆ A wish, a desire, or a prohibition

  Magari **vincessi**!   *If only **I won**!*
  Dio vi **benedica**!   *God **bless** you!*
  Che non **succeda** mai più! *May it never **happen** again!*

- ◆ An exclamation

  Vedessi come è bello il lago di Como!   *If you could only see how beautiful Lake Como is!*

  Sapessi che paura ho degli esami!   *If you only knew how scared I am of finals!*

ESERCIZIO
14·5

Using the verbs in parentheses, complete the following sentences with the correct forms of the subjunctive.

1. Tu _____ come sono belle le Hawaii! (sapere)

2. Tu _____ quanta gente c'è in piazza! (vedere)

3. (Voi) _____ pazienza con i vecchi! (avere)

4. _____ signora! Il dottore viene subito. (accomodarsi)

5. Loro _____ zitti! (stare)

6. _____ agli affari suoi! (pensare)

7. Che Dio vi _____! (aiutare)

8. Magari _____! (io-dormire)

Uses of the subjunctive in dependent clauses

It is necessary to use the subjunctive after the following subordinating conjunctions and expressions:

a condizione che	*on condition that*	nonostante	*despite*
affinchè	*so that*	perchè	*so that*
appena che	*as soon as*	prima che	*before*
benchè	*although*	purchè	*provided that*
come se	*as if*	sebbene	*although*
dopo che	*after*	senza che	*without*
nel caso che	*on condition that*		

Lo dico **affinchè** tutti lo sappiano.   *I am saying it, **so that** everybody knows.*
Vado al cinema, **benchè** piova.   *I am going to the movies, **although** it is raining.*
Abbiamo saputo la notizia **prima che** lo   *We knew the news **before** others found out.*
   sapessero gli altri.

The subjunctive is also used with these indefinite pronouns and adjectives:

chiunque	*whoever*	qualunque	*any*
dovunque	*wherever*	qualunque cosa	*whatever*
qualsiasi	*any*		

Chiunque lo voglia, potrà prendere lezioni   ***Whoever** wants to can take skiing lessons.*
   di sci.
Dovunque siate, verrò a visitarvi.   ***Wherever** you are, I will visit you.*
Qualunque cosa vogliano, gliela   ***Anything** they want, we will buy it for her.*
   compriamo.

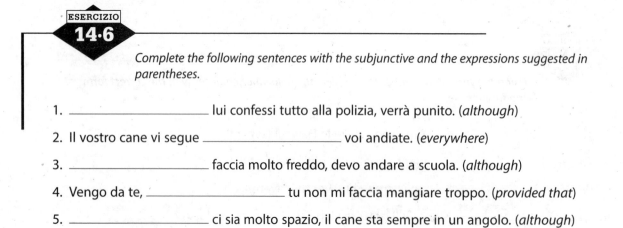

ESERCIZIO
14·6

Complete the following sentences with the subjunctive and the expressions suggested in parentheses.

1. _____ lui confessi tutto alla polizia, verrà punito. (*although*)

2. Il vostro cane vi segue _____ voi andiate. (*everywhere*)

3. _____ faccia molto freddo, devo andare a scuola. (*although*)

4. Vengo da te, _____ tu non mi faccia mangiare troppo. (*provided that*)

5. _____ ci sia molto spazio, il cane sta sempre in un angolo. (*although*)

6. _____ voi abbiate detto niente, hanno scoperto il modo di aprire la porta. (*though*)

7. _____ loro venissero, abbiamo pulito la casa. (*before*)

8. Abbiamo chiuso la porta _____ nessuno senta quel che diciamo. (*so that*)

The subjunctive is used after impersonal expressions. These expressions appear only in the third person singular, and they are formed by using the verb **essere** + **an adverb**:

essere + adverb + che + subjunctive + object

È impossibile che tu abbia finito il tuo lavoro.	*It is impossible that you finished your work.*

È bene/male che	*It is good/bad that*	È necessario che	*It is necessary that*
È giusto che	*It is fair that*	È opportuno che	*It is convenient that*
È impossibile che	*It is impossible that*	È possibile che	*It is possible that*
È meglio che	*It is better that*	È utile/inutile che	*It is useful/useless that*

È meglio che voi **aspettiate** l'autobus.	***It is better that** you **wait** for the bus.*
È necessario che lui **vada** dal dottore.	***It is necessary that** he **go** to the doctor.*
È giusto che lo **paghino** per il suo lavoro.	***It is right that** they **pay** him for his work.*

The subjunctive is also used with verbs that express necessity. The verbs in this instance are always used in the third person singular.

avere bisogno	*to need*	convenire	*to be worth*
bastare	*to be enough*	occorrere	*to need*
bisognare	*to be necessary*	valere la pena	*to be worth*

Bisogna che voi **andiate** dal calzolaio.	***It is necessary that** you **go** to the shoemaker.*
Occorre che lei **parli** con il padrone.	***It is necessary that** she **speak** with the landlord.*
Vale la pena che tu **compri** una macchina usata.	***It is worth it** for you **to buy** a used car.*

ESERCIZIO
14·7

Complete the following sentences with the appropriate forms of the subjunctive, using the verbs in parentheses.

1. È impossibile che voi _____ a ballare bene. (imparare)

2. Era impossibile che tu _____ a ballare bene. (imparare)

3. È meglio che voi _____ lontano da me. (stare)

4. Sarebbe stato meglio che lei _____ lontano da lui. (stare)

5. È bene che noi _____ le istruzioni prima di cominciare. (ascoltare)

6. Non è giusto che il professore mi _____ un brutto voto. (dare)

7. Bisogna che tu _____ tua sorella. (chiamare)

8. È necessario che lui _____ a letto la bambina. (mettere)

The subjunctive is used after verbs that express a command, a wish, hope, fear, permission, emotion, doubt, expectation, or uncertainty.

aspettare	*to wait*	desiderare	*to wish*
aspettarsi	*to expect*	dubitare	*to doubt*
augurarsi	*to wish*	essere contento	*to be happy*
avere paura	*to be afraid*	ordinare	*to order*
consentire	*to allow*	sperare	*to hope*
credere	*to believe*	temere	*to fear*

Ci **auguriamo** che tutto vada bene.   *We hope that everything goes well.*
Spero che voi mi telefoniate.   *I hope that you will call me.*
Desidero che tu rimanga da me.   *I wish that you would stay at my house.*

ESERCIZIO
14·8

Complete the following sentences with the appropriate forms of the subjunctive.

1. Bisogna che _____ .

2. Spero che _____ .

3. Tutti pensano che _____ .

4. Temiamo che _____ .

5. Ho paura che _____ .

6. Mi auguro che _____ .

7. Aspetto che _____ .

8. Sono contenti che _____ .

Subjunctive after the conjunction *se*

The subjunctive is used after the conjunction **se** (*if*) if the clause that follows expresses a condition that cannot be true or if it refers to something that is impossible to realize. The example sentences shown below are the same in meaning, except the first expresses a wish that cannot be realized in the present, while the second expresses the same wish that could not be realized in the past.

se + imperfect subjunctive + present conditional

Se potessi viaggerei con te.   *If I could, I would travel with you.*

se + pluperfect subjunctive + past conditional

Se avessi potuto avrei viaggiato con te.   *If I had been able, I would have traveled with you.*

| Se avessi i soldi, comprerei una casa in Italia. | *If I had the money, I would buy a home in Italy.* |
| Se me l'avessi detto, ti avrei aspettato. | *If you had told me, I would have waited for you.* |

When the condition being expressed is a known fact, the **se** clause is followed by a tense in the indicative instead of the subjunctive.

| Se studi, impari. | *If you study, you will learn.* |
| Se hai sete, bevi l'acqua. | *If you are thirsty, drink water.* |

Subjunctive in relative clauses

The subjunctive is used in relative clauses introduced by negatives such as **niente**, **nessuno**, or **non c'è**.

| **Non c'é niente** che mi sorprenda. | *There is nothing that will surprise me.* |
| **Non trovo nessuno** che mi possa aiutare. | *I cannot find anybody who can help me.* |

It is also used with a relative clause introduced by an adjective or a superlative such as **primo**, **supremo**, **ultimo**, or **unico**.

| Luisa è l'**unica amica** che mi abbia scritto. | *Luisa is the only friend who wrote to me.* |
| Tu sei la persona **più gentile** che io conosca. | *You are the kindest person (whom) I know.* |

The indefinite expressions **uno**, **una**, **qualcuno**, and **qualcosa** can be used with the subjunctive.

| Cerco **uno che** sappia l'inglese. | *I am looking for someone who knows English.* |
| Hai **qualcosa** che mi faccia passare il mal di testa? | *Do you have anything that will help get rid of my headache?* |

ESERCIZIO

14·9

Complete the following sentences with the appropriate forms of the subjunctive, using the verbs in parentheses.

1. Se _____, sarei venuto. (potere)

2. Se mi _____, sarei venuta ad aiutarti. (chiamare)

3. Se _____ i soldi, comprerei una macchina a mio figlio. (avere)

4. Se _____ i soldi, avrei comprato una macchina a mio figlio. (avere)

5. Se voi _____, imparereste. (studiare)

6. Se loro _____, avebbero imparato. (studiare)

7. Non credo ci sia nessuno che _____ l'arabo. (parlare)

8. Non c'è niente che mi _____. (piacere)

PROBLEM SOLVER

Introduction to Part V

In this final part, you will learn how to become more aware of when and why errors occur. As your awareness increases, you will begin to identify gaps and errors and gradually build language proficiency and accuracy.

Each chapter is dedicated to a particular grammatical topic. The exercises have been designed to keep you focused and interested as you tackle and overcome each problem.

Nouns, gender, and number

The English language distinguishes biological gender in humans and animals, but these words are not marked in any way for gender. For example, *woman* and *man*, *sister* and *brother* are different genders, but the final -n and -r are common to both. There are a few remnants of gender markers in English, such as **-or** for masculine nouns (*actor*) and **-ess** for feminine nouns (*actress*), but these endings are slowly becoming obsolete.

In Italian, the last letter of nouns and adjectives indicates gender (masculine and feminine) and number (singular and plural). Nouns ending in **-o** are generally masculine singular, and nouns ending in **-a** are feminine singular. To form the plural, the final **-o** changes to an **-i** in the masculine form, and the final **-a** changes to an **-e** in the feminine form.

MASCULINE NOUNS	FEMININE NOUNS
zi**o** → zi**i**	zi**a** → zi**e**
fratell**o** → fratell**i**	sorell**a** → sorell**e**
nonn**o** → nonn**i**	nonn**a** → nonn**e**
gatt**o** → gatt**i**	donn**a** → donn**e**

These nouns all refer to animate beings of the masculine and feminine genders. But nouns that refer to inanimate things or ideas also have gender in Italian, and this gender has nothing at all to do with biological gender. In fact, the gender of some nouns varies within romance languages. The words for *sea* and *flower*, for example, are masculine in Italian (**il mare**, **il fiore**) but feminine in French.

Categories of masculine and feminine words

There are some categories of words that tend to be masculine.

- ◆ Trees

il melo	l'arancio	il pero
apple tree	*orange tree*	*pear tree*

  Exceptions:

la quercia	la palma
oak tree	*palm tree*

- ◆ Metals, minerals, and elements

l'oro	l'argento	l'ossigeno
gold	*silver*	*oxygen*

◆ Mountains, seas, rivers, and lakes

il Monte Bianco	l'Arno	il Mediterraneo
Mont Blanc	*Arno river*	*Mediterranean sea*

The following categories are generally feminine.

◆ Fruits

la mela	l'arancia	la pera
apple	*orange*	*pear*

Exceptions:

il limone	il fico	il pompelmo
lemon	*fig*	*grapefruit*

◆ Arts and sciences

la fisica	la chimica	la matematica	la musica
physics	*chemistry*	*mathematics*	*music*

◆ Continents, countries, regions, and cities

l'Europa	l'Italia	la Toscana	la Roma antica
Europe	*Italy*	*Tuscany*	*ancient Rome*

Most nouns ending in **-tà** and **-tù** are feminine.

l'età	la città	l'università	la gioventù
age	*city*	*university*	*youth*

Those ending in **-i**, **-ione**, **-ice**, **-ie**, and **-ine** and are generally feminine.

la stazione	la scrittrice	la specie	l'origine
station	*writer*	*species*	*origin*

Nouns ending in **-i** in the singular (usually cognates of Greek origin that end in *-is* in English) are feminine and do not change spelling in the plural.

l'analisi	la crisi	la tesi	la metropoli	la diagnosi
analysis	*crisis*	*thesis*	*metropolis*	*diagnosis*

Nouns that have been abbreviated keep the gender of the original.

la fot**o**	*from* la fotograf**ia**
la bic**i**	*from* la biciclet**ta**
il cinem**a**	*from* il cinematograf**o**
la mot**o**	*from* la motoclet**ta**
la radio	*from* la radiotrasmittente

Nouns of foreign origin ending in consonants are generally masculine.

lo sport	il bar	il tennis	il computer

Many words of Greek origin ending in **-a** are masculine.

il problema	il sistema	il melodramma	il poema
problem	*system*	*melodrama*	*poem*

Nouns ending in **-e** can be either masculine or feminine, but those ending in **-one**, **-ore**, **-ale**, and **-ile** are generally masculine (except for **automobile**).

il sapone	il colore	il giornale	il campanile
soap	*color*	*newspaper*	*bell tower*

Nota bene

Many nouns from Greek or Latin have similar stems in English and are called *cognates*. Recognizing cognates will increase your vocabulary by hundreds of words! With a little practice you can recognize them instantly and use them to form other related words. For example, most English nouns ending in *-tion* are cognates and are feminine.

nazione	situazione	illustrazione
nation	*situation*	*illustration*

Other cognates include words in Italian ending in **-or** or **-er**, which are usually masculine.

dottore	trattore	attore	promotore
doctor	*tractor*	*actor*	*promotor*

ESERCIZIO
1·1

Provide the definite article for each of the following singular nouns.

1. _____ giornale

2. _____ lezione

3. _____ sport

4. _____ solitudine

5. _____ stazione

6. _____ dilemma

7. _____ frigo

8. _____ portale

9. _____ crisi

10. _____ virtù

Masculine and feminine suffixes

Some nouns that refer to humans and animals change gender simply by changing the endings **-o** or **-e** to an **-a**: **-e** / **-ore** → **-ice** / **-essa**. Others, however, add a suffix, as shown in the table on the next page. Notice how the nouns that have a double **tt** in the masculine favor the suffix **-rice** in the feminine.

MASCULINE	FEMININE	
principe	princip**essa**	*prince/princess*
professore	professor**essa**	*professor*
studente	student**essa**	*student*
scrittore	scritt**rice**	*writer*
direttore	dirett**rice**	*director*
attore	att**rice**	*actor/actress*

Some nouns have slightly different masculine and feminine forms.

dio	*god*	dea	*goddess*
re	*king*	regina	*queen*
cane	*dog*	cagna	*female dog*
gallo	*rooster*	gallina	*hen*

Other nouns have different roots.

padre	*father*	madre	*mother*
fratello	*brother*	sorella	*sister*
marito	*husband*	moglie	*wife*
genero	*son-in-law*	nuora	*daughter-in-law*
maschio	*male*	femmina	*female*
uomo	*man*	donna	*woman*

Finally, there is a group of nouns that has only one form for both masculine and feminine. The gender for these nouns will be marked only by an article, adjective, or context.

♦ **-e**

il nipote	la nipote	*nephew / niece, grandson / granddaughter*
il parente	la parente	*relative*

♦ **-ista**

il pianista	la pianista	*pianist*
l'artista	l'artista	*artist*
il socialista	la socialista	*socialist*

♦ **-a**

il collega	la collega	*colleague*
l'atleta	l'atleta	*athlete*
il maratoneta	la maratoneta	*roadrunner*

♦ **-ante** or **-ente** (These nouns are generally derived from verbs.)

il cantante	la cantante	*singer*
l'amante	l'amante	lover
l'insegnante	l'insegnante	teacher
il presidente	la presidente	president
il dirigente	la dirigente	*executive*

The following sentences are examples of how a noun's gender is revealed at the end of the sentence by the adjective. To reduce ambiguity, native speakers may include a proper name or a relative clause that will clarify the gender earlier on in the sentence.

L'insegnante di matematica è simpatic**a**.	*The math teacher is nice.*
L'insegnante di storia è altissim**o**.	*The history teacher is very tall.*

Nota bene

As we have seen, nouns that refer to living things often change their endings from **-o** to **-a** to indicate gender. Watch out for nouns that seem to have a masculine and feminine form but are actually unrelated words of totally different meaning. Associating these words with an adjective may help you connect gender with meaning; for example, **la porta aperta** vs. **il porto marino**.

il caso	*case*	la casa	*house*
il colpo	*hit*	la colpa	*fault*
il filo	*thread*	la fila	*line, cue*
il modo	*way*	la moda	*fashion*
l'oro	*gold*	l'ora	*hour*
il porto	*seaport*	la porta	*door*

Professions

Although many professions are open to all genders, some professions still lack a feminine form. In these cases, the article is masculine and the gender can be understood from the context: **il soprano Maria Callas, il ministro Rosy Bindi**. As more and more female ministers, lawyers, architects, and engineers emerge, these words gain a feminine form, and it is not so uncommon to see written or to hear **la ministra, l'avvocatessa**, or **l'architetta**. In prescriptive grammar, there is a preference for the following nouns to remain masculine, regardless of gender.

l'avvocato	*lawyer*	il soprano	*soprano*
il medico	*physician*	il mezzosoprano	*mezzo-soprano*
l'ingegnere	*engineer*	il contralto	*alto*
l'architetto	*architect*	il maestro	*teacher*

In professions ending in **-ente**, which are derived from verbs, the article changes according to the gender.

il/la presidente	*the president*
il/la conoscente	*the acquaintance*
il/la sovrintendente	*the superintendent*

ESERCIZIO

1·2

Indicate the missing nouns.

MASCULINE	FEMININE
signore	_____
_____	dottoressa
padre	_____
_____	professoressa
studente	_____
_____	scrittrice

nipote   _____

_____   sorella

uomo   _____

ESERCIZIO
1·3

Add the definite article to the following words, and then match them with their English equivalents.

1. _____ gallina   a. *row*

2. _____ porto   b. *engineer*

3. _____ casa   c. *hen*

4. _____ nipote   d. *nephew/niece*

5. _____ filo   e. *port*

6. _____ colpa   f. *home*

7. _____ ingegnere   g. *fashion*

8. _____ moda   h. *thread*

9. _____ fila   i. *fault*

10. _____ medico   j. *physician*

ESERCIZIO
1·4

Change the gender of the following articles and nouns. **Attenzione!** Some nouns are invariable.

1. la nipote _____

2. la scrittrice _____

3. il presidente _____

4. la collega _____

5. l'uomo _____

6. la moglie _____

7. la dottoressa _____

8. il dio _____

9. la nuora _____

10. l'insegnante _____

Number: Singular or plural

Nouns in Italian change their final letters to indicate number (singular or plural). Most nouns follow this simple formula:

- Masculine nouns ending in **-o** → **-i**

  ragazzo → ragazzi

- Feminine nouns ending in **-a** → **-e**

  ragazza → ragazze

- All nouns ending in **-e** (regardless of gender) → **-i**

  (*m.*) signore → signori
  (*f.*) nipote → nipoti

Some nouns are invariable:

- Nouns that end in a consonant (usually foreign words)
- Monosyllables (**il re → i re**)
- Feminine nouns ending in **-i** (**la tesi → le tesi**)
- Feminine nouns ending in **-ie** (**la serie → le serie**)
- Nouns ending in an accented vowel (**il caffè → i caffè, la città → le città**)

Nouns that end **-o** or **-e** form the plural by changing the **-o** or **-e** to an **-i**, regardless of gender. When two **-i**'s result, one is dropped unless it is accented.

padre → padri   madre → madri   moglie → mogli   zio → zii

Feminine nouns that end in **-a** form the plural by changing the **-a** to an **-e**.

donna → donne   mamma → mamme

However, feminine nouns ending in **-ca** or **-ga** add an **h** in the plural to maintain the hard **c** or **g** sound. (See **c** and **g** sounds in Chapter 1.)

amica → amiche   biologa → biologhe

Feminine nouns ending in **-ccia** and **-ggia** with an unaccented **i** drop the **i** in the plural, as it is no longer needed to soften the **c** or **g**.

focaccia → focacce   pioggia → piogge

However, if the **-cia** or **-gia** ending is preceded by a vowel, the softening **i** is retained.

camicia → camicie   valigia → valigie

Masculine nouns ending in **-co** or **-go** (with very few exceptions) add an **h** to keep the hard **c** or **g** sound in the plural.

lago → laghi   albergo → alberghi   parco → parchi   affresco → affreschi

Exception:

amico → amici   greco → greci

When accented on the third-to-last syllable, most masculine nouns do not add an **h** in the plural and the **c** or **g** softens.

sindaco → **sin**daci   bi**o**logo → bi**o**logi

Masculine nouns ending in a monosyllabic **-io** form the plural with a single **-i**.

negoz**io** → negoz**i**   stad**io** → stad**i**   figl**io** → figl**i**

When the **-i** of the diphthong is accented, both **i**'s are retained in the plural.

z**io** → z**íi**

1·5

Indicate which column each singular noun belongs to and add the plural forms.

stadio   università   sport   parco   medico

camicia   film   focaccia   zio   tesi

MASCULINE SINGULAR	MASCULINE PLURAL	FEMININE SINGULAR	FEMININE PLURAL
_____	_____	_____	_____
_____	_____	_____	_____
_____	_____	_____	_____
_____	_____	_____	_____
_____	_____	_____	_____

Articles

The definite (*the*) or indefinite article (*a*) precedes the noun and indicates the gender (masculine or feminine) and the number (singular or plural) of the noun. The definite article is used with known and specific nouns (*the book*), while the indefinite article is used with unknown and unspecific nouns (*a book*).

The indefinite article

The indefinite article (**un**, **uno**, **un'**, **una**, **un'**) varies depending on the gender and first letter of the word that follows. It is used with singular nouns that are unspecific or unknown and corresponds to *a/an* or *one* in English.

- ◆ With masculine nouns that begin with most consonants or a vowel, **un** is used:

    un libro   *a book*   un amico   *a friend*

- ◆ With masculine nouns starting with a **z**, **ps**, or **gn**, **s** + consonant, **y**, or **io**, **uno** is used to create a smoother sound:

    uno zio   *uncle*   uno psicologo   *psychologist*   uno gnocco   *type of pasta*
    uno studente   uno yoghurt

- ◆ With feminine nouns that begin with all consonants, **una** is used:

    una musica   una studentessa   *female student*

- ◆ With feminine nouns that begin with a vowel, **un'** is used:

    un'aria   un'automobile

Nota bene

The apostrophe is used only with the feminine article to substitute for the dropped final -**a**. The pronunciation of **un** and **un'** is identical. When an adjective precedes the noun, the first letter of the adjective will determine the form of **un** to be used.

    un'amica   **una** bella amica   *a pretty friend*
    un libro   **uno** strano libro   *a strange book*

Change the following nouns to the singular, and then add the indefinite article.

1. stadi _____

2. insalate _____

3. psicologi _____

4. automobili _____

5. città _____

6. stazioni _____

7. mani _____

8. serie _____

9. alberghi _____

10. tedeschi _____

The definite article

The definite article (**il**, **lo**, **l'**, **la**, **i**, **gli**, **le**) varies according to the gender and number of the noun, and the first letter of the word that follows. It has four singular and three plural forms.

STARTS WITH	MASCULINE SINGULAR	MASCULINE PLURAL
a consonant	il cantante (*singer*), il violino	i cantanti, i violini
s + consonant, **z**, **x**, **gn**, **ps**, **y**, or **io**	lo studente, lo zio (*uncle*), lo yoghurt, lo iodio (*iodine*)	gli spaghetti, gli zii, gli gnocchi, gli psicologi, gli Stati Uniti
a vowel	l'amico (*friend*), l'albero (*tree*)	gli amici, gli alberi

STARTS WITH	FEMININE SINGULAR	FEMININE PLURAL
a consonant studentesse	la sorella (*sister*), la matematica	le sorelle, le
a vowel	l'amica, l'America	le amiche, le Americhe

The definite article is used more frequently in Italian than in English. Following are some examples that demonstrate when the definite article is needed in Italian but not in English.

◆ With abstract nouns

la paura	la sete	il bisogno
fear	*thirst*	*need*

◆ With nouns that indicate matter or the elements

il legno	l'acqua	l'aria	il ferro
wood	*water*	*air*	*iron*

◆ With nouns that indicate a category, a species, or a group

la vita	l'uomo	i fiori	i pomodori	i violinisti
life	*mankind*	*flowers*	*tomatoes*	*violinists*

Nota bene

Since in English the definite article may be omitted, it is helpful to repeat these nouns and their articles in Italian as one inseparable unit.

Proverbi

L'abito non fa **il** monaco.	*The habit does not make the monk.*
La notte porta consiglio.	*Night brings (good) advice.*

Articles and proper names

The definite article is used before names of continents, countries, large islands, lakes, mountains, and rivers but not with cities. (Exceptions include Israel and Cuba, where the article is dropped.)

l'Italia   gli Stati Uniti   il Canada   la Sardegna   l'Europa   gli Appennini

The definite article often precedes the last names of famous men but is optional. When using both first and last names, no article is used.

il Petrarca   Petrarca   Francesco Petrarca

However, with women's last names the definite article must be used.

la Callas (*or* Maria Callas)   **la** Loren (*or* Sophia Loren)   **la** Morante (*or* Elsa Morante)

When referring to a family or a married couple, the family name remains unaltered and the plural definite article is used.

i Simpson   **i** Medici   **gli** Sforza

When using titles such as **signora**, **signore**, **dottore**, **avvocato**, and **professore/essa**, the definite article is used when referring to a third person.

la signora Rossi   **la** professoressa Mancini

The article is omitted, however, when speaking directly to the person.

Buongiorno, avvocato Agnelli!   Buonasera, dottor Rossi.

Nota bene

Titles in Italian are not capitalized as they are in English. Neither are days of the week, months, and adjectives of nationality.

Il professor Orlando, che insegna martedì e giovedì, è siciliano.
Professor Orlando, who teaches on Tuesdays and Thursdays, is Sicilian.

Cities do not take a definite article, unless it is part of the name. In this case, the article is capitalized.

| L'Aquila | **La** Spezia | **Il** Cairo |

When referring to literary, artistic, or musical works, the definite article is used and is lower case.

| *la* Divina Commedia | *le* Nozze di Figaro | *l'* Aida |

The definite article is generally used before possessive adjectives.

| il mio amico | la loro casa | i tuoi vestiti |
| *my friend* | *their home* | *your clothes* |

The adjectives **tutto** (*all*) and **ambedue** (*both*) are followed by the definite article.

| tutto **il** giorno | ambedue **le** amiche | tutti e quattro **gli** studenti |

The definite article is used with seasons, days of the week, parts of the day, and specific hours of the day.

| Amo **la** primavera. | **La** mattina mi alzo presto. | Sono **le** otto. |
| *I love spring.* | *I wake up early in the morning.* | *It is 8 o'clock.* |

Lavoro sempre **la** domenica.
I always work on Sundays.

In certain prepositional phrases, the definite article is omitted. These set phrases are better learned as one unit so that the omission of the article becomes automatic.

| a casa | a scuola | a teatro | a letto |
| in campagna | in città | in montagna | in giardino | in spiaggia |

However, there are some exceptions:

al mare

With the verb **parlare** + a language, the article may be omitted, while with other verbs followed by a language such as **studiare**, **ricordare**, **amare**, etc., using the article is preferred.

Studio l'italiano da un mese. *I have been studying Italian for a month.*
Si parla catalano in Sardegna? *Is Catalan spoken in Sardinia?*

ESERCIZIO
2·2

Add the definite article to the following phrases where necessary.

1. _____ signora Bianchi

2. _____ Maria Callas

3. _____ scienze politiche

4. _____ Stati Uniti

5. _____ Canada (*m.*)

6. _____ New York

7. _____ autunno

8. _____ otto di mattina

9. _____ Alpi

10. _____ Cuba

Add definite the articles to the following singular nouns, and then change them to the plural form.

1. _____ sport _____

2. _____ aria _____

3. _____ tesi (*f.*) _____

4. _____ film _____

5. _____ foto _____

6. _____ auto _____

7. _____ estate (*f.*) _____

8. _____ papà _____

9. _____ psichiatra _____

10. _____ parentesi (*f.*) _____

Adjectives

Adjectives have a close relationship to the nouns they modify. They generally appear close to that noun, usually following it. They agree with the noun in gender and number. This is often problematic for speakers of English, where adjective-noun agreement does not occur. For example, in English we say:

> *Those paintings are very beautiful.*

In English, the adjectives *those* and *beautiful* are invariable. Here is the same sentence in Italian:

> Quest**i dipinti** sono molto bell**i**.

Notice the words in the sentence that agree with the subject (**dipinti**) by changing their last letter to **-i**. The adjectives have changed their endings to agree with the noun, which is masculine plural. This is known as adjective-noun agreement.

Adjectives describe the quality of a noun (color, shape, size, psychological, physical and moral characteristics, etc.) as well as the quantity, nationality, possession, and so on.

There are four types of adjectives in Italian: four-form adjectives (the most frequent), two-form adjectives, three-form adjectives, and one-form, or invariable adjectives (the least frequent).

How important is it to make the agreement between the noun and the adjective? Mismatching gender does not usually interfere with communication, but one of the distinctions between a beginner and an intermediate or advanced learner lies in the ability to make the agreement automatically and consistently. Every time you use the wrong form, you reinforce it in your memory, and chances are you will make the same error again. If you practice the more difficult adjectives (the one-, two- and three-form adjectives) and repeat the the noun and adjectives as one chunk, your memory of the sounds will help you when the time comes to use them.

Four-form adjectives

There are several different types of adjectives in Italian, and they are distinguished by the base form of the masculine singular and by the way number and gender agreement is formed. The most frequently encountered is the four-form adjective. When consulting the dictionary, you will find the base form of the adjective, always the masculine singular form, which ends in **-o**.

italian**o**   ross**o**   larg**o**   poc**o**

The four-form adjective agrees with the noun in gender and in number by changing its ending to:

- **-a** for feminine singular

    italian**a**   ross**a**   larg**a**   poc**a**

- **-i** for masculine plural

    italian**i**   ross**i**   largh**i**   poch**i**

- **-e** for feminine plural

    italian**e**   ross**e**   largh**e**   poch**e**

In **poco** and **largo**, notice how in the plural an **-h** is added to keep the hard sound of the letters **c** and **g**.

Change the following nouns and adjectives from the singular to the plural.

1. libro giallo _____

2. studente universitario _____

3. piazza romana _____

4. buona regola _____

5. seta leggera _____

6. vestito chiaro _____

7. pizzeria antica _____

8. quadro famoso _____

9. cara amica _____

10. strada silenziosa _____

Two-form adjectives

The second most common type of adjective is the two-form adjective, which ends in an **-e** in both the feminine and masculine singular.

    elegant**e**   verd**e**   frances**e**   possibil**e**

In the plural, both feminine and masculine forms end in **-i**.

SINGULAR	PLURAL
uno studente frances**e**	due studenti frances**i**
una studentessa frances**e**	due studentesse frances**i**

Nota bene

As you can see, the masculine and feminine forms are identical, which means that they are not marked for gender, only for number. There are always other factors in a sentence that will be marked for gender, such as the nouns, articles, other adjectives, and of course, context. In the following sentence, the words **verdi** and **eleganti** could be either gender, but **quell<u>e</u>** and **scarp<u>e</u>** both indicate a feminine subject.

Quelle scarpe verdi sono eleganti.
Those green shoes are elegant.

Change the following phrases from the plural to the singular. All the adjectives are two-form.

1. ragazze intelligenti _____

2. libri interessanti _____

3. città affascinanti _____

4. attrici francesi _____

5. sport internazionali _____

6. domande difficili _____

7. bambini vivaci _____

8. vestiti eleganti _____

9. lezioni importanti _____

10. film francesi _____

Three-form adjectives

The three-form adjectives often correspond to English cognates that end in **-ist**, such as *optimist, feminist, violinist,* etc. Three-form adjectives have one form in the singular that ends in **-a** and two forms in the plural.

SINGULAR (-**ISTA**)	PLURAL (-**ISTI** MASCULINE/-**ISTE** FEMININE)
un amico ottim**ista** (*m.*)	due amici ottim**isti** (*m.*)
un'amica ottim**ista** (*f.*)	due amiche ottim**iste** (*f.*)

Although these two-form and three-form singular adjectives do not always indicate gender, other adjectives and articles surrounding the nouns, as well as context, will usually clarify it.

One-form, or invariable, adjectives

One-form, or invariable, adjectives include foreign words and the names of colors.

scarpe **blu**	fiori **viola**	ristorante **chic**
blue shoes	*purple flowers*	*chic restaurant*

Any time adjectives are combined with a noun or another adjective, they become one-form, or invariable.

guanti verd**e** bottiglia	scarpe ross**o** fiamma	fiore **rosa** pallido
dark green gloves	*bright red shoes*	*pale pink flower*

ESERCIZIO 3·3

Identify each adjective as four-form, three-form, two-form, or one-form.

1. rosso _____

2. rosa _____

3. verde _____

4. blu _____

5. importante _____

6. pari _____

7. pessimista _____

8. viola _____

9. difficile _____

10. arancione _____

ESERCIZIO 3·4

Match the noun in the first column with the adjective from the second column that agrees in gender and number.

NOUN	ADJECTIVE
1. _____ il libro	a. francesi
2. _____ la casa	b. deliziosi
3. _____ l'automobile	c. ricco
4. _____ le amiche	d. interessante
5. _____ i mesi	e. tropicale
6. _____ gli studenti	f. spaziosa
7. _____ gli spaghetti	g. nuovo
8. _____ lo zio	h. italiane
9. _____ l'anno	i. veloce
10. _____ l'isola	j. invernali

Indefinite adjectives and pronouns

The following four-form adjectives are used to describe an indefinite quantity, and as we saw earlier, their endings change to agree with the noun.

poco	molto	troppo	tutto	altro
little	*much*	*too much*	*all*	*other*

Ho **molta** fame.	Ci sono **troppe** macchine.	Ci vediamo un'**altra** volta!
I'm very hungry.	*There are too many cars.*	*We'll see each other another time!*

Tutto means *all, whole* and is always followed by the definite article.

Tutti i giorni.	**Tutta** l'estate.	**Tutto** il tempo.
Every day.	*The whole summer.*	*The whole time.*

These adjectives are often used as pronouns, in which case the number and gender of the noun being replaced is used.

Avete mangiato **tutta** la torta?
Sì, l'abbiamo mangiata **tutta**!

Nessuno means *none* or *no one* and is always singular.

Non c'è ness**uno**?

Adjectives describing more than one noun

In general, when one adjective is being used to describe more than one noun of the same gender, the plural form of the common gender is used.

Anna e Mara sono italian**e**.
Roberto e Marco sono stanch**i**.

When two or more nouns do not share the same gender, the modifying adjective will be in the masculine plural form.

Roberto e Anna sono italian**i**.

The position of adjectives

Adjectives are generally placed *after* the noun in Italian, in a more emphatic position that makes the noun distinct from other nouns. This type of emphasis in English is achieved by stressing the adjective with the voice.

Il musicista **giovane** mi ha invitato al suo concerto.
*The **young** musician invited me to his concert.* (as opposed to the older one)

Quell'attrice porta gli occhiali da sole **molto grandi**.
*That actress is wearing **very large** sunglasses.*

Lo studente **italiano** parla bene l'inglese.
*The **Italian** student speaks English well.*

The same adjective before the noun is less important within the phrase and acquires a less restrictive and more descriptive function. Possessive, interrogative, demonstrative, and indefinite adjectives generally precede the noun.

il **mio** amico   **Quanti** corsi segui?   **queste** ragazze   un'**altra** volta

Pre-noun placement occurs frequently in idiomatic or everyday expressions and is often redundant.

il piccolo bambino	il ricco banchiere	la brava cantante
the small child	*the rich banker*	*the good singer*

un buon lavoro	un brutto affare	una buon'idea
a good job	*a terrible ordeal*	*a good idea*

Some adjectives actually change meaning depending on their positions.

un uomo grande	un grand'uomo
a big man	*a great man*

un prodotto caro	un caro amico
an expensive product	*a dear friend*

Nota bene

Although adjectives generally follow the noun, when they are modified by the adverb **molto**, they *always* follow the noun they modify.

ESERCIZIO 3·5

Match the adjectives with the opposite meanings.

1. buono _____
2. povero _____
3. piccolo _____
4. magro _____
5. leggero _____
6. dinamico _____
7. bello _____
8. vicino _____
9. caldo _____
10. famoso _____

a. lontano
b. pigro
c. grasso
d. pesante
e. freddo
f. ricco
g. sconosciuto
h. cattivo
i. grande
j. brutto

Possessive adjectives

Possessive adjectives are used to denote possession and precede the noun they modify. Since the agreement is with the noun, the gender of the owner is not indicated by the adjective. Notice how **loro** is invariable and how all the possessives are regular except for the ones highlighted.

il mio	la mia	i **miei**	le mie
il tuo	la tua	i **tuoi**	le tue
il suo	la sua	i **suoi**	le tue
il nostro	la nostra	i nostri	le nostre

il vostro   la vostra   i vostri   le vostre
il loro   la loro   i loro   le loro
Il cane di Maria. → Il su**o cane**.   La giacca di Luigi. → La **sua** giacca.

If the article is preceded by **a**, **di**, **su**, or **in**, they combine into one word.

Il libro **di** + **la** mia professoressa. → Il libro **della** mia professoressa.

With singular and unmodified close relatives, the definite article is dropped, with the exception of the adjective **loro**.

mia sorella → **la** mia sorella minore → **le** mie sorelle → **la loro** sorella

Nota bene

The possessive adjectives are dropped with common possessions, such as **casa** (*home*), **la macchina** (*car*), **la bicicletta** (*bicycle*), **gli amici** (*friends*), and parts of the body, especially when used with reflexive verbs.

Tuo fratello si è messo **i guanti**?   *Did your brother put on (his) gloves?*
Quando ho aperto **gli occhi** . . .   *When I opened (my) eyes . . .*
Ti sei fatto male **al braccio**?   *Did you hurt (your) arm)?*

I miei, **i tuoi**, and **i suoi**, when used without a noun, refer to one's parents.

Quando arrivano i tuoi?   *When are your (parents) getting back?*
I miei si sono conosciuti a Roma.   *My parents met in Rome.*

Comparative and superlative uses of the adjective

When making a comparison of inequality between two nouns, **più** or **meno** are placed before the adjective, which is generally followed by the preposition **di**. The subject generally appears at the beginning of the sentence, and the noun or pronoun it is being compared to follows the preposition **di**, with or without the article as the case may be.

Gaia è **più alta di** Susanna.   *Gaia is taller than Susanna.*
Venezia è **meno caotica delle** altre città   *Venice is less chaotic than the other cities I visited.*
che ho visitato.

Carlo studia **più dei** suoi amici   *Carlo studies more than his friends Giovanni and*
Giovanni e Marco.   *Marco.*

Notice that in these sentences the comparison is followed by **di** + a noun, and two nouns are being compared in terms of the same quality or action.

In sentences where the comparison is being made between two adjectives, two pronouns, two adverbs, or two prepositional phrases (or any two terms that are the same parts of speech) in reference to one subject, **che** is used rather than **di**.

Marta è **più alta** *che* magra.   *but*   Marta è **più alta** *di* Gaia.
Ho cantato meno **in America** *che* in Italia.   *but*   Ho cantato **meno forte** *di* lei.
Mi piace più **leggere** *che* **giocare** a calcio.   *but*   Leggo **più** *di* Francesco.

Nota bene

When you're not sure whether to use **di** or **che**, remember that **di** will be preceded by an adjective and followed by a noun or pronoun, while **che** will link two words or phrases of the same part of speech.

ESERCIZIO
3·6

*Complete each sentence with **che** or **di** + article when needed.*

1. Anna è meno alta _____ Maria.

2. È più difficile guidare _____ prendere il treno.

3. Secondo me, il mare è più rilassante _____ stimolante.

4. In agosto la montagna è più tranquilla _____ spiaggia.

5. L'Italia ha più alberghi al nord _____ al sud.

6. Gli spaghetti ingrassano più _____ verdure.

7. Gli americani hanno meno ferie (*vacation*) _____ italiani.

8. Roma è più antica _____ New York.

9. Mi piace più cucinare _____ lavare i piatti.

10. Una Ferrari costa molto più _____ una Fiat.

Nota bene

If the second part of the comparison is a subordinate clause (it has another subject and conjugated verb), then **di quanto** + the subjunctive must be used. This type of sentence is rather complex and may be useful to more advanced speakers.

La campagna marchigiana è più bella **di quanto** immaginassi.
The Marche countryside is more beautiful than I imagined.

Equal comparisons

To make a comparison between two nouns that are equal, use:

> **(tanto)** + adjective + **quanto**
>
> *or*
>
> **(così)** + adjective + **come**

The first adverb has been put in parentheses because it is optional. The adjective must agree with the subject and not with the noun it is being compared to, and the adverb, as always, is invariable.

Isabella è **tanto** alta **quanto** Roberto. → Isabella è alta **quanto** Roberto.
Isabella è **così** alta **come** Roberto. → Isabella è alta **come** Roberto.

*Make comparisons of equality (=) or inequality (**più** +, **meno** −) using the appropriate form of the verb **essere** and the adjectives provided.*

1. Mario / + simpatico / Giacomo

   _____

2. le montagne / + alto / le colline

   _____

3. Giovanna / = studioso / sua sorella

   _____

4. Quell'attore / + bello / intelligente

   _____

5. autobus / = veloce / tram

   _____

6. spagnolo / + facile / francese

   _____

7. cani / + affettuosi / pescirossi (*goldfish*)

   _____

8. Cina / − grande / Russia

   _____

9. leggere la *Divina commedia* / + difficile / leggere *il Decameron*

   _____

10. Kobe Bryant / + famoso / Vasco Rossi

    _____

Absolute superlatives

Absolute superlatives are adjectives that are used to describe the quality of a noun without comparing it to any other noun. In English, this is done by placing words such as *very* or *extremely* before the adjective. In Italian, words such as **molto**, **assai**, and **estremamente** have similar meaning and function.

Superlatives with -issimo/a/i/e

There is another form that is even more common in everyday speech, which is formed by adding the suffix **-issimo/a/i/e** to the adjective after dropping the final letter.

bello → bellissimo   elegante → elegantissimo*   largo → larghissimo**
simpatico → simpaticissimo**

---

*Notice that two-form adjectives, those ending with **-e** in the masculine and feminine singular, become four-form when the **-issimo** suffix is used.

The **c or **g** sound preceding the **-issimo** suffix acquires the same sound as the masculine plural form of the adjective, regardless of gender or number.

largo → lar**ghi** → lar**ghi**ssimo/a/i/e
simpatico → simpati**ci** → simpati**ci**ssimo/a/i/e

Irregular superlatives

In everyday speech, the following adjectives are used to describe physical or material qualities of people or animals. In writing and in more figurative descriptions, the following irregular forms are also possible.

BASE ADJECTIVE	COMPARATIVE	SUPERLATIVE
alto	superiore	sommo
basso	inferiore	infimo
buono	migliore	ottimo
cattivo	peggiore	pessimo
grande	maggiore	massimo
piccolo	minore	minimo

ESERCIZIO
3·8

Reword the sentences, using the irregular form of the adjective with a similar meaning.

1. I cornetti in quel bar sono **buoni**.

   _____

2. Roberto è il fratello **più piccolo**.

   _____

3. Salieri fu un compositore **poco importante**.

   _____

4. Maradona è stato il calciatore **più bravo**.

   _____

5. Abitano al piano di **sopra**.

   _____

6. Quel film è di **cattivo** gusto.

   _____

7. Quell'avvocato ha una **brutta** reputazione.

_____

8. Dante Alighieri è considerato il **più grande** poeta italiano.

_____

9. Gli spaghetti alla carbonara sono **buonissimi**!

_____

10. L'Orvieto Classico è **più buono** del vino della casa.

_____

Reword the sentences, using an adjective of the opposite meaning.

1. La casa è **piccola**.

_____

2. Questo pacco è **leggero**.

_____

3. Giovanni è un ragazzo **pigro**.

_____

4. Roberto è più **grasso** di Antonio.

_____

5. Questa strada è **stretta**.

_____

6. L'esame di chimica è **difficilissimo**!

_____

7. Nel negozio ho visto delle sedie **antiche**.

_____

8. La mia bici è **nuovissima**.

_____

9. Le mie amiche sono **tranquille**.

_____

10. Il **vecchio** professore è bravissimo.

_____

Adverbs

·V-4·

There are numerous types of adverbs that describe how, when, where, how much, or how often something is done and are often used in questions. They are much easier to use than adjectives because they are not marked for gender or number, and, therefore, have only one form. Adverbs can modify:

- A verb

    Francesco guida **velocemente**.   *Francesco drives **fast**.*

- An adjective

    Alida è un'attrice **estremamente**   *Alida is an **extremely** gifted*
    brava.   *actress.*

- An adverb or adverbial phrase

    Canta **molto** bene.   *He sings **very** nicely.*
    Sfortunatamente devo partire.   ***Unfortunately** I have to leave.*

Adverbs can be one word (**oggi**, **qui**, **quando**, **come**, etc.), compound words (that is, single words that are combined—**perché**, **soprattutto**, etc.), words that are derived from adjectives (**veramente**, **generalmente**, **probabilmente**), and adverbial phrases (**in fretta**, **di corsa**, etc.). Adverbs often describe how something is done.

As you can see from the earlier examples, many adverbs end in -**mente**, which generally corresponds to the English suffix -*ly*. The stem of these adverbs is always an adjective, which can be turned into an adverb by following these simple rules:

- Four-form adjectives: change the adjective to the feminine form and add the suffix -**mente**.

    vero → vera + mente →   allegro → allegra + mente →
    veramente   **allegramente**

- Two-form adjectives not ending in -**le** or -**re**: simply add -**mente**.

    breve + mente →   semplice + mente →
    brevemente   **semplicemente**

- Adjectives ending in -**le** and -**re**: simply drop the final -**e** and add -**mente**.

    naturale → **naturalmente**   speciale → **specialmente**
    probabile → **probabilmente**

521

There are a few exceptions, the most common being:

leggero → **leggermente**   violento → **violentemente**

Some important adverbs are not derived from an adjective.

bene   male   insieme   così   volentieri

Some adverbs and adjectives share the same form. Look at these two examples:

La musica **forte** non mi piace. (adj.)
Parla **piano**! (adv.)

Different types of adverbs

Some adverbs answer questions starting with *where?* *when?* and *how much?* Here is a list of common adverbs that answer questions starting with:

+ **Dove** (*Where*)?

Dove siete?	*Where are you?*	Siamo qui!	*We're over here!*
qui, qua	*here*	lì, là	*there*
giù	*down*	su	*up there*
vicino	*near*	lontano	*far*
dentro	*inside*	fuori	*outside*
davanti	*in front of*	dietro	*behind*
sopra	*above*	sotto	*beneath*

+ **Quando** (*When*)?

Quando andiamo?	*When are we going?*	Domani sera.	*Tomorrow night.*
oggi	*today*	domani	*tomorrow*
ieri	*yesterday*	dopodomani	*the day after tomorrow*
ora, adesso	*now*	fra poco	*in a little while*
prima	*before*	dopo	*later*
sempre	*always*	mai	*never*
presto	*soon*	tardi	*late*

+ **Quanto** (*How much*)?

Quanto costa?	*How much does it cost?*	Costa molto.	*It costs a lot.*
molto, tanto	*a lot*	un po', un poco, poco	*a little*
più	*more*	meno	*less*
abbastanza, piuttosto	*rather, enough*	troppo	*too much*
quasi	*almost*		

Nota bene

The words listed in bold above can also function as adjectives. Remember, when used as adjectives, they must agree with the noun they are describing. With **molto**, remember that if **molto** means *very* (adv.), it "doesn't vary."

Ho **molti** amici italiani. (adj.)	Sono **molto** stanca. (adv.)
I have a many Italian friends.	*I am very tired.*
Scrivo **poche** lettere. (adj.)	Pollini lo suona **un poco** più velocemente. (adv.)
I write few letters.	*Pollini plays it a little faster.*

Some adverbs replace the simple affirmative **sì**.

> Vuoi andare a vedere un film?   ***Certo!***
> *Do you want to go see a movie?*   *Sure!*

Some adverbs indicate agreement.

esattamente	precisamente	appunto	davvero
exactly	*precisely*	*right*	*really*

The adverbs **mica**, **niente**, and **mai** make negative phrases more emphatic.

non è vero	*it's not true*	non è **mica** vero	*it's not true **at all***
non c'entra	*it doesn't have to do with*	non c'entra **niente**	*it doesn't have **anything** to do with it*
non ho detto questo	*I didn't say this*	non ho **mai** detto questo	*I **never** said this*

Adding these adverbs to your conversation is not difficult and will make it sound more native. As you see from the examples, they almost always follow the verb in the present tense, and they follow the auxiliary in the compound tenses.

Proverbi che usano avverbi

Chi va **piano** va sano e **lontano**.
He who goes slowly goes healthy and far.

Lontano dagli occhi, **lontano** dal cuore.
Far from the eyes, far from the heart.

ESERCIZIO
4·1

Change the following adjectives into adverbs.

1. relativo   _____
2. breve   _____
3. esatto   _____
4. vero   _____
5. semplice   _____
6. possibile   _____
7. raro   _____
8. franco   _____
9. diretto   _____
10. probabile   _____

Match each question with its answer. Note any adverbs you find in the questions or answers.

1. Quando vanno in vacanza? _____
2. Abiti ancora a Milano? _____
3. Perché studi l'italiano? _____
4. Come guida tuo fratello? _____
5. Quanto vuole per questa sedia? _____
6. Ha già trovato un lavoro? _____
7. Come si chiama quella ragazza? _____
8. Vai spesso a teatro? _____
9. Siete mai andati in montagna? _____
10. Mi presti cento euro? _____

a. Perché voglio andare a Roma.
b. Fortunatamente sì.
c. Ci siamo andati spessissimo.
d. Generalmente in agosto.
e. Non ci abito più da un anno.
f. La vendo a poco . . . 40 euro.
g. Ci vado raramente.
h. Certamente!
i. Corre troppo.
j. Veramente non l'ho mai vista.

The following sentences each answer a question introduced by the adverbs **quando**, **perché, quanto, dove***, or* **come***. Give the most logical question to each answer, using no more than four words.*

1. L'inverno comincia in dicembre.

_____

2. Claudia è alta e bionda.

_____

3. Il pane costava pochissimo.

_____

4. Non so perché si arrabbia.

_____

5. Tornerà la settimana prossima.

_____

6. Le lezioni vanno benissimo, grazie.

_____

7. Abitava a Venezia.

_____

8. Mette la macchina in un garage vicino a casa sua.

_____

Change the boldfaced phrases in the following sentences into one of the adverbs from the list with the same meaning. There are two extra words.

velocemente	veramente	sempre	pochissimo	seriamente
spesso	divinamente	piano	raramente	sfortunatamente

1. Vado al cinema **una volta l'anno**.

_____

2. Con la mia Ferrari guido **a 100 chilometri all'ora**.

_____

3. Mangia la pasta **a pranzo e a cena**.

_____

4. Amedeo **non** parla **forte**.

_____

5. Giacomo studia **il meno possibile** ma prende sempre 100!

_____

6. Vado in palestra **tre o quattro volte a settimana**.

_____

7. Paola studiava **con molta serietà**.

_____

8. Suona il violino **in modo divino**.

_____

Complete the answers with the opposite adverb.

1. Guidi troppo **velocemente**!

   Ma no, guido _____!

2. Parli **sempre** al telefono!

   Ma no, non parlo _____!

3. Sei così **fortunata**!

   Ma no, sono _____!

4. Ti sta **malissimo** l'arancione!

   Ma no, mi sta _____!

5. Mangiamo **fuori**?

   Ma no, mangiamo _____!

6. Studi **poco**!

   Ma no, studio _____!

7. Ceniamo **prima** del concerto?

   Ma no, ceniamo _____!

8. Arrivi sempre **tardi**!

   Ma no, arrivo sempre _____!

Present and present perfect tenses

·V-5·

The three conjugations are recognizable from the last three letters of the verb. Regular verbs follow the patterns presented in this chapter and do not change their stems or roots. Irregular verbs change their stems and follow patterns that are generally determined by their Latin origins. The two most important irregular verbs are **avere** and **essere**.

Regular -are verbs

Verbs of the first conjugation end in -**are** and are the most common verb type in Italian. In regular -**are** verbs, the person, or subject, is indicated by the suffix, or ending, which is added to the stem. The present tense (**il presente**) form is as follows:

parlare (*to speak*)			
(io)	**parl**-o	(noi)	parl-**ia**mo
(tu)	**parl**-i	(voi)	parl-**a**te
(lei/lui)	**parl**-a	(loro)	**parl**-ano

The syllables in bold show where the stress falls. This pattern is the same in all three conjugations. The stem is stressed in all persons except for the **noi** and **voi** forms. It may be easier to remember that all the forms are stressed on the penultimate, or second-to-last, syllable, except for the third person plural, which is stressed on the third-to-last syllable.

> ### Nota bene
> When practicing the verbs, remember that the *third* person plural is stressed on the *third*-to-last syllable.

Notes on -are verbs

Verbs ending in -**care** and -**gare** always retain their hard **c** and **g** sounds, so an -**h** is added when the suffix starts with the softening vowels -**i** or -**e**.

pago	pag**h**iamo
pag**h**i	pagate
paga	pagano

Verbs that end in -**ciare**, -**giare**, or -**sciare** drop the initial -**i** of the stem when the ending begins with an -**e** or -**i**.

comincio   cominciamo
cominci   cominciate
comincia   cominciano

In the participle form, the soft sound is kept and, therefore, the -**i** remains.

cominciato   festeggiato   mangiato   lasciato

In verbs that have an accented -**i**, such as **invio** or **scio** (rhymes with **mio**), the extra -**i** is kept when a suffix beginning with an -**i** is added.

invii   scii

One -**i** is dropped when it falls on an unaccented syllable.

inviamo   sciamo

The verbs ending in -**gliare** drop the -**i** of the stem before endings that start with -**i** but keep it if the ending begins with -**a**, -**e**, or -**u**.

sbagli   consigli   sbadigli   *but*   sbaglierò   consiglierei   sbadiglieranno

Regular -ere verbs

Most irregular verbs belong to this (second) conjugation. The stress pattern in -**ere** verbs can be of two types. In the infinitive form, some verbs have the stress on the penultimate syllable (**vedere**, **temere**) similar to the -**are** verbs, but most have the stress on the stem (**vendere**, **prendere**, **spendere**), or the third-to-last syllable.

prendere (*to take*)			
(io)	**prend**-o	(noi)	prend-**iamo**
(tu)	**prend**-i	(voi)	prend-ete
(lei, lui)	**prend**-e	(loro)	**prend**-ono

Pronunciation tips

Contrary to the -**are** verbs, verbs ending in -**cere**, -**gere**, or -**scere** harden the soft -**c**, -**g**, and -**sc** of the infinitive when followed by a suffix beginning with a letter other than -**e** or -**i**.

leggere (*to read*)			
(io)	**legg**-o	(noi)	legg-**iam**o
(tu)	**legg**-i	(voi)	legg-ete
(lei/lui)	**legg**-e	(loro)	**legg**-ono

Therefore, the first person singular and the third person plural are pronounced with the hard **c** or **g**, while the remaining forms retain the soft sound of the infinitive. In regular verbs, such as **conoscere** and **piacere**, an -**i** is added to the participle to keep the soft sound.

conoscere → conosciuto   piacere → piaciuto

Regular -ire verbs

Verbs of the third conjugation share the same endings as -**ere** verbs, except for the **voi** form.

dormire (*to sleep*)

(io)	**dorm**-o	(noi)	dorm-**ia**mo
(tu)	**dorm**-i	(voi)	dorm-ite
(lei/lui)	**dorm**-e	(loro)	**dorm**-ono

-isc verbs

There is a group of -**ire** verbs that adds -**isc** between the stem and the ending in first, second, and third person singular and third person plural. Most verbs of this type (**capire, finire, ferire, preferire, pulire**) tend to have one consonant and vowel just before the -**ire** ending.

finire (*to finish*)

(io)	fin-**isc**-o (sk)	(noi)	fin-**ia**mo
(tu)	fin-**isc**-i (sh)	(voi)	fin-ite
(lei/lui)	fin-**isc**-e (sh)	(loro)	fin-**isc**-ono (sk)

Nota bene

Remember that in -**isc** verbs, the **c** sound is pronounced as a *k* in the first person singular and third person plural, and as *sh* in all the other forms.

The -**isc** is added only in the present tense but not in the participial or the gerund.

capito   finito   ferito   preferendo

Proverbi nel tempo presente (*Proverbs that feature the present tense*)

Il tempo porta consiglio.	*Time brings advice.*
Troppi cuochi guastano la minestra.	*Too many cooks spoil the soup.*
Il cane che abbaia non morde.	*The dog that barks doesn't bite.*

ESERCIZIO 5·1

Indicate the correct forms of the missing verbs.

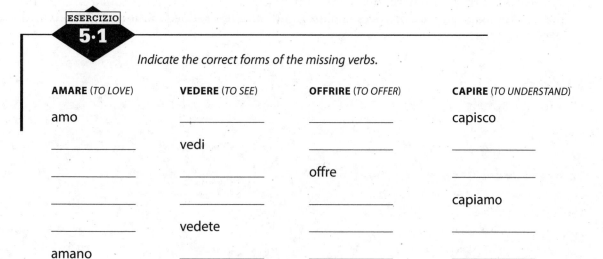

AMARE (*TO LOVE*)	**VEDERE** (*TO SEE*)	**OFFRIRE** (*TO OFFER*)	**CAPIRE** (*TO UNDERSTAND*)
amo	_____	_____	capisco
_____	vedi	_____	_____
_____	_____	offre	_____
_____	_____	_____	capiamo
_____	vedete	_____	_____
amano	_____	_____	_____

Present tense irregular verbs

The verbs listed below include some frequently used irregular verbs from each conjugation. A complete list can be found on the many Italian language websites by searching *irregular Italian verbs*.

ANDARE (to go)	FARE (to do)	AVERE (to have)	ESSERE (to be)	RIMANERE (to remain)	TENERE (to keep)
vado	faccio	ho	sono	**rimango**	**tengo**
vai	fai	hai	sei	rimani	**tieni**
va	fa	ha	è	rimane	**tiene**
andiamo	facciamo	abbiamo	siamo	rimaniamo	teniamo
andate	fate	avete	siete	rimanete	tenete
vanno	fanno	hanno	sono	**rimangono**	**tengono**

DIRE (to say)	USCIRE (to go out)	VENIRE (to come)
dico	**esco**	**vengo**
dici	esci	**vieni**
dice	esce	**viene**
diciamo	usciamo	veniamo
dite	**uscite**	**venite**
dicono	**escono**	**vengono**

Some students learn irregular verb forms through memorization, while others prefer to learn them in context. I recommend a combination of both. As you read and study these verbs, try to make a mental note and analyze the patterns you see, grouping together verbs with similar patterns. For example, if you look at the first and last person of these verbs, what do you notice? Here are three patterns that will help you use these verb forms correctly:

1. The first person singular and the third person plural are almost always identical except for the last syllable (**-no**) of the third person plural.

2. The **voi** form always uses the regular infinitive stem, except for **essere**.

3. The verbs **venire** and **tenere** follow the same pattern with the letter **g** added in the first person singular and the third person plural, and the letter **i** added in the second and third person singular.

Complete the chart with the missing forms of the irregular verbs.

ANDARE		FARE		AVERE	
vado	_____	faccio	_____	_____	abbiamo
_____	_____	_____	fate	_____	_____
_____	vanno	_____	_____	ha	hanno

ESSERE		TENERE		BERE	
_____	_____	tengo	_____	_____	_____
_____	siete	_____	_____	bevi	_____
è	_____	_____	_____	_____	bevono

DIRE		USCIRE		VENIRE	
_____	_____	esco	_____	vengo	_____
dici	dite	_____	uscite	_____	_____
_____	_____	_____	_____	_____	vengono

Uses of the present tense (il presente)

The use of the present tense in Italian and English is for the most part very similar. It is important to remember, however, that in English the present continuous (*I am working*) and the simple present (*I work, I do work*) correspond to the just one tense in Italian. This means that the question **"Che cosa fai?"** in Italian can be translated as either "What are you doing?" or "What do you do?" Depending on the context, the answers to the question may vary. Below is a list of situations in which the present tense is commonly used.

◆ An event happening in the present or the near future

> Torno a Roma.
> *I am returning to Rome.*

◆ A repeated or ongoing action

> Di solito studio in biblioteca.
> *I usually study in the library.*

◆ A current state of being and condition

> Sono americana e vivo a Venezia.
> *I am American and I live in Venice.*

The following words and phrases often accompany or trigger the use of verbs in the present tense:

| di solito | *usually* |
| domani | *tomorrow* |

fra poco	*soon*
oggi	*today*
ora, adesso	*now*
stasera	*this evening, tonight*

ESERCIZIO 5·3

Compose sentences using the correct form of the irregular verbs in parentheses.

1. Anna (andare) . . .

_____

2. Gli italiani (essere) . . .

_____

3. Io (bere) . . .

_____

4. Rob e Cecilia (venire) . . .

_____

5. Tu e Marco (rimanere) . . .

_____

6. Io e Susanna (dire) . . .

_____

7. Lei, Signora Rossellini, (uscire) . . .

_____

8. Tu, Maria, (fare) . . .

_____

Proverbi con verbi irregolari

L'unione **fa** la forza.	*Unity makes strength.*
L'occasione **fa** l'uomo ladro.	*Opportunity makes the man a thief.*
Una rondine non **fa** primavera.	*One swallow doesn't make spring.*
Le bugie **hanno** le gambe corte.	*Lies have short legs. (They don't run very far.)*
Al buio tutti i gatti sono bigi.	*In the dark all cats are grey.*

The present perfect tense (il passato prossimo)

The present perfect (**il passato prossimo**) is used to describe actions completed in the recent past. It is a compound tense made up of an auxiliary verb (**essere** or **avere**) and the past participle of the main verb. The **passato prossimo** corresponds to two tenses in English.

Ho studiato l'italiano can be translated as:

> *I studied Italian.* (simple past)

or

> *I have studied Italian.* (present perfect)

The auxiliary verb combines with the past participle of the main verb form to form compound tenses, such as the present perfect (**ho mangiato**, **sono andato/a**), the past conditional (**avrei mangiato**, **sarei andato**), the future perfect (**avrò mangiato**, **sarò andato**), and others.

Knowing which auxiliary the verb requires can be difficult at first, but through frequent use and repetition this will become automatic. When in doubt, however, it may help to remember that the great majority of verbs use **avere**.

Nota bene

You will be able to use the auxiliaries more fluently if you review the simple tenses before learning each new compound tense.

avere as an auxiliary verb

Most verbs are transitive verbs, can be used with an object, and take the auxiliary verb **avere**. It is used:

- ◆ With compound forms of **avere**

  | abbiamo avuto | avevo avuto | avresti avuto |
  | *we had* | *I had had* | *you would have had* |

- ◆ With all transitive verbs

  Ho mangiato una mela.   Hai letto un libro.
  I ate an apple.   *You read a book.*

- ◆ With a few intransitive verbs

  Ho lavorato.   Hanno viaggiato.   Avresti dormito.
  I worked.   *They traveled.*   *You would have slept.*

Nota bene

Although these verbs cannot be used with an object, and are therefore intransitive, they are unusual in that they use **avere** as the auxiliary. Here is a list of some other intransitive verbs that use **avere** in compound tenses:

ballare
pranzare
cenare
dormire
piangere
ridere
lavorare
camminare
passeggiare
nuotare
viaggiare

Using the two model sentences, compose sentences using the **presente** and **passato prossimo** of the given verb. All the verbs are transitive and will use **avere** as their auxiliary.

ESEMPIO   studiare

Oggi studio l'italiano.

Anche ieri ho studiato l'italiano.

1. parlare con il professore

_____

_____

2. telefonare alla zia

_____

_____

3. capire la lezione

_____

_____

4. vendere qualcosa su eBay

_____

_____

5. avere freddo

_____

_____

6. guardare la TV

_____

_____

7. ascoltare la radio

_____

_____

8. finire la lezione

_____

_____

9. ballare il tango

_____

_____

10. preferire il cappuccino

_____

_____

Modals and auxiliaries

In standard Italian, modal verbs take the auxiliary of the verb that follows the modal.

> Main verb takes **avere** → **Hai** dovuto **lavorare** fino a tardi?
> *Did you have to work until late?*

> Main verb takes **essere** → **Sei** dovuto **rimanere** fino a tardi?
> *Did you have to stay late?*

In everyday speech, however, this rule is often disregarded. This is another example of how *prescriptive grammar*, where rules are prescribed by grammarians, does not always match *descriptive grammar*, where rules are based on forms that speakers actually use.

> Descriptive grammar → **Hai** dovuto **rimanere** fino a tardi? *Did you have to stay late?*

Nota bene

The written language tends to be more conservative and does not always reflect the changes that occur in the spoken language. In academic or literary speech, prescriptive forms are preferred and should be used whenever there is any doubt.

More on modals

A modal verb followed by a reflexive verb takes **essere** as the auxiliary when the pronoun precedes the modal, as in the following example:

> **Si sono dovuti** salutare alla stazione.
> *They had to say good-bye at the station.*

But it takes **avere** when the pronoun is attached to the infinitive:

> **Hanno dovuto salutarsi** alla stazione.
> *They had to say good-bye at the station.*

Transitive verbs

If a verb can be used with an object, it generally uses the auxiliary **avere** in compound tenses. The verb **bere** (*to drink*) is an example of a transitive verb. The object in this case answers the question *What* do you drink? The direct object **acqua** answers that question.

Bevo l'acqua.	*I drink the water.*
Ho bevuto l'acqua.	*I drank the water.*
Avevo bevuto l'acqua.	*I had drunk the water.*
Avrei bevuto l'acqua.	*I would have drunk the water.*
Avrò bevuto l'acqua.	*I will have drunk the water.*

Intransitive verbs

If a verb *cannot* be used with an object, then it generally takes **essere** as the auxiliary in all compound tenses, with the last letter of the participle changing to agree in gender and number with the subject. The following sentences in the **passato prossimo** (*present perfect*) illustrate the agreement of the participle with the subject.

> Sono andat**o**.   (masculine singular)
> *I went.*

> Sono andat**a**.   (feminine singular)
> *I went.*

> Siamo andat**i**.   (masculine plural)
> *We went.*

> Siamo andat**e**. (feminine plural)
> *We went.*

> Vado a casa.
> *I am going home.*

> **Sono** andato/andata a casa.
> *I went home.*

> **Ero** andato/andata a casa.
> *I had gone home.*

> **Saremmo** andati/andate a casa.
> *We would have gone home.*

> **Saranno** andati/andate a casa.
> *They will have gone home.*

Idioms with the present perfect

When asking how something went and there is no inherent subject in the sentence, the participle generally has a feminine ending. If there is a subject, then the regular agreement occurs.

Com'è **andata**?	*How did it go?*
Com'è **andato** il viaggio?	*How did **the trip** go?*

essere as an auxiliary verb

The auxiliary **essere** requires agreement of the participle in gender and number with the subject. It is used:

◆ With compound forms of **essere**

È stat**o** un malinteso.	Isabella sarà stat**a** qui un'ora fa.
It was a misunderstanding.	*Isabella must have been here an hour ago.*

◆ With reflexive and pronominal verbs (verbs that are preceded by a pronoun)

Mi sono svegliato.	Ci siamo ricordati.
I woke up.	*We remembered.*

- With most intransitive verbs

    Siamo partiti presto.
    We left early.

    È uscito poco fa.
    He went out a while ago.

- With the passive voice

    È **stato** costruito in tre anni.
    It was built in three years.

    I ragazzi **sono stati** invitati.
    The kids were invited.

ESERCIZIO 5·5

Create two sentences using the **presente** and the **passato prossimo** of the given verbs, following the model. All the following verbs take **essere**, so be careful to make the agreement.

ESEMPIO   Maria / andare
                Oggi Maria va a scuola.
                Anche ieri è andata a scuola.

1. Antonio (tornare) tardi

    _____

    _____

2. Amelia (svegliarsi) presto

    _____

    _____

3. Tu e Amedeo (partire) per Napoli

    _____

    _____

4. Paola e Francesca (andare) a scuola

    _____

    _____

5. Voi (uscire) alle 7.30

    _____

    _____

6. Io e i miei amici (andare) al cinema

    _____

    _____

7. I ragazzi (restare) a casa

    _____

    _____

8. Paola (passare) a casa mia

_____

_____

9. Guglielmo non (tornare) a New York

_____

_____

10. Regina (partire) con Sandro

_____

_____

ESERCIZIO
5·6

*Change the following sentences from the **presente** to the **passato prossimo**, remembering the agreement for the intransitive verbs.*

1. Anna deve andare a New York.

_____

2. Puoi telefonare a Marco?

_____

3. Amelia vuole venire a casa.

_____

4. I ragazzi possono tornare.

_____

5. Devo lavorare fino a tardi.

_____

6. Vogliono andare al mare.

_____

7. Non posso venire a cena.

_____

8. Te e Anna dovete leggere questo libro.

_____

Verbs that can take either **essere** or **avere**

Some verbs can function as either transitive or intransitive verbs, and their auxiliary changes accordingly. These include: **cominciare, finire, cambiare, passare**. If the subject is a person and takes an object, the verb is transitive and takes **avere**. If the subject is a thing or cannot take an object, then it is intransitive and takes **essere**. Notice that in the left column, there are no objects, while on the right, the verbs are followed by a direct object.

INTRANSITIVE	TRANSITIVE
Il film **è cominciato** tardi. *The film started late.*	Susanna **ha cominciato** il libro ieri. *Susanna started the book yesterday.*
L'inverno **è passato**. *Winter has passed.*	Gaia **ha passato** l'estate in Grecia. *Gaia passed the summer in Greece.*
Lo stile di Armani non **è cambiato**. *Armani's style has not changed.*	Susanna **ha cambiato** l'abito. *Susanna changed her dress.*
L'acqua bolle! *The water is boiling!*	**Ho bollito** le uova per tre minuti. *I boiled the eggs for three minutes.*
Il tempo **è cambiato**. *The weather has changed.*	Marco **ha cambiato** lavoro. *He changed jobs.*
Il film **è finito** a mezzanotte. *The film ended at midnight.*	**Ho finito** il libro ieri sera. *I finished the book yesterday.*

Nota bene

Verbs related to the weather can take either **essere** or **avere**.

Ieri **ha** piovuto. *Yesterday it rained.*	Ieri **è** piovuto. *Yesterday it rained.*

ESERCIZIO
5·7

Decide whether the following sentences are transitive or intransitive and change them to the **passato prossimo**, *using either* **avere** *or* **essere**.

1. L'opera finisce tardi.

   _____

2. Maria comincia il lavoro.

   _____

3. La situazione cambia.

   _____

4. Marco passa davanti a casa mia.

   _____

5. Lucia e Bob ritornano sabato.

   _____

6. Riporto il libro in biblioteca.

_____

7. Il tempo cambia in autunno.

_____

8. La musica finisce.

_____

9. Il presidente comincia il suo discorso.

_____

10. Passiamo l'estate in Italia.

_____

Irregular participles

Most **-are** verbs have regular participles, but some **-ere** and **-ire** verbs change the stem slightly in forming the participle. The best way to learn these irregular forms is to look closely at the patterns and to use them in writing and speaking. They have been divided according to their conjugation and pattern similarities. Try to identify in what way they are irregular and why they are grouped the way they are.

-are
fare → fatto
dare → dato
stare → stato

-ere (remember that most -ere verbs are stressed on the third-to-last syllable)
accendere → acceso
offendere → offeso
chiudere → chiuso
decidere → deciso
dividere → diviso
prendere → preso
scendere* → sceso
bere → bevuto
chiedere → chiesto
rimanere** → rimasto
rispondere → risposto
vedere → visto
essere** → stato
nascere** → nato
correre* → corso
perdere → perso

_____

*Verbs that take **essere** or **avere**
Verbs that take **essere

leggere → letto
rompere → rotto
scrivere → scritto
mettere → messo
vivere* → vissuto
succedere** → successo
spegnere → spento
vincere → vinto

-ire

aprire → aperto
offrire → offerto
dire → detto
morire** → morto
venire** → venuto
tradurre → tradotto
produrre → prodotto

*Verbs that take **essere** or **avere**
Verbs that take **essere

ESERCIZIO
5·8

Create ten sentences about yourself, using only irregular participles. If your experiences do not include some verbs, use them in a negative sentence. Be careful to use the correct auxiliary!

ESEMPIO   *Sono nata a Roma.*

Ho visto Parigi, Vienna e Budapest.

Ho letto un libro di Michela Murgia.

1. _____
2. _____
3. _____
4. _____
5. _____
6. _____
7. _____
8. _____
9. _____
10. _____

Imperfect and past perfect tenses

In this chapter, we will look at the imperfect tense, which is used frequently in Italian but does not have a corresponding tense in English, and the past perfect, which does exist in English. In English, the imperfect is usually expressed with *would* + main verb and indicates a repeated or customary action.

> After school, I **would go** to the café to meet my friends. (This action occurred frequently.)

Nota bene

In English, the imperfect is easily confused with the conditional. Notice the difference in meaning between the above sentence and the following one, even though the verb tense seems to be identical:

> I **would go** to the café if I had the money. (This action has not occurred and is dependent on a condition. In Italian, the conditional tense would be used.)

The past perfect, or **trapassato prossimo**, is used to express an action in the past that took place before another action in the past, and therefore clarifies the order in which these actions occurred. This tense exists in English but is not often used in everyday speech.

The imperfect (l'imperfetto)

Learning the different forms of the imperfect (**l'imperfetto**) is not difficult, since it is a tense that has few irregular forms. Since English does not have a tense for recurring or continuous actions in the past, it can prove challenging to know how and when to use it. While other past-tense forms are used to describe completed events, the **imperfetto** tends to describe how things were or used to be. Let us look at some examples illustrating when this tense is used.

In the first example, a recurring event is being described, and the use of the imperfect is accompanied by the phrase "in the summer." We do not know how many times this event occurred; the **imperfetto** indicates it was not a single event but a recurring event in the summertime. If "in the summer" were omitted, the **imperfetto** alone would be enough to express that this was not one isolated event but one that recurred many times.

> D'estate **andavamo** al mare.   *In the summer we would go to the beach.*

The **imperfetto** is also used to describe an ongoing event that was occurring when another single event occurred. In this sentence, the act of studying can be imagined as a continuous line (**imperfetto**), while Jim's call, in the present perfect (**passato prossimo**), is represented by the slash that interrupts the continuous line. The act of studying may have continued before and after the phone call.

Mentre **studiavo** (continuous)   Jim ha preparato la cena. (completed event)
While I was studying   *Jim prepared dinner.*

_____/_____

However, with both verbs in the **imperfetto**, the actions are simultaneous but incomplete and can be depicted as two parallel lines.

Mentre studiavo (continuous)   Jim ascoltava la musica. (continuous)
While I studied   *Jim listened to music.*

The **imperfetto** is also used with:

◆ References to the time of day, the weather, and age in the past

Erano solo le 5.30 di mattina e **faceva** già caldo.
It was only 5:30 in the morning and it was already hot.

◆ Descriptions of physical and psychological states of being

Anna **era** una bambina molto vivace.
Anna was a very active child.

Avevamo paura delle grandi stanze buie.
We were afraid of the large dark rooms.

The following words and phrases tend to trigger the **imperfetto**:

da piccolo	*as a child*
di solito	*usually*
sempre	*always*
generalmente	*generally*
ogni giorno, estate	*every day, summer, etc.*
mentre	*while*

Other words tend to trigger the **passato prossimo** because they imply a completed event:

un giorno	*one day*
una volta	*once*
dieci anni fa	*ten years ago*

Forms of the **imperfetto**

The **imperfetto** suffix is formed by the first letter of the infinitive ending (**-are**, **-ere**, or **-ire**) followed by the **imperfetto** suffixes, which, after that first vowel, are the same for all three conjugations.

AMARE		LEGGERE		CAPIRE	
amavo	amavamo	leggevo	leggevamo	capivo	capivamo
amavi	amavate	leggevi	leggevate	capivi	capivate
amava	amavano	leggeva	leggevano	capiva	capivano

Most verbs are regular in the **imperfetto**—the few irregular verbs have the same stem as their irregular present tense, which then combines with the regular **imperfetto** suffixes as shown earlier.

INFINITIVE	PRESENT ROOT	IMPERFECT FIRST PERSON
bere	**bev**o	**bev**evo
dire	**dic**o	**dic**evo
fare	**facc**io	**fac**evo (Note: only one **c**)

The **imperfetto** form of **avere** is regular, but **essere** is irregular, as shown here. Notice how each form begins with **er** and that the suffix endings are similar but not the same as the **-are** conjugation. Take care to memorize this auxiliary verb correctly. The most common problem generally occurs with the forms that have no **v**.

ero	eravamo
eri	eravate
era	erano

Nota bene

Besides those previously described, there are several other uses of the **imperfetto**, such as after **ho visto** or **ho sentito** with a relative clause.

Ho sentito un programma **che parlava** di economia.
I heard a program that talked about economics.

Ho visto gli studenti **che studiavano** per l'esame.
I saw the students who were studying for the exam.

The **imperfetto** is also used to ask questions politely.

Volevo farLe una domanda.
I wanted to ask you (formal) a question.

Ti telefonavo per chiederti un favore.
I was calling to ask you a favor.

Mi domandavo se . . .
I was wondering if . . .

Imperfect or present perfect?

The use of the imperfect or the present perfect often depends on the nuances and meaning a speaker wants to express. Both of the following sentences are correct, but the different tenses convey a slightly different meaning.

Sapevo che Marco non era felice.	**Ho saputo** che Marco non era felice
I knew Marco wasn't happy.	*I found out that Marco wasn't happy.*

Change the following verbs from the **presente** into the **imperfetto**.

ESEMPIO   parla   *parlava*

1. diciamo   _____

2. bevete   _____

3. fanno   _____

4. sei   _____

5. faccio   _____

6. prende   _____

7. vieni   _____

8. c'è   _____

9. andiamo   _____

10. (loro) sono _____

Complete the sentences with the **imperfetto** or the **passato prossimo** of the given verb.

1. Da piccola io _____ (essere) molto timida.

2. Noi _____ (avere) un cane per molti anni.

3. _____ (fare) sempre caldo d'estate.

4. Di solito mia nonna _____ (andare) al mare.

5. Nell'estate del 2006 (io) _____ (vedere) la Tour Eiffel.

6. La casa _____ (sembrare) disabitata.

7. Charlie Chaplin _____ (fare) molti film.

8. Mio padre _____ (dire) sempre quello che _____ (pensare).

The past perfect (il trapassato prossimo)

The past perfect (**trapassato prossimo**) tense is used for activities that occurred before another activity in the past. This compound tense combines the auxiliary **avere** or **essere** in the imperfect tense with the past participle of the verb. Adverbs of frequency, such as **ancora** (*yet*), **già** (*already*), and **sempre** (*always*), are often used with this tense and are placed between the auxiliary and the participle.

Transitive verbs combine the auxiliary **avere** in the **imperfetto** + the past participle.

> A otto anni non **avevo** ancora **imparato** a nuotare.
> *At eight I **had not** yet **learned** how to swim.*

Intransitive verbs combine the auxiliary **essere** in the **imperfetto** + the past participle of the verb.

> Quando sono arrivata alla stazione di Milano, il treno per Como **era** già **partito**.
> *When I arrived at the Milan station, the train for Como **had** already **left**.*

ESERCIZIO
6·3

*Change the following verbs from the **presente** to the **trapassato prossimo**.*

ESEMPIO   arrivano   *erano arrivati*

1. partono   _____

2. mangiate   _____

3. ritorna   _____

4. sei   _____

5. va   _____

6. prendete   _____

7. dice   _____

8. chiediamo   _____

9. mettono   _____

10. studio   _____

Future and future perfect tenses

The future tense (**il futuro**) is used for actions that will take place in the future or may be taking place in the present (future of probability).

-ARE	-ERE	-IRE
parlerò	spenderò	dormirò
parlerai	spenderai	dormirai
parlerà	spenderà	dormirà
parleremo	spenderemo	dormiremo
parlerete	spenderete	dormirete
parleranno	spenderanno	dormiranno

Notice that the **-are** verbs change the **-a** of the infinitive to an **-e**, and that the suffixes are the same for all types of regular verbs. The first and third person singular is written with an accent on the final syllable in each conjugation.

The following words are commonly used with the **futuro**.

domani	*tomorrow*
dopodomani	*the day after tomorrow*
presto	*soon*
la settimana prossima	*next week*
il mese / l'anno prossimo	*next month / next year*
fra un anno	*in a year*
quando	*when*
appena	*as soon as*

The future of probability (**futuro di probabilità**) is used when speaking of an action that is possible or probable but not verified. It is used when making a guess or conjecture. This corresponds to the use of *must* in English.

Dove sono le tue chiavi?	*Where are your keys?*
Saranno vicino alla porta.	*They **must be** near the door.*

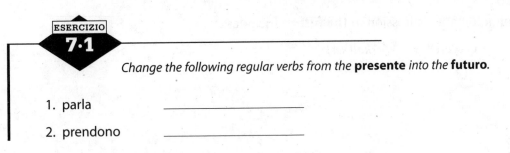

ESERCIZIO

7·1

*Change the following regular verbs from the **presente** into the **futuro**.*

1. parla   _____

2. prendono   _____

3. capite　　　_____

4. arrivo　　　_____

5. leggiamo　　_____

6. paga　　　　_____

7. mangiate　　_____

8. metto　　　 _____

9. arriviamo　 _____

10. dormono　　_____

Irregular verbs in the future tense (il futuro)

There are some verbs that change their stems in the future tense but have the same suffixes as the regular **futuro**. The best way to learn these is to carefully notice how the infinitive and the irregular stems compare.

Here is a list of common irregular verbs with a short description of their patterns:

DROPS THE THIRD-TO-LAST LETTER OF THE INFINITIVE	DROPS THE THIRD- AND FOURTH-TO-LAST LETTER OF THE INFINITIVE AND DOUBLES THE **R**
avere → avr-	rimanere → rimarr-
andare → andr-	tenere → terr-
cadere → cadr-	venire → verr-
dovere → dovr-	volere → vorr-
potere → potr-	
vedere → vedr-	
vivere → vivr-	
sapere → sapr-	

The **futuro** of the verbs **essere**, **dare**, **fare**, and **stare** is slightly irregular and is another subgroup that follows the same pattern.

essere (*to be*)	
sarò	saremo
sarai	sarete
sarà	saranno

dare → darò, etc.
fare → farò, etc.
stare → starò, etc.

Nota bene

A common idiomatic expression in the **futuro** includes:

Staremo a vedere!　　*We shall see!*

Un proverbio

Se son rose fioriranno.   *If they are roses, then they will bloom.* (This means that if something has promise it will eventually prove itself. The English version of this proverb is "time will tell.")

*Change the following sentences from the **presente** to the **futuro**.*

1. Lavoro domani.

   _____

2. Quando arriva l'inverno, andiamo in Sicilia.

   _____

3. Domani comincia la scuola.

   _____

4. Tu e Giovanni tornate l'anno prossimo?

   _____

5. Stasera resto a casa.

   _____

6. La settimana prossima arriva mia sorella!

   _____

7. Non vuole andare al concerto.

   _____

8. Sei qui per la festa?

   _____

9. Cosa fa quando finisce l'università?

   _____

10. Devo trovare un lavoro.

    _____

The future perfect tense (il futuro anteriore)

The future perfect (**il futuro anteriore**) is used to express an action in the future that will have already occurred by the time a second action takes place. It specifies which of two actions in the future happened first. In English, the present or future is often used, and which action precedes the other is understood through logic or context rather than a specific verb tense.

Quando avrò ventun'anni **mi sarò laureato**.
When I am twenty-one, ***I will have graduated***.

Since the **futuro anteriore** is unusual in English, most native English speakers would simply say:

Quando avrò ventun'anni, **mi laureerò**.
When I am twenty-one, ***I will graduate***.

The sentence using the **futuro anteriore** means:

When I turn twenty-one (**futuro**), *I will have* <u>already</u> *graduated* (**futuro anteriore**).

In the second example, the graduation occurs during the twenty-first year, while in the first example, the graduation will have already occurred by the twenty-first year. The second example is simpler, and in most cases is perfectly adequate to communicate an action in the future.

The **futuro anteriore** can also express a past action that is likely to have occurred. In English, this can be expressed with *must have* + verb.

Dove sono andati Roberto e Paolo?   *Where did Roberto and Paolo go?*
Saranno andati al cinema.   ***They must have gone** to the movies.*

ESERCIZIO
7·3

*Translate the following sentences into Italian, using the **futuro di probabilità**. When referring to a possibility in the present, use the **futuro** of the main verb. When referring to a possibility that may have already occurred, use the **futuro anteriore**.*

ESEMPIO   *They must be happy to be in Rome.*   <u>*Saranno contenti di essere a Roma.*</u>

    They probably missed the train.   <u>*Avranno perso il treno.*</u>

1. *Maria must be happy with her new job.*

   _____

2. *You probably met a lot of interesting people.* (**la gente**, singular)

   _____

3. *I must have left my book on the train.*

   _____

4. *The student must have missed the bus.*

   _____

5. *We must have seen a hundred films!*

   _____

6. *The Italian team must have won the game.*

   _____

7. *She probably has a lot of questions.*

   _____

8. He'll probably be back by 8:00.

_____

9. How much could I have slept?

_____

10. How much do you think it costs?

_____

Present and perfect conditional tenses

In English, the conditional is constructed with the auxiliary *would* + verb, while in Italian, it is a separate tense. **Vorrei** is probably the most frequently used conditional verb, and it is used to make polite requests. In Italian, the conditional has a present form (one word) and a past form (two words).

The present conditional (il condizionale)

The present conditional (**condizionale**) is used to express a wish, to give advice, and to make polite requests or suppositions. As with the **futuro**, the first letter of the **-are** ending changes to an **-e**, and the six suffixes are the same for all regular and irregular **-are**, **-ere**, and **-ire** verbs.

-ARE	-ERE	-IRE
parlerei	spenderei	dormirei
parleresti	spenderesti	dormiresti
parlerebbe	spenderebbe	dormirebbe
parleremmo	spenderemmo	dormiremmo
parlereste	spendereste	dormireste
parlerebbero	spenderebbero	dormirebbero

Study tip

When learning a new tense, look carefully at the patterns of the suffixes, noticing the details that distinguish it from other tenses. In the conditional, for example, the first person does not end in an **-o** (as it does in the present, imperfect, and future); the suffixes all start with the letter **-e**, and the third person singular and plural forms contain a double **b**. The patterns you notice yourself will help you anchor each tense in your memory, making them easier to retrieve and use automatically and without stopping to think as you speak.

Irregular verbs in the conditional

There are many verbs that change their stem in the **condizionale** and then combine with the regular suffix endings. The best way to learn these is to carefully notice how the infinitive and the irregular stem compare. Also remember that the **futuro** and the **condizionale** share the same irregular verbs.

Here is a list of the common irregular verbs in the **condizionale**, divided according to their distinctive patterns.

DROPS THE THIRD-TO-LAST LETTER OF THE INFINITIVE	DROPS THE THIRD- AND FOURTH-TO-LAST LETTER OF THE INFINITIVE AND DOUBLES THE **R**
avere → avr- andare → andr- cadere → cadr- dovere → dovr- potere → potr- vedere → vedr- vivere → vivr- sapere → sapr-	rimanere → rimarr- tenere → terr- venire → verr- volere → vorr-

Essere, dare, fare, and **stare** are another set of verbs that share a distinctive pattern. **Dare, fare**, and **stare** do *not* change the infinitive ending **-a** to an **-e**.

essere → sa + suffix

sarei	saremmo
saresti	sareste
sarebbe	sarebbero

dare → darei, etc.
fare → farei, etc.
stare → starei, etc.

Idiomatic expressions in the conditional

Come **sarebbe** a dire?
What do you mean? What are you talking about?

Ti **andrebbe** di andare al cinema?
How would you feel about going to the movies?

Faresti meglio a studiare un po' di più.
You would be better off studying a little more.

ESERCIZIO
8·1

*Change the following sentences from the **presente** to the **condizionale**.*

1. Voglio un bicchiere di acqua minerale per favore.

   _____

2. Va a studiare.

   _____

3. Andiamo in Francia.

   _____

4. È facile.

   _____

5. Vogliamo andare in vacanza.

_____

6. Sono contenti. (third person plural)

_____

7. Partite subito?

_____

8. Vai in Canada?

_____

9. Non faccio niente.

_____

10. Quando torni?

_____

The perfect conditional (il condizionale passato)

The perfect conditional (**condizionale passato**) is used for actions that would, could, or should have occurred in the past. It combines the auxiliary **avere** or **essere** in the **condizionale** + the participle of the verb.

> **Avrei telefonato** ma non avevo il tuo numero.
> *I **would have called** (you) but I didn't have your number.*

> **Avrebbero comprato** una casa più spaziosa.
> ***They would have bought** a more spacious home.*

> **Sarei arrivata** prima ma ho perso il treno.
> *I **would have arrived** earlier but I missed the train.*

To express *should have* + past or *could have* + past use the **condizionale passato** of **dovere** (*should*) and **potere** (*could*). The auxiliary of the main verb should be used to form compound tenses, although this distinction is not always made in common informal speech.

Avrei dovuto telefonare.	*I **should have** phoned.*
Sarei dovuto/a andare.	*I **should have** gone.*
Avrei potuto vincere.	*I **could have** won.*
Sarei potuto/a arrivare prima.	*I **could have arrived** earlier.*

For each phrase in column 1, choose the letter of the most logical conclusion from column 2.

1. Sarei andato al cinema _____
2. Avremmo mangiato una pizza _____
3. Avrei comprato una BMW _____
4. Ti saresti divertita alla festa _____
5. Sarebbero stati felici insieme _____
6. Avrebbe potuto vincere _____
7. Ti avrei telefonato _____
8. Avremmo voluto avvertirti _____
9. Ti avrei salutato _____

a. ma non ti ho riconosciuto.
b. ma non avevamo il cellulare.
c. ma non avevo il tuo numero.
d. ma era troppo distratto.
e. ma lui era troppo geloso.
f. ma il film era già cominciato.
g. ma la pizzeria era già chiusa.
h. ma costava troppo.
i. ma sei arrivata troppo tardi.

Choose the appropriate verb from the following list and change it to the **condizionale passato** to complete each sentence. There are two extra verbs.

andare   dovere   fare   vendere   cambiare

essere   avere   volere   rimanere   studiare

1. Stefania _____ economia ma non è molto brava in matematica.
2. Cameriere, _____ un caffè macchiato, per favore.
3. Giovanni _____ colazione al bar dietro casa, ma oggi è chiuso.
4. Io _____ al mercato, ma ormai è troppo tardi.
5. I miei amici _____ casa, ma si trovano bene in quel quartiere.
6. Senti, Marco, _____ studiare di più se vuoi superare il corso.
7. Scusi, _____ da cambiare 100 euro?
8. Tu e Valentina _____ liberi sabato sera per una cena da noi?

Make the following sentences more polite by using the **condizionale** *without changing the register (formal/informal).*

1. Mi dai una mano?

_____

2. Mi fa lo sconto, signora?

_____

3. Dottore, mi dà un appuntamento per domani?

_____

4. Signori, possono tornare domani?

_____

5. Marco, puoi chiamarmi domani?

_____

6. Vieni con me in Italia?

_____

7. Professore, è possibile rimandare l'esame fino a domani?

_____

8. Può ripetere la domanda, per favore?

_____

The subjunctive

·V-9·

The subjunctive construction is not used much any more in English, but in Italian it is used frequently in academic, political, or formal situations. There are certain phrases and words that trigger the use of the subjunctive and can easily be avoided by speakers who do not wish to use it until they are ready.

The subjunctive (il congiuntivo) with subordinate clauses

The subjunctive (**congiuntivo**) is used in subordinate clauses that express emotion, judgment, necessity, opinion, possibility, wishes, doubt, or an action that has not occurred. The independent clause is identifiable as a clause that can stand on its own. Here are some verbs and expressions that trigger, or make necessary, the use of the **congiuntivo**.

INDEPENDENT CLAUSE	SUBORDINATE CLAUSE
Penso	che Roberto **suoni** in un'orchestra.
I think	*that Roberto **plays** in an orchestra.*
Spero	che gli amici non **facciano** tardi.
I hope	*that my friends **are** not **late**.*
Sembra	che il tempo **migliori**.
It seems	*that the weather **is improving**.*
Dubito	che Gina **arrivi** puntuale.
I doubt	*that Gina **will be arriving** on time.*
Credo	che gli studenti **debbano** prima dare un esame.
I believe	*that the students **must** first take an exam.*
Temo	che Gianni **perda** il lavoro.
I fear	*that Gianni **will lose** his job.*
Ho paura	che il regalo non gli **piaccia**.
I am afraid	*that she doesn't **like** the gift.*

All the verbs in the independent clause indicate uncertainty, emotion, opinion, or doubt. The subordinate clause is always introduced by **che**, with the verb that follows in the **congiuntivo**.

The following expressions also trigger the subjunctive:

sebbene	*although*
purché	*as long as*
a condizione che	*provided that*
a meno che non	*unless*
senza che	*without*
è possibile che	*it is possible that*
è probabile che	*it is probable that*
senza che	*without + verb*
prima che	*before + verb*

Important: If the main clause uses a verb that expresses *certainty*, then the indicative is used. Here are some verbs that use the indicative rather than the **congiuntivo**.

So che il treno parte alle 3.00.	*I know the train is departing at 3:00.*
È certo che arriva domani.	*It is certain that he is arriving tomorrow.*
Ricordo che ha una casa molto bella.	*I remember that he has a beautiful home.*
È vero che torna stasera?	*Is it true that he's returning tonight?*
Dicono tutti che beve troppo.	*Everyone says he drinks too much.*

The four subjunctive tenses are present (**presente**), past (**passato**), imperfect (**imperfetto**), and past perfect (**trapassato**).

The present subjunctive is used after a main clause in the present tense if the action of both clauses occurs at the same time.

Penso che Luca **canti** molto bene.	*I think Luca sings very well.*

The first, second, and third person of the present subjunctive are identical, ending in **-i** for **-are** verbs and in **-a** for **-ere** and **-ire** verbs. As a result of the three identical forms, the subject pronoun can be added for clarity if the subject is not already in the sentence.

Penso che **lui** cant**i** molto bene.	*I think **he sings** very well.*

As you can see, the stems used in the present subjunctive are the same as those used in the present indicative.

-ARE	-ERE	-IRE
parl**i**	spend**a**	dorm**a**
parl**i**	spend**a**	dorm**a**
parl**i**	spend**a**	dorm**a**
parl**iamo**	spend**iamo**	dorm**iamo**
parl**iate**	spend**iate**	dorm**iate**
parl**ino**	spend**ano**	dorm**ano**

ESERCIZIO
9·1

Indicate the correct form of the present subjunctive in each sentence, and then translate the sentences into English.

1. Credo che Mara (parli / parla) il francese.

2. Penso che Letizia (insegni / insegno) l'inglese.

_____

3. Dubito che Eleonora mi (chiede / chieda) scusa.

_____

4. Non è possibile che tu (dici / dica) sempre le bugie (*lies*)!

_____

5. Sebbene Maria (guadagni / guadagna) molto, è sempre senza soldi.

_____

6. Credo che quel ragazzo si (chiama / chiami) Andrea.

_____

7. Penso che Gaia e Jim (vedono / vedano) molti film francesi.

_____

8. Voglio parlarti prima che tu (decidi / decida) di lasciare il lavoro.

_____

9. Sembra che Sandro (parla / parli) spesso di te.

_____

10. Non voglio che (pagate / paghiate) sempre voi!

_____

Present subjunctive of irregular verbs

The three irregular verbs **essere**, **dare**, and **stare** have similar forms in the present subjunctive, so they are more easily learned together. As with the regular present subjunctive verbs, the first, second, and third person singular are the same.

ESSERE	DARE	STARE
sia	**dia**	**stia**
siamo	diamo	stiamo
siate	diate	stiate
siano	diano	stiano

Avere and **andare** are also irregular in the present subjunctive and, as all verbs in this tense, the first three persons are the same. Notice how the subjunctive of **andare** and **capire** use the same stems as the present indicative. This similarity with the present indicative also applies to **-isc** verbs, which omit it in the first and second person plural.

AVERE	ANDARE	CAPIRE
abbia	vada	capisca
abbiamo	andiamo	capiamo
abbiate	andiate	capiate
abbiano	vadano	capiscano

ESERCIZIO
9·2

Complete the chart with the missing forms of the present subjunctive.

ESSERE	AVERE	PARLARE	PRENDERE	FINIRE
sia	_____	_____	_____	finisca
_____	abbiamo	_____	_____	_____
_____	_____	parliate	_____	_____
_____	_____	_____	prendano	_____

The past subjunctive

If the action of the subordinate clause has taken place *before* the action of the independent clause, the past subjunctive will be used. In both sentences below, the subordinate clause describes an event that has already occurred.

> Penso che Lucia **sia andata** a Roma.   (Remember the agreement!)
> *I think Lucia **has gone** to Rome.*
>
> Penso che Paolo **abbia fatto** l'esame.
> *I think Paolo **took** the exam.*

Similar to other compound tenses, the past subjunctive combines the present subjunctive of **avere** (if transitive) or of **essere** (if intransitive), followed by the past participle of the verb. As always, with **essere**, the participle agrees with the subject in gender and number.

The imperfect subjunctive (**congiuntivo imperfetto**) is used when the main clause is not in the present but in the past, imperfect, or conditional tenses. Look at the regular forms below and notice how all the suffixes after the **-a**, **-e**, or **-i** of the stem are the same for the three conjugations (**-ssi**, **-sse**, **-ssimo**, **-ste**, **-ssero**). The stress of the **congiuntivo imperfetto** always falls on the **-a**, **-e**, or **-i** before the suffix.

-ARE	-ERE	-IRE
parlassi	spendessi	dormissi
parlassi	spendessi	dormissi
parlasse	spendesse	dormisse
parlassimo	spendessimo	dormissimo
parlaste	spendeste	dormiste
parlassero	spendessero	dormissero

The auxiliaries **avere** and **essere**

Avere is regular and **essere** is irregular in the imperfect subjunctive. Notice how the irregular stem **fo-** is combined with the **congiuntivo imperfetto** endings **-ssi**, **-sse**, **-ssimo**, **-ste**, **-ssero**.

Verbs such as **bere**, **dire**, and **fare** (with only one **c**) use the same stem as in the present indicative.

ESSERE

fossi	fossimo
fossi	foste
fosse	fossero

The past perfect (or pluperfect) subjunctive (il congiuntivo trapassato)

This is formed with the **congiuntivo imperfetto** of the auxiliary verbs **essere** (if intransitive) or **avere** (if transitive) and the past participle of the verb. It is used in subordinate clauses following the independent clause in the imperfect indicative (**l'imperfetto**), conditional (**il condizionale**), or any past tense. Since the first and second person singular forms are identical, there are only five forms to learn.

(io, tu)	avessi parlato	avessi veduto	avessi capito
(lui/lei, Lei)	avesse parlato	avesse veduto	avesse capito
(noi)	avessimo parlato	avessimo veduto	avessimo capito
(voi)	aveste parlato	aveste veduto	aveste capito
(loro)	avessero parlato	avessero veduto	avessero capito

As always, the intransitive verbs **andare**, **essere**, **venire**, **tornare**, etc., use the auxiliary **essere** and the participle ending agrees with subject in gender and number.

(io, tu)	fossi andato/a
(lui/lei, Lei)	fosse andato/a
(noi)	fossimo andati/e
(voi)	foste andati/e
(loro)	fossero andati/e

When the main clause is in the conditional or any past tense, the following subordinate clause must be either in the **imperfetto** or **congiuntivo trapassato**. The chart that follows will clarify the relationship between the two clauses.

MAIN CLAUSE	SUBORDINATE CLAUSE	TENSE
present, future, imperative	same time	present subjunctive
	already occurred	past subjunctive
past tense, imperfect, conditional	same time	imperfect subjunctive
	already occurred	past perfect subjunctive

In English, the subjunctive is often used with the verb *to wish*, and the time relationship (whether or not the action of the subordinate clause is simultaneous or has already occurred) is also expressed. The following chart illustrates the time relationship between the two clauses. The base sentences in English are:

INDEPENDENT CLAUSE	SUBORDINATE CLAUSE
I wish	*that Roberto **were** in Rome.*
I wish	*that Roberto **had been** in Rome.*

I wished	*that Roberto **were** in Rome.*	
I wished	*that Roberto **had been** in Rome.*	

Now let us look at the Italian version of a similar sentence:

INDEPENDENT CLAUSE	SUBORDINATE CLAUSE	TENSE
Penso	che Roberto **sia** a Roma.	C. presente (*present subjunctive*)
	che Roberto **sia stato** a Roma.	C. passato (*past subjunctive*)
Pensavo	che Roberto **fosse** a Roma.	C. imperfetto (*imperfect subjunctive*)
	che Roberto **fosse stato** a Roma.	C. trapassato (*past perfect subjunctive*)

Nota bene

Remember that if the action in the two clauses is simultaneous, the subordinate clause *will not* include the past participle. When expressing a prior action, the subordinate clause will include the past participle. There are often other clue words in the sentence that will indicate whether the action has already occurred (**già** *already*), time references such as **la settimana, il mese, l'anno scorso, stamattina, ieri** (*last week, last month, last year, this morning, yesterday*), or that the action has yet to occur (**domani, la settimana, il mese, l'anno prossimo** *tomorrow, next week, next month, next year*).

Also, remember that if the main clause expresses certainty (*I know, I was told, I am sure*, etc.), the subjunctive mood is not to be used.

◆ ESERCIZIO
9·3

Complete the sentences with the appropriate verbs. Some sentences state a fact and will use the indicative.

1. Pensavo che Riccardo Muti _____ (venire) a Chicago l'anno scorso.

2. Mi hanno detto che (tu) _____ (partire) presto stamattina.

3. Tutti sanno che _____ (vincere) la Roma.

4. Speravo che _____ (vincere) i Cubs (plurale).

5. Sai che Nina _____ (partire) domani?

6. Vorrei che mi (loro) _____ (dire) tutto.

7. Pensi che loro _____ (andare) in l'Italia l'anno scorso?

8. Pensavo che l'università _____ (essere) più difficile.

9. Ho paura che domani _____ (piovere).

10. Non immaginavo che tu _____ (avere) paura di volare.

The imperative

·V-10·

The imperative (**imperativo**) is most commonly used to make a suggestion or to give advice and to issue a warning or a command. An imperative sentence is often written with an exclamation point and may consist of only one word. It is common to add **per favore**, **per piacere**, or **per cortesia**, all of which mean *please*, to make the command more courteous.

The following chart illustrates the imperative forms. Notice that the imperative is never use in the first-person singular.

(tu)	Guarda!	Prendi!	Senti!
(Lei, *formal*)	Guardi!	Prenda!	Senta!
(noi)	Guardiamo!	Prendiamo!	Sentiamo!
(voi)	Guardate!	Prendete!	Sentite!
(loro)*	Guardino!	Prendano!	Sentano!

---

*The use of the third-person plural formal is rare in current Italian. The **voi** form is preferred.

When using the **imperativo** with a direct- or indirect-object pronoun, it attaches to the end of the verb in all cases *except* for the formal, where it precedes the verb.

> Prendi i libri! → Prendi**li**!
> *Take the books! → Take them!*

but

> Signorina, prenda i libri! → **Li** prenda!

The negative imperative (**imperativo negativo**) in the **tu** form is very simple. **Non** precedes the infinitive form of the verb.

> Non fumare!   *Don't smoke!*

In all other persons, the negative is expressed by placing **non** before the conjugated verb.

> Non partiamo domani, partiamo   *Let's not leave tomorrow,*
>   oggi!   *let's leave today!*
> Vi prego, non lasciate la cucina   *I'm begging you, don't leave*
>   in disordine!   *the kitchen in a mess!*

Nota bene

Common idioms that use the imperative:

IDIOMATIC PHRASE	
Non mi seccare!	*Don't bother me!*
Non ci provare!	*Don't you dare!*

ESERCIZIO
10·1

*A friend is having a dinner party and needs your advice. Use the **imperativo** to make suggestions, with direct-object pronouns whenever necessary.*

1. Posso invitare il tuo ex? Per favore, non _____!

2. Che cosa preparo da mangiare? _____ gli spaghetti alla carbonara!

3. Chi posso invitare? _____ Marco ed Elena!

4. Che cosa mi metto? _____ il tuo vestito nero!

5. Cosa dico al mio compagno di stanza? _____ di venire anche lui!

6. Quando faccio i compiti? _____ domani mattina!

7. Faccio anche una torta alla cioccolata? Sì, _____!

8. Beviamo lo champagne? Sì, _____!

ESERCIZIO
10·2

*Change the following verbs from the informal to the formal **imperativo**.*

1. Prendi il telefono! _____

2. Compra il latte! _____

3. Non tornare tardi! _____

4. Salutate i nostri amici! _____

5. Non ti preoccupare! _____

6. Fa' pure! _____

7. Entra! _____

8. Torna presto a trovarmi! _____

9. Accomodati! _____

10. Calmati! _____

Using the informal **imperativo**, make these suggestions to a friend.

1. Let's have a party! _____

2. Don't eat all the pizza! _____

3. Come back! _____

4. Let's study together! _____

5. Call your mother! _____

6. Close the door! _____

7. Open the window! _____

8. Be careful! _____

9. Don't be late! _____

10. Write soon! _____

Suggest to your Italian professor the following, using the formal **imperativo**.

1. Please speak more slowly.

_____

2. Please repeat the question.

_____

3. Please give me two more days.

_____

4. Please be patient! (**avere pazienza**)

_____

5. Please don't get angry with the students.

_____

6. Please speak a little louder.

_____

7. Please open the window.

_____

8. *Please show us that movie.*

   _____

9. *Please don't smoke in class!*

   _____

10. *Please answer our messages!*

    _____

Prepositions

Prepositions are words placed before (pre-posed) words or phrases to show how they are related. In Italian there are simple prepositions (one word) and combined prepositions (preposition + article).

> Sono andata **al** cinema **con** le mie amiche **in** bicicletta.
> *I went **to** the movies **with** my friends **on** my bike.*

Simple prepositions

Simple prepositions clarify the relationship between two elements in a phrase. There are eight simple prepositions:

> a
> su
> da
> di
> in
> per
> con
> tra / fra

The first five, when followed by a definite article, combine with the article to form combined prepositions. We will look first at how and when simple prepositions are used.

Most prepositions have several meanings and their use differs from one language to another. Learning them in the context of small phrases will help you use them fluently and correctly.

The preposition a

The preposition **a** is used:

♦ before an indirect object

dare **a** Cesare	scrivere **a** Roberto
to give to Caesar	*to write to Roberto*

♦ after verbs indicating being or movement toward or within places

Abito **a** Roma.	Andiamo **a** Napoli.	Quando arrivate **a** Venezia?
I live in Rome.	*Let's go to Naples.*	*When are you arriving in Venice?*

567

◆ to link the conjugated verb *to go* with an infinitive verb

Oggi Mario non va **a** lavorare. Andiamo **a** vedere Mamma Roma!
Today Mario is not going to work. *Let's go see Mamma Roma!*

Nota bene

When the preposition **a** is followed by a vowel, it may be changed to **ad**, especially when that vowel is an **–a**, so as to make both **a**'s audible. This is optional, but in central and northern Italy, it is still preferred.

Lavoro **ad** Ancona. Hanno telefonato **ad** Alessandra.

The preposition **con**

The preposition **con** is used to combine elements in a phrase, just as *with* is used in English.

Prendo il gelato **con** le fragole. Andiamo al mare **con** Isabella.
I'll take the ice cream with strawberries. *We're going to the beach with Isabella.*

The preposition **da**

The preposition **da** is used:

◆ to express movement away from or distance from a place

Il treno parte **da** Roma alle 2.00. *The train is leaving from Rome at 2:00.*
Abito a un chilometro **da** Firenze. *I live a kilometer away from Florence.*

◆ with verbs in the present tense to indicate an amount of time from the past to the present

Abito a Roma **da** cinque anni. *I have been living in Rome for five years.*

◆ with a proper name, meaning *at*, to indicate a restaurant or someone's home

da Giordano **da** Cipriani **da** mamma
Giordano's *Cipriani's* *to mom's house*

◆ with articles of clothing to describe their particular use

scarpe **da** tennis tuta **da** ginnastica costume **da** bagno
tennis shoes *gym clothes* *swimsuit*

◆ with **niente** or **qualcosa** + infinitive

niente **da** fare qualcosa **da** mangiare
nothing to do *something to eat*

The preposition **di**

The preposition **di** is used:

◆ to indicate possession and city of origin

il libro **di** Davide la voce **di** mia madre
David's book *my mother's voice*

Sono **di** Roma.
I am from Rome.

◆ with a specific quantity (after the container, volume, weight, etc.)

una bottiglia **di** vino bianco	un litro **di** latte
a bottle of white wine	*a liter of milk*

◆ for quantities of a million or billion

un milione **di** euro	un miliardo **di** anni fa
a million euros	*a billion years ago*

◆ to describe what something is made of (a material or fabric)

un vestito **di** lino	un cucchiaio **d'**argento	una giacca **di** pelle
a linen dress	*a silver spoon*	*a leather jacket*

The preposition **in**

The preposition **in** is used before a country, region, continent, rooms of the house, street names, piazzas, means of transportation, seasons, and months and to indicate institutional buildings.

in Francia	in Toscana	in Europa
in France	*in Tuscany*	*in Europe*

in giugno	in estate	in cucina
in June	*in the summer*	*in the kitchen*

The preposition **per**

The preposition **per** is used to express purpose or function.

Sono in Italia **per** studiare la musica.	Usiamo la macchina **per** viaggiare.
I am in Italy to study music.	*We use the car to travel.*

The preposition **su**

The preposition **su** is generally used in reference to a location, as in English.

Vorrei abitare **su** un isola.	Ho messo le foto **su** Facebook.
I want to live on an island.	*I put the pictures on Facebook.*

The prepositions **tra / fra**

The prepositions **tra / fra** are interchangeable and mean *between* when indicating location or a time in the future.

La banca è **tra** la libreria e il supermercato.
The bank is between the bookstore and the supermarket.

Arrivo **fra** due ore.
I'll be arriving in two hours.

Proverbio

Tra il dire e il fare c'è di mezzo il mare.
Between saying and doing there is the sea.

What is the closest English version of this proverb?

Match the phrases with the most logical prepositional phrases to complete each sentence.

1. Ogni estate vado _____   a. per studiare architettura.

2. Lavoro a Roma, ma abito _____   b. tra il ristorante e la libreria.

3. Ieri sera sono tornato _____   c. di Roberto.

4. Questo libri sono _____   d. a Firenze.

5. Il mio ufficio è _____   e. in Italia per un mese.

6. Marco è italiano, _____   f. a casa tardi.

7. Sono a Venezia _____   g. ma vive a New York.

8. Questa camicia è _____   h. di Carla fa la cantante.

9. La madre _____   i. da Roma?

10. Viterbo è lontano _____   j. di cotone.

Complete the sentences with the appropriate prepositions.

1. Mia sorella abita _____ via Mantova 16, _____ un palazzo elegante.

2. Quando sono _____ Italia, preferisco viaggiare _____ treno.

3. Quell'attrice è _____ Glasgow, ma vive _____ New York _____ il marito e il figlio.

4. Mamma, c'è qualcosa _____ mangiare e _____ bere _____ casa?

5. Perché vuoi andare _____ America? _____ lavoro?

6. Tuo nonno ha cominciato _____ lavorare _____ dodici anni!

7. Quest'estate vado _____ Capri e _____ Sardegna, e poi parto _____ il Brasile.

8. Mio marito insegna _____ settembre _____ giugno.

9. L'aereo parte _____ mezzora!

10. Ho telefonato _____ Marco un'ora fa.

Prepositions in other roles

Some prepositions can also function as adverbs, adjectives, and verbs. The following words are prepositions only when they are followed by a noun, an adjective, or another preposition. As prepositions, they are invariable.

attraverso	*through*
durante	*during*
entro	*by (a certain amount of time)*
salvo, tranne	*except*
meno	*less*
secondo	*according*
lungo	*along*
malgrado	*despite*

Since some of the preceding prepositions also double as adjectives, it is important to identify what is being described in order to use them correctly.

Cammino **lungo** (prep.) la strada.   Il Pò è il fiume più **lungo** (adj.) d'Italia.
I walk along the road.   *The Pò is the longest river in Italy.*

The following prepositions are generally followed by a noun, either explicitly or implied:

contro il muro   **dentro** casa   **dietro** il ristorante
against the wall   *inside the house*   *behind the restaurant*

senza sale   **verso** sera
without salt   *towards evening*

When these prepositions are followed by a personal pronoun, **di** is added before the pronoun.

contro di me   **dentro** di noi   **dietro** di te   **senza** di me   **verso** di lui
against me   *inside us*   *behind you*   *without me*   *toward him*

Other prepositions require **a**, **da**, or **di** when followed by a noun or pronoun. I recommend learning these as phrases rather than as separate words.

accanto a	*next to*
davanti a	*in front of*
rispetto a	*regarding*
grazie a	*thanks to*
insieme a / con	*together with*
fino a	*until*
vicino a	*near to*
lontano da	*far from*
prima di	*before*
invece di	*instead of*

Some prepositional phrases consist of two prepositions. These too are better learned as phrases.

in mezzo a	*in the midst of*
in base a	*based on*
in cima a	*at the top of*
in seguito a	*following*
al di là di	*beyond*
a causa di	*because of*
a destra / sinistra di	*to the right / left of*
a eccezione di	*except for*

Combined prepositions (le preposizioni articolate)

When the prepositions **di**, **in**, **a**, **da**, and **su** are followed by a definite article, they combine with the article and form a single word, as shown in this table:

	il	lo	l'	la	i	gli	le
a	al	allo	all'	alla	ai	agli	alle
di	del	dello	dell'	della	dei	degli	delle
da	dal	dallo	dall'	dalla	dai	dagli	dalle
in	nel	nello	nell'	nella	nei	negli	nelle
su	sul	sullo	sull'	sulla	sui	sugli	sulle
con	col				coi		

Nota bene

1. The prepositions **a**, **da**, and **su** do not change their spelling when they combine.
2. The prepositions **di** and **in** change to **de** and **ne** before combining with the definite article.
3. All the other articles simply combine with the proposition, and whenever the article begins with **-l**, it is doubled.
4. The preposition **con** may combine with the article by dropping the **-n**; however, this form is slowly disappearing in spoken Italian. It appears mainly in opera librettos or literary works.

Prepositions and idiomatic expressions

Prepositional phrases are often used idiomatically and seem to be more difficult to translate into English than other words. They cannot always be translated literally into English. These phrases are said to be "crystalized," or fixed, since they cannot be changed. They are typical of native and informal speech, and you should try to use them whenever possible. Here is a list to get you started. A close Italian equivalent is given in the second column.

IDIOMATIC EXPRESSION	EQUIVALENT EXPRESSION	ENGLISH TRANSLATION
di buon'ora	presto	*early*
di gran lunga	moltissimo	*by far*
di punto in bianco	all'improvviso	*suddenly*
a bruciapelo	velocemente	*point-blank*
andare a finire	concludersi	*to end up*
a lungo andare	dopo molto tempo	*in the long run*
a mala pena	con difficoltà	*barely*
a quattr'occhi	privatamente	*in private*
alla buona	semplicemente	*simply*
in gamba	con molte qualità	*to have your act together*
con le mani in mano	senza fare niente	*idle, not lifting a finger*
su due piedi	immediatamente	*at once, quickly*
su per giù	all'incirca	*more or less*
sulle spine	nervoso, preoccupato	*worried*
darsi da fare	prendere iniziativa	*to get busy*
faccio per dire	voglio dire	*I mean*
stare per	accingersi a	*to be about to*

ESERCIZIO
11·3

Combine the prepositions with the articles.

1. L'albergo è vicino (a + la) _____ chiesa.

2. Non mettere i gomiti (*elbows*) (su + il) _____ tavolo!

3. Quel negozio apre (a + le) _____ 9.00.

4. E chiuso (da + le) _____ 14.00 (a + le) _____ 16.00.

5. La pensione è aperta (da + il) _____ mese di giugno.

6. Dante nacque (in + il) _____ 1265.

7. Non camminare (su + i) _____ fiori!

8. Gli animali non stanno bene (a + lo) _____ zoo.

ESERCIZIO
11·4

Fill in the blanks with the correct simple or combined prepositions, as needed.

1. Vado _____ casa presto perché sono stanca.

2. Ci vediamo _____ stazione?

3. C'è un bel film _____ cinema Rialto _____ mezzanotte.

4. Vado _____ lavoro in autobus, ma quando fa bello vado _____ piedi.

5. Se vuoi spendere di meno è meglio andare _____ pizzeria.

6. Ci sono moltissime fontane _____ Roma.

7. Vuoi venire _____ Sicilia con noi? Possiamo andare tutti _____ mia zia.

8. Voglio stare _____ spiaggia _____ mattina _____ sera!

Problematic prepositions

It is an unfortunate truth that the smaller words such as articles and prepositions tend to cause the most problems for learners of Italian. Memorizing common prepositions in the context of short phrases will help them "stick," and as you notice new phrases you can make a list so that they will come to mind more easily as you speak.

a casa	*at home*
a teatro	*to the theater*
a piedi	*on foot*
a scuola	*to school*
a letto	*to bed*
in Italia	*to Italy*
in treno	*by train*
in cucina	*in the kitchen*

in realtà	*actually*
in effetti	*actually*
in ogni caso	*in any case*
tra noi/fra noi	*between us*
da Giovanni	*to Giovanni's place, home*
da piccolo/a	*as a child*
scarpe da tennis	*tennis shoes*
molto da fare	*a lot to do*
qualcosa da bere	*something to drink*
di Roberto	*Roberto's*
di mattina	*in the morning*
di sera	*in the evening*
di solito	*usually*
di niente	*don't mention it*

ESERCIZIO 11·5

Review the preceding list, and then translate the following common phrases from English to Italian on your own. Check the answer key; mark the ones you missed and review them again.

1. *I am going by bike.*

_____

2. *I usually eat early.*

_____

3. *I live in Rome.*

_____

4. *Let's go to Silvio's place.*

_____

5. *I am going on foot.*

_____

6. *It's 8:00 in the morning.*

_____

7. *I have a lot to do.*

_____

8. *I actually prefer sparkling water.*

_____

9. *Don't mention it!*

_____

10. *He was very blonde as a child.*

_____

The following sentences contain a number of incorrect prepositions (number noted in parentheses). Find the errors and correct them. Check the answer key for accuracy. For extra practice, translate them into English and then back into Italian. Compare your translations with the answer key and indicate the errors.

1. Abito in Roma, e vado a lavoro nella metropolitana (*subway*). (2)

   _____

   _____

2. Studia quasi sempre nel salotto. (1)

   _____

   _____

3. Sei tornata alla casa tardi? (1)

   _____

   _____

4. Stasera andiamo al teatro. (1)

   _____

   _____

5. Parto a Roma nell'aereo. (2)

   _____

   _____

6. Vado in casa della mia sorella. (2) (**Nota:** Sentence can be reduced to four words.)

   _____

   _____

7. Perché hai messo le scarpe per tennis? (1)

   _____

   _____

8. Domani pomeriggio ho un appuntamento al dentista. (1)

   _____

   _____

9. Gli italiani non vanno sempre nella chiesa. (1)

   _____

   _____

10. Vuoi qualcosa per mangiare? (1)

_____

_____

Read aloud the following sentences several times. Prepositions and idioms that often cause errors are in boldface. You can expand this exercise by repeating the sentences in the negative and changing the tenses and subjects, until the highlighted elements become automatic.

1. **Fanno** colazione a casa.　　　　　　_They have breakfast at home._

2. **Faccio** un bagno caldo.　　　　　　_I take a hot bath._

3. Perché **fai** sempre tardi?　　　　　　_Why are you always late?_

4. **Escono di** casa presto.　　　　　　_They leave the house early._

5. **Prendo** un caffè la mattina.　　　　_I have a coffee in the morning._

6. Ho **un sacco da** fare.　　　　　　_I have a lot of stuff to do._

7. **Finisce di** lavorare tardi.　　　　　_She finishes work late._

8. **Andiamo in** palestra?　　　　　　_Shall we go to the gym?_

9. Come **va**?　　　　　　　　　　　_How is it going?_

10. Mi vesto **in fretta**.　　　　　　　_I get dressed in a hurry._

Translate the following words and phrases, but be careful!

1. _something to drink_

_____

2. _usually_

_____

3. _by train_

_____

4. _in Venice_

_____

5. _a lot to do_

_____

6. *actually*

_____

7. *between us*

_____

8. *in any case*

_____

9. *on foot*

_____

10. *at my place*

_____

Pronouns

There are many types of pronouns, and their main function is to replace nouns (*pronoun* means "in place of" or "for the noun") to avoid repetition and to simplify the discourse. In this section, we will discuss subject and object pronouns in their unstressed forms, which generally precede the verb, as well as the emphatic forms, which generally follow the verb or preposition.

Subject pronouns

In English, the subject pronoun is almost always expressed, since most regular verbs do not conjugate at all, except for the third person singular.

In Italian, however, the subject pronoun is generally omitted, since the subject is also expressed through the verb ending. Having both the subject pronoun and the verb ending, therefore, is redundant and is simplified by dropping the pronoun.

io	*I*	noi	*we*
tu	*you*	voi	*you (plural)*
lui/lei, Lei (*formal*)	*she, he, it, you (formal)*	loro, Loro	*they, you (formal)*

There are, however, some cases when the subject pronoun is used:

1. when the pronoun is being emphasized or to avoid ambiguity or confusion. In English speech, this is done by emphasizing the pronoun with the voice, and in writing, it is underlined or put it in italics.

2. after the word **anche**, which means *also*

   Anch'**io** vengo al cinema!

3. in questions—the pronoun is sometimes added at the end of the sentence

4. to replace a whole verb phrase

   Vengo anch'*io!*   No, tu no!
   I'm coming, too!   *No, you're not!*

   Sto bene, e **tu**?
   I'm well, and you?

If you leave out the subject pronouns in the following Italian sentences, the meaning and emphasis change slightly. Emphasis is frequently used in irony and humor, and learning when to use the pronouns will make your Italian more native and idiomatic. When the pronouns are used, they can be emphasized further as follows:

♦ by putting them after the verb, as in example 2, or at the end of a question, as in example 3

    1. **Io** cucino, mentre **lui** si rilassa.   *I cook, while **he** takes it easy.*
    2. Sono stati **loro** a farlo.   *They're the ones who did it.*
    3. Francesco, sei proprio **tu**?   *Francesco, is it really **you**?*

♦ after **come** or **quanto** (**io** and **tu** are replaced by **me** and **te**)

    Ho studiato quanto **lui**.   Siamo partiti presto come **voi**.
    *I studied as much as **he**.*   *We left as early as **you**.*

♦ after the words **anche** (**pure**), **neanche** (**neppure**), **nemmeno**, and **proprio**

    Anch'**io** parto con quel volo.   Neanche **lui** vuole andare alla festa.
    I'm also leaving on the same flight.   *He doesn't want to go to the party either.*

♦ in exclamations and phrases without a verb (**io** and **tu** are replaced by **me** and **te**)

    Beato **lui**! Povera **te**!   Chi ha vinto? **Lui**.
    Lucky him! Poor me!   *Who won? He did.*

When using the formal **Lei** or **Loro** in writing, it is generally capitalized for clarity. The plural formal **Loro** is gradually disappearing and being replaced by **voi**.

ESERCIZIO
12·1

Add the correct subject pronoun in the following sentences.

1. Anche _____ vogliono fare un viaggio in Messico.

2. Neanch' _____ uso macchina. Preferisco andare a piedi o in bicicletta.

3. Questa volta offro _____!

4. Vieni alla festa anche _____?

5. Perché non vanno anche _____ in Italia?

6. Come state _____ e tuo marito?

7. È vero che _____ è una scrittrice molto famosa?

8. Come si chiama _____? Si chiama Marcello.

9. Scusi, ma _____ come si chiama? (*formal*)

Direct-object pronouns

A direct object is a noun that is directly affected by the action of the verb. It usually follows the verb directly, without a preposition, and identifies the thing or person being acted upon. It answers the question *What . . . ?* or *Whom . . . ?* (in colloquial English *Who . . . ?*)

    *What are you reading? I am reading an **article** by my professor.*
    *Whom (who) are you inviting? I am inviting **Giorgia**.*

The nouns that immediately follow the verbs in the above examples are direct objects of the verb. When referring back to these nouns, instead of repeating them again and again, one can replace them with direct-object pronouns. This avoids useless repetition of the nouns and greatly simplifies communication. Look at the following conversation and notice how the noun **articolo** *(article)* is referred to in the second sentence.

> **Cosa** leggi?
> *What are you reading?*

> Leggo un **articolo** del mio professore. (**Articolo** is the direct object.)
> *I'm reading an **article** by my professor.*

> Anch'io **lo** voglio leggere. (The pronoun **lo** replaces the noun **articolo**.)
> *I want to read **it**, too.*

> **Chi** inviti a cena?
> *Who/whom are you inviting to dinner?*

> Invito **Giorgia**. (**Giorgia** is the direct object.)
> *I'm inviting **Giorgia**.*

> **La** inviti anche al cinema? (The direct-object pronoun **la** replaces the direct object **Giorgia**.)
> *Are you inviting **her** to the movies, too?*

For many learners, replacing the object with a pronoun can be challenging. In English, *it* replaces all inanimate things, and speakers do not have to think of these nouns as feminine or masculine. Another problem is how the word order changes when object pronouns are introduced. In English, the direct-object pronoun always comes after the verb. As you can see in the Italian examples above, the object pronoun goes before the verb. Practice and repetition will eventually lead to a smooth and automatic use of these pronouns.

A good way to learn the direct-object pronouns is to observe them carefully and to look for patterns. First of all, you may notice that they are two letters long, and that the first and second person pronouns **mi**, **ti**, **ci**, and **vi** all end with the letter **-i** and are identical to the reflexive pronouns. You may also notice that only the third person pronouns reflect gender and number, with the same final vowels used in nouns and adjectives, **-o**, **-a**, **-i**, and **-e**. By noticing these patterns and finding others on your own, you will find that they will be securely anchored in your memory and will be there when you need to use them.

mi	*me*
ti	*you*
lo/la	*it, her/him*
ci	*us*
vi	*you*
li/le	*them*

When used with an infinitive verb, the pronoun attaches to the end of the verb, which drops the final **-e**.

> È importante studiare i pronomi.   È importante studiar**li**.   *It is important to study them.*

But with the modal verbs **dovere**, **volere**, and **potere** + infinitive, the pronoun can either precede the conjugated modal or attach to the infinitive.

> Voglio salutar**lo**.   *or*   **Lo** voglio salutare.   *I want to greet him.*

Only the singular pronouns **lo** and **la** may elide with a word that starts with a vowel or a silent **h**.

> Romeo l'ama.   L'hanno visto a Verona.
> *Romeo loves her.*   *They saw him in Verona.*

Extra challenge

When used with a compound tense, the participle must agree with the third person direct-object pronouns **lo**, **la**, **li**, **le**, and **ne** in gender and number. The agreement with the other persons is optional and is gradually disappearing. Agreement does not occur with indirect-object pronouns.

Dove hai comprato quelle **scarpe**?
Where did you buy those shoes?

Le ho comprat**e** a Milano.
I bought them in Milan.

Hai invitato Liliana?
Did you invite Liliana?

Sì, l'ho invitat**a**, ma non **le ho detto** che veniva il suo ex.
Yes, I invited her, but didn't tell her that her ex-boyfriend was coming.

ESERCIZIO
12·2

Answer the questions using a direct-object pronoun. For an extra challenge, recast the question in the **passato prossimo**, *remembering the agreement with the participle in the response.*

ESEMPIO   Compri la pasta?
Sì, _la_ compro.
Hai comprato la pasta?
Sì, l'ho comprata.

1. Vedi le tue amiche questo weekend? Sì, _____ vedo.

_____? _____

2. Studi la matematica? No, non _____ studio.

_____? _____

3. Guardi la TV? No, non _____ guardo.

_____? _____

4. Parli il cinese in classe? Sì, _____ parlo.

_____? _____

5. Leggi i giornali italiani? Sì, _____ leggo.

_____? _____

Indirect-object pronouns

In some sentences, the noun object indicates not what but *to whom* or *for whom* the action is being carried out. In Italian, the indirect-object nouns are preceded by the prepositions **a** or **per**, which indicate the object as indirect. As recipients, indirect objects are usually people or living things. The pronouns that replace them are identical to the direct-object pronouns, except for the third person forms as shown below. Like the other pronouns, they precede the conjugated verb and attach to the infinitive verb. When used with the modal verbs **dovere**, **potere**, and **volere**, the pronouns can either go before the conjugated verb or attach to the infinitive.

to me	mi	to us	ci
to you	ti	to you all	vi
to him	gli (*m.*)	to them	gli (*m.* + *f.*) (*loro)
to her	le (*f.*)		

*In contemporary speech, the third person plural form **loro** has been replaced by **gli**.

How important is it to be able to distinguish a direct object from an indirect object? Since both types of pronouns share the same forms in the first and second person, unless you are using the third person pronouns, it may not seem to matter. Noticing that certain verbs commonly use a preposition before the object, and memorizing verb + preposition as one (**parlare con, comprare per,** etc.) will lead to a deeper understanding of Italian sentence structure, will improve comprehension, and, most importantly, will give you more confidence.

The following is a list of verbs that take direct objects, indirect objects, or both.

DIRECT		INDIRECT		DIRECT AND INDIRECT	
amare	*to love*	mancare a	*to be missing*	chiedere	*to ask*
ascoltare	*to listen*	parere a	*to seem to*	dare	*to give*
bere	*to drink*	piacere a	*to be pleasing to*	dire	*to say*
chiamare	*to call*	rispondere a	*to answer*	fare	*to do*
conoscere	*to know*	sembrare a	*to seem to*	leggere	*to read*
guardare	*to look at*			mandare	*to send*
invitare	*to invite*			offrire	*to offer*
mangiare	*to eat*			portare	*to bring*
perdere	*to lose*			regalare	*to give a gift*
prendere	*to take*			scrivere	*to write*
sentire	*to hear*			vendere	*to sell*
studiare	*to study*				
trovare	*to find*				
vedere	*to see*				

Nota bene

There are some verbs that take a direct object in English but an indirect object in Italian.

INDIRECT	DIRECT
chiedere a	*to ask*
dire a	*to tell*
rispondere a	*to answer*
telefonare a	*to phone*
piacere a	*to please*

There are also those that take a direct object in Italian but an indirect object in English.

DIRECT	INDIRECT
ascoltare	*to listen to*
aspettare	*to wait for*

Identify the object in each sentence as direct or indirect and rewrite the questions using the appropriate pronoun.

1. Bevi l'acqua minerale?

   _____

2. Parli spesso con Susanna?

   _____

3. Telefoni alla tua amica?

   _____

4. Mangi gli spaghetti?

   _____

5. Ai tuoi genitori piace il tuo ragazzo?

   _____

6. Conosci quel cantante bravissimo?

   _____

7. Vuoi scrivere ad Annamaria e Letizia?

   _____

8. Cosa dici alla tua amica?

   _____

Stressed pronouns (i pronomi tonici)

Stressed pronouns are used after a preposition, and unlike the direct- and indirect-object pronouns, they follow the verb. Except for the first and second person singular, they are the same as the subject pronouns.

me	noi
te	voi
lui/lei	loro

The reflexive stressed pronouns are the same as the preceding except for the third person singular and plural, which is **sé**. When stressing the reflexive pronoun, it is common to follow the reflexive pronoun with **stesso** or to use the preposition **da** before the pronoun.

Conosci **te stesso**.	*Know yourself.*
Mio figlio di tre anni si lava **da sé**.	*My three-year-old son washes himself on his own.*

When **da** is used to indicate someone's home, office, or place, it is always followed by either a proper name or a stressed pronoun.

Andiamo da lei!	*We're going to her place.*
Venite da me per un caffè.	*Come to my place for a coffee.*

Stressed pronouns can be used for emphasis, but one should be careful not to overuse them. The unstressed forms occur much more frequently in native speech, and although stressed pronouns happen to follow the same word order as English, they do not have the same meaning. Here are some sentences that illustrate the difference:

Ti chiamo domani. (unstressed pronoun)
I'll call you tomorrow.

Chiamo **te** domani. (stressed pronoun)
*I'll call **you** tomorrow. (as opposed to someone else)*

Mi dica, signora Rossi. (unstressed pronoun)
Tell me, Mrs. Rossi.

Dica **a me,** signora Rossi. (stressed pronoun)
*Tell **me**, Mrs. Rossi. (as opposed to someone else)*

Nota bene

When emphasizing a pronoun, one must be careful to use the correct type of pronoun, which may be an object, subject, or reflexive pronoun. The subject pronoun often follows the verb when emphasized.

Sono io. *It's me (I).*
Paghi tu? *Are you paying?*

ESERCIZIO
12·4

Translate the following sentences using stressed object or subject pronouns.

1. *I speak with him every day.*

   _____

2. *You always pay!*

   _____

3. *Come (sing.) to my place!*

   _____

4. *I'm going out with them tonight.*

   _____

5. *Do you need me tomorrow?*

   _____

6. *Can I count on you (plural)?*

   _____

7. *He always talks about himself!*

   _____

8. *There's a message for you.*

_____

9. *I fell in love with him.* (**innamorarsi**)

_____

10. *According to him they are arriving tomorrow.*

_____

Prepositions + di + pronouns

The following prepositions add **di** before a pronoun. The same prepositions, when followed by a noun, omit **di**. In English, these prepositions stand alone, whether they are followed by a pronoun or a noun. It is important to make this distinction when using the following prepositions.

contro *against*	Hai qualcosa **contro di me?** *Do you have something against me?*	Metti lo scaffale **contro il muro.** *Put the bookshelf against the wall.*
dietro *behind*	C'è un uomo strano **dietro di noi.** *There is a strange man behind us.*	**Dietro la porta** c'e la scopa. *Behind the door there is a broom.*
dopo *after*	**Dopo di me** c'è la signora. *The lady is after me.*	Arriverò **dopo le due.** *I will arrive after 2.*
fra / tra *in / between*	C'è tensione **fra di loro.** *There's tension between them.*	La lampada è **fra i due letti.** *The lamp is between the two beds.*
senza *without*	Non posso vivere **senza di te!** *I can't live without you!*	Mangi la pasta **senza il parmigiano?** *Do you eat pasta without parmigiano?*
sopra *above*	**Sopra di noi** ci sono degli studenti. *Above us there are some students.*	Lo specchio è **sopra il lavandino.** *The mirror is above the sink.*
sotto *underneath*	**Sotto di noi** non c'è nessuno. *Underneath us there is no one.*	Il cane va sempre **sotto il letto.** *The dog always sleeps under the bed.*
su *on*	Puoi contare **su di** me! *You can count on me!*	Il giornale è **sul tavolo.** *The newspaper is on the table.*

Non voglio parlare **di lui** stasera. *I don't want to talk **about him** tonight.*
Ho comprato un regalo **per loro.** *I bought a gift for them.*

ci

Ci is used most frequently as a direct, indirect, or reflexive pronoun.

Volete venire a cena?	*Do you want to come to dinner?*
Che cosa **ci** prepari?	*What will you make for us?*
Arriveder**ci**!	*Until we see each other again.*
Io e mio fratello **ci** svegliamo (reflexive) sempre tardi.	*My brother and I always get up late.*

Ci is frequently used to express the general idea of existence or being in the verb **esserci.**

Pronto, **c'è** Paola?	*Hello, **is Paola there?***
C'è qualche problema?	***Is there** some problem?*

Before the vowels **e** or **i**, **ci** is usually elided. In writing it is never elided to a letter that will change its pronunciation, but in speaking it is often pronounced without the **i** sound.

C'erano molte persone al concerto.	*There were a lot of people at the concert.*
Mi dispiace, non **ci ho** pensato.	*I'm sorry, I didn't think about it.*

Ci can be used to replace a prepositional phrase introduced by **a, in, su,** or **da** followed by a place or location. In this case, **ci** functions as an adverb of place, meaning *there*. It either precedes the conjugated verb or follows the infinitive or gerund.

Siete andati **all'opera**?	*Did you go to the opera?*
Sì, **ci** siamo stati ieri sera.	*Yes, we went (there) last night.*
Vai spesso in palestra?	*Do you often go to the gym?*
Cerco di **andarci** almeno tre volte a settimana.	*I try to go (there) at least three times a week.*

Ci can be used to replace **a, di,** or **con** followed by a noun.

Ripensando **alla mia carriera**, forse avrei dovuto studiare ingegneria.
Thinking back on my career, maybe I should have studied engineering.

Ripensando**ci**, forse avrei dovuto studiare ingegneria.
Thinking back on it, maybe I should have studied engineering.

Non capisco **l'economia.**	*I don't understand economics.*
Anch'io non **ci capisco** niente.	*I don't understand anything (about it) either.*

Ho visto la mia professoressa di italiano e **ci** ho parlato a lungo.
I saw my Italian professor and talked with her a long time.

Ci can be used to replace **a** followed by an infinitive phrase.

Riesci **a vedere** la strada?	*Can you see the road?*
Non **ci** riesco, c'è troppa nebbia.	*No, I can't see it, there's too much fog.*

Some verbs used with the particle **ci** take on an alternate meaning:

◆ **entrarci** (*to have to do with*)

Mia sorella **non c'entra** niente!	*My sister has **nothing to do with** this!*

◆ **metterci** (*to take time*)

Quanto **ci metti** a scrivere questa tesi?	*How long **is it taking you** to write this thesis?*

◆ **volerci** (*to take [time, money, etc.]*)

Quante **ore ci vogliono**?	**Ci vuole** una mezza giornata.
How many hours does it take?	*It takes a half a day.*

With **volerci** the amount becomes the subject. It takes **essere** as an auxiliary, and therefore, the participle agrees with the subject (the amount of time, money, etc.):

Per andare da Roma a Chicago **ci sono volute** otto ore.
To go from Rome to Chicago it took us eight hours.

Quanto **ci vuole** per comprare un appartamento a Venezia?
How much do you need to buy an apartment in Venice?

Ci vogliono almeno duecentomila euro.
At least 200,000 euros (are needed.)

Proverbi

Non **c'è** rosa senza spine.
There is no rose without the thorns.

Non **c'è** due senza tre.
There is no two without a three. (Things come in threes.)

ne

Ne is another small word that is very useful. It is important to know that **ne** is not a negative! Like **ci,** it is invariable and is used as a partitive pronoun to express quantity or number. In English, a number can be used alone to express quantity, but in Italian, expressions of quantity are generally followed by a noun. These phrases of quantity can be replaced by the object pronoun **ne,** which means *of it/them.*

Quante rosette desidera?	*How many rolls do you want?*
Ne vorrei tre, per favore.	*I would like three (of them), please.*
Quanti pomodori vuole?	*How many tomatoes do you want?*
Ne prendo un chilo.	*I'll take two pounds (of them).*

In the responses, **ne** replaces the object modified by an expression of quantity.
   Ne can also be used with an indefinite quantity.

Hai amici italiani?	*Do you have Italian friends?*
Ne ho moltissimi.	*I have a lot of them.*

Ne can replace a prepositional phrase introduced by **di** or **da.**

Parli **di politica** con i tuoi genitori?	*Do you talk about politics with your parents?*
Non, non **ne** parlo.	*No, I don't talk (about it).*
Hai bisogno **di** questo libro?	*Do you need this book?*
No, grazie. Non **ne** ho bisogno.	*No, thanks. I don't have a need (of it).*
Appena l'ho visto, **ne** sono rimasta innamorata. (di lui)	*As soon as I saw him, I fell in love (with him).*
Quando è uscito **dall'aula**?	*When did he come out of the classroom?*
Ne è uscito poco fa. (dall'aula)	*He came out (of it) a little while ago.*

With transitive verbs in a compound tense, **ne** is treated like a direct-object pronoun, and the participle agrees in gender and in number with the noun being replaced.

Quanti **libri** hai comprato?	*How many books did you buy?*
Ne ho comprat**i** tre.	*I bought three (of them).*

ESERCIZIO
12·5

Answer the following questions using **ci** *or* **ne**.

1. Quando vai a Roma? _____ vado in giugno.

2. Quanto anni ha tuo fratello? _____ ha 23.

3. Parli mai della tua adolescenza? Non _____ parlo quasi mai.

4. Quando arriviamo a Pisa? _____ vorranno almeno due ore.

5. Hai più sentito Luigi? Non _____ parlo da almeno tre anni.

6. Prenderai una BMW? Non _____ penso nemmeno, costa troppo.

7. Quando è uscito dal cinema? _____ è uscito poco fa.

8. Hai paura dei ragni? _____ ho una paura estrema!

9. Quando torni a Como? _____ tornerò l'estate prossima.

10. Credi nella telepatia? Sì, _____ credo.

Double-object pronouns

Leggi **le favole** <u>al tuo fratellino</u>?   *Do you read **fairy tales** <u>to your little brother</u>?*

In the preceding sentence, there is a direct object (*fairy tales*) followed by the recipient, or indirect object (*your little brother*).

Many verbs can be followed by both a direct and indirect object. The indirect object can be singular or plural (**mi, ti, gli, le, ci, vi, gli**), while the direct object will always be third person singular or plural (**lo, la, li, le**). Both objects can be replaced by double-object pronouns, which combine the indirect and the direct-object pronouns into one word or phrase, as we will see later, and can be placed before the conjugated verb or attached to the infinitive verb.

The first and second person indirect-object pronouns (**mi, ti, ci, vi**) always precede the direct-object pronouns, and when combined, change to **me, te, ce,** and **ve**. The direct-object pronouns **lo, la, li, le,** and **ne** will follow as a separate word unless the infinitive is being used, in which case, they are combined and attached to the end of the infinitive. To help you distinguish them, the direct objects are in bold and the indirect objects are underlined.

<u>Mi</u> passi **il sale**?
*Can you pass **the salt** <u>to me</u>?*

<u>Me</u> **lo** passi?
*Can you pass **it** <u>to me</u>?*

<u>Ti</u> mando **una mail**.
*I'll send <u>you</u> **an e-mail**.*

<u>Te</u> **la** mando oggi.
*I'll send **it** <u>to you</u> today.*

<u>Ci</u> date **i vostri indirizzi**?
*Can you give <u>us</u> **your addresses**?*

<u>Ce</u> **li** date?
*Can you give **them** <u>to us</u>?*

Dove possiamo mandar<u>vi</u> **dei fiori**?
*Where can we send <u>you</u> **some flowers**?*

Dove possiamo mandar<u>ve</u>**li**?
*Where can we send **them** <u>to you</u>?*

When the third person, indirect-object pronouns **le** and **gli** combine with the direct-object pronouns, they both change to **glie-**, to which **lo, la, li, le,** or **ne** attach and form one word.

Gli or **le** + **lo, la, li, le** → glielo, gliela, glieli, gliele

This is the form of all four possible indirect-object pronouns in the third person (*to her, to him, to you* [formal], and *to them*).

Hai dato **la foto** a Sofia?
*Did you give **the photo** to Sofia?*

Sì, <u>glie</u>**lo**'ho data.
*Yes, I gave **it** <u>to her</u>.*

Mandiamo **una cartolina**
   a Marina e Roberto?
Sì, <u>glie</u>**la** mandiamo da Roma.

*Shall we send a **postcard** to
   Marina and Roberto?*
Yes, we'll send it from Rome.

Agreement of third person direct-object pronouns in compound tenses

When using object pronouns in compound tenses such as **passato prossimo**, **condizionale passato**, etc., the participle must agree with the direct-object pronouns **lo**, **la**, **li**, **le**, and **ne** in gender and number.

Ti ho mandato **le ricette**?
*Did I send you **the recipes**?*

Te le ho mandate?
*Did I send **them to you**?*

Ti hanno dato **la promozione**?
*Did they give you **the promotion**?*

Te l'hanno data?
*Did they give **it to you**?*

ESERCIZIO
12·6

Simplify the sentences using double-object pronouns, as in the example. If it helps you, indicate the indirect object in the sentence. Remember the agreement between the direct-object pronouns and the participle.

ESEMPIO   Hai preparato <u>la pasta</u> per gli amici ? <u>*Glie l'hai preparata?*</u>

1. Hai comprato i libri per la tua amica? _____

2. Hai riportato il libro al professore? _____

3. Dai il giornale alla nonna, per favore? _____

4. Hai prestato la macchina ai tuoi amici? _____

5. Consiglieresti l'ultimo film di Woody Allen ai tuoi genitori? _____

6. Puoi prendermi una bottiglia di acqua minerale? _____

7. Tuo padre ti regala una Fiat 500 per il tua compleanno? _____

8. Marina vi ha dato i biglietti per l'opera? _____

9. Hai regalato tre DVD a tuo cugino? (Use ne) _____

10. Hai insegnato quell'aria di Mozart alla tua studentessa? _____

APPENDIX

Irregular verbs

The following verbs are irregular in one or more tenses as shown. Verbs conjugated with **essere** in compound tenses are indicated by a notation in parentheses.

andare (essere) *to go*

	PRESENT INDICATIVE	FUTURE	IMPERATIVE	CONDITIONAL	PRESENT SUBJUNCTIVE
io	vado	andrò	—	andrei	vada
tu	vai	andrai	va'	andresti	vada
lui/lei	va	andrà	—	andrebbe	vada
Lei	va	andrà	vada	andrebbe	vada
noi	andiamo	andremo	andiamo	andremmo	andiamo
voi	andate	andrete	andate	andreste	andiate
loro; Loro	vanno	andranno	vadano	andrebbero	vadano

aprire *to open*
Past participle: aperto

avere *to have*

	PRESENT INDICATIVE	PAST ABSOLUTE	FUTURE	IMPERATIVE	CONDITIONAL	PRESENT SUBJUNCTIVE
io	ho	ebbi	avrò	—	avrei	abbia
tu	hai	avesti	avrai	abbi	avresti	abbia
lui/lei	ha	ebbe	avrà	—	avrebbe	abbia
Lei	ha	ebbe	avrà	abbia	avrebbe	abbia
noi	abbiamo	avemmo	avremo	abbiamo	avremmo	abbiamo
voi	avete	aveste	avrete	abbiate	avreste	abbiate
loro; Loro	hanno	ebbero	avranno	abbiano	avrebbero	abbiano

bere *to drink*
Past participle: bevuto

	PRESENT INDICATIVE	IMPERFECT	PAST ABSOLUTE	FUTURE	IMPERATIVE	CONDITIONAL	PRESENT SUBJUNCTIVE	IMPERFECT SUBJUNCTIVE
io	bevo	bevevo	bevvi (bevetti)	berrò	—	berrei	beva	
tu	bevi	bevevi	bevesti	berrai	bevi	berresti	beva	
lui/lei	beve	beveva	bevve (bevette)	berrà	—	berrebbe	beva	
Lei	beve	beveva	bevve (bevette)	berrà	beva	berrebbe	beva	
noi	beviamo	bevevamo	bevemmo	berremo	beviamo	berremmo	beviamo	
voi	bevete	bevevate	beveste	berrete	bevete	berreste	beviate	
loro; Loro	bevono	bevevano	bevvero (bevettero)	berranno	bevano	berrebbero	bevano	

Gerund: bevendo

cadere (essere) *to fall*

	PRESENT INDICATIVE	IMPERFECT	PAST ABSOLUTE	FUTURE	IMPERATIVE	CONDITIONAL	PRESENT SUBJUNCTIVE	IMPERFECT SUBJUNCTIVE
io			caddi	cadrò		cadrei	cada	
tu			cadesti	cadrai		cadresti	cada	
lui/lei			cadde	cadrà		cadrebbe	cada	
Lei			cadde	cadrà		cadrebbe	cada	
noi			cademmo	cadremo		cadremmo	cadiamo	
voi			cadeste	cadrete		cadreste	cadiate	
loro; Loro			caddero	cadranno		cadrebbero	cadano	

chiedere *to ask for*
Past participle: chiesto

	PRESENT INDICATIVE	IMPERFECT	PAST ABSOLUTE	FUTURE	IMPERATIVE	CONDITIONAL	PRESENT SUBJUNCTIVE	IMPERFECT SUBJUNCTIVE
io			chiesi					
tu			chiedesti					
lui/lei			chiese					
Lei			chiese					
noi			chiedemmo					
voi			chiedeste					
loro; Loro			chiesero					

chiudere *to close*
Past participle: chiuso

	PRESENT INDICATIVE	IMPERFECT	PAST ABSOLUTE	FUTURE	IMPERATIVE	CONDITIONAL	PRESENT SUBJUNCTIVE	IMPERFECT SUBJUNCTIVE
io			chiusi					
tu			chiudesti					
lui/lei			chiuse					
Lei			chiuse					
noi			chiudemmo					
voi			chiudeste					
loro; Loro			chiusero					

conoscere *to know*

	PRESENT INDICATIVE	IMPERFECT	PAST ABSOLUTE	FUTURE	IMPERATIVE	CONDITIONAL	PRESENT SUBJUNCTIVE	IMPERFECT SUBJUNCTIVE
io			conobbi					
tu			conoscesti					
lui/lei			conobbe					
Lei			conobbe					
noi			conoscemmo					
voi			conosceste					
loro; Loro			conobbero					

dare *to give*
Past participle: dato

	PRESENT INDICIATIVE	IMPERFECT	PAST ABSOLUTE	FUTURE	IMPERATIVE	CONDITIONAL	PRESENT SUBJUNCTIVE	IMPERFECT SUBJUNCTIVE
io	do	davo	diedi	darò	—		dia	dessi
tu	dai	davi	desti	darai	da'		dia	dessi
lui/lei	dà	dava	diede	darà	—		dia	desse
Lei	dà	dava	diede	darà	dia		dia	desse
noi	diamo	davamo	demmo	daremo	diamo		diamo	dessimo
voi	date	davate	deste	darete	date		diate	deste
loro; Loro	danno	davano	diedero	daranno	diano		diano	dessero

Gerund: dando

decidere   *to decide*
Past participle: deciso

	PRESENT INDICATIVE	IMPERFECT	PAST ABSOLUTE	FUTURE	IMPERATIVE	CONDITIONAL	PRESENT SUBJUNCTIVE	IMPERFECT SUBJUNCTIVE
io			decisi					
tu			decidesti					
lui/lei			decise					
Lei			decise					
noi			decidemmo					
voi			decideste					
loro; Loro			decisero					

dire   *to say, tell*
Past participle: detto

	PRESENT INDICATIVE	IMPERFECT	PAST ABSOLUTE	FUTURE	IMPERATIVE	CONDITIONAL	PRESENT SUBJUNCTIVE	IMPERFECT SUBJUNCTIVE
io	dico	dicevo	dissi	dirò	—	direi	dica	dicessi
tu	dici	dicevi	dicesti	dirai	di'	diresti	dica	dicessi
lui/lei	dice	diceva	disse	dirà	—	direbbe	dica	dicesse
Lei	dice	diceva	disse	dirà	dica	direbbe	dica	dicesse
noi	diciamo	dicevamo	dicemmo	diremo	diciamo	diremmo	diciamo	dicessimo
voi	dite	dicevate	diceste	direte	dite	direste	diciate	diceste
loro; Loro	dicono	dicevano	dissero	diranno	dicano	direbbero	dicano	dicessero

Gerund: dicendo

dovere   *to have to*

	PRESENT INDICATIVE	IMPERFECT	PAST ABSOLUTE	FUTURE	IMPERATIVE	CONDITIONAL	PRESENT SUBJUNCTIVE	IMPERFECT SUBJUNCTIVE
io	devo			dovrò		dovrei	deva (debba)	
tu	devi			dovrai		dovresti	deva (debba)	
lui/lei	deve			dovrà		dovrebbe	deva (debba)	
Lei	deve			dovrà		dovrebbe	deva (debba)	
noi	dobbiamo			dovremo		dovremmo	dobbiamo	
voi	dovete			dovrete		dovreste	dobbiate	
loro; Loro	devono			dovranno		dovrebbero	devano (debbano)	

essere (essere) *to be*
Past participle: stato

	PRESENT INDICATIVE	IMPERFECT	PAST ABSOLUTE	FUTURE	IMPERATIVE	CONDITIONAL	PRESENT SUBJUNCTIVE	IMPERFECT SUBJUNCTIVE
io	sono	ero	fui	sarò	—	sarei	sia	fossi
tu	sei	eri	fosti	sarai	sii	saresti	sia	fossi
lui/lei	è	era	fu	sarà	—	sarebbe	sia	fosse
Lei	è	era	fu	sarà	sia	sarebbe	sia	fosse
noi	siamo	eravamo	fummo	saremo	siamo	saremmo	siamo	fossimo
voi	siete	eravate	foste	sarete	siate	sareste	siate	foste
loro; Loro	sono	erano	furono	saranno	siano	sarebbero	siano	fossero

fare *to do, make*
Past participle: fatto

	PRESENT INDICATIVE	IMPERFECT	PAST ABSOLUTE	FUTURE	IMPERATIVE	CONDITIONAL	PRESENT SUBJUNCTIVE	IMPERFECT SUBJUNCTIVE
io	faccio	facevo	feci	farò	—	farei	faccia	facessi
tu	fai	facevi	facesti	farai	fa'	faresti	faccia	facessi
lui/lei	fa	faceva	fece	farà	—	farebbe	faccia	facesse
Lei	fa	faceva	fece	farà	faccia	farebbe	faccia	facesse
noi	facciamo	facevamo	facemmo	faremo	facciamo	faremmo	facciamo	facessimo
voi	fate	facevate	faceste	farete	fate	fareste	facciate	faceste
loro; Loro	fanno	facevano	fecero	faranno	facciano	farebbero	facciano	facessero

Gerund: facendo

leggere *to read*
Past participle: letto

	PRESENT INDICATIVE	IMPERFECT	PAST ABSOLUTE	FUTURE	IMPERATIVE	CONDITIONAL	PRESENT SUBJUNCTIVE	IMPERFECT SUBJUNCTIVE
io			lessi					
tu			leggesti					
lui/lei			lesse					
Lei			lesse					
noi			leggemmo					
voi			leggeste					
loro; Loro			lessero					

mettere *to put*
Past participle: messo

	PRESENT INDICATIVE	IMPERFECT	PAST ABSOLUTE	FUTURE	IMPERATIVE	CONDITIONAL	PRESENT SUBJUNCTIVE	IMPERFECT SUBJUNCTIVE
io			misi					
tu			mettesti					
lui/lei			mise					
Lei			mise					
noi			mettemmo					
voi			metteste					
loro/Loro			misero					

nascere (essere) *to be born*
Past participle: nato

	PRESENT INDICATIVE	IMPERFECT	PAST ABSOLUTE	FUTURE	IMPERATIVE	CONDITIONAL	PRESENT SUBJUNCTIVE	IMPERFECT SUBJUNCTIVE
io			nacqui					
tu			nascesti					
lui/lei			nacque					
Lei			nacque					
noi			nascemmo					
vio			nasceste					
loro; Loro			nacquero					

perdere *to lose*
Past participle: perso

	PRESENT INDICATIVE	IMPERFECT	PAST ABSOLUTE	FUTURE	IMPERATIVE	CONDITIONAL	PRESENT SUBJUNCTIVE	IMPERFECT SUBJUNCTIVE
io			persi					
tu			perdesti					
lui/lei			perse					
Lei			perse					
noi			perdemmo					
voi			perdeste					
loro; Loro			persero					

piacere (essere) *to like, be pleasing to*
Past participle: piaciuto

	PRESENT INDICATIVE	IMPERFECT	PAST ABSOLUTE	FUTURE	IMPERATIVE	CONDITIONAL	PRESENT SUBJUNCTIVE	IMPERFECT SUBJUNCTIVE
io	piaccio		piacqui				piaccia	
tu	piaci		piacesti				piaccia	
lui/lei	piace		piacque				piaccia	
Lei	piace		piacque				piaccia	
noi	piacciamo		piacemmo				piacciamo	
voi	piacete		piaceste				piacciate	
loro; Loro	piacciono		piacquero				piacciano	

potere *to be able to*

	PRESENT INDICATIVE	IMPERFECT	PAST ABSOLUTE	FUTURE	IMPERATIVE	CONDITIONAL	PRESENT SUBJUNCTIVE	IMPERFECT SUBJUNCTIVE
io	posso			potrò		potrei	possa	
tu	puoi			potrai		potresti	possa	
lui/lei	può			potrà		potrebbe	possa	
Lei	può			potrà		potrebbe	possa	
noi	possiamo			potremo		potremmo	possiamo	
voi	potete			potrete		potreste	possiate	
loro; Loro	possono			potranno		potrebbero	possano	

prendere *to take*
Past participle: preso

	PRESENT INDICATIVE	IMPERFECT	PAST ABSOLUTE	FUTURE	IMPERATIVE	CONDITIONAL	PRESENT SUBJUNCTIVE	IMPERFECT SUBJUNCTIVE
io			presi					
tu			prendesti					
lui/lei			prese					
Lei			prese					
noi			prendemmo					
voi			prendeste					
loro; Loro			presero					

salire (essere) *to go up*

	PRESENT INDICATIVE	IMPERFECT	PAST ABSOLUTE	FUTURE	IMPERATIVE	CONDITIONAL	PRESENT SUBJUNCTIVE	IMPERFECT SUBJUNCTIVE
io	salgo				—		salga	
tu	sali				sali		salga	
lui/lei	sale				—		salga	
Lei	sale				salga		salga	
noi	saliamo				saliamo		saliamo	
voi	salite				salite		saliate	
loro; Loro	salgano				salgono		salgano	

sapere *to know*

	PRESENT INDICATIVE	IMPERFECT	PAST ABSOLUTE	FUTURE	IMPERATIVE	CONDITIONAL	PRESENT SUBJUNCTIVE	IMPERFECT SUBJUNCTIVE
io	so		seppi	saprò	—	saprei	sappia	
tu	sai		sapesti	saprai	sappi	sapresti	sappia	
lui/lei	sa		seppe	saprà	—	saprebbe	sappia	
Lei	sa		seppe	saprà	sappia	saprebbe	sappia	
noi	sappiamo		sapemmo	sapremo	sappiamo	sapremmo	sappiamo	
voi	sapete		sapeste	saprete	sappiate	sapreste	sappiate	
loro; Loro	sanno		seppero	sapranno	sappiano	saprebbero	sappiano	

scegliere *to choose, select*
Past participle: scelto

	PRESENT INDICATIVE	IMPERFECT	PAST ABSOLUTE	FUTURE	IMPERATIVE	CONDITIONAL	PRESENT SUBJUNCTIVE	IMPERFECT SUBJUNCTIVE
io	scelgo		scelsi		—		scelga	
tu	scegli		scegliesti		scegli		scelga	
lui/lei	sceglie		scelse		—		scelga	
Lei	sceglie		scelse		scelga		scelga	
noi	scegliamo		scegliemmo		scegliamo		scegliamo	
voi	scegliete		sceglieste		scegliete		scegliate	
loro; Loro	scelgono		scelsero			scelgano	scelgano	

scendere *to descend, go down*
Past participle: sceso

	PRESENT INDICATIVE	IMPERFECT	PAST ABSOLUTE	FUTURE	IMPERATIVE	CONDITIONAL	PRESENT SUBJUNCTIVE	IMPERFECT SUBJUNCTIVE
io			scesi					
tu			scendesti					
lui/lei			scese					
Lei			scese					
noi			scendemmo					
voi			scendeste					
loro; Loro			scesero					

scrivere *to write*
Past participle: scritto

	PRESENT INDICATIVE	IMPERFECT	PAST ABSOLUTE	FUTURE	IMPERATIVE	CONDITIONAL	PRESENT SUBJUNCTIVE	IMPERFECT SUBJUNCTIVE
io			scrissi					
tu			scrivesti					
lui/lei			scrisse					
Lei			scrisse					
noi			scrivemmo					
voi			scriveste					
loro; Loro			scrissero					

stare (essere) *to stay*
Past participle: stato

	PRESENT INDICATIVE	IMPERFECT	PAST ABSOLUTE	FUTURE	IMPERATIVE	CONDITIONAL	PRESENT SUBJUNCTIVE	IMPERFECT SUBJUNCTIVE
io	sto	stavo	stetti	starò	—	starei	stia	stessi
tu	stai	stavi	stesti	starai	sta'	staresti	stia	stessi
lui/lei	sta	stava	stette	starà	—	starebbe	stia	stesse
Lei	sta	stava	stette	starà	stia	starebbe	stia	stesse
noi	stiamo	stavamo	stemmo	staremo	stiamo	staremmo	stiamo	stessimo
voi	state	stavate	steste	starete	state	stareste	stiate	steste
loro; Loro	stanno	stavano	stettero	staranno	stiano	starebbero	stiano	stessero

Gerund: stando

tenere *to hold, keep*

	PRESENT INDICATIVE	IMPERFECT	PAST ABSOLUTE	FUTURE	IMPERATIVE	CONDITIONAL	PRESENT SUBJUNCTIVE	IMPERFECT SUBJUNCTIVE
io	tengo		tenni	terrò	—	terrei	tenga	
tu	tieni		tenesti	terrai	tieni	terresti	tenga	
lui/lei	tiene		tenne	terrà	—	terrebbe	tenga	
Lei	tiene		tenne	terrà	tenga	terrebbe	tenga	
noi	teniamo		tenemmo	terremo	teniamo	terremmo	teniamo	
voi	tenete		teneste	terrete	tenete	terreste	teniate	
loro; Loro	tengono		tennero	terranno	tengano	terrebbero	tengano	

uscire (essere) *to go out*

	PRESENT INDICATIVE	IMPERFECT	PAST ABSOLUTE	FUTURE	IMPERATIVE	CONDITIONAL	PRESENT SUBJUNCTIVE	IMPERFECT SUBJUNCTIVE
io	esco				—		esca	
tu	esci				esci		esca	
lui/lei	esce				—		esca	
Lei	esce				esca		esca	
noi	usciamo				usciamo		usciamo	
voi	uscite				uscite		usciate	
loro; Loro	escono				escano		escano	

vedere *to see*
Past participle: visto

	PRESENT INDICATIVE	IMPERFECT	PAST ABSOLUTE	FUTURE	IMPERATIVE	CONDITIONAL	PRESENT SUBJUNCTIVE	IMPERFECT SUBJUNCTIVE
io			vidi	vedrò		vedrei		
tu			vedesti	vedrai		vedresti		
lui/lei			vide	vedrà		vedrebbe		
Lei			vide	vedrà		vedrebbe		
noi			vedemmo	vedremo		vedremmo		
voi			vedeste	vedrete		vedreste		
Loro; Loro			videro	vedranno		vedrebbero		

venire (essere) *to come*
Past participle: venuto

	PRESENT INDICATIVE	IMPERFECT	PAST ABSOLUTE	FUTURE	IMPERATIVE	CONDITIONAL	PRESENT SUBJUNCTIVE	IMPERFECT SUBJUNCTIVE
io	vengo		venni	verrò	—	verrei	venga	
tu	vieni		venisti	verrai	vieni	verresti	venga	
lui/lei	viene		venne	verrà	—	verrebbe	venga	
Lei	viene		venne	verrà	venga	verrebbe	venga	
noi	veniamo		venimmo	verremo	veniamo	verremmo	veniamo	
voi	venite		veniste	verrete	venite	verreste	veniate	
loro; Loro	vengono		vennero	verranno	vengano	verrebbero	vengano	

vincere *to win*
Past participle: vinto

	PRESENT INDICATIVE	IMPERFECT	PAST ABSOLUTE	FUTURE	IMPERATIVE	CONDITIONAL	PRESENT SUBJUNCTIVE	IMPERFECT SUBJUNCTIVE
io			vinsi					
tu			vincesti					
lui/lei			vinse					
Lei			vinse					
noi			vincemmo					
voi			vinceste					
loro; Loro			vinsero					

volere *to want*

	PRESENT INDICATIVE	IMPERFECT	PAST ABSOLUTE	FUTURE	IMPERATIVE	CONDITIONAL	PRESENT SUBJUNCTIVE	IMPERFECT SUBJUNCTIVE
io	voglio		volli	vorrò		vorrei	voglia	
tu	vuoi		volesti	vorrai		vorresti	voglia	
lui/lei	vuole		volle	vorrà		vorrebbe	voglia	
Lei	vuole		volle	vorrà		vorrebbe	voglia	
noi	vogliamo		volemmo	vorremo		vorremmo	vogliamo	
voi	volete		voleste	vorrete		vorreste	vogliate	
loro; Loro	vogliono		vollero	vorranno		vorrebbero	vogliano	

Italian-English Glossary

A

a at, to
a casa mia at my house
a che ora at what time
a destra to the right
a domani see you tomorrow
a meno che unless
a presto see you soon
a sinistra to the left
abbastanza enough
abitare to live, to dwell
abito suit
acceleratore (*m.*) gas pedal
acqua minerale mineral water
acqua water
adesso now
affare (*m.*) business transaction
affatto not at all
affinché so that
affittare to rent an apartment, house, etc.
agosto August
albergo hotel
albero tree
alcuni (*m.*) / **alcune** (*f.*) some, several
alla moda in style, fashionable
allacciare to fasten
allegare to attach
allora then, thus
alto tall
altro anything else, other
alzarsi to get up
amare to love
americano American
amichevole friendly
amico (*m.*) / **amica** (*f.*) friend
amore (*m.*) love
analisi (*f.*) analysis
anche (**anche io** *or* **anch'io**) also, too
ancora still, yet
andare (*ess.*) to go
andare via to go away
andata e ritorno round-trip
anello ring
anno year
annoiarsi to become bored

antipasto appetizer
antropologo anthropologist
anzi as a matter of fact
appena just, barely
appuntamento appointment, date
aprile April
aprire to open
arancia (*noun*) orange
aranciata orange drink
arancio orange tree
arancione (*inv.*) orange
architetto (*m./f.*) architect
arcobaleno rainbow
aria air
arrabbiarsi to become angry
arrivare (*ess.*) to arrive
arrivederci good-bye (*informal*)
arrivederLa good-bye (*formal*)
arrivo arrival
ascensore (*m.*) elevator
ascoltare to listen (to)
asino donkey
aspettare to wait for
assai quite, rather
assoluto absolute
atletica leggera track and field
atrio lobby
attore (*m.*) / **attrice** (*f.*) actor/actress
attraversare to cross
augurare to wish
autista (*m./f.*) driver
autobus (*m., inv.*) bus
automobile (*f.*) automobile
automobilismo car racing
autore (*m.*) / **autrice** (*f.*) author
autunno autumn, fall
avere to have
avere… anni to be … old
avere bisogno di to need (to have need of)
avere fame to be hungry
avere ragione to be right
avere voglia di to feel like
avventura adventure
avvocato lawyer
azzurro blue

B

babbo dad
baciare to kiss
bacio kiss
baffi (*m., pl.*) mustache
bagaglio baggage
bagno bathroom
ballare to dance
bambino (-a) little boy/girl, child
banca bank
bancomat (*m.*) automatic teller
bar coffee place, bar
barbiere (*m.*) barber
barista (*m./f.*) bartender
basso short
bastare (*ess.*) to be enough
bello beautiful
benché although
bene well
benevolo benevolent
bere to drink
bianco white
bibita soft drink, soda
bicchiere glass
bigliettaio (-a) ticket agent
biglietto bill, ticket
binario track
biologia biology
biologo biologist
biondo blond
bisognare to be necessary
blu (*inv.*) dark blue
borsa purse
bottiglia bottle
braccio arm
bravo good
brindisi (*m.*) drinking toast
bruno dark-haired
brutto ugly
bue (*m.*) ox
bugia lie
Buon compleanno! Happy birthday!
buon pomeriggio good afternoon
buona notte good night
buonasera good evening
buongiorno good morning, good day, hello
buono good

C

cacciavite (*m.*) screwdriver
cadere (*ess.*) to fall
caffè coffee
caffellatte (*m.*) coffee with milk (a "latte")
calcio soccer
caldo hot, warm
calmarsi to stay calm
cambiare to change, to exchange
camera bedroom
cameriere (-a) waiter

camerino change room
camicetta blouse
camicia shirt
campionato championship, playoffs
cane (*m.*) dog
cantante (*m./f.*) singer
cantare to sing
capelli (*m., pl.*) hair (on the head)
capire (-isc) to understand
capoluogo capital of a region
caporeparto head of a department
cappotto coat
cappuccino cappuccino
carino cute
carne (*f.*) meat
caro dear
carota carrot
carta d'imbarco boarding pass
carta di credito credit card
casa house
cassaforte (*f.*) safe (for valuables)
cattivo bad
celeste sky blue
cellulare cell phone
centimetro centimeter
centro downtown, center of town
cercare to search for, to look for
certo certainly, of course
che what, that, who, which
che cosa what
Che ore sono?/Che ora è? What time is it?
chi who
chiamare to call
chiamarsi to call oneself, to be named
chiave (*f.*) key
chiedere to ask for
chiesa church
chilo kilogram
chimica chemistry
chiudere to close
chiunque whoever
ci vediamo See you
ciao hi, bye
ciliegia cherry
ciliegio cherry tree
cinema (*m., inv.*) cinema, movies
cinematografo (**il cinema**) movie theater
cintura belt
cintura di sicurezza seat belt
cioccolato chocolate
circa around, nearly
città (*f.*) city
clacson (*m., inv.*) car horn
classe (*f.*) class
classico classic
cliente (*m./f.*) customer
cognata sister-in-law
cognato brother-in-law
cognome (*m.*) surname, family name

colazione (*f.*) breakfast
coltello knife
comandante (*m./f.*) captain
come how, like
come se as if
Come si chiama? (*pol.*) What is your name?
Come stai? (*fam.*)/sta? (*pol.*) How are you?
Come ti chiami? (*fam.*) What's your name?
Come va? How's it going?
cominciare to begin, to start
commemorativo commemorative
commesso (-a) clerk
compito task, homework assignment
compiuto completed
compleanno birthday
comprare to buy
computer (*m.*) computer
comune common
con with
condominio condo
conoscere to know, be familiar with
consiglio advice
contento happy, content
conto account, bill, check
contorno side dish
controllare to check, to control
convenire (*ess.*) to be better to
copione (*m.*) script
cordone (*m.*) rope
cornetto croissant
corpo body
corretto correct, coffee with a drop
   of alcohol
cosa thing
così so, thus
costare (*ess.*) to cost
costoso costly, expensive
cotoletta cutlet
cravatta tie
creare to create
credere to believe
crescere (*ess.*) to grow
crisi (*f.*) crisis
cucchiaino teaspoon
cucchiaio spoon
cucina kitchen
cugino (-a) cousin
cui which, whom
cuore (*m.*) heart

D

d'accordo fine, I agree
da from (for)
da leggere to read
da portare via to take out
dare to give
dare su to look onto
data date
davanti in front

decidere to decide
decimo tenth
decollo takeoff
denaro money
dentista (*m./f.*) dentist
depositare to deposit
desiderare to desire, to want
dessert (*m., inv.*) dessert
destra right (direction)
devo andare I have to go
di of
di nuovo again
di solito usually
diagramma (*m.*) diagram
dicembre December
difficile difficult
dimenticare to forget
dimenticarsi to forget
dire to tell, to say
diritto straight ahead
discoteca disco
dispositivo device
dito finger
ditta company (business)
divano sofa
diventare (*ess.*) to become
diverso diverse, various, several
divertire to entertain
divertirsi to enjoy oneself
divorziarsi to get divorced
dolce sweet
dollaro dollar
domanda question
domani tomorrow
domenica Sunday
donna woman
dopo after
doppio double
dormire to sleep
dottore (*m.*) Dr./doctor
dottoressa (*f.*) Dr./doctor
dove where
dovere to have to, must
dovunque wherever
dozzina dozen
dramma (*m.*) drama
dubitare to doubt
durare (*ess.*) to last

E

e and
eccezionale exceptional
ecco here is
edicola newsstand
educato well-mannered
egli he
elefante (*m.*) / elefantessa (*f.*) elephant
elegante elegant
elettricista (*m./f.*) electrician

ella she
enorme enormous
entrare (*ess.*) to enter
equipaggio crew
esame (*m.*) exam
esperienza experience
espresso espresso
esserci to be there
essere (*ess.*) to be
essere innamorato to be/fall in love
essere nato (-a) to be born
essere pregato to be asked
essere previsto to be expected
essere sposato (-a) to be married
esso it
estate (*f.*) summer
euro euro

F

fa ago
faccia face
facile easy
fagiolino string bean
fagiolo bean
fame (*f.*) hunger
famiglia family
farcela to be able to take/manage it
fare to do, to make
fare il biglietto to buy a (travel) ticket
fare il footing to jog
farmacia pharmacy
farmacista (*m./f.*) pharmacist
faro car headlight
fastidioso fussy
favore (*m.*) favor
febbraio February
felice happy
ferrovia railroad
festa feast, holiday, party
fetta slice
fico fig, fig tree
figlia daughter
figlio son
film (*m.*) movie, film
finestra window
finestrino passenger window
finire (-isc) to finish
finora until now
firmare to sign
fisica physics
foglia leaf
forbici (*f., pl.*) scissors
forchetta fork
formaggio cheese
forse maybe
forte strong, hard
fortunato fortunate, lucky
foto(grafia) photo(graph)
fra between, within

fragola strawberry
francese (*m./f.*) French
francobollo stamp
fratello brother
freddo cold
freno brake
fresco fresh
frigorifero refrigerator
frutta fruit
funzionare to work (function)

G

gallo rooster
garage (*m.*) garage
gatto cat
gelato ice cream
generi alimentari groceries
genero son-in-law
generoso generous
genitore (*m.*) parent
gennaio January
gente (*f.*) people
geografia geography
geometra (*m./f.*) draftsperson
già already
giacca jacket
giallo yellow
ginocchio knee
giocare to play (a sport)
gioco game
giornale (*m.*) newspaper
giorno day
giovane young
giovedì Thursday
gioventù (*f.*) youth
girare to turn
giro tour
giugno June
giusto right (correctness), just
gnocco dumpling
gomma tire
gonna skirt
grande big
grasso fat
grazie thank you
greco Greek
grigio gray
griglia grill
guardare to look at, to watch
guardia guard
guarire (*type 2*) to get better, heal, cure
guida guide
guidare to drive

I

idea idea
ieri yesterday
immaginare to imagine
imparare to learn

impermeabile (*m.*) raincoat
impiegato (-a) office worker
importante important
impossibile impossible
in in
in anticipo early
in ferie on vacation
in fretta in a hurry
in orario on time
in punto on the dot
in saldo on sale
incontrare to meet, run into
indicare to indicate
indirizzo address
infermiere (*m.*) / infermiera (*f.*) nurse
informatica computer, informatics
inglese (*m./f.*) English
ingresso entrance
insalata salad
insegnante (*m./f.*) teacher
insieme together
intelligente intelligent
interessante interesting
intero entire
intervista interview
invece instead
inventare to invent
inverno winter
io I
ipotesi (*f.*) hypothesis
isola island
isolato block
italiano Italian

L

là over there
labbro lip
laggiù down there, over there
lago lake
lamentarsi to complain
lasagne (*f., pl.*) lasagne
latte (*m.*) milk
laurea degree
lavare to wash
lavarsi to wash oneself
lavorare to work
lavoro work, job
leggere to read
leggero light
lei she
Lei you (*pol.*)
lento slow
leone (*m.*) / leonessa (*f.*) the lion
letto bed
lì there
libretto opera libretto, bankbook
libricino little book
libro book
lieto delighted

limonata lemonade
limone (*m.*) lemon, lemon tree
lingua language
locale notturno nightclub
lontano far
Loro (*pol., pl.*) your
loro they, their
lotta wrestling
luglio July
lui he
lunedì Monday
lungo long
luogo place

M

ma but
Macché! No way!
macchiato with a dash of steamed milk
macchina car
madre mother
maggio May
maggiore bigger, greater, major, older
maglia sweater
magnifico magnificent
magro skinny
mai ever
mail (*f.*) e-mail
mal di denti toothache
mal di gola sore throat
mal di stomaco stomachache
mal di testa headache
male bad(ly)
mamma mom
mancia tip (gratuity)
mandare to send
mandarino mandarin, mandarin tree
mangiare to eat
mano (*f.*) hand
mare (*m.*) sea
marito husband
marrone (*inv.*) brown
martedì Tuesday
marzo March
mascalzone (*m.*) rascal, scoundrel
matematica mathematics
mattina morning
mattone (*m.*) brick
meccanico mechanic
medico medical doctor
meglio better
mela apple
melo apple tree
meno less
Meno male! thank goodness!
mentre while
menù (*m., inv.*) menu
mercato market
mercoledì Wednesday
meridionale southern

mese (*m.*) month
messaggino text, message
metro meter
mettere to put
mettersi to put on, to wear
mezzanotte (*f.*) midnight
mezzo half
mezzogiorno noon
mi chiamo my name is
mi presento let me introduce myself
Mi può aiutare? (*pol.*) Can you help me?
Mi puoi aiutare? (*fam.*) Can you help me?
mica not really/quite
migliore better
milione million
mille thousand
minestra soup
minestrone (*m.*) minestrone
minore smaller, minor
minuto minute
mio my
mobile (*m.*) piece of furniture
mobile mobile
moderno modern
modulo form
moglie wife
molto very, much, a lot
momento moment
monaco monk
mondo world
montagna mountain(s)
motocicletta (**moto**) motorcycle
musica music
musicista (*m./f.*) musician
mutande (*f., pl.*) underwear

N

nascere (*ess.*) to be born
Natale (*m.*) Christmas
natalizio of Christmas
navigare to navigate
navigare in Internet to surf the Internet
nazione (*f.*) nation
né neither, nor
neanche neither
negozio store
nel caso che in the event that
nel frattempo in the meantime
nemmeno not even
neppure not even
nero black
nessuno no one
neve (*f.*) snow
nevicare to snow
niente nothing
nipote (*m./f.*) grandson/granddaughter, nephew/niece
no no
noi we, us
noioso boring, fussy

noleggiare to rent a vehicle, a movie, etc.
nome (*m.*) name
non not
non... affatto not at all
non c'è problema no problem
non importa it doesn't matter
nonna grandmother
nonno grandfather
nono ninth
nonostante che despite
normale normal
nostro our
notte (*f.*) night
novembre November
nulla nothing
numero number
nuora daughter-in-law
nuoto swimming
nuovo new

O

o or
occhiali (*m., pl.*) (eye)glasses
occhio eye
occidentale western
odiare to hate
oggi today
oggigiorno nowadays
ogni each, every
opinione (*f.*) opinion
ora hour, time
orario schedule, timetable
orientale eastern
ormai by now
orologio watch
orzo barley
ottavo eighth
ottimista optimistic
ottimo excellent
ottobre October

P

pace (*f.*) peace
padre father
pagare to pay
paio pair
palestra gym
pallacanestro basketball
pane (*m.*) bread
panino bun sandwich
pantaloni (*m., pl.*) pants
papà (*m., inv.*) dad
parabrezza (*m.*) windshield
parecchio several, quite a few
parete (*f.*) wall (partition)
parlare to speak
partenza departure
partire (*ess.*) to leave, to depart
partita game, match

Pasqua Easter
passeggero (-a) passenger
pasta pasta
pasto meal
patata potato
patatina french fry
patente (f.) driver's license
pattinaggio skating
pazienza patience
peggiore worse
penna pen
pensare to think
pepe (m.) pepper
per for, through
per caso by chance
per favore please
pera pear
perché why, because
perdere to lose
pero pear tree
persona person
pesante heavy
pesca peach
pesce (m.) fish
pesco peach tree
pezzo piece
piacere (ess.) to like, to be pleasing to, a pleasure
Piacere di conoscerti. A pleasure to know you.
Piacere di fare la Sua (pol.) conoscenza. A pleasure to make your acquaintance.
pianeta planet
pianista (m./f.) pianist
piano floor
pianoforte (m.) piano
pianta plant
piatto plate, dish
piazza city square
piccolo little, small
piede (m.) foot
pieno full
piovere to rain
piscina swimming pool
pisello pea
pittore (m.) / pittrice (f.) painter
più more
piuttosto rather
pizzicheria delicatessen
plurale plural
poco little, few
poi then
poltrona armchair
pomeriggio afternoon
pomodoro tomato
popolare popular
porco pig
porta door
portare to wear
portatile (m.) laptop
possibile possible

posto seat
posto al corridoio aisle seat
posto al finestrino window seat
potere to be able to, can
povero poor
pratico practical
preciso precise (precisely)
preferire (-isc) to prefer
prego you're welcome
prelevare to withdraw
prendere to take
prenotazione (f.) reservation
preoccuparsi to worry
prepararsi to prepare oneself
presentare to present, to introduce
prestare to lend
presto soon, early
prezzo price
prima first, before
prima che before
primavera spring
primo first
probabile probable
problema (m.) problem
professore (m.) professor
professoressa (f.) professor
programma (m.) program
Pronto! Hello!
proporre to propose
proprio just, right, really
prosciutto prosciutto ham
prossimo next
provare to try
provarsi to try on
psicologo (m.) / psicologa (f.) psychologist
pugilato boxing
pulire to clean
purché provided that
purtroppo unfortunately

Q

qua right over here
qualche some
qualcosa something
qualcuno someone
quale which, what
qualsiasi whichever, any
qualunque whichever, any
quando when
quanto how much
quarto fourth
quasi almost
quello che that which, whatever
qui here
quinto fifth

R

radio (f.) radio
ragazzo (-a) boy (girl), youth

ragioniere (*m.*) / **ragioniera** (*f.*) accountant (bookkeeper)
ragù (*m.*) meat sauce
raro rare
regione (*f.*) region
regolare regular
ricco rich
ricordare to remember
rientrare (*ess.*) to get back, return home
riga straight ruler
rimanere (*ess.*) to remain
riso rice
rispondere to answer
ristorante (*m.*) restaurant
ristretto short/strong
riunione (*f.*) meeting
rivista magazine
romantico romantic
romanzo novel
rosa pink
rosso red

S

sabato Saturday
sala da pranzo dining room
salame (*m.*) salami
sale (*m.*) salt
salire (*ess.*) to go up
salotto living room
salvagente (*m.*) life jacket
sapere to know
sbagliare to make a mistake
sbaglio mistake
sbocciare to blossom
scarpa shoe
scatola box
scegliere to choose, select
scendere to descend
sciare to ski
sciarpa scarf
scienza science
sconto discount
scorso last
scrivere to write
scultore (*m.*) / **scultrice** (*f.*) sculptor
scuola school
scusi excuse me (*pol.*)
se if
sebbene although
secondo according to, second, main course
sedia chair
segnale (*m.*) sign
semaforo traffic lights
sembrare (*ess.*) to seem
semplice simple
sempre always
sentire to hear, to feel
senza without
senz'altro without doubt, likely
sera evening

serie series
servire to serve
sesto sixth
sete (*f.*) thirst
settembre September
settentrionale northern
settimana week
settimo seventh
sì yes
siciliano Sicilian
sicuro sure
signora Mrs., madam, lady
signore Mr., sir, gentleman
signorina Miss, Ms.
simpatico nice, charming
sincero sincere
sindaco (*m./f.*) mayor
singolo single
sinistra left
sistema (*m.*) system
SMS (*m.*) text message
soldi money
sole (*m.*) sun
solo only, alone
sopra over, on top
soprano soprano
sorella sister
sotto under, below
spagnolo Spanish
speciale special
sperare to hope
spesa food shopping
spesso often
spia spy
spicciolo coin, small change
sporco dirty
sport (*m.*) sport
sportello door
sposarsi to marry, get married
stamani this morning
stanco tired
stanza room
stare (*ess.*) to stay, to be
stare bene a to look good on
stare zitto to be quiet
stasera tonight
stato civile marital status
stazione station
stazione (*f.*) **di servizio** service station
stella star
stesso same
stivale boot
storia history
strada road, street
studente (*m.*) male student
studentessa (*f.*) female student
studiare to study
stufo fed up
stupido stupid

su on
subito right away
succo di frutta fruit juice
Suo (*pol., sing.*) your
suo his, her, its
suocera mother-in-law
suocero father-in-law
suonare to play (an instrument)
supermercato supermarket
svegliarsi to wake up

T

taglia size
tanto many, a lot
tardi late
tassì (*m.*) taxi
tavolo table
tazza cup
tè (*m.*) tea
teatro theater
tedesco German
telefonare to phone
televisione (*f.*) television
tempo time (abstract), weather
tenere to keep, hold
tennis (*m., inv.*) tennis
teologo theologian
teorema (*m.*) theorem
terribile terrible
terzo third
tesi (*f.*) thesis
testa head
timido shy, timid
tipo type
tirare vento to be windy
tornare (*ess.*) to return, to come back
torta cake
tovagliolo napkin
tra within
tram (*m.*) streetcar, trolley
treno train
triste sad
troppo too, too much
trota trout
trovare to find
tu (*fam., sing.*) you
tuo your (*fam.*)
turista (*m./f.*) tourist (*male or female*)
tutti everyone
tutti e due both
tutto everything
TV (*f.*) TV

U

ufficiale official
ultimo last
un po' a bit
università (*f.*) university

uomo man
uscire (*ess.*) to go out
uscita exit, gate
utile useful
uva grapes

V

va bene OK
vacanza vacation
vaglia (*m.*) money order
valigia suitcase
vecchio old
vedere to see
veloce fast
vendere to sell
venerdì Friday
venire (*ess.*) to come
vento wind
verde green
verdura vegetables
vergognarsi to be ashamed, be embarrassed
verità (*f.*) truth
vero true, right
vestirsi to get dressed
vestito dress
vetrina store window
via street
viaggio trip
vicino near
vigile (*m.*) traffic policeman
vincere to win
vino wine
viola (*inv.*) purple
violento violent
virgola comma
virtù (*f.*) virtue
visitare to visit
vitello veal
vivace lively, vivacious
vivere (*ess.*) to live
voi (*fam., pl.*) you
volante (*m.*) steering wheel
volentieri gladly
volere to want
volere bene a to care for, to love
volo flight
volta time (occurrence)
vorrei I would like
vostro (*fam., pl.*) your

Z

zabaione (*m.*) egg custard
zaino backpack
zero zero
zia aunt
zio uncle
zucchero sugar

English-Italian Glossary

A

a bit un po'
a lot molto, tanto
A pleasure to know you. Piacere di conoscerti.
A pleasure to make your acquaintance. Piacere di fare la Sua (*pol.*) conoscenza.
absolute assoluto
according to secondo
account conto
accountant ragioniere (*m.*) / ragioniera (*f.*)
actor/actress attore (*m.*) / attrice (*f.*)
address indirizzo
adventure avventura
advice consiglio
after dopo, poi
afternoon pomeriggio
again ancora, di nuovo
ago fa
I agree d'accordo
air aria
aisle seat posto al corridoio
all tutto
almost quasi
alone solo
already già
also anche (anche io or anch'io)
although benché, sebbene
always sempre
American americano
among fra, tra
analysis analisi (*f.*)
and e
to answer rispondere
anthropologist antropologo (*m.*) / antropologa (*f.*)
any qualsiasi, qualunque
anything else, other altro
appetizer antipasto
apple mela
apple tree melo
appointment appuntamento
April aprile
architect architetto (*m./f.*)
arm braccio
armchair poltrona

around circa
arrival arrivo
to arrive arrivare (*ess.*)
as come, così
as a matter of fact anzi
as if come se
to ask (for) chiedere
at my house a casa mia
at what time a che ora
at a, in
to attach allegare
August agosto
aunt zia
author autore (*m.*) / autrice (*f.*)
automatic teller bancomat (*m.*)
automobile automobile (*f.*)
autumn autunno

B

backpack zaino
bad cattivo
bad(ly) male
baggage bagaglio
bank banca
bankbook libretto
bar bar
barber barbiere (*m.*)
barely appena
barley orzo
bartender barista (*m./f.*)
basketball pallacanestro
bathroom bagno
to be essere (*ess.*), stare (*ess.*)
to be able to potere
to be able to take/manage it farcela
to be ashamed vergognarsi
to be asked essere pregato
to be better to convenire (*ess.*)
to be called chiamarsi
to be born essere nato (-a), nascere (*ess.*)
to be embarrassed vergognarsi
to be enough bastare (*ess.*)
to be expected essere previsto
to be familiar with conoscere
to be hungry avere fame

to be in love essere innamorato

to be married essere sposato (-a)

to be named chiamarsi

to be necessary bisognare

to be . . . old avere... anni

to be pleasing to, a pleasure piacere (*ess.*)

to be quiet stare zitto

to be right avere ragione

to be there esserci

to be windy tirare vento

bean fagiolo

beautiful bello

because perché

to become diventare (*ess.*)

to become angry arrabbiarsi

to become bored annoiarsi

bed letto

bedroom camera

before prima, prima che

to begin cominciare

to believe credere

belt cintura

below sotto

benevolent benevolo

better meglio, migliore

between fra, tra

big grande

bigger maggiore

bill biglietto

biologist biologo

biology biologia

bill conto

birthday compleanno

black nero

block isolato

blond biondo

to blossom sbocciare

blouse camicetta

blue azzurro

boarding pass carta d'imbarco

body corpo

book libro

boot stivale (*m.*)

boring noioso

both tutti e due

bottle bottiglia

box scatola

boxing pugilato

boy (girl) ragazzo (-a)

brake freno

bread pane (*m.*)

breakfast colazione (*f.*)

brick mattone (*m.*)

to bring portare

brother fratello

brother-in-law cognato

brown marrone (*inv.*)

bun sandwich panino

bus autobus (*m., inv.*)

business transaction affare (*m.*)

but ma

to buy comprare

to buy a (travel) ticket fare il biglietto

by di, da

by chance per caso

by now ormai

bye ciao

C

cake torta

to call chiamare

to call oneself chiamarsi

can potere

Can you help me? Mi puoi aiutare? (*fam.*), Mi può aiutare? (*pol.*)

capital of a region capoluogo

cappuccino cappuccino

captain comandante (*m./f.*)

car macchina

car headlight faro

car horn clacson (*m., inv.*)

car racing automobilismo

to care for volere bene a

carrot carota

cat gatto

cell phone cellulare (*m.*)

centimeter centimetro

center of town centro

central centrale

certainly certo

chair sedia

championship campionato

change room camerino

to change cambiare

charming simpatico

check conto

to check controllare

cheese formaggio

chemistry chimica

cherry ciliegia

cherry tree ciliegio

child bambino (-a)

chocolate cioccolato

to choose scegliere

Christmas Natale (*m.*), natalizio (*of Christmas*)

church chiesa

cinema cinema (*m., inv.*)

city città (*f.*)

city square piazza

class classe (*f.*)

classic classico

to clean pulire (type 2)

clerk commesso (-a)

to close chiudere

coat cappotto

coffee caffè (*m.*)

coffee place bar

coffee with a drop of alcohol corretto

coffee with milk (a "latte") caffellatte (*m.*)
coin spicciolo
cold freddo
to come venire (*ess.*)
to come back tornare (*ess.*)
comma virgola
commemorative commemorativo
common comune
company (business) ditta
to complain lamentarsi
completed compiuto
computer computer (*m.*), informatica (*informatics*)
condo condominio
content contento
to control controllare
correct corretto
to cost costare (*ess.*)
costly costoso
cousin cugino (-a)
to create creare
credit card carta di credito
crew equipaggio
crisis crisi (*f.*)
croissant cornetto
to cross attraversare
cup tazza
to cure guarire (type 2)
customer cliente (*m./f.*)
cute carino
cutlet cotoletta

D

dad papà (*m., inv.*), babbo
to dance ballare
dark blue blu (*inv.*)
dark-haired bruno
date data, appuntamento
daughter figlia
daughter-in-law nuora
day giorno
dear caro
December dicembre
to decide decidere
degree laurea
delicatessen pizzicheria
delighted lieto
dentist dentista (*m./f.*)
to depart partire (*ess.*)
departure partenza
to deposit depositare
to descend scendere
to desire desiderare
despite nonostante che
dessert dessert (*m., inv.*)
device dispositivo
diagram diagramma (*m.*)
difficult difficile
dining room sala da pranzo

dirty sporco
disco discoteca
discount sconto
dish piatto
diverse diverso
to do fare
doctor/Dr. dottore (*m.*), dottoressa (*f.*)
dog cane (*m.*)
dollar dollaro
donkey asino
door porta, sportello
double doppio
to doubt dubitare
down there laggiù
downtown centro
dozen dozzina
draftsperson geometra (*m./f.*)
drama dramma (*m.*)
dress vestito
to drink bere
drinking toast brindisi (*m.*)
to drive guidare
driver autista (*m./f.*)
driver's license patente (*f.*)
dumpling gnocco
to dwell abitare

E

each ogni
early presto, in anticipo
Easter Pasqua
eastern orientale
easy facile
to eat mangiare
egg custard zabaione (*m.*)
eighth ottavo
electrician elettricista (*m./f.*)
elegant elegante
elephant elefante (*m.*) / elefantessa (*f.*)
elevator ascensore (*m.*)
e-mail mail (*f.*)
English inglese (*m./f.*)
to enjoy oneself divertirsi
enormous enorme
enough abbastanza
to enter entrare (*ess.*)
to entertain divertire
entire intero
entrance ingresso
espresso coffee espresso
euro euro
evening sera
ever mai
every ogni
everyone tutti
everything tutto
exam esame (*m.*)
excellent ottimo
exceptional eccezionale

to exchange cambiare
excuse me (*pol.*) scusi
exit uscita
expensive costoso
experience esperienza
eye occhio
eyeglasses occhiali (*m., pl.*)

F

face faccia
fall (*autumn*) autunno
to fall cadere (*ess.*)
to fall in love essere innamorato
family famiglia
family name cognome (*m.*)
far lontano
fashionable alla moda
fast veloce
to fasten allacciare
fat grasso
father padre
father-in-law suocero
favor favore (*m.*)
feast festa
February febbraio
fed up stufo
to feel sentire
to feel like avere voglia di
female student studentessa (*f.*)
few poco
fifth quinto
fig, fig tree fico
film film (*m.*)
to find trovare
fine (*I agree*) d'accordo
finger dito
to finish finire (-isc) (type 2)
first primo, prima
fish pesce (*m.*)
flight volo
floor piano
food shopping spesa
foot piede (*m.*)
for per
to forget dimenticare, dimenticarsi
fork forchetta
form modulo
fortunate fortunato
fourth quarto
French francese (*m./f.*)
french fry patatina
fresh fresco
Friday venerdì
friend amico (*m.*) / amica (*f.*)
friendly amichevole
from (for) da
fruit frutta
fruit juice succo di frutta
full pieno

fussy fastidioso, noioso

G

game gioco, partita
garage garage (*m.*)
gas pedal acceleratore (*m.*)
gate uscita
generous generoso
gentleman signore
geography geografia
German tedesco
to get back rientrare (*ess.*)
to get better guarire (type 2)
to get divorced divorziarsi
to get dressed vestirsi
to get married sposarsi
to get up alzarsi
girl (boy) ragazza (-o)
to give dare
gladly volentieri
glass bicchiere
(eye)glasses occhiali (*m., pl.*)
to go andare (*ess.*)
to go away andare via
to go out uscire (*ess.*)
to go up salire (*ess.*)
good buono, (*at something*) bravo
good afternoon buon pomeriggio
good-bye (*informal*) arrivederci, arrivederLa
    (*formal*)
good day buongiorno
good evening buonasera
good morning buongiorno
good night buona notte
grandfather nonno
grandmother nonna
grandson/granddaughter nipote (*m./f.*)
grapes uva
gratuity mancia
gray grigio
greater maggiore
Greek greco
green verde
grill griglia
groceries generi alimentari
to grow crescere (*ess.*)
guard guardia
guide guida
gym palestra

H

hair (on the head) capelli (*m., pl.*)
half mezzo
hand mano (*f.*)
handsome bello
happy felice, contento
Happy birthday! Buon compleanno!
hard forte
to hate odiare

to have avere
to have to dovere
he egli, lui
head testa
head of a department caporeparto
headache mal di testa
to heal guarire (type 2)
to hear sentire
heart cuore (*m.*)
heavy pesante
Hello! Pronto!, Buongiorno!
her suo
here qui
here (it is) ecco
hi ciao
his suo
history storia
to hold tenere
holiday festa
homework assignment compito
to hope sperare
hot caldo
hotel albergo
hour ora
house casa
how come
How are you? Come stai? (*fam.*)/sta? (*pol.*)
how much quanto
How's it going? Come va?
hunger fame (*f.*)
husband marito
hypothesis ipotesi (*f.*)

I

I io
I have to go devo andare
I would like vorrei
ice cream gelato
idea idea
if se
to imagine immaginare
important importante
impossible impossibile
in in
in a hurry in fretta
in front davanti
in style alla moda
in the event that nel caso che
in the meantime nel frattempo
to indicate indicare
informatics informatica
instead invece
intelligent intelligente
interesting interessante
interview intervista
to introduce presentare
to invent inventare
island isola
it esso

it doesn't matter non importa
Italian italiano
its suo

J

jacket giacca
January gennaio
job lavoro
to jog fare il footing
July luglio
June giugno
just (*barely*) appena, proprio, giusto (*correctness*)

K

to keep tenere
key chiave (*f.*)
kilogram chilo
kiss bacio
to kiss baciare
kitchen cucina
knee ginocchio
knife coltello
to know sapere, (*be familiar with*) conoscere

L

lady signora
lake lago
language lingua
laptop portatile (*m.*)
lasagne lasagne (*f., pl.*)
last scorso, ultimo
to last durare (*ess.*)
late tardi
lawyer avvocato
leaf foglia
to learn imparare
to leave partire (*ess.*)
left sinistra
lemon, lemon tree limone (*m.*)
lemonade limonata
to lend prestare
less meno
let me introduce myself mi presento
lie bugia
life jacket salvagente (*m.*)
light leggero
like come
to like piacere (*ess.*)
likely senz'altro
lion leone (*m.*) / leonessa (*f.*)
lip labbro
to listen (to) ascoltare
little poco, piccolo (*small*)
little book libricino
little boy/girl bambino (-a)
to live vivere (*ess.*), abitare
lively vivace
living room salotto

lobby atrio
long lungo
to look at guardare
to look for cercare
to look good on stare bene a
to look onto dare su
to lose perdere
love amore (*m.*)
to love amare, volere bene a
lucky fortunato

M

madam signora
magazine rivista
magnificent magnifico
main course secondo
to make fare
major maggiore
to make a mistake sbagliare
male student studente (*m.*)
man uomo
mandarin, mandarin tree mandarino
many tanto
March marzo
marital status stato civile
market mercato
to marry sposarsi
match partita
math(ematics) matematica
May maggio
maybe forse
mayor sindaco (*m./f.*)
meal pasto
meat carne (*f.*)
meat sauce ragù (*m.*)
mechanic meccanico
medical doctor medico
to meet incontrare
meeting riunione (*f.*)
menu menù (*m., inv.*)
message messaggino
meter metro
midnight mezzanotte (*f.*)
milk latte (*m.*)
million milione
mineral water acqua minerale
minestrone minestrone (*m.*)
minor minore
minute minuto
Miss, Ms. signorina
mistake sbaglio
mobile mobile
modern moderno
mom mamma
moment momento
Monday lunedì
money denaro, soldi
money order vaglia (*m.*)
monk monaco

month mese (*m.*)
more più
morning mattina
mother madre (*f.*)
mother-in-law suocera
motorcycle motocicletta (moto)
mountain(s) montagna
movie film (*m.*)
movies cinema (*m., inv.*)
movie theater cinematografo (il cinema)
Mr. signore
Mrs. signora
Ms. signorina
much molto, tanto
music musica
musician musicista (*m./f.*)
must dovere
mustache baffi (*m., pl.*)
my mio
my name is mi chiamo

N

name nome (*m.*)
napkin tovagliolo
nation nazione (*f.*)
to navigate navigare
near(by) vicino
nearly circa
necktie cravatta
to need (*to have need of*) avere bisogno di
neither neanche, né
nephew nipote (*m.*)
new nuovo
newspaper giornale (*m.*)
newsstand edicola
next prossimo
nice simpatico
niece nipote (*f.*)
night notte (*f.*)
nightclub locale notturno
ninth nono
no no
no one nessuno
no problem non c'è problema
No way! Macché!
noon mezzogiorno
nor né
normal normale
northern settentrionale
not non
not at all affatto, non... affatto
not even nemmeno, neppure
not really mica
nothing niente, nulla
novel romanzo
November novembre
now adesso
nowadays oggigiorno
number numero

nurse infermiere (*m.*) / infermiera (*f.*)

O

October ottobre
of di
of course certo
office worker impiegato (-a)
official ufficiale
often spesso
OK va bene
old vecchio
older maggiore
on su
on sale in saldo
on the dot in punto
on time in orario
on top sopra
on vacation in ferie
only solo
to open aprire
opera libretto libretto
opinion opinione (*f.*)
optimistic ottimista
or o
orange arancione (*inv.*), arancia (noun)
orange drink aranciata
orange tree arancio
our nostro
over there là, laggiù
over sopra
ox bue (*m.*)

P

painter pittore (*m.*) / pittrice (*f.*)
pair paio
pants pantaloni (*m., pl.*)
parent genitore (*m.*)
party festa
passenger passeggero (-a)
passenger window finestrino
pasta pasta
patience pazienza
to pay pagare
pea pisello
peace pace (*f.*)
peach pesca
peach tree pesco
pear pera
pear tree pero
pen penna
people gente (*f.*)
pepper pepe (*m.*)
person persona
pharmacist farmacista (*m./f.*)
pharmacy farmacia
to phone telefonare
photo(graph) foto(grafia)
physics fisica
pianist pianista (*m./f.*)

piano pianoforte (*m.*)
piece pezzo
piece of furniture mobile (*m.*)
pig porco
pink rosa
place luogo
planet pianeta
plant pianta
plate piatto
to play (a sport) giocare
to play (an instrument) suonare
playoffs campionato
please per favore
plural plurale
poor povero
popular popolare
possible possibile
potato patata
practical pratico
precise(ly) preciso
to prefer preferire (-isc) (type 2)
to prepare oneself prepararsi
to present presentare
price prezzo
probable probabile
problem problema (*m.*)
professor professore (*m.*), professoressa (*f.*)
program programma (*m.*)
to propose proporre
prosciutto ham prosciutto
provided that purché
psychologist psicologo (*m.*) / psicologa (*f.*)
purple viola (*inv.*)
purse borsa
to put mettere
to put on mettersi

Q

quarter quarto
question domanda
quite assai, mica
quite a few parecchio

R

radio radio (*f.*)
railroad ferrovia
to rain piovere
rainbow arcobaleno
raincoat impermeabile (*m.*)
rare raro
rascal mascalzone (*m.*)
rather piuttosto, assai
to read leggere
really proprio
red rosso
refrigerator frigorifero
region regione (*f.*)
regular regolare
to remain rimanere (*ess.*)

to remember ricordare
to rent an apartment, house, etc. affittare
to rent a vehicle, a movie, etc. noleggiare
reservation prenotazione (*f.*)
restaurant ristorante (*m.*)
to return tornare (*ess.*)
to return home rientrare (*ess.*)
rice riso
rich ricco
right proprio, vero, (*correctness*) giusto, (*direction*) destra
right away subito
right over here qua
ring anello
road strada
romantic romantico
room stanza
rooster gallo
rope cordone (*m.*)
round-trip andata e ritorno
to run into incontrare

S

sad triste
safe (*for valuables*) cassaforte (*f.*)
salad insalata
salami salame (*m.*)
salt sale (*m.*)
same stesso
Saturday sabato
to say dire
scoundrel mascalzone (*m.*)
scarf sciarpa
schedule orario
school scuola
science scienza
scissors forbici (*f., pl.*)
screwdriver cacciavite (*m.*)
script copione (*m.*)
sculptor scultore (*m.*) / scultrice (*f.*)
sea mare (*m.*)
to search for cercare
seat posto
seat belt cintura di sicurezza
second secondo
to see vedere
see you soon a presto
see you tomorrow a domani
to seem sembrare (*ess.*)
to select scegliere
to sell vendere
to send mandare
September settembre
series serie
to serve servire
service station stazione (*f.*) di servizio
seventh settimo
several diverso, parecchio, alcuni (*m.*) / alcune (*f.*)
she ella, lei

shirt camicia
shoe scarpa
short basso
short/strong coffee ristretto
shy timido
Sicilian siciliano
side dish contorno
sign segnale (*m.*)
to sign firmare
simple semplice
sincere sincero
to sing cantare
singer cantante (*m./f.*)
single singolo
sir signore
sister sorella
sister-in-law cognata
sixth sesto
size taglia
skating pattinaggio
to ski sciare
skinny magro
skirt gonna
sky blue celeste
to sleep dormire
slice fetta
slow lento
small piccolo
small change spicciolo
smaller minore
snow neve (*f.*)
to snow nevicare
so that affinché
so così
so that affinché
soccer calcio
sofa divano
soft drink, soda bibita
some qualche, alcuni (*m.*) / alcune (*f.*)
someone qualcuno
something qualcosa
son figlio
son-in-law genero
soon presto
soprano soprano
sore throat mal di gola
soup minestra
southern meridionale
Spanish spagnolo
to speak parlare
special speciale
spoon cucchiaio
sport sport (*m.*)
spring primavera
spy spia
stamp francobollo
star stella
to start cominciare
station stazione

to stay stare (*ess.*)
to stay calm calmarsi
steering wheel volante (*m.*)
still ancora
stomachache mal di stomaco
store negozio
store window vetrina
straight ahead diritto
straight ruler riga
strawberry fragola
street via, strada
streetcar tram (*m.*)
string bean fagiolino
strong forte
strong coffee ristretto
student student (*m.*) / studentessa (*f.*)
to study studiare
stupid stupido
sugar zucchero
suit abito
suitcase valigia
summer estate (*f.*)
sun sole (*m.*)
Sunday domenica
supermarket supermercato
sure sicuro
to surf the Internet navigare in Internet
surname cognome (*m.*)
sweater maglia
sweet dolce
swimming nuoto
swimming pool piscina
system sistema (*m.*)

T

table tavolo
to take prendere
to take out da portare via
takeoff decollo
tall alto
task (*homework assignment*) compito
taxi tassì (*m.*)
tea tè (*m.*)
teacher insegnante (*m./f.*)
teaspoon cucchiaino
television televisione (*f.*)
to tell dire
tennis tennis (*m., inv.*)
tenth decimo
terrible terribile
text messaggino
text message SMS (*m.*)
thank goodness! meno male!
thank you grazie
that che
that which quello che
to the left a sinistra
to the right a destra
theater teatro

then poi, allora
their loro
theologian teologo
theorem teorema (*m.*)
there lì
thesis tesi (*f.*)
they loro
thing cosa
to think pensare
third terzo
thirst sete (*f.*)
this morning stamani
thousand mille
through per
Thursday giovedì
thus allora, così
ticket biglietto
ticket agent bigliettaio (-a)
tie cravatta
time (of day) ora, (*abstract*) tempo, (*occurrence*)
    volta
timetable orario
timid timido
tip (*gratuity*) mancia
tire gomma
tired stanco
to a, in
today oggi
together insieme
tomato pomodoro
tomorrow domani
tonight stasera
too troppo, anche (anche io or anch'io)
too much troppo
toothache mal di denti
tour giro
tourist (*male or female*) turista (*m./f.*)
track binario
track and field atletica leggera
traffic lights semaforo
traffic policeman vigile (*m.*)
train treno
tree albero
trip viaggio
trolley car tram (*m.*)
trout trota
true vero
truth verità (*f.*)
to try provare
to try on provarsi
Tuesday martedì
to turn girare
TV TV (*f.*)
type tipo

U

ugly brutto
uncle zio
under sotto

to understand capire (-isc) (type 2)
underwear mutande (*f., pl.*)
unfortunately purtroppo
university università (*f.*)
university graduate dottore (*m.*) / dottoressa (*f.*)
unless a meno che
until now finora
useful utile
us noi
usually di solito

V

vacation vacanza
various diverso
veal vitello
vegetables verdura
very molto
violent violento
virtue virtù (*f.*)
to visit visitare
vivacious vivace

W

to wait (for) aspettare
waiter/waitress cameriere (-a)
to wake up svegliarsi
wall (*partition*) parete (*f.*)
to want volere, desiderare
warm caldo
to wash lavare
to wash oneself lavarsi
watch orologio
to watch guardare
water acqua
we noi
to wear portare, mettersi
weather tempo
Wednesday mercoledì (*m.*)
week settimana
well bene
well-mannered educato
western occidentale
what che, che cosa, quale
whatever quello che
What's your name? Come ti chiami? (*fam.*), Come si chiama? (*pol.*)
What time is it? Che ore sono?/Che ora è?
when quando
where dove
wherever dovunque

which quale, cui
whichever qualsiasi, qualunque
while mentre
white bianco
who che, chi
whoever chiunque, chi
whom cui
why perché
wife moglie
to win vincere
wind vento
window finestra
window seat posto al finestrino
windshield parabrezza (*m.*)
wine vino
winter inverno
to wish augurare
with con
with a dash of steamed milk macchiato
to withdraw prelevare
within tra, fra
without senza
without doubt senz'altro
woman donna
to work lavorare, (*function*) funzionare
work lavoro
world mondo
to worry preoccuparsi
worse peggiore
wrestling lotta
to write scrivere

Y

year anno
yellow giallo
yes sì
yesterday ieri
yet ancora
you tu (*fam., sing.*), Lei (*pol., sing.*), voi (*fam., pl.*)
you're welcome prego
young giovane
young lady signorina
your tuo (*fam., sing.*), Suo (*pol., sing.*), vostro (*fam., pl.*), Loro (*pol., pl.*)
your (*fam.*)
youth gioventù (*f.*), ragazzo (-a)

Z

zero zero

Answer key

Part I: Conversation

I-1 Making contact

1·1
1. uomo 2. Mr. Verdi 3. sì 4. Professor Marchi 5. A presto 6. Dr. Bruni 7. e
8. Professor Santucci 9. Lei 10. Mrs. (Ms.) Marchi 11. donna 12. Dr. Santucci
13. certo 14. how 15. domani 16. thank you 17. tu 18. very 19. bene
20. Buongiorno. 21. Buon pomeriggio. 22. A domani. 23. ArrivederLa.
24. Arrivederci./Ciao. 25. Come va? 26. Ciao. 27. Buongiorno, signora Verdi.
28. Buonasera, signor Marchi. 29. Buon pomeriggio, professoressa Santucci. 30. Ciao,
Marcello. 31. Buonanotte.

1·2
1. Molto lieto. 2. Piacere di fare la Sua conoscenza. 3. italiana 4. americano
5. sono 6. sei 7. è 8. Come si chiama? 9. Come ti chiami? 10. Piacere di
conoscerti. 11. (Io) sono italiano (-a). 12. Devo andare.

1·3
1. Che (cosa) è? 2. Chi è? 3. Dov'è (Dove è) il commesso? 4. Perché non mi puoi
aiutare? 5. isolati 6. libri 7. italiani 8. romanzi 9. uomini 10. dottori
11. professori 12. ho 13. hai 14. ha 15. abbiamo 16. avete 17. hanno
18. Mi piace il nuovo romanzo. 19. Mi piacciono i libri. 20. Mi piace il dottore.
21. Mi piacciono i professori. 22. Ho bisogno di un nuovo libro da leggere. 23. Le
piacciono i romanzi d'avventura? 24. Il libro è in vetrina. 25. Ecco un romanzo
d'avventura. 26. Va bene. 27. Scusi, mi può aiutare? 28. Scusa, mi puoi aiutare?
29. Via Nazionale è qui a sinistra, non a destra. 30. Certo, signorina. 31. È a due
isolati. 32. Non c'è problema. 33. Maria non è americana. 34. È italiana, Maria?/Maria è
italiana?

I-2 Numbers, time, dates

2·1
1. i francobolli 2. i cornetti 3. i libri 4. i panini 5. i romanzi 6. una casa
7. una nuova casa/una casa nuova 8. una donna bella 9. due euro 10. tre panini
11. quattro romanzi 12. cinque cornetti 13. sei espressi/sei caffè espressi 14. sette
uomini 15. otto libri belli 16. nove euro 17. dieci francobolli commemorativi
18. tredici uomini belli 19. quattordici donne belle 20. quindici case belle 21. sedici,
diciassette, diciotto 22. diciannove, trentotto 23. duecento cinquantatré 24. novecento
sessantadue 25. duemila ottanta 26. Vorrei un caffè espresso, per favore. 27. Altro?
28. Vorrei due o tre cornetti subito. 29. Ho molta fame. 30. Va bene, vorrei comprare due
panini da portare via. 31. C'è una festa a casa mia stasera. 32. Prego. 33. C'è un nuovo
bar/un bar nuovo in via Nazionale. 34. Non ci sono nuovi libri/libri nuovi in
vetrina. 35. Ecco un espresso. 36. Quanto costano i francobolli? 37. Ogni panino costa
undici euro. 38. Allora, ne prendo solo dodici.

2·2
1. È l'una e dieci del pomeriggio./Sono le tredici e dieci. 2. Sono le tre e trenta/mezzo del
pomeriggio./Sono le quindici e trenta. 3. Sono le quattro e dodici del pomeriggio./Sono le
sedici e dodici. 4. Sono le nove e dieci della mattina. 5. Sono le dieci e quindici/un quarto
della mattina. 6. Sono le sette e trentacinque della sera./Sono le diciannove e
trentacinque. 7. Sono le nove e quarantotto della sera./Sono le ventuno e quarantotto.
8. È mezzogiorno. 9. È mezzanotte. 10. Tu torni alle diciannove e quindici/un quarto.
11. La donna comincia alle otto e trentotto. 12. Noi cominciamo alle dieci e trenta/mezzo.
13. Voi tornate alle ventidue e venti. 14. Loro cominciano alle undici e dieci. 15. Io
comincio alle tredici e cinque. 16. Che ora è?/Che ore sono? 17. No, non è tardi. 18. (Io)

ho un appuntamento alle quattro precise del pomeriggio/alle sedici precise col professore.   19. Maria torna alle otto in punto della sera/alle venti in punto.   20. Quando finisce?   21. Finisce alle dieci della sera/alle ventidue circa.   22. Il giro comincia troppo tardi.   23. C'è un giro che comincia a mezzogiorno?   24. Allora, (io) torno domani alla stessa ora.

2·3 1. Oggi è lunedì, il primo gennaio.   2. Oggi è martedì, l'otto febbraio.   3. Oggi è mercoledì, il dieci marzo.   4. Oggi è giovedì, il dodici aprile.   5. Oggi è venerdì, il ventotto maggio.   6. Oggi è sabato, il ventitré giugno.   7. Oggi è domenica, il quattro luglio.   8. Quanti   9. Quanti   10. Quanto   11. Quante   12. Alessandro è nato nel 1994.   13. La moglie è nata nel 1987.   14. Il marito è nato nel 1984.   15. Quanti ne abbiamo (oggi)?   16. Se non sbaglio, è il compleanno di Maria.   17. Buon compleanno!   18. Quanti anni hai?   19. Quanti anni ha?   20. (Io) ho trentasei anni.   21. (Tu) sembri ancora un bambino.   22. Che giorno è?   23. È terribile!   24. Il marito dimentica sempre tutto.   25. Ma anche noi dimentichiamo sempre tutto.   26. Ricordo in che anno è nato (-a).

I-3 Getting information

3·1 1.americani   2. appuntamenti   3. avventure   4. bambini   5. bambine   6. dottoresse   7. romanzi   8. sere   9. mogli   10. dottori   11. Come sta tuo fratello?   12. Come state (voi)?   13. Come sta (Lei)?   14. Come stanno i bambini?   15. (io) vengo, so, conosco   16. (tu) vieni, sai, conosci   17. (lui/lei) viene, sa, conosce   18. (noi) veniamo, sappiamo, conosciamo   19. (voi) venite, sapete, conoscete   20. (loro) vengono, sanno, conoscono   21. Dove abiti adesso?   22. Dove abita adesso, signora Marchi?   23. (Io) abito a Firenze.   24. La signora Marchi abita in Italia.   25. Il signor Verdi abita in via Dante.   26. (Io) abito vicino a Maria.   27. (Io) abito negli Stati Uniti.   28. Qualcuno ha detto che (io) sono sposato (-a).   29. Per adesso, mi piace la libertà.   30. Il romanzo che leggo è nuovo.   31. Come sta tuo fratello?   32. È sposato e ha bambini.   33. Non sono sicuro (-a) quando verrà la prossima volta.   34. (Lui) viene spesso a Roma.   35. (Io) so leggere in italiano.   36. (Io) non conosco il professore d'italiano.

3·2 1. devi, vai, dici, fai, puoi   2. deve, va, dice, fa, può   3. dobbiamo, andiamo, diciamo, facciamo, possiamo   4. dovete, andate, dite, fate, potete   5. devono, vanno, dicono, fanno, possono   6. devo, vado, dico, faccio, posso   7. un semaforo   8. una strada   9. uno studente   10. una studentessa   11. uno zio   12. una zia   13. i bambini belli   14. la donna bella   15. i vigili alti   16. la madre alta   17. le case grandi   18. il bambino grande   19. (Scusi), mi sa dire dov'è via Dante?   20. Vada a destra per un isolato e poi giri a sinistra al semaforo.   21. Devo attraversare la strada?   22. Vada diritto per ancora tre isolati.   23. Lì c'è via Macchiavelli?/C'è via Macchiavelli lì?   24. Ecco il/un bancomat.   25. Come si fa per andarci?   26. Vada a nord per un po'.   27. È vicino alla chiesa.   28. È proprio davanti alla chiesa.   29. Non può sbagliare.   30. Vada a sud e poi a est per un po'.

3·3 1. i bambini   2. la strada   3. gli studenti   4. l'avventura   5. gli anni   6. l'euro   7. i caffè *(Recall that nouns ending in an accented vowel do not change.)*   8. l'uomo   9. voglio   10. vogliono   11. vuoi   12. vuole   13. vogliamo   14. volete   15. Giovanni, ti chiamo stasera col (mio) cellulare.   16. È meglio mandarmi un SMS/un messaggino.   17. Non ho un dispositivo mobile.   18. Pronto!   19. Chi parla?   20. Sono io.   21. Laura, che vuoi?   22. Signora Verdi, che vuole?   23. Non c'è.   24. Non importa.   25. Chiamo/Telefono più tardi.

I-4 People

4·1 1. questo uomo sicuro   2. quello studente stupido   3. questi commessi bassi   4. quegli uomini belli   5. questo signore stupido   6. quell'americano grande   7. quegli italiani bassi   8. questa donna brutta   9. queste bambine timide   10. quella casa piccola   11. quelle case brutte   12. quell'americana bassa   13. quelle americane alte   14. al semaforo   15. dai commessi   16. dello zio   17. nell'occhio   18. sul SMS   19. alle donne   20. nella strada   21. dei bambini   22. degli uomini   23. Guarda che uomo bello!   24. Guarda che donna bella!   25. L'uomo è troppo alto per me.   26. Mi piacciono gli uomini biondi con gli occhi blu.   27. Non mi piacciono gli uomini bruni che sono troppo alti.   28. Non sembra intelligente, ma sembra molto simpatico.   29. (Tu) sei troppo fastidiosa.   30. Allora, che cosa aspetti?   31. Va bene, ci provo.   32. Questa donna qui è proprio bella.   33. Quella donna è senz'altro sposata, perché porta l'anello.   34. Forse la donna è un po' timida.   35. Non ci credo, perché lei è sempre sicura di sé.

4·2 1. (Lui) capisce molto.   2. (Noi) finiamo alle cinque e poi andiamo da Maria/alla casa di Maria.   3. Il fratello di Maria dorme fino a mezzogiorno.   4. capiscono   5. dormono   6. finiscono   7. capisci   8. il mio amico; i miei amici   9. tua zia; le tue zie *(With family and relatives, the article is dropped only in the singular, not the plural.)*   10. tuo zio; i tuoi zii   11. la sua amica; le sue amiche *(Recall that **suo** translates as both "his" and "her," but the form must agree with the noun.)*   12. la sua amica; le sue amiche *(Same as above.)*   13. nostro padre; i nostri padri   14. il nostro professore; i nostri professori   15. vostro fratello; i vostri fratelli   16. la Sua casa; le Sue case   17. la loro zia; le loro zie *(Recall that the exception to the article being dropped is **loro**.)*   18. il loro amico; i loro amici.   19. Mio fratello è noioso, ma è assai carino.   20. (Io) trovo la mia amica simpatica e vivace.   21. (Io) non conosco l'amico di mio fratello.   22. Il fratello della mia amica sembra un ragazzo sincero e educato.   23. Capisco!   24. (Tu) sei innamorata?   25. (Tu) sei innamorato?   26. (Voi) siete tutti e due innamorati?   27. Mi piacciono i ragazzi felici e ottimisti.

28. Mi piacciono anche le ragazze felici e ottimiste. (*Remember that the plural of an adjective ending in* **-e**, *like* **felice**, *is* **-i**, *even in the feminine.*)

4·3 1. Vorrei degli anelli. 2. Vorrei dei cellulari. 3. Vorrei dei francobolli. 4. Vorrei dei libri. 5. Vorrei dei panini. 6. la sua moglie bella 7. il suo fratello carino 8. il loro figlio grande 9. la loro figlia alta 10. il nostro nonno simpatico 11. la tua mamma vivace 12. il mio papà educato 13. il suo marito bello 14. la nostra cugina piccola/la nostra piccola cugina 15. il loro cugino basso 16. Alessandro, mi presti dei soldi? 17. (Io) non posso. 18. Sei proprio come il papà! 19. Sei proprio come la mamma! 20. Perché non chiedi al nonno o alla nonna? 21. Hai ragione e sei molto generosa. 22. La nostra piccola cugina è nata ieri? 23. (Lei) assomiglia a sua madre. 24. Tutta la mia famiglia è simpatica.

I-5 Jobs and homes

5·1 1. i buoni zii (*Don't forget to change the article form* **gli** *to fit before* **buoni**, *not* **zii**.) 2. le belle ragazze 3. la bella signora 4. la bell'amica 5. i begli amici 6. il bell'uomo 7. il buon uomo 8. il bello zio 9. il buon panino 10. qualche amica 11. degli studenti 12. qualche cornetto 13. dei libri 14. Marco, parla italiano! (**tu**-*form*) 15. Signor Verdi, parli italiano! (**Lei**-*form*) 16. Giovanni e Maria, aspettate qui! (**voi**-*form*) 17. Signorine, aspettino qui! (**Loro**-*form*) 18. Conosci un bravo avvocato o un bravo dentista? 19. Hai mal di denti? 20. Voglio diventare un medico o forse un architetto. 21. (È) impossibile. 22. È forse meglio fare qualcosa di più pratico? 23. Secondo me, tu sei nato per essere un insegnante. 24. (Io) preferisco fare il meccanico/essere un meccanico piuttosto che (un) impiegato (-a). 25. Fa' quello che vuoi!

5·2 1. hai aspettato 2. ha lavorato 3. ha mandato 4. abbiamo prestato 5. avete sbagliato 6. hanno telefonato 7. Maria, leggi il bel romanzo! /leggi il romanzo bello! 8. Signora Verdi, chieda un caffè! 9. Marco e Maria, prendete un po' di caffè! 10. Signori, leggano il nuovo libro. 11. (Scusi), cerco (un) lavoro nella Sua ditta. 12. Non ho mai lavorato in una ditta di informatica. 13. (Io) ho una laurea in matematica. 14. (Io) ho creato diversi programmi all'università. 15. (Io) ho qualche esperienza di lavoro. 16. (Io) ho lavorato per una banca diversi anni fa. 17. Torni la prossima settimana per un'intervista ufficiale. 18. Eccomi di nuovo. 19. Quanti anni ha? 20. (Io) voglio fare/Le faccio una serie di domande. 21. Qual è il Suo indirizzo? 22. Abito/Vivo in centro. 23. Qual è il Suo stato civile? 24. Mi piacciono quei bei programmi. 25. Cerchi la banca?

5·3 1. Giovanni, dormi! 2. Signora Verdi, dorma! 3. Marco e Maria, finite il caffè! 4. Signorine, finiscano il libro! 5. Bruna, finisci il cornetto! 6. Signora Verdi, finisca il panino! 7. Marco e Maria, dormite fino a tardi! 8. Questa casa è molto piccola, ma ha una bella cucina, una bella camera, e un bagno grande. 9. La casa ha un salotto magnifico e una sala da pranzo eccezionale. 10. Il garage, però, è molto piccolo. 11. L'entrata è assai grande. 12. (Io) devo comprare tanti nuovi mobili. 13. (Io) ho già un bel divano e una bella poltrona. 14. (Io) voglio comprare un nuovo frigorifero, un nuovo letto per la camera e un nuovo tavolo. 15. Conviene rimanere nel mio condominio.

I-6 Daily life

6·1 1. Vorrei delle fragole. 2. Vorrei dei piselli. 3. Vorrei delle pere. 4. Vorrei delle pesche. 5. Vorrei dei fagioli. 6. Vorrei del formaggio. 7. Vorrei del prosciutto. 8. Vorrei della carne. 9. Vorrei del pesce. 10. Vorrei del pane. 11. Vorrei dell'acqua. 12. Vorrei del latte. 13. Vorrei del vino. 14. Vorrei della frutta. 15. Vorrei della verdura. 16. Maria, non tornare domani! 17. Signor Marchi, non faccia questo! 18. Marco, non fare quella domanda al professore! 19. Giovanni e Bruna, non siate vivaci! 20. Maria, non avere fretta! (*Maria, don't be in a hurry!*) 21. Quante fragole desidera? 22. Vorrei una dozzina di mele e un chilo di pesche. 23. Queste fragole sono più fresche. 24. Basta così. 25. Desidera? 26. Vorrei una dozzina di fette di prosciutto. 27. Vorrei anche un po' di salame. (*Note the spelling in Italian.*) 28. Il formaggio è buonissimo/molto buono e freschissimo/molto fresco. 29. Vorrei comprare del prosciutto alla pizzicheria in via Nazionale. 30. Vorrei comprare il pane al panificio in via Dante.

6·2 1. Professor Giusto, vada in centro! 2. Marco e Bruna, andate in centro! 3. Maria, di' la verità! 4. Dottoressa Marinelli, dica la verità! 5. Giovanni e Maria, dite la verità! 6. Marco, vieni qui! 7. Signora Martini, venga qui! 8. Marco e Maria, venite qui! 9. Ieri ho comprato una camicetta bianca e una cintura gialla. 10. Ieri ho comprato due maglie grigie e una camicia marrone. 11. Ieri ho comprato una cravatta viola, una borsa rossa, un abito verde e una giacca nera. 12. Il professore non ha avuto tempo. 13. (Noi) non abbiamo dovuto comprare quell'abito. 14. (Voi) non avete potuto comprare quegli stivali. 15. (Tu) non hai voluto leggere quel libro. 16. (Io) non ho capito la verità. 17. (Tu) non hai dormito fino a tardi. 18. Il ragazzo non ha preferito il cornetto. 19. (Noi) non abbiamo finito di lavorare. 20. (Voi) non avete capito il libro. 21. Vorrei comprare una giacca alla moda. 22. Che taglia porta? 23. Vuole provarsi un vestito azzurro? 24. Vorrei (dei) pantaloni che vanno insieme con la (colla) giacca verde. 25. Dov'è il camerino? 26. Vada lì, a destra. 27. Quanto costano gli stivali e le scarpe? 28. Le scarpe sono in saldo. 29. Che numero porta? 30. Le stanno proprio bene.

6·3 1. (Io) non sono andato (-a) al supermercato. 2. (Tu) non sei venuto (-a) con loro in centro. 3. Quell'uomo non è tornato dal centro. 4. Quella donna non è tornata dal centro. 5. (Noi) non siamo stati (-e) in Italia. 6. (Voi) non siete venuti (-e) in centro. 7. Gli studenti non sono rimasti in classe. 8. Le donne non sono state al bar. 9. Quegli stivali non sono costati molto. 10. Quelle scarpe non sono costate tanto. 11. Marco non ha chiesto quelle domande al professore. (*Be careful! This verb is conjugated with* **avere**.)   12. Maria non ha detto la verità.   13. (Io) non ho fatto la spesa ieri.   14. Mio fratello non ha letto quel libro. 15. (Io) non ho preso il caffè al bar.   16. (Tu) non hai visto Maria ieri.   17. (Loro) non sono venuti (-e) con noi.   18. Vorrei depositare dei soldi/del denaro nel mio conto.   19. Vorrei prelevare dei soldi/del denaro dal mio altro conto.   20. Firmi questo modulo.   21. Vorrei (dei) biglietti di taglio piccolo.   22. Mi può cambiare questi biglietti in spiccioli?

I-7   Weather, seasons, and holidays

7·1   1. Il tuo amico non va mai al cinema.   2. La sua amica non sa niente/nulla.   3. Loro non vanno più in montagna.   4. Maria non conosce nessuno.   5. Io non voglio né la carne né il pesce.   6. Maria non ti chiama mai.   7. Maria non ci chiama mai.   8. Maria non vi chiama mai.   9. Maria non lo chiama mai.   10. Maria non la chiama mai.   11. Maria non li chiama mai.   12. Maria non le chiama mai.
13. (Io) non esco mai.   14. Le ragazze sono già uscite/sono uscite già.   15. Marco, esci con Maria!   16. Signora Verdi, esca con Suo marito!   17. Mio fratello è uscito qualche momento fa.   18. Marco, esci spesso? 19. Fa troppo freddo.   20. Fa troppo caldo.   21. Preferisco andare in montagna piuttosto che andare al mare.   22. Nevica sempre d'inverno.   23. Non sei mai contento (-a).   24. Vieni in centro con me. 25. Non voglio andare in centro perché piove forte.   26. Ho voglia di uscire.   27. Andiamo al cinema.

7·2   1. Maria non ti ha parlato.   2. Maria non ci ha parlato.   3. Maria non vi ha parlato.   4. Maria non gli ha parlato.   5. Maria non le ha parlato.   6. Maria non gli ha parlato.   7. Maria non gli ha parlato.   8. Maria è uscita con te.   9. Maria ha parlato a noi.   10. Maria è uscita con voi.   11. Maria ha parlato a lui. 12. Maria è uscita con lei.   13. Maria ha parlato a loro.   14. Maria è uscita con loro.   15. Amo la primavera ma odio l'inverno.   16. Preferisco l'estate perché amo il caldo.   17. A primavera sbocciano le piante. 18. Sei romantico (-a).   19. Il mio amore per te è molto forte.   20. Mi piace la neve.   21. Amo l'autunno perché cadono le foglie.

7·3   1. Io lo ho (l'ho) preso a quel bar.   2. Noi lo abbiamo letto già.   3. Mia sorella le ha comprate ieri. 4. La sua amica la ha (l'ha) fatta ieri.   5. Mia cugina non li ha voluti.   6. Non lo ho (l'ho) ancora finito. 7. Maria non la ha (l'ha) mai detta.   8. Li ho finiti.   9. Non le ho mai preferite.   10. Io te li ho comprati. 11. Mio fratello gliele ha chieste ieri.   12. Mio fratello glieli ha comprati ieri. (*Note that* **le** + **li** *becomes* **glieli**.)   13. Tu ce li hai mandati, vero?   14. Io ve lo ho preso, va bene?   15. È già Natale!   16. Amo le feste natalizie.   17. Non mi piace la Pasqua perché piove sempre.   18. Amo la primavera perché fa bel tempo e tutto comincia a crescere.   19. Tutti vanno in vacanza in agosto.   20. Purtroppo (io) devo lavorare.   21. Sei un vero amico/una vera amica!

I-8   Traveling

8·1   1. arriverà 2. parleremo 3. pagheremo 4. mangerete 5. comincerò 6. cercherai 7. chiederai 8. crederò 9. prenderemo 10. pioverà 11. leggeranno 12. capirò 13. finiranno 14. partiremo 15. dormirete 16. uscirà 17. Vorrei fare il/un biglietto di andata e ritorno per Roma.   18. Vorrei un biglietto di prima classe.   19. Il treno partirà dal binario numero dodici.   20. (Io) arriverò alla stazione in orario.   21. Il mio amico/La mia amica arriverà in anticipo di qualche minuto.   22. La partenza dell'autobus è alle quattordici e l'arrivo è alle diciassette.   23. (Io) ho ancora tempo.   24. C'è un'edicola qui vicino?

8·2   1. diamo 2. do 3. dai 4. dà 5. date 6. danno 7. (Io) ho dato quelle scarpe a mio fratello. 8. (Tu) davi molte cose a tua sorella.   9. (Lui) mi darà dei soldi/del denaro per uscire stasera.   10. Loro mi darebbero dei soldi/del denaro, ma non possono.   11. lui mangerebbe 12. io cercherei 13. noi partiremmo 14. tu verresti 15. voi sapreste 16. io pagherei 17. tu saresti 18. lei avrebbe 19. io vorrei 20. loro direbbero 21. io farei 22. Non ho fatto la prenotazione.   23. Vorrei una camera che dà sulla piazza.   24. Vorrei una camera singola, non una camera doppia.   25. A quanto viene a/per notte? 26. Potrei avere due chiavi?   27. L'ascensore non funziona.   28. Potrei avere una camera al sesto piano? 29. Dov'è l'atrio?   30. L'uscita è qui.   31. Dov'è l'entrata dell'albergo?   32. Non tornerò mai più in quest'albergo.   33. La colazione non è quasi mai buona.   34. La mia camera è sporca.   35. Vorrei uno sconto.

8·3   1. Eccolo. 2. Eccoli. 3. Eccole. 4. Eccola. 5. Ne prendo. 6. Ne ho mangiati. 7. Ci vado domani. 8. Ci andrò nel pomeriggio.   9. Si deve dire sempre la verità.   10. Si comprano quelle cose in centro. 11. Ecco il mio biglietto.   12. Il volo partirà tra/fra mezz'ora.   13. Meno male!   14. Ecco la Sua (*pol.*)/la tua (*fam.*) carta d'imbarco.   15. Dov'è l'uscita?   16. È laggiù, davanti a quel segnale.   17. Vorrei un posto al finestrino, non al corridoio.   18. Signore e signori, siete pregati di allacciare la cintura/le cinture di sicurezza.   19. Il decollo è previsto tra/fra qualche minuto.   20. Il comandante e l'intero equipaggio vi augurano un buon viaggio.

Part II: Complete Italian Grammar

II-1   Nouns and titles

1·1   **A.** 1. zii 2. ragazzo 3. libri 4. gatto 5. figli 6. zia 7. ragazze 8. penna
9. figlie 10. casa 11. cani 12. cellulare 13. padri 14. parete 15. madri

16. nazione   17. notti   18. cosa   19. case   20. anno   21. giorni   22. vestito
23. cravatte   24. donna   25. gonne   26. macchina   27. chiavi   28. cognome
29. giornali   30. nome   31. copioni   32. riunione   33. cordoni   34. mattone

B. 1. A suo nipote piace la matematica.   2. L'amore conquista tutto.   3. Quella donna ha chiamato mia nipote.   4. Marco è un caro amico.   5. La mia amica vive in periferia.   6. I miei amici hanno comprato un televisore plasma.   7. L'italiano è una lingua facile.   8. Lui è italiano, ma lei è americana.   9. Dov'è quella regione?
10. A che ora c'è la riunione?

C. 1. Quei due uomini sono italiani.   2. La gente parla troppo.   3. Sara è siciliana.
4. Alessandro parla francese.

1·2 **A.** 1. americano, americana   2. italiano, italiana   3. amico, amica   4. soprano, soprano
5. guardia, guardia   6. stella, stella   7. spia, spia   8. persona, persona   9. inglese, inglese   10. francese, francese   11. cantante, cantante   12. infermiere, infermiera

B. 1. il nipote   2. gli americani   3. le italiane   4. la nipote   5. i camerieri   6. le cameriere   7. il signore   8. la signora

1·3 **A.** 1. luoghi   2. tedeschi   3. antropologi   4. greci   5. amici   6. giochi   7. biologi
8. laghi   9. monaci   10. fichi   11. sindaci   12. porci   13. righe   14. greche
15. banche   16. camicie

B. 1. bacio   2. occhio   3. zio   4. orologio   5. farmacia   6. bugia   7. faccia
8. valigia

1·4 **A.** 1. (lo) zucchero   2. (gli) occhiali   3. (i) baffi   4. (il) latte   5. (l') uva

B. 1. (il) sale e (il) pepe   2. (la) carne, (il) pane e (il) riso   3. (la) fame e (la) sete
4. (l') acqua   5. le acque del mare   6. (i) pantaloni e (le) mutande   7. (le) forbici e (gli) occhiali

1·5 **A.** 1. Paola   2. Franco   3. Alessandra   4. Giovanni   5. nipote   6. signore
7. professoressa   8. dottore   9. geometra   10. ragioniere   11. la dottoressa Totti
12. il professor Nardini   13. architetto   14. avvocato

B. 1. Luca, Andrea e Nicola sono amici.   2. Amo (il) Natale e (la) Pasqua in Italia.
3. Il signor Rossi è un amico della famiglia.   4. «Salve, signor Rossi.»   5. La signora Rossi è un'amica della famiglia.   6. «Buongiorno, signora Rossi.»

C.

	Common	Proper	Count	Mass	Masc.	Fem.	Sing.	Pl.
1.	X	—	X	—	X	—	X	—
2.	—	X	—	—	—	X	X	—
3.	X	—	X	—	X	—	—	X
4.	X	—	X	—	—	X	—	X
5.	—	X	—	—	X	—	X	—
6.	X	—	X	—	—	X	X	—
7.	X	—	—	X	X	—	X	—
8.	X	—	X	—	X	—	—	X

D. 1. La signora Binni è italiana.   2. Maria e Paola sono due donne.   3. Le ragazze sono francesi.   4. Il professor Jones è americano.   5. Pasquale è mio zio.

1·6 1. Trento è il capoluogo del Trentino-Alto Adige.   2. La Sardegna, l'Umbria e la Valle d'Aosta sono regioni.   3. Venezia è il capoluogo del Veneto. / Torino è il capoluogo del Piemonte.   4. Firenze e Aosta sono capoluoghi.   5. La Basilicata è una regione.

II-2   More about nouns

2·1 **A.** 1. pianista   2. dentista   3. farmacista   4. musicista

B. 1. attrice   2. scultore   3. autrice   4. pittore   5. farmacista   6. dottore   7. leonessa   8. professore
9. elefantessa   10. avvocato   11. studentessa

C. 1. ciliegia   2. pero   3. mela   4. arancio   5. pesca   6. limone   7. mandarino   8. fico

2·2 **A.** 1. ipotesi   2. tesi   3. programmi   4. problemi   5. sistemi

B. 1. brindisi   2. crisi   3. diagramma   4. teorema   5. dramma   6. analisi

2·3 **A.**

	Masculine	Feminine
1. città	—	X
2. lunedì	X	—
3. papà	X	—
4. tè	X	—

5. menù	X	—
6. ragù	X	—
7. caffè	X	—
8. gioventù	—	X
9. virtù	—	X
10. università	—	X
11. tassì	X	—
12. tram	X	—
13. autobus	X	—

B. 1. caffè 2. città 3. foto 4. cinema 5. moto 6. computer 7. vaglia 8. mail 9. dita 10. braccio 11. paia 12. ginocchio 13. i bracci della croce 14. il labbro della ferita 15. buoi 16. radio 17. mani 18. pianeta 19. clacson 20. sport

2·4 **A.** 1. asinello, asinone 2. ragazzina (ragazzetta), ragazzona 3. libricino, librone 4. manina, manona

B. 1. un braccione 2. un corpaccio 3. una manetta 4. un problemino 5. un problemone 6. un problemaccio 7. un affaraccio 8. un affarone 9. Mariuccia

2·5 **A.** 1. arcobaleni 2. salvagente 3. ferrovie 4. cassaforte 5. pianoforti

B. 1. il caporeparto 2. il cacciavite 3. il francobollo 4. il pianoforte 5. il capoluogo

C. 1. a 2. b 3. a 4. b 5. a 6. a 7. b 8. a

D. 1. pianista, pianisti, pianista, pianiste 2. farmacista, farmacisti, farmacista, farmaciste 3. attore, attori, attrice, attrici 4. scultore, scultori, scultrice, scultrici 5. elefante, elefanti, elefantessa, elefantesse 6. studente, studenti, studentessa, studentesse

E. 1. caffè 2. città 3. foto 4. sport 5. tennis 6. autobus 7. dita 8. paia

2·6 1. b 2. a 3. a 4. b 5. a

II-3 Articles

3·1 **A.** 1. un americano 2. un'americana 3. uno studente 4. una zia 5. una studentessa 6. un'ora 7. uno gnocco 8. un portatile 9. una tesi 10. un brindisi 11. un problema 12. un programma 13. un caffè 14. una foto 15. un computer 16. una mano 17. una radio 18. un pianoforte 19. un'isola 20. una porta 21. uno psicologo 22. una psicologa 23. un orologio

B. 1. una cara amica 2. un piccolo zio 3. una brava figlia 4. un bravo cantante 5. una grande professoressa 6. un bravo signore 7. una brava musicista 8. un grande scultore

3·2 **A.** 1. il vestito, i vestiti 2. la studentessa, le studentesse 3. lo psicologo, gli psicologi 4. la psicologa, le psicologhe 5. la tesi, le tesi 6. il tedesco, i tedeschi 7. lo sport, gli sport 8. il problema, i problemi 9. l'orologio, gli orologi 10. l'ora, le ore 11. l'amico, gli amici 12. l'amica, le amiche 13. lo zio, gli zii 14. la zia, le zie 15. il bambino, i bambini 16. la bambina, le bambine 17. lo gnocco, gli gnocchi 18. lo studente, gli studenti

B. 1. gli zii 2. il vaglia 3. le valige 4. la virtù 5. gli uomini 6. il tè 7. gli gnocchi 8. il sistema 9. gli scultori 10. il programma 11. le radio 12. l'università 13. le paia 14. l'orologio 15. i musicisti 16. l'infermiera

3·3 **A.** 1. Mia madre aveva mal di denti ieri. 2. Anch'io ho mal di gola. 3. Che bella musica! 4. Mio padre ha mal di testa o mal di stomaco. 5. Che bella macchina! 6. In questa classe conosco solo uno studente e una studentessa. 7. Lui è una persona simpatica; e anche lei è una persona simpatica. 8. Io studio sempre un'ora ogni giorno.

B. 1. (Io) ho solo una zia e uno zio. 2. (Io) ho comprato una macchina / un'automobile. 3. Che bella casa! / Che casa bella! 4. Che grande film!

3·4 **A.** 1. L'acqua è necessaria per vivere. 2. Il caffè è buono. 3. Gli italiani sono simpatici. 4. La pazienza è la virtù più importante. 5. Anche gli americani sono simpatici. 6. Mi piacciono le lingue e la storia. 7. La Sicilia è una bella regione. 8. L'anno prossimo vado in Piemonte. 9. Forse vado nell'Italia settentrionale. 10. Mia zia vive a Roma. 11. Lei si mette sempre la giacca per andare in centro. 12. Il venerdì, io gioco sempre a tennis. 13. La domenica vado regolarmente in chiesa. 14. Il martedì o il mercoledì guardo la televisione. 15. Il giovedì o il sabato vado in centro. 16. Come si chiama la professoressa d'italiano? 17. Come sta, professoressa Bianchi? 18. Mi fa male la testa.

B. 1. (Io) bevo solo (il) tè. 2. (Io) amo gli spaghetti. 3. (Io) ho solo uno zio e una zia in Italia. 4. Lui vive nell'Italia meridionale. 5. Lei vive negli Stati Uniti orientali. 6. Io invece vivo negli Stati Uniti occidentali. 7. Mi piacciono la biologia, la chimica, la scienza, la geografia, la matematica e la fisica. 8. Lei è molto brava in musica e nelle lingue. 9. Il mese scorso ho comprato la/una macchina.

10. L'anno prossimo vado in Italia.   11. La settimana prossima vado in centro.   12. Lui vive a sinistra e lei a destra.

C. 1. il ragazzo 2. un anno 3. la settimana 4. un mese 5. il caffè 6. uno psicologo

D. 1. i ragazzi 2. gli spagnoli 3. le scienze 4. le giacche 5. gli amici 6. le amiche 7. i cellulari 8. le virtù

E. 1. Che bel film! 2. Ho mal di stomaco. 3. Loro hanno un cane e un gatto. 4. Sono la zia e lo zio dall'Italia. 5. Io amo la carne. 6. Gli italiani sanno vivere. 7. Loro vanno spesso in Italia. 8. La Francia è un bel paese. 9. Oggi vado in centro con lo zio. 10. Il venerdì vanno spesso al cinema. 11. Conosci il professor Martini? 12. Mio fratello ama la matematica. 13. Lei è andata al cinema la settimana scorsa. 14. Loro vivono a destra.

F. 1. f 2. e 3. a 4. g 5. b 6. c 7. d

3·5   1. il 2. X; X 3. X 4. il 5. X

II-4 Adjectives

4·1 **A.** 1. la bambina ricca 2. i ragazzi alti 3. la casa grande 4. le case grandi 5. gli uomini stanchi 6. le donne povere 7. la bambina bella 8. i cantanti brutti 9. le cantanti magre 10. la giacca rossa 11. le giacche blu 12. le sciarpe verdi 13. le sciarpe viola 14. la camicia bianca 15. le camicie marrone 16. gli zaini celesti 17. le gonne grige 18. i vestiti rosa 19. l'impermeabile azzurro 20. gli impermeabili gialli 21. i cappotti arancione 22. la camicia e la sciarpa bianche 23. la gonna e il cappotto rossi

B. 1. gli zii vecchi 2. la studentessa intelligente 3. le valige grandi 4. la città piccola 5. gli uomini ricchi 6. la donna stanca 7. i ragazzi simpatici 8. la cantante simpatica 9. i vestiti lunghi 10. la sciarpa lunga

C. 1. la macchina vecchia 2. gli uomini bassi 3. le donne ricche 4. il cane piccolo 5. i cantanti magri 6. i professori brutti 7. le ragazze ricche 8. il vestito bianco

4·2 **A.** 1. Lui è un simpatico studente. 2. È uno zaino nuovo. 3. Ho comprato un nuovo orologio. 4. Marco e Maria sono simpatici amici. 5. Lei è una ricca amica.

B. 1. a 2. b 3. a 4. b 5. a 6. b 7. b 8. a

4·3 **A.** 1. buono zio 2. buona zia 3. buon amico 4. buon'amica 5. buon padre 6. buoni ragazzi 7. buone amiche 8. bello zaino 9. bel libro 10. bell'orologio 11. begli zaini 12. bei libri 13. begli orologi 14. bella donna 15. belle donne 16. bell'attrice 17. belle attrici

B. 1. uno zaino bello 2. degli scultori grandi 3. un caffè buono 4. dei ragionieri buoni 5. un uomo bello 6. un portatile buono 7. dei programmi belli 8. uno psicologo buono 9. una psicologa buona 10. un problema grande 11. una pesca buona 12. delle autrici grandi 13. un orologio buono 14. un musicista grande 15. una donna bella 16. un affare buono

C. 1. San Marco 2. Sant'Isabella 3. San Bernardo 4. San Francesco 5. Sant'Agnese 6. Sant'Alessio

4·4 **A.** 1. a. Giovanni è così alto come Maria. / Giovanni è tanto alto quanto Maria. b. Giovanni è così intelligente come Maria. / Giovanni è tanto intelligente quanto Maria. c. Giovanni è così simpatico come Maria. / Giovanni è tanto simpatico quanto Maria. d. Giovanni è così felice come Maria. / Giovanni è tanto felice quanto Maria. 2. a. Il signor Sabatini è più felice degli studenti. b. Il signor Sabatini è più ricco degli studenti. c. Il signor Sabatini è più simpatico degli studenti. d. Il signor Sabatini è più stanco degli studenti. 3. a. La signora Sabatini è meno felice degli studenti. b. La signora Sabatini è meno ricca degli studenti. c. La signora Sabatini è meno simpatica degli studenti. d. La signora Sabatini è meno stanca degli studenti. 4. a. Le giacche sono più costose/care dei cappotti. b. Le giacche sono più lunghe dei cappotti. c. Le giacche sono più belle dei cappotti. d. Le giacche sono più nuove dei cappotti. 5. a. Gli impermeabili sono meno costosi/cari dei vestiti. b. Gli impermeabili sono più lunghi dei vestiti. c. Gli impermeabili sono meno belli dei vestiti. d. Gli impermeabili sono più vecchi dei vestiti.

B. 1. Lui è il professore più bravo dell'università. 2. Lei è la più intelligente di tutti. 3. Giovanni è più bravo che intelligente. 4. Giovanni è più bravo di Pasquale. 5. Gli studenti sono più simpatici che intelligenti. 6. Maria è più intelligente di quello che crede.

C. 1. migliori 2. maggiore 3. peggiore 4. minori 5. maggiori 6. ricchissimo 7. rossissimi 8. facilissimo/facilissima 9. bellissime 10. simpaticissimi 11. simpaticissime 12. buonissima

D. 1. la donna intelligente 2. l'amico elegante 3. la zia alta 4. il bello studente 5. la sorella simpaticissima 6. il buon amico 7. la ragazza francese 8. un bravissimo professore 9. una buona zia 10. un bel ragazzo 11. una bell'amica 12. San Mario

E. 1. b 2. b 3. b 4. a 5. b 6. a

4·5   1. Fa caldo e/ed è piovoso. 2. Fa sempre freddo qui e/ed è sempre nuvoloso. 3. Il tempo è bello oggi. / Fa bel tempo oggi. È sereno e fa fresco. 4. È piovoso / Piove oggi. Il tempo è cattivo. / Fa cattivo tempo.

II-5 Pronouns

5·1 **A.** 1. Anch'io voglio andare in Italia.   2. Devi chiamare tu, non io!   3. Non è possibile che siano stati loro.   4. Mio fratello guarda sempre la TV. Lui guarda sempre programmi interessanti.   5. Mia sorella legge molto. Lei vuole diventare professoressa d'università.   6. Anche noi siamo andati in centro ieri.   7. Siete proprio voi?   8. Galileo era un grande scienziato. Egli era toscano.   9. Elsa Morante è una grande scrittrice. Ella è molto famosa.   10. Maria, vai anche tu alla festa?   11. Signora Marchi, va anche Lei al cinema?   12. Signore e signori, anche voi/Loro siete/sono felici?

B. 1. Anche essi sono (dei) problemi importanti.   2. Anche esse sono (delle) tesi interessanti.   3. Noi andremo in Italia quest'anno.   4. Loro sono italiani.   5. Loro sono italiane.

5·2 **A.** 1. a. Giovanni mi chiama ogni sera. b. Giovanni mi ha dato la sua penna.   2. a. La sua amica ti ha telefonato, non è vero? b. Lui vuole che io ti chiami stasera.   3. a. Professoressa, La chiamo domani, va bene? b. Professoressa, Le do il mio compito domani, va bene?   4. a. Conosci Marco? Mia sorella gli telefona spesso. b. Sì, io lo conosco molto bene.   5. a. Ieri ho visto Maria e le ho dato il tuo indirizzo. b. Anche tu hai visto Maria, no? No, ma forse la chiamo stasera.   6. a. Marco e Maria, quando ci venite a visitare? b. Signor Verdi e signora Verdi, quando ci telefonerete?   7. a. Claudia e Franca, vi devo dire qualcosa. b. Claudia e Franca, non vi ho dato niente ieri.   8. a. Conosci quegli studenti? No, non li conosco. b. Scrivi mai a quegli studenti? No, non gli scrivo mai.   9. a. Conosci quelle studentesse? No, non le conosco. b. Scrivi mai a quelle studentesse? No, non gli scrivo mai.

B. 1. Marco la guarda sempre ogni sera.   2. Anche lei lo preferisce.   3. Li mangeremo volentieri in quel ristorante.   4. Anche Maria le vuole.   5. Le compreremo domani.   6. Loro li compreranno in centro.   7. Anch'io lo prendo, va bene?   8. La vuoi anche tu?

5·3 **A.** 1. a. Claudia chiama solo me ogni sera, non la sua amica. b. Giovanni ha dato la sua penna a me, non al suo amico.   2. a. Claudia ha telefonato a te, non è vero? b. Lui vuole che io chiami anche te stasera.   3. a. Dottor Marchi, chiamo Lei, non l'altro medico, domani, va bene? b. Professoressa Verdi, do il mio compito a Lei domani, va bene?   4. a. Conosci il professor Giusti? Mia sorella telefona solo a lui per studiare per gli esami. b. Sì, io conosco proprio lui molto bene.   5. a. Ieri ho visto la tua amica e ho dato il tuo indirizzo anche a lei. b. Anche tu hai visto Paola, no? No, ma forse esco con lei stasera.   6. a. Marco e Maria, quando uscirete con noi? b. Signor Verdi e signora Verdi, quando telefonerete a noi?   7. a. Marco e Maria, parlerò di voi alla professoressa. b. Claudia e Franca, non ho dato niente a voi ieri.   8. a. Conosci quegli studenti? Sì, e domani parlerò di loro al professore. b. Scrivi mai a quegli studenti? No, non scrivo mai a loro.   9. a. Conosci quelle studentesse? Sì, e domani parlerò di loro al professore. b. Scrivi mai a quelle studentesse? No, non scrivo mai a loro.

B. 1. Marco darà il tuo/Suo indirizzo a me, non a lui!   2. Ieri (io) ho scritto a te, e solo a te!   3. Maria viene con noi, non con loro, al cinema domani.   4. Il professore / La professoressa parla sempre di voi, non di noi!   5. Maria, l'ho fatto per te!   6. Signora Verdi, l'ho fatto per Lei!

5·4 **A.** 1. Sì, ne comprerò.   2. Mio fratello ne comprerà domani.   3. Ne devo guardare due stasera.   4. Di solito ne leggo molte ogni settimana.   5. Anche lei ne ha parlato.   6. Ci andiamo domani.   7. Mia sorella ci vive da molti anni.   8. Loro ne arrivano tra poco.

B. 1. Mio fratello mangia assai/molto/tanto.   2. Dorme molto tua sorella?   3. Ieri abbiamo mangiato troppo.   4. Solo alcuni vanno in Italia quest'anno. Ma molti sono andati l'anno scorso. (The masculine plural forms are the appropriate ones for the pronouns when the gender is unmarked.)   5. Di quelle donne, molte sono italiane e alcune sono americane.

C. 1. a 2. b 3. a 4. a 5. a 6. b 7. b

D. 1. Claudia lo darà a me domani.   2. Io le darò a te dopo.   3. Io le ho dato le scarpe.   4. Li voglio anch'io.   5. Lui li chiama spesso.   6. Lui ne vuole.   7. Non la voglio.   8. Ne prendo due.   9. Marco ci andrà domani.   10. Lei ne comprerà molte per la festa.   11. Ne prendo quattro di solito.

5·5 1. Gina, ti chiamo domani, va bene?   2. Professore, Le ho dato il regalo per Natale.   3. Gina e Claudia, partite anche voi domani?   4. Signore, chi è Lei?   5. Professoressa, ho dato quella cosa a Lei ieri.

II-6 More pronouns

6·1 **A.** 1. Mio fratello l'ha (lo ha) comprato ieri.   2. Gli abbiamo dato quello zaino.   3. Loro li hanno presi ieri.   4. Gli ho dato quegli stivali ieri.   5. Mia sorella l'ha (la ha) comprata ieri.   6. Mia madre le ha dato quella borsa.   7. Le abbiamo viste in centro.   8. Gli abbiamo dato quelle scarpe ieri.   9. Ne ho mangiate tre.   10. Ne abbiamo comprate molte in centro ieri.

B. 1. Sì, l'ho (lo ho) preso.   2. Sì, le ho comprate.   3. Sì, l'ho (la ho) vista.   4. Sì, li ho chiamati.   5. Sì, ne ho mangiate.

6·2 **A.** 1. Mia sorella me l'ha (lo ha) comprato ieri.   2. Gliel'ho (Glielo ho) dato ieri.   3. Loro te li hanno presi ieri.   4. Glieli ho dati ieri.   5. Nostra madre ce l'ha (la ha) comprata qualche anno fa.   6. Mia madre gliel'ha (gliela ha) data.   7. Ve le abbiamo comprate in centro.   8. Gliele abbiamo date ieri.   9. Gliene ho date tre.   10. Gliene abbiamo comprate molte in centro ieri.

B. 1. Sì, ve l'ho preso.   2. Sì, gliele ho comprate.   3. Sì, me le hai date.   4. Sì, gliele ho dette.   5. Sì, te ne ho prese.

6·3   **A.** 1. Prima di berla, voglio mangiare. 2. Vedendoli, li ho chiamati. 3. Eccole. 4. Eccoteli. 5. Non voglio mangiarli. / Non li voglio mangiare. 6. Potremo andarci tra poco. / Ci potremo andare tra poco. 7. Vogliamo scrivergliene molte. / Gliene vogliamo scrivere molte. 8. Giovanni, bevilo! 9. Alessandro dammela! 10. Maria, faglielo! 11. Signora Marchi, me la dica! 12. Franco, dimmela!

       B. 1. Giovanni, da' la penna a me! / Giovanni, dammi la penna! Non darla a lei! / Non dargliela! / Non la dare a lei! / Non gliela dare! 2. Dottor/Dottoressa Verdi, gli dica la verità! Ma non la dica a loro! / Ma non gliela dica! 3. Mamma, fa' quel compito per me! / Mamma, fammi quel compito! Ma non farlo per lui! / Ma, non lo fare per lui! / Ma non farglielo! / Ma non glielo fare! 4. Marco, fammi un favore! Ma non farlo a loro! / Ma non lo fare a loro! / Ma non glielo fare! / Ma non farglielo! 5. Maria, va' in centro con noi! Non andarci con lui! / Non ci andare con lui! 6. Signora Verdi, vada in centro con noi! Non ci vada con lei!

       C. 1. Marco me lo darà domani. 2. Io te le ho date ieri. 3. Loro gliele hanno date. 4. Prima di mangiarli, voglio mangiare l'antipasto. 5. Eccoli. 6. Lui le ha comprate ieri. 7. Non voglio mangiarla. / Non la voglio mangiare. 8. Claudia, mangiale! 9. Giovanni, dammene due! 10. Mio fratello ci è andato ieri. 11. Lei ne ha comprate molte ieri. 12. Ce ne sono quattro nello zaino.

       D. 1. Bruno me lo ha comprato. Bruno mi ha comprato quegli orologi. Bruno me li ha comprati. 2. Marco, mangiala! Marco, mangia quelle mele! Marco, mangiale! 3. Paola ve lo darà domani. Paola vi darà quei libri domani. Paola ve li darà domani. 4. Anche tu me l'hai (la hai) comprata nello stesso negozio, vero? Anche tu mi hai comprato quelle camicie nello stesso negozio, vero? Anche tu me le hai comprate nello stesso negozio, vero? 5. Lui l'ha (lo ha) bevuto volentieri. Lui ha bevuto quei caffè volentieri. Lui li ha bevuti volentieri.

6·4   1. Gina, non me la dare! 2. Luca, non andarci! 3. Ti posso dare questo libro? 4. Voglio chiamarti subito.

II-7 Demonstratives

7·1   **A.** 1. questi affari 2. queste attrici 3. questi biologi 4. queste bugie 5. questi camerieri 6. queste cameriere

       B. 1. questo diagramma 2. questo dito 3. questo francese 4. questa francese 5. questo giornale

7·2   **A.** 1. quegli architetti 2. quelle autrici 3. quelle braccia 4. quelle cameriere 5. quegli zaini 6. quelle ipotesi 7. quelle macchine 8. quei simpatici bambini 9. quei bei ragazzi 10. quelle belle ragazze

       B. 1. quel programma 2. quel problema 3. quell'inglese 4. quell'inglese 5. quel nome 6. quella notte 7. quell'occhio 8. quel paio 9. quello spagnolo simpatico 10. quel teorema e quella tesi

7·3   **A.** 1. quello 2. quelle 3. quello 4. quelli 5. quello 6. quelli 7. quelli 8. quelli 9. quelle 10. questa 11. questa 12. queste 13. questo 14. questo 15. questi 16. questi

       B. 1. No, quello. 2. No, quelli. 3. No, quella. 4. No, quelle. 5. No, quello. 6. No, quelli. 7. No, quello. 8. No, quella.

7·4   **A.** 1. No, quell'orologio lì. 2. No, quegli impermeabili lì. 3. No, quella camicia là. 4. No, quelle sciarpe là. 5. No, quel libro lì. 6. No, quegli zaini là.

       B. 1. Ecco la penna. 2. Sì, c'è (un'americano qui). / No, non c'è (un'americano qui). 3. Sì, è uno studente d'italiano. / No, non è uno studente d'italiano. 4. Ecco quelle persone. 5. Sì, ci sono (persone italiane lì). / No, non ci sono (persone italiane lì). 6. Sì, sono amici. / No, non sono amici.

       C. 1. quel ragazzo 2. questa nuova macchina 3. quello qui/qua 4. questi studenti lì 5. quelle amiche simpatiche 6. questi simpatici psicologi 7. quegli gnocchi là 8. queste paia di pantaloni

       D. 1. Io, invece, voglio quell'impermeabile. 2. Io, invece, voglio quei libri. 3. Io, invece, voglio quella camicia. 4. Io, invece, voglio quelle giacche. 5. Io, invece, voglio quello zaino. 6. Io, invece, voglio quegli orologi. 7. Io, invece, voglio quelle foto.

       E. 1. Giovanni e Maria non ci sono. / Giovanni e Maria non sono qui. 2. Dove sono quelle camicie? Ecco le camicie. 3. Che cosa è? / Che cos'è? È una macchina nuova. / È una nuova macchina. 4. Dove sono gli studenti? Ecco gli studenti. 5. Sono qua? No, sono là.

7·5   1. Ecco perché (lui) non l'ha fatto. 2. Ecco, questa è la verità. 3. Ecco tutto. Non c'è altro da dire. 4. Eccoci (qui) finalmente.

II-8 Possessives

8·1   **A.** 1. la mia bibita, la tua bibita, la nostra bibita, la loro bibita 2. il mio cappuccino, il tuo cappuccino, il nostro cappuccino, il loro cappuccino 3. i miei bicchieri, i tuoi bicchieri, i nostri bicchieri, i loro bicchieri 4. le mie braccia, le tue braccia, le nostre braccia, le loro braccia 5. il mio cappotto, il tuo cappotto, il nostro cappotto, il loro cappotto 6. la mia cravatta, la tua cravatta, la nostra cravatta, la loro cravatta 7. le mie dita, le tue dita, le nostre dita, le loro dita 8. i miei diagrammi, i tuoi diagrammi, i nostri diagrammi, i loro diagrammi

B. 1. No, è il loro espresso.   2. No, sono i suoi figli.   3. No, sono le sue figlie.   4. No, è il loro giornale.   5. No, è la tua professoressa.   6. No, sono i suoi amici.   7. No, sono le mie chiavi.

8·2   **A.** 1. Sì, è la sua macchina.   2. Sì, è il suo caffè.   3. Sì, è il suo caffè.   4. Sì, sono i suoi amici.   5. Sì, sono i suoi amici.   6. Sì, sono le sue amiche.   7. Sì, sono le sue amiche.   8. Sì, è la sua foto.   9. Sì, sono le sue foto.

B. 1. Maria, è il tuo caffè?   2. Signora Rossi, è il Suo caffè?   3. Gino, è il tuo cappuccino?   4. Signor Bruni, è il Suo cappuccino?   5. Claudia, sono le tue amiche?   6. Signorina Verdi, sono le Sue amiche?   7. Giovanni, sono le tue forbici?   8. Professor Marchi, sono le Sue forbici?   9. Maria e Claudia, è il vostro caffè?   10. Signora Rossi e signorina Verdi, è il Loro caffè?   11. Gino e Marco, è il vostro cappuccino?   12. Signor Bruni e dottor Rossini, è il Loro cappuccino?   13. Claudia e Maria, sono le vostre amiche?   14. Signorina Verdi e dottoressa Dini, sono le Loro amiche?   15. Giovanni e Claudia, sono le vostre forbici?   16. Professor Marchi e dottoressa Bruni, sono le Loro forbici?

8·3   **A.** 1. a. Marco è mio cugino. b. Marco è il suo fratello minore / più piccolo / più giovane. c. Marco è tuo padre. d. Marco è il nostro zio italiano. e. Marco è il loro amico.   2. a. Maria è mia cugina. b. Maria è la sua sorella maggiore / più grande / più vecchia. c. Maria è tua madre. d. Maria è vostra zia. e. Maria è la loro amica.   3. a. Il signor Verdi e la signora Verdi sono mio nonno e mia nonna. b. Il signor Verdi e la signora Verdi sono il suo zio e la sua zia italiani. c. Il signor Verdi e la signora Verdi sono tuo suocero e tua suocera. d. Il signor Verdi e la signora Verdi sono vostro genero e vostra nuora. e. Il signor Verdi e la signora Verdi sono il loro cognato e la loro cognata italiani.

B. 1. i miei cugini   2. le mie nonne   3. i tuoi fratelli   4. le tue sorelle   5. i suoi zii   6. le sue zie   7. i nostri generi   8. le nostre suocere   9. i vostri cognati   10. le vostre cognate   11. i loro fratelli   12. le loro sorelle

8·4   **A.** 1. Sì, è la mia.   2. Sì, è la loro.   3. Sì, sei il nostro.   4. Sì, sono la sua.   5. Sì, è il suo.   6. Sì, è il loro.   7. Sì, sono i miei.   8. Sì, sono le nostre.

B. 1. È la mia.   2. È il suo.   3. È la sua.   4. È il nostro.   5. Sono i loro.   6. Sono le mie.   7. Sono i suoi.   8. Sono le sue.

C. 1. i miei orologi   2. la nostra amica   3. le mie camicie   4. il nostro libro   5. i tuoi cani   6. la vostra amica   7. le tue macchine   8. il vostro amico   9. i suoi gatti   10. la sua amica   11. i loro amici   12. la loro casa

D. 1. Lui è mio fratello.   2. Lei è la nostra sorella maggiore.   3. Quel ragazzo è il loro figlio.   4. Lei è la sua figlia più grande.   5. Signora Marchi, come si chiama Sua figlia?   6. Signora e signor Marchi, come si chiama il Loro figlio?   7. Lui è un mio amico, tra molti amici.   8. Anche lei è una mia amica, tra molte amiche.   9. Questo libro è mio. Dov'è il tuo?

8·5   1. (Lei) è mia sorella, non la mia amante!   2. Ecco il mio ragazzo e tuo fratello.   3. (Lei) è la mia ragazza, non ancora la mia fidanzata.   4. Mia sorella è anche la mia amica.

II-9   Partitives

9·1   **A.** 1. dei coltelli   2. uno sbaglio   3. delle forchette   4. un salotto   5. degli zii   6. una cucina   7. degli psicologi   8. un bagno   9. delle camere   10. una bottiglia   11. delle sedie   12. una tavola   13. dei bicchieri   14. un cucchiaio   15. dei cucchiaini   16. una forchetta   17. dei coltelli   18. uno gnocco   19. delle automobili   20. un amico

B. 1. Sono delle automobili italiane.   2. Sono delle nuove sedie. / Sono delle sedie nuove.   3. Sono dei bravi psicologi. / Sono degli psicologi bravi.   4. Sono dei vecchi amici. / Sono degli amici vecchi.   5. Sono delle vecchie amiche. / Sono delle amiche vecchie.   6. Sono dei bagni grandi.   7. Sono delle camere piccole.   8. Sono dei bei salotti. / Sono dei salotti belli.   9. Sono delle belle cucine. / Sono delle cucine belle.

9·2   **A.** 1. alcuni coltelli   2. alcune sedie   3. alcuni gnocchi   4. alcune automobili   5. alcuni cucchiai   6. alcuni amici

B. 1. qualche cucchiaino   2. qualche tavola   3. qualche zaino   4. qualche automobile   5. qualche bicchiere   6. qualche sbaglio

C. 1. Alcuni amici nostri sono italiani.   2. Qualche amico nostro è italiano.   3. Alcune ragazze sono americane.   4. Qualche ragazza è americana.

9·3   **A.** 1. un po' d'insalata   2. dell'uva   3. un po' di pesce   4. della carne   5. un po' di minestra   6. del riso   7. un po' di zucchero   8. dell'orzo   9. un po' di pasta   10. dell'acqua

B. 1. Voglio del pesce e dei fagioli.   2. Voglio dell'insalata e delle carote.   3. Voglio della pasta e dei fagiolini.   4. Voglio della carne e delle mele.   5. Voglio del caffè e dello zucchero.   6. Voglio dell'uva e delle patate.

9·4   **A.** 1. Mario non mangia patate.   2. Io non voglio fagiolini.   3. Il ragazzo non prende carne.   4. La ragazza non vuole zucchero.   5. Anch'io non voglio biglietti.   6. Maria non prende pomodori.

B. 1. nessuna carota   2. nessun fagiolino   3. nessun cucchiaio   4. nessuna patata   5. nessuno zaino   6. nessun'arancia

9·5 **A.** 1. l'ultima donna 2. pochi studenti 3. tutta la minestra 4. parecchi bambini 5. una certa signora 6. qualsiasi città 7. qualunque ristorante 8. abbastanza soldi 9. assai studenti 10. ogni settimana

B. 1. Ho bisogno di poche patate. 2. Ho bisogno di tutti i fagioli. 3. Ho bisogno di tante carote. 4. Ho bisogno di molti fagiolini. 5. Ho bisogno di poche mele. 6. Ho bisogno di tutta la minestra. 7. Ho bisogno di tanta pasta. 8. Ho bisogno di molti cucchiai.

C. 1. dei bambini, alcuni bambini, qualche bambino 2. delle patate, alcune patate, qualche patata 3. dei fagioli, alcuni fagioli, qualche fagiolo 4. delle mele, alcune mele, qualche mela 5. degli zaini, alcuni zaini, qualche zaino 6. delle forchette, alcune forchette, qualche forchetta

D. 1. b 2. b 3. b 4. b 5. a 6. a

9·6 1. Amo / Mi piace l'uva. 2. (Lei) mi ha mandato/inviato delle/alcune comunicazioni/informazioni ieri. 3. Questo chicco è azzurro! 4. (Lui) mi manda/invia sempre poche informazioni.

II-10 Present tenses

10·1 **A.** 1. a. (io) arrivo, (tu) arrivi, (lui/lei) arriva, (Lei) arriva, (noi) arriviamo, (voi) arrivate, (loro) arrivano, (Loro) arrivano b. (io) cerco, (tu) cerchi, (lui/lei) cerca, (Lei) cerca, (noi) cerchiamo, (voi) cercate, (loro) cercano, (Loro) cercano c. (io) comincio, (tu) cominci, (lui/lei) comincia, (Lei) comincia, (noi) cominciamo, (voi) cominciate, (loro) cominciano, (Loro) cominciano d. (io) mangio, (tu) mangi, (lui/lei) mangia, (Lei) mangia, (noi) mangiamo, (voi) mangiate, (loro) mangiano, (Loro) mangiano e. (io) pago, (tu) paghi, (lui/lei) paga, (Lei) paga, (noi) paghiamo, (voi) pagate, (loro) pagano, (Loro) pagano 2. a. (io) chiedo, (tu) chiedi, (lui/lei) chiede, (Lei) chiede, (noi) chiediamo, (voi) chiedete, (loro) chiedono, (Loro) chiedono b. (io) rispondo, (tu) rispondi, (lui/lei) risponde, (Lei) risponde, (noi) rispondiamo, (voi) rispondete, (loro) rispondono, (Loro) rispondono c. (io) vendo, (tu) vendi, (lui/lei) vende, (Lei) vende, (noi) vendiamo, (voi) vendete, (loro) vendono, (Loro) vendono d. (io) leggo, (tu) leggi, (lui/lei) legge, (Lei) legge, (noi) leggiamo, (voi) leggete, (loro) leggono, (Loro) leggono e. (io) chiudo, (tu) chiudi, (lui/lei) chiude, (Lei) chiude, (noi) chiudiamo, (voi) chiudete, (loro) chiudono, (Loro) chiudono 3. a. (io) apro, (tu) apri, (lui/lei) apre, (Lei) apre, (noi) apriamo, (voi) aprite, (loro) aprono, (Loro) aprono b. (io) dormo, (tu) dormi, (lui/lei) dorme, (Lei) dorme, (noi) dormiamo, (voi) dormite, (loro) dormono, (Loro) dormono c. (io) parto, (tu) parti, (lui/lei) parte, (Lei) parte, (noi) partiamo, (voi) partite, (loro) partono, (Loro) partono 4. a. (io) capisco, (tu) capisci, (lui/lei) capisce, (Lei) capisce, (noi) capiamo, (voi) capite, (loro) capiscono, (Loro) capiscono b. (io) finisco, (tu) finisci, (lui/lei) finisce, (Lei) finisce, (noi) finiamo, (voi) finite, (loro) finiscono, (Loro) finiscono c. (io) preferisco, (tu) preferisci, (lui/lei) preferisce, (Lei) preferisce, (noi) preferiamo, (voi) preferite, (loro) preferiscono, (Loro) preferiscono

B. 1. Neanche io capisco la lezione. 2. Anche noi partiamo domani. 3. Anche tu giochi a calcio da molti anni. 4. Neanche voi aspettate mai. 5. Anche Luigi telefona spesso a mia sorella. 6. Anche le mie amiche giocano sempre a tennis.

C. 1. Signor Verdi, capisce la lezione? 2. Sara, cerchi qualcosa? 3. Signori, partono domani? 4. Ragazze, cominciate a studiare la matematica?

10·2 **A.** 1. (io) voglio, (tu) vuoi, (lui/lei) vuole, (noi) vogliamo, (voi) volete, (loro) vogliono 2. (io) vengo, (tu) vieni, (lui/lei) viene, (noi) veniamo, (voi) venite, (loro) vengono 3. (io) esco, (tu) esci, (lui/lei) esce, (noi) usciamo, (voi) uscite, (loro) escono 4. (io) tengo, (tu) tieni, (lui/lei) tiene, (noi) teniamo, (voi) tenete, (loro) tengono 5. (io) sto, (tu) stai, (lui/lei) sta, (noi) stiamo, (voi) state, (loro) stanno 6. (io) so, (tu) sai, (lui/lei) sa, (noi) sappiamo, (voi) sapete, (loro) sanno 7. (io) posso, (tu) puoi, (lui/lei) può, (noi) possiamo, (voi) potete, (loro) possono 8. (io) faccio, (tu) fai, (lui/lei) fa, (noi) facciamo, (voi) fate, (loro) fanno 9. (io) sono, (tu) sei, (lui/lei) è, (noi) siamo, (voi) siete, (loro) sono 10. (io) devo, (tu) devi, (lui/lei) deve, (noi) dobbiamo, (voi) dovete, (loro) devono 11. (io) dico, (tu) dici, (lui/lei) dice, (noi) diciamo, (voi) dite, (loro) dicono 12. (io) do, (tu) dai, (lui/lei) dà, (noi) diamo, (voi) date, (loro) danno 13. (io) bevo, (tu) bevi, (lui/lei) beve, (noi) beviamo, (voi) bevete, (loro) bevono 14. (io) ho, (tu) hai, (lui/lei) ha, (noi) abbiamo, (voi) avete, (loro) hanno 15. (io) vado, (tu) vai, (lui/lei) va, (noi) andiamo, (voi) andate, (loro) vanno

B. 1. Marco: Ciao, Maria, come stai?

2. Maria: Ciao, Marco, io sto molto bene. E tu?

3. Marco: Io sto così, così. Anzi, sto male.

4. Maria: Perché?

5. Marco: Sto male quando fa cattivo o brutto tempo. Ho freddo!

6. Maria: Domani, per fortuna, dovrebbe fare bel tempo.

7. Marco: Meno male! E allora spero di avere caldo!

C. 1. Signor Rossi, dove va? 2. Maria, come stai? 3. Signorina Verdi, cosa vuole? 4. Giovanni, quando vieni alla festa? 5. Signor Verdi e signora Verdi, quando escono stasera?

Part III: Verb Tenses

III-1 More on the present tense (*presente indicativo*)

1·1
1. sta preparando
2. sta leggendo
3. sta facendo
4. sta vendendo
5. sta facendo
6. sta andando
7. stanno arrivando
8. sta partendo
9. sta piovendo
10. sto mangiando
11. stai salendo
12. sta bevendo
13. stiamo finendo
14. sta camminando
15. state ascoltando

1·2

A.
1. sto andando
2. state cucinando
3. sta arrivando
4. stiamo portando
5. state finendo
6. stanno facendo
7. sto mangiando
8. sta parlando
9. stanno ritornando

B.
1. sto partendo per Firenze
2. stai dormendo in albergo
3. sta scrivendo la lettera
4. sta finendo di mangiare
5. stiamo scrivendo un libro
6. state parlando al telefono
7. stanno ascoltando la musica
8. non sto mangiando la carne
9. non stai arrivando con il treno

1·3
1. siamo/We are at Maria's.
2. sono/They are happy because they can travel.
3. sono/I am anxious because I don't understand well.
4. sono/There are many people in the house.
5. sei/Where are you?
6. sono/The pears are green.
7. è/The cat is sick.
8. è/The woman is tall.
9. sei/You are very beautiful.

1·4
1. Sono a scuola io? Io non sono a scuola.
2. Sei al cinema? Tu non sei al cinema.
3. È con i suoi amici lui? Lui non è con i suoi amici.
4. È molto bella lei? Lei non è molto bella.
5. Siamo ricchi noi? Noi non siamo ricchi.
6. Siete a casa voi? Voi non siete a casa.
7. Sono ammalati loro? Loro non sono ammalati.

1·5
1. Quanti anni hai?
2. Io ho vent'anni.
3. Tu hai dodici anni.
4. Quanti anni ha lei?
5. Lidia ha trent'anni.
6. Il mio gatto ha sette
7. Suo fratello ha quindici anni.
8. Quanti anni hanno i ragazzi?
9. Hanno nove anni.
   anni.

1·6
1. Ho fame.
2. Tu hai fame.
3. Lui ha sonno.
4. Lei ha paura.
5. Abbiamo freddo.
6. Tu hai fretta.
7. Loro hanno fortuna.
8. Ho molta fame.
9. Tu hai molta sete.
10. Lui ha molto sonno.
11. Lei non ha paura.
12. Non abbiamo freddo.
13. Hai fretta?
14. Non hanno fortuna.

1·7
1. fai
2. faccio
3. fai
4. fa
5. fanno
6. fa
7. fate
8. fanno
9. facciamo

1·8
1. Faccio
2. Fa
3. fa
4. fa
5. facciamo
6. fate
7. fanno
8. fare
9. fare

1·9
1. sai
2. so
3. sai
4. sa
5. sa
6. sappiamo
7. sapete
8. sanno

1·10
1. Conosco Maria.
2. Conosco un buon allenatore di tennis.
3. Mio fratello conosce molte persone.
4. Lei conosce mia sorella.
5. Noi non conosciamo il tuo amico.
6. Voi conoscete Mary e Albert.
7. Lo conosci molto bene.
8. Li conosci bene?
9. Io conosco New York.
10. Non conosco Chicago.
11. Conosci bene l'Africa.
12. Lei conosce l'Africa?
13. Conosciamo la nostra città.
14. Voi conoscete bene questo ristorante.
15. Conoscono la sua storia.
16. Non conoscono la sua storia.

III-2 The imperative (*imperativo*)

2·1
1. scrivi
2. Prendiamo
3. leggete
4. scrivete
5. parlate
6. non parlate
7. Guarda
8. Non guardare

2·2
1. Sii gentile con le persone anziane!
2. Non dire bugie!
3. Non dite bugie!
4. Stai zitto!
5. State zitti!
6. Dà il pane ai poveri!
7. Stai a casa, fa troppo freddo!
8. Sii paziente con gli studenti!
9. Non essere troppo paziente con gli studenti!

2·3
1. Non venire a casa!
2. Non venite a casa!
3. Non mangiare tutta la pasta!
4. Non leggere il libro!
5. Non dormire di più!
6. Non dormite di più!
7. Non guardare la televisione!
8. Non mangiamo in fretta!
9. Non vendere la tua casa!

2·4 Next Sunday is your father's birthday, and you want to have a party. Here is what I have to do to help you:
1. Manda gli inviti agli amici!
2. Va al supermercato!
3. Compra le bibite!
4. Prepara i panini!
5. Metti tutto nel frigorifero!
6. Fà la torta!
7. Metti le sedie nel giardino!
8. Ricevi gli ospiti!
9. Dopo la festa, pulisci tutto!

2·5
1. Abbi
2. Stai
3. Stai
4. essere
5. Fai
6. dare
7. Sii
8. Fai
9. dare

2·6
1. Dimentica!/Non dimenticare!
2. Spendi!/Non spendere!
3. Spendiamo!/Non spendiamo!
4. Lavora!/Non lavorare!
5. Lavorate!/Non lavorate!
6. Ricordiamo!/Non ricordiamo!
7. Leggi!/Non leggere!
8. Entra!/Non entrare!
9. Entriamo!/Non entriamo!
10. Pulisci!/Non pulire!

2·7
1. Signora, mi guardi!
2. Signor Smith, non dorma troppo!
3. Signora Smith, finisca tutta la medicina!
4. Per favore, mi canti una canzone!
5. Parli con il manager!
6. Non venda la frutta marcia!
7. Non guardi sempre dalla finestra!
8. Signor e signora Smith, mi aspettino!
9. Signor e signora Smith, aprano le finestre!

2·8
1. Mangia in quel ristorante!
2. Ritorna a casa presto!
3. Non ballare!
4. Non ballate!
5. Impacchiamo!
6. Sii paziente!
7. Siate pazienti!
8. Mangia in fretta!
9. Mangiamo in fretta!

2·9
1. Dì tutto!
2. Telefonate tardi!
3. Leggete il giornale!
4. Sii sgarbato!
5. Ritorna tardi!
6. Urla!
7. Urliamo!
8. Scrivi a mia nonna!
9. Bevete acqua ghiacciata!

2·10
1. Non parlare piano!
2. Non parli piano!
3. Non parlate piano!
4. Non parlino piano!
5. Non stare zitto!
6. Non fare il caffè!
7. Non fate il caffè!
8. Non darmi la mano!
9. Non dargli i soldi!

2·11
1. Venga qui!
2. Scriva la lezione!
3. Creda in se stesso!
4. Parli poco!
5. Si svegli presto!
6. Finisca la colazione!
7. Lavori di più!
8. Scenda dalle scale!
9. Mi dia quella mela!

2·12
1. Hai bisogno di soldi. Vai in banca!
2. Hai un mal di testa. Prendi un'aspirina!
3. Hai paura di viaggiare in aereo. Vai in treno!
4. È il compleanno di tua mamma. Comprale un regalo!

5. Tu cammini dieci minuti al giorno. Cammina di più!
6. Tu mangi troppo tardi alla sera. Mangia più presto!
7. Ti alzi troppo tardi il sabato. Alzati più presto!
8. Sei stanco. Riposati!
9. Non hai fame. Non mangiare!

2·13

Ascolta	dammi	chiama	bevi
dimenticare	metti	siediti	vai
dimenticare	Preparami	chiama	

III-3 Reflexive verbs (*verbi riflessivi*)

3·1
1. ti alzi/si alza/vi alzate
2. si sveglia/ci svegliamo/si svegliano
3. si addormentano/mi addormento/ ti addormenti
4. si lava/si lava/si lavano
5. mi vesto/ti vesti/si vestono
6. si riposa/si riposa/ci riposiamo
7. si sveglia
8. ci divertiamo
9. si vestono

3·2
1. Mi devo svegliare presto. Devo svegliarmi presto.
2. Ci dobbiamo svegliare presto. Dobbiamo svegliarci presto.
3. Ti vuoi divertire con i tuoi amici. Vuoi divertirti con i tuoi amici.
4. Si vuole fare la doccia tutte le mattine. Vuole farsi la doccia tutte le mattine.
5. Si deve pettinare. Deve pettinarsi.
6. Mi devo vestire. Devo vestirmi.
7. I bambini si possono svegliare tardi. I bambini possono svegliarsi tardi.
8. Vi dovete lavare spesso le mani. Dovete lavarvi spesso le mani.
9. Non si possono addormentare. Non possono addormentarsi.

3·3
1. ci vediamo
2. ci incontriamo
3. si sposano
4. si vogliono bene
5. si aiutano
6. vi vedete
7. vi conoscete
8. ci visitiamo
9. si amano

3·4
1. mi
2. ti
3. ———
4. si
5. ———
6. ———
7. ci
8. ———
9. si

3·5

mi alzo	mi preparo	visitarci
mi alzo	ci mettiamo	ci divertiamo
mi vesto	si occupa	ci riuniamo

On Sundays I always get up late. I like to sleep very much. When I get up I take a shower, I get dressed, and I get ready to go out to the park with my small dog. When I go back home, my family and I sit down to eat. My mother prepares lunch, and my father takes care of the wine. After lunch, our relatives come to visit us. We have a lot of fun when we gather and are all together.

3·6
1. si veste
2. ti ricordi
3. mi lavo
4. si divertono
5. riposati
6. ci incontriamo
7. si trucca
8. si fa
9. mi alzo

III-4 The future tense (*futuro semplice*)

4·1
1. suonerà
2. guarderemo
3. studierò
4. porterai
5. comprerà
6. ascolterà
7. leggerò
8. arriverà
9. dormirete
10. pranzerete
11. finiremo
12. prenderete
13. parleranno
14. canterò

4·2
1. Domani riceverò il libro.
2. Mangeremo in un buon ristorante.
3. Risponderò alla tua lettera la prossima settimana.
4. A che ora arriverai?
5. A che ora partirai?
6. Venderai la casa.
7. Non venderai la casa.
8. Quante persone inviterai?
9. Inviterò solo i miei amici.
10. Visiterò molte città.

4·3
1. arriveranno
2. andremo
3. visiterai
4. vedremo
5. verrai
6. andrò
7. spenderete
8. verranno
9. farà

4·4
1. Le ragazze saranno al parco.
2. Quando andrai in Italia?
3. Quando andrò in Italia, vedrò il Vaticano.
4. Quando arriveranno i turisti, i ristoranti avranno da fare.
5. Se tu visiterai tua madre, sarà contenta.
6. Quando andrò a casa, mi metterò il pigiama.
7. Se verrai a casa tardi, la cena sarà fredda.
8. Quando arriveremo, saranno tutti a letto.
9. Se nevicherà, faremo un pupazzo di neve.

4·5
1. mangerò
2. noleggerai
3. viaggerà
4. comincerà
5. cercherò
6. cercheremo
7. pagherete
8. cercheranno
9. pagherò

4·6
1. Saranno in casa.
2. Saranno le 13,30.
3. No, costerà poco.
4. Rientrerò tardi.
5. Saranno al cinema.
6. Avrà vent'anni.
7. Ce ne saranno venti.
8. Farà brutto tempo.
9. Ne imparerò molte.

4·7
1. Domani andremo a visitare nostra zia.
2. Il prossimo anno i miei genitori andranno in Italia.
3. Avrai un lavoro importante.
4. Li vedrò domani.
5. Vivremo in Italia.
6. Vedremo i nostri amici fra qualche giorno.
7. Lui verrà a casa mia.
8. Lei rimarrà per una settimana.
9. Non berranno molta birra.
10. Vivrò per molti anni.
11. Terry verrà in ufficio tardi.
12. Berremo acqua minerale.
13. Vedrai molti monumenti.

4·8
1. sarò
2. sarai
3. sarà
4. saremo
5. sarete
6. saranno
7. sarò
8. sarai
9. sarai

4·9
andremo
andrò
prenoterò
costerà

starò
andrò
Vedrò

sarà
rimarrò
farò

Farò
starò
ritornerò

III-5   The present perfect tense (*passato prossimo*)

5·1
1. ho parlato
2. hai cantato
3. ha provato
4. ha giocato
5. abbiamo provato
6. avete camminato
7. hanno preparato
8. ho ballato
9. hanno giocato

5·2
1. ho tradotto
2. hai composto
3. ha preso
4. ha letto
5. abbiamo riso
6. avete chiuso
7. hanno conosciuto
8. hanno vinto
9. non ho letto
10. non hai chiuso

5·3
1. Ho risposto alla tua lettera.
2. Hai bevuto un bicchiere di vino.
3. Hai cotto una buona cena.
4. Abbiamo eletto un nuovo presidente.
5. Ha letto il giornale.
6. Il cane ha nascosto la palla.
7. Ha pianto tutto il giorno.
8. Non ha risposto alla mia lettera.
9. Ha riso tutto il giorno.
10. Avete spento la televisione.
11. Abbiamo vinto la partita di pallone.

5·4
1. Maria ha cantato bene.
2. Abbiamo letto il libro.
3. Ho mangiato con i miei genitori.
4. Avete scritto una storia molto lunga.
5. Il bambino ha pianto sempre.
6. Abbiamo fatto molte cose.
7. Avete capito bene la lezione.
8. Hanno ballato tutta la sera.
9. Non hai acceso la luce.
10. Lui ha preso il raffreddore.

5·5
1. Non l'ho mai visto.
2. Li hai visti.
3. Lui l'ha vista.
4. Lui non l'ha vista.
5. Hai ricevuto la lettera? No, non l'ho ricevuta.
6. Ho salutato le mie zie. Le ho salutate.
7. Abbiamo aperto le finestre. Le abbiamo aperte.
8. Non ci hanno portato il pane. Non l'hanno portato.
9. Ho comprato molte mele. Tu ne hai comprate alcune.
10. Le abbiamo mandato un fax.

5·6	ho dormito	abbiamo giocato	ha pulito
	Ho fatto	ha guardato	ha telefonato
	ho ascoltato	ha letto	ha preparato
	è andato	abbiamo lavato	

On Saturday I slept late. I ate breakfast, then I listened to country music. My brother went to the pool, and my sister and I went to play tennis. My father watched television and read the newspaper. In the afternoon we washed our car. My mother cleaned the house, called grandmother, and prepared a special dinner for all of us.

5·7
1. Sono andato/a al cinema.
2. Sei arrivato/a tardi.
3. È entrato al ristorante.
4. È morta il mese scorso.
5. Io sono nato/a in una piccola città.
6. Siamo partiti con la nave.
7. Voi siete diventati cittadini americani.
8. Sono ritornati a casa in tempo per la cena.
9. Sono andati sull'autobus.

5·8
1. Paola è andata al mercato.
2. Tu non sei uscito/a con i tuoi amici.
3. È ritornato/a a casa sua.
4. Maria è entrata nel negozio.
5. Siete partiti per l'Africa.
6. Siamo stati dagli zii.
7. Le ragazze sono arrivate alla stazione.
8. Sono molto cresciuti/e.
9. Non sei caduto quando hai pattinato.

5·9
1. Non so che cosa è accaduto a Peter.
2. Mi è sembrato troppo tardi per chiamarti.
3. Siamo andati a sciare, ma non c'era molta neve.
4. I prezzi della frutta sono molto aumentati.
5. Ci sono volute tre ore per arrivare a casa.
6. Ieri è nevicato tutto il giorno.
7. Ci siamo molto divertiti sulla spiaggia.
8. Sono andati sull'aereo.
9. I miei parenti sono andati via alle tre.

5·10 L'estate scorsa sono andato/a in Italia con alcuni amici. Una volta in Italia, abbiamo preso il treno da una città all'altra. Ci è piaciuto viaggiare in treno. È molto comodo e non abbiamo dovuto cercare un parcheggio. Abbiamo camminato molto. Abbiamo visitato molti musei e abbiamo mangiato molti gelati italiani. I gelati italiani sono famosi in tutto il mondo. Abbiamo passato due settimane in Italia. Ci siamo molto divertiti e ci ricorderemo di questo viaggio per molto tempo!

5·11
1. Angela è andata negli Stati Uniti.
2. È partita da Milano alle otto.
3. È rimasta a New York per qualche giorno.
4. È andata a visitare le chiese e i musei di New York.
5. La sera è andata a teatro.
6. Dopo tre o quattro giorni è andata a Chicago.
7. Ha fatto delle piacevoli camminate lungo il lago.
8. Ha visitato i musei ed è andata a fare molte spese.
9. Da Chicago è andata a San Francisco.
10. San Francisco è (stata) la città che ha preferito.
11. È ritornata in Italia dopo tre settimane.
12. Le è piaciuta molto la vacanza negli Stati Uniti.

III-6   The imperfect tense (*imperfetto*)

6·1
1. Di solito Maria cenava presto.
2. I ragazzi andavano spesso in biblioteca.
3. I bambini piangevano sempre.
4. Ogni tanto andavo al cinema.
5. Andavo in spiaggia tutti i giorni.
6. Andavate spesso a sciare.
7. Il lunedì andavo a scuola.
8. La domenica andavamo sempre in chiesa.
9. Mentre mangiavate, guardavate la televisione.

6·2
1. La bambina era brava.
2. Gli insegnanti erano pazienti.
3. Le camice erano sporche.
4. Le strade erano larghe.
5. Tu eri stanco.
6. Voi eravate alti.
7. Eri molto magro.
8. Ero molto studiosa.
9. Il cielo era nuvoloso.

6·3
1. Avevo sedici anni.
2. C'era molto vento.
3. Che tempo faceva?
4. Quanti anni aveva tuo nonno?
5. Aveva novant'anni.
6. Faceva brutto tempo.
7. Era presto.
8. Era molto tardi.
9. Nevicava molto forte.

6·4
1. sapevamo
2. vinceva
3. eravamo
4. piangeva
5. viveva
6. studiavi
7. viaggiavano
8. andava
9. funzionava

6·5
1. Sì, leggevamo dei bei libri in classe.
2. Sì, uscivo di frequente con i miei amici.
6. Capivano bene l'italiano.
7. Visitavamo spesso i nostri parenti.

3. Andavo al mare ogni estate.
4. Preferivamo il mare.
5. Avevo molti amici.
8. Mi piaceva giocare al calcio.
9. Andavamo spesso in Italia.

6·6 Cara Maria,

Sono appena ritornata da una vacanza a Roma. Faceva bel tempo e il sole splendeva ogni giorno. Mi alzavo e camminavo nel parco. La città era molto quieta al mattino. In fondo al parco c'era un bel caffè e mi fermavo a prendere un cappuccino caldo. Mi sedevo e leggevo il giornale italiano. Non mi piaceva leggerlo perché era pieno di cattive notizie. Dopodichè ritornavo in albergo, facevo la doccia, e andavo a visitare i musei e le chiese. Quando ero stanca, ritornavo in albergo, mi sedevo sotto l'ombrellone accanto alla piscina, e scrivevo cartoline. Era una vacanza molto bella e indimenticabile, ma troppo breve.

6·7
1. Ho mangiato al ristorante./Mangiavo al ristorante.
2. Ho viaggiato molto./Viaggiavo molto.
3. Sono andato dal dottore./Andavo dal dottore.
4. Sabato hai chiamato Marco./Tutti i sabati chiamavi Marco.
5. Hanno finito tardi di lavorare./Di solito finivano di lavorare tardi.
6. Ho nuotato tutta la mattina./Nuotavo tutte le mattine.
7. Ieri sera siamo andati a una festa./Andavamo a una festa tutti i fini settimana.
8. L'estate scorsa è andato allo zoo./Andava allo zoo ogni estate.
9. Siete andati nel parco./Andavate nel parco.

6·8
1. andava/l'ha fermato
2. mangiavo/ho trovato
3. eri/ho chiamato
4. faceva/sei uscito/a
5. avevi/hai cominciato
6. studiavo/hanno suonato/hanno portato
7. Avevo/ho cominciato
8. avevo/ho potuto
9. Erano/ho chiamato

6·9
1. Mangiavamo il dolce quando tu sei arrivato/a.
2. Mentre studiavo, qualcuno ha suonato il campanello.
3. Eri stanco quando sei venuto/a a casa?
4. Che tempo faceva in Italia?
5. Non pioveva quando sono uscito/a.
6. Faceva la doccia quando l'ho chiamata.
7. Giocavano a golf quando ha cominciato a piovere.
8. Mentre studiavo, tu sei andato/a al cinema.
9. Aspettavi l'autobus quando ti ha visto/a?

6·10 Era una bella giornata. Il sole splendeva, ed era una calda giornata primaverile. Carlo era felice perchè aveva un appuntamento con una bella ragazza. Voleva portarla alla partita di pallone e poi in un bel ristorante.

Sfortunatamente, la ragazza non è venuta, il tempo è cambiato, e ha cominciato a tuonare e a piovere molto forte. Si è bagnato tutto. È ritornato a casa, ha acceso la televisione, e ha guardato la partita alla televisione. La sua squadra ha perso. Questo giorno non è andato molto bene. È andato a letto di cattivo umore.

III-7 The preterite (*passato remoto*)

7·1
1. -ai
2. -asti
3. -ò
4. -ò
5. -ò
6. -aste
7. -ammo
8. -asti
9. -aste

7·2
1. invitai
2. camminasti
3. comprò
4. preparammo
5. pagaste
6. cenarono
7. andai
8. telefonasti
9. ascoltaste

7·3
1. Tu viaggiasti molto.
2. Io mangiai con le mie sorelle.
3. Lei aspettò suo marito.
4. Lui visitò il museo.
5. Noi telefonammo a Carlo.
6. Voi compraste molti libri.
7. Loro comprarono una casa nuova.
8. Io non preparai il letto per gli ospiti.
9. Tu non lavasti la maglia.

7·4
1. sedei (sedetti)
2. ripetesti
3. dovè (dovette)
4. vendè (vendette)
5. ricevemmo
6. credeste
7. ripeterono
8. battemmo
9. crederono (credettero)

7·5
1. Io ricevei (ricevetti) la lettera da mio figlio.
2. Tu vendesti la tua casa.
3. Lei sedè (sedette) da sola nel suo grande giardino.

4. Noi credemmo a tutti.
5. Il pappagallo ripeté quello che sentiva.
6. Voi riceveste una bella notizia.
7. Loro abbatterono (abbattettero) l'albero.
8. Giovanni e Carla venderono (vendettero) la loro casa.
9. Lo studente dové (dovette) studiare molto.

7·6

1. lessi
2. passasti
3. andarono
4. venisti
5. venne
6. partirono
7. andai
8. vidi
9. riposai

7·7

1. caddero
2. chiesi
3. chiudesti
4. decise
5. discusse
6. prendemmo
7. leggeste
8. scrissero
9. vissi

7·8

1. conobbi
2. cadde
3. volli
4. seppe
5. rompemmo
6. doveste
7. tennero
8. conoscesti
9. volle

7·9

1. dissi
2. dicesti
3. venne
4. vennero
5. venimmo
6. veniste
7. divennero
8. dicemmo
9. venne

7·10

1. nacqui
2. nascesti
3. nacque
4. piacque
5. dispiacque
6. fecero
7. piacque
8. facesti
9. piacque

7·11

1. nacque
2. andammo
3. fu
4. piacque
5. facesti
6. foste
7. facemmo
8. ebbi
9. facemmo

7·12

1. Io risposi alla tua lettera.
2. Tua madre comprò una collana di perle.
3. Lui ruppe molti bicchieri.
4. Gli studenti seppero la poesia.
5. Tu comprasti un bel paio di scarpe.
6. I nonni vollero restare a casa.
7. Maria non venne a scuola.
8. I bambini piansero tutto il giorno.
9. Le giornate furono molto lunghe.

7·13

1. Arrivai ieri sera alle nove.
2. Visitammo il museo due giorni fa.
3. Andai in montagna a sciare.
4. Non finisti la minestra.
5. Non comprai la borsa al mercato.
6. Arrivammo tardi alla stazione.
7. Mi chiesero di andare alla partita con loro.
8. Carlo passò le sue vacanze nelle Hawaii.
9. Si divertì molto.

7·14

1. Sei arrivato molto stanco.
2. Nessuno ci ha aiutato.
3. Leonardo è stato un genio.
4. Noi non abbiamo visto niente di bello.
5. Non ricordano dove hanno messo le chiavi.
6. Ho aperto la finestra, ma faceva freddo.
7. Giovanna ha risposto subito alla sua lettera.
8. Sono andato/a a comprare due francobolli.
9. L'estate scorsa ha fatto molto caldo.

7·15

Nel 1954 la televisione arrivò in Italia. Lentamente, piano piano, venne in tutte le case. Tutti vollero comprarla. Alcuni programmi ebbero un grande successo. Alla gente piacquero i programmi di varietà e i programmi di quiz. I notiziari furono molto popolari. La televisione permise alla gente di riunirsi e incontrarsi nelle case e nei bar. Gli italiani fecero dei sacrifici per comprare un televisore proprio. L'arrivo della televisione cambiò la vita di tutti.

III-8 The past perfect (*trapassato prossimo*), preterite perfect (*trapassato remoto*), and future perfect (*futuro anteriore*)

8·1

1. Avevano parlato con lui.
2. Avevano mangiato.
3. Avevano già mangiato.
4. Non era ancora ritornato.
5. Erano arrivati/e tardi.
6. Non avevo ancora finito.
7. Rita aveva confermato il suo volo.
8. Avevamo viaggiato.
9. Avevano già mangiato.

8·2

1. I have seen.
2. You had seen.
3. He had gone.
4. They had read.
5. I have played.
6. I had played.
7. We have not read.
8. They had not finished.
9. Had you already eaten?

8·3
1. Io ebbi letto i libri.
2. Tu fosti partito alle tre.
3. Gli ospiti furono partiti.
4. Voi aveste cantato bene.
5. Appena fui arrivato/a, spensi la luce.
6. Noi fummo usciti presto.
7. Lei ebbe piantato molti fiori.
8. Noi avemmo creduto nel futuro.
9. Loro ebbero mangiato troppo.

8·4
1. Gli ospiti ebbero mangiato.
2. Io ebbi dormito.
3. Tu avesti parlato.
4. Quando furono arrivati/e, li salutammo.
5. Appena ebbe finito i compiti, andò fuori a giocare.
6. Dopo che avemmo scritto le cartoline, le spedimmo.
7. Dopo che avesti fatto il bagno, ti vestisti.
8. Dopo che ebbi visto i bambini, fui felice.
9. Appena tu fosti ritornato/a, molte cose andarono male.

8·5
1. Avrò finito.
2. Sarai arrivato.
3. Si sarà sposato.
4. Tutto sarà cambiato.
5. Saremo andati.
6. Avranno chiuso la porta.
7. Niente sarà cambiato.
8. Lei avrà finito.
9. Tu avrai pulito.

8·6
1. Io sarò andato/a a casa.
2. Tu avrai studiato.
3. Lui avrà parlato con il direttore.
4. Lei sarà andata in Italia.
5. Noi saremo partiti.
6. Voi avrete avuto molti bambini.
7. Loro avranno costruito la casa.
8. Noi non saremo arrivati/e tardi.
9. Gli astronauti saranno andati sulla luna.

8·7
Dopo che abbiamo visitato Roma, ritorneremo negli Stati Uniti. Se non avremo speso tutti i soldi, ci ritorneremo la prossima estate. Quando avremo visto tutte le regioni del Nord Italia, cominceremo a visitare la parte centrale del paese.

Quando siamo andati in precedenza, abbiamo visitato Venezia e dintorni. Siamo andati nella bella regione vitivinicola nei dintorni di Verona e laghi. Non mi ero mai sognata di vedere panorami così belli. Molte persone ci avevano detto che l'Italia era molto bella e avevamo desiderato di vederla, ed ora non ci stanchiamo mai di ritornarci.

III-9 The present conditional (*condizionale presente*)

9·1
1. canterei
2. visiteresti
3. comprerebbe
4. preparerebbe
5. parlereste
6. cenerebbero
7. ballerei
8. laveresti
9. camminerebbe

9·2
1. leggerei
2. apriresti
3. capirebbe
4. ripeterebbe
5. finiremmo
6. friggerebbero
7. vendereste
8. servirei
9. chiuderesti

9·3
1. comincerei
2. parleresti
3. non parleresti
4. mangerebbe
5. pulirebbe
6. non arriveremmo
7. non penserebbe
8. nuoteremmo
9. guarderebbero

9·4
1. mangerei
2. viaggeresti
3. giocherebbe
4. pagherebbe
5. mangeremmo
6. comincereste
7. viaggerebbero
8. mangeresti
9. cominceresti

9·5
1. I would buy a lot of bread.
2. You would see all your friends and relatives.
3. He would hear the latest news.
4. She would buy many dresses.
5. We would like to go to the movies.
6. You and Paolo would take many walks.
7. They would play ball.
8. You would not read only the newspaper.
9. They would not always cry.
10. Would you come to the theater with us?
11. Would you be happy to come home?
12. Wouldn't you be tired?
13. Wouldn't we be too many?
14. Would you do the lady a favor?
15. As far as I am concerned, it would be better to sleep.

9·6
1. Mi piacerebbe andare in montagna.
2. Sì, viaggerei da solo.
3. No, non avrei bisogno di aiuto per fare le prenotazioni.
4. Io potrei partire fra una settimana.
5. Sì, vorrei noleggiare una macchina.
6. Io preferirei un agriturismo.
7. Vorrei stare in vacanza due settimane.
8. Vorrei incontrare degli italiani.
9. Vorrei mangiare in tipici ristoranti della montagna.

1. Quest'estate io e la mia amica vorremmo studiare l'italiano in Italia.
2. Verremmo all'inizio dell'estate.
3. Vorremmo stare a Firenze per due mesi.
4. Vorremmo trovare un piccolo albergo.
5. Se fosse possibile, vorremmo abitare con una famiglia italiana.
6. Vorremmo stare con una famiglia dove nessuno parla l'inglese.
7. Quando dovremmo iscriverci?
8. Quanti studenti ci sarebbero in ogni classe?
9. Quanto costerebbe tutto compreso?
10. Dove potremmo mandare il pagamento per i corsi?
11. Quando potremmo chiamarvi/telefonarvi?
12. Avremmo bisogno di un permesso speciale per stare in Italia?
13. Quando comincerebbero i corsi?

9·8 I should study, but I don't feel like it. I am thinking about summertime and where I could go on vacation. While I am making plans for the holidays, and I am thinking where I would prefer going, I would like to have something cool to drink. There isn't a thing in the refrigerator. It would be good to make some iced tea. My parents would like to go to the mountains; I would prefer going camping. We could go to Puglia or Calabria. My father could come with his van because my mini car is too small and we cannot fit in it. My parents are very nice, and it would be very pleasant going on vacation with them. When they come home from work, I will ask them. Now it would be better to study because there is still plenty of time before summer arrives.

III-10 The past conditional (*condizionale passato*)

10·1
1. Io avrei mangiato una mela.
2. Tu avresti parlato col dottore.
3. Lui avrebbe pensato di venire domani.
4. Lei avrebbe firmato il documento.
5. Noi avremmo risposto al telefono.
6. Voi avreste scritto una cartolina.
7. Loro sarebbero usciti/e presto.
8. Io non avrei comprato le scarpe.
9. Saresti venuto/a con noi?
10. Non avrebbe invitato molti amici.
11. Avrebbero invitato anche noi?

10·2
1. Avrei preso l'autobus.
2. Avresti ballato tutta la notte.
3. Lui avrebbe saputo.
4. Avremmo risposto.
5. Lei avrebbe capito la lezione.
6. Voi avreste aspettato.
7. Avrebbero viaggiato.
8. Non avresti dovuto rispondere.
9. Avrebbe dovuto scrivere lei?
10. Non avrebbero saputo.
11. Avrebbero dovuto sapere?

10·3
1. sarebbe andata in centro
2. sarebbero arrivati/e in ritardo
3. sarei andato/a a dormire
4. sareste andati/e a nuotare
5. avrebbe cantato
6. saremmo andati/e a ballare
7. sareste entrati/e
8. avrei riso
9. avresti riparato

10·4
avrebbe dovuto
sarebbe ritornata
avrebbe aiutato
Avrebbe dovuto
sarebbe stato
avrebbe portato

Mussolini was a very ambitious politician. According to him, Italy should have gone back to the glorious past of the ancient Roman Empire. He was convinced that under his rule, Italy would have gone back to being a great empire. He believed that an alliance with Germany would have helped him with his ambitious idea. Mussolini has done many wonderful things for Italy, like building schools, roads, and hospitals. He should have listened to who was suggesting to him that it would have been a mistake to ally himself with Germany. He was too self-confident. Many Italians followed him, and they were sure that Mussolini knew what he was doing and that he would take Italy and the Italians to the glory of the past.

He came into power in 1924. In 1943, when the war was over and Italy had lost, his dictatorship fell and he was hanged along with his lover in Piazzale Loreto in Milano.

III-11 Compound reflexive verbs (*verbi riflessivi composti*)

11·1
1. Carlo si è fatto la barba tutte le mattine.
2. I ragazzi si sono alzati tardi.
3. Io mi sono messa il vestito nuovo.
6. Paolo si è alzato presto tutte le mattine.
7. Pietro e Anna si sono sposati.
8. Giovanna si è divertita molto.

4. Paola si è lavata le mani.
5. Io mi sono seduto vicino alla porta.

9. Giovanna e Teresa si sono divertite.

11·2
1. I ragazzi si erano divertiti molto.
2. Carlo si era vestito molto bene.
3. Giovanna si era pettinata.
4. Pietro e Anna si erano innamorati.
5. Io non mi ero sentito molto bene.

6. Le ragazze si erano coperte perchè faceva freddo.
7. I bambini si erano divertiti al parco.
8. Il signore si era pulito le scarpe.
9. Le signore si erano pulite le scarpe.

11·3
1. Io mi sarò seduto sulla poltrona.
2. Carlo si sarà fatto la barba.
3. Il bambino si sarà addormentato.
4. Pietro e Anna si saranno sposati.
5. Noi ci saremo vestiti.

6. Voi vi sarete laureate.
7. Loro si saranno spogliati.
8. Giovanna non si sarà svegliata.
9. Carlo si sarà dimenticato.

11·4
1. Quei ragazzi si sarebbero alzati alle otto.
2. Luigi si sarebbe svegliato presto.
3. Tu ti saresti laureato in medicina.
4. Lei si sarebbe fatta la doccia.
5. Noi ci saremmo divertiti/e molto.

6. Voi vi sareste vestite di bianco.
7. Giovanna e Paola si sarebbero messe il cappotto.
8. Noi ci saremmo scusati/e.
9. Noi non ci saremmo scusati/e.

III-12   The subjunctive mood (*modo congiuntivo*)

12·1
1. apra
2. scriva
3. cada
4. chiami
5. senta
6. balli
7. guardiate
8. camminino
9. spenda

12·2
1. paghi
2. cominci
3. mangi
4. mangino
5. giochino
6. cerchi
7. tocchi
8. paghi
9. cominciate

12·3
1. È possibile che vengano subito.
2. Carlo vuole che voi facciate i tuoi compiti.
3. Penso che tu capisca la lezione.
4. Non voglio che tu tenga la porta aperta.
5. Lui spera che noi veniamo a casa sua.

6. Lei vuole che lei si sieda.
7. Penso che devano (debbano) andare.
8. Lui spera che noi diciamo la verità.
9. Penso che sia ora che loro vadano a casa.

12·4
1. sappia
2. dia
3. portiate
4. sappia
5. abbiate
6. abbiate
7. stiate
8. stiano
9. sia

12·5
1. Spero che lui abiti qui vicino.
2. Spero che lui scriva una cartolina.
3. Spero che lei cammini molto.
4. Spero che noi arriviamo presto.
5. Spero che voi studiate all'università.

6. Spero che Carlo impari a suonare il piano.
7. Spero che Maria non perda l'autobus.
8. Spero che Carlo e Maria non litighino.
9. Spero che tu giochi al tennis.

12·6
1. Mi dispiace che tu stia poco bene.
2. Mi dispiace che lui sia troppo impegnato.
3. Mi dispiace che lei abbia il raffreddore.
4. Mi dispiace che noi non possiamo venire da te.

5. Mi dispiace che voi siate molto stanchi.
6. Mi dispiace che loro mangino troppo.
7. Mi dispiace che tu non giochi al tennis.
8. Mi dispiace che il bambino pianga sempre.
9. Mi dispiace che voi non possiate venire a visitarci.

12·7
1. Preferisco che tu metta questo vestito.
2. Preferisco che lei studi il francese.
3. Preferisco che lui parli con il direttore.
4. Preferisco che noi andiamo al cinema.
5. Preferisco che voi dormiate e vi riposiate.

6. Preferisco che tu ti alzi presto.
7. Preferisco che voi andiate in vacanza al mare.
8. Preferisco che voi veniate da noi.
9. Preferisco che loro viaggino in macchina.

12·8
1. Io voglio che tu vada.
2. Dubitiamo che lui arrivi.
3. Speri che io vi visiti.
4. Speriamo che lui capisca.
5. Penso che tu possa.
6. Dubito che tu possa.

7. Carlo vuole che io ascolti.
8. Penso che Mario compri la frutta.
9. Dubito che voi studiate.
10. Spero di finire.
11. Speriamo di partire.
12. Dubitate di finire.

12·9
1. scriva
2. ritorni
4. siate
5. stia
7. io ti dia
8. mangiate
10. parliamo
11. volete

		3. partiamo	6. sia	9. veniamo	12. piace

12·10
1. sia
2. nevichi
3. sia
4. voglia
5. parta/venga
6. faccia
7. siate
8. andiate
9. arrivino

12·11
1. svegli
2. apra
3. piaccia
4. disturbi
5. valga
6. protegga
7. faccia
8. aiuti
9. sappia

12·12
1. ha
2. faccia
3. studiano
4. studino
5. miagola
6. abbiano
7. venda
8. vende
9. vada
10. conosca
11. esista
12. sia

12·13
abbiano
ascoltino
esageri
possono
aiutino

Almost every day in Italy, there is a strike. I have the impression that the Italians don't want to work anymore. With the strikes, the people hope to get raises in their salaries. It is necessary that the government and the unions listen to the workers. People are saying that they work a lot and don't make enough money. It is possible that they exaggerate, but one thing is for sure: they cannot keep on increasing the cost of merchandise without increasing the salaries. It seems that strikes might help people to obtain what they want, but, in reality, one doesn't obtain anything or enough to justify these strikes and the loss of working hours.

12·14
1. dicessero
2. andassi
3. tornaste
4. leggessero
5. fumassero
6. rimanesse
7. regalassi
8. giocassero
9. comprassero
10. comprassi
11. arrivasse
12. finisse
13. facessi
14. lavassi
15. potesse

12·15
1. Volevo che tu venissi.
2. Speravo che tu venissi.
3. Credevo che scrivesse delle lettere.
4. Lui pensava che lei pulisse.
5. Non sapevo che venisse anche lei.
6. Sarebbe necessario che partissero.
7. Mio padre voleva che noi lavorassimo tutto il giorno.
8. Desiderava dormire tutto il giorno.
9. Tu volevi che noi andassimo a casa.
10. Voleva chiederlo al dottore.
11. Tu pensavi che lui venisse.
12. Tu pensavi che lui potesse studiare.
13. Volevano che io cucinassi.
14. Speravo che stesse bene per il matrimonio.
15. Vorrei dormire tutto il giorno.

12·16
1. Sperava che voi studiaste.
2. Desideravano che li chiamassimo.
3. Proibivano che noi fumassimo in ufficio.
4. Avevo paura che tu lo vedessi.
5. Preferivo che loro venissero a casa mia.
6. Insistevo che tu finissi i compiti.
7. Pensavo che voi vi ricordaste.
8. Credevo che tu venissi.
9. Speravo che tu parlassi.
10. Speravo che tu non dicessi niente.
11. Dubitavo che comprassero la casa.
12. Pensavo che lui fosse americano.
13. Immaginavo che voi foste stanchi.
14. Non credeva che voi viaggiaste in macchina.
15. Non pensavo che voi vi ricordaste.

12·17
1. fosse
2. venissero
3. fosse
4. avesse
5. fossi
6. portassi
7. facessi
8. suonassi
9. chiamasse
10. avesse

12·18
avessi
fosse
costasse
Comprerei
fosse
avessi
fosse
avesse
fossero
sapessero

Yesterday Giovanna went downtown with her friend Maria. They stopped in front of the shop windows and they dreamed. Giovanna said, "If I had a lot of money, I would buy a silk blouse. I think that if it were possible and didn't cost a lot, I would also buy a modern fashionable skirt. I would buy the shoes, too. I would do all this if it were possible, but I can't because I am a student and I don't have many resources." Maria said, "If I had a lot of money, I would go to a travel agency and I would ask for some brochures to go to an island, away from everything and everybody. I would like to rent a villa. I would like this villa to be near the beach but have a swimming pool, too. I would like it to have many rooms so that I could invite some of my friends. I would hire people who would know how to cook well. I would go around and get to know the island. In short, I would have a lot of fun and I would rest."

12·19
1. siano arrivati/e
2. siate stati/e
3. siate alzati/e
4. abbiate bussato
5. abbia svelato
6. siate andati/e
7. abbia fatto
8. abbiamo capito
9. siate arrivati/e
10. abbia lavorato
11. abbiano rubato
12. abbia detto

12·20
1. sia venuto
2. è venuta
3. ha parlato
4. abbia parlato
5. avete nuotato
6. abbiate nuotato
7. sia partito
8. è partito
9. ha ricevuto
10. abbia ricevuto
11. hanno capito
12. abbiano capito

12·21
avesse messo
avesse dimenticato
scherzassi

venisse
avesse lasciato
avesse messo

Yesterday afternoon, I had to make a photographic presentation of my last trip. I had prepared everything the night before, and I thought that my husband had put in the box all the necessary cables. The cables were not there! I didn't think that he would have forgotten such an important thing. My friends thought I was joking when I told them I did not have the cables. I took the car and I went home to get what I needed. When I got there, I rang the doorbell and I waited for someone to come to open the door. Nobody was at home! I hoped my husband had left the garage door open. It was locked. I hoped he had put an extra key outside. Not a chance. I was desperate! At that moment, I heard a car coming. It was my son. I took what I needed, and I went back to my friend's house where I could finally give my presentation!

12·22
1. avessero capito
2. fossero arrivati/e
3. fossi venuto/a
4. foste andati/e
5. avessi saputo
6. foste entrati/e
7. avesse cercato
8. avesse imparato
9. fosse arrivata
10. avessimo chiesto

12·23
1. Dubitavo che Maria fosse venuta.
2. Speravo che tu avessi trovato le chiavi.
3. Era possibile che fosse arrivato tardi.
4. Lei pensava che tu avessi preso i soldi.
5. Voi dubitavate che io avessi cercato lavoro.
6. Avevo sperato che lui avesse venduto il suo motor scooter.
7. Mi sembrava che tu lo avessi già letto.
8. Non volevo che gli operai fossero già andati via.
9. Era il libro più lungo che io avessi mai letto.

12·24
fosse stata
avessi invitati
avessi chiesto

fossero rimasti
fossero venuti
avessero dormito

avessero mangiato
avessero sciato

If your house had been near a ski resort, you would have had many guests. Your friends would have expected you to invite them to your house and that you would ask them to stay there to sleep. They had hoped that you would invite them to go to ski on the wonderful ski runs where you go. Your house is not near a ski resort. You could not have invited your friends, but I think that your parents would not have been very happy if your friends had come, had slept, had eaten, and had skied for a week at your house.

12·25
1. Se avessimo preso il rapido, adesso saremmo già a casa.
2. Se tu fossi stato/a pronto, non avremmo perso il treno.
3. Se fosse stato onesto, non avrebbe mentito.
4. Maria sarebbe uscita, se non fosse piovuto.
5. Se avesse trovato la persona giusta, si sarebbe sposato.
6. Se avessero voluto venire, avrebbero potuto chiamarci.
7. Saresti venuto/a se ti avessero telefonato?
8. Se mi avessero aspettato, sarei stato molto felice.
9. Se avessi scritto a mia madre, l'avrei sorpresa.

12·26
1. se ti avessi chiesto un favore
2. se avessi visto un extraterrestre
3. se avessi avuto una casa grande
4. se lui avesse capito
5. se lei avesse letto
6. se noi avessimo bevuto il vino rosso
7. se voi aveste aspettato
8. se avessero mangiato
9. se non avessero capito

12·27
1. Sì, se tu mi avessi chiesto un favore te lo avrei fatto.
2. Sì, se avesse visto un cane, avrebbe avuto paura.
3. Sì, se fossimo andati a sciare, avremmo avuto tutto il necessario.
4. Sì, se avessimo avuto bisogno, avremmo telefonato.
5. Sì, se avessero parlato lentamente, li avrei capiti.
6. Sì, se tu avessi ordinato il cappuccino, lo avrei bevuto.
7. Sì, se fossimo andati al mare, ci saremmo divertiti.
8. Sì, se lui fosse caduto sul ghiaccio, si sarebbe fatto male.
9. Sì, se mi fossi sentito bene, sarei venuto a lavorare.

III-13   The passive voice (*forma passiva*)

13·1
1. Il conto è stato pagato ieri.
2. La Divina Commedia è stata scritta da Dante Alighieri.
3. I ragazzi sono stati svegliati tardi.
4. Queste scarpe sono state fatte in Italia.
5. Sono state scattate molte fotografie.
6. Questo libro è stato pubblicato in America.
7. L'America è stata scoperta nel 1492.
8. I quadri sono stati portati in cantina.

13·2
1. La nuova statua verrà ammirata nell'entrata del museo.
2. Le opere di Alessandro Manzoni vengono studiate da tutti gli studenti italiani.
3. La squadra di pallone verrà onorata per l'eccellente stagione.
4. Il tetto della scuola verrà riparato durante l'estate.
5. Il contratto verrà firmato questa sera.
6. La dichiarazione delle tasse verrà finita per la metà di aprile.
7. Il museo verrà chiuso per tre mesi per restauri.
8. Le tende vennero tolte per essere pulite.
9. La casa venne venduta tanto tempo fa.

13·3
1. Il contratto deve essere firmato.
2. Il contratto dovrà essere firmato dai tuoi genitori.
3. Il contratto venne firmato da tutti.
4. Il contratto venne firmato in tribunale.
5. Siamo sorpresi che il contratto non sia stato ancora firmato.
6. Il biglietto aereo sarà rimborsato.
7. Il biglietto aereo è già stato rimborsato.
8. Il biglietto aereo verrà rimborsato appena possibile.
9. La casa verrà costruita in sei mesi.
10. Questo museo resterà chiuso tutto l'inverno.

13·4
1. Nei ristoranti si spreca molto cibo.
2. Molto spesso si vedono dei cartelli che dicono: "È stato perso un cane".
3. Va ricordato che non si può pescare senza permesso.
4. Va ricordato che è proibito fumare nei gabinetti degli aerei.
5. Tutti i rifiuti della riparazione del tetto dovranno essere raccolti e messi nei contenitori.
6. Tutti i miei documenti sono stati rubati.
7. Tutti quei pettegolezzi dovranno essere ascoltati con discrezione.
8. Molto spazio è sprecato nella sua casa!
9. Tutte queste idee dovranno essere prese in considerazione.

13·5
1. Polenta is eaten today.
2. Where does one find tomatoes?
3. The problems have multiplied.
4. The work should be finished.
5. School has to be reformed.
6. When do we go on the excursion?
7. Credit cards are not accepted.
8. English is spoken here.
9. That tree has to be cut down.

13·6   Next Sunday, more than 36,000 people in Milan will have to leave their houses for an entire day. The main station will be closed, and the trains will not arrive or depart. The railway tracks into the city will be blocked, with serious repercussions on the national and international train traffic. All this to allow the specialists to neutralize and remove a bomb fallen from a plane in World War II, still unexploded under the city streets. The bomb was found when some workers were excavating the street to replace the sewers and had to go to some depth. It is believed to be one of the biggest bombs still unexploded ever found in Milan. The zone will be protected by experts and by the city police.

III-14   Idiomatic expressions (*espressioni idiomatiche*)

14·1
1. Ho bisogno di un ombrello.
2. Tu hai sempre fretta.
3. Lui ha freddo.
4. Lei ha mal di testa.
5. Abbiamo sete.
6. Avevo torto.
7. Hanno bisogno di scarpe nuove.
8. Avevo mal di testa.
9. Tu hai vergogna.
10. Voi avete sonno.
11. Abbiamo molto caldo.
12. Hanno ragione.

14·2
1. Lui fa attenzione.
2. Facciamo colazione.
3. Faranno delle fotografie.
8. Lui farà un discorso.
9. Faremo alla romana.
10. Lui mi fa un favore.

4. Ho fatto un viaggio.
5. Fa uno spuntino.
6. Io faccio una visita.
7. Faceva molto freddo.

11. Faremo una crociera.
12. Faccio la spuntino.
13. Lei fa attenzione.
14. Voi fate una domanda.

14·3
1. L'hanno fatta lavorare troppe ore.
2. Mi sono fatta portare dal dottore da mio marito.
3. Mia nonna mi faceva asciugare i piatti tutti i giorni.
4. Ci faranno guardare le fotografie per due ore.
5. Ha fatto andare a letto i bambini molto presto.
6. Non lo lascerà andare in casa.
7. I nonni lasciano fare tutto quello che vogliono ai nipotini.
8. La scuola lascia andare gli studenti a casa presto.
9. Lasciala ridere!
10. Lasciali giocare!
11. Ci vorranno diversi anni finché gli alberi crescano.
12. Quanto tempo ci vorrà per fare questa traduzione?
13. Mi ci sono voluti solo tre giorni.
14. Quanti giorni ci mette una lettera per arrivare dall'Italia?
15. Ci mette una settimana.

14·4
I have a beautiful house in the country, but it is old. I would like to have it remodeled. I already have the plan and the estimate being done for me by an architect well known in this area. I will have the job done by a construction company that I have known for a long time. Many months will be needed to complete this project. I will not go to see it until it is finished. I will let the masons work in peace. They know how to do their work.

I have already had the fireplace fixed, but it cannot be used for two or three more weeks. As soon as the work is done, I'll invite my friends for a party.

14·5
1. Devo dare da mangiare al cane.
2. Non dargli fastidio, stanno dormendo.
3. Mi ha dato il benvenuto con affetto.
4. Mia sorella dà sempre la colpa ai suoi amici.
5. In Italia la gente dà la mano.
6. Non dargli ascolto!
7. Domani gli studenti daranno gli esami finali.
8. La casa di Georgia dà sulla spiaggia.
9. Ho dato un urlo quando ho visto il topo.
10. Ci danno un passaggio per'aeroporto.
11. Ai bambini piace dare calci alla palla.
12. Ho dato un sospiro di sollievo quando ho finito il libro in orario.
13. Non gli abbiamo ancora dato una risposta.
14. Devo darmi da fare, perchè parto fra due settimane.
15. Mio figlio non vuole darsi per vinto.

14·6
1. La gente in Italia spesso va a braccetto.
2. Carlo vuole andare a pescare con suo nonno.
3. I loro bambini vanno sempre d'accordo.
4. Vorrei andare a cavallo nel West.
5. Oggi, tutto quello che ho fatto è andato bene.
6. Lei ha paura di andare in aereo.
7. Lei preferisce andare in treno.
8. Perchè non andiamo di sera?
9. Tutto andrà in vendita domani.

14·7
The boys were in the park playing soccer. All of a sudden, one of them kicked a player of the opposite team. The boy screamed with pain and fell on the ground. Everybody surrounded him to see if he was really hurt. The coach wanted them to stay away, but nobody was listening. They wanted to help their friend. The adults talked it over for a while and they agreed with the boy who had been hurt. When they asked the other boy the reason for his behavior, he did not give an answer. The coach suspended him from the game for two weeks. Maybe the next time he will try to be kinder, more respectful, and more sportsmanlike with his fellow players.

14·8
1. Quel vestito le sta a pennello.
2. Aspetteremo a vedremo chi prenderà il premio per il quadro migliore.
3. Giovanni è a letto. Non sta affatto bene.
4. Erica non sta mai ferma.
5. Perchè stai in piedi?
6. Sono stato dal dentista per tre ore.
7. State fermi e zitti. Sono stanca.
8. Fa troppo freddo. Starò a casa.
9. Stai attenta a non scivolare sulla strada ghiacciata.

14·9
This morning I woke up early and I was going to the station to meet Giovanna, when she called me to tell

me that her baby-sitter was not well and she could not go to her house to stay with the children. She also told me that her children were sick with the flu and they had to stay quietly in bed. When the children are well and the weather is good we will go horseback riding all together. For now Giovanna has to stay home to keep the children still. What a pity!

III-15   Verbs and expressions followed by a preposition

15·1
1. Credono a tutti.
2. Cerco di non dare fastidio a mia sorella.
3. I bambini non danno ascolto alla maestra.
4. Il gatto dà la caccia al topo.
5. Per favore fai attenzione alla strada.
6. Il bambino ha dato un pugno a sua sorella sul naso.
7. Tu farai piacere a tua madre.
8. Lui pensa sempre a te.
9. A loro piace giocare alle carte.
10. Lei assomiglia a suo padre.
11. Lui non stringe la mano al suo amico.
12. Dobbiamo dare da mangiare ai nostri animali.

15·2
1. Mi devo abituare al posto nuovo.
2. Si affretta a mangiare.
3. Ti aiuterò a allacciarti le scarpe.
4. Si è deciso a studiare l'italiano.
5. Ci divertiamo molto a guardare le scimmie allo zoo.
6. Fai meglio a non sposarti.
7. Dobbiamo imparare a sciare.
8. La madre insegna al bambino a camminare.
9. Ci invitano a ballare.
10. Io penso sempre a comprare qualche cosa per i miei figli.
11. Questo strumento serve a bloccare la porta.
12. Dovete rinunciare al vostro viaggio.
13. Non continuare a ridere!
14. Mi manderanno a prendere il pacco alla posta.
15. Riprenderemo a imparare l'italiano domani.

15·3
1. Andiamo al cinema.
2. Sono andato al cimitero.
3. Corre a casa perchè ha fame.
4. Si ferma a comprare il giornale.
5. Ci fermeremo a casa tua.
6. Sono ritornati/e a casa molto tardi.
7. Andiamo a scuola con i nostri amici.
8. Maria e Carlo vengono a visitarci oggi pomeriggio.
9. Corre a prendere l'autobus.
10. Mi fermo a guardare i fiori nel prato.
11. Staranno a casa tutto il giorno.
12. È ritornata a casa con molti libri.

15·4
1. Non mi sono accorto/a di lei.
2. Tu hai bisogno dei tuoi amici.
3. Maria si nutre solo di frutta.
4. Abbiamo paura dei gatti.
5. Vi siete dimenticati di me a casa.
6. Si preoccupavano dei loro vecchi genitori.
7. Mi fido di te.
8. Non si ricorda affatto di te.
9. Lei si è innamorata di lui.
10. Ridono di lui.
11. Ci meravigliamo delle sue capacità.
12. Lei soffre di emicranie.
13. Si lamentano di tutto.
14. Non potete vivere solo di pane e acqua.

15·5
1. Ammetto di sbagliare.
2. Hai finito di parlare al telefono.
3. Ha ordinato alle sue truppe di ritirarsi.
4. Pensa di mangiare una bistecca.
5. Ti auguro di vivere una vita lunga e felice.
6. Abbiamo bisogno di dormire.
7. Ti prego di venire subito.
8. Lei ti proibisce di toccare la torta.
9. Ti chiediamo di chiudere la porta.
10. Conto di arrivare in orario.
11. Mi hanno promesso di portarmi un bel giocattolo.
12. Vi ringraziamo di aver annaffiato le piante.
13. Crede di uscire dall'ospedale fra quattro giorni.
14. Mi sono dimenticato di spegnere la luce.
15. Tu hai deciso di viaggiare in treno.

15·6
1. Puoi contare su di me.
2. Sto riflettendo sul da farsi.
3. Il presidente giura sulla Bibbia.
4. Desidero avere un bel giardino.
5. Permettiamo ai bambini di guardare la televisione.
6. Preferiamo mangiare fuori.
7. Amo avere una bella casa.
8. Tu sai vivere bene.
9. Basta parlare.
10. Bisogna parlare con il direttore.

15·7
1. Impariamo a sciare.
2. Comincio a capire.
3. Penso di venire.
4. Ha bisogno di studiare.
5. Ritorneranno in Italia.
6. Tu hai paura del buio.
7. Non ci fidiamo di lui.
8. Smetti di parlare!
9. Staremo a casa.
10. Hanno dimenticato di studiare.
11. Ho bisogno di te.
12. Ha promesso di venire.
13. Ringraziano di tutto.
14. Insegnava scuola di guida.
15. Chiamami prima di partire.

Part IV: Sentence Building

IV-1 Declarative sentences and word order

1·1   1. P   2. S   3. S   4. P   5. P   6. S   7. S   8. S

1·2   1. Mio fratello è molto giovane.   2. Ha solo diciotto anni.   3. Si chiama Marco.   4. Ho parlato con lui ieri.   5. Lui è sempre puntuale.   6. Lui ti chiamerà presto.   7. Lei legge molti libri.   8. A noi (ci) piace Roma.   9. Vogliamo visitare posti nuovi.   10. Voi siete interessati ad imparare una lingua nuova.

1·3   1. Maria vive in questo palazzo.   2. Lucia, è la moglie di Pietro?   3. La casa di Marco è sulla spiaggia.   4. Lucia e suo marito rientrano dalle vacanze.   5. Abbiamo letto la notizia del tuo matrimonio sul giornale.   6. Ti piacciono i film di fantascienza.   7. Guardate la televisione alla sera?   8. Quando glielo portate?   9. Non andiamo, ma telefoniamo spesso.   10. La tazza del caffè è sul tavolino.

1·4   1. Oggi studiamo l'italiano.   2. Parliamo bene l'italiano.   3. Abbiamo già finito di leggere.   4. Studio raramente.   5. Glielo porterò questa sera.   6. Parliamo sempre dell'Italia.   7. Mi dà anche il caffè.   8. Porto un libro a mia sorella.   9. Ci incontriamo spesso per fare una festa.   10. Vivi in campagna ma ami la città.

1·5   1. A   2. N   3. A   4. A   5. N   6. N   7. N   8. A   9. A   10. N

1·6   1. The palms are tall and beautiful.   2. The moon is not shining today.   3. I see many stars in the sky.   4. At night the birds sleep in the trees.   5. I will never ever stay and sleep in this hotel.   6. Nobody says anything.   7. I do not like people who smoke.   8. He is afraid of traveling by plane.   9. We have a lot to do.   10. There is nothing I want to buy.

1·7   1. Mai   2. mai   3. nessuno   4. nè   5. nessuno   6. niente   7. nessuno   8. niente   9. Non   10. Mai, Non

1·8   1. Io non compro il vino in questo negozio.   2. L'impiegato mai è molto disponibile.   3. Maria non gioca con qualcuno.   4. Non mi piace guardare il baseball o il football alla televisione.   5. Nessuno di noi due sta bene.   6. Tu mai giochi a tennis.   7. I bambini di questo quartire mai sono fuori a giocare.   8. Gli studenti nelle scuole italiane non hanno sport o teatro.   9. Questa città non è vicina al mare o alle montagne.   10. Mai il mio lavoro è noioso.

IV-2 Interrogative sentences

2·1   *Sample answers are provided.*   1. Cantano i ragazzi?   2. Lavora Luisa?   3. È grande la casa?   4. Viaggiano molto loro?   5. Dormite sempre voi?   6. Giocano a tennis le ragazze?   7. Piangono i bambini?   8. Fumi troppo tu?   9. È andata a casa Maria?   10. È ammalata la tua amica?

2·2   *Sample answers are provided.*   1. Giochi a pallacanestro?   2. Fumi tanto?   3. Abita qui Luigi?   4. Parli l'inglese?   5. Le signore giocano a bridge il mercoledì?   6. Viaggia in treno lei?   7. Sei felice in questa casa?   8. Tuo padre è l'uomo che ho incontrato l'altra sera?   9. Hai molto stress nella tua vita?   10. Hai viaggiato in molte parti del mondo?

2·3   *Sample answers are provided.*   1. Tu studi molto, giusto?   2. Suo marito è un campione di tennis, non è vero?   3. Loro sono in vacanza, no?   4. Il concerto è sabato, non è vero?   5. Preferisci il gelato al dolce, vero?   6. Loro vanno in chiesa la domenica, non è vero?   7. È molto scoraggiante perdere sempre, vero?   8. Se uno non paga le tasse, potrebbe andare in prigione, no?   9. I parchi americani sono molto belli, vero?   10. Bisogna viaggiare molte ore per attraversare gli Stati Uniti, giusto?

2·4   1. Per chi ha un libro Luisa?   2. Di chi è la casa?   3. A chi porti il pane?   4. Con chi vai al cinema?   5. Chi vogliono visitare?   6. Da chi stai quando vai in Florida?   7. A chi pensi spesso?   8. Chi viene domani?

2·5   1. a. Quando mangi il gelato? b. Quale gelato mangi? c. Perchè mangi il gelato? d. Mangi il gelato, non è vero?   2. a. Quando bevi il succo di frutta? b. Quale succo di frutta bevi? c. Perchè bevi il succo di frutta? d. Bevi il succo di frutta, giusto?   3. a. Quando mangi il formaggio? b. Quale formaggio mangi? c. Perchè mangi il formaggio? d. Mangi il formaggio, vero?   4. a. Quando mangi la pasta? b. Quale pasta mangi? c. Perchè mangi la pasta? d. Mangi la pasta, non è vero?   5. a. Quando bevi la cioccolata calda? b. Quale cioccolata calda bevi? c. Perchè bevi la cioccolata calda? d. Bevi la cioccolata calda, giusto?   6. a. Quando mangi la torta? b. Quale torta mangi? c. Perchè mangi la torta? d. Mangi la torta, vero?

2·6   1. Quante   2. Quando   3. Come   4. Quale   5. Chi   6. Quanti   7. Dove   8. Come   9. Da dove   10. Di dove

2·7   1. Chi   2. Di chi   3. A chi   4. Con chi   5. Da chi   6. Per chi   7. Di chi   8. Per chi   9. Di chi   10. A chi

2·8   *Sample answers are provided.*   1. Quando   2. Che cosa   3. Da dove   4. Quale   5. Che cosa   6. Quanti   7. Quante   8. Quali   9. Quando   10. Come

IV-3 Questions and answers

3·1   1. a. Chi vuole andare in Italia? b. Dove vuole andare la vostra insegnante?   2. a. Quando sono chiuse le banche? b. Chi chiude il sabato e la domenica?   3. a. Che cosa costa troppo?   4. a. Che cosa annaffi tu?   5. a. Chi è seduto accanto alla sua padrona? b. Dove è seduto il cane?   6. a. Quando vai al cinema? b. Con chi vai al cinema domani?   7. a. Chi vuole visitare i figli?   8. a. Che cosa è parcheggiata davanti alla casa? b. Dov'è parcheggiata la macchina?   9. a. Chi vuole guardare il torneo di tennis? b. Che cosa vuole guardare tuo marito?   10. a. Chi ti telefona tutti i giorni? b. Che cosa fa tua sorella?

3·2   1. Vengo da Roma.   2. Oggi ne abbiamo dodici.   3. I ladri hanno rubato la televisione.   4. I miei amici viaggiano in macchina.   5. Mia sorella viene a visitarmi la prossima settimana.   6. Prima di andare in Italia, studio l'italiano.   7. Questi documenti sono dei miei genitori.   8. L'aereo arriva fra un'ora.   9. Ogni giorno leggo due giornali.   10. Faccio tutti questi costumi per le cantanti d'opera.

3·3   1. Che cosa devono lavarsi i bambini?   2. Chi deve aspettare Maria?   3. Chi deve aspettare Maria?   4. Che cosa ha comprato lei?   5. Che cosa hai letto?   6. Che cosa ha perso tuo zio?   7. Che cosa ha dimenticato tua zia?   8. A che cosa pensi?   9. Chi ha freddo in classe?   10. Che cosa ha lasciato in classe Margherita?

3·4   1. La nonna abita con mio nonno.   2. Mia nonna guarda la televisione tutto il giorno.   3. Oggi ha telefonato il falegname.   4. Maria mi ha detto che non viene a casa mia.   5. Carlo va al mercato venerdì mattina.   6. Eric balla molto bene.   7. Il figlio della mia amica suona molto bene il piano.   8. Questa sera voglio mangiare gli spaghetti.

3·5   1. Lui viene al cinema con sua sorella?   2. Perchè non giochi con i bambini?   3. Quanti metri di stoffa ha comprato la sarta?   4. Quanto costa il nuovo CD?   5. Quale macchina hai comprato?   6. Che cosa avete mangiato questa sera?   7. Siete andati a mangiare al ristorante?   8. Da dove è venuto questo libro?

3·6   *Sample answers are provided.*   1. a. Quando vai al parco? b. Ci vado quando ritorno a casa dal lavoro.   2. a. Perchè devi partire così presto? b. Perchè non mi piace viaggiare con il buio.   3. a. Da dove viene quel dottore famoso? b. Viene da Firenze.   4. a. Chi hai portato a casa ieri? b. Ho portato il mio ragazzo.   5. a. Come vai all'aereoporto? b. Devo prendere un tassì.   6. a. Da quanto tempo studiate in Italia? b. Da diversi anni.   7. a. Quale delle due ragazze conosci meglio? b. Quella vicina alla porta.
8. a. Quanto tempo ci vuole per arrivare in Australia? b. Ci vogliono più di venti ore di areo.

IV-4 Imperatives

4·1   1. Bevi!, beva!, bevano!   2. aspetta!, aspetti!, aspettino!   3. ordina!, ordini!, ordinino!   4. sta'!, stia!, stiano!   5. vota!, voti!, votino!   6. leggi!, legga!, leggano!   7. mangia!, mangi!, mangino!   8. sappi!, sappia!, sappiano!   9. sii!, sia!, siano!   10. metti!, metta!, mettano!

4·2   1. Spingere!   2. Tirare!   3. Non toccare!   4. Non calpestare l'erba!   5. Non parlare all'autista!   6. Non fare fotografie!   7. Non oltrepassare!   8. Non parcheggiare!   9. Non dar da mangiare agli animali!   10. Tenere la porta chiusa!

4·3   1. Let's go to the movies!   2. Let him travel to Europe!   3. Let her speak!   4. Let's write a letter to Grandmother!   5. Let him do what he wants!   6. Let me speak!   7. Let's go get a coffee!   8. Let me eat!   9. Let's read!   10. Let's take a picture! 11. Let the others speak! 12. Let me stay!

4·4   1. Non mangiate tutti i cioccolatini!   2. Non compriamo le ciliege!   3. Non fate la doccia!   4. Non salutare il professore!   5. Non facciamo gli esercizi!   6. Non chiamare un tassì!   7. Non parlare lentamente!   8. Non mettete la giacca!   9. Non comprate una giacca pesante!   10. Non imparare a usare il computer!

4·5   1. parli 2. Scrivi 3. chiudete 4. provi 5. Studiate 6. Prepara 7. Cuocia 8. Compra 9. Aspettino 10. Controlla

4·6   1. riposarti 2. alzarti 3. Fermatevi 4. si rivolga 5. pettinati 6. svegliatevi 7. Copritevi 8. Si accomodino 9. dimenticatevi 10. si porti

4·7   1. Dille che lui l'ama!   2. Stammi vicino!   3. Dicci chi viene alla festa!   4. Dammi la borsa!   5. Dacci un colpo di telefono!   6. Facci un favore!   7. Fagli un regalo per il suo compleanno!   8. Non dargli un orologio!   9. Dalle la macchina nuova!   10. Non darle la macchina fotografica!

IV-5 Coordinating conjunctions

5·1   *Sample answers are provided.* 1. e 2. ma 3. ma 4. o 5. e 6. ma 7. perciò 8. quindi 9. e 10. per questo

5·2   *Sample answers are provided.* 1. Ci sono tanti nostri amici e vorremmo che venissi anche tu.   2. Ti ammonisco, ma fa quel che vuoi.   3. Segui il tuo istinto, ma non venire a piangere da me.   4. Filippo non è generoso, infatti è molto tirchio.   5. Franco è un ragazzo molto intelligente, infatti è un genio.   6. Tu vuoi andare al cinema, ma io non voglio andarci.   7. I miei genitori non vogliono comprarmi un cane e neppure un gatto.   8. Se tutto va bene mi comprerò la moto, e mi comprerò la macchina l'anno prossimo.
9. Abbiamo comprato la frutta e la carne, però abbiamo dimenticato il pane.   10. Lui non sta molto bene, per questo deve andare dal dottore per un controllo.

5·3   1. però 2. e 3. quindi 4. perciò 5. però 6. e 7. però 8. ma 9. e 10. e

5·4   *Sample answers are provided.* 1. Entrambi Luigi ed io andremo alla festa.   2. I soldi e il potere non portano la felicità.   3. Ci ha dato dei regali, e ci ha invitati a casa sua.   4. Era stanco, e non si sentiva bene.   5. Ho finito i miei compiti, quindi posso andare fuori a giocare. 6. Vi vedrò tutti fra due settimane o per Natale. 7. Il ladro si mosse velocemente e silenziosamente. 8. Nè io nè te, possiamo andare al matrimonio. 9. Oggi ha fatto freddo, infatti ha nevicato. 10. Uscirai con i tuoi amici o con i tuoi parenti?

IV-6 Subordinating conjunctions

6·1 Sample answers are provided. 1. perchè 2. benchè 3. prima che 4. dopo che 5. a patto che 6. Se 7. che 8. perchè

6·2 1. come 2. Benchè 3. perchè 4. perchè 5. così... che 6. perchè 7. sebbene 8. Benchè

6·3 1. Se 2. Benchè 3. ma 4. quindi 5. perchè 6. Dopo che 7. perchè 8. Dato che

6·4 1. e 2. Benchè 3. benchè, perchè, così 4. sebbene 5. e, ma, perchè 6. e, anche 7. o 8. Benchè, e

IV-7 Relative pronouns

7·1 1. che 2. che 3. che 4. che 5. che 6. chi 7. chi 8. chi

7·2 1. di cui 2. da cui 3. il cui 4. in cui 5. per cui 6. in cui 7. a cui 8. di cui

7·3 1. che 2. chi 3. quello che 4. di cui 5. Chi 6. in cui 7. da cui 8. che

7·4 1. quanto 2. dove 3. Chi 4. chiunque 5. Chi 6. Quelli che 7. Chiunque 8. quello che

7·5 1. che 2. che 3. chi 4. chi 5. di cui 6. a cui 7. con cui 8. quello che

7·6 1. Chi 2. che 3. cui 4. che 5. cui 6. Chiunque 7. chi 8. dove (in cui)

IV-8 Present and past participles

8·1 1. assistente (*assistant*) 2. commovente (*emotionally moving*) 3. dirigente (*directing, director*) 4. mancante (*missing*) 5. obbediente (*obedient*) 6. perdente (*losing*) 7. riposante (*restful, resting*) 8. tollerante (*tolerant*) 9. uscente (*exiting*) 10. vivente (*living*)

8·2 1. bollente 2. corrente 3. sorridente 4. obbedienti 5. assistente 6. sconvolgente 7. divertente 8. seguente

8·3 1. governanti 2. dipendente 3. emigranti 4. conducenti 5. passanti 6. dissetante 7. partecipanti 8. abbaglianti

8·4 1. fritte 2. mosso 3. preceduto 4. accaldato 5. depurate 6. ridotta 7. amata 8. conosciuto

8·5 1. fermata 2. permesso 3. visto 4. invitati 5. soffritto 6. candidati 7. ammalati 8. udito

8·6 1. Quando sarà finito il concerto, ti riporteremo a casa. 2. Appena saranno spente le luci, la bambina si addormenterà. 3. Quando avranno finito il corso, gli studenti andranno al mare. 4. Quando saranno saliti sull'autobus, troveranno senz'altro un posto a sedere. 5. Appena avranno lavato i piatti, puliranno la cucina. 6. Quando avranno preso la patente, potranno guidare. 7. Quando saranno arrivati a destinazione, si riposeranno. 8. Appena finiti i compiti, potranno andare fuori a giocare.

8·7 1. Finitala, mi sono sentita sollevata. 2. Riposatosi, viene a visitarvi. 3. Cercava la palla dappertutto, trovatala è uscito a giocare. 4. Le ho lette tutte in questi giorni. 5. Li vedo sempre quando ritornano dal lavoro. 6. La cioccolata calda era squisita, ne ho bevute due tazze. 7. Ne ho mangiata una, ma era acerba. 8. Ne ho comprate tante.

IV-9 Adjectives

9·1 *Sample answers are provided.* 1. lungo, interessante, triste 2. giallo, piccolo, estivo 3. grande, bianca, stretta 4. nero, robusto, piccolo 5. alta, pericolosa, vasta 6. quotidiano, interessante, diurno 7. bianca, fredda, nuova 8. intelligente, felice, longilineo

9·2 1. Ho visto una povera donna bloccata nella neve. 2. Sono bambini americani. 3. Lui è un cittadino austriaco. 4. Mi piacciono i tavoli quadrati. 5. Nel Michigan si trova terreno sabbioso dappertutto. 6. Lei indossa solo scarpe nere. 7. Ho una sciarpa rossa. 8. Lei è una persona malata.

9·3 1. incertezza 2. bellezza 3. fioritura 4. difficoltà 5. velocità 6. novità 7. calore 8. realtà 9. veleno 10. profumo 11. freschezza

9·4 1. i rosso·neri 2. il futuro 3. i mondiali 4. stranieri 5. I ricchi, i belli 6. gli studiosi 7. i temerari, deboli 8. I timidi

9·5 1. Gli sportivi 2. chiaro, tondo 3. toscano, fiorentina 4. piano, sano, lontano 5. il peggio 6. gli stranieri 7. le cinesi, duro 8. il futuro

9·6 1. più alto di 2. molto alto 3. meno di 4. pochissimo 5. più, della 6. molto salata 7. più, della 8. molto fredda

9·7   1. a. Il gatto è più piccolo del cane nero. b. Il gatto è il più piccolo di tutti. c. Il gatto è piccolissimo.   2. a. Il dolce è più buono del gelato. b. Il dolce è il migliore di tutti. c. Il dolce è buonissimo.   3. a. L'uomo è più alto di sua moglie. b. L'uomo è il più alto di tutti. c. L'uomo è altissimo.   4. a. L'inverno è più freddo dell'autunno. b. L'inverno è la stagione più fredda di tutte. c. L'inverno è freddissimo.

9·8   1. giovanissima   2. molto vecchia   3. molto interessante   4. molto indaffarata   5. più ambizioso che   6. molto vecchia   7. vecchissimi   8. molto ricchi

9·9   1. piovana   2. nudo   3. sereno   4. insipida   5. disoccupato   6. primaverile   7. arida   8. orfano

IV-10   Adverbs

10·1   1. esattamente   2. doppiamente   3. ordinatamente   4. freddamente   5. velocemente   6. attivamente   7. allegramente   8. pacificamente

10·2   1. felici   2. felicemente   3. esatta   4. ordinatamente   5. freddo   6. freddamente   7. attiva   8. attivamente

10·3   *Sample answers are provided.*   1. a dirotto   2. fuori   3. davanti   4. fortunatamente   5. poi   6. molto   7. dintorni   8. circa

10·4   *Sample answers are provided.*   1. profondamente   2. attentamente   3. diligentemente   4. velocemente   5. molto   6. attentamente   7. continuamente   8. frequentemente

10·5   1. più diligentemente   2. moltissimo   3. benissimo   4. più tardi   5. più volentieri   6. peggio   7. malissimo   8. molto elegantemente

IV-11   Pronouns

11·1   1. a. La portano al cinema. b. Portano lei al cinema.   2. a. Luisa li porta in piscina tutti i giorni. b. Luisa porta loro in piscina tutti i giorni.   3. a. Lo contatterò appena posso. b. Contatterò lui appena posso.   4. a. Lo portiamo all'aereoporto, poi torniamo a casa. b. Portiamo lui all'aereoporto poi torniamo a casa.   5. a. Ci inviti a cena a casa tua. b. Inviti noi a cena a casa tua.   6. a. Luigi li porta in vacanza. b. Luigi porta loro in vacanza.   7. a. Li vediamo al mare. b. Vediamo loro al mare.   8. a. Lo rivedo con molto piacere. b. Rivedo lui con molto piacere.

11·2   1. uno (In treno ho parlato con uno che non conoscevo.)   2. Uno (Uno non sa mai cosa dire ai parenti dei morti.)   3. una (Abbiamo conosciuto una che parla bene l'inglese.)   4. Uno (Uno ha avuto problemi di cuore mentre era in aereo.)   5. uno (Ho parlato con uno dell'anagrafe.)   6. uno (Non c'è uno che capisca la matematica.)   7. una (Ho parlato con una che non mi piaceva affatto.)   8. una (Maria è una che sa il fatto suo.)   9. una (Teresa è una delle mie migliori amiche.)

11·3   1. chiunque   2. Ognuno   3. Chiunque   4. Qualcuno   5. Chiunque   6. ognuno   7. qualcuno   8. qualcuno

11·4   *Sample answers are provided.*   1. niente   2. niente   3. qualcosa   4. Nessuno   5. qualcosa   6. nessuno   7. qualcosa   8. nulla

11·5   1. mi, ti   2. si   3. si   4. ci   5. vi   6. mi   7. Mi   8. si

IV-12   Infinitives

12·1   1. a. Prima di comprare, chiediamo il prezzo. b. Dopo aver chiesto il prezzo, compriamo.   2. a. Prima di telefonare a Marco, chiamo un taxi. b. Dopo aver telefonato a Marco, chiamo un taxi.   3. a. Prima di passare di qui, vado in chiesa. b. Dopo essere passato di qui, vado in chiesa.   4. a. Prima di mangiare, mi lavo le mani. b. Dopo essermi lavato le mani, mangio.   5. a. Prima di agire, pensa. b. Dopo aver pensato, agisce.   6. a. Prima di andare a lavorare, mi vesto. b. Dopo essermi vestito, vado a lavorare.   7. a. Prima di andare alla posta, scrive la lettera. b. Dopo aver scritto la lettera, va alla posta.   8. a. Prima di giocare, studiamo. b. Dopo aver studiato, giochiamo.

12·2   1. vedere   2. essere   3. giocare   4. fumare   5. bere   6. andare   7. fare   8. vedervi

12·3   1. vedere   2. averci pensato   3. arrivare   4. chiamare   5. aver finito   6. comprare   7. passare   8. passare

12·4   1. aver appreso   2. diventare   3. aver letto   4. andare   5. aver finito   6. aver telefonato   7. guardare   8. diventare

12·5   1. Sua madre non può bere vino.   2. La ragazza non può mai leggere.   3. Dopo pranzo possiamo andare a riposare.   4. Lei non può aprire la porta a nessuno.   5. Noi possiamo parlare con i nostri amici.   6. Lei ha potuto comprare i biglietti per l'aereo.   7. Voi siete potuti andare dal dottore.   8. Io posso farmi la barba tutte le mattine.

12·6   1. parlare   2. camminare   3. suonare   4. comprare   5. pulire   6. arrivare   7. vedere   8. ascoltare

IV-13 Passive voice

13·1   1. Il programma televisivo è guardato dai bambini.   2. Il bar è gestito da Giovanni.
3. La casa nuova è comprata da mia figlia.   4. Il libro è scritto dal professore di italiano.   5. Il nuovo
romanzo giallo è letto dagli studenti.   6. Questo bel palazzo è costruito da un famoso architetto.   7. Il
viaggio in Asia è fatto dai miei amici.   8. La birra è bevuta da Luigi.

13·2   1. Da chi viene prenotato l'albergo?   2. Da chi vengono indirizzate le lettere?   3. Da chi viene interpretato il
film?   4. Da chi viene organizzata la festa?   5. Da chi vengono inviati questi pacchi?   6. Da chi viene firmato
il documento?   7. Da chi viene pagato il conto?   8. Da chi viene preparata la cena?

13·3   1. L'albergo viene prenotato da mio fratello.   2. Le lettere vengono indirizzate dalla segretaria.
3. Il film viene interpretato da Sofia Loren.   4. La festa viene organizzata dai miei amici.   5. Questi pacchi
vengono inviati dalla mamma.   6. Il documento viene firmato dal notaio.   7. Il conto viene pagato da mio
padre.   8. La cena viene preparata dalla cuoca.

13·4   1. va spenta   2. va spalata   3. va buttato   4. vanno asciugati   5. va controllato   6. vanno
lodati   7. vanno aiutati   8. vanno lavati

13·5   1. Si lavora per vivere.   2. Si è lavorato per tanti anni per avere un certo benessere.   3. Si sono piantati tanti
fiori per avere un bel giardino.   4. Di notte, si vedono tante stelle.   5. Si porteranno tante cose in Italia per le
nostre nipoti.   6. In America si vive bene.   7. In questa casa si parla solo l'italiano.   8. Negli aeroporti si
vedono tante cose strane.

IV-14 Subjunctive mood

14·1   1. faccia   2. stia   3. esca, vada   4. sia   5. arrivi   6. faccia   7. ritorniate   8. dormiamo

14·2   1. abbia fatto   2. abbiano vinto   3. abbia conosciuto   4. abbiate mangiato   5. abbia
trascurato   6. abbiate letto   7. abbia nevicato   8. abbiate ricevuto

14·3   1. facessi   2. vincessero   3. avessi   4. mangiaste   5. trascurasse   6. piacesse
7. nevicasse   8. ricevessi

14·4   1. avesse studiato   2. aveste fatto   3. foste venuti   4. fossero, andati   5. io fossi arrivato   6. avessi
venduto   7. fossi partito   8. fosse piaciuto

14·5   1. sapessi   2. vedessi   3. abbiate   4. Si accomodi   5. stiano   6. Pensi   7. aiuti   8. dormissi

14·6   *Sample answers are provided.*   1. Benchè   2. dovunque   3. Sebbene   4. purchè
5. Benchè   6. Benchè   7. Prima che   8. affinchè

14·7   1. impariate   2. imparassi   3. stiate   4. fosse stata   5. ascoltiamo   6. dia   7. chiami   8. metta

14·8   *Sample answers are provided.*   1. tu ti prepari in fretta   2. il bambino si addormenti presto   3. tu parli bene
l'inglese   4. venga un temporale   5. tu non finisca gli esercizi   6. si laureino presto   7. mi mandino un
messaggio   8. possiate visitarci

14·9   1. avessi potuto   2. avessi chiamato   3. avessi   4. avessi avuto   5. studiaste   6. avessero
studiato   7. parli   8. piaccia

Part V: Problem Solver

V-1 Nouns, gender, and number

1·1   1. il   2. la   3. lo   4. la   5. la   6. il   7. il   8. il   9. la   10. la

1·2

Masculine	Feminine
	signora
dottore	
	madre
professore	
	studentessa
scrittore	
	nipote
fratello	
	donna

1·3   1. la / c   2. il / e   3. la / f   4. il/la / d   5. il / h   6. la / i   7. l' / b   8. la / g   9. la / a   10. il / j

1·4   1. il nipote   2. lo scrittore   3. la presidente   4. il collega   5. la donna   6. il marito
7. il dottore   8. la dea   9. il genero   10. l'insegnante

1·5	Masculine singular	Masculine plural	Feminine singular	Feminine plural
	stadio	stadi		
			università	università
	sport	sport		
	parco	parchi		
	medico	medici		
			camicia	camicie
	film	film		
			focaccia	focacce
	zio	zii		
			tesi	tesi

V-2 Articles

2·1 1. uno stadio   2. un'insalata   3. uno psicologo   4. un'automobile   5. una città   6. una stazione   7. una mano   8. una serie   9. un albergo   10. un tedesco

2·2 1. la   2. X   3. le   4. gli   5. il   6. X   7. l'   8. le   9. le   10. X

2·3 1. lo, gli sport   2. l', le arie   3. la, le tesi   4. il, i film   5. la, le foto   6. l', le auto   7. l', le estati   8. il, i papà   9. lo, gli psichiatri or la, le psichiatre   10. la, le parentesi

V-3 Adjectives

3·1 1. libri gialli   2. studenti universitari   3. piazze romane   4. buone regole   5. sete leggere   6. vestiti chiari   7. pizzerie antiche   8. quadri famosi   9. care amiche   10. strade silenziose

3·2 1. ragazza intelligente   2. libro interessante   3. città affascinante   4. attrice francese   5. sport internazionale   6. domanda difficile   7. bambino vivace   8. vestito elegante   9. lezione importante   10. film francese

3·3 1. 4   2. 1   3. 2   4. 1   5. 2   6. 1   7. 3   8. 1   9. 2   10. 2

3·4 1. d   2. f   3. j   4. h   5. k   6. a   7. b   8. c   9. g   10. e

3·5 1. h   2. f   3. i   4. c   5. d   6. b   7. j   8. a   9. e   10. g

3·6 1. di   2. che   3. che   4. della   5. che   6. delle   7. degli   8. di   9. che   10. di

3·7
1. Mario è più simpatico di Giacomo.
2. Le montagne sono più alte delle colline.
3. Giovanna è tanto (così) studiosa quanto (come) sua sorella.
4. Quell'attore è più bello che intelligente.
5. L'autobus è tanto (così) veloce quanto (come) il tram.
6. Lo spagnolo è più facile del francese.
7. I cani sono più affettuosi dei pescirossi.
8. La Cina è meno grande della Russia.
9. Leggere *la Divina commedia* è più difficile che leggere *il Decameron*.
10. Kobe Bryant è più famoso di Vasco Rossi.

3·8
1. I cornetti in quel bar sono ottimi.
2. Roberto è il fratello minore.
3. Salieri fu un compositore minore.
4. Maradona è stato il calciatore migliore.
5. Abitano al piano superiore.
6. Quel film è di pessimo gusto.
7. Quell'avvocato ha una pessima reputazione.
8. Dante Alighieri è considerato il sommo/massimo poeta italiano.
9. Gli spaghetti alla carbonara sono ottimi!
10. L'Orvieto Classico è migliore del vino della casa.

3·9
1. La casa è grande.
2. Questo pacco è pesante.
3. Giovanni è un ragazzo dinamico.
4. Roberto è più magro di Antonio.
5. Questa strada è larga.
6. L'esame di chimica è facilissimo!
7. Nel negozio ho visto delle sedie moderne.

8. La mia bici è vecchissima.
9. Le mie amiche sono nervose (stressate).
10. Il giovane professore è bravissimo.

V-4 Adverbs

4·1
1. relativamente   2. brevemente   3. esattamente   4. veramente   5. semplicemente
6. possibilmente   7. raramente   8. francamente   9. direttamente   10. probabilmente

4·2
1. d / quando   2. e / ancora   3. a / perché   4. i / come   5. f / quanto   6. b / già   7. j / come
8. g / spesso   9. c / mai   10. h

4·3
1. Quando comincia l'inverno?
2. Com'è Claudia?
3. Quanto costava il pane?
4. Perché si arrabbia?
5. Quando torna?
6. Come vanno le lezioni?
7. Dove abitava?
8. Dove mette la macchina?

4·4
1. raramente
2. velocemente
3. sempre
4. piano
5. pochissimo
6. spesso
7. seriamente
8. divinamente

4·5
Answers may vary.
1. piano
2. mai
3. sfortunata
4. benissimo
5. dentro
6. tanto, molto
7. dopo
8. puntuale, in anticipo

V-5 Present and present perfect tenses

5·1

amare (*to love*)	vedere (*to see*)	offrire (*to offer*)	capire (*to understand*)
	vedo	offro	
ami		offri	capisci
ama	vede		capisce
amiamo	vediamo	offriamo	
amate		offrite	capite
	vedono	offrono	capiscono

5·2

andare		fare		avere	
	andiamo		facciamo	ho	
vai	andate	fai		hai	avete
va		fa	fanno		

essere		tenere		bere	
sono	siamo		teniamo	bevo	beviamo
sei		tieni	tenete		bevete
	sono	tiene	tengono	beve	

dire		uscire		venire	
dico	diciamo		usciamo		veniamo
		esci		vieni	venite
dice	dicono	esce	escono	viene	

5·3
Answers will vary.
1. Anna va . . .
2. Gli italiani sono . . .
3. Io bevo . . .
4. Rob e Cecilia vengono . . .
5. Tu e Marco rimanete . . .
6. Io e Susanna veniamo . . .
7. Lei, signora Rossellini, esce . . .
8. Tu, Maria, fai . . .

5·4
1. Oggi parlo con il professore.
2. Oggi telefono alla zia.
3. Oggi capisco la lezione.
4. Oggi vendo qualcosa su eBay.
5. Oggi ho freddo.
6. Oggi guardo la TV.
7. Oggi ascolto la radio.

Anche ieri ho parlato con il professore.
Anche ieri ho telefonato alla zia.
Anche ieri ho capito la lezione.
Anche ieri ho venduto qualcosa su eBay.
Anche ieri ho avuto freddo.
Anche ieri ho guardato la TV.
Anche ieri ho ascoltato la radio.

8. Oggi finisco la lezione. Anche ieri ho finito la lezione.
9. Oggi ballo il tango. Anche ieri ho ballato il tango.
10. Oggi preferisco il cappuccino. Anche ieri ho preferito il cappuccino.

5·5
1. Oggi Antonio torna tardi. Anche ieri è tornato tardi.
2. Oggi Amelia si sveglia presto. Anche ieri Amelia si è svegliata presto.
3. Oggi tu e Amedeo partite per Napoli. Anche ieri siete partiti per Napoli.
4. Oggi Paola e Franca vanno a scuola. Anche ieri sono andate a scuola.
5. Oggi voi uscite alle 7.30. Anche ieri siete usciti alle 7.30.
6. Oggi io e i miei amici andiamo al cinema. Anche ieri siamo andati al cinema.
7. Oggi i ragazzi restano a casa. Anche ieri i ragazzi sono restati a casa.
8. Oggi Paola passa a casa mia. Anche ieri è passata a casa mia.
9. Oggi Guglielmo non torna a New York. Anche ieri non è tornato a New York.
10. Oggi Regina parte con Sandro. Anche ieri è partita con Sandro.

5·6
1. Anna è dovuta andare a New York.
2. Hai potuto telefonare a Marco?
5. Ho dovuto lavorare fino a tardi.
6. Sono voluti andare al mare.
3. Amelia è voluta venire a casa.
4. I ragazzi sono potuti tornare.
7. Non sono potuto/a venire a cena.
8. Tu e Anna avete dovuto leggere questo libro.

5·7
1. L'opera è finita tardi.
2. Maria ha cominciato il lavoro.
3. La situazione è cambiata.
4. Marco è passato davanti a casa mia.
5. Lucia e Bob sono ritornati sabato.
6. Ho riportato il libro in biblioteca.
7. Il tempo è cambiato in autunno.
8. La musica è finita.
9. Il presidente ha cominciato il suo discorso.
10. Abbiamo passato l'estate in Italia.

5·8 *Answers will vary.*

V-6 Imperfect and past perfect tenses

6·1
1. dicevamo
2. bevevate
3. facevano
4. eri
5. facevo
6. prendeva
7. venivi
8. c'era
9. andavamo
10. erano

6·2
1. ero
2. abbiamo avuto
3. Faceva
4. andava
5. ho visto
6. sembrava
7. ha fatto
8. diceva, pensava

6·3
1. erano partiti
2. avevate mangiato
3. era ritornato/a
4. eri stato/a
5. era andato/a
6. avevate preso
7. aveva detto
8. avevamo chiesto
9. avevano messo
10. avevo studiato

V-7 Future and future perfect tenses

7·1
1. parlerà
2. prenderanno
3. capirete
4. arriverò
5. leggeremo
6. pagherà
7. mangerete
8. metterò
9. arriveremo
10. dormiranno

7·2
1. Lavorerò domani.
2. Quando arriverà l'inverno, andremo in Sicilia.
3. Domani comincerà la scuola.
4. Tu e Giovanni tornerete l'anno prossimo?
5. Stasera resterò a casa.
6. La settimana prossima arriverà mia sorella!
7. Non vorrà andare al concerto.
8. Sarai qui per la festa?
9. Cosa farà quando finisce l'università?

10. Dovrò trovare un lavoro.

7·3   1. Maria sarà felice con il nuovo lavoro.
2. Avrai conosciuto molta gente interessante.
3. Avrò lasciato il mio libro sul treno.
4. Lo studente avrà perso l'autobus.
5. Avremo visto cento film!
6. La squadra italiana avrà vinto la partita.
7. Avrà molte domande.
8. Tornerà entro le 8.00.
9. Quanto avrò dormito?
10. Quanto costerà?

V-8 Present and perfect conditional tenses

8·1   1. Vorrei un bicchiere di acqua minerale, per favore.
2. Andrebbe a studiare.
3. Andremmo in Francia.
4. Sarebbe facile.
5. Vorremmo andare in vacanza.
6. Saranno contenti.
7. Partireste subito?
8. Andresti in Canada?
9. Non farei niente.
10. Quando torneresti?

8·2   1. f   2. g   3. h   4. i   5. e   6. d   7. c   8. b   9. a

8·3

1. studierebbe	5. cambierebbero
2. vorrei	6. dovresti
3. farebbe	7. avrebbe
4. andrei	8. sareste

8·4   1. Mi daresti una mano?
2. Mi farebbe lo sconto, signora?
3. Dottore, mi darebbe un appuntamento per domani?
4. Signori, potrebbero tornare domani?
5. Marco, potresti chiamarmi domani?
6. Verresti con me in Italia?
7. Professore, sarebbe possibile rimandare l'esame fino a domani?
8. Potrebbe ripetere la domanda, per favore?

V-9 The subjunctive

9·1   1. parli
   I believe that Mara speaks French.
2. insegni
   I think that Letizia teaches English.
3. chieda
   I doubt that Eleonora will apologize to me.
4. dica
   It isn't possible that you always tell lies!
5. guadagni
   Even though Maria earns a lot, she is always without money.
6. chiami
   I believe that student is named Andrea.
7. veda
   I think that Gaia and Jim see many French films.
8. decida
   I want to talk to you before you decide to quit your job.
9. parli
   It seems that Sandro often speaks of you.

10. paghi
I don't want you to pay all the time!

9·2

essere	avere	parlare	prendere	finire
sia	abbia	parli	prenda	**finisca**
siamo	**abbiamo**	parliamo	prendiamo	finiamo
siate	abbiate	**parliate**	prendiate	finiate
siano	abbiano	parlino	**prendano**	finiscano

9·3
1. fosse venuto
2. sei partito
3. vince
4. vincessero
5. parte
6. dicessero
7. siano andati
8. fosse
9. piova
10. avessi

V-10 The imperative

10·1
1. invitarlo
2. Prepara
3. Invita
4. Mettiti
5. Digli
6. Falli
7. falla
8. beviamolo

10·2
1. Prenda
2. Compri
3. Non torni
4. Salutate, Salutino
5. Non si preoccupi
6. Faccia
7. Entri
8. Torni
9. Si accomodi
10. Si calmi

10·3
1. Facciamo una festa!
2. Non mangiare tutta la pizza!
3. Torna!
4. Studiamo insieme!
5. Chiama tua madre!
6. Chiudi la porta!
7. Apri la finestra!
8. Stai attento/a!
9. Non fare tardi!
10. Scrivi presto!

10·4
1. Parli più lentamente, per favore.
2. Ripeta la domanda, per favore.
3. Mi dia ancora due giorni, per favore.
4. Abbia pazienza, per favore!
5. Non si arrabbi, per favore.
6. Parli più forte, per favore.
7. Apra la finestra, per favore.
8. Ci mostri quel film, per favore.
9. Non fumi in classe, per favore!
10. Risponda ai nostri messaggi, per favore!

V-11 Prepositions

11·1   1. e   2. d   3. f   4. c   5. b   6. g   7. a   8. j   9. h   10. i

11·2
1. a, in
2. in, in
3. di, a, con
4. da, da, in
5. in, Per
6. a, a
7. a, in, per
8. da, a
9. tra / fra
10. a

11·3
1. alla
2. sul
3. alle
4. dalle, alle
5. dal
6. nel
7. sui
8. allo

11·4   1. a   2. alla   3. al, a   4. a, a   5. in   6. a   7. in, da   8. in, dalla, alla

11·5   *Answers may vary.*
1. Vado in bici.
2. Di solito mangio presto.
3. Abito a Roma.

4. Andiamo da Silvio.
5. Vado a piedi.
6. Sono le otto di mattina.
7. Ho molto da fare.
8. In realtà preferisco l'acqua frizzante.
9. Di niente!
10. Da piccolo era biondissimo.

11·6
1. Abito a Roma, e vado a lavoro in metropolitana.
I live in Rome, and I go to work by subway.
2. Studia quasi sempre in salotto.
She/He always studies in the living room.
3. Sei tornata a casa tardi?
Did you (f.) get home late?
4. Stasera andiamo a teatro.
Tonight we are going to the theater.
5. Parto da Roma in aereo.
I'm leaving Rome by plane.
6. Vado da mia sorella.
I'm going to my sister's.
7. Perché hai messo le scarpe da tennis?
Why did you wear tennis shoes?
8. Domani pomeriggio ho un appuntamento dal dentista.
Tomorrow afternoon I have an appointment at the dentist's.
9. Gli italiani non vanno sempre in chiesa.
Italians don't always go to church.
10. Vuoi qualcosa da mangiare?
Do you want something to eat?

11·7 *No answers; read-aloud practice.*

11·8
1. qualcosa da bere
2. di solito
3. in treno
4. a Venezia
5. molto da fare
6. in realtà
7. tra/fra noi
8. in ogni caso
9. a piedi
10. da me

V-12 Pronouns

12·1 1. loro 2. io 3. io 4. tu 5. loro 6. tu 7. lei 8. lui 9. Lei

12·2
1. le / Hai visto le tue amiche? Sì, le ho viste.
2. la / Hai studiato la matematica? No, non l'ho studiata.
3. la / Hai guardato la TV? No, non l'ho guardata.
4. lo / Hai parlato cinese in classe? Sì, l'ho parlato.
5. li / Hai letto i giornali italiani? Sì, li ho letti.

12·3
1. direct / La bevi?
2. indirect / Le parli spesso?
3. indirect / Le telefoni?
4. direct / Li mangi?
5. indirect / Gli piace?
6. direct / Lo conosci?
7. indirect / Gli vuoi scrivere?
8. indirect / Cosa le dici?

12·4
1. Parlo con lui ogni giorno.
2. Paghi sempre tu!
3. Vieni da me!
4. Esco con loro stasera.
5. Hai bisogno di me domani?
6. Posso contare su di te?
7. Parla sempre di sé!
8. C'è un messaggio per te.
9. Mi sono innamorata di lui.
10. Secondo lui arrivano domani.

12·5 1. ci 2. Ne 3. ne 4. ci 5. ci 6. ci 7. Ne 8. Ne 9. Ci 10. ci

12·6
1. Glieli hai comprati?
2. Glielo hai riportato?
3. Glielo dai, per favore?
4. Gliela hai prestata?
5. Glielo consiglieresti?
6. Me la puoi prendere?
7. Te la regala?
8. Ve li ha dati?
9. Gliene hai regalati tre?
10. Gliela hai insegnata?